Public
& Private
Families

Public & Private Families

AN INTRODUCTION

ANDREW J. CHERLIN
Johns Hopkins University

7e

McGraw Hill

Connect
Learn
Succeed™

PUBLIC AND PRIVATE FAMILIES: AN INTRODUCTION, SEVENTH EDITION

Published by McGraw-Hill, a business unit of The McGraw-Hill Companies, Inc., 1221 Avenue of the Americas, New York, NY, 10020. Copyright © 2013 by The McGraw-Hill Companies, Inc. All rights reserved. Printed in the United States of America. Previous editions © 2010, 2008, and 2005. No part of this publication may be reproduced or distributed in any form or by any means, or stored in a database or retrieval system, without the prior written consent of The McGraw-Hill Companies, Inc., including, but not limited to, in any network or other electronic storage or transmission, or broadcast for distance learning.

Some ancillaries, including electronic and print components, may not be available to customers outside the United States.

This book is printed on acid-free paper.

2 3 4 5 6 7 8 9 0 DOW/DOW 1 0 9 8 7 6 5 4 3

ISBN: 978-0-07-8026676
MHID: 0-07-8026679

Senior Vice President, Products & Markets: *Kurt L. Strand*
Vice President, General Manager, Products & Markets: *Michael Ryan*
Vice President, Content Production & Technology Services: *Kimberly Meriwether David*
Managing Director: *Gina Boedeker*
Brand Manager: *Patrick Brown*
Executive Director of Development: *Liso Pinto*
Development Editor: *Amy Mittelman*
Marketing Specialist: *Alexandra Schultz*
Director, Content Production: *Terri Schiesl*
Lead Project Manager: *Jane Mohr*
Buyer: *Laura Fuller*
Cover Designer: *Studio Montage, St. Louis, MO*
Cover Image: *Royalty-free/CORBIS*
Media Project Manager: *Sridevi Palani*
Typeface: *10/12 ITC Garamond Std Book*
Compositor: *Laserwords Private Limited*
Printer: *R. R. Donnelley*

All credits appearing on page or at the end of the book are considered to be an extension of the copyright page.

Library of Congress Cataloging-in-Publication Data

Cherlin, Andrew J., 1948-
    Public & private families : an introduction/Andrew J. Cherlin. — 7th ed.
        p. cm.
    ISBN 978-0-07-802667-6 (alk. paper)
    1. Families—United States. 2. Families. 3. Family policy. I. Title. II.
Title: Public and private families.
    HQ536.C442 2013
        306.850973—dc23   2012022811

The Internet addresses listed in the text were accurate at the time of publication. The inclusion of a website does not indicate an endorsement by the authors or McGraw-Hill, and McGraw-Hill does not guarantee the accuracy of the information presented at these sites.

www.mhhe.com

For Claire and Reid

About the Author

Andrew J. Cherlin is Benjamin H. Griswold III Professor of Public Policy and Sociology at Johns Hopkins University. He received a B.S. from Yale University in 1970 and a Ph.D. in sociology from the University of California at Los Angeles in 1976. His books include *The Marriage-Go-Round: The State of Marriage and the Family in America Today* (2009), *Marriage, Divorce, Remarriage* (revised and enlarged edition, 1992), *Divided Families: What Happens to Children When Parents Part* (with Frank F. Furstenberg, Jr., 1991), *The Changing American Family and Public Policy* (1988), and *The New American Grandparent: A Place in the Family, A Life Apart* (with Frank F. Furstenberg, Jr., 1986). In 1989–1990 he was chair of the Family Section of the American Sociological Association. In 1999 he was president of the Population Association of America, the scholarly organization for demographic research.

In 2005 Professor Cherlin was awarded a John Simon Guggenheim Memorial Foundation Fellowship. He received the Distinguished Career Award in 2003 from the Family Section of the American Sociological Association. In 2001 he received the Olivia S. Nordberg Award for Excellence in Writing in the Population Sciences. In 2009 he received the Irene B. Taeuber Award from the Population Association of America, in Recognition of Outstanding Accomplishments in Demographic Research. He has also received a Merit Award from the National Institute of Child Health and Human Development for his research on the effects of family structure on children. His recent articles include "The Deinstitutionalization of American Marriage," in the *Journal of Marriage and Family;* "The Influence of Physical and Sexual Abuse on Marriage and Cohabitation," in the *American Sociological Review;* and "American Marriage in the Early Twenty-First Century," in *The Future of Children*. He also has written many articles for *The New York Times, The Washington Post, The Nation, Newsweek,* and other periodicals. He has been interviewed on *ABC News Nightline,* the *Today Show,* network evening news programs, National Public Radio's *All Things Considered,* and other news programs and documentaries.

Contents in Brief

Part One Introduction, 1
1 Public and Private Families, 3
2 The History of the Family, 39

Part Two Gender, Class, and Race-Ethnicity, 79
3 Gender and Families, 81
4 Social Class and Family Inequality, 109
5 Race, Ethnicity, and Families, 139

Part Three Sexuality, Partnership, and Marriage, 175
6 Sexualities, 177
7 Cohabitation and Marriage, 207
8 Work and Families, 249

Part Four Links across the Generations, 271
9 Children and Parents, 273
10 Older People and Their Families, 305

Part Five Conflict, Disruption, and Reconstitution, 339
11 Domestic Violence, 341
12 Divorce, 373
13 Stepfamilies, 405

Part Six Family and Society, 431
14 The Family, the State, and Social Policy, 433

Contents

List of Boxes, xxiii
Preface, xxv

Part One | Introduction, 1

Chapter 1 | Public and Private Families, 3

Looking Forward, 4

MARRIAGE AND INDIVIDUALISM, 6

WHAT IS A FAMILY?, 9
The Public Family, 10
The Private Family, 13
Two Views, Same Family, 15

HOW DO FAMILY SOCIOLOGISTS KNOW WHAT THEY KNOW?, 17

SOCIOLOGICAL THEORY AND FAMILIES, 22
Four Widely Used Perspectives, 22
   The Exchange Perspective, 22
   The Symbolic Interaction Perspective, 23
   The Feminist Perspective, 26
   The Postmodern Perspective, 27

GLOBALIZATION AND FAMILIES, 30

A SOCIOLOGICAL VIEWPOINT ON FAMILIES, 33

Looking Back, 34
Study Questions, 35
Key Terms, 35
Thinking about Families, 36
Families on the Internet, 36

Boxed Features
   FAMILIES AND THE GREAT RECESSION: Introduction, 18
   HOW DO SOCIOLOGISTS KNOW WHAT THEY KNOW?: The National Surveys, 24

Chapter 2 | The History of the Family, 39

Looking Forward, 40

WHAT DO FAMILIES DO?, 42
The Origins of Family and Kinship, 42

THE AMERICAN FAMILY BEFORE 1776, 45
American Indian Families: The Primacy of the Tribe, 45
European Colonists: The Primacy of the Public Family, 47
Family Diversity, 48

THE EMERGENCE OF THE "MODERN" AMERICAN FAMILY: 1776–1900, 49
From Cooperation to Separation: Women's and Men's Spheres, 51

AFRICAN AMERICAN, MEXICAN AMERICAN,
AND ASIAN IMMIGRANT FAMILIES, 53
African American Families, 53
    An African Heritage?, 53
    The Impact of Slavery, 54
Mexican American Families, 56
Asian Immigrant Families, 58
    The Asian Heritage, 58
    Asian Immigrants, 58

THE RISE OF THE PRIVATE FAMILY: 1900–PRESENT, 60
The Early Decades, 60
The Depression Generation, 64
The 1950s, 66
The 1960s through the 1990s, 68

THE CHANGING LIFE COURSE, 71
Social Change in the Twentieth Century, 71
The Emergence of Early Adulthood, 72
    The Role of Education, 72
    Constrained Opportunities, 73
    Declining Parental Control, 73
Early Adulthood and the Life-Course Perspective, 74
What History Tells Us, 74

Looking Back, 75
Study Questions, 76
Key Terms, 77
Thinking about Families, 77
Families on the Internet, 77

Boxed Features

    FAMILIES AND PUBLIC POLICY: Divorce Reform: Have We Been Here Before?, 62
    FAMILIES AND THE GREAT RECESSION: Lessons from the Great Depression, 65

Part Two   Gender, Class, and Race-Ethnicity, 79

Chapter 3   Gender and Families, 81
Looking Forward, 82

THE TWO-SPIRIT PEOPLE, 82

THE GESTATIONAL CONSTRUCTION OF GENDER, 85

THE CHILDHOOD CONSTRUCTION OF GENDER, 88
Parental Socialization, 88
The Media, 89
Peer Groups, 89

THE CONTINUAL CONSTRUCTION OF GENDER, 91
Doing and Undoing Gender, 92

GENDER AS SOCIAL STRUCTURE, 95

THINKING ABOUT GENDER DIFFERENCES TODAY, 98
Causes at Multiple Levels, 98
The Slowing of Gender Change, 99
The Asymmetry of Gender Change, 100
Gender, Class, and Race, 100

MEN AND MASCULINITIES, 101

THE CONTRIBUTIONS OF GENDER STUDIES, 102

Looking Back, 104
Study Questions, 105
Key Terms, 105
Thinking about Families, 105
Families on the Internet, 106

Boxed Features

   HOW DO SOCIOLOGISTS KNOW WHAT THEY KNOW?: Feminist
Research Methods, 92
   FAMILIES AND PUBLIC POLICY: Do Employers Discriminate Against Women?, 96

Chapter 4   Social Class and Family Inequality, 109

Looking Forward, 110

FAMILIES AND THE ECONOMY, 111
The Growing Importance of Education, 113
Diverging Demographics, 114
   Age at Marriage, 114
   Childbearing Outside of Marriage, 114
   The Marriage Market, 116
   Divorce, 116
   Differences in Early Adulthood, 116
Family Life and the Globalization of Production, 118
Developed Countries, 118
Developing Countries, 119

DEFINING SOCIAL CLASS, 120
Bringing in Gender and Family, 121
Social Classes and Status Groups, 122
   The Four-Class Model, 122
   Three Status Groups, 124

SOCIAL CLASS DIFFERENCES IN FAMILY LIFE, 126
Assistance from Kin, 126
Kinship among the Poor and Near Poor, 126
Chronic Poverty and Kin Networks, 127
The Limits of Kin Networks, 128
Kinship among the Nonpoor, 128
Social Class and Child Rearing, 130
Social Class and Parental Values, 130
Concerted Cultivation versus Natural Growth, 132

SOCIAL CLASS AND THE FAMILY, 133

Looking Back, 135
Study Questions, 136
Key Terms, 137
Thinking about Families, 137
Families on the Internet, 137

Boxed Features
FAMILIES AND THE GREAT RECESSION: Job Losses and Financial Strain, 112
FAMILIES AND PUBLIC POLICY: Homelessness, by the Numbers, 124

Chapter 5 # Race, Ethnicity, and Families, 139

Looking Forward, 140

RACIAL-ETHNIC GROUPS, 141
Constructing Racial-Ethnic Groups, 142
"Whiteness" as Ethnicity, 145

AFRICAN AMERICAN FAMILIES, 147
Marriage and Childbearing, 148
Marriage, 148
Childbearing Outside of Marriage, 148
Single-Parent Families, 149
Explaining the Trends, 149
Availability, 150
Culture, 151
Reconciling the Explanations, 153
Gender and Black Families, 154
The Rise of Middle-Class Families, 154

HISPANIC FAMILIES, 156
Mexican Americans, 157
Puerto Ricans, 159
Cuban Americans, 160

ASIAN AMERICAN FAMILIES, 163

SOCIAL CAPITAL AND IMMIGRANT FAMILIES, 164

AMERICAN INDIAN FAMILIES, 166

RACIAL AND ETHNIC INTERMARRIAGE, 167
Variation in Intermarriage, 168
Intersectionality and Intermarriage, 169

RACE, ETHNICITY, AND KINSHIP, 169

Looking Back, 171
Study Questions, 172
Key Terms, 172
Thinking about Families, 173
Families on the Internet, 173

Boxed Feature
    FAMILIES AND PUBLIC POLICY: How Should Multiracial Families Be Counted?, 144

Part Three   Sexuality, Partnership, and Marriage, 175

Chapter 6   # Sexualities, 177

Looking Forward, 178

SEXUAL IDENTITIES, 180
The Emergence of Sexual Identities, 181
    Sexual Acts versus Sexual Identities, 181
    The Emergence of "Heterosexuality" and "Homosexuality", 181
The Determinants of Sexual Identities, 182
    The Social Constructionist Perspective, 182
    The Integrative Perspective, 186
    Points of Agreement and Disagreement, 188
Questioning Sexual Identities, 188
    Queer Theory, 189
    Strengths and Limitations, 189

NEW FAMILIES AND BEYOND?, 190
Beyond the Family?, 191
Networks of Friends, 191
Living Apart Together, 192
Blurred Boundaries, 194

MARITAL AND NONMARITAL SEXUALITY, 195
Nonmarital Sexual Activity, 196
Marital and Extramarital Sex, 197

ADOLESCENT SEXUALITY AND PREGNANCY, 198
Changes in Sexual Behavior, 198
The Teenage Pregnancy "Problem", 199
The Consequences for Teenage Mothers, 200

SEXUALITY AND FAMILY LIFE, 202

Looking Back, 204
Study Questions, 205
Key Terms, 205
Thinking about Families, 205
Families on the Internet, 205

Boxed Features
HOW DO SOCIOLOGISTS KNOW WHAT THEY KNOW?: Asking about Sensitive Behavior, 184
FAMILIES AND PUBLIC POLICY: The Rise and Fall of the Teenage Pregnancy Problem, 202

Chapter 7 # Cohabitation and Marriage, 207

Looking Forward, 208

FORMING A UNION, 209
American Courtship, 210
The Rise and Fall of Dating, 211
Hooking Up, 212
Independent Living, 213

COHABITATION, 214
Cohabitation and Class, 217
College-Educated Cohabitants, 217
Moderately-Educated Cohabitants, 218
The Least-Educated Cohabitants, 219
Summing Up, 220
Cohabitation Among Lesbians and Gay Men, 221

MARRIAGE, 222
From Institution To Companionship, 222
The Institutional Marriage, 222
The Companionate Marriage, 224
From Companionship to Individualization, 225
Toward the Individualistic Marriage, 225
The Influence of Economic Change, 226
The Globalization of Love, 227

THE CURRENT CONTEXT OF MARRIAGE, 230
Why Do People Still Marry?, 230
Marriage as the Capstone Experience, 231
The Wedding as a Status Symbol, 232
Marriage and Religion, 233
Is Marriage Good for You?, 235
The Marriage Market, 236
The Specialization Model, 237
The Income-Pooling Model, 238

SOCIAL CHANGE AND INTIMATE UNIONS, 240
Changes in Union Formation, 240
Marriage as an Ongoing Project, 242

Looking Back, 244
Study Questions, 245
Key Terms, 245
Thinking about Families, 245
Families on the Internet, 246

Boxed Features
  FAMILIES AND PUBLIC POLICY: Domestic Partnerships, 215
  FAMILIES AND THE GREAT RECESSION: Putting Plans on Hold, 223

Chapter 8 Work and Families, 249

Looking Forward, 250

FROM SINGLE-EARNER TO DUAL-EARNER MARRIAGES, 251
Behind the Rise, 251
A Profound Change, 252
The Current Situation, 253

THE DIVISION OF LABOR IN MARRIAGES, 255
Rethinking Caring Work, 255
    Breaking the Work/Family Boundary, 255
    Valuing Caring Labor, 255
    Toward an Ethic of Care, 257
Who's Doing the Care Work?, 257
Wives' Earnings and Domestic Work, 259
The Current State of Sharing, 259

WORK-FAMILY BALANCE, 261
Overworked and Underworked Americans, 262
When Work Interferes with Family Life, 263
    Task Size, 264
    Task Stress, 264
Nonstandard Work Hours, 264
Toward a Responsive Workplace?, 265

Looking Back, 269
Study Questions, 269
Key Terms, 270
Thinking about Families, 270
Families on the Internet, 270

Boxed Features
  FAMILIES AND THE GREAT RECESSION: What Long-Term
  Unemployment Does to Marriage, 254
  FAMILIES AND PUBLIC POLICY: Paid Parental Leave, 267

Part Four   **Links across the Generations, 271**

Chapter 9   Children and Parents, 273

Looking Forward, 274

WHAT ARE PARENTS SUPPOSED TO DO FOR CHILDREN?, 274
Socialization as Support and Control, 275
Socialization and Ethnicity, 275
Socialization and Social Class, 276
Socialization and Gender, 277
Religion and Socialization, 278
What's Important?, 278
What Difference Do Fathers Make?, 279
Adoption, 281
　　Domestic Adoption, 281
　　Transnational Adoption, 282
Lesbian and Gay Parenthood, 283

WHAT MIGHT PREVENT PARENTS FROM DOING
WHAT THEY ARE SUPPOSED TO DO?, 285
Unemployment and Poverty, 286
　　Unemployment, 286
　　Poverty, 287
Family Instability, 287
　　Different Kinds of Households, 288
　　Multiple Transitions, 289
Family Complexity, 289
Mass Incarceration, 291
Time Apart, 292
　　How Parents Compensate for Time Apart, 292
　　The Consequences of Nonparental Care, 292

TRANSNATIONAL FAMILIES, 293
Immigrant Caregivers, 293
The Effects on Children, 294

THE WELL-BEING OF AMERICAN CHILDREN, 295
Which Children?, 297
Diverging Destinies, 298
　　Poor and Wealthy Children, 298
　　Children in the Middle, 298

Looking Back, 300
Study Questions, 301
Key Terms, 302
Thinking about Families, 302
Families on the Internet, 302

Boxed Features
　　HOW DO SOCIOLOGISTS KNOW WHAT THEY KNOW?: Measuring the
　　Well-Being of Children, 296

　　FAMILIES AND PUBLIC POLICY: Do Children Have Rights?, 299

Chapter 10 Older People and Their Families, 305

Looking Forward, 306

THE MODERNIZATION OF OLD AGE, 308
Mortality Decline, 308
   The Statistics, 308
   The Social Consequences, 308
Fertility Decline, 310
Rising Standard of Living, 311
   Variations by Age, Race, and Gender, 311
   Social Consequences, 312
Separate Living Arrangements, 314
Contact, 317

INTERGENERATIONAL SUPPORT, 318
Mutual Assistance, 318
   Altruism, 319
   Exchange, 319
Moving in with Grandparents, 322
   Multigenerational Households, 322
   Skipped-Generation Households, 323
   Rewards and Costs, 323
The Return of the Extended Family?, 323
Care of Older Persons with Disabilities, 325
The Rewards and Costs of Caregiving, 326

THE QUALITY OF INTERGENERATIONAL TIES, 327
Intergenerational Solidarity, 327
Intergenerational Conflict and Ambivalence, 330
The Effects of Divorce and Remarriage, 332

THE FAMILY NATIONAL GUARD, 333

Looking Back, 335
Study Questions, 336
Key Terms, 337
Thinking about Families, 337
Families on the Internet, 337

Boxed Features
   FAMILIES AND PUBLIC POLICY: Financing Social Security and Medicare, 312
   FAMILIES AND THE GREAT RECESSION: Still, or Once Again, Living at Home, 320

Part Five Conflict, Disruption, and Reconstitution, 339

Chapter 11 Domestic Violence, 341

Looking Forward, 342

DOMESTIC VIOLENCE IN HISTORICAL PERSPECTIVE, 343

Early History, 343
The Twentieth Century, 344
    The Political Model of Domestic Violence, 344
    The Medical Model of Domestic Violence, 344

INTIMATE PARTNER VIOLENCE, 346
Two Kinds of Violence?, 346
Prevalence and Trends in Intimate Partner Violence, 349
    Prevalence, 349
    Intimate Partner Rape, 350
    A New Definition of Rape, 351
    Trends, 352
Which Partnerships Are at Risk?, 352
    Marital Status, 352
    Social Class, 352
Child Abuse, 353
    Incidence, 354
    Sexual Abuse and Its Consequences, 356
    Physical Abuse and Its Consequences, 357
    Poly-victimization, 357
    Poverty or Abuse?, 358
Elder Abuse, 360

SEXUAL AGGRESSION AND VIOLENCE IN YOUNG ADULT RELATIONSHIPS, 361
Prevalence, 362
The Intimate Setting, 363

EXPLANATIONS, 364
Social Learning Perspective, 365
Frustration–Aggression Perspective, 365
Social Exchange Perspective, 366

DOMESTIC VIOLENCE AND PUBLIC POLICY, 367
Diminished Policy Debates, 367
Social Programs, 368

Looking Back, 369
Study Questions, 370
Key Terms, 371
Thinking about Families, 371
Families on the Internet, 371

Boxed Features
    HOW DO SOCIOLOGISTS KNOW WHAT THEY KNOW?: Advocates and Estimates:
    How Large (or Small) Are Social Problems?, 350
    FAMILIES AND PUBLIC POLICY: The Swinging Pendulum of Foster Care Policy, 358

Chapter 12 Divorce, 373

Looking Forward, 374

THREE ERAS OF DIVORCE, 376
The Era of Restricted Divorce, 377

The Era of Divorce Tolerance, 378
The Era of Unrestricted Divorce, 379
Diverging Divorce Rates in the United States, 381

FACTORS ASSOCIATED WITH DIVORCE, 382
Societal Risk Factors, 383
    No-Fault Divorce Legislation, 383
    Cultural Change, 383
    Men's Employment, 383
    Women's Employment, 384
    Summing Up, 384
Individual Risk Factors, 385
    Age at Marriage, 385
    Race and Ethnicity, 386
    Premarital Cohabitation, 386
    Parental Divorce, 387
    Spouse's Similarity, 387

HOW DIVORCE AFFECTS CHILDREN, 388
Child Custody, 389
Contact and Co-Parenting, 389
Economic Support, 391
    Single-Father Families, 393
Psychosocial Effects, 394
    Parental Conflict, 394
    Multiple Transitions, 395
After the Crisis Period, 396
    Long-Term Adjustment, 396
    Glass Half-Empty/Half-Full, 397
    Genetically-Informed Studies, 398
    In Sum, 399

Looking Back, 400
Study Questions, 401
Key Terms, 402
Thinking about Families, 402
Families on the Internet, 402

Boxed Features
    HOW DO SOCIOLOGISTS KNOW WHAT THEY KNOW?: Measuring the Divorce Rate, 375
    FAMILIES AND PUBLIC POLICY: Enforcing Child Support Obligations, 392

Chapter 13 Stepfamilies, 405

Looking Forward, 406

AN INCOMPLETE INSTITUTION?, 407

WHAT IS A STEPFAMILY?, 409
Stepfamily Diversity, 410
Doing the Work of Kinship, 411

Stepfamilies in Later Life, 412
The Demography of Stepfamilies and Remarriages, 413
　　Who Remarries?, 414
　　Divorce Rates among the Remarried, 415

BUILDING STEPFAMILIES, 416
The Transitional Period, 417
　　The Stepparent as Affinity-Seeker, 417
　　The Stepparent as Polite Outsider, 417
　　Adjustment of the Stepchildren, 418
　　Drawing Boundaries, 418
The Stabilization Period, 419
Differences Between the Roles of Stepmother and Stepfather, 421

THE EFFECTS OF STEPFAMILY LIFE ON CHILDREN, 422
Cohabiting v. Married Stepfamilies, 423
Age at Leaving Home, 424

DIVORCE, REMARRIAGE, AND STEPFAMILIES: SOME LESSONS, 424
The Primacy of the Private Family, 425
New Kinship Ties, 426
The Impact on Children, 428

Looking Back, 429
Study Questions, 430
Key Terms, 430
Thinking about Families, 430
Families on the Internet, 430

Boxed Features
　　FAMILIES AND PUBLIC POLICY: The Rights and Responsibilities of Stepparents, 408
　　The Origins of the Wicked Stepmother, 420

Part Six　　Family and Society, 431

Chapter 14　The Family, the State, and Social Policy, 433

Looking Forward, 434

THE DEVELOPMENT OF THE WELFARE STATE, 437
The Welfare State, 438
The Rise and Fall of the Family Wage System, 438

FAMILY POLICY DEBATES, 440
The Conservative Viewpoint, 440
The Liberal Viewpoint, 443
Which Families Are Poor?, 444

PRACTICAL COMPROMISES, 445
The Earned Income Tax Credit, 445

The 1996 Welfare Reform Law, 446
> *Reasons for the Policy Reversal, 448*
> *The Effects of Welfare Reform, 449*

CURRENT DEBATES, 453
Marriage Promotion, 453
Same-Sex Marriage, 454
Nonmarital Childbearing, 455
Single-Parent Families, 456
National Health Insurance, 457
Responsible Fatherhood, 457
Work–Family Balance, 458

FAMILY POLICY IN THE 2010s, 460

Looking Back, 461
Study Questions, 462
Key Terms, 463
Thinking about Families, 463
Families on the Internet, 463

Boxed Features

   FAMILIES AND PUBLIC POLICY: The Abortion Dilemma, 442

   FAMILIES AND THE GREAT RECESSION: "The Safety Net", 450

Glossary, 464
References, 470
Acknowledgments, 500
Photo Credits, 502
Name Index, 504
Subject Index, 512

List of Boxes

Families and Public Policy

Chapter
2 Divorce Reform: Have We Been Here Before?, 62
3 Do Employers Discriminate Against Women?, 96
4 Homelessness, by the Numbers, 124
5 How Should Multiracial Families Be Counted?, 144
6 The Rise and Fall of the Teenage Pregnancy Problem, 202
7 Domestic Partnerships, 215
8 Paid Parental Leave, 267
9 Do Children Have Rights?, 299
10 Financing Social Security and Medicare, 312
11 The Swinging Pendulum of Foster Care Policy, 358
12 Enforcing Child Support Obligations, 392
13 The Rights and Responsibilities of Stepparents, 408
14 The Abortion Dilemma, 442

Families and the Great Recession

Chapter
1 Introduction, 18
2 Lessons from the Great Depression, 65
4 Job Losses and Financial Strain, 112
7 Putting Plans on Hold, 223
8 What Long-Term Unemployment Does to Marriage, 254
10 Still, or Once Again, Living at Home, 320
14 The Safety Net, 450

How Do Sociologists Know What They Know?

Chapter
1 The National Surveys, 24
3 Feminist Research Methods, 92
6 Asking about Sensitive Behavior, 184
9 Measuring the Well-Being of Children, 296
11 Advocates and Estimates: How Large (or Small) Are Social Problems?, 350
12 Measuring the Divorce Rate, 375

Preface

The sociology of the family is deceptively hard to study. Unlike, say, physics, the topic is familiar (a word whose very root is Latin for "family") because virtually everyone grows up in families. Therefore, it can seem "easy" to study the family because students can bring to bear their personal knowledge of the subject. Some textbooks play to this familiarity by mainly providing students with an opportunity to better understand their private lives. The authors never stray too far from the individual experiences of their readers, focusing on personal choices such as whether to marry and whether to have children. To be sure, giving students insight into the social forces that shape their personal decisions about family life is a worthwhile objective. Nevertheless, the challenge of writing about the sociology of the family is also to help students understand that the significance of families extends beyond personal experience. Today, as in the past, the family is the site of not only private decisions but also activities that matter to our society as a whole.

These activities center on taking care of people who are unable to fully care for themselves, most notably children and the elderly. Anyone who follows social issues knows of the often-expressed concern about whether, given developments such as the increases in divorce and childbearing outside of marriage, we are raising the next generation adequately. Anyone anxious about the well-being of the rapidly growing elderly population (as well as the escalating cost of providing financial and medical assistance to the elderly) knows the concern about whether family members will continue to provide adequate assistance to them. Indeed, rarely does a month pass without these issues appearing on the covers of magazines and the front pages of newspapers.

In this textbook, consequently, I have written about the family in two senses: the *private family,* in which we live most of our personal lives, and the *public family,* in which adults perform tasks that are important to society. My goal is to give students a thorough grounding in both aspects. It is true that the two are related—taking care of children adequately, for instance, requires the love and affection that family members express privately toward each other. But the public side of the family deserves equal time with the private side.

Organization

This book is divided into 6 parts and 14 chapters. Part One ("Introduction") introduces the concepts of public and private families and examines how sociologists and other social scientists study them. It also provides an overview of the history of the family. Part Two ("Gender, Class, and Race-Ethnicity") deals with the three key dimensions of social stratification in family life: gender, social class, and race-ethnicity. In Part Three ("Sexuality, Partnership, and Marriage"), the focus shifts to the private family. The section examines the emergence of the modern concept of sexuality, the formation of partnerships, and the degree of persistence and change in the institution of marriage. Finally, it covers the complex connections between work and family.

Part Four ("Links across the Generations") explores how well the public family is meeting its responsibilities for children and the elderly. Part Five ("Conflict, Disruption, and Reconstitution") deals with the consequences of conflict and disruption in family life. It first studies violence against wives and children. Then divorce, remarriage, and stepfamilies are discussed. Finally, in Part Six ("Family and Society") social and political issues involving the family and the state are discussed.

Special Features

Public and Private Families is distinguishable from other textbooks in several important ways.

First and foremost, it explores both the public and the private family. The public/private distinction that underlies the book's structure is intended to provide a more balanced portrait of contemporary life. Furthermore, the focus on the public family leads to a much greater emphasis on government policy toward the family than in most other textbooks. In fact, every chapter except the first and last includes a short, boxed essay under the general title, "Families and Public Policy," to stimulate student interest and make the book relevant to current political debates.

In addition to this unique emphasis on both the *Public and Private Families,* the text:

- **Highlights the connectedness of family lives across cultures.** Although the emphasis in the book is on the contemporary United States, no text should ignore the important cross-national connections among families in our globalized economy. Consequently, this edition features expanded coverage of the effects of the globalization and automation of production on families in the developed and developing world.
- **Includes distinctive chapters.** The attention to the public family led me to write several chapters that are not included in some sociology of the family textbooks. These include Chapter 14, "The Family, the State, and Social Policy," Chapter 9, "Children and Parents," and Chapter 10, "Older People and Their Families." These chapters examine issues of great current interest, such as income assistance to poor families, the effects of out-of-home child care, the costs of the Social Security and Medicare programs, and the extension of marriage to same-sex couples. Throughout these and other chapters, variations by race, ethnicity, and gender are explored.
- **Gives special attention to the research methods used by family sociologists.** To give students an understanding of how sociologists study the family, I include a section in Chapter 1 titled, "How Do Family Sociologists Know What They Know?" This material explains the ways that family sociologists go about their research. Then in other chapters, I include boxed essays under a similar title on subjects ranging from national surveys to feminist research methods.
- **Includes essays on the effects of the Great Recession.** I explore the effects on family life of the Great Recession that began in 2007. Seven boxed essays examine topics such as the effects of long-term unemployment on marriage, the postponement of the transition to adulthood, and how well the safety net of government assistance programs functioned.

- **Features "Families on the Internet" sections.** Since I wrote the first edition of this textbook, the World Wide Web has changed from a pleasant diversion to an essential information-gathering tool. Almost every chapter contains information that I gathered from the Web, including the most up-to-date demographic statistics from government statistical sites such as the Bureau of the Census Web pages. But the Internet is also a powerful instructional tool. Consequently, at the end of each chapter is a section titled "Families on the Internet," in which I list Web sites that students may find useful.

Pedagogy

Each chapter begins in a way that engages the reader: the neither-men-nor-women two-spirit people of many Native American tribes; the courtship of Maud Rittenhouse in the 1880s; the case of Danny Henrikson, taken from a stepfather who raised him and awarded by a judge to a father he did not know; and so forth. And each of the six parts of the book is preceded by a brief introduction that sets the stage.

- I have added several *Quick Review* boxes in each chapter that include bulleted, one-sentence summaries of the key points of the preceding sections.
- Each chapter includes the following types of questions:
  - *Looking Forward*—Questions that preview the chapter themes and topics.
  - *Ask Yourself*—Two questions, which appear at the end of each of the three types of boxes.
  - *Looking Back*—Looking Forward questions reiterated at the end of each chapter, around which the chapter summaries are organized.
  - *Thinking about Families*—Two questions, which appear at the end of each chapter and are designed to encourage critical thinking about the "public" and the "private" family.

What's New in Each Chapter?

As in previous revisions, I have updated all statistics and charts using the latest numbers available. I have also added findings from 20 recent books (listed at the end of this section) and numerous recent articles.

CHAPTER 1. PUBLIC AND PRIVATE FAMILIES

- Added an introduction to a set of boxed essays throughout the book, under the title "Families and the Great Recession," that explore the consequences of the severe recession of the late 2000s and early 2010s on family life.
- Added a section on "Globalization and Families," which introduces the process of globalization and its importance for family life in both the developed and developing world. It lists facets of globalization that will be explored in later chapters. Globalization receives much more attention in this edition than in previous editions.

- Deleted the functionalist perspective and the conflict perspective in the section on sociological theories and families. These two perspectives had been trending downward in previous editions and were grouped as "two other perspectives that are worth knowing" in the sixth edition. That designation was unsatisfactory. With few current references to these perspectives in the literature, I have dropped them to make room for new material.

CHAPTER 2. THE HISTORY OF THE FAMILY

- Expanded the discussion of recent historical scholarship on the increasing role of romantic love within marriage in the seventeenth and early eighteenth centuries.
- Deleted boxed essay on the Chinese minority society Na, in which the roles of husbands and fathers are absent. Instructors wishing to include material on this society should read the recent information in Chapter 5 of Judith Stacey's 2011 book, *Unhitched* (New York University Press). The "Families in Other Cultures" boxes are deleted in this edition, with some of the material incorporated into new discussions of the consequences of globalization.
- Added new boxed essay, "Families and the Great Recession: Lessons from the Great Depression."

CHAPTER 3. GENDER AND FAMILIES

- Undoing gender: Added to the discussion of West and Zimmerman's classic "doing gender" article a discussion of a more recent article which argues that some social interactions today may serve to un-do gender differences.
- Replaced the "Gender and Male Domination" section, with its dated discussions of gender differences under capitalism and socialism, with "Gender as Social Structure," the title of Barbara Risman's influential 2004 article. I first discuss the contention of Risman and others that gender is a basic part of social structure, like race and class; and then I add Cecilia Ridgeway's argument that the cultural frame of gender is also a part of the structural support for gender differences.
- Added a section title, "Thinking About Gender Differences Today," with several sub-sections covering recent developments:
  - The growing consensus that gender differences are produced at multiple levels; i.e., no single approach to explaining gender differences is sufficient.
  - The slowing of gender change in recent years.
  - The asymmetry of gender change: how women's lives have changed more than men's lives.
  - The prevalent view that gender, race, and class should all be considered together.
- Deleted the box on "Asia's Missing Girls." Some of the material has been shifted to Chapter 9.

CHAPTER 4. SOCIAL CLASS AND FAMILY INEQUALITY

- This is the most heavily revised and reorganized chapter of the new edition. The old title was "Social Class and Families." The new title reflects a great emphasis on family inequality and globalization.
- New opening section on the stagnating income of the average worker and the polarization of the labor market.
- Families and the Great Recession box: "Job Losses and Financial Strain."
- New section on "Family Life and the Globalization of Production," with sub-sections on the effects of the globalization of production on family life in (1) the developed countries, most notably the United States, in which I show the effects are more positive for the college-educated; and (2) the developing countries, where there has been a mixture of positive and negative effects.
- New studies cited on the differences in the amounts and types of assistance from kin that are received by low-income families and middle-income families.

CHAPTER 5. RACE, ETHNICITY, AND FAMILIES

- New section on "Intersectionality and Intermarriage," which addresses the relatively low marriage rates for college-educated African American women, a topic that has received a great deal of attention recently (see Banks, 2011; Clarke, 2011).
- The box on transnational families in the previous edition has been deleted, and a greatly expanded discussion of transnational families is now presented in Chapter 9, "Children and Parents." This widespread phenomenon is no longer just a racial or ethnic topic.
- Updated information from the 2010 Census on multiracial responses and other topics, where available.

CHAPTER 6. SEXUALITIES

- Detailed data on sexual life from the 2006–2010 continuous round of the National Survey of Family Growth.
- New data on the growing acceptance by Americans of diverse family forms, including same-sex couples with children.
- New summary discussion.

CHAPTER 7. COHABITATION AND MARRIAGE

- New research on hooking up.
- Greatly revised cohabitation section focusing on social class differences in the meaning of cohabitation.
- Section on multiple-partner fertility moved to Chapter 9.
- New Families and the Great Recession boxed essay: "Putting Plans on Hold."
- Expanded section on the globalization of love. (Replaces boxed essay in previous editions.)

CHAPTER 8. WORK AND FAMILIES

- New Families and the Great Recession box: "What Long-Term Unemployment Does to Marriage."
- New statistics on wives' and husbands' market and domestic labor from national time use surveys (see Figure 8.3).
- Arlie Hochschild's assessment that while the "second shift" has not been eliminated, it has been cut in half.
- The Families and Globalization box on the child care crisis in low-income countries has been incorporated into the text of Chapter 9.

CHAPTER 9. CHILDREN AND PARENTS

- A new section on family instability. I have used this increasingly prominent concept (the number of transitions in living arrangements to which a child is exposed), in discussing children's living arrangements, rather than focusing solely on the more static concepts of single parent households, or cohabiting unions.
- A new section on family complexity. It incorporates the material on multiple-partner fertility that previously was in Chapter 7. It presents the growing complexity as a consequence of the growing instability.
- A new section on transnational families. It describes the growing number of families that extend across national borders due to the migration of mothers to wealthy countries, often to care for the children of dual-career families in wealthy countries such as the United States. It discusses the experiences of both the mothers in the receiving countries and the children in the sending countries.

CHAPTER 10. OLDER PEOPLE AND THEIR FAMILIES

- New Families and the Great Recession box: "Still, or Once Again, Living at Home."
- New section, "The Return of the Extended Family?" with updated statistics and a new chart showing the percentage of households that contained various kinds of extended families (multigenerational households, young adults in their late twenties or older living in their parents' home, skipped-generation grandparents and grandchildren) from 1900 to 2009.
- Expanded discussion of intergenerational ambivalence, a topic on which much recent research has been done.
- More discussion of implications of divorce and remarriage for intergenerational support of the older population.

CHAPTER 11. DOMESTIC VIOLENCE

- A question mark has been added to the section heading "Two Kinds of Violence?" Recent research suggests that Michael Johnson's influential typology is more useful as a conceptual model than as a guide to assessing any particular couples, as I now explain in more detail.
- New definition of rape to be used in the FBI Uniform Crime Report.
- Data from the recently-released fourth administration of the National Incidence Study of Child Abuse and Neglect.

CHAPTER 12. DIVORCE

- More evidence of the growing divergence in divorce risks by social class.
- A recent study suggesting that the increased behavior problems among children whose parents have divorced may be due to an interaction of genetic predispositions and whether they live with two parents or not.

CHAPTER 13. STEPFAMILIES

- A brief reflection on the concept of an "incomplete institution" more than three decades after my 1978 article.
- New demographic information from the American Community survey.
- Discussion of research suggesting that cohabiting stepfamilies may be particularly disadvantageous family environments for children.

CHAPTER 14. THE FAMILY, THE STATE, AND SOCIAL POLICY

- Expanded discussion of the conservative and liberal positions on the role of the state with respect to families.
- Greatly expanded presentation of seven contemporary family issues: marriage promotion, same-sex marriage, nonmarital childbearing, single-parent families, national health insurance, responsible fatherhood, and work-family balance.
- New table summarizing the liberal and conservative positions on the contemporary issues that have been discussed.
- New Families and the Great Recession box, "The Safety Net," examines how well government assistance programs functioned during the Great Recession.

Books newly-cited in the seventh edition:

Banks, R. R. (2011). *Is marriage for white people? How the African American marriage decline affects everyone.* New York: Dutton.

Clarke, A. Y. (2011). *Inequalities of love: College-educated black women and the barriers to romance and family.* Durham: Duke University Press.

Dreby, J. (2010). *Divided by borders: Mexican migrants and their children.* Berkeley: University of California Press.

Gerson, K. (2010). *The unfinished revolution: How a new generation is reshaping family, work, and gender in America.* New York: Oxford University Press.

Hochschild, A. (2012). *The second shift: Working families and the revolution at home. Revised and with a new afterword.* New York: Penguin.

Kalleberg, A. L. (2011). *Good jobs, bad jobs: The rise of polarized and precarious employment systems in the United States, 1970s to 2000s.* New York: Russell Sage Foundation.

Klinenberg, E. (2012). *Going solo: The extraordinary rise and surprising appeal of living alone.* New York: Penguin Press.

Lee, J., & Bean, F. D. (2010). *The diversity paradox: Immigration and the color line in twenty-first century America.* New York: Russell Sage Foundation.

Murray, C. (2012). *Coming apart: The state of white America, 1960–2010.* New York: Crown Forum.

Nelson, T. J., & Edin, K. (2013). *Doing the best I can: Fathering in the inner city.* Berkeley: University of California Press.

Newman, K. (2012). *The accordion family: Boomerang kids, anxious parents, and the private toll of global competition*. Boston: Beacon Press.

Peters, H. E., & Dush, C. M. K. (Eds.). (2009). *Marriage and family: Perspectives and complexities*. New York: Columbia University Press.

Powell, B., Bolzendahl, C., Geist, C., & Steelman, L. C. (2010). *Counted out: Same-sex relations and Americans' definitions of family*. New York: Russell Sage Foundation.

Pugh, A. J. (2009). *Longing and belonging: Parents, children, and the consumer culture*. Berkeley: University of California Press.

Ridgeway, C. L. (2011). *Framed by gender: How gender inequality persists in the modern world*. Oxford: Oxford University Press.

Riley, N. E., & Van Vleet, K. E. (2012). *Making families through adoption*. Los Angeles: Pine Forge Press.

Risman, B. J. (Ed.). (2010). *Families as they really are*. New York: W. W. Norton.

Smart, C. (2007). *Personal life: New directions in sociological thinking*. Cambridge: Polity Press.

Trask, B. S. (2010). *Globalization and families: Accelerated systemic social change*. New York: Springer.

Williams, J. C. (2010). *Reshaping the work-family debate: Why men and class matter*. Cambridge, MA: Harvard University Press.

Supplements Package

McGraw-Hill offers an extensive array of supplements for students and instructors. This edition of *Public and Private Families* is accompanied by a comprehensive package:

FOR THE STUDENT

- *Public and Private Families: A Reader, 7th Edition*—Edited by the text's author and keyed to text chapters, this Reader includes articles and book excerpts by family sociologists and other writers on a variety of issues facing families today. A special discount is available when the textbook and Reader are ordered as a package.
- *Online Learning Center* (www.mhhe.com/cherlin7e)—This provides innovative, text-specific resources including quizzes with feedback that students can use to study for exams.

FOR THE INSTRUCTOR

- The *Online Instructor's Resource* manual provides access to a wide array of important ancillaries:
  - *Instructor's Manual/Testbank*—includes detailed chapter outlines, key terms, overviews, lecture notes, and a complete testbank
  - *Computerized Testbank*—easy-to-use computerized testing program for both Windows and Macintosh computers
  - *PowerPoint Slides*—complete, chapter-by-chapter slideshows featuring text, art, and tables

- *Course Management Systems*—whether you use WebCT, Blackboard, e-College, or another course management system, McGraw-Hill will provide you with a cartridge that enables you to either conduct your course entirely online or supplement your lectures with online material. And if your school does not yet have one of these course management systems, we can provide you with PageOut, an easy-to-use tool that allows you to create your own course Web page and access all material on the Online Learning Center.
- *Primis Online*—a unique database publishing system that allows instructors to create their own custom text from material in this text or elsewhere and deliver that text to students electronically as an e-book or in print format via the bookstore.

■ Acknowledgments

To write a book this comprehensive requires the help of many people. At McGraw-Hill, sponsoring editor Gina Boedeker provided initial support, managing editor Jessica Cannavo and freelance development editor Nadia Bidwell provided valuable editorial guidance, and Jane Mohr smoothly managed the production process. In addition, the following people read the sixth edition and provided me with helpful suggestions for this revision:

Valerian DeSousa, West Chester University

Bahira Trask, University of Delaware

Johnathan Varhola, Wright State University

Julia Wilson, Emory & Henry College

Part One

Introduction

The family has two aspects. It is, first, the place where we experience much of our private lives. It is where we give and receive love, share our hopes and fears, work through our troubles, and relax and enjoy ourselves. Second, it is a setting in which adults perform tasks that are of importance to society, particularly raising children and assisting elderly parents. To be sure, people undertake these tasks not to perform a public service but rather to express love, affection, and gratitude. Nevertheless, family caretaking benefits us all by raising the next generation and by reducing our collective responsibility for the elderly. Indeed, people today frequently express concern over whether changes in the family have reduced parents' abilities to raise their children well. This book is about both the private and public aspects of families. It examines the contributions of family life not only to personal satisfaction but also to public welfare. The first two chapters provide an introduction to this perspective. • Chapter 1 explores the most useful ways to think about families. It reviews the debates about family life today, and it examines the approaches that sociologists and other social scientists use to study families. • Chapter 2 provides an overview of the history of the family. Over the past half-century family historians have produced many studies that provide useful insights. A knowledge of family life in the past can help us to understand families today.

Chapter One

Public and Private Families

Looking Forward

Marriage and Individualism

What Is a Family?

The Public Family

The Private Family

Two Views, Same Family

How Do Family Sociologists Know What They Know?

Sociological Theory and Families

Four Widely Used Perspectives

The Exchange Perspective

The Symbolic Interaction Perspective

The Feminist Perspective

The Postmodern Perspective

Globalization and Families

A Sociological Viewpoint on Families

Looking Back

Study Questions

Key Terms

Thinking about Families

Families on the Internet

Boxed Features

FAMILIES AND THE GREAT RECESSION: *Introduction*

HOW DO SOCIOLOGISTS KNOW WHAT THEY KNOW?: *The National Surveys*

Looking Forward

1. How do Americans feel about marriage and families?

2. What do families do that is important for society? What do families do that is important for the individuals in them?

3. How do sociologists go about studying families?

4. What are the leading theoretical approaches to studying families?

5. How is globalization changing family life?

I recently taught a seminar on family sociology to a small group of undergraduates at Johns Hopkins. During the first class, I gave them a questionnaire that included two questions about how the American family is faring. The first question asked whether they agreed or disagreed with this statement: "I think the American family is in trouble these days." Nine out of 14 agreed that the American family is in trouble. Then they were asked whether they agreed or disagreed with the statement "I think my family is in trouble." Since a majority of them had just said that American families were in trouble, you might expect many of them to say that their own families were in trouble. But only one out of 14 agreed that their own family was in trouble. On the face of it, these responses don't make sense. After all, if families in general are having trouble, then *someone's* family must be having this trouble. You might counter that, well, these are middle-class college students from privileged backgrounds whose families have escaped the problems that are prevalent among others. Yet when the American public was asked two similar questions, their answers followed the same pattern. In a 1999 national telephone survey by *The New York Times,* people were asked, "In general, do you think that because of such things as divorce, more working mothers, or single parents, etc., family ties in the U.S. are breaking down—or don't you think so?"[1] Seventy-seven percent responded that, yes, they thought family ties were breaking down—an even more negative assessment than my students gave. The next question was, "What about in your own family? Are family ties breaking down, or not?" Eighty-two percent responded that their family ties were not breaking down. Apparently, most Americans think that family life in general is in decline, but not their own families.

These opposing answers—American families are having a terrible time except for my family—reflect widespread ambivalence about the enormous changes in American family life over the past several decades. On the one hand, many people share the concern about family decline voiced by commentators who bemoan changes such as the increase in divorce, childbearing outside of marriage, and couples who live together outside of marriage. Sometimes called "traditionalists," they view childrearing as the central purpose of marriage. They charge that parents today are doing a poorer job

[1] The data that I cite from the survey come from unpublished tabulations. For an overview, see Cherlin (1999).

of bringing up children due to the increase in single-parent families and a higher percentage of mothers working outside the home. They favor public policies that encourage marriage. (In fact, Congress passed a controversial bill in 2006 that included $150 million per year for promoting marriage.) They also tend to believe that marriage should be between a man and a woman; about 30 states have passed constitutional amendments stating as much.

Still, many Americans also sympathize with what we might call a "modern" view that focuses less on childrearing and more on the personal rewards that family life provides to adults. According to this view, adults should be free to choose the style of life they find most satisfying. Its advocates argue that society can adjust to the new family forms, such as two-earner couples and single-parent households, by changing the ways in which the workplace and the school are organized. They assert that there is little evidence to back up the claim that having a working mother hurts children. And they argue that single-parent families can be just as good for children as married-couple families if children receive the support they need. They back public policies that support families of all types, whether headed by a married couple or not. For instance, many favor extending the legal protections of marriage to same-sex couples because they believe that gay and lesbian couples experience the same kind of intimacy and commitment as opposite-sex couples and therefore deserve the same kind of rights and recognition. In 2004, Massachusetts became the first state to legalize same-sex marriage, and as of 2012 it was also legal in six other states and the District of Columbia. It is also legal in at least ten other countries.

Yet although the political activists have taken sides, most Americans are of two minds about the great changes in family life. People are concerned about the effects of day care on children, but they approve of decisions by women in their own families to work outside the home. They are worried about the consequences of divorce, but they don't expect their relatives to remain in unhappy marriages. They believe that, ideally, children should be born to married couples, but they accept the occurrence of non-marital births in their families. In other words, many people share both the concern about family decline voiced by traditionalists and the defense of newer family forms voiced by modernists. Although they may endorse old-style values, such as the superiority of the stable, two-parent family, they reserve the right to deviate from those values in their own lives. And they are loath to tell others how to live their family lives. They may value the traditional family, but they accept family diversity as inevitable, and perhaps beneficial. In fact, when Alan Wolfe (1998) conducted interviews to learn whether Americans could be divided into "traditionalists" and "modernists" in their beliefs about family life, he concluded that they could not. Rather, he found that many people agreed with some of what both groups were saying. "The divisions over the family do not take place between camps of people," he wrote; "instead, they take place within most individuals." That is to say, many of us hold parts of both positions. This chapter will examine the sources of that ambivalence. It will then consider several questions raised by the debate: What is a family? What do families do that is important to society? And what do families do that is meaningful to individuals?

■ Marriage and Individualism

A family life centered on marriage remains the preference of most Americans. When young adults are asked their plans for the future, the overwhelming majority respond that they plan to marry and to have children. But it is a different kind of marriage than it used to be. In most societies at most times in the past, marriage was the only acceptable setting for sexual activity and childbearing. As recently as the mid-twentieth century, marriage, childbearing, and sexual activity overlapped to a great extent, possibly even greater than in prior times. Sexual intercourse, for the majority of women at least, was restricted to marriage (or to the men they were engaged to); consequently, few children were born outside marriage. Cohabitation was rare except among the poor. Marriage was more nearly universal than at any other time in the twentieth century. The probability that a marriage would end in divorce, although substantially higher than in the nineteenth century, was much less than it is today. To be respectable, it was necessary to be married before living with a partner or having a child; to stay respectable, it was necessary to avoid divorce if at all possible.

Today, even though nearly 90 percent of whites and about two-thirds of African Americans eventually marry, the power of marriage to regulate people's personal lives is much weaker. Cohabitation before marriage has become common and acceptable to most people. Although childbearing outside marriage is still frowned upon by many, it is tolerated by most. Divorce is considered to be unfortunate but acceptable if a partner wishes to end a marriage. Lifelong singlehood, although still uncommon, is also acceptable. In general, there is a greater acceptance of nonmarried adults.

There are several reasons for the lesser role of marriage and the greater tolerance of those who are not married. Marriage is less economically necessary than when most people needed to pool their labor and earnings with a spouse in order to subsist. Moreover, the movement of married women into the paid workforce—a major trend of the past half-century—has lessened women's economic dependence on men. Even though women's wages remain, on average, lower than men's, it is less difficult now for a woman to support herself and her children. Also, the job prospects for young men without college educations have worsened as jobs are transferred overseas or lost to automation, discouraging young adults from marrying.

But in addition, the decline of marriage and greater tolerance for alternative lifestyles reflect the rise of a more individualized view of family and personal life. By **individualism,** I mean a style of life in which individuals pursue their own interests and place great importance on developing a personally rewarding life. Individualism in American life is of two types (Bellah, Madsen, Sullivan, Swidler, & Tipton, 1985). The older, more-established type is **utilitarian individualism:** a style of life that emphasizes self-reliance and personal achievement, especially in one's work life. Benjamin Franklin was the quintessential utilitarian individualist. In his *Poor Richard's Almanack* he advised that "early to bed and early to rise, makes a man healthy, wealthy, and wise" and that "God helps them that help themselves." Today, this is the style of the person determined to succeed on his or her own or to get to the top of the corporate ladder. It is also the style of a single mother who works two jobs to pay for her children's college tuition. The second type, newer

individualism a style of life in which individuals pursue their own interests and place great importance on developing a personally rewarding life

utilitarian individualism a style of life that emphasizes self-reliance and personal achievement, especially in one's work life

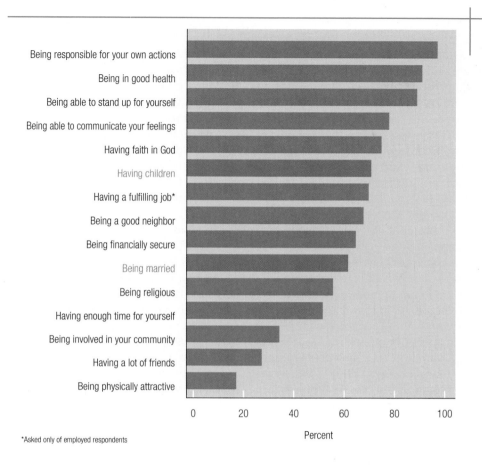

Being responsible for your own actions
Being in good health
Being able to stand up for yourself
Being able to communicate your feelings
Having faith in God
Having children
Having a fulfilling job*
Being a good neighbor
Being financially secure
Being married
Being religious
Having enough time for yourself
Being involved in your community
Having a lot of friends
Being physically attractive

0   20   40   60   80   100

Percent

*Asked only of employed respondents

FIGURE 1.1
Percentage of adults replying "very important" when asked how important each of these values is to them. (*Source:* Cherlin, 1999)

on a large scale, is **expressive individualism:** a style of life that emphasizes developing one's feelings and emotional satisfaction. This is the style of the person who wants to connect emotionally with a romantic partner, express his or her innermost thoughts to a trusted friend, and develop a good body at the health club.

The 2003 Supreme Court decision overruling a Texas law against gay sexual acts exemplifies American individualism and its tolerance of diverse lifestyles. Writing for the majority, Justice Anthony Kennedy stated:

> *Liberty presumes an autonomy of self that includes freedom of thought, belief, expression, and certain intimate conduct.* (*Lawrence v. Texas, 2003*)

An autonomy of self: Kennedy argues that liberty cannot be attained unless individuals can maintain an independent sense of who they are. *Freedom of thought, belief, expression, and certain intimate conduct:* Individuals must also be free to express their feelings through their intimate lives. This sentence seems to say that expressive individualism is an essential component of liberty.

Here is another example of American individualism: In the same *New York Times* telephone survey, adults were presented with a list of value statements and asked how important each one was to them. The list is displayed in Figure 1.1 in order of the percentage replying "very important." What is most interesting is the relative ranking of these value statements. The first four reflect either utilitarian individualism ("Being responsible for your actions,"

expressive individualism
a style of life that emphasizes developing one's feelings and emotional satisfaction

"Being able to stand up for yourself") or expressive individualism ("Being in good health," "Being able to communicate your feelings"). Note that "Having children" ranked sixth and "Being married" ranked tenth. In fact, the proportion of people who replied that "Being married" was very important was less than the proportion who replied that "Being a good neighbor" was very important. Overall, the rankings suggest that Americans value independent action and self-expression more highly than playing the roles of parent or spouse.

This is not to say that Americans don't value family life. In the same survey, people often reported that family and children were the most fulfilling and satisfying aspects of their lives. But in an individualistically oriented society, adults are expected to construct their family lives in ways that are consistent with their self-development. Today, most Americans still want to marry, but they have less of a need to do so than in the past. Marriage must compete with alternatives such as staying in school longer to obtain a higher degree, taking more time to develop a career, living with a partner without marrying, or having children outside of marriage. Some people may be ambivalent about marriage, at once drawn by its promise of intimacy and wary of its commitments and constraints. Family life therefore becomes much more diverse than it was a half-century ago. Even though most Americans choose to marry and a majority choose to have children within a marriage, they tend to respect the choices that other, freely acting individuals may make.

Compared to a half-century ago, what's most notable is that people have so many choices. They don't have to be married in the sense that adults at midcentury did. Predictably, people spend less of their lives married and fewer children are raised by two married parents. Moreover, people tend to marry at a later point in their lives than they did a half-century ago. Individuals used to get married prior to living together, having children, and establishing careers. Today, before marrying you may live with your future spouse or with someone else, you may spend several years establishing yourself in the labor market, and you may even have children. It is not a status to enter into lightly; rather, you wait until you're sure it's going to work. Marriage is a status you work toward, a personal achievement, a mark of distinction. In some ways, then, marriage's symbolic value has increased even as its practical significance has decreased. For instance, although you and your partner can have children without marrying and still be respectable, you may choose to marry to show everyone that you have achieved a successful personal life. For some people, then, marriage has become the ultimate family merit badge.

In fact, a key way in which family and personal life is different today than in the past is that not only *can* you make choices, but also you *must* make choices. You have to choose whether to live with someone, whether and when to have children, whether to marry, and sometimes whether to end a marriage. You must make these decisions yourself because your options are less constrained by parents and social norms. One's family life, according to two social theorists, becomes a permanent do-it-yourself project (Beck & Beck-Gernsheim, 2002). And so you get out your hammer and nails and construct a cohabiting relationship with someone, try it out, see how you like it, renovate or clean house, or maybe remodel with someone else. You construct it and reconstruct it; every person is his or her own architect. This is a very individualistic approach to marriage and family life because it centers on your personal evaluation of how much satisfaction you are getting, on your sense of whether you are growing and developing as a person, and on whether your partnership is meeting your emotional needs. It has led to the growth of what I will call later in this book the "individualistic marriage": a union based on individual rewards rather than on the approval of family, friends, and community. These are different criteria for judging whether your family life is a success from the criteria your grandparents' generation used. What this transformation means for the personal life of adults today, as well as for the lives of the children and elderly they care for, is the fundamental question that underlies this book. It is a vital concern because so much depends on it: the well-being of the next generation, the health and comfort of the growing older population, and the emotional rewards we so highly value.

Quick Review

- Families have become much more diverse over the past half-century.
- Some observers are concerned about the increasing proportion of children who are not being raised by two married, biological parents.
- Others argue that the alternative family forms are just as good as lifelong marriage.
- Americans tend to take individualistic perspectives on adult life.
- Utilitarian individualism emphasizes self-reliance and personal achievement.
- Expressive individualism emphasizes one's feelings and emotional satisfaction.
- People must choose the kind of family life they will have.

■ What Is a Family?

The growing diversity of families and the widespread ambivalence about them raise the question of how to define a family. At one extreme, some observers claim that families are so diverse that the concept may not even be useful anymore. At the other extreme are those who press politicians to use the singular form "family" (instead of the plural "families") to signify that there is only one proper kind of family—the married couple living with their biological children.

The definition of the family is also important economically. Rules specifying who is a "family member" determine billions of dollars of government and corporate benefits. For example, I am eligible for health insurance coverage through my employer for my "family," which is defined as a spouse and children under 18. If I were unmarried but living with a woman who was the mother of my children, I could insure the children but not their mother. If I had been living for years with a man whom I considered my lifelong partner, I probably could not insure him. Moreover, how one defines a family plays an important role in the debate over whether the family has declined.

I would argue that there is no single definition of a family that is adequate for all purposes. Rather, how you define a family depends on what questions you want to answer. Two key questions are

1. How well are family members taking care of children, the chronically ill, and the frail elderly?
2. How well are families providing the emotional satisfaction people value so highly—intimacy, love, personal fulfillment?

These questions address, respectively, the public responsibilities and the private pleasures the family is called upon to meet. For each of these questions, I submit, one of two definitions of the family will be helpful; I will call them the public family and the private family. These definitions provide two useful ways of looking at the same reality—and often the very same group of adults and children. Some observers may impose their own theological definitions of what constitutes a family from religious works such as the Bible or the Koran. But social science cannot determine the moral essence of the family, nor need it do so.

THE PUBLIC FAMILY

In examining the concept of the public family, it's useful to borrow a few terms from the field of economics. Economists who specialize in public welfare have introduced the notion of **externalities,** of which there are two types. First, **negative externalities** occur when an individual or a business produces something that is beneficial to itself but imposes costs on other individuals or businesses. For example, factories that release sulfur dioxide through smokestacks impose a cost on everyone else by polluting the air. The factory gains by producing goods without having to install expensive smokestack scrubbers, but everyone else loses. Second, **positive externalities** occur when an individual or business produces something that benefits others but for which the producers are not fully compensated. For example, a corporation may start an expensive job-training program in order to obtain qualified workers; but some of the workers may take jobs with rival firms after completing the training. The other firms obtain skilled workers without paying the cost of their training.

Some positive externalities involve the production of what are called **public goods.** These goods have a peculiar property: It is almost impossible to stop people who don't produce them from enjoying them. As a result, public goods are often produced in smaller quantities than is socially desirable. Suppose a town raises taxes to build a water filtration plant that cleans a polluted river. It cannot stop residents of other towns downstream from enjoying the cleaner water, yet these fortunate residents have paid nothing for the cleanup. In a situation like this, it is clearly in each town's interest to have some other town farther up the river produce the public good—the treatment plant. Yet if no town builds the plant, no one will enjoy cleaner water. One solution to this dilemma is for the county or state government to raise taxes in all the towns and then build the plant. Another is for the towns to reach an agreement whereby one will build the plant but all will contribute to the costs. Either solution compensates the producer of the public good for the benefits that others obtain.

Although it may seem like a long leap from factories to families, the concepts of externalities and public goods still apply. Families do produce valuable public goods—most notably, children (England & Folbre, 1999). For example, when I retire, I hope to receive a Social Security check from the government each month, just as all retired people do today. The funds for those checks will come from payroll taxes paid by workers. In a few years the many men and women born during the post–World War II baby boom will begin to reach retirement age; I hope to be one of them. Currently, there

externalities benefits or costs that accrue to others when an individual or business produces something

negative externalities the costs imposed on other individuals or businesses when an individual or business produces something of value to itself

positive externalities benefits received by others when an individual or business produces something, but for which the producer is not fully compensated

public goods things that may be enjoyed by people who do not themselves produce them

U.S. families are more diverse today than in earlier times because of the great changes that have occurred since the middle of the twentieth century. Single-parent families, extended families, and complex families formed by remarriages are among the kinds of families with which the two-parent, first-marriage family must share its spotlight.

are about five persons of working age for each retired person; but by 2030 there may be only three persons of working age for every retired person.[2] This means that the burden of supporting the elderly will increase greatly. It's in my interest, then, for families to have and rear children today who will pay taxes when they grow up.

More generally, it's in society's interest that today's children become good citizens with traits such as obeying the law, showing concern about others,

---

[2] Considering 20 to 64 as working age and 65 or older as retirement age. See U.S. Bureau of the Census (2011b), Table 8.

and being informed voters. It's also in society's interest that they be productive workers who are willing and able to fill the needs of the economy. To be sure, critics charge that families often raise children in ways that reproduce existing inequalities between women and men (see Chapter 3) or between the working class and middle class (see Chapter 4). Nevertheless, what they do is of great public value. They are greenhouses growing the workers and citizens of tomorrow.

But children are costly to raise, and I will receive the same Social Security check whether or not the workers were raised by me. Therefore, it's in my economic interest to remain childless and to have every other family except mine raise children. Yet if everyone followed this strategy there would be no next generation. This dilemma is sometimes known as the **free-rider problem:** the tendency for people to obtain public goods by letting others do the work of producing them—metaphorically, the temptation to ride free on the backs of others. Luckily, people have children for reasons other than economic self-interest. At the moment, however, they are barely having enough to replace the current generation of parents. Everyone benefits from the child rearing that parents do.[3]

In addition, families provide other services that have the character of public goods. As will be noted in Chapter 10, adult children still provide the bulk of the care for the frail elderly. If I am old and ill, I will benefit if I have adult children who will care for me. But others will also benefit from the care that my family provides. Without them, I would need more assistance from the government-funded medical insurance programs for the elderly (Medicare) and for the poor (Medicaid). Consequently, the care my family provides will keep government spending, and hence taxes, lower for everyone. The same logic applies to care that family members provide for the chronically ill.

The first definition, then, concerns the view of the family you take when you are concerned about the family's contribution to the public welfare—the useful services family members provide by taking care of one another. It is a definition of what I will call the **public family:** *one adult, or two adults who are related by marriage, partnership, or shared parenthood, who is/are taking care of dependents, and the dependents themselves.* Dependents are defined as children, the frail elderly, and the chronically ill. The family members usually reside in the same household, but that is not essential. For example, an elderly woman may live in her own apartment but still receive daily assistance from her daughter or son. Nor is it essential that the family members be married or of the opposite sex. The important fact is that they are taking care of dependents and, in doing so, producing public goods. This definition would include, of course, a married couple and their children or their elderly parents. But it would also include a divorced (or never-married) mother and her children, a cohabiting couple with children, a lesbian couple

free-rider problem the tendency for people to obtain public goods by letting others do the work of producing them—metaphorically, the temptation to ride free on the backs of others

public family one adult, or two adults who are related by marriage, partnership, or shared parenthood, who is/are taking care of dependents, and the dependents themselves

[3] This example holds only, however, for developed countries such as the United States, where the birthrate is at or below the level needed to replace the population. In developing countries with very high birthrates, children can impose negative externalities. Given the high death rates in the poorest developing countries, it is in the interest of a peasant farmer to have many children to ensure that at least one or two will still be alive when the farmer is too old to work. But if every family follows that logic, the land may become overpopulated and the country's development may slow. See Cain (1983).

who are jointly raising a child who was born to one of them, or a gay man caring for a partner with AIDS. Note also who would be excluded by this definition: a childless married couple with no dependent or elderly relatives, or opposite-sex or same-sex cohabitors without children, the elderly, or ill dependents.

The production of public goods invites public scrutiny, and public families are easily identifiable to outsiders by the presence of dependents. Because society has an interest in how well families manage the care of dependents, the law allows for some regulation of these families—despite strong sentiment in the United States against intervening in family matters. For example, we require families to send their children to school until age 16. And state social welfare agencies have the power to remove children from homes judged to be harmful. More recently, several states have required medical personnel to report suspected cases of physical abuse of children. The public family, then, is about caretaking and dependency. It points us toward the kinds of kinship ties that are important for nurturing the young and caring for the elderly and the ill. It is a useful perspective for answering questions such as: How adequately will our society raise the next generation? How will we care for the growing number of elderly persons?

THE PRIVATE FAMILY

At the same time, the family is much more than a public service institution. It also provides individuals with intimacy, emotional support, and love. Indeed, most people today think of the family and experience it in these private terms. Although some of the intimacy is expressed sexually, the family is also where we get hugs as children and back rubs as adults. It is where children form first attachments, teenagers take steps toward autonomy, and adults share their inner selves with someone else. The public family is not the most useful perspective in this regard because the central question is not how we will care for dependents or reproduce the workforce but, rather, how we will obtain the intimacy and emotional support we desire.

An appropriate definition of the private family must, therefore, encompass intimate relationships whether or not they include dependents. Yet if we are to maintain our focus on families, the definition still must encompass some rules for defining what kinds of intimate relationships constitute a family. It is difficult to know where to draw the line between private families and other kinds of intimate relationships, such as two people who live in separate apartments but consider themselves to be a couple. Where exactly is the boundary between family life and less intensive forms of intimacy? Rapid change has undermined the consensus among Americans about the norms of family life—the social rules about what constitutes a family and how people should behave when they are in one. Let me offer, then, a definition of the **private family** not as an authoritative statement but rather as a starting point for analyzing this uncertainty: *two or more individuals who maintain an intimate relationship that they expect will last indefinitely—or, in the case of a parent and child, until the child reaches adulthood—and who usually live in the same household and pool their incomes and household labor.* This definition allows for children to be part of the private family, although the character of the intimacy between parents and children is clearly different from

private family two or more individuals who maintain an intimate relationship that they expect will last indefinitely—or, in the case of a parent and child, until the child reaches adulthood—and who usually live in the same household and pool their incomes and household labor

that between adult partners. It does not require that the individuals be of opposite sexes. The relationship must be one in which the commitment is long term, in which the expectation is that the adult partners will stay together indefinitely. I do not require that they expect to stay together for life because it's not clear how many married couples even expect as much, given that nearly half of all marriages now end in divorce. The definition also includes the notion that the partnership usually is household-based and economic as well as intimate—shared residence, common budgets. This reflects my sense that intimate relationships in families are not merely erotic and emotionally supportive but also involve sharing the day-to-day details of managing one's life. Nevertheless, I have added the qualifier *"usually* live in the same household" to allow for couples who live apart but in other ways meet the criteria of the private family.

In fact, families are becoming so diverse and complex that it is hard to determine their boundaries from either the public or private perspectives. Suppose that after a divorce a father makes regular child support payments to his ex-wife and sees his children often. You might argue that he is still sharing parenthood and therefore part of the family. If he doesn't make regular payments, on the other hand, and sees his children sporadically, you might not consider him to be part of the family any longer. When families are very complex, even the people who are involved may disagree about who's in them. Take the example of a large national survey that asked the mothers of teenage children who else was living in their household. Several hundred mothers said that they were living with a man who was not the father of the teenager. In other words, according to the mothers' reports, these were what might be called "cohabiting stepfamilies" that were similar to stepfamilies except that the stepfather and mother were not married. The survey also asked the teenage children in these households who besides their mothers was living with them. Strikingly, nearly half of them did not mention the man at all, as if their mothers were single parents (Brown & Manning, 2009). Perhaps in some of those households the men were present only half the week and the children considered them to be visitors; or perhaps the children rejected them as father figures. The correct answer, then, to the question of who is in the family is sometimes unclear.

boundary ambiguity a state in which family members are uncertain about who is in or out of the family

This is an example of **boundary ambiguity,** a state in which family members are uncertain about who is in or out of the family (Carroll, Olson, & Buckmiller, 2007). It is more common now than it was a half-century ago, when rates of divorce, remarriage, and childbearing outside of marriage were substantially lower.

To be sure, individuals also receive emotional support and material assistance from kin with whom they are not in an intimate relationship. The word "family" is sometimes used in the larger sense of relationships with sisters, uncles, grandmothers, and so forth. These broader kinship ties are still an important part of the setting in which people embed their intimate relations to spouses, partners, and children. The usual definition of "kin" is the people who are related to you by descent (through your mother's or father's line) or marriage. Yet the concept of kinship is also becoming broader and harder to define. In settings as varied as sharing networks among low-income African Americans, friend-based support networks among lesbians and gay men, and middle-class networks of adults who are related only through the ties of broken marriages and remarriages, people are expanding the definition of kinship, creating kin, as it were, out of relationships that don't fit the old mold. In fact, throughout the book I will distinguish between what I will call **created kinship**—kinship ties that people have to construct actively—and **assigned kinship**—kinship ties that people more or less automatically acquire when they are born or when they marry.

Created kinship is particularly valuable to people who can't find adequate support among blood-based or first-marriage-based kin. Lesbians and gay men, for example, are sometimes rejected by their parents, although less often than in the past. Poor African American mothers who cannot find suitable spouses exchange help not only with their mothers and grandmothers but also with close friends, creating kinship-like relationships. A divorced mother whose ex-husband provides little support can receive assistance from a live-in partner or second husband.

Some observers look at all of these new forms of intimate relationships and conclude that the concept of family is outmoded. The strongest criticism is coming from scholars in Europe, where rates of marriage are lower than in the United States and where, in many countries, long-term cohabiting relationships are more common (Roseneil & Budgeon, 2004). Family is a "zombie category," said social theorist Ulrich Beck (Beck & Beck-Gernsheim, 2002), a dead body walking around that we mistakenly think is still alive. The critics note the boundary ambiguities of many families, and the ways in which people are constructing new forms of kinship. They point to phenomena such as couples in intimate, committed relationships who are living in separate households because they prefer to (one's a neatnik, the other a slob) or have to (each has a good job in a different city) (Levin, 2004). They note the family networks gays and lesbians construct from friends, former lovers, and relatives. Some conclude that we should give up on the term "family" and use a broader, more inclusive descriptor, such as "personal community" (Pahl & Spencer, 2004). But I think that in an American context, where marriage remains highly valued by heterosexuals and gays and lesbians alike, we are not at the point where we should give up on the concept of family. Its boundaries are fuzzy, it takes diverse forms, it is stressed and strained by social change, but for the current day it is, I suggest, still worth studying.

created kinship kinship ties that people have to construct actively

assigned kinship kinship ties that people more or less automatically acquire when they are born or when they marry

TWO VIEWS, SAME FAMILY

That there are two views—public and private—of the same reality may explain the paradox that Americans seem concerned about everyone else's families but not their own. When people are asked about whether "the American family is in trouble" or whether "family ties in the United States are breaking down," they tend to think in terms of the public family. That is to say, when Americans view other families, they see their public faces: how their children are behaving, how they are providing for their oldest members, and how they are contributing to the civility of neighborhoods and communities. They worry about the effects of divorce, about the difficulties that low-income single parents can have in raising children, about teenage childbearing, and about high school dropouts—the litany of problems we learn about in the media and see around us.

Table 1.1	Two Ways of Looking at the American Family	
	THE PUBLIC FAMILY	**THE PRIVATE FAMILY**
Examples	Married couple, cohabiting couple, or single parent with children Single person caring for ailing parent Gay person caring for partner with AIDS	Married or cohabiting couples without children Gay or lesbian couples without children
Main Functions	Raising the next generation Caring for the elderly Caring for the ill and disabled	Providing love and intimacy Providing emotional support
Key Challenge	Free-rider problem	Boundary problem

Lately they worry about the effects of the severe economic downturn that began in 2008. (See *Families and the Great Recession: Introduction.*) But when they are asked "What about in your own family? Are family ties breaking down, or not?" they think in terms of the love and companionship they get. That is, they see the family's private face. And they tend to be satisfied, by and large, with the emotional rewards they are obtaining at the moment. So they respond that, no, their families are fine. Cue people one way and they respond in terms of the public family, but cue them the other way and they respond in terms of the private family. The two perspectives, then, can be thought of as complementary and sometimes overlapping ways of looking at the same reality: the institution of the family.

Table 1.1 reviews the basic distinction between these two perspectives. The first row shows examples of families as seen through the public and private family perspectives. The second row shows the main functions of the family in the public and private domains. In raising the next generation of children—the workers, citizens, and parents of the future—parents and other caregivers are best viewed as carrying out the functions of the public family. The same can be said for caregivers of the frail elderly or for disabled individuals. In contrast, when providing love, intimacy, and emotional support, family members are carrying out the functions of the private family. The third row shows the key challenges families face in these two guises. It's in people's narrow self-interests to let others do the hard work of raising children or caring for the elderly—activities that benefit society as a whole. (And much of this care is provided by women outside of the paid workforce. See Chapter 8.) But if too many people try to ride free, our society may not invest enough time and effort in producing the next generation or in caring for the elderly. In fact, some social critics believe American society has already reached this point. As for the private family, its key challenge is maintaining its dominant position as the setting where people experience emotional gratification. With the decline of marriage, there are many kinds of relationships that provide intimacy, love, and sex. Will the private family continue to cohere as a social institution, or will its boundaries collapse into a sea of diverse, limited personal relationships?

In sum, to examine the contributions of families to the public welfare is to look at relationships through the lens of the public family. To examine the family's provisions of intimacy, love, and fulfillment is to look through the lens of the private family. Sometimes, both lenses apply to the same situation, as when a parent derives great emotional satisfaction from raising a child. Both perspectives are embedded in each of the chapters that follow. Which is better? Neither. They are two takes on the same reality. Many textbooks emphasize the private family by focusing primarily on interpersonal relationships, cohabitation, and marriage. In doing so, they pay less attention to the socially valuable work that families do. Although this book, too, will have much to say about the private family, it will also emphasize the public family. Each subsequent chapter will include a short essay on families and public policy; and the concluding chapter, "The Family, the State, and Social Policy," is directed primarily toward public issues.

Quick Review

- The primary family unit in the United States and most other Western nations is the small, household-based unit of parents and children.
- No single definition of the family is adequate for all purposes.
- This book takes two perspectives and proposes two definitions:
  - The "public family," which focuses on the care that family members provide for dependents.
  - The "private family," which focuses on the love and emotional satisfaction family members provide for each other.
- Both definitions can be applied to the same family unit because most families have both a public and a private dimension.

How Do Family Sociologists Know What They Know?

Sociologists collect and analyze data consisting of observations of real families and the people in them. For the most part, they strive to analyze their data using objective, scientific methods. **Objectivity** means the ability to draw conclusions about a social situation that are unaffected by one's own beliefs. But it is much more difficult for a sociologist to be objective than it is for a natural or physical scientist. Sociologists not only study families, but they also live in them. They often have strong moral and political views of their own (indeed, strong views about social issues are what lead many people to become sociologists), and it is difficult to prevent those views from influencing one's research. In fact, there are some sociologists who argue that objectivity is so difficult to achieve that sociologists shouldn't try. Rather, they argue, sociologists should acknowledge their values and predispositions so that others can better interpret their work (see *How Do Sociologists Know What They Know?: Feminist Research Methods*, in Chapter 3).

But most sociologists, although aware that their views can influence the way they interpret their data, model their research on the scientific method. For a detailed examination of the scientific method in sociology, consult any

objectivity the ability to draw conclusions about a social situation that are unaffected by one's own beliefs

Families and the Great Recession | Introduction

On October 24, 1929, a day known ever since as Black Thursday, prices plunged on the New York Stock Exchange, ending the economic boom of the Roaring Twenties. As prices continued to drop over the following weeks and months, the nation slid into the Great Depression, an economic slump that was longer and far more severe than anything the country had ever experienced. The stock market did not hit bottom until 1932, and the economy did not fully recover until the late 1930s. During the depths of the Great Depression, businesses went bankrupt, banks failed, and one-fourth of the work force was unemployed. Since then, the nation has experienced several much milder downturns that are known as recessions.

But in September of 2008, the nation came perilously close to another depression. Risky investments in the housing market had driven stock prices to new highs. Then a major investment firm, Lehman Brothers, failed after taking large losses on its mortgage-related investments. The stock market plummeted. It is possible that the nation would have experienced another depression had the federal government not provided funds to shore up several large investment firms, banks, and lenders whose failures would have been catastrophic. Yet, although the worst was averted, the nation subsequently experienced the deepest and longest economic downturn since the Great Depression. Its effects are still being felt, and many are calling it the Great Recession.

A committee of economists at the National Bureau of Economic Research determined that the recession officially ended in June of 2009 because that was when the economy bottomed out and began to expand. Yet the expansion has been so feeble that the recession can be said to have continued through 2012 for everyone in the country except the National Bureau of Economic Research. Even as of mid 2012, the unemployment rate was about eight percent.

Economic downturns don't just affect banks and businesses. They also affect individuals and families. The Great Recession has cost millions of Americans their jobs and, because they have been unable to make their mortgage payments, their homes. Parents have been unable to provide for their children. People who have lost their homes or who cannot afford to rent apartments have moved in with relatives. Grandparents have been pressed into service to help care for their grandchildren. Young adults, their faith in the future diminished, have postponed marrying or having children.

In fact, the Great Recession is causing the largest economic disruption of family life that any generation has experienced since the 1930s. If we wish to understand what's happening to families today, we need to examine the effects of this still-ongoing event. Consequently, in several subsequent chapters, boxed essays will address the effects of the Great Recession.

- In Chapter 2: "Lessons from the Great Depression," a historical look at what we can learn from studies of family stress during the Depression.
- In Chapter 4: "Job Losses and Financial Strain," how the downturn affected families economically.
- In Chapter 7: "Plans on Hold," how marriage and childbearing were being postponed.
- In Chapter 8: "What Long-Term Unemployment Does to Marriage," how long-lasting spells of unemployment can affect marriages.
- In Chapter 10: "Still, or Once Again, Living at Home," why more adult children are living with older parents.
- In Chapter 14: "The Safety Net," how has the safety net of government assistance programs helped families hit by the recession?

scientific method a systematic, organized series of steps that ensures maximum objectivity and consistency in researching a problem

hypothesis a speculative statement about the relationship between two or more variables

good introductory sociology textbook. For example, Schaefer (2007, p. 29) defines the **scientific method** as "a systematic, organized series of steps that ensures maximum objectivity and consistency in researching a problem." The essence of the scientific method is to formulate a hypothesis that can be tested by collecting and analyzing data. (A **hypothesis,** Schaefer writes, is "a speculative statement about the relationship between two or more variables" [p. 45].) It's easy to come up with a hypothesis (God is a woman), but the trick is to find one that can be shown to be true or false by examining data. Sociologists therefore tend to formulate very specific hypotheses about family life that can be confirmed or disconfirmed by observation. For example, sociologists have hypothesized that having a first child as a teenager lowers,

An interviewer goes door-to-door during the 2010 Census. Social scientists frequently use survey research to study families.

on average, the amount of education a woman attains; and statistical data are consistent with this claim.

Even so, there are inherent limitations in how well social scientists can use the scientific method. The best way to confirm or disconfirm a relationship between two factors is to conduct an experiment in which all other factors are held constant. Scientists do this by randomly assigning subjects to one of two groups: an experimental group and a control group. For example, doctors will study whether a new drug speeds recovery from an illness by assembling a group of volunteers, all of whom have the illness, and then randomly giving half of them (the experimental group) the new drug. By randomizing, the doctors hope that all other confounding factors (such as past medical history) will be equalized between the two groups. Then they compare the average recovery times of the experimental group and the control group (those who did not receive the drug).

But it is rarely possible for sociologists to conduct randomized experiments on families. Without randomization, there is always the possibility that another, unobserved factor, lurking just beneath the surface, is causing the relationship we see. Consider again teenage childbearing. Women who have a first child as a teenager tend to come from families that have less education and less money, on average, than do other women. So the reason that teenage mothers attain less education may reflect their disadvantaged family backgrounds rather than having a child; in other words, they might have had less education even if they hadn't had children as teenagers. To truly settle this issue, a truth-seeking but cold-blooded sociologist would want to obtain a list of all families with teenage girls in the United States and then to assign *at random* some of the girls to have children and others to remain childless until their twenties. Because of the random assignment, teenage childbearing would be about as likely to occur in middle-class families as in poor families. In this way, the social scientist could eliminate family background as a cause of any differences that emerge between teenage mothers and nonmothers.

For very good ethical and legal reasons, of course, sociologists simply cannot conduct this type of study. Without random assignment, we can't be sure that having a child as a teenager *causes* a woman to have less education. Still, the lack of randomized experiments does not mean that sociologists should abandon the scientific method. Astronomers, after all, can't do experiments either. But this limitation makes the task of deciding whether a sociological study confirms or disconfirms a hypothesis more difficult.

If not from experiments, where does the data that family sociologists use come from? Generally, from one of two research methods. The first is the **survey,** a study in which individuals or households are randomly selected from a larger population and asked a fixed set of questions. Sociologists prepare a questionnaire and give it to a professional survey research organization. The organization then selects a sample of households randomly from an area (a city, a state, or the entire nation) and sends interviewers to ask the questions of one or more family members in the households. The responses are coded numerically (e.g., a "yes" answer is coded 1 and a "no" is coded 0), and the coded responses for all individuals are made available to the sociologists as a computer file.

The random selection of households is done to ensure that the people who are asked the questions are representative of the population in the area. This kind of random selection of households shouldn't be confused with conducting a randomized experiment. A random-sample survey is not an experiment because the households that are selected are *not* divided into an experimental group and a control group. Nevertheless, data from surveys provides sociologists with the opportunity to examine associations among characteristics of a large number of individuals and families. (See *How Do Sociologists Know What They Know?:* The National Surveys, in this chapter.)

The advantage of the survey method (assuming that the households are randomly selected) is that its results are representative not only of the sample that was interviewed but also of the larger population in the area. The main disadvantage is the limited amount of information that can be gathered on each person or family. Most people won't participate in an interview that takes more than an hour or two. Moreover, the same set of questions is asked of everyone, with little opportunity to tailor the interview to each participant. Another disadvantage is that it's difficult to determine whether the people in the sample are responding honestly, especially if the questions touch upon sensitive issues. (See *How Do Sociologists Know What They Know?:* Asking about Sensitive Behavior, in Chapter 6.)

The second widely used research method is the **observational study,** also known as *field research,* in which the researcher spends time directly observing each participant in the study—often much more time than an interviewer from a survey organization spends. The researcher may even join the group she or he is studying for a period of time. The individuals and families to be studied are not usually selected randomly; rather, the researcher tries to find families that have a particular set of characteristics

survey a study in which individuals from a geographic area are selected, usually at random, and asked a fixed set of questions

observational study (also known as field research) a study in which the researcher spends time directly observing each participant he or she is interested in. For example, in a classic observational study of a low-income area of Boston, Herbert Gans (1962) moved into an Italian neighborhood for eight months and got to know many families well. He was able to argue that the stereotype of slum families as "disorganized" was not true. The strength of the observational method is that it can provide a much more detailed and nuanced picture of the individuals and families being studied than can the survey method. Sociologist-observers can view the full complexity of family behavior and can learn more about it.

The disadvantage of observational studies is that it is hard to know how representative the families being studied are of similar families. Because it takes a great deal of time to study a family in depth, observational studies typically are carried out with far fewer families than are surveys. Moreover, sociologists who do observational studies usually can't choose their families randomly by knocking on doors or calling on the telephone because they must win a family's cooperation and trust before the family will agree to be studied in such detail. So although observational studies may yield a great deal of information about a small number of families, we may be unsure that we can generalize this knowledge to other similar families that weren't in the observational study.

Surveys and observational studies, then, have complementary strengths and limitations. If the knowledge from sociological studies could be stored in a lake, a survey-based lake would be wide (because of the large number of people reached) but shallow (because of the limited time spent with each family), whereas an observationally based lake would be narrow but deep. Ideally, it would be best to employ both methods to study a problem, and some research projects attempt to do so. But to choose a large number of families randomly and then to send in sociologists to observe each family intensively over weeks and months is too expensive to be feasible. Moreover, the set of skills necessary to do survey research versus observational research is so distinct that sociologists tend to specialize in one or the other.

Sociologists sometimes use other research methods as well. For some topics, it is useful to examine historical sources. Chapter 7 describes a study in which magazine articles from 1900 to 1979 were used to study changing conceptions of marriage. Occasionally, it is even possible to do an experiment. In the 1990s, the Department of Housing and Urban Development conducted an experiment in which some low-income families living in public housing in five cities were randomly selected to receive a voucher that they could use to subsidize their rent if they moved to nonpoor neighborhoods. These "treatment-group" families were compared to "control-group" families that received less assistance. Four to seven years later, families that had received the vouchers were living in safer neighborhoods and were less poor; in addition, the daughters in these families had better mental health than daughters in the control-group families. Sons in the treatment-group families, however, unexpectedly had poorer health and engaged in more risky behavior than sons in the control-group families (Kling, Liebman, & Katz, 2007).

These are the major methods that sociologists use to study families. In several of the chapters of this book, we will examine the methodology of key studies so that you may better understand how family sociologists develop their research findings.

Table 1.2   Comparing Survey Studies and Observational Studies

WHO IS STUDIED	HOW THEY ARE STUDIED	STRENGTHS	LIMITATIONS
SURVEY STUDY			
Large, random sample of individuals or familes	An interviewer asks questions from a predesigned questionnaire and records the answers	Results can be generalized to the population of interest	Only limited knowledge can be obtained; hard to judge honesty of responses
OBSERVATIONAL STUDY			
Small, purposefully chosen sample of individuals or families	A researcher observes them in depth over a long period of time, sometimes participating in their daily activities	Detailed knowledge is obtained	Findings may not be representative of other, similar individuals or families

Quick Review

- Survey research and observational research are the two methods most commonly used by sociologists.
- The two methods have complementary strengths and limitations.
- Table 1.2 summarizes the differences between the two methods.

Sociological Theory and Families

The methods sociologists use and the questions they ask are influenced by sociological theory. Let me present a brief introduction to four perspectives that I think are most actively used by family researchers today. I will draw on these perspectives often in this book.

FOUR WIDELY USED PERSPECTIVES

exchange theory
a sociological theory that views people as rational beings who decide whether to exchange goods or services by considering the benefits they will receive, the costs they will incur, and the benefits they might receive if they were to choose an alternative course of action

The Exchange Perspective   The sociological approach known as **exchange theory** is similar to the model of human behavior that economists use. People are viewed as rational beings who decide whether to exchange goods or services by considering the benefits they will receive, the costs they will incur, and the benefits they might receive if they chose an alternative course of action. In the rational choice-based theory of the family that won Gary Becker the 1992 Nobel Prize in economics, women often choose rationally to exchange the performance of household and child care services in return for receiving the benefits of a man's income. If men are more "efficient" at market production—meaning they can earn higher wages—and women are more "efficient" at home production—meaning they are better at raising small children—then both partners gain from this exchange, argues

Becker (1991). Thus, Becker's model was used to explain the prevalence in the mid-twentieth century of the **breadwinner-homemaker family**—a married couple with children in which the father worked for pay and the mother did not. His theory implied that the division of labor in this type of family is best for both husband and wife.

But in the hands of others, exchange theory can lead to very different conclusions. Many sociologists maintain that exchanges take on a different character if the two actors come to the exchange with unequal resources. Richard Emerson and his colleagues developed a version of exchange theory that is useful in studying families (Cook, O'Brien, & Kollock, 1990; Emerson, 1972). According to Emerson, if person A values goods or services person B has to offer, and if person A has few alternative sources of obtaining these goods or services, then person A is said to be dependent on person B. The degree of dependency is greater the more highly A values these goods or services and the fewer alternative sources A has. For example, if a husband (person B in this case), by virtue of his greater earning power, can offer to purchase many goods and services, and if his wife (person A) values these goods and services but can't purchase them on her own because she can't earn as much, then she is said to be dependent on her husband. Her dependency is greater if she has fewer alternative sources of income, perhaps because she took time away from paid work to have children and now finds it hard to find a good job. Moreover, according to Emerson, the more A is dependent on B, the greater is B's power over A. When one person is more powerful than another, he or she may be able to shape the exchange so that he or she receives greater benefits and incurs fewer costs than does the other person. Husbands, many writers have suggested, are in a stronger bargaining position when they are the sole earners in their families because their wives have fewer alternative sources of income. According to exchange theory, when wives earn money on their own, their dependence decreases and therefore their husbands' power over them decreases. They can drive a better bargain for who does the housework.

The Symbolic Interaction Perspective   Exchange theorists tend to see the social world as a concrete reality with easily perceived costs and benefits and they view individuals as rational, calculating beings, as if we each had a personal computer in our head, taking in data, calculating costs and benefits, and deciding how to act. The adherents of **symbolic interaction theory,** however, see the social world as a much more fragile and unstable place, in which individuals are continually creating and sustaining meanings, often without much conscious thought to costs and benefits (Stryker & Vryan, 2003). The major figure in symbolic interaction theory was philosopher George Herbert Mead, who taught at the University of Chicago early in the twentieth century. His foremost interpreter in sociology was Herbert Blumer (1962). According to these theorists, people do not react to the world like computers respond to mouse clicks, but rather they *interpret* what others do based on shared understandings they may take for granted. We interpret symbols—gestures, words, appearances—whose meanings we have come to understand. This interpretation occurs in situations in which we interact with someone. It is this process of the interpretation of symbols during social interaction that the symbolic interactionists study.

breadwinner-homemaker family a married couple with children in which the father worked for pay and the mother did not

symbolic interaction theory a sociological theory that focuses on people's interpretations of symbolic behavior

How Do Sociologists Know What They Know?

The National Surveys

Sociologists who study the family in the United States draw many of their findings from a series of national surveys that have been conducted over the past few decades. These surveys interview randomly selected samples of the U.S. population. They are similar to the opinion-poll surveys you see in the newspapers (e.g., what percent of the public thinks the president is doing a good job?), but they differ in several important ways:

- *They are larger* The surveys in the newspapers typically interview 500 to 1,500 individuals. The social scientific surveys typically interview 5,000 to 10,000 individuals or more. Because of this larger size, the social scientific surveys can provide reliable information on subgroups of the population, such as couples who are living together outside of marriage, currently divorced individuals, and never-married adults.
- *They are carried out using in-person interviews* In contrast, most of the news-paper polls are conducted by randomly dialing telephone numbers and speaking to people over the telephone. In-person interviews can be longer and more detailed (because people tire of telephone conversations more quickly than in-person conversations) and can be more flexible (e.g., the interviewer can give the subject a self-administered questionnaire for her husband or partner to fill out). But in-person interviews are also much more expensive to carry out.
- *They are longitudinal* Whereas the typical newspaper poll is a one-time activity, social scientists prefer a **longitudinal survey,** meaning a survey in which interviews are conducted several times at regular intervals. This design allows social scientists to study social change. The surveys typically select families or individuals at random and then reinterview them annually or biennially about how their lives are changing.
- *They are intended to be public resources* Most newspaper polls are meant for **primary analysis,** meaning they are analyzed by the people who collected the information. The data from these polls are then forgotten. The social scientific studies are designed for **secondary analysis,** meaning analysis of the data by people other than the group that collected it. The questionnaires are intentionally broad so that the interviewers can collect a wide range of information that will be of interest to many researchers. The results are coded numerically into electronic files and made available to anyone who wants to analyze them.
- *They are conducted by academic research centers rather than by commercial polling firms* The academic centers, such as the National Opinion Research Center at the University of Chicago and the Survey Research Center at the University of Michigan, typically take extra steps in designing and carrying out a survey so that the results are of better quality (e.g., the data conforms better to the statistical theory underlying random

longitudinal survey a survey in which interviews are conducted several times at regular intervals

primary analysis analysis of survey data by the people who collected the information

secondary analysis analysis of survey data by people other than those who collected it

For instance, when women and men interact with each other, they vary the way they dress, the gestures they use, and the tone of voice they employ according to whether the situation is a friendly conversation or a potentially romantic encounter. Each person in the interaction picks up on the symbols used by the other in order to understand which type of situation is being experienced. Most of the time the symbols are so clear and so routine that we don't even think about what's happening. In fact, we rely on not having to think about what kind of social situation we are in—we don't have the mental energy to continually scrutinize the basic facts of our social encounters. Instead, we rely on taken-for-granted symbols and meanings.

But these symbols and meanings can reinforce inequalities between women and men in subtle ways. When a man holds a door open for a woman, both people may see this as merely a display of courtesy. Yet a woman is much less likely to hold a door open for a man. Does this mean that women are less courteous than men? Of course not. Rather, the symbol of a man holding a door open has an additional meaning: It reinforces the cultural message that men are physically stronger than women and should take care of them, like gallant medieval knights ushering their ladies through

sample surveys; a greater percentage of the selected subjects are reached and interviewed).

Because of the large sample size, longitudinal design, use of in-person rather than telephone interviews, and extra care in the fieldwork, the social scientific surveys are very expensive. Most are sponsored by U.S. government agencies such as the National Institutes of Health, the National Science Foundation, or the Bureau of Labor Statistics. The agencies support those large surveys to provide information on many research questions so that hundreds of researchers can analyze the data.

One such project is the Fragile Families and Child Wellbeing Study, which was designed to learn more about unmarried parents and their children. Interviews were conducted between 1998 and 2000 in urban hospitals around the country with nearly 5,000 mothers, about three-fourths of them unmarried, just after their child's

birth. The researchers also interviewed the fathers of the children when possible, and they have followed these so-called fragile families for nine years. They found that half of the unmarried mothers were living with the fathers of their children at the time of birth (McLanahan et al., 2003).

Another study is the Panel Study of Income Dynamics. In 1968, researchers at the University of Michigan interviewed 5,000 American households selected at random. They have reinterviewed the members of these households every year or two since then. When children grew up and left home, or adults divorced and moved out, the study followed them and interviewed them in their new households. The Panel Study of Income Dynamics greatly increased our knowledge of the economic fortunes of families over time. For example, the results indicate that few families are poor every year, but over the course of a decade many families, perhaps one-fourth, experience at least a year in which they are poor (Duncan, 1984).

Throughout the book, findings from these and other national surveys will be presented. Although not without limitations (see Chapter 6, *How Do Sociologists Know What They Know?:* Asking about Sensitive Behavior), they constitute a valuable resource to everyone interested in families, households, parents, and children. The "Families on the Internet" feature at the end of this chapter lists the World Wide Web addresses at which information about these surveys can be obtained.

Ask Yourself

1. Besides researchers, who else might be interested in the results of social scientific surveys? Can you think of any practical use for this information?
2. Why do you think researchers would want to see survey results for particular racial and ethnic groups or specific types of families?

www.mhhe.com/cherlin7e

the castle gates. In this way, the simple gesture of holding the door becomes a symbol of the cultural differences between men and women. And done again and again on a daily basis, it reinforces gender differences. There are many such interactions. For example, husbands who don't want to change their babies' diapers may make a display of fumbling at the changing table when called upon by their wives, thus exhibiting their male "inferiority" at the task.

The interactionist perspective is also useful in analyzing situations in which family relations seem less institutionalized, less set in concrete—such as in newly formed stepfamilies or dual-career marriages. How a stepfather acts toward his stepchildren when they misbehave, for instance, is a symbol of his emerging role: Does he speak loudly and angrily and admonish them, or does he leave that kind of language to the children's mother and avoid the role of disciplinarian? In general, the interactionist perspective helps sensitize us to the ways in which people create shared understandings of how family members should act toward one another. These shared understandings become the bases of the social roles people play in families—spouse, parent, breadwinner, homemaker, child, and so forth.

feminist theory a sociological theory that focuses on the domination of women by men

gender the social and cultural characteristics that distinguish women and men in a society

The Feminist Perspective **Feminist theory** is a perspective developed to better understand, and to transform, inequalities between women and men. It draws upon both the exchange and the symbolic interaction perspectives. The central concept in feminist theory is **gender,** which is usually defined as the social and cultural characteristics that distinguish women and men in a society (see Chapter 3). Feminist theorists argue that nearly all the gender differences we see in the roles of women and men are of cultural origin and have been socially constructed. By socially constructed, they mean arising not from biological differences but rather from culturally accepted rules, from relationships of power and authority, and from differences in economic opportunities. For example, the culture might include a rule that women should not work outside the home (as was the case among the American middle class from the mid-nineteenth to the mid-twentieth centuries). Or the opportunities for women might be limited to jobs that tend to pay less than comparable jobs in which most workers are men.

Moreover, feminist theorists assert that these cultural differences are constructed in ways that maintain the power of men over women (Thorne, 1992). For instance, feminist theorists criticize the notion that the breadwinner–homemaker family provided an exchange that was equally beneficial to women and men. Rather, like Emersonian exchange theorists, they note that women's direct access to money through paid employment was restricted in this type of family, which maintained women's dependence on men. They also note that men's relationships with their children were often limited. The cultural belief that "women's place is in the home" and the lower wages paid to women employed outside the home compelled married women to give up the idea of paid employment. Under these constraints, their best strategy may indeed have been to trade household services for a male income; but it was a forced choice set up by a social system that favored men.

In addition, feminist theorists argue that the kinds of work that women tend to do are valued less highly in our culture than the kinds that men do. In particular, they say, the work of caring for other people is undervalued because we value individualism and autonomy from others more than we value connections with others (Tronto, 1993). Women have historically done much of the work of maintaining connections with kin and caring for young children and the frail elderly. They have done much of it for free as part of their family responsibilities; in fact, we may not even consider a mother who is raising children full time to be "working." But today women also constitute most of the employees at hospitals, nursing homes, day care centers, and other settings where people are cared for. Their pay tends to be low: As we will see in Chapter 8, aides at child care centers make less, on average, than gas station attendants. Their low wages reflect, at least in part, the devaluing of caring work, sociologists say (England, 2005). Until we value care more highly, they say, we will continue to have less caring labor than is optimal. For instance, the low pay of child care workers will continue to cause high job turnover and less stable caregiving to young children.

Some feminist theorists maintain that the family is itself an artificial creation that has been organized to maintain male dominance. They would deny that there are any deep-seated predispositions among people that would lead to the formation of the kinds of families that we see. In fact, some would argue that we shouldn't even try to study the family anymore because to do so accepts as "natural" the inequalities built into it. Rather, we should merely study households and the relations among people within them. Needless to say, these critics would reject the contention that there is any biological basis for the ways in which men and women act in families. At the extreme, some maintain that even sexual intercourse, pregnancy, and giving birth are best viewed as, in the words of two anthropologists, "cultural facts, whose form, consequences, and meanings are socially constructed in any society" (Yanagisako & Collier, 1987).

Whether or not you think it's useful to study the family (as I obviously do), there is an important insight to be gained from feminist theory. It makes us aware that the experience of living in a family is different for women than it is for men. Arrangements that make men happiest don't necessarily make women happiest. A husband might prefer that his wife stay home to care for their children and do household work full time. His wife might prefer to combine a paying job with housework and child care, and she might wish that he would share more of the household tasks. In other words, women's interests in the family are not necessarily the same as men's interests. The breadwinner–homemaker bargain may have been great for men (except for those who wanted an active role in raising their children), and it may have been great for women who wished to raise children and do housework full time, but it frustrated other women by restricting the possibility of developing a satisfying career outside the home. Feminist theory urges us to view families through a prism that separates the experiences of men and women rather than just considering what's best for the family as a whole. It is a view that I will take repeatedly in this book.

The Postmodern Perspective   A number of theorists of modernity claim that personal life has changed fundamentally over the last several decades. They argue that the modern era—the long period that began with the spread of industrialization in the mid-to-late nineteenth century— effectively ended in the last half of the twentieth century. It has been replaced, they state, by what they call the **late modern era** (Giddens, 1991) or sometimes the postmodern era. Looking back at the modern era, they emphasize that individuals moved through a series of roles (student, spouse, parent, housewife, breadwinner) in a way that seemed more or less natural. Choices were constrained. In mill towns, two or three generations of kin might work at the same factory. Getting married was the only acceptable way to have children, except perhaps among the poor. Young people often chose their spouses from among a pool of acquaintances from their neighborhood, church, or school. Life's stages flowed in a way that one accepted and didn't have to question.

late modern era the last few decades of the twentieth century and the present day

But in the late modern era, the theorists maintain, individuals must make choices about nearly all aspects of their lives (Beck & Beck-Gernsheim, 2002). You can't get a job in the factory where your father and grandfather worked because overseas competition has forced it to close, so you must choose an-other career. You get little help from relatives in finding a partner, so you sign on to an Internet dating service and review hundreds of personal profiles. As other lifestyles become more acceptable, you must choose whether to get married and whether to have children. In ways such as these, your identity in

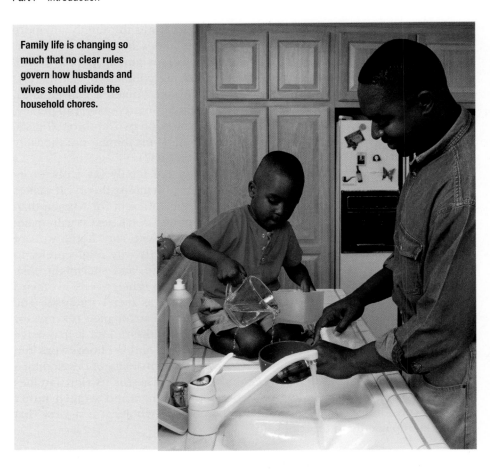

Family life is changing so much that no clear rules govern how husbands and wives should divide the household chores.

the late modern age is transformed from a "given" to a "task" you must undertake (Bauman, 1992, 2002).

As these choices are made, it is said, questions of self-identity become more important. By **self-identity,** I mean a person's sense of who he or she is and of where he or she fits in the social structure. In societies such as ours, individuals must construct their self-identities; they cannot rely on tradition or custom to order their daily lives. "We are not what we are," wrote social theorist Anthony Giddens (1991), "but what we make of ourselves." Developing one's self-identity becomes an important project that individuals must work on. People do the work of developing their identities through **reflexivity,** the process through which individuals take in knowledge, reflect on it, and alter their behavior as a result (Beck, Giddens, & Lash, 1994). In other words, people pay attention to their experiences and regularly ask themselves: How am I feeling? Do I find my life fulfilling? How do I want to live the rest of it? Depending on the answers to questions such as these, people may change the way they are living their lives. The postmodern theorists believe that the rise of reflexive change is a key characteristic of what they call the late modern era: the last few decades of the twentieth century and the beginning of the twenty-first. Table 1.3 compares the current era with the modern era that began with industrialization and ended in the mid-twentieth century (although, in a broader sense, modernization can be traced back to the

self-identity a person's sense of who he or she is and of where he or she fits in the social structure

reflexivity the process through which individuals take in knowledge, reflect on it, and alter their behavior as a result

Table 1.3 Aspects of Personal Life in the Late Modern Era		
	MODERN ERA	**LATE MODERN ERA**
Time period	Industrialization to mid-twentieth century	Since mid-twentieth century
Behavior	Rule-directed	Rule-altering
Lifestyle choices	Restricted	Mandatory
Kinship ties	Assigned	Created

Note: The table is the author's, but it is based on Giddens (1991, 1992), Beck & Beck-Gernsheim (1995, 2002), and Beck, Giddens, & Lash (1994).

Enlightenment in eighteenth-century Europe). In reality, the periods are not quite as distinct, and the differences not as sharp, as the table suggests.

Behavior, according to the theorists, was *rule-directed* in the earlier era, meaning that (1) rules such as social norms, laws, and customs strongly influenced personal life, and (2) the actions of individuals did not change those rules. Marriage was the only acceptable context for having children. Divorce was frowned upon and harder to obtain. Despite occasional movements to liberalize divorce laws, the norms and customs did not change much. In the current era, behavior is *rule-altering* to a much greater extent because the lifestyle choices individuals make can alter the laws and customs pertaining to families. For instance, as more gay and lesbian couples began to live openly together, a decade or two ago, many municipalities, in reaction, enacted domestic-partnership laws that gave same-sex couples privileges similar to those of married couples (such as requiring that employers who offer health insurance benefits that cover the spouses of their employees also cover their same-sex partners). These new laws altered the rules about what constituted a legally valid partnership. And as privileges and acceptability increased, gay men and lesbians found it even easier to live together in marriage-like partnership, leading to more recent changes, such as the legalization of same-sex marriage in several states.

Lifestyle choices, as Table 1.3 suggests, were *restricted* in the earlier era. For example, people were much less likely to choose a spouse of a different religion or racial-ethnic group. In the current era, choices are not only greater but also *mandatory:* You must make choices in nearly all aspects of personal life. Having to make so many decisions has its good and bad points. It opens the possibility of developing a self-identity that is deeply fulfilling; and it allows people to seize the opportunities that may be before them. On the other hand, choices can bring insecurity and doubt. The risk of making the wrong ones can weigh on you, creating a burden as well as a boon.

Finally, kinship ties tend to shift from being assigned to being *created*. In the past, you acquired your relatives at birth; then, when you married, you acquired a spouse and in-laws. There was little choice in the matter. Today, people in a variety of settings are more likely to choose their own kin and create their own kinship networks. What all these settings have in common is that they are defined outside the boundaries of lifelong heterosexual marriage.

People who cannot rely on, or choose not to rely on, lifelong marriage must construe kinship differently. They must do the hard work of constructing a group of kin, a broader family, that they can rely on. These ties

Table 1.4   Theoretical Perspectives on the Family

THEORETICAL PERSPECTIVE	MAIN THEME	APPLICATION TO FAMILIES
Exchange	Individuals with greater resources and more alternatives can drive better bargains.	Husbands' power over wives is greater when wives do not earn money on their own.
Symbolic interaction	Individuals interpret the actions of others and act in ways consistent with their interpretations.	Individuals give, and look for, symbolic cues about how to conduct the activities of everyday family life.
Feminist	Society is organized in ways that privilege men over women.	A system of male dominance gives husbands more power than their wives.
Postmodern	Individuals reflexively influence their social environments.	Individuals choose how they will act in new family forms such as stepfamilies.

require continual attention to maintain. In contrast, relations of blood and first marriage are supported by strong social norms and the law. Lacking this support, people must actively keep up created kinship ties. If they are allowed to lapse, there is no guarantee that they can be revived.

Postmodern theory is consistent with a view of families as diverse, changing, and developing in unpredictable directions. It can help us make sense of family life at a time when individuals must continually make choices in uncertain circumstances, for which there are no clear rules. For instance, two-career marriages are new enough that no general agreement exists on how spouses should divide up the tasks of work at home and in the labor market. (We will examine the work/family dilemma in Chapter 8.) Divorce and remarriage are new enough on a large scale that stepparents and stepchildren have little guidance on who is part of their family and how they should act toward them. (We will examine stepfamilies in Chapter 13.) These new circumstances bring both opportunities for fashioning mutually beneficial arrangements and the costs of the anxiety and conflict that working out new rules can cause.

Quick Review

- Four widely used theoretical perspectives are exchange, symbolic interaction, feminist, and postmodern.
- Table 1.4 summarizes the main theme of each perspective and its application to studying families.

Globalization and Families

globalization the increasing flow of goods and services, money, migrants, and information across the nations of the world

These days, many sociologists are applying their theories to the study of a major social trend that has occurred over the past few decades: **globalization,** the increasing flow of goods and services, money, migrants, and information across the nations of the world.

Globalization is evident in the movement of factory work overseas so that, for instance, virtually every piece of clothing you own was probably made outside of the United States. You face it when you call the technical service line for help with a laptop problem and are connected to someone in India. You have seen it if you know one of the many middle-class families that have hired women from countries such as Mexico or the Philippines to help care for their children while the parents work. You have experienced it on news sites where Twitter feeds and cellphone videos keep you apprised of uprisings in distant lands. Globalization is tying together the lives of people around the world in a way that was not possible before late-twentieth-century advances in computing, communications, and transportation. It has been aided by the ascendency of a political viewpoint known as neo-liberalism that supports free movement of investment funds and free trade of goods across nations, open borders, and individual initiative.

No national government controls this trend. Rather, globalization operates at world level above the nation state, as money, people, and information transit the globe. It is affecting family life in nearly every region of the world, although its effects differ from region to region (Trask, 2010). In developing countries, the new factories have created millions of low-wage jobs that have drawn mothers into the paid work force. As in the United States, the employment of mothers with young children can create child care problems, which are often worsened by the lack of any government child care assistance and by workers' inability to pay for care. But the jobs, modest in pay though they are, have also provided women with a greater degree of independence in their family lives, increasing their bargaining power with their husbands and allowing some to escape abusive marriages. Therefore, globalization is changing the relations between women and men in areas where manufacturing work has grown. In addition, the style of romantic love and companionship to be found in the United States and other wealthy countries seems to be spreading across much of the developing world.

The effects of globalization on family life can also be seen in the **Western nations,** the countries of Western Europe and the non-European, English-speaking countries of the United States, Canada, Australia, and New Zealand. This book's main focus will be on the family in the United States, but there are strong similarities between the American family and the family in other Western nations.

Western nations the countries of Western Europe and the non-European, English-speaking countries of the United States, Canada, Australia, and New Zealand

In the United States, the movement of manufacturing jobs overseas has made it more difficult for high-school educated young adults to find decent jobs. As a result they frequently are hesitant to marry, and they form short-term cohabiting relationships instead. Meanwhile, college-educated young adults, who have an easier time finding the kinds of well-paying professional and technical jobs that still remain in the United States, finish their education, marry, and enjoy a higher standard of living. In this way, globalization is creating a gap between the family lives of the college graduates and those with less education.

Moreover, international migration is creating family forms that span the developed and developing countries in ways that have never been seen before. Whereas in the past most people who migrated from their home country to another country were men, today half of all international migrants are women (United Nations, 2009). Many of them are mothers who leave their children at home. For instance, the women who migrate to the United States to care for the children of working parents often leave their own children in the care of others in their home countries. They typically send back most of their salary to pay for the children's school fees, better clothes, or a nicer house. A grandmother may be minding the children during the years that the mother is gone, or the family may be paying someone else to do the caring. In this way, the immigrant nannies create transnational families in which mothers and children can be thousands of miles apart and yet keep in touch through phone calls, text messages, and Skype sessions.

Globalization, then, can influence family life both positively and negatively. In less developed countries it can induce parents to work long hours for wages that are low by Western standards and it can create childcare crises. But the increase in household income does represent a step up in the families' economic fortunes, and it elevates the position of women. In the home countries of the women who migrate to the Western countries to do caring work, children are separated from their mothers by hundreds or thousands of miles; yet their opportunities are increased by the money their mothers send home. In the West, globalization has improved the economic prospects of highly educated young adults, most of whom are still forming marriage-based families, while eroding the ability of young adults with less education to form stable, long-term family bonds.

In subsequent chapters, we will explore these and other facets of globalization. Topics we will study include:

- The growing social class gap in American family life; the increase in women's employment in factories and home-production in developing countries. (Chapter 4)
- The spread of romantic love in the developing world. (Chapter 7)
- The childcare problems caused by women's employment in developing countries. (Chapter 8)
- The transnational families of the immigrant caregivers of children in the United States and other wealthy countries; the transnational adoption and surrogate mother markets. (Chapter 9)
- The influx of immigrant caregivers of the older population in Western Europe. (Chapter 10)
- How the earnings of women in developing countries may protect them against domestic violence. (Chapter 11)
- Changes in women's autonomy and divorce rates around the world. (Chapter 12)

The world is too interconnected to consider what is happening to families in the United States without also considering what is happening elsewhere.

Quick Review

- During the past few decades the international flows of goods and services, money, migrants, and information have increased greatly, in a process known as globalization.
- Globalization has affected family life throughout the world, although its effects are different in Western countries than in other regions.

A Sociological Viewpoint on Families

As noted earlier, some sociologists would argue that no one can conduct completely objective research. Therefore, they say, one must examine, reflexively, how one approaches the subject. Only by frankly examining and stating one's viewpoint can one provide a framework others can use to properly evaluate one's own research. In that spirit, let me briefly discuss the viewpoint I bring to the writing of this textbook. In reading this book, you should keep these convictions in mind. I believe that families perform services of value to society and therefore should be publicly supported when necessary. Despite their increasing diversity, families, in my opinion, still constitute a coherent social category worth studying. I believe that, other things being equal, stable, long-term partnerships—opposite-sex or same-sex—provide the best environment for raising children. These partnerships need not be marriages, but getting married seems to enhance the chances of long-term stability and to increase the investments parents make, at least in the United States. I also believe that alternative family forms, with adequate support, can provide good environments for children.

In addition, I think it is likely that our evolutionary history has produced some inherent differences between the ways that women and men go about finding partners and building family lives. But I don't believe these differences are significant enough to prevent equality for women and men, which is a goal that I think we should strive for in the early twenty-first century. Biologically based differences, if any, would stem from the different roles that men and women played in the hunter-gatherer bands in which most humans and their evolutionary predecessors lived until about 8,000 B.C. Women, on average, may be predisposed to value sex in the context of relationships and commitment more than men, whereas men may be predisposed to value sex outside of relationships and to behave aggressively more than women. But even if we do have biological predispositions toward some behaviors and away from others, whether we exhibit these behaviors depends on the social circumstances of our lives: the upbringing we received from our parents; the cultural influences we absorbed from peers, neighbors, ministers, and the media; and the economic constraints or racial prejudices we may have faced. These social factors may exaggerate whatever biological differences there may be between women and men, so that the differences we see are greater than biology alone would create. Biological predispositions, then, would not determine a person's behavior. Rather, they would create tendencies and leanings. On average, a group of people who share a predisposition (toward, say, aggressive behavior) would be likely to show more of it than would a group who does not share it; but it is difficult to predict how any single member of the group would behave.

In this book, I will use the singular form "the family" rather than the plural form "families" when discussing the family as a **social institution.** This term refers to a set of roles and rules that define a social unit of importance to society. The roles give us positions such as parent, child, spouse, ex-spouse, stepfather, partner, and so forth. The rules offer us guidance about how to act in these roles. But the use of the singular is not meant to imply that there is only one kind of family. On the contrary, there are many forms. Similarly, one might write about "the corporation" in a textbook on social organizations without implying that there is no difference between ExxonMobil and

social institution a set of roles and rules that define a social unit of importance to society

a chain of grocery stores. Or an author might discuss "the hospital" in a text on medical sociology while recognizing the difference between a giant teaching hospital in a central city and a community hospital out in the suburbs. In addition, referring to "the family" is not meant to imply that the interests of wives, husbands, and children are always identical—any more than that the interests of workers and managers in corporations are identical.

In all of these cases, the use of the singular would signal the study of a social institution rather than just a set of relationships. An institution can grow stronger or weaker over time; it can take on somewhat different forms at different times and places; and it can be difficult to define at its margins. But it is a visible structure that people can recognize and understand. It also does something important for society. I think the "family" still fits this description. Its important functions include rearing children, caring for the elderly, and providing comfort and emotional support to its members. Nevertheless, people's actions are greatly changing the family and eroding its institutional basis. Stability and change in the family are the subject matter of this book.

Currently, most Americans seem to view their own families primarily in emotional, personal terms—the terms of the private family—and to pay less attention to the commitments and obligations of the public family. This emphasis on sentiment and self-fulfillment might lead one to assume that the private family is the older, more established perspective. But that isn't so. The emergence of the private family is a relatively new development in history. Its origins lie in the upper-class and merchant families of Western Europe in the 1600s and 1700s. It did not spread to the masses until the late 1800s and 1900s. Most people have used the public perspective in thinking about families throughout most of history. The historical development of the family is the subject of the next chapter.

Looking Back

1. **How do Americans feel about marriage and families?** Some people are concerned about the diversity of American families, while others are pleased by it. Those who are concerned support public policies that support marriage, whereas those who defend diversity urge support for all types of families. Many Americans are ambivalent and agree with some of the positions taken by both sides. In general, Americans take an individualistic perspective toward family life, which emphasizes self-reliance and achievement but also feelings and emotional satisfaction.

2. **What do families do that is important for society? What do families do that is important for the individuals in them?** Families contribute to society by raising the next generation and caring for the ill and the elderly. On an individual level, families are settings in which people give and receive love, intimacy, and social support. This book proposes two definitions of the family—one for each of these questions. The public family perspective defines the family in terms of the presence of caregivers and dependents. The private family perspective defines the family in terms of an indefinite, intimate relationship between two or more individuals who live in the same household and share the fruits of their labor. These two perspectives constitute different views of the same reality; a given family unit might fit both of them.

3. **How do sociologists go about studying families?** Sociologists observe real families and the people in them, and for the most part, they try to analyze their data

objectively using the scientific method. Sociologists formulate hypotheses that can be tested, although there are limits to their use of the scientific method. The two most common research methods sociologists use are (1) the survey, a study in which a randomly selected group of individuals or families are asked a fixed set of questions; and (2) the observational study, in which the researcher spends time directly observing each participant in the study.

4. **What are the leading theoretical approaches to studying families?** Four widely used perspectives are exchange theory, which examines how family members bargain based on their resources and their alternatives;

symbolic interaction, which focuses on how individuals interpret the social world; feminist theory, which analyzes the sources of gender inequality in families; and post-modernism, which emphasizes the choices individuals must make in constructing family lives.

5. **How is globalization changing family life?** In developing nations, it has created factory jobs that have drawn mothers into the paid workforce, creating childcare problems for those women, but also giving mothers more bargaining power within marriage. In the developed, Western nations, it has opened a gap between the marriage-based family lives of the college-educated and the family lives of the less-educated.

Go to the Online Learning Center at www.mhhe.com/cherlin7e to test your knowledge of the chapter concepts and key terms.

Study Questions

1. How do people rate their own family's troubles compared to the average family?
2. What are the two components of American individualism?
3. Why might children be considered a "public good"?
4. What kinds of daily activities are better analyzed by thinking of the family as a public rather than a private institution?
5. Conversely, what daily activities are better analyzed by thinking of the family as a private institution?
6. Are there daily activities that could be viewed as having both a public and a private component?
7. Why can't sociological research be as objective as research in physics or chemistry?
8. How do people develop their self-identities today?
9. Give an example of a social institution other than the family.

Key Terms

assigned kinship 15
boundary ambiguity 14
breadwinner–homemaker
  family 23

created kinship 15
exchange theory 22
expressive individualism 7
externalities 10

feminist theory 26
free-rider problem 12
gender 26
globalization 30

hypothesis 18	primary analysis 24	social institution 33
individualism 6	private family 13	survey 20
late modern era 27	public family 12	symbolic interaction
longitudinal survey 24	public goods 10	theory 23
negative externalities 10	reflexivity 28	utilitarian individualism 6
objectivity 17	scientific method 18	Western nations 31
observational study 20	secondary analysis 24	
positive externalities 10	self-identity 28	

Thinking about Families

The Public Family	The Private Family
What are some of the ways that your family has carried out its "public" functions?	How has your family carried out its "private" functions?

Families on the Internet   www.mhhe.com/cherlin7e

Note: While all the URLs listed were current as of the printing of this book, these sites often change. Please check our Web site (www.mhhe.com/cherlin7e) for updates.

The Internet is a great source of information about family issues. Throughout this book, the "Families on the Internet" section will provide you with suggested World Wide Web sites. Keep in mind that Web sites come and go on the Internet and that the contents of each Web site change often. This flux means that you might occasionally not find a Web site or specific piece of information within a site that is listed in this section. I will attempt, however, to suggest sites that are likely to be long-lived.

In addition, the publishers of this book have established a Web site (www.mhhe.com/cherlin7e) where up-to-date links to useful sites will be posted.

The first way to obtain information on the family is to enter a phrase in a search engine such as Google. As you know, the phrase can't be too broad: Entering "family" will cause the search engine to return a blizzard of links. But a more focused entry can be useful: Typing "feminist theory" or "gay marriage," for example, should return a number of useful links. It may also, however, return some not-so-useful links; and it can be difficult and time-consuming to distinguish the good sites from the bad, or simply irrelevant, sites.

Consequently, it helps to have some suggested links to broader Web sites that provide issue-oriented information on a number of topics. A good place to start for issues involving children is the Center on Children and Families at the Brookings Institution, www.brookings.edu/ccf.

The organizations that maintain the major national surveys have Web sites. Information on the Fragile Families and Child Wellbeing Study is available at www.fragilefamilies.princeton.edu. Information on the Panel Study of Income Dynamics is available at www.psidonline.isr.umich.edu.

Chapter Two

The History of the Family

Looking Forward

What Do Families Do?

The Origins of Family and Kinship

The American Family before 1776

American Indian Families: The Primacy
of the Tribe

European Colonists: The Primacy of the
Public Family

Family Diversity

**The Emergence of the "Modern"
American Family: 1776–1900**

From Cooperation to Separation: Women's
and Men's Spheres

**African American, Mexican American,
and Asian Immigrant Families**

African American Families

An African Heritage?

The Impact of Slavery

Mexican American Families

Asian Immigrant Families

The Asian Heritage

Asian Immigrants

**The Rise of the Private Family:
1900–Present**

The Early Decades

The Depression Generation

The 1950s

The 1960s through the 1990s

The Changing Life Course

Social Change in the Twentieth
Century

The Emergence of Early
Adulthood

The Role of Education

Constrained Opportunities

Declining Parental Control

Early Adulthood and the Life-Course
Perspective

What History Tells Us

Looking Back

Study Questions

Key Terms

Thinking about Families

Families on the Internet

Boxed Features

FAMILIES AND PUBLIC POLICY: *Divorce Reform:
Have We Been Here Before?*

FAMILIES AND THE GREAT RECESSION: *Lessons
from the Great Depression*

Looking Forward

1. What functions have families traditionally performed?

2. How did American families change after the United States was founded?

3. How have the family histories of major ethnic and racial groups differed?

4. How did the emotional character of the American family change during the early twentieth century?

5. What important changes occurred in marriage and childbearing in the United States in the last half of the twentieth century?

6. How does the life course perspective help us to understand social change?

The serious study of the history of the family began in 1960, when the manager of a tropical fruit importing firm in France, a self-described "Sunday historian," published a book about the history of childhood (Ariès, 1960). Philippe Ariès, curious about family life in the Middle Ages, had examined works of art dating back 1,000 years. Any artist will tell you that children's heads are larger in proportion to the rest of their bodies than adults' heads. Yet many early medieval artists used adult proportions when painting children's heads and bodies, as if their subjects were, in fact, small adults. Moreover, the artists dressed children in the same clothes as adults. From such evidence, Ariès concluded that the concept of childhood was a modern invention.

Of course, there always had been children, but until the 1700s, wrote Ariès, the long stage of life we call childhood wasn't recognized by most people. American historian John Demos put forth a similar argument about the Puritans in Plymouth Colony in the 1600s: "Childhood as such was barely recognized in the period spanned by Plymouth Colony. There was little sense that children might somehow be a special group, with their own needs and interests and capacities" (Demos, 1970). According to historians such as Ariès and Demos, parents withheld love and affection from infants and toddlers because so many of them died. The great French essayist Montaigne wrote in the late 1500s, "I have lost two or three children in their infancy, not without regret, but without great sorrow."[1] *Two or three*—Montaigne couldn't even remember how many. If children survived, wrote Ariès and Demos, they were treated as little adults. By age seven, boys and girls performed useful work—helping fathers in the fields or mothers at the hearth—and played the same games and attended the same festivals as adults.

Ariès argued that it was only with the spread of schooling and the decline in child deaths—neither of which occurred on a large scale until the 1800s outside the noble and middle classes—that the notion of a protected, extended stage of childhood emerged.

Ariès's influential book launched a new generation of historians who studied ordinary families rather than royal families. His contribution is still

---

[1] From vol. 2, no. 8, of Montaigne's *Essais*. Quoted on p. 39 of Ariès (1960).

Marriage of Giovanni Arnolfini and Giovanna Cenami, Jan van Eyck's famous painting of the wedding vows of a wealthy couple in 1434, shows a late medieval view of marriage. Wives were valued primarily for their childbearing and domestic roles: The bride is shown holding her long gown over her womb, as if she were pregnant. In back of her is a statuette of St. Margaret, the patron saint of childbearing women. Arnolfini stands straight, his facial expression stern, as if ready to assume his role as head of the household. His wife's pose is more submissive: her head slightly bowed, her eyes slightly downcast. A dog symbolizes the faithfulness expected of the couple.

respected even though many historians now believe that he underestimated parents' appreciation of childhood as a stage of life. For every Montaigne, the revisionist historians have found a Martin Luther, who wrote in the 1500s after the death of his infant daughter, "I so lamented her death that I was exquisitely sick, my heart rendered soft and weak; never had I thought that a father's heart could be so broken for his children's sake."[2] When historian Linda Pollock located and read 68 diaries written by American and British parents in the 1600s and 1700s, she found that most of them were aware that children were different from adults and that they needed parental guidance and support. The diarists frequently referred to their children as "comforts" and showed pride in their accomplishments. "I doe not think one child of 100 of his age durst doe so much," wrote one proud father (Pollock, 1983). (See also Nicholas [1991], Ozment [2001].) Nevertheless, parents of this period did seem less saddened by the death of an infant than that of an older child.

The family history industry that Ariès spawned has produced thousands of books and articles. During the same period, a related field, the history of women and gender, has grown just as fast. Together, these fields provide an anchor for the study of the contemporary family. They describe the context in which the contemporary family has developed. Among other things, they tell us that the public family is as old as human civilization but that

---

[2] Quoted in Ozment (1983).

the private family blossomed only during the past few hundred years. For the sociologist studying the contemporary family, the historical literature is a wonderful source of insights. This chapter will provide a brief guided tour of that literature. Of necessity, it will be a highly selective tour, one that provides a foundation for the detailed study of the modern family in the remaining chapters of this book.

First, we must go back even further in time than the historians have traveled in order to understand the origins of family and kinship. Then we will look at what the colonial and American Indian families were like prior to 1776. Afterward, we will follow the changes in the American family that took place between 1776 and the start of the twentieth century. We will then study the diversity of racial and ethnic American families in the twentieth century and the rise of what I call "the private family." Then we will consider the changing "life course" and an emerging life stage, early adulthood.

What Do Families Do?

THE ORIGINS OF FAMILY AND KINSHIP

We have all seen pictures of a new colt, minutes after birth, standing on its four legs. My local newspaper printed a photograph of a one-day-old dolphin swimming with its mother. In contrast, the average human baby cannot sit up until about six months and cannot walk until about age one. This difference in maturation time between humans and other animals is not an accident of nature; rather, it reflects the evolution of our species. Throughout most of their existence, human beings have been **hunter-gatherers:** They wandered through the forests in small bands, hunting animals and gathering edible plants. According to the theory of evolutionary biology, humans evolved from four-legged primates to beings that could walk upright and hunt or gather with two arms. But humans are born smaller (relative to their adult size) than most other mammals and need prolonged, intensive care in order to survive. In hunter-gatherer societies, as in nearly all other known societies, mothers provide most of the care during the first few years of children's lives. Anthropologists who have studied the few remaining hunter-gatherer societies report that mothers carry their young with them during the first year and continue to breastfeed them for several years (Howell, 1979). As a result, women specialize in finding plants and hunting small animals within a limited area, whereas men range farther afield in search of larger animals.

About 10,000 years ago, humans discovered the advantage of remaining in one place and planting crops. Settled agriculture revolutionized human organization because it allowed humans to accumulate surpluses of grain that could support larger kinship groups than was possible in hunter-gatherer societies. Indeed, human societies were often organized around large kinship groups. In societies in which a tribe ruled a territory and no other strong government existed, people often traced descent through either the father's or the mother's line, but not both. What resulted were kinship groups called **lineages: patrilineages** if descent is traced through the father's line; **matrilineages** if traced through the mother's line. These groups seem odd, at first, to people in Western nations, who trace descent through both the father's and

hunter-gatherers people who wander through forests or over plains in small bands, hunting animals and gathering edible plants

lineage a form of kinship group in which descent is traced through either the father's or the mother's line

patrilineage a kinship group in which descent is through the father's line

matrilineage a kinship group in which descent is through the mother's line

Multigenerational households have been more common in China than in the West.

mother's line; but the structure serves a purpose. Among other virtues, lineages limit the number of people who are related to a person and with whom that person must share land, water, animals, and other resources. In a patrilineage, my sons will marry women from outside the lineage; then the couples will live near me (sometimes with me) and remain in my lineage. My grandsons will do the same. But my daughters and granddaughters will marry men from other lineages, move to their land, and leave my lineage. Consequently, I need to share my resources with, and to defend, only those persons related to me through my father, my brothers, and my sons. If a maternal uncle needs assistance, that's his lineage's problem; I am not my mother's brother's keeper.

Kinship, as one anthropologist has written, developed as "a weapon in the struggle for survival" (Fox, 1967). In tribal societies, family ties provide the structure that holds the society together: You are a member of the tribe not because you are a citizen (a concept that can't exist without a state) but rather because you are related to the other members. You obey rules set by the tribal elders, not laws set by a government. You tend farmland not because you purchased it but because the tribe lets you use it. Kinship groups ensure order, recruit members from outside the group (usually through marriage), defend against other outsiders, provide labor at harvesttime, and assist the less fortunate. Anthropologists who study social organization in tribal societies focus on family and kinship because, to a large extent, that *is* social organization.

In most societies, kinship groups are made up of smaller family units, consisting of a mother and children always, a husband usually, and other household members sometimes. In many of the Western nations, the larger kinship groups have been weak and the smaller husband-wife-children unit has dominated. This smaller unit of husband, wife, and children is referred to as the **conjugal family** (the word "conjugal" is from the Latin term for joining together in marriage). If any other relatives—such as a grandparent or uncle—are present in the household, it is said to contain an **extended family.** Many Americans assume that in the past Grandma, Grandpa, Mom, Dad, and the kids sat around the hearth, swapping stories and enjoying one another's company. To be sure, there were substantial numbers of extended families in many European nations (Kertzer, 1991). But there were fewer families like that in the United States, England, and northern France, for two reasons. First, young people in those areas typically waited until they could start a new household before they married. That might mean waiting for the father to retire and turn over his land or moving to the city to work for a merchant. Second, Grandma and Grandpa often didn't live long enough to share a household with their grandchildren, although most elderly people continued to live with one child, often unmarried at first, who remained at home (Ruggles, 1994).

In other parts of the world, larger family units have been more common. The traditional Chinese family was patrilineal, and the cultural ideal was for five male generations (and their wives and children) to live under one roof, ruled by the oldest male. There, too, few families reached the ideal, because the oldest generations rarely lived long enough, and because a family had to be affluent to support such a large dwelling. Nevertheless, households containing extended families were more common in China than in Western nations. In many African societies, men were allowed (and in some countries still are allowed) to have more than one wife, a practice known as **polygyny** (literally, in Greek, "many women"). A wealthy man might take a second or third wife and establish each of them in separate dwellings in the same compound. All the wives and children might cook and eat together, under the direction of the senior wife. In a much smaller number of societies, women were allowed to practice **polyandry,** having more than one husband.

In sum, family and kinship systems were developed to provide for people's fundamental needs, such as producing sufficient food and defending against outsiders. Although kin often shared strong emotional bonds, families did not develop primarily out of people's desire for love and intimacy; rather, they developed out of their will to survive, prosper, and raise children. Thus the origins of family and kinship are best analyzed from the perspective of the public family introduced in Chapter 1: the view of families as settings in which people take care of one another and depend on one another. In contrast, the perspective of the private family, which emphasizes intimacy and personal fulfillment, is less useful; its utility is greater for analyzing contemporary families, as will be noted later.

conjugal family a kinship group comprising husband, wife, and children

extended family a kinship group comprising the conjugal family plus any other relatives present in the household, such as a grandparent or uncle

polygyny a form of polygamy in which a man is allowed to have more than one wife

polyandry a form of polygamy in which a woman is allowed to have more than one husband

Quick Review

- For most of our history, humans were hunter-gatherers.
- Lineages offered a number of advantages to humans after settled agriculture began.
- In the Western nations, the smaller, conjugal family has dominated.

In most American Indian tribes, families were organized into lineages in which descent was traced through either the father's or the mother's line.

The American Family before 1776

There were several American families prior to the Revolution. There were, first of all, the families of the indigenous people who would become known as American Indians. There were the families of the European colonists. And there were the families of the African slaves, who were transported involuntarily to the Americas beginning in the 1500s. I will discuss the history of African American families later in this chapter. For now, let us examine the American Indian family and the European colonists' family before 1776.

AMERICAN INDIAN FAMILIES: THE PRIMACY OF THE TRIBE

Although there is little direct evidence about American Indian societies before the 1800s, scholars think that most American Indians lived in tribal societies based on lineages. (The term **American Indian** is often used for a subset of the original, indigenous people who had settled in North America thousands of years before Columbus, namely, those who had settled in the territory that later became the 48 contiguous United States [Snipp, 1989]. Indeed, it was because Columbus mistakenly believed that he had reached India that he gave this aboriginal population the misnomer "Indian.") We do know that the American Indian population was devastated by diseases brought by Europeans, such as smallpox—diseases to which the native population had developed no immunities. Moreover, we know that large numbers of American Indians were killed in wars and massacres (Shoemaker, 1991). How these catastrophic events modified family and kinship is unclear. In the absence of direct evidence, scholars have assumed that the numerous accounts of American

American Indian the name used for a subset of all Native Americans, namely, those who were living in the territory that later became the 48 contiguous United States

Indian societies in the 1800s and early 1900s can be generalized back in time. Although the assumption that present arrangements accurately reflect the past ignores the historical changes that occurred to American Indian societies after the arrival of the Europeans, the outlines of American Indian family and kinship seem clear.

Both patrilineal and matrilineal tribes existed. Related lineages were often organized into larger clans that provided the basis for social organization and governing. In matrilineal tribes such as the Hopi, for example, a person traced his or her relatives through his or her mother's line.[3] If you were a child, your father was a guest in your mother's home. Although strong bonds existed between wives and husbands, a woman's ties to her maternal kin—her mother, her mother's brothers, her maternal cousins—were generally stronger. Consequently, your maternal uncles played an important role in your upbringing. They, not your father, had to approve your choice of spouse. Still, if you were a boy, you did learn many of the skills of an adult male—growing crops, herding animals—from your father. It was as if you had two kinds of fathers: a biological father who taught you skills and an uncle-father who held greater authority over you. If you were a girl, you spent less time with your father.

When Hopi boys reached puberty, they moved out of the household, sleeping in the men's ceremonial house and eventually marrying into another clan. Girls, on the other hand, remained in or near their mothers' homes throughout their lives, bringing husbands from other clans into their dwellings. In general, American Indian children were more independent than European American children: They were given more freedom and experienced less physical punishment (Mintz, 2004). In all tribal societies, the common requirement that individuals marry someone outside their clan forged alliances across clans. If clan A and clan B frequently exchanged young adults as marriage partners, the two clans would likely consider themselves as allies in any disputes with other clans in the tribe. Thus, the lineage and clan organization of American Indian societies served to strengthen the social order and to protect individuals against unfriendly outsiders.

Kinship was also matrilineal among the Apache of Arizona. Soon after a girl's first menstruation (which probably occurred several years later in her life than is the case today), her lineage held a four-day Sun Rise ceremony, after which she was eligible to marry (Joe, Sparks, & Tiger, 1999). Marriages were typically arranged by elders from the prospective bride's and groom's lineages. (Marrying someone from the same lineage was forbidden.) A series of gifts was exchanged by the bride's and groom's families, which culminated in the groom's family bringing him to the home of the bride. The bride's family then constructed a separate home for the couple. The gifts between families symbolized the importance of establishing an alliance with a family in another lineage. It's not that love between the young couple was necessarily lacking, but their marriage also served the larger purpose of tying together members of two lineages who could provide assistance in times of trouble or need.

---

[3] This account of Hopi kinship draws from Queen, Habenstein, and Quadagno (1985).

EUROPEAN COLONISTS: THE PRIMACY
OF THE PUBLIC FAMILY

Among the European colonists, there were no lineages. But the conjugal family of husband, wife, and children provided services that were of great value to the community. Consider education. In Plymouth Colony, children received their basic education from their parents or, if they were working as servants, in another family's home. Parents and masters were required by law to teach reading to their children and young servants, so they could at least "be able to duely read the scriptures" (Demos, 1970). Why weren't these children learning to read in school? Because there was no school—or rather, because the family *was* school. In addition to providing schooling, all Plymouth Colony families were expected to provide vocational training. Through apprenticeship and service, working next to an adult, children and youths learned the skills they needed to farm, trade, garden, cook, and make clothes. All families were also expected to supplement church services by engaging in "family worship," praying and meditating daily.

Selected Plymouth Colony families also functioned as

- *Hospitals*   Some adults who supposedly had specialized knowledge took sick persons into their homes for treatment.
- *Houses of correction*   Judges ordered some idle or criminal persons to live in the homes of upstanding families to learn how to change their ways.
- *Orphanages*   Children whose parents had died—a far more common occurrence than today—were taken in by a relative or family friend.
- *Nursing homes*   Frail elderly parents were cared for in their homes by their children.
- *Poorhouses*   Families sometimes took in poor relatives who needed food and shelter. (Demos, 1970)

Today, all these activities, with the exception of caring for the elderly, are carried out primarily outside the home, mostly by publicly supported institutions. In Plymouth Colony, then, the family's public role was much broader than it is now.

In contrast, the family's private role was much smaller. The kind of privacy that Westerners today take for granted hardly existed a few hundred years ago, as is apparent to anyone who visits the Puritan houses that still stand in Massachusetts. The downstairs area of a typical house contained one or two rooms. The larger of them was an all-purpose room called the "hall," in which the members of the household spent most of their indoor waking hours. It was dominated by a huge fireplace used for heating and cooking. In smaller houses, the second downstairs room would contain little except bedding. Most houses also had one or two second-story lofts with beds. Often, only the hall contained furniture for any activity other than sleeping. In this one room, fathers, mothers, children (Plymouth families had an average of seven or eight children), servants or apprentices, and perhaps a grandparent ate, cooked, talked, prayed, sewed clothing, relaxed, and received visitors. Individuals simply could not find a place to get away from other household members.

Not only did individuals have difficulty maintaining privacy but the conjugal family also had difficulty maintaining privacy from other households.

The colonists did not regard the conjugal family as separate from society, but rather as an integral part of it. To a great extent, a family's affairs were considered public business. For example, Puritan laws required that married couples maintain harmonious relations and raise their children properly—and imposed fines on those who didn't. Friends and neighbors commonly called at one another's houses without advance notice. Given all the ways in which privacy was prevented, the idea of a private, conjugal family with its own separate space—and of individual privacy within the family—may not have been in the mind-set of most people. At best, privacy was probably dismissed as unattainable.

FAMILY DIVERSITY

But not all colonial families fit the ideal of two married, biological parents and their children. Particularly outside of New England, families were diverse. For one thing, death rates were so high that children commonly lost a parent and lived in a stepfamily after their remaining parent remarried (Uhlenberg, 1980). In addition, people sometimes proclaimed themselves married in front of family or friends, without the participation of clergy, and were accepted as married by their communities. Europeans, it turns out, had a long tradition of informal marriage. Until the Council of Trent in 1563, the Catholic Church accepted as a marriage any public statement by a couple that they considered themselves married to each other, as long as neither partner coerced the other and their marriage did not violate church laws about who could marry whom. Until 1753 the Church of England, which had broken with the Catholic Church during the reign of Henry VIII, recognized informal marriage (Therborn, 2004). Even as late as 1850, informal marriage was common in England among the poorer classes (Gillis, 1985). People used the phrase "living tally" to describe couples living as married but who had never wed in the church.

Informal marriage was particularly common in the Middle Colonies (New York, New Jersey, Pennsylvania, Delaware, and Maryland) and the Southern Colonies (Virginia, North Carolina, South Carolina, and Georgia), where the Anglican Church (the American wing of the Church of England) did not provide enough clergy, and in frontier areas where social control was looser. An Anglican minister in eighteenth-century Maryland said, "if . . . no marriage should be deemed valid that had not been registered in the parish book, it would I am persuaded bastardize nine-tenths of the People in the Country."[4] As in England, informal marriage persisted into the nineteenth century. In 1833, the Chief Justice of the State of Pennsylvania wrote that if the state truly enforced its marriage laws, the "vast majority" of the state's children would be considered illegitimate. A form of bigamy also sometimes occurred: A man who left his wife and migrated to a faraway state or territory was unlikely to be followed, so he could marry anew without much fear of prosecution (Hartog, 2000). In the nineteenth and early twentieth centuries, in contrast, families probably became *less* diverse over time, as churches established control of marriage and as fewer parents died while their children were young.

[4] Quoted in Cott (2000). The Anglican minister is quoted on p. 32; the Chief Justice, on p. 39.

Quick Review

- Lineages and clans constituted the main social organization of American Indian tribal societies.
- In American colonial society, families had many public functions but a smaller private role than today.
- Parental death and informal marriage produced diverse types of families.

The Emergence of the "Modern" American Family: 1776–1900

Pinpointing the beginnings of social change is always difficult; rarely can we discern a great divide between an older way of life and an emerging one. Nevertheless, the decades surrounding the American Revolution seem to have been a watershed in the history of the American family. Between 1776 and 1830, the outlines emerged of a kind of family that would remain prominent well into the twentieth century. Clearest among the white middle class, it had four new characteristics:

- Marriage was increasingly based on affection and mutual respect rather than on male authority and custom. As a consequence, women experienced increasing autonomy in the family. (But, I would add, they were increasingly restricted to the home.)
- The primary role of the wife became the care of children and the maintenance of the home. Women came to be seen as morally superior to men, and the home came to be seen as "women's sphere."
- The attention and energy of the husband and wife were increasingly centered on their children. Children came to be seen as needing not only discipline and economic support, but also attention, affection, and loving care.
- The number of children per family declined, in part as a consequence of the greater investment of emotion and time that they were seen to need.

Moreover, some historians believe that the idea of individualism gained greater currency during the 1700s. Lawrence Stone's (1977) influential account of British family history claims that individualism gained ground among the British middle and upper classes in the 1700s. Individualism, Stone wrote, had two meanings where the family was concerned. The first was a greater consideration of one's own self and, in particular, one's own sense of self-satisfaction. This led, in turn, to an increased emphasis on personal gratification in family relationships. The second meaning was of autonomy—individual freedom from constraints imposed by others. Consequently, Stone called this phenomenon the rise of "affective individualism," a concept very similar to "expressive individualism," defined in Chapter 1. Since the work of Stone, Ariès (whose theory of childhood was described at the beginning of the chapter), and other historians of what has become known as the "sentiments school" appeared, however, many historians have argued that sentiment and affection had been present for centuries prior to the 1700s (Cooper, 1999; Ozment, 2001).

Under the ideology of "separate spheres" that developed in the 1800s, caring for children was seen as a central part of women's lives.

Nevertheless, there probably was a movement toward greater individualism and sentiment in American family life in the 1700s and early 1800s. The role of romantic love increased within marriage during this period, at least among the middle and upper classes who left diaries and letters that historians can read today (Bloch, 2003). But romantic love needed to be tempered by a careful judgment of whether a potential spouse was a reliable and dependable person—someone with whom one could build a family. These practical considerations were particularly important for women, who became legally and socially bound to their husband's authority upon marrying. During courtship, women needed to assure themselves that feelings of love were leading to a safe choice of husband (Blauvelt, 2007). To be sure, young adults today still care about a partner's character, but the stakes are not as high as in the past because it is possible for women to lead independent adult lives and because ending an unhappy marriage through divorce is much more acceptable. In the early 1800s, then, both emotion and practicality played important roles in choosing a spouse.

Despite these changes, marriage retained a moral basis in custom and law through the nineteenth century. According to historian Nancy Cott (2000), political philosophers argued that lifetime marriage with the husband as the head was similar to American governance: It involved democratic rule by a leader (the husband) with the voluntary consent of the governed (the wife). Preserving marriage was seen as essential to maintaining a democratic moral order. Consequently, government support for marriage—such as laws that made obtaining a divorce difficult—was viewed as necessary and proper. Cott's thesis suggests that the family's contribution to public welfare was conceived more broadly than today. I defined the "public family" in terms of its valuable care for dependents. Prior to the twentieth century, many Americans also thought that marriage served as the foundation of national morality. This view of marriage as the moral and political backbone of society would erode during the twentieth century, although it has reemerged among some traditionalists in the twenty-first.

FROM COOPERATION TO SEPARATION: WOMEN'S AND MEN'S SPHERES

Another spur to family change was the transition from subsistence farming to wage labor. Instead of growing crops and tending animals, more husbands took paying jobs. It began sometime in the 1700s and early 1800s, with the growth of commercial capitalism—an economic system that emphasizes the buying, selling, and distribution of goods such as grain, tobacco, or cotton. Commercial capitalism created jobs for merchants, clerks, shippers, dock-workers, wagon builders, and others like them, who were paid money for their labor. The opportunity to earn money outside the home undermined the authority of fathers. Because sons had alternatives to farming, fathers no longer had a near monopoly on the resources needed to make a living. This greater economic independence facilitated the growth of individualism. The transition accelerated in the mid-1800s with the spread of industrial capitalism, which created factory work for the great masses of immigrants and their descendants.

The heart of this change was the movement of men's work out of the home. Instead of working together in a common household enterprise, husbands and wives now worked on separate enterprises—he exchanging his labor for wages, she maintaining the home and raising the children. Instead of working in close proximity, the two were physically separated during the workday. Moreover, wage work held no intrinsic value for most men, and in nineteenth-century factories it was frequently exhausting and dangerous.

The sharp split between a rewarding home life and an often alienating work life led to the emergence of the idea of "separate spheres": men's sphere being the world of work and, more generally, the world outside the home; and women's sphere being the home, relatives, and children. Whereas men's sphere was seen as being governed by the rough ethic of the business world, women's sphere came to be seen as morally pure, a place where wives could renew their husbands' spirituality and character. And whereas men's sphere was seen as providing no reward other than a paycheck, women's sphere was the center of affection and nurturing, the emotional core for husbands and children.

Thus developed a nineteenth-century ideology, a set of beliefs, which historian Barbara Welter (1966) named "the cult of True Womanhood." The True Woman was, first of all, a pious upholder of spiritual values. She was also pure: She was to have no sexual contact before marriage—although men might try to tempt her—and none afterward except with her husband. Moreover, the True Woman was submissive to men, particularly her husband. And finally, she was domestic: Her proper place was in the home, comforting her husband, lovingly raising her children.

Woman's sphere at once limited women's opportunities and glorified their domestic role. It was a more restricted role than wives in the colonial era had experienced. To be sure, the Puritan wife was also home most of the day, but she was collaborating with her husband in the family economy; without her contribution, her husband might not have been able to feed and clothe their children. Then the movement to wage labor separated women from paid work. Men went out every morning into the wider social world, but their wives could not follow. In a culture that had begun to celebrate individualism, women were supposed to give up much of their individualism to care for their husbands and children. Seen from this vantage point, one might argue that women's lives were worse than they had been before the Revolution—more restricted, less productive, more dependent and more isolated. Indeed, many historians have argued as much.

But other historians, while acknowledging the restrictions and dependency inherent in the domestic sphere, argue that it nevertheless offered some benefits. Appointing women the guardians of moral values and giving them the major role in rearing children provided them with substantial influence. However circumscribed, it may have allowed wives to counter the authority of their husbands, which had been so pervasive in the colonial period. Moreover, the ideology of women's sphere may have created a self-consciousness of, and an identification with, women as a group. Women established and maintained deep friendships with other women, reinforced by the segregation of their lives and by female rituals surrounding childbirth, weddings, illnesses, and funerals (Smith-Rosenberg, 1975). Some joined together in public associations to promote values consistent with domesticity, such as greater devotion to religion, assistance for the poor, or enlightened child-rearing. These friendships and associations may have been a prerequisite for the development of feminist organizations in the nineteenth and twentieth centuries. Historian Nancy Cott captured the dual nature of women's sphere in the title of her book, *The Bonds of Womanhood* (1977), for the bonds that tied women to the domestic sphere also bound them together in a subculture of sisterhood that prefigured their social and political movements decades later.

Quick Review

- In the late 1700s and early 1800s, American marriage seemed to change.
  - Greater importance was given to affection and mutual respect rather than male authority.
  - Increasing attention was paid to the loving care of (a declining number of) children.
- Under the emerging doctrine of "separate spheres," men's sphere was the world outside the home, women's, the home, relatives, and children.
- Women's sphere restricted their opportunities but also fostered friendships and participation in public organizations.

African American, Mexican American, and Asian Immigrant Families

Europeans, of course, were not the only immigrants to the United States. Three other groups were present early in the nation's history. Africans had been forced to immigrate—captured or bought in West Africa, transported across the ocean under horrible conditions that killed many, and sold as slaves upon arrival. Mexicans, in search of grazing land, had pushed north into the area that is now the Southwest. Asian immigrants first arrived in large numbers in the mid-nineteenth century, when they were used as laborers by the railroads and other enterprises. The family lives of all three groups differed from those of the Europeans. Like white working-class women, those from racial and ethnic minority groups had to contribute economically outside, as well as inside, the home (Dill, 1988).

AFRICAN AMERICAN FAMILIES

An African Heritage? As later chapters will document, African American families have long been distinct from white families: Historically, they have maintained stronger ties to extended kin such as uncles, aunts, and cousins and have borne a higher percentage of children outside marriage. The extent to which these differences reflect the lasting influence of African culture has been hotly debated (Herskovits, 1990). But the similarities between the old and the new cultures are striking enough to consider whether some continuities may exist.

Traditionally, African society was organized by lineages, which I have defined as large kinship groups that trace their descent through the male or female line. Members of the lineage cooperated and shared resources with others, and adults carefully controlled and monitored courtship and marriage among the young. What mattered most was not the happiness of the married couple, but the birth of children who could be retained by the lineage. In the Western nations, we are used to thinking of marriage as an event that occurs at a particular time: On the appointed date, two people participate in a ceremony and register their intentions with the state government. But in Africa, marriage was much more of a process, a series of steps that occurred over a long period of time (Bledsoe, 1990). Childbearing could occur before the ceremony, but the clear expectation was that marriage would follow within a few years.

When Africans brought these cultural patterns to the United States, the institution of slavery stripped their elders of authority over the marriage process. Their lineages, as anthropologist Niara Sudarkasa (1980, 1981) has written, were reduced to extended families. In Africa, elders had had substantial authority over individuals because they controlled crucial resources, most notably land. An African who was disowned by a lineage faced a terrible future. But in the United States, the wider kinship group no longer controlled the allocation of land, livestock, or jobs. Thus, among many African Americans, the extended kinship groups were limited to serving as social support networks. Extended families were important to individuals who belonged to them, but they had less control over their members' actions.

Historically, African American families have placed more emphasis on ties to extended kin than have European American families.

The Impact of Slavery   Until the appearance of new scholarship in the 1970s, in fact, most historians thought that the oppression and harsh conditions of slavery had destroyed most of the culture African slaves brought with them, leaving little in its place. The writings of both white and black scholars emphasized the losses imposed by slavery: the uprooting from Africa, the disruption of families through sales of family members to new owners, the inability of fathers to protect their families from the abuses imposed by masters. In an influential 1939 book, E. Franklin Frazier, a sociologist and an African American, argued that white masters had destroyed all social organization among the slaves. As a result, he wrote, slave family life was disorganized; the only stable bond was between mothers and their children:

> *Consequently, under all conditions of slavery, the Negro mother remained the most dependable and important figure in the family. (Frazier, 1939)*

From Frazier and others, then, came the idea that both during and after slavery, most African American families were headed by women and that African American men were relatively powerless in and outside the home. But in 1976, historian Herbert Gutman published a comprehensive study of plantation, local government, and census records that suggested a much different picture (Gutman, 1976). Gutman found substantial evidence that

A family history chart from about 1880, "designed for the colored people of America" according to the artist, W. H. Cowell, shows scenes from before and after the Civil War.

whenever possible, slaves had married and lived together for life and that they knew and kept track of uncles, aunts, cousins, and other kin. He cited letters such as one the field hand Cash sent to relatives on a Georgia plantation after he, his wife, Phoebe, and some of their children were sold away:

> *Clairissa your affectionate Mother and Father sends a heap of love to you and your Husband and my Grand Children. Mag. & Cloe. John. Judy. My aunt sinena . . . Give our Love to Cashes brother Porter and his Wife Patience. Victoria sends her Love to her Cousin Beck and Miley. (Gutman, 1976)*

Moreover, Gutman argued, before and after slavery, in both the North and the South, most African American families included two parents. These family ties were forged despite the frequent sale of husbands, wives, and children to other masters, despite the sexual abuse of slave women by owners, and despite high rates of disease and death.

Still, there were some differences, both before and after the Civil War, between black and white families. For example, young slave women often had a first child before marrying; if so, they were usually married within a few years, although not necessarily to the father (Jones, 1985). This pattern may have occurred in part because slave owners valued women who had many children, increasing the owner's wealth. Yet as we have seen, it is also consistent with custom in Africa. Moreover, the disruption of slave families may have been more severe on smaller plantations. In the Appalachian area, where landowners had fewer slaves, the frequent hiring out of slaves to other landowners disrupted marriages. Sales of slaves—often to cotton farmers in the lower South—may have been more common than in the larger plantations, with perhaps one-third of Appalachian slave marriages broken by sales (Dunaway, 2003).

Another difference between black and white families was that after the Civil War, wives in rural black families worked seasonally in the fields, whereas rural white women didn't. According to 1870 census figures for the Cotton Belt states, about 4 in 10 African American wives had jobs, almost all as field workers. In contrast, 98 percent of white wives said they were "keeping house" and had no other job (Jones, 1985). Here again, the differences reflect a mixture of economic pressure and culture. The plots of land African American sharecroppers farmed in the late nineteenth century provided such a marginal standard of living that men and women (and often children) were needed in the fields, at least at harvesttime. Historian Jacqueline Jones (1985) has also noted that "the outlines of African work patterns endured among the slaves," in that African women often bore the major responsibility for cultivating food.

Moreover, although most black families still had two parents, black mothers were more likely to be living without a male partner than white mothers. This racial difference stemmed partly from the high mortality rates of black men; by one estimate, 42 percent of black wives were widowed by ages 45 to 50 around 1900 (Preston, Lim, & Morgan, 1992). But a difference still remains after mortality is taken into account (Morgan, McDaniel, Miller, & Preston, 1993). A much larger racial difference in household structure would emerge after about 1960 (see Chapter 5).

When black families migrated to Northern cities in the twentieth century, black women continued to work outside the home in larger numbers than white women. About one-third of married nonwhite women worked outside the home in the 1920s and 1930s, compared with less than one-tenth of married white women (Goldin, 1977). Because of discrimination, black men were offered only low-paying, physically challenging jobs that couldn't support a family, such as stoking a blast furnace in a steel factory. Staying home simply was not an option for most black wives, who also faced discrimination and found work mainly as domestic servants. Not until the 1960s did black women break out of domestic service into occupations previously reserved for white women. Today, women of both races still lag behind men in earnings, and black men's employment situation, though improved, remains difficult.

MEXICAN AMERICAN FAMILIES

Like African Americans, Mexican Americans established a presence early in the history of what is now the United States—although unlike African Americans, the descendants of these early residents are now vastly outnumbered by recent immigrants. In the early nineteenth century, well before migrants from the eastern United States arrived, Mexicans settled the frontier of what was then northern Mexico (Moore & Cuéllar, 1970). These pioneers crossed deserts and fought with American Indians to reach as far west as California and as far north as Colorado. Their early settlements generally included an elite landowning family and poorer farmer-laborer settlers. The landowning elite tended to be (or claimed to be) of nearly pure Spanish descent. Some owned vast tracts of land on which they grazed cattle or sheep. They arranged their children's marriages with care and celebrated elaborate weddings and feasts, so as to preserve or merge their holdings with other wealthy families or with wealthy Anglo (non-Mexican) immigrants (Griswold del Castillo, 1979).

More numerous were the laborers who worked the great estates or farmed or grazed animals on their own smaller holdings. They tended to be **mestizos,** people whose ancestors included both Spanish settlers and Native Americans from Mexico. There is some evidence that informal marriages were more common among this group (Griswold del Castillo, 1979). Informal marriages allowed couples to evade the control of their parents and other kin; and with fewer resources to protect than among the elite, the *mestizo* classes had less reason to control who married whom. These small landholders and laborers attempted to enlist the sponsorship and support of the well-to-do through the tradition of **compadrazgo,** a godparent relationship in which a wealthy or influential person outside the kinship group became the *compadre,* or godparent, of a newborn child, particularly at its baptism. The godfather and godchild were expected to retain a special relationship, and the godparent was supposed to assist his godchild, for example, by providing or finding a job for him (Camarillo, 1979).

mestizo a person whose ancestors include both Spanish settlers and Native Americans

compadrazgo in Mexico, a godparent relationship in which a wealthy or influential person outside the kinship group is asked to become the *compadre,* or godparent, of a newborn child, particularly at its baptism

This social structure was disrupted by a series of wars, revolts, and land grabs by U.S. troops and immigrants during the 1830s and 1840s. When it was over, the United States had acquired, by conquest, the current Southwest. Soon thereafter, most of the Spanish elite lost their land to taxes, drought, and Anglo squatters. Instead of ranchers and farmers, Mexicans became more of a working-class community, employed by the growing numbers of Anglos (Camarillo, 1979). Census statistics for the Los Angeles district in the last half of the nineteenth century show a rising number of households headed by women (Griswold del Castillo, 1979). Some of these women were probably married to men who migrated from harvest to harvest, picking crops; others were informally married. But many were probably unmarried, their numbers reflecting the economic changes of the time. Mexican American women, like African American women, could find low-paying but steady work as domestics and launderers for wealthier Anglos, whereas Mexican American men were losing their established positions as small ranchers and farmers.

As the number of Anglo immigrants rose, Mexican Americans were forced into **barrios,** segregated neighborhoods in the city. Residents of the *barrios* faced high unemployment or low income if they provided low-wage labor to Anglo employers. During economic expansions, waves of new Mexican immigrants were drawn into the country, further depressing their wages (Camarillo, 1979). Mexican immigrant families often were highly male-dominant: Husbands were supposed to be powerful, respected, and in charge; wives were supposed to submit to their authority (Queen et al., 1985). But the traditional male dominance eroded under the low wages of urban employment and the separation of migrant workers from their families. Today, Mexican American

barrio a segregated Mexican-American neighborhood in a U.S. city

families in the barrios still show the effects of poverty and unemployment. Yet they remain distinctive in other respects, such as their high birthrates (see Chapter 5).

ASIAN IMMIGRANT FAMILIES

The Asian Heritage   Before the middle of the twentieth century, most Asian American families in the United States consisted of immigrants from China and Japan and their descendants. Family systems in East Asia (where China and Japan are located) were sharply different from those in the United States and other Western countries, although these differences are currently diminishing (Goode, 1963; Hong, 1999; Queen et al., 1985). In the traditional East Asian family, fathers had more authority over family members than is true in the West. For example, fathers usually controlled who their children would marry and when. In addition, kinship was patrilineal, or traced through the father's line. In China, the ideal was that a man's sons (and eventually his grandsons) would bring their wives into his growing household. Daughters would be sent at marriage to live in their in-laws' households. When parents grew old, sons and their wives were expected to live with them and care for them. In Japan, the oldest son carried the main responsibility for the care of elderly parents. Thus, East Asian cultures placed a greater emphasis on children's loyalty to their parents than Western culture. For a son or daughter, happiness in marriage was less important than fulfilling obligations to parents and other kin.

Asian Immigrants   Chinese immigrants first began to arrive during the California gold rush in the 1850s. After the Civil War, they were hired to build the railroads of the Southwest. Because the vast majority of these immigrant laborers were men, relatively few new families were formed. In fact, about half left wives behind (Glenn, 1983). Many of the men fulfilled the obligations they felt toward kin by sending **remittances,** or cash payments, to family members such as spouses or elderly parents in their country of origin. In California and most other western states, laws prohibited Chinese (and later Japanese) immigrants from marrying white Americans or becoming citizens. In fact, American sentiment against Chinese immigrants was so strong that in 1882 Congress passed the Chinese Exclusion Act, which restricted Chinese immigration until after World War II (Olson, 1979). By the mid-twentieth century, Chinese immigrants could more easily bring over their wives. Many immigrant families started small businesses such as laundries or restaurants in which all family members worked (Glenn, 1983).

remittances cash payments sent by immigrants to family members in their country of origin

In the 1880s, significant numbers of Japanese immigrants began to arrive in Hawaii (which the United States would soon annex) and the mainland United States. The ratio of women to men was more balanced among the Japanese than among Chinese immigrants, so more families were formed. Both Chinese and Japanese families were patrilineal. The father's authority was strong, and ties to extended family members were important. Traditionally, parents or other relatives arranged their children's marriages (Wong, 1988). Since immigrants usually left their extended families behind, they developed other ways of building family-like ties in the United States. For example, people from the same region of China or Japan formed mutual aid societies, and wealthy merchants sometimes played the supervisory roles village elders had in Asia (Olson, 1979).

Like the Chinese, Japanese immigrants faced discrimination. After the war with Japan began in 1941, some Americans warned that Japanese immigrants might be disloyal, even though many had lived in the United States for decades. Bowing to these fears, the government rounded up Japanese immigrants, most of whom lived in California, and sent them to internment camps. Aside from the imprisonment, humiliation, and economic losses the Japanese suffered there, the camps eroded the traditional authority of Japanese parents (Kitano & Daniels, 1988). They had little to offer children who were exposed to American activities such as dancing to the music of the latest bands. Young Japanese American men could even volunteer to join a much-decorated U.S. Army unit that fought in Europe. After the war, the autonomy children had experienced in the camps contributed to sharp changes in Japanese American marriage patterns. Whereas the older generation's marriages had been arranged by relatives who stressed obligations to kin and emotional restraint, the younger generation much more often chose their own spouses based on romantic love and companionship (Yanagisako, 1985).

Overall, Asian immigration was modest until Congress passed the **1965 Immigration Act,** which ended restrictions that had blocked most Asian immigration and substituted an annual quota. Since then, the Asian population of the United States has expanded rapidly. There were 17.3 million people of Asian origin in the United States in 2010, a 46 percent increase from 2000 (U.S. Bureau of the Census, 2012a). The two largest groups were Chinese and Filipinos.

Filipino immigration began as a small stream of mostly students after the United States captured the Philippines in the Spanish-American War of 1898. After 1965, many Filipino immigrants were professionals, most notably nurses. Unlike Chinese and Japanese families, Filipino families trace descent through both the father's and mother's line, a system called **bilateral kinship** (the system followed in the United States). Such a system usually provides women more independence than patrilineal kinship, so Filipino American women have been more likely to work outside the home than women in Chinese or Japanese families (Kitano & Daniels, 1988).

1965 Immigration Act act passed by the U.S. Congress which ended restrictions that had blocked most Asian immigration and substituted an annual quota

bilateral kinship a system in which descent is reckoned through both the mother's and father's lines

Quick Review

- The family lives of groups that emigrated from Africa (through slavery), Mexico, and Asia differed from the family lives of European immigrants.
- The women in all immigrant families were more likely to contribute economically than were middle-class women.
- African American families have maintained stronger ties to extended kin and borne a higher percentage of children outside of marriage than have European American families.
- Most African American families had two parents, even during slavery.
- Early Mexican settlers included a landed elite and a larger population of *mestizos.*
- Mexican families use the tradition of *compadrazgo* to obtain assistance for children.
- Chinese immigration was heavily male at first, and immigrants sent home remittances to family.
- Japanese families were sent to internment camps during World War II.
- Both Chinese and Japanese families were traditionally patrilineal, with arranged marriages.

The Rise of the Private Family: 1900–Present

THE EARLY DECADES

An increase in premarital sex. A drop in the birthrate. A new youth culture rebelling against propriety, dressing outrageously, and indulging in indecent dance steps. And a rapidly rising divorce rate. These were the concerns of American moralists, politicians, and social scientists during the first few decades of the twentieth century. The flourishing new youth culture was exemplified in the 1920s by the "flapper" girls. Independent, often employed outside the home, and brazen enough to bob their hair and wear lipstick and eyeliner in public, the flappers patronized dance halls and movie theaters with their male companions. Historian Stephanie Coontz (2005) notes that interest in and openness about sexuality grew during this period. A good marriage, people increasingly thought, required a good sex life, although the husband's satisfaction still seemed to matter more than the wife's. By the 1920s, birth control pioneers such as Margaret Sanger had opened clinics, and public discussion about ways to prevent births was widespread.

Perhaps the greatest source of concern, the divorce rate had risen to the point where a marriage begun in 1910 had about a 1-in-7 chance of ending in divorce. This may seem like a small risk today, but it represented a substantial increase over the 1-in-12 chance in 1880 or the 1-in-20 chance at the end of the Civil War (Cherlin, 1992). Yet the period from the 1890s through the 1920s was generally one of increasing prosperity—which raises the question of why an increase in divorce would occur. In part, it was made possible by the growing economic independence of women, who were now better educated, had fewer children, had likely worked outside the home before marrying, and therefore had greater potential to find work outside the home if their marriages ended (O'Neill, 1967). But that is not the whole story, for the marriage rate kept rising right along with the divorce rate. What had occurred, in addition, is that both women and men came to expect a greater amount of emotional satisfaction from marriage (May, 1980). More than ever before, they sought happiness, companionship, and romantic love in marriage. If they found their marriages fell short of their expectations, they were more likely to ask for a divorce. (See *Families and Public Policy:* Divorce Reform: Have We Been Here Before?) As Coontz (2005) writes, the trend had begun in the latter part of the 1800s:

> *The people who took idealization of love and intimacy to new heights during the nineteenth century did not intend to shake up marriage or unleash a new preoccupation with sexual gratification. . . . In the long run, however, they weakened it. The focus on romantic love eventually undercut the doctrine of separate spheres for men and women and the ideal of female purity, putting new strains on the institution of marriage.*

The emphasis on love and companionship, and the accompanying strain on marital bonds, spread in the early 1900s.

And so women and men came to see marriage and family as central to their quest for an emotionally satisfying private life. Before the twentieth century,

In the 1920s, greater numbers of independent young women were employed outside the home.

emotional satisfaction had been less important to both husbands and wives, but not because they were ignorant of the concept—no Ariès-like claim is made here that people of the twentieth century discovered happiness. Rather, before the twentieth century the standard of living had been so low that most people needed to concentrate on keeping themselves clothed, housed, and fed. Before 1900, pursuing personal pleasure was a luxury few could indulge in. Most were too busy just trying to get by.

Even after 1900, large segments of the American population—immigrants and racial and ethnic minorities—had little time to invest in private life. My grandparents immigrated from Eastern Europe just after the turn of the century, started a grocery store, and raised 10 children. Had I been around to ask them whether their marriage was satisfying, they would have said "of course"—they were raising a big family. They would not have answered in terms of companionship, romance, sexual pleasure, excitement, or personal growth. Yet these were the ways in which more and more Americans came to define a successful marriage in the twentieth century.

Still, Americans (and the citizens of other Western nations) were gradually enlarging the scope of the *private family*. They were defining marital success in emotional terms, not material terms, and were beginning to derive their greatest satisfaction not from the roles they played (breadwinner, homemaker, father, mother) but from the quality of the relationships they had with their spouses and children. This process had certainly begun long ago among the more prosperous classes, and it continued throughout the twentieth century. But in some eras its ascendancy was more noticeable than in others, and the first few decades of the twentieth century were such an era.

Divorce Reform: Have We Been Here Before?

At current rates, nearly one out of two marriages begun in the United States today will end in divorce (Bramlett & Mosher, 2002). As noted, the divorce rate has been increasing since at least the Civil War. The most recent burst occurred between the early 1960s and mid-1970s, during which time the probability that a marriage would end in divorce doubled. Since then, the rate has declined (Cherlin, 1992). Nevertheless, the rise in divorce has alarmed some commentators, who fear that it is undermining the institution of the family. (The effects of divorce will be discussed in detail in Chapter 12.)

Some writers have called for a toughening of divorce laws, which were relaxed in the 1970s and 1980s, when all states enacted "no fault" divorce legislation. About half of Americans in a national survey say that divorce should be more difficult to obtain (Davis & Smith, 2010). Yet this is not the first time a debate has emerged about the consequences of divorce, and restrictive legislation has been proposed. In fact, the divorce debates of the Progressive Era (1890–1930) bear an uncanny resemblance to the current discourse. As in the 1960s and 1970s, a rise in the divorce rate during that era caused concern. So did a fall in the birthrate among native-born whites. John Watson, a leading psychologist, voiced the fears of many when he predicted that "in fifty years there will be no such thing as marriage" (Mintz & Kellogg, 1988). Arthur Calhoun, the leading historian of the family, acknowledged the sweeping changes, but wrote approvingly that "we are in the midst of a social revolution" which would make a new, more democratic family "inevitable" (Calhoun, 1919).

Divorce had been available in most states since the colonial era but at first on a very restricted basis. Through most of the 1800s, it was stigmatizing and granted only on limited grounds such as adultery. According to a legal historian, "Divorce was not a right, only a remedy for a wrong" (Hartog, 2000). Nevertheless, in the 1890s and 1900s, rising divorce rates led many legislatures, especially in the eastern states, to tighten divorce laws. According to historian Elaine Tyler May, between 1889 and 1906 state legislatures enacted more than 100 restrictive marriage and divorce laws. For instance, 15 states forbade remarriage until one or two years after a final divorce decree, and 6 eliminated certain grounds for divorce. New York permitted divorce only in the event of adultery, and South Carolina prohibited it altogether (May, 1980).

The Progressive Era was also a time of great and varied action by groups seeking reform in order to increase democracy, governmental efficiency, and the quality of life. So-called social progressives sought improvements in industrial working conditions and in the lives of parents and children (Skocpol, 1992). Many social progressives, including those interested in the family, sought reform through the passage of new laws. For example, an InterChurch Conference led by Episcopal Bishop William Doane convinced President Theodore Roosevelt to order the Bureau of the Census to carry out a new study on marriage and divorce.

In Roosevelt's message to Congress in 1905, he wrote:

As these developments were occurring, the family was becoming less of a dominant force in people's lives. The many public goods the colonial family had provided gradually diminished: Compulsory schooling replaced education at home; hospitals replaced sickbeds; department stores replaced home crafts; and so forth. As marriage became less necessary economically and materially, it was redefined as a means of gaining emotional satisfaction. A well-known text on the family described this transformation as a shift "from institution to companionship" (Burgess & Locke, 1945). (See Chapter 7.) In this process, marriage became more fragile, for the bonds of sentiment were weaker than the ties forged by working a family farm or the unchallenged authority of the patriarch. Soon, an institution that had been designed to enhance survival and security began to creak under the weight of expectations that it provide so much emotional satisfaction. One result was a more or less continuous increase in the divorce rate, which reached a high plateau about 1980.

There is widespread conviction that the divorce laws are dangerously lax and indifferently administered in some of the states, resulting in a diminished regard for the sanctity of the marriage relation.[1]

To eliminate overly liberal state laws, Roosevelt called for uniform divorce legislation in all states.

Yet despite all this activity, despite numerous conferences on uniform divorce laws and attempts in Congress to tighten state provisions, little was accomplished, and the divorce rate continued to rise. Why did reformers have so little success? Historians who have studied the era argue that the reformers were fighting against powerful cultural changes in the nature of marriage. Marriage was becoming more of a companionship, more of a relationship among equals. Increasingly, people sought personal satisfaction through marriage.[2] I would add that the rising standard of living in the early decades of the twentieth century allowed people to focus less on food and shelter and more on emotional satisfaction. Because of this new emphasis, people who found their marriages lacking in satisfaction were more likely to consider divorce (see Chapter 12). Moreover, the increasing employment of women decreased their economic dependence on men, making marriage less necessary.

Given the strength of these cultural and economic forces, the social progressives were unable to enact their program of divorce reform. Advances in one state would be stymied by setbacks in others. Resistance to more restrictive divorce legislation remained firm. The failures of the reformers may hold lessons for those who today urge public action to reduce the divorce rate. The same cultural and economic forces have continued to influence marriage and divorce throughout the twentieth century. Indeed, one could argue that they are more powerful now: The quest for personal fulfillment has led to widespread cohabitation outside of marriage; the loosening of cultural constraints has led to a toleration of childbearing outside of marriage; and the economic independence of women has grown as a majority of wives now work outside the home. A look backward at the entire century, and particularly at the Progressive Era, suggests that today's divorce reformers have few promising strategies to follow. Lowering the divorce rate through political action and moral suasion is a very difficult task.

Ask Yourself

1. Think back over the last two or three generations in your family. Has the divorce rate increased from one generation to the next? What about marital happiness and personal fulfillment—does it seem to have increased?

2. Should the law be changed so it is more difficult to obtain a divorce? From the family's point of view, what might be the advantages and disadvantages of doing so?

[1] Quoted in O'Neill (1967).
[2] Mintz and Kellogg, May, and O'Neill all present arguments along these lines.

www.mhhe.com/cherlin7e

Privacy also increased after 1900. Two demographic trends contributed to this increase. First, the birthrate declined, which meant, among other things, fewer persons per room. Second, adult life expectancy increased due to advances in medicine and a rising standard of living. As a result of these trends, parents were younger when they finished the child-rearing stage of life, and they lived longer after their last child left home. Consequently, a new stage of family life, the "empty nest" phase of married life after all children have left home, became common. Between 1900 and 2000 the proportion of 45–64 year olds who were empty nesters tripled from 11 to 34 percent (Fischer & Hout, 2006).

Greater prosperity also meant that more apartments were built, and more people could afford to live on their own. And the rise in individualism probably made more unmarried people *wish* to live on their own. Consequently, boarding and lodging went from commonplace to rarity during the first half of the century (Laslett, 1973). In 1950, 9 percent of all households contained one person; by 1970 the figure was 17 percent; and by 2010 it was 27 percent (Kobrin, 1976; U.S. Bureau of the Census, 2010b). Even so, during the first few decades of the century, about two-thirds of young women and perhaps 40 percent of young men did not leave home until they married. If they did, it was often because their parents lived in rural areas, where young adults couldn't find jobs. Later, in the 1940s and 1950s, the age at which young adults left home fell sharply, both because of earlier marriage and because many young men left home to join the military during World War II and the Korean War (Goldscheider & Goldscheider, 1994).

The first few decades of the twentieth century, then, were an important time of change in the American family. The basis for marriage moved away from an economic partnership and toward emotional satisfaction and companionship. Men and women became more economically independent of each other. As a result of these developments, the bonds of marriage became weaker, and divorce became more common. In addition, prosperity, lower birthrates, and longer life expectancy accelerated the trend toward privacy, as exemplified by child-free older couples and people living alone.

THE DEPRESSION GENERATION

The prosperity of the early decades of the century was interrupted by the Great Depression, which began in 1929 and continued until the late 1930s. In addition to its severe effects on family finances, the Depression also undermined the authority and prestige of the father. If he lost his job, his family might view him as having failed in his role as breadwinner. If his wife or his children were forced to find jobs, as many were, their labor was a constant reminder of his inability to fulfill their expectations. The experiences of families during the Great Depression can help us understand the strains families are facing today as the United States struggles to surmount the Great Recession. (See *Families and the Great Recession:* Lessons from the Great Depression.)

The economic hardships forced many young adults to postpone marriage and childbearing. The Depression was so long and so severe that some couples never had the opportunity to have children. As a result, lifetime childlessness was more common among women who reached their peak childbearing years in the 1930s than in any other generation of women in the twentieth century: About one in five never had a child (Rindfuss, Morgan, & Swicegood, 1988). In contrast, only about one in ten of the women who reached their peak reproductive years during the 1950s baby boom never had a child.

As fathers and mothers struggled to make a living, their children helped out. Teenage boys took whatever jobs they could find; teenage girls took over more of the household work for mothers who were forced to work outside the home. The result was what Glen Elder, Jr., called "the downward extension of adultlike experience": Girls took on the role of homemaker; boys took on the role of breadwinner. Elder (1974) examined the records of a group of children who were first observed in 1932, at age 11, and then followed through adulthood. He found that when they reached adulthood, the men and women in the group who came from economically

Families and the Great Recession

Lessons from the Great Depression

In times of economic crisis, Americans turn to their families for support. The question is how much weight their families will bear and how resilient their spouses and partners will be. As we seek to understand the likely effects of today's Great Recession on family life, we can learn some lessons from studies of what happened to divorce rates during the Great Depression of the 1930s.

You might expect that divorce would have increased during the Depression because of the marital stress caused by widespread unemployment. Yet the divorce rate, which had been rising slowly since the Civil War, suddenly dropped in 1930, the year after the Depression began. By 1932, when one-quarter of the workforce was unemployed, it had declined by 25 percent. It's very unlikely that people were suddenly happier with their marriages. Rather, with incomes plummeting and jobs insecure, unhappy couples often couldn't afford to get divorced. They feared that if they split their families in two, neither spouse would be able to manage.

Economic constraints aren't the whole story of why divorce rates dropped in the early 1930s. Studies of natural disasters such as hurricanes and floods show that when crises occur, family members do whatever they can to help each other and their communities. Morale is high. Relatives take in kin who have lost their homes. This is also the way people initially respond to financial disasters, as the Depression showed. In her book, *The Unemployed Man and His Family*, sociologist Mirra Komarovsky (1940) told of a family in which the husband initially reacted to losing his job "with tireless search for work." He was always active, looking for odd jobs or washing windows for neighbors. Another unemployed man initially enjoyed spending more time with his young children. These men's spirits were up, and their wives were supportive, despite the devastating blow of having lost their jobs. The Depression at first brought families together rather than splitting them apart.

The problem, however, is that it's hard to sustain extraordinary activity and spirited support. Eventually the adrenaline rush goes away, the impulse to help fades, and people simply tire of trying so hard. Over time the men Komarovsky studied grew discouraged, their efforts lessened, and their relationships with their wives and teenage children often deteriorated. Across the country, many similar families were unable to sustain any boost in morale they may have established just after unemployment hit. For some, the tensions and hardships of life without steady work eventually overwhelmed their attempts to keep their families together. The divorce rate began to rise again in 1934 when employment picked up, providing some unhappy couples with the income they needed in order to separate. It rose during the rest of the decade as the recovery took hold.

If this two-stage pattern of solidarity followed by distress is still applicable, millions of Americans who experienced job losses in today's Great Recession may have worked together with their families and supported one another through the early months of unemployment. During the Depression this stage seemed to last a year at most. Today, it might last longer. Wives now share with their husbands the burden of earning money, and the government provides more assistance through programs such as Unemployment Insurance and Supplemental Nutrition Assistance (formerly food stamps).

At first, then, we might expect the divorce rate to decline. And that is indeed what appears to have happened early in the current Great Recession. A survey of married Americans in late 2010 reported that among all individuals who said they had been considering divorce prior to the recession 38 percent said that the recession had caused them to put aside their thoughts. But it is likely that toward the end of the Great Recession, as was the case toward the end of the Great Depression, marital solidarity will be strained, financial constraints will ease, and the recession-induced drop in divorce rates will end.

---

deprived families valued marriage and family life more highly than those whose families hadn't experienced hardship. Women from deprived families married at younger ages than other women. Perhaps the difficulties their families had faced when they were adolescents made the deprived group eager for a secure marriage, or perhaps they viewed families as an important resource in hard times. In any event, when they reached adulthood, these young men and women turned inward to build their own family lives.

The hardships of the Great Depression strained many families in the 1930s. Dorothea Lange photographed this migrant mother and her children in their makeshift home.

Quick Review

- In the twentieth century, people increasingly viewed family life through the perspective I have called the *private family*.
  - People began to derive their greatest pleasure from the quality of their personal relationships.
  - People increasingly viewed marriage primarily as a means of obtaining emotional satisfaction.
  - Divorce became more common.
  - Privacy itself increased as standards of living rose, birthrates dropped, and life expectancy rose.
- The hardship of the Great Depression forced a generation to alter their family lives by, for example, delaying or forgoing marriage and childbearing.

THE 1950s

In fact, when the young adults of the Depression generation began to marry and have children after World War II, they created the most unusual and distinctive family patterns of the century. They married younger and had more children than any other twentieth-century generation. Figure 2.1 shows the percentage of 20- to 24-year-old men and women who had never been married, from 1890 to 2010. This is the age group that is most sensitive to variations in age at marriage. Note the percentage is highest at the beginning and end of this chart, indicating that young men and women were most likely to be single (and therefore to marry at an older age) in the late 1800s and the current era. The percentage who had never been married declined slowly during the first

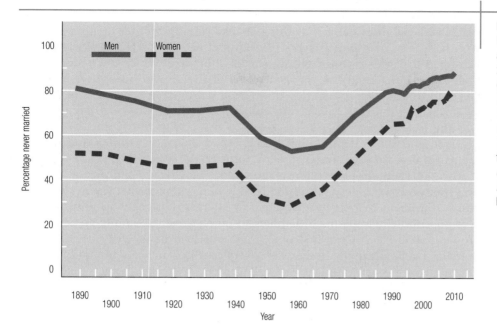

FIGURE 2.1
Percentage never married among men and women aged 20 to 24, 1890 to 2010. (*Sources:* for 1890–1960, *U.S. Bureau of the Census, 1995, Historical Statistics of the United States, Colonial Times to 1970*, pp. 20–21; for 1970–2010, *U.S. Bureau of the Census, Current Population Reports*, Series P20, various issues.)

half of the twentieth century and then plunged to its lowest point during the 1950s. After 1960, it rose sharply especially for women, who by the turn of the century were marrying later than at any time in the previous 100 years.

The years after World War II were also the time of the great **baby boom.** Couples not only married at younger ages but also had children faster—and had more of them—than their parents' generation or, as statistics would later show, than even their children's generation. Indeed, the late 1940s through the 1950s was the only period in the past 150 years during which the American birthrate rose substantially. It spiked dramatically just after the war, as couples had babies they had postponed having during the war. After a few years it dropped, but then began to climb again, peaking in 1957. Women who married during the 1950s had an average of slightly more than three children, the highest fertility rate of the century (Evans, 1986).

Although the causes of the baby boom are not fully clear, a strong post-World War II economy and a renewed cultural emphasis on marriage and children were certainly contributing factors. One explanation focuses on the unique circumstances of the young adults who married during the 1950s. Since most of them were born during the Depression, when birthrates were low, they constituted a relatively small **birth cohort,** as demographers call all the people born during a given year or period of years. After the bad luck of growing up during the Depression and the war, they had the good fortune to reach adulthood just as the economy was growing rapidly. The Allied victory in World War II had left the United States with the strongest economy in the world. Employers needed more workers, but the small size of the cohort meant there were fewer workers to hire (especially given the widespread preference during the 1950s that married women forgo work outside the home). In this tight labor market wages rose for young men, allowing them to support larger families.[5]

baby boom the large number of people born during the late 1940s and 1950s

birth cohort all people born during a given year or period of years

[5] The relative-cohort-size theory was expounded by Easterlin (1980).

This explanation, however, is incomplete. Birthrates rose not only among newlyweds in their early twenties but also among women in their thirties who had been married for years (Rindfuss et al., 1988). These older women belonged to larger cohorts, so the small-cohort-size theory can't account for their behavior. Rather, the pervasiveness of the rise in births suggests that the preferred family size shifted during the baby boom. The cultural emphasis on getting married and having children seems to have been greater than was the case before or since—perhaps as a result of the trauma of the Depression and the war. The shift had a broad effect on women and men in their twenties, thirties, and even early forties.

Together, the strong economy and the marriage-and-childbearing orientation produced the high point of the breadwinner–homemaker family. The federal government helped by granting low-interest mortgages to armed forces veterans, allowing millions of families to purchase single-family homes in the growing suburbs. For the first time, the "American dream" of marriage, children, and a single-family home was within reach of not only the middle class, but many in the working class as well (Laslett, 1973). Yet some homemakers missed the world of paid work and school they had left behind and felt constrained by their economic dependence on their husbands (Weiss, 2000).

Moreover, overlooked during the 1950s because of all the attention given to the baby boom was a countercurrent that would loom large later in the century. Increasingly, homemakers went back to work outside the home after their children were of school age. They took jobs that had been typed as women's work—jobs that were relatively low paying, but still required some education, such as secretary, nurse, or salesclerk. And some urged their daughters to postpone marriage in order to pursue higher education and professional careers (Weiss, 2000).

THE 1960s THROUGH THE 1990s

Just as social commentators confidently announced a return to large families, the roller-coaster car reached the top of its track and hurtled downward. The birthrate plunged from the heights of the baby boom to an all-time low in the 1970s, from which it has risen slightly since then. Women who were in their peak childbearing years in the 1970s had an average of 1.8 children. Women in their peak childbearing years today are having an average of 2.1 children (U.S. National Center for Health Statistics, 2010). The baby boom had begotten the baby bust. In addition, young women and men were marrying at later and later ages; between the mid-1950s and 2000, the age at which half of all first marriages occur increased by about five years for men and women (U.S. Bureau of the Census, 2010c). So the percentage of young adults who had never married, as Figure 2.1 shows, surpassed the levels of the early twentieth century.

What were they doing during these five additional years before marriage? In part, they were living on their own. In the first half of the twentieth century, it was rare for an unmarried person in his or her twenties to be living alone. Either you remained with your parents or you rented a room in another family's house. Young people couldn't afford to live on their own; there was a shortage of adequate housing; and anyway it was morally questionable, especially for an unmarried woman, to live alone. But by 2000 the

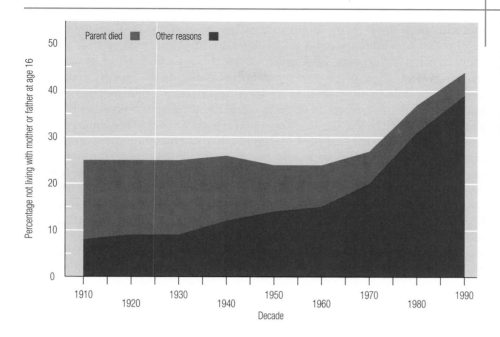

FIGURE 2.2
Percentage of children not living with own mother and father at age 16 because a parent died or for other reasons, 1910s to 1990s. (*Source:* Ellwood & Jencks, 2004, Figure 1.1)

proportion of unmarried twenty-somethings heading their own households had risen to 36 percent for women and 28 percent for men (Rosenfeld, 2007). Not all of these young household heads, however, were *truly* alone. After about 1970, **cohabitation**—the sharing of a household by unmarried persons in a sexual relationship—accounted for some of the postponement of marriage (Smock, 2000). In other words, some young adults substituted cohabiting relationships for early marriages. Moreover, they were increasingly having children prior to marrying. In 1950 only 4 percent of births occurred outside of marriage; but by 2000, 33 percent did (U.S. National Center for Health Statistics, 2005). Most of these births occurred among less-educated women. In 2000, 70 percent of unmarried high school dropouts aged 25 to 44 had already given birth, as had 53 percent of comparable high school graduates. But only 9 percent of unmarried college-educated women in the same age range had given birth (Fischer & Hout, 2006). Although the conventional path of marrying before having children is still prevalent among the college-educated, many of the less-educated are having children prior to marrying.

Change occurred not only in how and when people entered marriage but also in how and when they ended marriage. The divorce rate, which had been stable during the 1950s, doubled during the 1960s and 1970s. Since then, divorce rates have diverged by educational level: the rate has declined for the college-educated, remained stable for people with high school degrees or a few years of college, and increased for people without high school degrees (Martin, 2006). According to recent estimates, about one-third of the marriages of college graduates would end in separation or divorce, whereas over half of the marriages of people without college degrees would end in separation or divorce (Raley & Bumpass, 2003). Here again, a person's level of education has become an important marker of the kind of family life she or he leads.

What all of these developments have meant for the living arrangements of children during the twentieth century is shown in Figure 2.2. It is based

cohabitation the sharing of a household by unmarried persons who have a sexual relationship

on the answers of people of differing ages to the question "Were you living with both your own mother and father around the time you were 16?" in a series of national surveys. If they said no, they were asked whether they weren't living with both parents due to a parent dying or for other reasons—most often, divorce or separation but also, as the century progressed, being born outside of marriage. In 1900, according to the answers to these questions, about 25 percent of children were not living with both parents around age 16. Note that by far the most common reason for not living with both parents was that a parent had died. A fair number of children experienced family disruption a century ago but mostly because of parental death. The percentage not living with both parents stayed relatively stable for the first two-thirds of the century, although the reasons changed: By mid-century parental death rates had declined but disruptions for other reasons had increased. The percentage not living with both parents even declined temporarily in the 1950s, by which time the likelihood of losing a parent by death had fallen substantially but divorce rates were steady. Yet beginning in the 1960s, the percentage not living with both parents began to rise, and by 2000 it exceeded the level a century earlier, even though it was quite uncommon to have a parent die. Over the century, then, the reasons why adolescents weren't living with both parents changed dramatically from the death of a parent to divorce or separation or being born to an unmarried parent.

After the 1950s, married women continued to work outside the home in ever larger numbers. Even women with pre-school-aged children joined the workforce in large numbers. By 2000, 77 percent of all married women with school-aged children and 63 percent of married women with pre-school-aged children were working outside the home (U.S. Bureau of the Census, 2011b). Whereas in the 1950s, married women tended to drop out of the paid workforce when they were raising small children, today married women are much more likely to remain at their jobs throughout the child-rearing years. This change in women's work lives has had a powerful effect on the family.

The most recent period in the history of the family—from about 2000 to the present—will be the main subject matter of this book. As a prelude to understanding the present, future chapters will examine in detail the recent history of marriage, childbearing, divorce, cohabitation, and women's labor force participation in the United States and elsewhere.

Quick Review

- The 1950s produced the most distinctive family patterns of the twentieth century, notably early marriage and larger numbers of children.
- Rising wages and a cultural shift toward home and family may have caused the 1950s baby boom.
- Family trends reversed in the 1960s: Young adults married later; birthrates fell; divorce rates rose.
- In addition, married women with young children began to enter the workforce in large numbers in the 1960s.
- The percentage of children not living with both parents rose toward the end of the century because of increases in marital separation and divorce and births to unmarried parents.

The Changing Life Course

We have seen that family and personal life changed greatly during the twentieth century. One way to understand these changes is to compare the experiences of groups of individuals who were born in different time periods. This approach is known as the **life-course perspective:** the study of changes in individuals' lives over time and how those changes are related to historical events.

life-course perspective
the study of changes in individuals' lives over time, and how those changes are related to historical events

SOCIAL CHANGE IN THE TWENTIETH CENTURY

Consider Figure 2.3. In the middle of the figure is a time line for the twentieth century, divided into 10-year intervals. The top half shows the time lines for three different birth cohorts born 30 years apart. The first group was born in 1920; I have labeled them the "depression cohort" because they were nine years old when the Great Depression began in 1929. The second group, "the baby boom cohort," was born in 1950, at the start of the baby boom. The third group, born in 1980, is more difficult to label. Some social commentators have noted that people born in the 1980s and 1990s are very roughly the tenth generation of Americans born since the country was founded. I will call the third group the "tenth generation cohort." The bottom half of Figure 2.3 shows time lines for the occurrence of major historical events and trends that have changed family and personal life. For example, the Great Depression lasted from 1929 until about 1940, and the baby boom occurred from the late 1940s to the early 1960s.

One can think of the top and bottom halves of Figure 2.3 as showing two kinds of time. The top half displays what we might call "individual time": the passing of time in people's lives as they age. This is the usual way we think of time. The bottom half displays what might be called "historical time": the beginning and ending of key events and social trends that have influenced

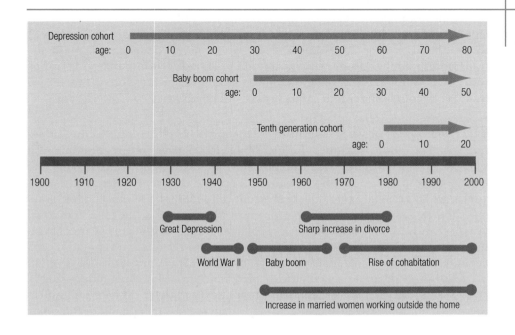

FIGURE 2.3
A life-course perspective on social change in the twentieth century.

family life during the century. The figure's usefulness is that it allows a comparison of individual time and historical time; or put another way, it places the course of an individual's life in historical context.

For example, the figure shows that in 1950, as the baby boom started, members of the depression cohort were still in their childbearing years; therefore, they became the parents of the baby boomers. The figure also shows that by the time the baby boom cohort reached age 30 in 1980, a sharp rise in divorce had occurred. As a result, the baby boomers have had a much higher rate of divorce than the depression cohort. In addition, the figure shows that the tenth generation cohort is the first to have lived their early childhood years after the sharp rise in divorce. That is why far more tenth generation cohort members have experienced the breakup of their parents' marriages than have previous cohorts.

This way of looking at changes in family and personal life is an example of the life-course perspective. Rather than study families as an undifferentiated group, sociologists and historians who use this perspective tend to study the lives of individuals within families. They examine how historical developments affect the course of these individuals' personal and family lives. Elder's work on the depression cohort (defined in his case as people born in 1921) is probably the most influential study of this genre (Elder, 1974). The life-course perspective is particularly attractive to scholars who wish to study social change over time. And as this chapter has made clear, the twentieth century was a time of great change in the kinds of family lives individuals led.

THE EMERGENCE OF EARLY ADULTHOOD

Recently, sociologists have used the life-course perspective to suggest the emergence of a new stage of life: **early adulthood** (Settersten, Furstenberg, & Rumbaut, 2005). I will define it as the period between the mid-teens and about age 30 when individuals finish their education, enter the labor force, and begin their own families. (The **labor force** is defined as all people who are working for pay or who are looking for paid work.) It is the stage of life when one makes the transition from adolescence (itself only a century old, as we will see in Chapter 7) to adulthood. As I noted earlier in this chapter, most young people made the transition to adulthood quickly in the mid-twentieth century, marrying at historically young ages and having children soon afterwards. Today, this transition has become longer and more varied and complex.

> **early adulthood** period between mid-teens and about age 30 when individuals finish their education, enter the labor force, and begin their own families
>
> **labor force** all people who are working for pay or who are looking for paid work

The Role of Education   The main factor in the lengthening of early adulthood is education. Changes in the labor force have put a premium on schooling: Employment opportunities have improved much more for the college-educated than for those without a college degree. Consequently, early adults are increasingly pursuing higher education. Some are enrolling in graduate and professional schools that promise great rewards but take additional years of study. Others are completing college, even if that means years of part-time study. In the early 1990s, it was unusual for a twenty-five-year-old to still be in school; but today perhaps one out of six whites and one out of eight blacks of that age are enrolled at least part-time (Fussell & Furstenberg, 2005). Early adults who are still in school are more likely to defer decisions about careers and families. Given the increasing acceptance of cohabitation, they may live with a partner until they finish their educations rather than marry. Or they may marry but postpone having children. Although they may be working for pay to help defray the costs of their education, they delay starting on a career ladder until after they have the appropriate degree in hand.

Constrained Opportunities   Early adults with more limited education take other, usually shorter, paths to reach the traditional markers of adulthood. Most of those who don't graduate from high school, or who graduate but don't go on to college, enter the job market well before their college-bound peers. Some take college courses but don't achieve a bachelor's degree. Their opportunities are more constrained than were the opportunities of similarly educated individuals a half-century ago (Hill & Yeung, 1999). As I will explain in Chapter 4, the movement of manufacturing jobs overseas and the growth of automation have reduced the demand for non-college-educated workers. The kinds of decent-paying blue-collar factory jobs that sustained a generation of workers and their families a half-century ago are in short supply. Sociologists argue that non-college-educated entrants into the labor force often must take "stopgap jobs"—short-term, often part-time jobs such as working at a fast-food restaurant—that give them a modest income for a short time but don't help to develop a career (Oppenheimer, Kalmijn, & Lim, 1997).

Consequently, some non-college-educated adults are postponing marriage not because they are still studying but rather because they (or their prospective marriage partners) don't think their economic prospects are good enough to support a marriage. But forgoing marriage no longer means one must forgo having children because childbearing outside of marriage has become more acceptable. Some early adults father, or give birth to, children without marrying. In 2000, 5 percent of white 25-year-olds and 28 percent of black 25-year-olds were unmarried parents. They have made more progress toward traditional markers of adulthood than their childless contemporaries still in school because they have had children and are often working. But their work lives are erratic and usually consist of a series of low- and moderate-paying jobs rather than a career. And they may not marry for a long time, if ever.

Many early adults are living independently of their parents, a situation we will examine more closely in Chapter 7. But the probability that an independent early adult will move back in with his or her parents—if, for example, he or she loses a job or breaks up with a partner—has increased since the mid-twentieth century (Goldscheider, 1997). This trend toward returning to the nest is another reason why early adults often achieve lasting independence—and full adulthood—in fits and starts over a longer period of time. Nevertheless, by age 30 the differences between the college-educated and the less-educated in marriage, parenthood, and employment are smaller. Most have married, most are working, and a majority have children. What education does is make a difference in how they got there—how they experience early adulthood.

Declining Parental Control   A century ago, when most people lived with their parents until they married, parents had more control over their young adult children. Today, when most early adults live separately, parents have less control. As a result, parents have less influence over whom their children marry or live with. For example, Rosenfeld (2007) hypothesized that early adults who have moved away from their parents will have marriages and cohabiting unions that are less conventional because their parents aren't around to object. He examined records for 20- to 29-year-olds from the U.S. Census, which asks people not only for their current state of residence but also for the state where they were born. He found that the more unconventional the marital or cohabiting union that early adults were in, the more likely they were to have moved away from the state where they were born. People who were cohabiting were a bit more likely to have moved away than people who were married. People who were in interracial unions, married or cohabiting, were more likely to have moved away than people in same-race unions; people in same-sex unions were even more likely to have moved away; and those in interracial same-sex unions were most likely of all to have moved away.

EARLY ADULTHOOD AND THE LIFE-COURSE PERSPECTIVE

The growing literature on early adulthood is a good example of the life-course perspective for several reasons. It focuses on a key transition in the lives of individuals—in this case the lengthening period from adolescence to adulthood. It demonstrates the substantial social changes that have occurred in this stage of life. And importantly, it places that transition in historical perspective by showing the influences of the decline in manufacturing jobs, the growing employment opportunities for the well-educated, and the greater acceptance of cohabitation and childbearing outside of marriage. As they make the transition today, early adults steer a course in a different sea than was sailed in the past. Many reach their destinations later, and by different routes, than their parents and grandparents.

Quick Review

- The life-course perspective seeks to study the course of individual lives in historical context.
- Early adulthood is the term for an emerging life stage between adolescence and adulthood.
- The pursuit of higher education is the main factor lengthening early adulthood.
- Early adults without college degrees start the transition to full adulthood sooner.

WHAT HISTORY TELLS US

The history of the family tells us that Americans come from regions of the world that have different family traditions. To some extent, the American mixing bowl blends those traditions together and reduces the differences. The result is that the family lives of today's ethnic and racial groups have more in common than not. Still, the historical record can help us understand some of the variation we see today.

Americans of European ancestry hail from a system that has emphasized the conjugal unit of the married couple and children more than have family systems in other regions of the world. In the nineteenth and early twentieth centuries, European-American conjugal families developed a sharp division of labor between the husband, who worked outside the home, and the wife, who by and large worked inside the home. That sharp division, however, broke down in the last half of the twentieth century as more married women entered the workforce. And during the twentieth century, Americans placed increasing weight on personal satisfaction as the standard people should use in judging the quality of their relationships. European-American family traditions are important because they have been the basis for American law and custom. For example, American law gives parents nearly exclusive rights over children and gives far less authority to grandparents or other kin.

The family systems of American Indians and of Americans from other regions (such as Latin America, Asia, and Africa) have traditionally placed more emphasis on kin beyond the conjugal family. Sometimes these family systems consisted of tightly organized lineages. Think of the matrilineal tribes of the Hopi. At other times and places, they consisted of extended families in which grandparents, uncles, aunts, and others from both sides of a person's family might contribute to her or his well-being and even share a home. And as the Mexican tradition of *compadrazgo* showed, sometimes individuals without any ties of blood or marriage were recruited into a person's kin network.

Marriage was still central to most of these systems, although less so in Africa. But married couples were embedded in larger family structures that could provide assistance and support. This tradition of support is important because marriage declined among all American racial and ethnic groups during the last half of the twentieth century. The weakening of marriage left European-American families in a particularly vulnerable position because they had less of a tradition of extended family support to fall back on. The story of recent changes in marriage and family life, and their impact on Americans with different heritages, will be told in subsequent chapters.

Looking Back

1. **What functions have families traditionally performed?** Family and kinship emerged as ways of ensuring the survival of human groups, which were organized as bands of hunter-gatherers until about 10,000 years ago. Until the past 250 years or so, most families performed three basic activities: production, reproduction, and consumption. Most American Indian tribes were organized into lineages and clans that provided the basis for social organization and governing. Colonial American families performed functions such as education that are now performed by schools and other institutions. These kinds of families can be said to follow the familial mode of production. The colonial American family performed many activities that are now done mainly outside the family: educating children, providing vocational training, treating the seriously ill, and so forth.

2. **How did American families change after the United States was founded?** Between 1776 and about 1830, a new kind of family emerged among the white middle class in the United States, one in which marriage was based on affection rather than authority and custom. Over time, the primary role of women in these families became the care of children and the maintenance of the home. Children came to be seen as needing continual affection and guidance, which mothers were thought to be better at providing than fathers. As families became more centered on children, the number of children they raised declined. At the same time, a movement toward greater individualism weakened parents' influence over their children's marriage decisions and family lives. Working-class families, because of difficult economic circumstances, did not change as much.

3. **How have the family histories of major ethnic and racial groups differed?** Before the Civil War, African slaves married and lived together for life, wherever possible, and knew and kept track of other kin. After the Civil War, discrimination shaped their family lives. For example, out of economic necessity, rural black wives worked in the fields, and urban black wives worked for wages outside the home, more than white wives did. As for Mexican Americans, after U.S. troops and immigrants seized their land, they became more of a working-class community, increasingly confined to *barrios.* Over time, more and more women headed households, in part because their husbands often worked as migratory farm workers. Chinese and Japanese families also faced discrimination. Traditionally patrilineal, their authority over their children has declined over the generations. Filipinos, the second largest Asian immigrant group in the United States today, are descended mostly from people who immigrated in the twentieth century. Filipinos have a bilateral kinship structure more similar to the kinship system of Europeans.

4. **How did the emotional character of the American family change during the early twentieth century?** During the early decades of the twentieth century, rising standards of living allowed for greater attention to an emotionally satisfying private life. As the search for emotional satisfaction through family life became an important goal, the private family emerged. Eventually, the success of marriage came to be defined more in emotional terms than in material terms. People experienced more privacy in their personal lives through the increasingly common empty nest phase of marriage and the rise in the number of individuals living alone.

5. **What important changes occurred in marriage and childbearing in the second half of the twentieth century?** In the 1950s, young adults married at earlier ages and the birthrate rose to a twentieth-century high. The baby boom was caused in part by the small cohort size and good economic fortune of the cohort that reached adulthood in the 1950s. In addition, a greater cultural emphasis on marriage and childbearing seems to have been present. The 1950s was the high point of the breadwinner–homemaker family, which was dominant only during the first half of the twentieth century. Since then the trends in marriages, divorces, and births all reversed: Age at marriage increased sharply, the divorce rate doubled, and the birthrate reached its lowest level. Cohabitation became common. Moreover, married women were increasingly likely to work outside the home even when their children were young.

6. **How does the life-course perspective help us to understand social change?** Sociologists examine how the course of individuals' lives is affected by historical events such as the Great Depression of the 1930s or the large rise in divorce rates in the 1960s and 1970s. Because young adults today have better job opportunities if they obtain a college degree, many are postponing marriage and childbearing until they finish their studies. Life-course scholars now use the term "early adulthood" for this emerging life stage.

 Go to the Online Learning Center at www.mhhe.com/cherlin7e to test your knowledge of the chapter concepts and key terms.

Study Questions

1. How did belonging to a lineage help a family in a tribal, agricultural society?
2. What did the colonial family do that modern families do not? What do modern families do that the colonial family did not?
3. How did marriage change during the late 1700s and early 1800s?
4. What were the costs and benefits to women of their restriction to the "women's sphere"?

5. In what ways did the scope of the "private family" increase after 1900?
6. In what ways was family life in the 1950s distinctive compared to earlier or later in the century?
7. Why didn't the decline of parental death lead to an increase in children living with both parents?
8. What does it mean to take a "life-course perspective" on the study of social change?
9. Why is the concept of "early adulthood" emerging now rather than 50 or 100 years ago?

Key Terms

1965 Immigration Act   59
American Indian   45
baby boom   67
barrio   57
bilateral kinship   59
birth cohort   67
cohabitation   69
compadrazgo   57
conjugal family   44
early adulthood   72
extended family   44
hunter-gatherers   42
labor force   72
life-course perspective   71
lineage   42
matrilineage   42
mestizo   57
patrilineage   42
polyandry   44
polygyny   44
remittances   58

Thinking about Families

The Public Family	The Private Family
Why were the American family's public responsibilities much broader in the colonial period than is the case today?	Why are emotional satisfaction, intimacy, and romantic love more important in American family life today than they were 100 years ago?

Families on the Internet   www.mhhe.com/cherlin7e

Note: While all the URLs listed were current as of the printing of this book, these sites often change. Please check our Web site (www.mhhe.com/cherlin7e) for updates.

Although it's the most modern of media, the Internet is also a great resource for historians. In fact, it is transforming historical research by providing access to millions of sources. For example, the Library of Congress maintains the Web site "American Memory" (http://memory.loc.gov/ammem/index.html). It contains searchable links to more than 9 million digital items—photos, pamphlets, films, etc.—from over 100 collections. A search on "marriage" returned 1,518 items such as a 1923 letter from anthropologist Margaret Mead to her grandmother explaining why she intended to retain her maiden name after marrying.

"History Matters" (http://americanhistory.about.com) is a Web site maintained for high school and college students. Clicking on "Eras of American History," "Great Depression," and then "Great Depression Photos" returns harrowing photographs of families enduring the hardships of the Depression.

The University of Rochester has placed online several monthly issues of *Godey's Lady's Book* from 1850, one of the most popular magazines of the nineteenth century. You can view articles, poems, and engravings (www.history.rochester.edu/godeys). Go to the February 1850 issue and read "The Elopement," a story about a young woman whose father saves her from a tragic elopement at the last minute. What is the message to young women about obeying family versus their own hearts when choosing a husband?

Part Two

Gender, Class, and Race-Ethnicity

Families are affected by the larger social structures in which they are embedded. Three main axes of social stratification are gender, class, and race-ethnicity. How gender is structured greatly affects the ways that men and women relate to each other in families. Social class differences influence the ways that family life is organized. Racial and ethnic groups also differ in their family lives. Moreover, gender, class, and race-ethnicity are linked because all three are structures in which a more powerful group (men, the wealthier classes, whites) dominate the less powerful; and all three can affect a family simultaneously. Consequently, the content of the next three chapters should be seen as overlapping and interlocking, even though for educational purposes it is useful to have one chapter focus on each of these core constructs of sociology. • Chapter 3 examines the construction and maintenance of gender differences, a core source of differentiation in family life. It presents several different approaches to understanding gender. • Chapter 4 explores differences in family life among social classes. It includes an examination of how trends in the economy have affected families. • Chapter 5 considers the consequences for families of the divisions in society along racial-ethnic lines. The family patterns of African Americans are discussed. The chapter also examines commonly used categories such as "Hispanic" and "Asian," which include groups that vary greatly in their family patterns.

Chapter Three

Gender and Families

Looking Forward

The Two-Spirit People

The Gestational Construction of Gender

The Childhood Construction of Gender

Parental Socialization

The Media

Peer Groups

The Continual Construction of Gender

Doing and Undoing Gender

Gender as Social Structure

Thinking about Gender Differences Today

Causes at Multiple Levels

The Slowing of Gender Change

The Asymmetry of Gender Change

Gender, Class, and Race

Men and Masculinities

The Contributions of Gender Studies

Looking Back

Study Questions

Key Terms

Thinking about Families

Families on the Internet

Boxed Features

HOW DO SOCIOLOGISTS KNOW WHAT THEY KNOW?: *Feminist Research Methods*

FAMILIES AND PUBLIC POLICY: *Do Employers Discriminate Against Women?*

Looking Forward

1. How do sociologists distinguish between the concepts of "sex" and "gender"?

2. How might fetal development affect the behavior of women and men?

3. How do children learn how women and men are supposed to behave?

4. How does everyday life reinforce gender differences?

5. Are gender differences built into the structure of society?

6. Overall, how should we think about gender differences?

7. Is there more than one kind of masculinity?

The Two-Spirit People

In 1841, the American traveler and artist George Catlin published his monumental *Manners, Customs, and Conditions of the North American Indians*. The result of his eight years of traveling among Native Americans in the West, it included about 300 engravings. One of them, titled "Dance to the Berdache," is shown on page 83. It depicts warriors of the Sauk and Fox Indians dancing around a man wearing a woman's clothing. "For the extraordinary privileges he is known to possess," wrote Catlin of the man, "he is . . . looked upon as medicine and sacred, and a feast is given to him annually." Men like him, who dressed like women, performed women's work, and behaved like women, were called "berdaches" by the French colonists. Today that term is considered pejorative (it is derived from Arabic or Persian words that meant "kept boy" or "male prostitute"), and the term two-spirit is preferred (Jacobs, Thomas, & Lang, 1997; Leland, 2008). According to some scholars, **two-spirit people** existed in more than 100 Native American cultures, while others claim they were less common. In many tribes they were accepted members of adult society, although attitudes toward them "varied from awe and reverence through indifference to scorn and contempt" (Callendar & Kochems, 1983). In a smaller number of these cultures, female two-spirit people, who dressed and worked like men, were also found.

> **two-spirit people** in Native American societies, men or women who dressed like, performed the duties of, and behaved like a member of the opposite sex

Most individuals became two-spirit people in one of two ways. First, some children displayed what their parents thought were two-spirit-like characteristics. In some of the Native American cultures, parents might develop a male child as a two-spirit if he showed "a gentle, androgynous [having characteristics of both sexes] nature" and showed great interest in the work of the other sex (Williams, 1986). Second, some men and women experienced spiritual visions at adolescence or even later that they took as signs to become two-spirits. These visions usually involved some supernatural intervention, such as instructions from the female moon deity. In many cultures they were credited with supernatural powers and exceptional skill at carrying out the other sex's work. The dance at the annual feast that Catlin sketched indicated that the Sauk and Fox respected the powers of the two-spirits. As neither ordinary men nor ordinary women, two-spirits could undertake special tasks that women and men could not perform as

George Catlin's "Dance to the Berdache," from Catlin's *Manners, Customs, and Conditions of the North American Indians,* 1841. Original sketch at the National Museum of American Art, Smithsonian Institution, Washington, D.C.

easily, such as negotiating a marriage bargain between a woman's family and a man's family or settling a dispute between a man and a woman.

In many cultures, a two-spirit person could marry a person of the same sex who was not a two-spirit. Male two-spirits typically engaged in homosexual intercourse, while the sexual relations of married female two-spirits were lesbian. But many two-spirits also had heterosexual relations; the Navaho, for example, permitted male two-spirits any form of sexual intercourse with either sex (Callendar & Kochems, 1983). Moreover, a male two-spirit could renounce his role and return to being an ordinary male. By some accounts, non-two-spirit males could have sex with a two-spirit without being considered primarily homosexual.

Female two-spirits, who were less common, were found in Native American cultures in which relationships between men and women were relatively egalitarian and in which women owned and distributed the goods they produced. But in cultures with strong lineages, they were very rare. For instance, in matrilineal cultures, the children of a man's sister remained in his lineage under his control. Under these circumstances, females of reproductive age were too valuable to the men of the lineage to be allowed to take on the two-spirit role. But in less hierarchical cultures, some women could take on a male role without threatening the male social order (Blackwood, 1984). Put simply, female two-spirits were more likely to be found in societies in which men had less control over women.

As the influence of European culture on Native Americans grew during the nineteenth century, the number of two-spirits declined rapidly; by the end of the century there were very few. Nevertheless, the story of the two-spirits can help to answer some important questions that will be addressed in this chapter.

1. *What is the difference between sex and gender?* The social situation of the two-spirit people illustrates the distinction sociologists make between sex and gender. In most sociological writing, **sex** refers to the

sex the biological characteristics that distinguish men and women biological characteristics that distinguish women and men: sex chromosomes, reproductive organs, sex-specific hormones, and physical characteristics. A very small number of people are born with ambiguous sex characteristics, but for the vast majority there is a clear sexual identification as either woman or man. **Gender,** in most sociological writing, refers to the social and cultural characteristics that distinguish women from men (Coltrane & Adams, 2008). In our society, such characteristics include the different clothing that men and women wear or the expectation that boys shouldn't cry when they are hurt. Gender is said to be a social creation; sex is said to be a biological creation.

The distinction between sex and gender will be useful in examining many of the topics in this book. Nevertheless, drawing a line that separates the two is occasionally more difficult than this definition at first suggests. For example, the literature on the two-spirits indicates that parents sometimes perceived qualities in their young sons that were more typical of daughters and then raised them as two-spirits. If sexual orientation is partly biologically determined, as evidence suggests (see Chapter 6), these parents may have recognized a predisposition in their sons toward a homosexual orientation (Williams, 1986).

2. *How many genders are there?* The story of the two-spirits shows that gender need not be confined to two sexes. Just what gender were the two-spirits? Did a male two-spirit who dressed, acted, and married like a woman take on the female gender? Not quite, for he could not give birth, often had greater physical strength, was sometimes taken along on hunts, and differed in other ways from women (Williams, 1986). Rather, the two-spirit appears to have occupied an intermediate position between male and female—a third gender, of sorts. He was called not a "man" or a "woman" but a "halfman-halfwoman," a "man-woman," or a "would-be-woman." Reflecting this mixture, the Zuni buried male two-spirits in women's dress but men's trousers, on the men's side of the graveyard (Callendar & Kochems, 1983).

In the blurring of the difference between male and female, the status as an in-between gender, the two-spirit people, demonstrates how society and culture created gender categories. Recently, a number of adults who were born with ambiguous sexual organs have formed an organization, calling themselves **intersexuals** (Weil, 2006). As children, most had surgery and long-term treatments with sex hormones to make their genitals and secondary sex characteristics more like those of males or females. Their goal is to convince doctors and parents not to reassign a child's sex until the individual is old enough to make an informed choice.

3. *Can a person's gender identity be modified?* In some tribes Native American men were allowed to become two-spirits in adolescence or even later if a supernatural event guided them to do so. They were also allowed to shed the status and return to the male gender. Clearly, under some cultural circumstances, gender identity can be established after middle childhood and modified in adulthood. Yet even in this extraordinary case, the modification is not from male to female, but rather from male to an in-between third gender. Research shows that most children develop a gender identity during their preschool years, that it is reinforced during middle

gender the social and cultural characteristics that distinguish women and men in a society

intersexual a person who is born with ambiguous sexual organs

childhood and adolescence, that it becomes a central part of the child's self-definition, and that it is altered in only a small number of cases.

4. *How much do gender differences reflect men's attempts to retain power over women?* We have learned that male two-spirits were tolerated in many Native American cultures throughout western North America, but female two-spirits were more restricted. Women had the freedom to modify their gender only in cultures in which they had substantial resources relative to men and in which the power of male-dominated lineages was weak. In cultures in which men had greater control over women, they blocked women's moves toward a male role. Do similar forces still operate today? As a social creation, notions of gender are likely to reflect the existing power relationships in a society. In fact, some scholars would restrict the definition of gender to sex-linked characteristics that reflect male power over women or would argue even more broadly that all gender differences reflect gender politics (Scott, 2000). Others would argue for a looser connection between gender and power. We will examine the connection between gender differences and male domination later in this chapter.

Overall, the story of the two-spirits shows a surprising flexibility and variability in gender. Yet even in this instance, as well as in the current controversy over sex reassignment, we can see evidence that both cultural norms and biological predispositions may influence a person's gender identity, that a shift in gender identity from male to female or vice versa occurs only rarely, and that gender differences can be influenced by the degree of power men have over women. Although the two-spirits and the intersexuals show that alternative ways of organizing the culture and biology of sex and gender are possible, their rarity underscores how widespread is the familiar two-sex, two-gender model most of us take for granted. I will assume this model holds throughout this chapter.

The distinction between women and men, female and male, is basic to the study of the family because of the sharp differentiation, in nearly all societies, between what women and men do in families. Exactly what they do differs from one society to the next, but almost universally, they tend to do different things. To understand families, we must understand gender. And to understand gender, we must begin before birth, for the paths of male and female begin to diverge in the womb. The origins and consequences of gender differences in childhood, and their maintenance in adulthood through social interaction and social structure constitute the subject of this chapter. (A more general examination of how parents raise their children will be the subject of Chapter 9.)

The Gestational Construction of Gender

For the first several weeks of **gestation** (the term for the nine-month development of the fetus inside the mother's uterus), the external sex organs of soon-to-be girls and boys are identical. These primitive genitals can develop into either a clitoris, vagina, and ovaries or a penis, scrotum, and testes. But soon

gestation the nine-month development of the fetus inside the mother's uterus

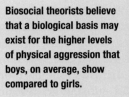

Biosocial theorists believe that a biological basis may exist for the higher levels of physical aggression that boys, on average, show compared to girls.

male embryos begin to develop testes. In the second trimester (the middle three months) of gestation, the testes in soon-to-be boys produce male sex hormones called androgens. These hormones cause the genitals to develop into the male form. In the absence of high levels of androgens, the genitals develop into the female form. After only a few months, then, the developing child's genital sex is determined by the level of male sex hormones.

Some scientists believe that the androgens that circulate in male fetuses do more than cause the genitals to take on the male form. They claim that parts of the fetus's brain develop differently depending on the level of androgen that is present. In other words, the brains of males and females may be organized somewhat differently because of the presence or absence of high levels of male sex hormones during the second trimester of gestation (Leaper & Friedman, 2007). If so, then some of the gender differences we recognize in women and men could be influenced by differences in prenatal (before birth) hormone levels (Udry, Morris, and Kovenock, 1995).

biosocial approach (to gender differences) the theory that gender identification and behavior are based in part on people's innate biological differences

Those who believe that both biology and society have important influences on gender differences are said to be taking the **biosocial approach** to human behavior (Painter-Brick, 1998). The biosocial perspective does not suggest that hormones and chromosomes are destiny nor that biology always wins out over social influences. In fact, those who believe biological influences do affect gendered behavior would add at least three qualifications. First, biologically based differences in gendered behavior exist only "on average"; individuals can show a wide range of behavior. If we were to select a large group of women and another large group of men at random and measure the incidence of some biologically influenced behavior, we would find the behavior occurred more frequently among one group than the other. For example, if the behavior were physical aggression, we might find that, on average, aggression levels were higher among the men than among the women. But not all men, nor all women either, would show the same level of aggression. A modest number of women would be very aggressive, and a modest number of men not at all aggressive. To take another example, even if, on average, women are more predisposed than men to engage in nurturing behavior, as some observers suggest, in any randomly selected group, some women will not be very nurturing and some men quite nurturing.

Second, whether biological predispositions lead to actual behaviors depends on the environment in which a person is raised. For example, a child who is predisposed to be physically aggressive may not behave aggressively if his or her parents provide supportive but firm guidance and control. But a comparably predisposed child might behave very aggressively if his or her parents are neglectful. Biology and environment—nature and nurture—work together to produce behavior. It makes little sense, therefore, to attempt to determine how much of children's observed behavior is "genetic" or "environmental" because the interaction of nature and nurture is what produces the behaviors we see (Handel, Cahill, & Elkin, 2007).

Third, social influences can counteract biological predispositions. For instance, even if, on average, men are predisposed to be more physically aggressive than women, our society can control overly aggressive behavior through moral education, public pressure, and, for extreme aggression, law enforcement. Why, then, should biological predispositions matter at all? Because counteracting the influence of genes or hormones on human behavior is a bit like rolling a stone uphill: It can be done, but it takes continuing effort. If society were to decide that all biologically based gender differences in behavior should be eliminated, strong, deliberate steps would need to be taken to achieve that goal. And the stronger the biological predisposition, the stronger those steps would need to be. Understanding the biological bases of behavior, then, can help us to understand persistent differences between women and men and to estimate the ease or difficulty of bringing about social change.

Quick Review

- Some researchers think that the brains of male and female fetuses may be organized somewhat differently by the presence or absence of high levels of male sex hormones.
- Sociologists taking the biosocial approach to human behavior believe that both biologically based predispositions and social experiences influence gendered behavior.
- Biologically based differences, if any, exist only "on average."
- Social influences can counteract biologically based predispositions.

As part of the socialization process, children learn appropriate gendered behavior from their parents.

The Childhood Construction of Gender

Once born, children face multiple influences on their behavior. The most obvious influence comes from their parents, who typically treat girls and boys differently. In addition, children receive messages about gender from television and other media. And when they play together at a day care center or in their neighborhood or at school, they again are taught lessons about how girls and boys are supposed to behave.

PARENTAL SOCIALIZATION

socialization the processes by which we learn the ways of a given society or social group so as to adequately participate in it

socialization approach (to gender differences) the theory that gender identification and behavior are based on children's learning that they will be rewarded for the set of behaviors considered appropriate to their sex but not for those appropriate to the other sex

Researchers have argued that people first learn how women and men act through socialization during childhood. **Socialization,** according to the definition in one widely cited book, encompasses "the processes by which we learn and adapt to the ways of a given society or social group so as to adequately participate in it" (Handel, Cahill, & Elkin, 2007). It is how individuals learn to take on the attitudes and behaviors considered culturally appropriate for them. The emphasis in the **socialization approach** to gender differences is on conscious, social learning: Children are rewarded for behavior adults think is appropriate for their gender and admonished or punished for behavior that is not considered appropriate. By watching parents, teachers, television actors, and others, children learn the behavior of both genders, but they soon learn that they will be rewarded for one set of behaviors and not for the other. For example, although at first little boys cry as much as little girls, they are admonished not to, so that as men they cry less often than women. More generally, men are encouraged to be competitive and independent, whereas women are encouraged to be more nurturing to children and adults, and better at enabling and maintaining personal relationships.

In the standard model of socialization, children passively learn lessons from their parents. Many researchers now think this model is too simplistic and that, in reality, both children and parents influence each other's behavior as socialization proceeds (Maccoby, 2007; McHale & Crouter, 2003). A brother and sister may respond differently to their parents' attempts at discipline because they have different predispositions for disruptive behavior or merely because the younger child is acting differently from the older one in order to compete for the parents' attention. The parents may then respond differently to the two children, perhaps becoming stricter with one than the other. This response, in turn, may encourage the two children to become even more different in their actions. Or parents may buy a toy building set as a birthday present for a son in response to his interest in playing with blocks; and this present may make him even more interested in stereotypically male toys than his sister. In other words, a feedback loop is created in which differences in siblings' predispositions, whether biologically based or based on earlier treatment, may make parents respond differently to each of them, which in turn will make their behaviors even more distinctive from each other.

THE MEDIA

Nor is gender socialization confined to parents; children learn lessons from books and television, among other sources. As recently as the 1960s, schools made little effort to balance the gender content in the books children were assigned to use. Publishers produced stories and histories that focused mainly on boys and men. Then, spurred by the feminist movement, school systems began to demand more balanced literature. As a result in most children's books, girls and boys receive much more equal treatment. Gooden & Gooden (2001) examined 83 picture books for young readers that had been designated as "notable" by the American Library Association between 1995 and 1999. They found that female main characters (human or animal) were just as common as male main characters, a sharp difference from the better than two-to-one edge that male main characters had in a similar study 25 years earlier. Still, male characters were rarely seen doing housework or child care.

Over the past few decades, books have lost ground to television and the Internet as a source of information for children. The average 4-year-old watches two hours of television per day; the average 12-year-old watches four hours (Comstock & Scharrer, 2001). Television programs generally have more male characters than female characters, and the male characters are shown in more adventurous, independent roles, while the female characters are more often shown as caring and romantic. As with picture-book content, however, the disparities between how men and women are portrayed on television may be narrowing (Handel, Cahill, & Elkin, 2007). Children who watch television extensively seem to have more stereotyped attitudes about gender than children who watch little television (Lippa, 2005).

PEER GROUPS

Researchers also suspect that much of the development of gender-specific behavior occurs from an early age in children's **peer groups**—similar-age children who play or perform other activities together. Between the ages of two and three, children begin to sort themselves into same-sex peer groups.

peer group a group of people who have roughly the same age and status as one another

Psychologist Eleanor Maccoby argues that these same-sex peer groups strongly influence the distinctive behavior patterns of boys and girls (Maccoby, 1998). In observing pairs of children who were on average 33 months old, Maccoby and her colleagues found that these youngsters were far more likely to show social behavior—offering or grabbing a toy, hugging or pushing, vocally greeting or protesting, and so forth—to children of the same sex than to children of the opposite sex. Maccoby suggests that boys' peer groups tend to reinforce a competitive, dominance-oriented interaction style that carries over into such adult male communication tactics as interrupting, boasting, contradicting, and threatening, which restrict conversation. Girls' groups, she suggests, reinforce a different style that carries over into adult female communication. Through expressing agreement or support, asking questions rather than making statements, and acknowledging other persons' comments, girls continue interactions rather than restricting them. These styles, Maccoby asserts, may influence adult, mixed-sex interactions in school, at the office, and in families.

Symbolic interactionists say that children develop a sense of self through activities such as peer group play—a "gendered" sense of self, in this instance. As a girl (or a boy) formulates what she will say or do in the group, she imagines how the others are likely to respond. This process of imagining how others will respond is what George Herbert Mead called "taking the role of the other" (Blumer, 1962). It is, interactionists say, how children develop an internalized sense of appropriate behavior.

Consider the same-sex peer groups that are formed in school settings by children somewhat older than the ones we have been considering. Children are socialized, in part, through playing games and sports in same-sex, school-age peer groups. In these groups, children learn the behaviors expected of them, try out these behaviors with their peers, get feedback on how well they are performing, and try again. Sociologists have studied how this interactive process produces and reinforces different behavior patterns in boys and girls. In a study of Little League baseball teams, Gary Alan Fine observed that boys were concerned with impression management—behaving in a way that met with approval from the other boys—as well as with winning or losing. They learned to control their emotions and not to cry; otherwise, they would risk ridicule from their peers. They also learned to value competition. Once, when an opposing team showed up with too few players, a coach offered his first-place team the options of winning by forfeit or playing the game anyway and taking the small risk that they would lose. All the best players argued for taking the forfeit; only two players argued in favor of going ahead with the game because they were supposed to be playing for fun. When the team voted overwhelmingly to take the forfeit, the boys learned a lesson about valuing competition over cooperative play—a lesson that is consistent with the expected behavior of men (Fine, 1987).

In the past, elementary school girls tended to play indoors more than boys, to engage more often in noncompetitive activities without a goal, and to play in smaller groups. These play settings reinforced the relational and emotional skills women are expected to have. In these small groups, girls showed more affection than boys and learned to pick up on nonverbal cues about their friends' moods. The traits that were reinforced by girls' play were consistent with an adult life that emphasized home, family, emotional closeness, and cooperation (Lever, 1976). But since the passage in 1972 of a law prohibiting discrimination against women and girls in federally funded athletic programs, women's participation in high school varsity sports has expanded dramatically (Harrison & Lynch, 2005). One would expect that the character of girls' play would now be different, but we still await a good study on the subject.

In any case, not all girls and boys follow these stereotypical scripts when at play. When Barrie Thorne (1993) observed children in elementary schools, she found that most play groups comprised either all girls or all boys. But a modest number of girls and boys played in groups with the other gender, and there was much crossing of the gender border—for example, when boys and girls chased one another or invaded the other gender's space. The degree of separation between girls' and boys' worlds, Thorne concluded, was overstated. Thorne's approach to her study reflects many of the principles of feminist research methods (see *How Do Sociologists Know What They Know?:* Feminist Research Methods).

In sum, studies of young children's preferences and activities suggest numerous influences on the different behaviors of girls and boys. Society's expectations about how to behave are transmitted to children through channels such as parents, books, television, and peer groups. In these ways, cultural differences between women and men are reproduced in the next generation. Yet the evidence also suggests that children may have innate predispositions that affect gender differences in their behavior. These predispositions appear to be stronger for boys than for girls. Boys seem to prefer blocks, trucks, and rough play more than girls, on average, regardless of their parents' opinions about how they should play. Thus the influence of same-sex peer groups may reflect both socialization and biological predispositions.

Quick Review

- Sociologists who take the socialization approach to gender differences believe that children learn they will be rewarded for some types of behavior but not others.
- Parents both act and respond to their children by rewarding them for behavior they think appropriate and withholding rewards for behavior they think inappropriate.
- The media—television, books, magazines, commercial Web sites—often portray boys and girls, and men and women, behaving in gender-stereotypical ways.
- Children's same-gender peer groups often reinforce gender-stereotypical behavior.
- Feminists have developed research methods that challenge key assumptions of the standard social scientific model. (See *How Do Sociologists Know What They Know?:* Feminist Research Methods.)

The Continual Construction of Gender

Over the past decade or two, sociological research on the construction of gender differences has moved away from studying socialization or predispositions formed in childhood. In this recent way of thinking, gender is more fluid, more fragile, and more in need of constant reinforcement. Scholars argue instead for an approach that focuses on the continual construction and maintenance of gender differences throughout adulthood.

How Do Sociologists Know What They Know?
Feminist Research Methods

Sociologist Barrie Thorne (1993) begins her influential book about children's play groups, *Gender Play: Girls and Boys in School*, by writing not about her subject but about herself. She recalls that the segregation of girls and boys on the playgrounds of the elementary school she attended was considered "natural." She tells the reader that her views on gender were transformed by the women's movement of the 1970s and 1980s, which argued that the differences between the genders are not natural but rather a social construction. She describes her commitment to raise her own children in a nonsexist way.

Thorne then discusses how, in her own research, she took pains to learn the terminology that the subjects themselves used: "kids" rather than "children." She explained, "I found that when I shifted to 'kids' in my writing, my stance toward the people in question felt more side-by-side than top-down" (p. 9). Using "kids" helped her to adopt the viewpoint of her subjects, as opposed to the viewpoint of an adult feminist scholar.

In fact, Thorne's entire first chapter consists of preliminary material about herself and her relationship with her subjects.

The chapter illustrates an orientation that is called *feminist research methods.* It emerged from the feminist movement of the 1970s and 1980s and is linked to feminist theory and to the postmodern perspective. Researchers are encouraged to *reflexively* examine the nature of the research process that they are undertaking. Two feminist methodologists write approvingly of "the tendency for feminists to reflect on, examine critically, and explore analytically the nature of the research process" (Fonow & Cook, 2005, p. 2218).

Researchers are also encouraged to learn the point of view of the subjects they are studying. This emphasis on entering into the subjects' perspective is known as "connected knowing" in feminist research methods (Belenky, Clinchy, Goldberger, & Tarule, 1997). They are also encouraged to minimize power differences between researchers and the groups they study (Harding & Norberg, 2005). That is why Thorne sought to use language and methods that made her more of a "side-by-side" observer than a "top-down" observer.

Researchers are also encouraged to conduct socially engaged research that may create social change, particularly by reducing the oppression of women—and also by ending the gender constraints placed on men (Reinharz, 1992; Harding & Norberg, 2005). Feminist researchers explicitly acknowledge this political agenda. More important, they argue that *all* social scientific research reflects the social and political beliefs of the researchers but that most social scientists hide their beliefs—sometimes even from themselves.

In contrast, most sociologists try to follow the *scientific method.* A key assumption of the scientific method as it is often practiced is that researchers are neutral figures who stand outside the phenomena they study. The researcher's point of view, it is said, should not influence the methods she or he uses or the conclusions that she or he makes. In this way, social scientists strive for objectivity—a way of viewing the social world that is independent of personal beliefs. Feminist methodologists sometimes describe this orientation as "separated knowing" because of the distant and impartial stance it implies (Belenky et al., 1997).

But feminist researchers argue that objectivity is nearly impossible to achieve (Ruddick, 1996). They argue that much supposedly

DOING AND UNDOING GENDER

Candace West and Don H. Zimmerman (1987) developed this approach in "Doing Gender," perhaps the most influential article on the sociology of gender in the past quarter century. Their perspective was so new and different that it took them ten years of rejections and revisions to find an academic journal that was willing to publish it (West and Zimmerman, 2009). To develop their framework, which is commonly known as the **interactionist approach,** the authors hearkened back to symbolic interaction theory (Blumer, 1962).[1] "We argue," West and Zimmerman (1987, p. 129) wrote, "that gender is not a set of traits, nor a role, but the product of social doings of some sort." These social doings occur through "situated conduct"—interactions between men and women in particular settings (such as a kitchen or a job interview).

interactionist approach (to gender differences)
the theory that gender identification and behavior are based on the day-to-day behavior that reinforces gender distinctions

[1]They actually adhere to a variant of the interactionist approach called ethnomethodology (Wickes & Emmison, 2007).

"objective" social scientific research actually reflects male bias. The very categories that social scientists use often reflect prevailing political agendas (Harding & Norberg, 2005). For example, they note that not long ago, the U.S. Bureau of the Census, in its surveys, defined the husband as the "head of household" in a married-couple family, no matter what the family's situation was. Similarly, violence against women by husbands and partners was greatly underreported in crime statistics until feminists focused attention on the problem (Reinharz, 1992).

Proponents of feminist research methods frequently try to show that there is substantial variation from person to person in the ways in which women and men act. They do so because they oppose generalizations about women that might be used to restrict their independence and equality (for example, the belief, prevalent at mid-century, that the husband should earn the money and the wife should stay home and care for the children). They sometimes carry out research with the intent of demonstrating that generalizations about women are wrong. Thorne warns, for instance: "One should be wary of what has been called 'the tyranny of averages,' a misleading practice of referring to average differences as if they are absolute" (pp. 57–58).

So Thorne ventured out to the elementary school playground to disprove the idea that boys and girls are inherently different in their play styles—boys more aggressive, more concerned with dominance in groups; girls more concerned with relationships with a small number of friends. On the playground, girls and boys did separate, for the most part, in the ways the generalizations about them predict. They were not, however, completely separate. Thorne provided an insightful analysis of contact between girls and boys during the "border work" that maintained their separation, such as invading the other gender's spaces and chasing one another. She also found that a few children defied the stereotype, such as a boy who played jump rope and an athletic girl who played sports with the boys. And she documented occasional mixed games of dodgeball and the like.

From evidence such as this, Thorne concluded that gender "has a fluid quality" (p. 159) and that the claim that boys and girls have separate cultures "has outlived its usefulness" (p. 108). However, as one reviewer noted, the number of times that boys and girls cross the gender boundaries "are a tiny minority of her observations" (England, 1994, p. 283). Consequently, claiming that the average differences between boys and girls aren't important because some individuals cross the boundaries may be an overstatement.

Even if one is not always convinced by the conclusions of researchers like Thorne, one can find useful lessons in feminist research methods. Perhaps the main lesson is that researchers should pay more attention to where they are coming from: the reasons they choose to study a particular topic, the assumptions they have going into a research project, and the beliefs they hold that might influence their conclusions. Feminist researchers have made a convincing case that in the study of family and gender, objectivity has its limits.

Ask Yourself

1. Does your gender affect the way you react to Barrie Thorne's research? Explain.
2. What are the advantages and disadvantages of feminist research methods and of the scientific method? Why?

www.mhhe.com/cherlin7e

Gender is an achieved property that is created through countless social interactions that reinforce gender differences.

For example, how do a wife and husband come to understand that she should do most of the housework? Socialization theory suggests that doing the housework is part of the behavior women learn beginning with the dolls and teacups they are given in childhood and the praise they get for helping their mothers wash the dishes. But the symbolic interactionists, while not denying that socialization occurs, emphasize that questions such as who does the housework are settled again and again in daily life. For example, in a study conducted by Sarah Fenstermaker (2002), a woman who was asked "What household work does your husband do?" replied:

> *He tries to be helpful. He tries. He's a brilliant and successful lawyer. It's incredible how he smiles after he sponges off the table and there are still crumbs all over. (p. 113)*

The interactionists suggest that gendered behavior is not only learned in child-hood but also reinforced day after day in adulthood.

Here the husband's smile—the symbol—indicates to his wife that he is incapable of sponging all the crumbs off the table, despite having enough brains to be a brilliant and successful lawyer. It is a way for the husband to express a feigned helplessness, which he and his wife both interpret as meaning that she's the only one who can do a good job of cleaning up after dinner. Daily scenes such as this, Berk and others argue, not only produce clean tables but also produce—and reproduce—gender distinctions. The interactionists focus on people's actions in concrete situations such as this one in order to determine how social meanings—in this case the shared understanding of who should do the housework—are produced.

According to this line of reasoning, people must continually "do" gender—do the work of creating a shared sense of what the relations between men and women should be (West & Zimmerman, 1987). Gender becomes a verb, usually in the passive voice: Housework is gendered, work for wages is gendered, childcare is gendered, over and over in hundreds of situations. The household, in Fenstermaker's phrase, becomes a gender factory that produces the shared reality of gender relations along with crumb-free tables (Fenstermaker, 2002).

In a sense, the interactionist approach turns the logic of the socialization approach on its head. The socialization view is that men offer to carry packages for women because men and women are taught to believe that women aren't strong enough to manage on their own; the interactionist view is that men and women believe that women can't manage on their own because men keep offering to carry their packages. The setting is a woman walking to her car in a supermarket parking lot carrying a manageable load of groceries; the interaction is that a male friend of hers approaches and offers to carry the bags for her; she smiles politely and accepts his offer with thanks, even though she could have made it to the car herself. The achievement is reinforcing and, in effect, re-creating gender differences—in other words, doing gender. You can think of many other daily situations that have similar properties; add them up and multiply by the thousands of days in the average life, say the interactionists, and you get a powerful mechanism for reproducing a society with gender differences so strong that people think they are natural.

A quarter century later, the idea of doing gender and the interactionist perspective that underlies it are still relevant. Yet not all interactions between women and men should be thought of as doing gender. The intention of West and Zimmerman was to examine interactions that reinforce inequality between women and men (Risman, 2009). But some interactions may narrow inequality between women and men. For instance, women who enter traditionally male occupations may have interactions with their male co-workers that will help them to accept women on the job. A couple who try to establish shared parenting may use their interactions to establish a more equal relationship to each other. One author suggests that we reserve the term "doing gender" for interactions that reproduce gender differences, and use a new term, "undoing gender," for interactions that reduce gender differences (Deutsch, 2007). After several decades of change in family and work lives, an increasing share of the daily interactions between women and men may be undoing gender.

Quick Review

- Sociologists who take the interactionist approach believe that gender is not a fixed role or trait but rather a social construction that must be actively maintained throughout adulthood.
- Through situated conduct—interaction in concrete settings—in everyday life, women and men unthinkingly reproduce and sustain gender differences.

Gender as Social Structure

Another body of writing about the construction and maintenance of gender differences focuses not only on social interaction or socialization, but also on the very structure of society: its hierarchies of dominance and power and its economic and political systems. According to this line of reasoning, gender differences are social creations deeply imbedded in society (Risman, 2004). Think of **social structure** as the fundamental set of positions that organize society as a whole. Social structure consists, in part, of the distribution of material resources such as wealth and education among individuals and groups. Those with more material resources tend to have power over those with fewer resources, the way the wealthy exercise power over the poor or whites exercise power over blacks. Resources and power are the bricks and mortar out of which social structure is built. Like class (see Chapter 4) and race (see Chapter 5), gender is said to be a basic part of social structure, a central way in which a society is stratified into more and less powerful groups.

social structure the fundamental set of positions that organize society as a whole

For instance, a study of 22 countries suggests that how a couple divides the housework is not just a matter of their personal beliefs. Rather, the degree of gender equality that exists at the national level also influences them. Consider two couples, A and B, who both believe that ideally housework should be divided equally. Suppose couple A lives in a country such as Russia or Japan, where few women are in parliament, few have powerful or prestigious occupations, and few earn high salaries. Suppose couple B, in contrast, lives in a country such as Sweden or Canada, where women have much more political and economic power at the national level. Then couple B will tend to divide the housework more equally than will couple A, even though their personal beliefs are the same. How they live their home lives, the study suggests, is

Families and Public Policy

Do Employers Discriminate Against Women?

In the late 1970s, the weekly earnings of the average woman who worked full-time were only about 63 percent of the weekly earnings of the average man who worked full-time. Progress has been made toward gender equality in earnings since then. In 2010, the average woman earned 81 percent of what the average man earned. But an earnings gap continues to exist (U.S. Bureau of Labor Statistics, 2011f). Why in nearly all occupations do women still earn less than men? And why are women workers still overrepresented in lower-paying jobs? Do employers discriminate against women? Are they less likely to hire a woman than a man, and do they pay women less? Or are other factors responsible for the differences between women and men in the labor market?

Some economists have argued that the earnings gap primarily represents the different social roles that women choose.

That is, they assume that women prefer to devote a larger share of their lives to raising children than do men. Consequently, according to this line of reasoning, women tend to choose jobs that they can leave for a period of time and then reenter, and they leave voluntarily when they have young children. These jobs tend to be in the lower-paying occupations and industries. In addition, they have less work experience and invest less in their careers (for example, by taking fewer job-training courses). Since employers pay lower wages to people with less work experience, they pay women less than men.

The evidence, however, suggests that this is not the whole story of the earnings gap. When two economists looked at the wage gap and took into account differences between women and men in education, work experience, and occupation and industry, they still could not explain a

substantial part of the gap (Blau & Kahn, 2007). It's possible, as they suggest, that some or all of the remaining gap in earnings is due to discrimination in how much employers pay women compared to men. We cannot be sure, however: The effect of discrimination on the earnings gap could be lower because of other unmeasured differences between women's and men's jobs; or it could be higher because employers are less likely to hire women for high-paying jobs in the first place.

A change in the world of classical music provided an unexpected window on the question of whether employers discriminate against women. Until the 1970s the conductors of the major symphony orchestras in the United States, all of whom were male, made decisions about hiring new players to fill vacancies based on recommendations from musicians they knew and on seeing and hearing the top candidates

influenced by the power and influence that women have in their national political and economic systems (Fuwa, 2004).

Or consider the way the economy runs. In Western nations, people must purchase the goods they need with money (as opposed to making their own clothes and building their own houses). Western societies are organized so that men have access to more money than women: Men are more likely to work for pay, and when they do, most earn considerably higher wages and salaries than women. To be sure, men tend to have more education and work experience than women, in part because many women withdraw from the paid workforce to bear and rear children. Gender theorists argue, however, that the wage gap is far wider than differences in education and work experience would predict—and recent economic studies suggest that their argument is probably correct. (See *Families and Public Policy:* Do Employers Discriminate Against Women?) In a number of ways—such as when parents encourage sons more than daughters to have careers, when employers discriminate against women in hiring or pay, and when long-established rules provide men with higher pay than women for comparable work—society creates and reinforces men's economic domination. Therefore, most women must depend on men if they wish to live in a household with a substantial income.

audition for the jobs. Nearly all of the new hires were men. Then in the 1970s most of the major orchestras switched to so-called blind auditions. Orchestras first advertised for vacancies; and then, in the preliminary round of auditions, a committee of orchestra members listened to the musicians from behind a screen. Since the committee members could not see the players, they could not determine their genders. Some symphonies went so far as to run a carpet from where the applicants entered the room to the screen so that the committee could not guess the gender of the musicians by the sound of their footsteps. The audition committee selected candidates for the final round of auditioning without knowing their names or genders—they relied purely on the sound of their playing. Conductors still made the final decision in most cases, but only among the candidates who made it through the preliminary round.

Did the introduction of the blind audition result in more hiring of women players? Yes, concluded Claudia Goldin and Cecilia Rouse, who obtained detailed information about auditions and rosters of players from 11 major American orchestras (Goldin & Rouse, 2000). They estimate that the screen increased the likelihood that a woman would advance beyond the preliminary rounds of auditions by 50 percent and sharply increased the likelihood that a woman would be hired to fill a vacancy. Since the 1970s, the percentage of women players in the major symphonies has increased greatly (about one-third of the players in the New York Philharmonic are women), and the authors estimate that 25 percent of that increase is the result of blind auditions.

It seems clear that discrimination in hiring was one of the factors that kept the percentage of women players low until the 1970s. Is there still discrimination in hiring today in other occupations? Without the possibility of blind job interviews, we can't be sure. Attitudes toward women in the workforce have become more favorable, and many employers may have changed their behavior. Yet it is possible that discrimination in hiring, as well as in pay, still exists.

Ask Yourself

1. Have you ever compared notes with your coworkers and discovered that the women in your group are being paid less than men? If so, how did you and the other employees interpret the earnings gap?

2. Can you think of reasons other than work experience and discrimination that would help explain the earnings gap?

www.mhhe.com/cherlin7e

Women still earn less than men in comparable jobs, on average, despite modest progress in the past decade or two.

Social structure also has a cultural component that contains the rules about how to act when relating to other people. In order to simplify the task of determining what's an appropriate way to act in everyday situations, individuals rely on simple mental models of behavior. Gender is one of the basic mental models, or cultural frames as Ridgeway (2011) calls them, that people use for this purpose. Others are age and race. When you meet someone, you almost instantaneously categorize them according to gender without even thinking about it; and that categorization affects how you act toward the other person. What's more, the cultural frame of gender contains inequalities: Men are expected to be more dominant and aggressive than women, and women are expected to be nicer and more nurturing. These mental models not only influence how we behave toward men and women but also reinforce and recreate stereotypical gender differences. An employer hiring for a management position may be predisposed to view male applicants more positively than women applicants, whereas an employer hiring for a child care center may be predisposed toward women. Thus, the sociological argument that gender is a basic part of social structure has two parts: First, men typically have material advantages (e.g., higher earning potential) that can lead to greater power over women (e.g., doing much less housework and child care). Second, the cultural frame of gender subtly influences men and women to interact in ways that reinforce male privilege. Even when men's material advantages erode, the cultural frame of gender may change more slowly, thus slowing the movement toward gender equality.

Quick Review

- Many theorists view gender as a basic part of the social structure, like class and race.
- Men tend to have material resources (money, education) that place them in positions of power over women.
- Mental models, or cultural frames, of the characteristic of women and men are also part of the social structure.

Thinking About Gender Differences Today

The huge outpouring of scholarship on the sociology of gender over the past several decades has transformed the way we view gender differences in family life and the workplace. Let's assess where knowledge, discussion, and debate are today.

CAUSES AT MULTIPLE LEVELS

The growing consensus among scholars is that gender differences are produced and reproduced at all the levels we have examined in this chapter: biosocial, childhood socialization, interactional, and social structural (England, 2009; Ridgeway, 2011). As for the biosocial level, there may be some biologically-based differences in personality or preferences between women and men that are relevant to gender differences, although there would also be a big overlap that included many women who are aggressive at work and many men who are nurturing at home. But even if biology plays a role, the social world greatly expands and amplifies these differences. It does so at the level of socialization by providing thousands of little lessons for children and adolescents to learn from sources as diverse as friends, teachers, and music videos. It does so at the level of the continual, daily interactions of men and women. In these interactions, women and men often do gender: They respond to each other using the cultural frame of stereotypical gender differences and in the process reinforce those differences. And it does so at the level of social structure, where the greater material resources of men often give them an advantage in hiring decisions or negotiations about housework. Because gender differences are created and strengthened at so many levels, they are deeply embedded in our view of the social world—so much so that we sometimes tend to see all gender differences as "natural." Yet gender relations that seemed natural in the 1950s don't seem natural today; and what we view as natural today probably won't seem so natural a generation or two from now.

THE SLOWING OF GENDER CHANGE

After rapid changes in the 1960s through the 1980s, the pace of gender change has slowed. The amount full-time female workers earn per every dollar full-time male workers earn—81 cents—hasn't increased since 2004 (U.S. Bureau of Labor Statistics, 2011f). As we will see in Chapter 8, married men increased the share of household work they did in the 1970s and 1980s but there has been no further increase since then. Why might change have slowed? One possibility is that women with dependent children remain at a disadvantage in a labor market that stills seems to assume that workers have a spouse at home to take most of the responsibility for child care. It remains difficult for the primary caregivers of children to work full-time, especially in lower-wage service and clerical jobs where a mother cannot take a personal phone call and can be fired for missing a day. The United States government provides less assistance to working parents than does any other wealthy country, as we will discuss in Chapter 8. Another possibility is that the cultural frame of gender has changed less than one might expect given the increases in mothers working outside the home—an instance of what sociologists have called **cultural lag** (Ogburn, 1964).

People tend to interpret new situations in ways that are consistent with their existing cultural expectations; they discount evidence of change and pay more attention to evidence of continuity until the evidence for change is overwhelming. The result is that gender stereotypes change more slowly than do material circumstances such as women's changing roles at work and at home (Ridgeway, 2011). Even the expansion of higher educational opportunities may have slowed the pace of gender change. As one's choice of a major comes to be seen as a way to express one's personal preferences, men's and women's senses of what are stereotypically "male" and "female" occupations may lead them to choose gender-typical majors. In the most economically advanced nations, such as the United States and Western European countries, women tend to cluster more highly in the social sciences and the humanities and men in the natural sciences than is the case in less wealthy countries (Charles and Bradley, 2009).

cultural lag the tendency for attitudes and values to change more slowly than the material circumstances that underlie them

THE ASYMMETRY OF GENDER CHANGE

When preteens at a middle school in a southeastern city were asked how a hypothetical girl who tried to start a girls' football team would be treated, a few expressed concerns that she would be teased, but most thought she would be accepted. When asked, however, about a hypothetical boy who tried to become a cheerleader, nearly all the students said that he would be the target of ridicule. Many said he would be called "gay," which was the worst insult a boy in the school could receive, according to the authors of the study (Risman & Seale, 2010). Yet the label of "gay" seemed to have less to do with sexual orientation than with acting outside of boundaries of expected behavior. Boys (and some girls) strictly policed the boundaries of masculinity by taunting boundary crossers. High school boys, other studies show, do the same (Pascoe, 2007). Yet girls at the middle school could easily cross the boundaries of femininity to be good athletes and to compete with boys for academic success in ways that their mothers and grandmothers could not. In other words, the changes in gender expectations in middle school seem to have made it OK for girls to act like boys but not for boys to act like girls.

asymmetry (of gender change) the greater change in women's lives than in men's lives

This is an example of the **asymmetry of gender change** over the past few decades. If change were symmetric, it would be the same on both sides: as much movement toward crossing the boundaries of traditional masculinity and femininity among men as among women. In contrast, there has been more change in women's behavior than in men's. To take another example, far more women than men have moved into occupations that were traditionally held by the opposite sex. Between 1975 and 2010, the percentage of physicians who were women increased from 13 percent to 32 percent; and yet the percentage of nurses who were men rose from 3 percent to only 9 percent. Over the same period, the percentage of college teachers who were women rose from 31 to 46 percent, while the percentage of men who were elementary and middle school teachers increased from 15 percent to only 18 percent (U.S. Bureau of Labor Statistics 2011b; Wootton, 1997). England (2009) argues that men's resistance to entering occupations staffed largely by women reflects the persistent devaluation in our culture of roles and activities that are seen as feminine. This devaluation may reflect deep-seated patterns of socialization as well as the "doings" of gender display. Gender differences may be reinforced by the taunting a boy knows he will receive if he steps outside the bounds of acceptable school-age male behavior. While today's school girls may be learning lessons that lead some of them to become doctors, today's school boys are still learning lessons that lead most of them to avoid becoming nurses.

GENDER, CLASS, AND RACE

The scholars who established the sociology of gender as a field of study in the 1960s and 1970s maintained that gender is not reducible to class differences, as earlier scholars had argued. They maintained that gender should be thought of in the same way scholars think of race and class—namely, as a primary basis of social stratification. By the 1980s, this view was widely accepted, and it remains so today. But in the 1980s and 1990s, some sociologists who studied minority groups criticized gender theorists for not linking gender with race (and its close cousin ethnicity) and class—essentially, for focusing heavily on the lives of white, middle-class women (Acker, 2000; Glenn, 2000b). The critics agreed that gender is as much a part of social stratification as race and class, but they noted that members of minority groups experience gender and race together, and often in combination with class. Therefore, one often needs to study a situation from these three overlapping lenses—gender, race, and class—at the same time in order to fully understand it.

For example, the number of workers who provide support and caring to middle-class families has increased in the past decade or two. (And, in fact, a new subfield of *care work studies* has developed around these workers, as we will discuss in Chapter 8.) They include nannies, house cleaners, home health care aides, day care center staff, and others. These jobs tend to be typed as women's work (when's the last time you saw a male nanny?), so issues of gender are clearly important in understanding their growth. But it is also true that a substantial number are African American, Hispanic, or Asian and that most are lower class or working class. A recent immigrant woman from Mexico or Jamaica who lacks proper documents may be channeled into the nanny business, where she will accept low pay and quite possibly send home part of her earnings to pay someone to care for her own children (Parreñas, 2002). To understand her story, you will need to see how her gender, ethnicity, and class position intersect to place her in a suburban American home.

Quick Review

- Gender differences are produced and reproduced at multiple levels, including the biosocial level, the socialization level, the level of interaction, and the social structural level.
- The pace of gender change has slowed in recent decades. Possible reasons include work-family conflict and the persistence of a cultural frame that supports gender stereotypes.
- Gender change has been asymmetric: There has been more change in women and girls' behavior than in men and boys' behavior.
- Women from minority racial and ethnic groups often experience inequalities that simultaneously involve their gender, class, and racial/ethnic position.

Men and Masculinities

Sociological writings on gender have commonly focused on the conditions under which women and girls live their lives. This orientation reflects the roots of gender studies in the feminist movement that began in the 1960s. Although men have not been absent from gender studies, they tended to be included mainly because of the ways in which they influence or control women. Beginning in the 1980s, however, both a scholarly and a popular literature emerged that was focused on men. This body of literature grew greatly in the 1990s and 2000s, as social movements aimed at men gained strength. The main topic of these writings was **masculinity**—the set of personal characteristics that society defines as being typical of men.

masculinity the set of personal characteristics that society defines as being typical of men

These writers reject the idea that masculinity has a singular essence (Coltrane, 1994). Instead, they argue that what we often think of as the "essence" of masculinity—aggressiveness, attempts to dominate, emotional detachment, aversion to homosexuality, and so forth—is merely a social construction. These authors write not of masculinity but of *masculinities,* the title of an influential book by R. W. Connell (1995) that implies that there is more than one way to be masculine. Connell and others argue that the social influences that prop up the Western version of masculinity are so pervasive they become invisible to us. Consequently, we assume incorrectly that the current version of masculinity is the way men naturally are.

Can men swim against the tide of the current construction of masculinity and be nurturing and caring? This is an important question because most mothers now work outside the home rather than caring for children full-time. Is it possible for fathers to become the principal caregivers in the home and do the kind of caring that mothers routinely do? Studies suggest that at least some fathers can do caregiving well (Coltrane & Adams, 2008). For instance, Andrea Doucet set out to interview fathers who were primary caregivers in and around Ottawa, Canada (Doucet, 2006). Through advertisements and word of mouth, she identified over 100 fathers. She found that these men cared for and nurtured their children in ways that resembled the kind of care mothers provided, but with a noticeable difference: Fathers emphasized playfulness, physical activity, risk taking, and autonomy more than mothers typically did. These kinds of activities have long been seen as part of fathers' repertoires (Parke, 1996). This doesn't mean that fathers aren't nurturing, Doucet argues, but rather that they tend to nurture in a somewhat different way than mothers typically do. If more fathers were to become primary caregivers in the coming years, we might see more of this style of nurturing.

Quick Review

- Feminist sociologists argue that the characteristics that comprise "masculinity" as we know it are socially constructed rather than natural.
- Fathers are capable of nurturing children but may do so in a somewhat different way from mothers.

■ The Contributions of Gender Studies ■

We have reviewed several approaches to the study of gender differences (Table 3.1, p. 103). Despite their different perspectives—or perhaps because of them—sociologists who have studied gender (along with their colleagues in anthropology, history, and psychology) have made important contributions to our understanding of the family. First, they have demonstrated that the roles men and women play in families are in large part socially and culturally constructed. Indeed, many sociologists would argue that such differences are almost entirely constructed by conscious social forces. But all would agree that biology cannot explain why the great 1950s liberal Adlai Stevenson told the 1955 graduating class of Smith College (a private liberal arts college for

Table 3.1 Approaches to the Study of Gender Differences

APPROACH	HOW GENDER IS CONSTRUCTED	EXAMPLES
Biosocial	Through biologically based (e.g., genetic, hormonal) differences that have evolved over the history of the human existence.	Boys will sometimes insist on playing with trucks and tools even if they are given dolls and stuffed animals.
Socialization	Through learning from adults, the media, peers, and teachers what kinds of behavior are expected of women and men.	Boys are given trucks and tools for birthday presents; girls are given dolls and stuffed animals. Boys are admonished not to cry; girls are allowed to cry.
Interactionist	Through continual reinforcement of gender differences because of the everyday behaviors of women and men.	Husbands who are very competent outside the home will claim they're not good at washing dishes or changing diapers, and their wives will agree with them and do these tasks.
Structural	Through the distribution of resources and power that favors men over women.	Women are paid less than men for working at the same job. Women who work outside the home are still expected to be the primary caregivers to children, even if they are married.

women) that their place in politics was to "influence man and boy" through the "humble role of housewife" (Chafe, 1972). Moreover, biology can't explain the social changes in family life that have occurred over the past few decades, or even the past few centuries, because evolutionary change is slow. Consequently, the biological approach may not be very useful to a sociologist who is trying to explain social change—although it might be helpful in determining the difficulty of bringing about social change. In this book the social and cultural construction of gender will be relevant to discussions of changing conceptions of sexuality (Chapter 6), patterns of courtship, dating, and spouse choice, and the relationships between married or cohabiting couples (Chapter 7).

Second, sociologists of gender have taught us that gender distinctions sometimes (some would say *always*) reflect differences in power between men and women. Adlai Stevenson's speech was meant to convey to the Smith graduates how important their restricted political role was. But women whose only political influence is through their husbands are not equal in political power to men. After the rise of the feminist movement in the 1960s and 1970s and the increases in the number of women elected to political office, no male politician would make Stevenson's statement. Feminist scholars argue, moreover, that power differences do not stop at the family's front door; rather, the roles women play within marriages often reflect their husbands' greater power—in particular, his greater economic power. Said differently, the lesson is that families are not islands isolated from the rest of society; rather, the relations of power and inequality that hold outside the home can also extend within it. Differences in power and the allocation of work within the household will be examined in Chapter 8. Other chapters will include discussions of the effects of male domination on domestic violence against women (Chapter 11), the economic circumstances of divorced women (Chapter 12), and family law and policy (Chapter 14).

Looking Back

1. **How do sociologists distinguish between the concepts of "sex" and "gender"?** Sociologists use the term *sex* to refer to biologically based differences between women and men and *gender* to refer to differences that are social and cultural, and therefore constructed by society. Gender differences often reflect male domination over women. Nevertheless, in some instances social and biological influences on gender differences are difficult to disentangle.

2. **How might fetal development affect the behavior of women and men?** There is some evidence that biological differences in the development of male and female fetuses could account for some of the gender differences in children's and adults' behavior. Studies have found a correlation between gender-typical behavior and exposure to higher levels of male sex hormones before birth. Biologically based differences only exist "on average"; individuals can show a wide range of behavior. And social influences such as parental upbringing and education can counteract biological predispositions.

3. **How do children learn how women and men are supposed to behave?** According to the socialization approach, young children learn stereotypical behavior from parents, peers, teachers, and the media. The emphasis in this approach is on conscious, social learning. In general, children are taught to think that boys and men are aggressive, competitive, and independent, whereas girls and women are less aggressive, more nurturing, and better at enabling and maintaining personal relationships. From these lessons, children mentally construct the concept of gender.

4. **How does everyday life reinforce gender differences?** Sociologists who take the interactionist approach believe that gender differences need continual reinforcement throughout life. In their view, gender differences are reproduced in daily interactions between women and men in settings such as the home and the workplace. Without being conscious of it, individuals do the work of maintaining gender differences.

5. **Are gender differences built into the structure of society?** Many gender theorists argue that gender differences are built into the social structure in a fundamental way like social class or race. Men tend to have material advantages which place them in positions in the social structure where they have power over women. People also use pervasive mental models, or cultural frames, of the characteristics of women and men that are built into the social structure. They use these cultural frames to guide their interactions. The cultural frames reinforce inequalities, such as the idea that men are more dominant and aggressive than women. Even if the material advantages of men decline, the cultural frames can remain strong enough to reinforce gender differences.

6. **Overall, how should we think about gender differences today?** Gender differences are created and maintained on many levels, which is why gender is such a strong factor in people's identities and in how societies are organized. Biosocial factors predispose people to act in gendered ways and childhood experiences socialize them to do so. Gender differences are reinforced in everyday interactions between women and men. And differences in power and influence are built into the social structure. After several decades of rapid change in gender differences, the pace of change has slowed; moreover, the amount of change in women's lives has been greater than in men's lives. The influences of gender often depend on the social class and racial context of a situation. Minority group women often experience gender, class, and racial or ethnic inequality simultaneously.

7. **Is there more than one kind of masculinity?** Sociologists suggest that the dominant kind of masculinity, with its aggressiveness, emotional detachment, and so forth, is socially constructed and is not the only kind of masculinity. They argue that many men can be nurturing caregivers to children, even though they may do the work of caring in a way that emphasizes physical activity, play, and autonomy more than mothers typically do.

Go to the Online Learning Center at www.mhhe.com/cherlin7e to test your knowledge of the chapter concepts and key terms.

Study Questions

1. What does the story of the two-spirit people teach us about sex and gender?
2. Let us suppose for the moment that prenatal male hormone levels influence aggressive behavior. Would we then expect all boys to be aggressive and all girls to be unaggressive?
3. The newest medium to which children and adolescents are exposed is the Internet. Do frequently visited Web sites impart messages about women's and men's proper behavior?
4. Is "doing gender" in daily life—the daily reinforcement of gendered behavior through social interaction—strong enough to maintain the gender differences we see in society?
5. Do you agree, as many feminist researchers do, that "connected knowing" is preferable to "separated knowing"?
6. Why might the pace of gender change have slowed?
7. Why has gender changed more for women than for men?
8. Are fathers capable of nurturing children?

Key Terms

asymmetry (of gender change)   100
biosocial approach (to gender differences)   86
cultural lag   99
gender   84
gestation   85
interactionist approach (to gender differences)   92
intersexual   84
masculinity   101
peer group   89
sex   83
social structure   95
socialization   88
socialization approach (to gender differences)   88
two-spirit people   82

Thinking about Families

The Public Family	The Private Family
Do parents, peers, and teachers prepare boys for success in the work world more than they prepare girls?	Does everyday life reinforce gender differences in families in ways we usually don't notice?

Families on the Internet   www.mhhe.com/cherlin7e

Note: While all the URLs listed were current as of the printing of this book, these sites often change. Please check our Web site (www.mhhe.com/cherlin7e) for updates.

Information on gender and on women's issues abounds on the Internet. On the liberal side, the Feminist Majority Foundation Online Web site (www.feminist.org) provides links to many sources of information. Click on "research center" and you will find a list of women's studies programs, journals, and feminist magazines. A conservative perspective is available from Concerned Women for America (www.cwfa.org).

For an abundance of factual information on labor force issues such as earnings differences between women and men, go to the home page of the Women's Bureau at the U.S. Department of Labor (www.dol.gov/wb). The Women's Bureau is concerned with working conditions, including equal pay, for women employed outside the home. Click on "Data and Statistics" and then "20 Leading Occupations of Employed Women." In how many of these occupations are 80 percent or more of the workers women? The Census Bureau maintains a list of news releases about reports on women's statistics (http://www.census.gov/Press-Release/www/releases/archives/women/index.html).

Chapter Four

Social Class and Family Inequality

Looking Forward

Families and the Economy

The Growing Importance of Education

Diverging Demographics

Age at Marriage

Childbearing Outside of Marriage

Marriage Market

Divorce

Differences in Early Adulthood

Family Life and the Globalization of Production

Developed Countries

Developing Countries

Defining Social Class

Bringing in Gender and Family

Social Classes and Status Groups

The Four-Class Model

Three Status Groups

Social Class Differences in Family Life

Assistance from Kin

Kinship among the Poor and Near Poor

Chronic Poverty and Kin Networks

The Limits of Kin Networks

Kinship among the Nonpoor

Social Class and Child Rearing

Social Class and Parental Values

Concerted Cultivation versus Natural Growth

Social Class and the Family

Looking Back

Study Questions

Key Terms

Thinking about Families

Families on the Internet

Boxed Features

FAMILIES AND THE GREAT RECESSION: *Job Losses and Financial Strain*

FAMILIES AND PUBLIC POLICY: *Homelessness, by the Numbers*

Looking Forward

1. How have changes in the American economy since the 1970s affected families?

2. How have the family lives of people with college degrees diverged from the family lives of those with less education?

3. How has the globalization of production affected family life in developed countries and in developing countries?

4. What factors determine the social class position of families?

5. Are there social class differences in kinship?

6. Are there social class differences in how parents raise children?

In the fall of 2011 the Census Bureau released its annual report on income and poverty (U.S. Bureau of the Census, 2011f). With the country still in the throes of the Great Recession, the numbers were predictably bad. Between 2007 and 2010 the income of the median household had declined by 7.1 percent. (The *median* household income is the midpoint: half of the other households had higher incomes and half had lower incomes.) As for poverty, 15.1 percent of Americans lived in households with incomes below the federal poverty line in 2010. Poverty was even worse for American children: 22.0 percent of them lived in households below the poverty line. But one other figure drew the attention of the media: The average male full-time worker earned less in 2010 than did his counterpart in 1973. A generation had gone by in which the size of the American economy grew and the productivity of the work force improved. And yet the average worker had made no progress.

Who is that average worker? It is typically someone with a high school degree but no college degree. A generation ago, we called these workers "blue collar," after the iconic chambray shirt that workers wore to their factory jobs. Today, many of those factory jobs are gone. Every old city has seen the closing of factories that had formerly provided fulltime jobs at good wages to workers without college educations. The Singer Sewing Machine Company dominated Elizabeth, New Jersey, from its founding in 1873 until it closed in 1982—its market reduced by ready-to-wear clothes and its competitive edge lost to plants in developing countries that paid workers far lower wages. One longtime worker told anthropologist Katherine Newman:

> I worked there forty-seven years and one month. I was one of many people in my family. My niece worked there. My two brothers, my father. You see, Singer's in the old days, it was a company that went from one generation to the other. (Newman, 1988)

Advances in communications and transportation allowed managers to close plants such as Singer and import their goods from factories in developing nations in Latin America, South Asia (for example, India), Southeast Asia (for example, Indonesia or the Philippines), or East Asia (for example, China) where wages were much lower. American factory workers lost their jobs, while opportunities grew for the well-educated managers who imported and marketed goods. In other industries, computers allowed employers to replace less-skilled workers with machines, including workers who used to answer the telephone. When I call Amtrak to make a train reservation, a perky voice answers by saying, "Hi, I'm Julie, Amtrak's automated agent," and continues to give me options until I yell "operator" several times and am finally connected to a human being. Julie could not function without a voice recognition system that depends upon fast, powerful computers and complex software that did not exist until about two decades ago. Before then, sales agents, most of whom did not have college degrees, answered the phones. Jobs like theirs are also disappearing. At the same time, jobs for the well-educated people who design systems like Amtrak's are increasing.

The result has been a **polarization** of the labor market since the 1970s: Job opportunities have increased for the most-educated workers and for the least-educated workers, while declining for workers with moderate levels of education and skill (Autor, Katz, & Kearney, 2006; Kalleberg, 2011). Managers (such as business executives) and professionals (such as lawyers) are still needed, as are the low-skilled service workers (such as restaurant staff) who cook their meals and the sales workers (such as cashiers) who sell them their clothes. Managers and professionals tend to have high salaries, while service and sales workers typically have low wages. Meanwhile the percentage of workers who have jobs in manufacturing has declined as plants like Singer closed. And the percentage who work in moderately-skilled white-collar jobs like the people who used to answer Amtrak's phones has declined, too. The American occupational structure looks more and more like an hourglass, bulging at the top and the bottom but narrow in the middle.

Employment has also become more precarious, with less security and shorter periods of employment. For example, employers increasingly contract out work to temporary agencies instead of hiring their own workers. They downsize quickly when demand for their products or services drops. Workers, in response, feel less loyalty to their employers and are more likely to change jobs when an opportunity arises. What some call the psychological contract between employers and employees—employers promise job security and advancement while employees promise loyalty and hard work—strengthened in the mid-twentieth century as American manufacturing prospered; but it has since broken down (Kalleberg, 2011). As a result of the greater polarization and precariousness of employment today, people feel anxious and insecure about jobs. Young people entering the labor market, especially those without college degrees, have less confidence that they can find a good job today. And that feeling of insecurity can lead them to postpone starting a family. These developments were made even worse in the late 2000s by the Great Recession. (See: *Families and the Great Recession:* Job Losses and Financial Strain.)

polarization (of the labor market) a growth of job opportunities at the top and bottom of the job market but a lessening of opportunities in the middle

Families and the Economy

In fact, since the 1960s, average wages have stayed the same or decreased for workers without a college education because of the movement of factory jobs overseas and the spread of automation. Only the college educated workers have experienced substantial wage growth since then (Katz & Autor, 1999). The result is a great increase in what I will call **family inequality,** the extent to which some families obtain more income and wealth than do others.

family inequality the extent to which some families obtain more income and wealth than do others

Families and the Great Recession

Job Losses and Financial Strain

Aₛ the Great Recession hit, the unemployment rate rose sharply, doubling between 2007 and 2009 and remaining near 9 percent through 2011. And if you had any doubt that the Great Recession caused a jump in unemployment among family members, a glance at the graph on this page will convince you. It shows the percentage of families with at least one member who was unemployed for each year from 1995 to 2010. The American economy was in good shape in the late 1990s, and the percentage dropped below six in the year 2000. It varied up and down after that until it rose in 2008—just as the recession hit—and then spiked to 12 percent in 2009. It increased further in 2010.

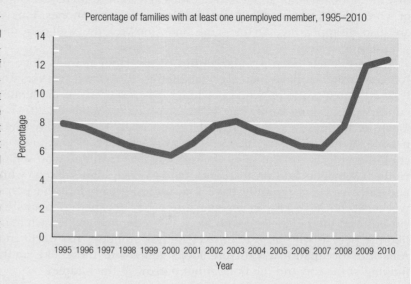

Percentage of families with at least one unemployed member, 1995–2010

What did unemployment mean for families? Sociologists Anne H. Gauthier and Frank F. Furstenberg, Jr., reported on the responses to a 2009 national survey of adults who had children under age 18 living with them (Gauthier and Furstenberg, 2010). The authors noted that many families were already stressed prior to the recession. As discussed elsewhere in this chapter, some of the jobs that used to support workers without college degrees have moved overseas or disappeared into computer chips. As a result, families in the middle of the American income distribution have had their share of the economic pie squeezed; in contrast, families near the top of the distribution have seen their share of the pie grow. Moreover, the amount of debt families owe has also risen, as credit card usage increased and as banks, in the run-up to the recession, offered home mortgages to families with limited means to pay them. Thus, when the recession struck, many families already were operating

with little margin for error. When asked, "If somebody in your household were to lose his/her job (including yourself), how many months do you think your family could manage without borrowing money?" 31 percent of individuals in the survey responded *none*.

So when unemployment increased, many already-stressed families took a hit. When individuals in the survey were asked, "Have the last 12 months been better, worse, or the same when it comes to the financial situation of your family?" half replied that it had been worse. Although people at all levels of education reported a rise in unemployment, the situation was worse for those with less education. For instance, individuals with a high school diploma were almost twice as likely to feel financially strained as were individuals with college degrees.

The consequences of financial strain were tangible. For example, 5 percent of those who reported financial strain

had experienced the foreclosure of their homes. Now, 5 percent may not seem like a lot, but it means that if you lived in a neighborhood where most residents felt the strain of the recession, one out of every twenty neighbors would have lost their homes. Another 5 or 10 percent, according to the survey, had put their house up for sale. And 2 to 5 percent declared bankruptcy. Multiply these effects across all of the distressed neighborhoods in America and you will quickly see how severe the financial effects of the recession were. And that was just in 2009. As the economic downturn lasted through 2012, many more American families lost their homes or went bankrupt. The Great Recession refused to leave. And two economists projected that the percentage of Americans living below the poverty line would remain above the pre-recession level until the end of this decade (Monea and Sawhill, 2011).

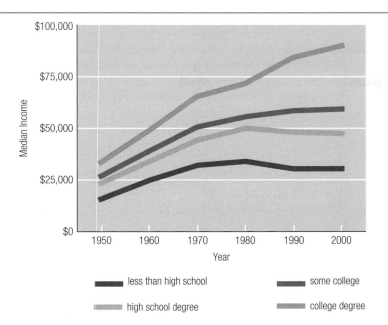

FIGURE 4.1
Adjusted family-of-four income medians, by education, 1950 to 2000. (*Source:* Fischer & Hout, 2006) Note: Income expressed in 1999 dollars and adjusted for family size (see Fischer & Hout, 2006).

Moreover, we will see that families that are doing well are increasingly headed by married, well-educated couples, whereas the ones that are not doing as well are increasingly headed by cohabiting couples or single parents, most of them without a college education.

THE GROWING IMPORTANCE OF EDUCATION

Over time, the amount of education that people obtain has become a stronger predictor of the types of families that they live in and how well-off they are. In contrast, education was a much less important factor in determining family income a half-century ago. Figure 4.1 shows the median income for a typical family of four, by education of the family head, for the period 1950 to 2000. You can see that the lines start closer together, and then in the 1970s they begin to move farther apart. As the lines diverge, the income advantage of families with college-educated family heads increases over families whose heads had less education; and the income disadvantage of families whose heads did not gradu-ate from high school grows. In 1950 a family whose head had a college degree earned about twice as much as a family whose head had not completed high school. In 2000 that family earned about three times as much.

There is another important reason why the families of the college-educated were pulling away from other families: they were more likely to have two par-ents in the household. Over the past several decades, single-parent families have increased in the United States due to rising rates of divorce and to more childbearing outside of marriage. But the increase has been faster among the less-educated. Of all families with children whose heads had a college degree in 2011, 13 percent were headed by an unmarried mother. In contrast, 30 percent of families with children whose heads did not have a college degree were headed by an unmarried mother (U.S. Bureau of the Census, 2011s). Single-parent families must rely on the money that one parent brings in;

moreover, women's earnings (most single-parent families are headed by women) are usually lower than men's. Two-parent families, in contrast, can pool the incomes of both adults. Since the 1980s, the median income of married-couple families in which both spouses work has increased much more rapidly than has the median income of other types of families (U.S. Bureau of the Census, 2011t). Because the families of the college educated could rely on two earners more than families with less education could, the gap between the incomes of the college educated and the less educated widened (Western, Bloome, & Percheski, 2008).

Quick Review

- Family inequality has increased over the past several decades.
- The kinds of jobs that used to allow high-school-educated adults to support a family have become scarce because of automation and the globalization of production.
- Widespread higher education is a recent phenomenon; high-school degrees were uncommon and college degrees rare in 1900. College attendance rose rapidly in the second half of the 1900s.
- The incomes of families, where the head of the family is college-educated, have risen more rapidly than the incomes of families when the head of the family is less educated.
- A person's education is a more important predictor of the kind of family life he or she leads than it was in the past.

DIVERGING DEMOGRAPHICS

Since about 1980, the family patterns of people with college degrees have moved in a different direction than those of people with less education. Today, college-educated Americans are more likely to marry (although they take longer to do it), more likely to wait until after marriage to have a first child, and less likely to divorce than are less-educated Americans.

Age at Marriage   People with four-year college degrees are displaying a pattern we might call catch-up marriage: Until age 25, relatively few of them marry, which is consistent with the societywide trend toward later marriage. But in their late twenties and thirties, their rates of marriage exceed those of the less educated (Martin, 2004). By the time they are in their forties, a higher proportion of them have married than is the case for people without college degrees (Goldstein & Kenney, 2001). In other words, if you just followed a group of young adults until their mid-twenties, you would conclude that college graduates have lower marriage rates, and you might even predict that fewer of them will ever marry. You would be missing, however, the action that occurs later on, after men and women have completed their higher education and begun to establish careers, which more than compensates.

Childbearing Outside of Marriage   Most college-educated women also wait to have children until after they are married—childbearing outside of marriage remains almost as uncommon among them as it was a half-century ago (Ellwood & Jencks, 2004). Among women without college degrees, however, and especially among women who have never attended college, far fewer

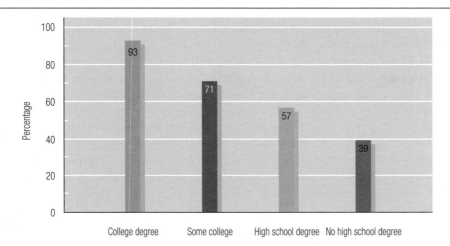

FIGURE 4.2
Percentage of women who were married when they gave birth, by education, 1997–2001. (*Source:* Kennedy & Bumpass, 2008)

wait until marriage to have children than was the case a half-century ago. Figure 4.2 shows how the percentage of women who are married when they give birth varies by education, based on a 2002 national survey. You can see how sharply the percentage falls as education decreases. It is as if marriage and childbearing—so closely linked in Western culture—have become separate phenomena among the least educated, with childbearing often preceding marriage by years. One way of thinking about this difference is to view Americans as following different ways of fitting childbearing into the life course.

A study of young women in low-income Philadelphia-area neighborhoods found that many of them think it unlikely that they could find suitable marriage partners (Edin & Kefalas, 2005). They see few men who are earning steady, decent incomes—still a requirement for a husband in the United States—and who are free of the problems such as substance abuse and illegal activity that often come with limited earning potential. Consequently, they think that to postpone having a child until one is married carries a high risk of never having children—a risk they are unwilling to take. And they do not think that having a child outside of marriage will hurt them subsequently in the marriage market. Moreover, they do not expect to attend college. So they often follow the strategy of having children at a relatively early age without marrying and then thinking seriously about marriage many years later. The authors, Kathryn Edin and Maria Kefalas (2005), write:

> Unlike their wealthier sisters, who have the chance to go to college and embark on careers—attractive possibilities that provide strong motivation to put off having children—poor young women grab eagerly at the surest source of accomplishment within their reach: becoming a mother.

Young women who are confident that they will graduate from college, on the other hand, can reasonably expect to find a suitable husband afterwards and to have children after they marry. Most of them can make the conventional strategy—finish your education, marry, and then have children—work successfully. Thus, the most- and least-educated groups tend to follow different strategies for ensuring that they will have children. The groups in the middle of the educational distribution ranges are somewhat more likely than the college educated to have children outside of marriage, and they increasingly do so in cohabiting unions rather than marriage. I will discuss the role of cohabitation in more detail in Chapter 7.

The Marriage Market   Education has become a more important factor in who marries whom over the past half-century or so. Sociologists call the tendency of people to marry others similar to themselves **assortative marriage.** In the 1930s, religion was a more important determinant of who marries whom than was education: A college-educated Protestant was more likely to marry a Protestant high school graduate than to marry a college-educated Catholic. But since the middle of the twentieth century, college graduates have become much more likely to marry each other than to marry people with the same religion but less education. Religion remains a factor, but the college educated have largely removed themselves from the rest of the marriage market (Kalmijn, 1991). And since the 1970s, people who did not complete high school have become less likely to marry people with more education; rather, they have become more isolated in the marriage market (Schwartz & Mare, 2005). In the middle of the educational distribution, on the other hand, more marriage across educational groups exists (for example, a marriage between a high school graduate who did not attend college and someone who attended college but did not get a bachelor's degree). In sum, the marriage market today seems to be stratified by education into three submarkets of people who choose partners primarily like themselves: people with college degrees; people who graduated from high school and may have attended college but did not get a bachelor's degree; and people who did not graduate from high school. To be sure, some marriages still cross these boundaries, but on the whole these divisions exist.

Divorce   The trends in divorce also show a divergence. In the 1960s and 1970s the risk of divorce was rising for all groups, but starting about 1980 the risk began to decrease. The drop was greatest for college graduates. By the 2000s, college graduates had a substantially lower lifetime risk of divorce than the less-educated; perhaps one-third of all marriages will end in divorce. Those with a high school degree but not a college degree may have the highest rates (Isen and Stevenson, 2001; National Center for Family and Marriage Research, 2011b). So, as is the case with marriage, the risk of divorce also seems to be stratified, with a college-educated group at the low end. We will consider divorce in more detail in Chapter 12.

Differences in Early Adulthood   To sum up this picture of diverging demographics, several trends in marriage, childbearing, and divorce suggest that the family patterns of individuals with different levels of education have moved in different directions in the past few decades:

- College graduates delay marriage but ultimately have a higher lifetime probability of marrying than do people without college degrees.
- People increasingly choose a spouse with a similar level of education.
- College graduates are much less likely to have a child without marrying.
- The chances of divorce have been declining for college graduates.

---

assortative marriage the tendency of people to marry others similar to themselves

A couple sees their children off to school before going to work. Dual-earner families have shown the greatest income gains in recent decades.

It is likely that the restructuring of the American economy, which improved the life chances of those with the most education and reduced them for those with the least education, influenced this divergence. But it did not act alone; rather, a broad cultural shift probably played a role: Alternatives to marriage (having a child as a single parent or cohabiting) have become more acceptable, and the meaning of marriage has changed. I will return to the theme of cultural change in marriages and partnerships in Chapter 7.

In any event, people with different levels of education increasingly experience the life stage of early adulthood in different ways. The college educated continue their schooling into their twenties, postpone both marriage and childbearing, but eventually marry and have a lower risk of divorce. Individuals who did not graduate from high school are increasingly isolated in the marriage market, and are much more likely to have a child prior to marrying. In addition, when and if they marry, their risk of divorce is high. Finally, individuals with a high school degree and perhaps some college credits are in the middle range with regard to marriage, childbearing outside of marriage, and may have the highest risk of divorce.

Quick Review

- Since about 1980, the family patterns of people with different levels of education have diverged in several ways.
- People with college degrees have been delaying marriage but ultimately marrying at higher rates, waiting until they are married to have children, and experiencing declining divorce risks.
- People who have not graduated from high school are more likely to have children prior to marrying, less likely to marry, and if they marry, more likely to divorce.
- Over the past several decades, people have become increasingly likely to choose a spouse with a similar level of education.
- The less educated are increasingly following a path of having children before marrying, whereas the well educated tend to follow the conventional path of finishing their education, marrying, and only then having children.

FAMILY LIFE AND THE GLOBALIZATION OF PRODUCTION

Overall, the globalization of production—the movement of manufacturing and clerical jobs to developing countries—has altered family life in the developed countries that have sent jobs elsewhere and in the developing countries that have received jobs. The effects are different but profound in both. They show that the globalization of production is having a world-wide effect on family life.

DEVELOPED COUNTRIES

In the developed countries that have lost jobs to the developing world, there is a growing economic gap between the college-educated and the less-educated, as shown by the diverging demographics we have just reviewed for the United States. A sharp educational differential in childbearing within marriage is also apparent in the United Kingdom and, to a lesser extent, other European countries (Kiernan, 2011). College-educated individuals still have access to the managerial and professional jobs that have remained in the developed nations even as factory and clerical work has left. As a result, this group is doing relatively well economically. In the United States, at least, the college-educated are increasingly living family lives that we might call **neo-traditional.** Marriage rates are high; and most children are born to married couples; and divorce rates have dropped. This marriage-centered style of life harks back to the mid-twentieth century, although with some differences: unlike the 1950s family, couples may cohabit before they marry, and most wives work outside the home. Far from being a cultural vanguard, college-educated young adults are leading more conventional family lives.

High school educated Americans, on the other hand, face a much weaker job market because the kinds of mid-level jobs that their parents used to take have moved to countries where workers earn far less. Consequently, they hesitate to marry and increasingly have children before marrying. Their risk of divorce is higher. Meanwhile, for Americans without high school degrees, globalization has not altered family life as much. As was true before globalization, their work opportunities are largely confined to low-level service jobs that do not pay well, have few fringe benefits, and are often insecure.

neo-traditional a style of family life centered on marriage but which may be preceded by cohabitation and in which wives work outside the home

Their levels of marriage remain low and a majority of them have children outside of marriage. In sum, college-educated adults and their families are emerging as the most advantaged group in the globalization of production in the United States and probably in other developed countries as well (although the Great Recession has hurt all young adults lately). In contrast, this great transformation of employment has constrained the family lives of less-educated adults and their families, leaving them disadvantaged by globalization.

DEVELOPING COUNTRIES

But what about family life in the developing countries that have been on the receiving end of the globalization of production? Here, too, family lives are changing. The most important factor is the increasing employment of women. Employers in many developing countries seem to think that women will work for lower wages than men and that they are easier to control than are men (for instance, less likely to complain or to go on strike) (Benería, 2003; Trask, 2010). Women dominate the work force in occupations such as assembling electronic goods or making clothes. Some women work in the **formal sector** of the economy, where jobs have characteristics such as long-term labor contracts, legal protections, and fringe benefits such as sick leave, and where the activities of employers are regulated by local or national law. But an increasing number of jobs are in what is called the **informal sector** of the economy. This term does not mean relaxed or laid-back; rather, it signifies that employment is precarious and outside of the law: jobs are based on verbal agreements rather than contracts; they are unregulated by local or national law; they are easily ended; and they do not have fringe benefits. Among women workers, some of these jobs are done at home, as when employers drop off parts for electronic devices or toys and later pick up the assembled products. It is generally less expensive for employers to use informal sector labor because wages are lower, there is no factory to be maintained, and work can be ended whenever demand for the products declines. Employers often subcontract tasks to middlemen who in turn hire a predominantly female, home-based work force.

> **formal sector** the part of the economy in which workers have labor contracts and legal protections and employers are regulated

> **informal sector** the part of the economy in which workers have no labor contracts, no legal protections, and no employer regulation

The great increase in women working for pay has brought both benefits and costs to family life in developing countries. As for the benefits: Women's wages, although very low by developed country standards, have allowed them to raise their family's standard of living, such as by improving their children's diet or purchasing a refrigerator. Studies show that when wives have control over money they tend to spend more of it on their children than when husbands have control of it (Lundberg, Pollak, & Wales, 1997). Women who are earning wages have been able to gain more independence and bargaining power in their households (as have employed women in developed countries— see Chapter 8). Their increased earnings have made their husbands less likely to physically abuse them, and in more extreme circumstances they have been able to use their earnings to escape abusive marriages (see Chapter 11). Moreover, working at home has allowed them to combine earning money with the childcare and household work that they are still expected to do.

Yet the costs have been substantial, too. The wages are so low, and employment so unstable, that a family may need multiple sources of income to subsist from day to day, entailing long hours of work by both parents. Especially when they are employed in the informal sector, women may have little control over when they work and how long they work. The lack of institutionalized child care centers or subsidies sometimes means that younger children are left in the care of older ones (see Chapter 8). A daughter may be forced to drop out of school in order to care for her siblings, thus ending her chance to get a good education (Trask, 2010). Many husbands have not increased their share of the domestic work, creating a crushing double burden for wives whose jobs may require long working hours and six- or seven-day work weeks (Heymann, 2006).

Unlike families in the United States and other developed countries, then, families in developing countries cannot easily be sorted into winners and losers in the globalization of production on the basis of characteristics such as education. Although one could undoubtedly find some families for whom the effects have been completely positive and others for whom the effects have been completely negative, there are many more for whom the effects have been both positive *and* negative. The ability to earn money through factory work or home production, even if wages are low, is an opportunity that women in low-income countries cannot easily pass up. It can increase their independence and boost their children's standard of living. But it can also make their lives increasingly harried by the long hours of paid and unpaid work that make up their day. It can leave their children without adult care and can cut short the education of caregiving daughters. It can leave women exploited by employers in the informal sector who are not bound by contracts and labor laws. The globalization of production is a decidedly mixed blessing for the families of the developing world.

Quick Review

- The globalization of production has had a world-wide effect on family life.
- In developed countries such as the United States, college-educated individuals are living a neo-traditional family life centered on marriage.
- Also in developed countries, the less-educated are marrying less, having more children outside of marriage, and divorcing more than the college-educated.
- In developing countries women are working for pay in both the formal and informal sectors of the economy.
- The great increase in women working for pay has brought both benefits (more independence and bargaining power) and costs (child care problems) in developing countries.

Defining Social Class

social class an ordering of all persons in a society according to their degrees of economic resources, prestige, and privilege

life chances the resources and opportunities that people have to provide themselves with material goods and favorable living conditions

It's clear from the previous sections that people who differ in the level of education they have attained also tend to experience the job market and family life differently. When sociologists think about differences in economic resources, they often use the concept of **social class,** an ordering of all persons in a society according to their degrees of economic resources, prestige, and privilege. All agree that income and wealth are core elements of this ordering. But the German sociologist Max Weber added other standards (Gerth & Mills, 1946). One is the broader idea of **life chances,** the resources and opportunities that people have to provide themselves with material goods and favorable living conditions. People's life chances may be augmented by the higher education

A manager at a fast-food restaurant chain both supervises workers and is supervised by higher-level executives.

they obtain or their family's contacts in the labor market. Their life chances may be limited by discrimination or racial segregation. So education can be considered an economic resource, too. A second concept is a more subjective category: the **status group,** a group of people who share a common style of life and often identify with each other. They are sometimes distinguished by prestige—the honor and status a person receives—such as the prestige of medical doctors or university professors. They often differ in their level of privilege—that is, their access to special advantages such as attendance at elite universities. Are the concepts of social class and status groups useful in helping us understand the variations in family life today?

status group a group of people who share a common style of life and often identify with each other

BRINGING IN GENDER AND FAMILY

The great theories of class were developed at a time when relatively few married women worked outside the home. Theorists focused on the kinds of jobs men typically did: physical labor, factory work, supervising, or managing. Therefore, these theories really refer to the class positions of individual men (Acker, 2000). But if you are interested in the pooling of resources and the sharing of living conditions, you might want to analyze the class location of a family. For instance, if your ultimate interest is children's living conditions, the family would be a more appropriate unit to study than the individual parent. In the days when most families had two parents and only one (almost always the husband) worked for wages, one could assign to a family the class location of the husband. One could speak of a "working-class" family and mean a family in which the husband worked in a factory and the wife did not work outside the home. (Note that wives' unpaid labor inside the home isn't counted as "work" in these theories; we will discuss this problem in Chapter 8.)

But this simple procedure doesn't work well any more. Because of the great increase in married women's work outside the home, both the husband and the wife work for pay in the majority of married-couple families. Studies in the United States and other Western nations suggest that, depending on the definition of social class, husbands and wives may belong to different classes in up to one-third of all two-parent, two-earner families (Sørensen, 1994). Moreover, many women work in the expanding service sector (i.e., sales, clerical, personal services) of the economy. It's harder to assign a class position to these jobs, in part because they tend to pay less than the jobs that men with comparable education obtain. Consider a woman who works as a salesclerk in a department store. She might be considered part of the "middle class" as long as she is married to a husband with a well-paying job. But if the marriage ends and she becomes a single parent, her standard of living is likely to drop. Whether she necessarily leaves the middle class is unclear—she has less income, but she retains the same level of education and many of the same friends and interests.

Yet when people are asked in surveys whether they are "working class" or "middle class," they give ready answers. How, in fact, do husbands and wives decide what social class they are in? Research suggests that both spouses consider the husband's and the wife's incomes and weigh them about equally when deciding what class they are in. But women and men diverge in their thinking about education and occupational prestige: Women tend to consider theirs and their husband's more or less equally, whereas men tend to weight their own more heavily (Davis & Robinson, 1988, 1998; Yamaguchi & Wang, 2002).

SOCIAL CLASSES AND STATUS GROUPS

Clearly, thinking about families in class terms is complex, but it also seems unavoidable. Let us examine the four social class categories commonly used in sociological research: upper class, middle class, working class, and lower class. But think of them as ideal types rather than concrete realities. Introduced by Weber, the **ideal type** refers to a hypothetical model that consists of the most significant characteristics, in extreme form, of a social phenomenon. It is useful for understanding social life, even though any real example of the phenomenon may not have all the characteristics of the ideal type.

ideal type a hypothetical model that consists of the most significant characteristics, in extreme form, of a social phenomenon

The Four-Class Model   Americans understand the four-category scheme, but they overwhelmingly say they are either middle class or working class. For instance, in the 2010 General Social Survey (GSS), a biennial national survey of adults, 3 percent of the respondents said they were upper class, 42 percent said middle class, 47 percent said working class, and 9 percent said lower class (Davis & Smith, 2010). Both extremes apparently sound unpleasant to people, probably because of the stigma of being "lower class" and the embarrassment of admitting to being "upper class." By most reasonable criteria, however, the lower class is larger than 9 percent. As noted earlier, 15.1 percent of Americans had incomes below the official poverty level in 2010.

There is little consensus on the size of the upper class or on just how to define it. In general, **upper-class families** are those that have amassed wealth and privilege and that often have substantial prestige as well. They tend to own large, spacious homes, to possess expensive clothes and furnishings, to have substantial investment holdings, and to be recognized as part of the social and cultural elite of their communities. Upper-class husbands tend to be owners or senior managers of large corporations, banks, or law firms. Their wives are less likely to work for pay outside the home than women

upper-class families families that have amassed wealth and privilege and that often have substantial prestige as well

Middle-class families have a secure, comfortable income and can afford privileges such as a lakeshore vacation.

in other social classes, and they may be instrumental in maintaining ties to wealthy kin.

Middle-class families are those whose connection to the economy provides them with a secure, comfortable income and allows them to live well above a subsistence level. Middle-class families can usually afford privileges such as a nice house, a new car, a college education for the children, fashionable clothes, a vacation at the seashore, and so forth. The jobs that middle-class men and women hold usually require some college education and are performed mainly in offices and businesses. Middle-class men tend to hold higher-paying jobs such as a lawyer, pharmacist, engineer, sales representative, or midlevel manager at a corporation. Jobs such as these usually have some prestige and include fringe benefits such as health insurance, paid vacations, paid sick leave, and retirement pensions. Women in general are underrepresented in the higher-paying professional and managerial occupations, although their numbers are growing. Women professionals still tend to be found in occupations that require a college education, such as nursing and teaching, but that don't pay as much as male-dominated professions.

middle-class families families whose connection to the economy provides them with a secure, comfortable income and allows them to live well above a subsistence level

Working-class families are those whose incomes can provide reliably for the minimum needs of what people see as a decent life: a modest house or an apartment, one or two cars, enough money to enroll children at a state or community college, and so forth. Working-class men tend to hold manual jobs in factories, automobile repair shops, construction sites, and so forth, that involve little or no authority over others. Layoffs are more common in manual occupations than in the office and business jobs middle-class men tend to have, so working-class men are more vulnerable to periods of unemployment. Moreover, working-class men and women are less likely to work a full week and have fringe benefits. Clerical jobs, such as secretary, or service jobs, such as cafeteria cashier or hospital orderly, are common among working-class women; a minority work in factories.

working-class families families whose income can reliably provide only for the minimum needs of what other people see as a decent life

Families and Public Policy | Homelessness, by the Numbers

Homelessness is the kind of issue that tugs at people's heartstrings. Whether they believe that poverty is the fault of the individual (the poor don't work hard enough) or of society (too little opportunity, too much discrimination), most people think that everyone ought to have a place to sleep. They are troubled by homelessness and at once appalled and fascinated by reports of individuals and families who live in the streets or in shelters. But although the problem has been long on empathy, it has been short on numbers. Ever since the issue gained currency a few decades ago, good information on the homeless population has been scarce. It is, after all, difficult to count people who sleep in alleyways and move in and out of shelters.

Only in the past several years can we finally get good estimates of the homeless. That's because the Department of Housing and Urban Development has now set up a system of reports from community institutions across the country. On a single night in January 2010, the report says, there were 649,917 homeless people sleeping in shelters or on the streets (U.S. Department of Housing and Urban Development,

2011). Nearly two-thirds of them were individuals, and more than one-third were in families. Homelessness is an urban phenomenon. For instance, in 2007 8 out of 10 homeless people in the state of New York were in New York City. One of every five homeless people in the country lived in New York City, Los Angeles, and Detroit.

The 2010 study also reported that 1,593,150 individuals used shelters for the homeless or transitional housing at some point during 2010. Of this total, 567,334 adults and children arrived in families; the rest arrived alone. Shelter families overwhelmingly consist of single mothers and their children. Single parents are more vulnerable to homelessness because they do not have a second adult earner to help pay the rent. The homeless parents who use shelters and their children tend to be young; over half of the parents are between 18 and 30. Forty-two percent of the sheltered homeless family population is African American, and 22 percent is Hispanic.

Figure 4.3 shows where families in shelters were living the night before they first entered. Despite the image of a homeless family walking into a shelter after a night

sleeping on the street, few families—only 3 percent—came to shelters from places "not meant for human habitation." Parents try hard not to live on streets or in abandoned buildings or in their cars because, if they are discovered, the child welfare agencies will sometimes take their children and put them into foster care. An additional 19 percent of families came from another shelter or transitional housing. This total of 22 percent of families represents the only ones that were actually homeless before arriving at the shelter. Twenty-one percent had stayed at their own apartments or houses; presumably they had just been evicted or left because they were unable to pay the rent or the mortgage. When they lose their own housing, parents try to double up with friends or relatives. In fact, 41 percent of the families in shelters had stayed with relatives or friends the previous night. But their presence can strain the already-stretched resources of their hosts' households; and after they have worn out their welcome, if they have no other options, they will enter a shelter.

Surprisingly, the number of homeless people counted in the single-night estimates

lower-class families families whose connection to the economy is so tenuous that they cannot reliably provide for a decent life

Lower-class families are those whose connection to the economy is so tenuous that they cannot provide reliably for a decent life, either because they work steadily at low-paying jobs (the so-called working poor) or because they are frequently unemployed. They may live in deteriorated housing in neighborhoods with high crime rates. They may not be able to afford adequate clothing for winter, and they may need government-issued food stamps to purchase enough food. They are susceptible to homelessness (see *Families and Public Policy: Homelessness, by the Numbers*). Lower-class men, who have little education and few occupational skills, can find jobs that pay only at or slightly above the minimum wage and that have few, if any, fringe benefits and little security.

Three Status Groups   Although these four categories seem ingrained in both social scientific research and popular thought, the definitions are so broad that it is very difficult to draw a clear distinction between middle-class and working-class families or between working-class families and lower-class families.

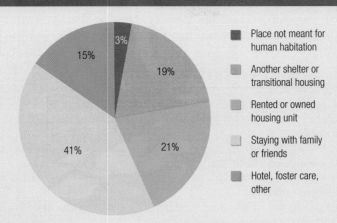

- Place not meant for human habitation
- Another shelter or transitional housing
- Rented or owned housing unit
- Staying with family or friends
- Hotel, foster care, other

FIGURE 4.3
Living arrangements of families the night before entering a homeless shelter, 2010. (*Source:* U.S. Department of Housing and Urban Development, 2011)

dropped between 2007 and 2010 despite the Great Recession, which might have been expected to increase homelessness. The lack of increase may reflect more effective government programs, which now emphasize putting individuals into supportive housing first and dealing with the personal or family problems after that (Lee, Tyler, and Wright, 2010). Or it could mean that the shelters were full to capacity and the counters missed some of the homeless who were on the street.

Either of the two estimates of the size of the homeless population, the number homeless on a night in January or the number who rely on a shelter during the course of the year, is a small percentage of the total population with incomes below the federal poverty line. This doesn't mean that homelessness isn't a serious problem or that we should ignore it. On the contrary, we should strengthen our efforts to combat it. But the numbers do suggest that for every poor homeless person there are many poor people who are precariously housed—behind on the rent or trying the patience of a friend whose living room couch they are sleeping on. Helping this larger number of people stay housed is an important part of the solution, for if the precariously housed lose their places to live, their numbers could overwhelm the already-stressed shelter system. The homeless problem and the larger poverty problem are not as separate as they may seem.

Ask Yourself

1. Has anyone in your family ever been forced to move into a friend's or relative's home, or perhaps into a homeless shelter? If so, what caused the crisis?

2. What can the government do to prevent families from becoming homeless? What can families themselves do?

www.mhhe.com/cherlin7e

Moreover, given the increasing importance of education, it may be more useful to group people by the amount of education they have. These groupings are more like Weber's status groups. The first group comprises people with a college degree. I will draw this boundary based on two arguments: First, the restructuring of the American economy has increased the life chances of those with college degrees to a much greater extent than those without college degrees; and second, the college educated form a status group, in the Weberian sense of sharing a common style of life, because their patterns of marriage, divorce, and childbearing appear to be diverging from the patterns of people without college degrees. About one-third of all adults between the ages of 25 and 54 have a four-year college degree. In addition, some individuals who have a two-year college degree are able to attain this style of life.

The second group comprises people who graduated from high school and most of those who have attended college but did not obtain a four-year degree; they are the most difficult to categorize in terms of social class because they sometimes share the characteristics of the groups above and below them. The third group comprises people who did not graduate from high school, whose family patterns in some respects are diverging from both groups above them. These three status groups are roughly equivalent to what people think of as the "middle class," "working class," and "lower class," respectively; but these labels are so imprecise that I will avoid them for the most part.

Quick Review

- Social scientists use the concept of social class to order all individuals in a society.
- Max Weber maintained that one needs to consider status groups as well as classes to understand how a society is stratified.
- Wives and husbands both consider each other's income, education, and occupation in identifying their social class, but wives do so more than husbands.
- Sociologists typically assume that four broad social classes exist: the upper class, middle class, working class, and lower class.
- Differences in life chances and styles of living suggest that three status groups defined by education may be as useful as the four broad social classes.

■ Social Class Differences in Family Life ■

Earlier in the chapter, Figure 4.1 showed that the median incomes of families with different levels of education have diverged since the 1970s: The incomes of families whose heads are college educated have risen compared to other families, and the incomes of families whose heads have not completed high school have fallen compared to other families. Subsequent sections showed that parallel patterns of marriage, divorce, and childbearing have diverged. There are other long-standing social class differences that are important but have not necessarily diverged. One is the kind of assistance family members received from relatives living in their household or elsewhere. A second is the way parents approach child rearing. They are not completely different, of course; similarities run across status groups that would be apparent to someone visiting from a non-Western culture where, for instance, parents are heavily involved in helping their children choose spouses, newly married couples move in with the husband's family, and adult children care for their aged parents in their homes.

ASSISTANCE FROM KIN

As differences in whether people have children before marrying show, there is variation around the norm of the two-parent-and-children conjugal family. Families differ not only in terms of marriage but also in terms of their ties to other kin, both the kin that a person is born to or acquires at marriage and the kin that some people construct from distant relatives, friends, partners, partners' families, and so forth. These kinship patterns differ by social class, although some of the class differences appear to be fading or overstated.

Kinship among the Poor and Near Poor   A large literature dating back to the Great Depression shows that a husband's place in the family is heavily dependent on whether he has a job. (See *Families and the Great Recession: Lessons from the Great Depression,* in Chapter 2.) In the cultures of all

Women-centered
kinship ties are an
important source of
strength among many
low-income families.

industrialized nations, men have been viewed as the main earners; providing a steady income has been seen as their responsibility. Rightly or wrongly, women's economic contribution has been viewed as secondary, although this perception may be changing as women increasingly work outside the home. When wives choose not to work for pay, or when they lose their jobs, they are not looked down upon. But when husbands lose their jobs, as happens frequently to husbands in poor and near-poor families, their authority in their homes decreases, their self-respect declines, and other family members treat them with less respect as well. Chapter 9 examines in more detail how a husband's unemployment affects a married couple and their children.

Chronic Poverty and Kin Networks   When a man's unemployment problems are chronic—when he is unable or unwilling to find steady employment over many years—he may be viewed, and may view himself, as having failed to fulfill a central role in his life. In a community with many chronically unemployed men, young mothers rely less on marriage and more on other kinship ties for support. Commonly, in poverty areas, young mothers, many of them unmarried, receive help from their own mothers in raising their children. They may also get money or assistance from sisters and brothers, friends, and, sometimes, the fathers of their children. The result is **women-centered kinship,** a kinship structure in which the strongest bonds of support and caregiving occur among a network of women, most of them relatives, who may live in more than one household. Mothers, grandmothers, sisters, and other female kin hold most of the authority over children and provide most of the supervision.

The extended kinship ties of the women-centered network help its members survive the hardships of poverty. If the members of a household have little to eat or are evicted from their homes, relatives and friends in their network will

women-centered kinship a kinship structure in which the strongest bonds of support and caregiving occur among a network of women, most of them relatives, who may live in more than one household

provide whatever assistance they can. Sisters or aunts who are themselves poor will nevertheless give food or money because they know that in the future they may need emergency help. In this way, the kinship networks of the poor spread the burdens of poverty, cushioning its impact on any one household and allowing its members to get by from day to day. In a widely cited study of The Flats, a low-income African American neighborhood in the Midwest, anthropologist Carol Stack found that individuals could draw upon a complex network of relatives and friends that extended over many households (Stack, 1974).

The Limits of Kin Networks   Yet membership in such a kinship network is not without cost. Because an individual's meager income must be shared with many others, it is difficult for her or him to rise out of poverty. Stack described what happened when an older couple unexpectedly inherited $1,500. At first, they wished to use the money for a down payment on a house. Then other members of their network, upon learning of the windfall, asked for help. Several relatives needed train fare to attend a funeral in another state; another needed $25 so her telephone wouldn't be turned off; a sister was about to be evicted because of overdue rent. Moreover, the public assistance office cut their children off welfare temporarily. Within six weeks, the inheritance was gone. The couple acquiesced to these requests because they knew they might need assistance in the future. Even someone who finds a good job may not withdraw from a network unless she is confident that the job will last a long time.

Moreover, it's not clear how widespread these networks are today. Studies show that very disadvantaged parents tend to receive less support from kin, either because the people in their networks have fewer resources to provide or because they are not in a network (Harknett & Hartnett, 2011). In general, low-income parents are more likely to receive practical support from their kin, such as child care assistance, than to receive financial support, whereas middle-class parents are more likely to receive financial support (Swartz, 2009). Assistance from kin takes different forms among the poor and nonpoor but seems to be important for both.

Kinship among the Nonpoor   The core of kinship among the nonpoor in the United States has been the conjugal family of wife, husband, and children, at least ideally (Schneider & Smith, 1973). The married couple is expected to spend their income on their children and themselves rather than to provide financial assistance to siblings or other relatives. Any assets or savings are passed from parents to children, rather than being spread throughout a kin network. Income sharing is not as necessary, to be sure, because the standards of living of kin tend to be higher than among the poor. Yet standards of living are higher in part *because* it is expected that the conjugal family will spend its savings on a down payment for a house rather than doling it out to relatives who need train fare to attend funerals or to pay bills and *because* it is expected that the family will move away from kin, if necessary, to pursue better job opportunities.

A clever survey of adults in the Boston area in 1984 and 1985 demonstrated people's beliefs about the restricted kinship obligations of the conjugal family (Rossi & Rossi, 1990). Alice and Peter Rossi presented 1,393 mostly white people whom they identified as "middle class" with a set of "vignettes": brief, hypothetical descriptions of relatives and friends who were experiencing

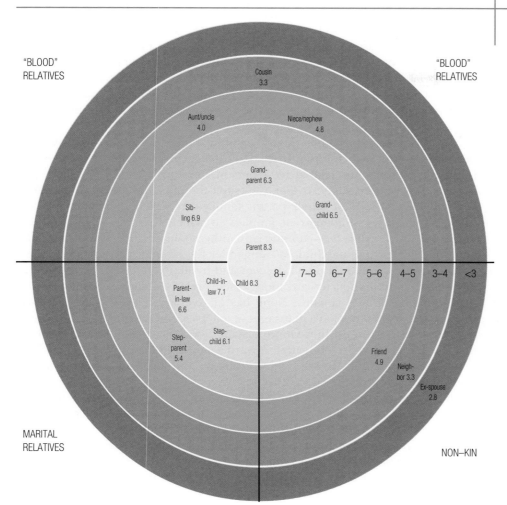

FIGURE 4.4
"Wheel of obligation": degree of obligation felt by survey respondents to various relatives and friends, for Boston-area adults, 1984–1985.
(*Source:* Rossi & Rossi, 1990)

crises that might require "some financial help" or "comfort and emotional support." For example: "Your unmarried sister has undergone major surgery and will be bedridden for a few weeks. This problem is straining her financial resources." From a list of relatives and friends (e.g., child, father-in-law, cousin, neighbor), eight crises (e.g., "run out of unemployment benefits and no job in sight"), and two obligations ("to offer some financial help," "to offer comfort and emotional support"), a computer program selected one relative or friend, one crisis, and one obligation at random and printed a vignette. The process was repeated until 26 crisis vignettes had been generated randomly to present to each of the survey respondents. We will focus on the vignettes for which the respondent was asked to rate "How much of an obligation would you feel to offer some financial help?" on a scale from 0 to 10, where 0 meant no obligation at all and 10 meant a very strong obligation.

The mean obligation scores for offering financial help, for 15 common relatives and friends, averaged across the various vignettes, was plotted by Rossi and Rossi on a "wheel of obligation," which is reproduced as Figure 4.4. The closer to the center of the wheel, the stronger the sense of obligation people felt:

A mean score of 10 would be plotted at the hub of the wheel, whereas a mean score lower than 3 would be plotted in the outer circle. Note first that most of the mean scores are close to the hub, indicating that people felt a moderate to high level of obligation to most kin. Only neighbors and ex-spouses had mean scores lower than four. (Of course, these are hypothetical obligations; we don't know whether people actually would provide financial assistance this freely.) Since it did not make sense to ask these kinds of questions about a person's current husband or wife, there is no score for spouses.

Note also that the highest levels of obligation were expressed toward a person's parents and children. Indeed, all the relatives in the two circles surrounding the hub are related to a person through a child, a parent, or a spouse. This pattern suggests that adults felt the most obligation to the members of the conjugal or single-parent families in which they grew up and to the conjugal or single-parent families in which they have had children. These vertical kinship ties—up and down the chain of generations from parents to children to grandchildren—engender the strongest feelings of obligation. They are created by direct descent and by marriage. Contrast the degree of obligation adults felt toward more distant relatives such as aunts, uncles, nieces, nephews, and cousins: None has an average score of five or above. Kinship ties from a person's marriage—even a second marriage—are stronger than kinship ties toward these more distant blood relatives. For instance, note that the adults felt more obligation toward a stepchild than toward a cousin or a nephew. Obligations to the conjugal family, and to one's parents, seem to take precedence over those to other relatives.

The image of middle-class kinship suggested by these findings is of a tall, solid tree trunk with skinny branches: The vertical axis is strong as one moves from parents to children to grandchildren, but the horizontal links are weaker as one moves from parents to uncles, or from children to nieces (Bengston, 2001). Resources are passed from a person's parents to his or her spouse and children, and then to the grandchildren. Assistance to elderly parents is likely to be much more substantial and more common than assistance to elderly aunts and uncles.

SOCIAL CLASS AND CHILD REARING

Families also differ by social class in how they raise their children. In general, college-educated parents often act in ways that encourage autonomy and independence, whereas less-educated parents more often encourage conformity and obedience to (and distrust of) authority. Not all parents fit this pattern, of course; there is substantial variation within social classes. Moreover, as the twentieth century progressed, parents in all social classes moved toward emphasizing independence (Alwin, 1988). On average, though, intriguing class differences remain.

Social Class and Parental Values   Beginning in the 1960s, Melvin Kohn pioneered a line of research showing the connections between the conditions a person experiences on the job and his or her child rearing values (Kohn, 1969). He noted that working-class employees (by which he meant blue-collar industrial workers), for the most part, are closely supervised, work with physical objects (as would carpenters), and perform simple tasks repetitively (as on an automobile assembly line). It is important for workers in these

In contrast to attitudes prevalent a half-century ago, wives (and their husbands) view working for pay outside the home as a necessary and proper activity.

jobs to obey their supervisors and to accept the discipline of doing repetitive tasks. In contrast, middle-class workers (by which he meant white-collar professional and technical workers), are less closely supervised, usually work with data (as would computer programmers) or people (as would personnel managers), and perform a variety of tasks (as would physicians). Middle-class jobs, Kohn argued, encourage more independence than working-class jobs and often reward creativity and individual initiative.

When working-class and middle-class parents are asked to select the most important characteristics that children should have, their preferences reflect their occupational positions. Working-class parents are more likely to select obedience to authority, conformity, and good manners, whereas middle-class parents are more likely to select independence, self-direction, curiosity, and responsibility (Alwin, 1990). Working-class parents emphasize the kinds of characteristics their children would need if they were to enter blue-collar jobs. To work on an assembly line for 40 years requires obedience and conformity; someone who is creative and independent might have a harder time tolerating the job. In contrast, to be a successful manager requires independence and initiative. Thus, each class socializes its children to fill the same positions their

Middle-class parents tend to actively enhance their children's skills.

parents have filled. Because of his or her conformist upbringing, a child from a working-class family may be less successful as a manager than a self-directed child from the middle class. In this way, socialization by parents both is influenced by and helps to perpetuate the social class divisions in the United States.

Concerted Cultivation versus Natural Growth   More recently, sociologist Annette Lareau intensively studied 12 families with third-graders and found class differences in the way parents view the task of raising children (Lareau, 2003, 2011). These differences, which are consistent with Kohn's research, applied to both African American and European American children in her sample; at least for these families, class, more than race, determined parents' approaches to child rearing. Lareau defined a group of families in which the parents had jobs requiring college or more advanced degrees as "middle class" and a group with jobs requiring less education as "working class" or "poor." Middle-class families tended to actively enhance children's talents, opinions, and skills, a cultural style she calls "concerted cultivation"—as if parents were cultivating a garden so its plants would grow as well as possible. Working-class (and poor) parents, on the other hand, did not focus on developing their children's special talents;

rather, they emphasized providing a safe environment and love and letting children grow on their own. Lareau calls this cultural pattern the "accomplishment of natural growth." In everyday life, these different styles affected children's time use, language use, and family ties. Middle-class parents filled their children's weeks with a whirlwind of formal activities such as lessons, sports, tutoring, and play dates, whereas working-class parents were often content to let their children hang out at home or in the neighborhood. Middle-class parents talked with their children more, reasoning with them rather than telling them what to do. Children from working-class and poor families had closer ties to uncles, aunts, and children than did middle-class children.

As a result, argues Lareau, middle-class children have advantages in school and, later, in the job market: They are more assertive with authority figures such as teachers and coaches, they are more verbal, and they have a more independent sense of self. Working-class and poor children (and their parents) are less likely to speak up for themselves and challenge authority; they are more deferential and less trusting of authority. Middle-class children gain a sense that they are entitled to a stimulating, rewarding daily life, whereas working-class and poor children get a sense that their opportunities are constrained. So as they grow up, middle-class children are in a better position to achieve a middle-class lifestyle themselves. The main point, for Lareau as for Kohn, is that the social class of the family you grow up in affects the way you think about school, authority figures, and work.

Quick Review

- Poor families often depend on women-centered kinship networks, in large part because men cannot consistently earn enough to support a family.
- Nonpoor families typically center on a wife, husband, and children who have obligations to their parents and their grandchildren but are otherwise independent of kin.
- Middle-class parents tend to emphasize independence and self-direction in raising children.
- Working-class parents tend to emphasize conformity and obedience to authority in raising children.

■ Social Class and the Family

A half-century ago, most families with children, rich or poor, had two parents and one earner. As recently as the early 1970s, half of all poor families consisted of married couples; by 2010 one-third were married-couple families (U.S. Bureau of the Census, 2011e). Meanwhile, a majority of well-off families have two parents and two earners. Thus, the association between the type of family you live in and your social class position is stronger today than in the past. This great sorting out of families by social class has occurred for both economic and cultural reasons. On the economic side, two developments stand out: the movement of married women into the workforce and the declining employment prospects of men without college educations. On the cultural side are the rise in expressive individualism and people's higher aspirations for material goods.

In the 1960s and 1970s, social commentators debated whether it was "necessary" for married women to work. After all, standards of living had been far lower in the first half of the twentieth century, and yet few married women had worked outside the home. However, the economic slide after 1973 more or less ended that debate. Among those without college educations, objections to married women working outside the home faded as decent-paying entry-level blue-collar jobs—the kind of jobs young husbands used to take—dwindled. Whereas in the 1970s wives' employment was seen by many as a sign of a husband's failure to provide adequately for his family, now it is seen as a necessary and acceptable contribution.

Among couples with college educations, the employment situation has been better; still, only two-earner couples have been beating inflation consistently. Moreover, the price of housing has risen far faster than wages, placing the American dream of homeownership out of reach of more and more single-earner couples. In the 1950s and 1960s, payments on a median-priced home required just 15 to 18 percent of the average 30-year-old man's income. That figure rose to 20 percent in 1973 and then doubled to 40 percent in 1987 (Levy & Michel, 1991). Housing affordability deteriorated further through the early 2000s (U.S. Bureau of the Census, 2009c). Consequently, for college-educated couples, too, wives' employment was seen as necessary and acceptable. (In the mid-2000s the availability of so-called subprime mortgage loans to families with modest incomes may have created the illusion that homes were more affordable, but many of the families that took out these loans defaulted on the payments, triggering the Great Recession of the late 2000s.)

Concurrently, adults in a more individualistic culture were freer to choose not to marry or to end marriages. Having children outside of marriage became more acceptable. People's expectations about what constitutes a good life also changed. Young middle-class couples could, in theory, aspire only to the standard of living of the late 1940s and early 1950s—which for many consisted of an apartment or a small, one-story home, one car, a clothesline in the backyard for drying the laundry, one telephone, no stereo system, few restaurant meals, no airplane travel, and, of course, no DVD players or computers—and still keep one parent home all day. This is not an appealing prospect in a country where people have gotten used to a higher standard of living that is promoted by advertising and reinforced by the media.

With regard to what women and men do in families, however, class differences may have lessened over the past few decades. To be sure, the women-centered kinship networks of low-income families remain distinctive. Yet not all low-income families have functioning networks, and the number of single-mother families has increased among the nonpoor as well. The distinctive working-class gender segregation and resistance to wives' employment, presented in several widely read mid-twentieth-century studies (Bott, 1957; Gans, 1962; Rubin, 1976), seems to have faded. Child-rearing patterns do still seem different, with college-educated parents instilling in their children a sense of independence and of entitlement to a rewarding life, while less-educated parents tend to stress obedience, safety, and natural growth. These class differences in child rearing could affect the quality of education that children obtain and the type of occupations they will eventually get.

Until the 1980s, families at all educational levels seemed to move in parallel as rates of marriage, divorce, and childbearing rose and fell in waves.

Extended families are more important to the working class than to the middle class.

Since then, however, we see evidence that families at the top and bottom of the social ordering are moving in different directions. The college educated appear to be consolidating their gains in the restructured economy: Young adults postpone marriage while obtaining advanced educations, then they marry spouses who also have college degrees, and only then do they have children. Their marriages have become more stable in recent years, quite possibly reflecting their improved economic position. In contrast, individuals without high school degrees seem increasingly marginalized. They are isolated in the marriage market, as if shunned by those with better economic prospects. They often have children years before marrying, if they marry at all. And their marriages still have a high risk of divorce. These are not encouraging trends in a nation that thinks of itself as a land of equal opportunity.

Social class is not the only way that American society classifies families. Racial and ethnic distinctions are also frequently made, and it is to these differences in family patterns that we now turn.

Looking Back

1. **How have changes in the American economy since the 1970s affected families?** The restructuring of the U.S. economy since the 1970s has caused a shortage of well-paid semiskilled and skilled jobs that do not require a college education—the kind of jobs less-educated young men used to rely on to support their wives and children—and has increased the importance of education. Since the 1970s, incomes have increased the most among families headed by college graduates and the least among families headed by persons who did not graduate from high school.

2. **How have the family lives of people at the top and bottom of the social order diverged recently?** People with college educations are more likely to marry than are people with less education, although they marry at later ages. Their marriages are less likely to end in divorce, and they are less likely to have a child outside of marriage. In general, people are more likely than in the past to marry someone with a similar level of education. The typical life course of people who obtain college degrees involves completing one's education, then marrying someone else

who is a college graduate, and then having children. For a person who does not graduate from high school, the life course may involve having children well before marrying, having a restricted choice of marriage partners, and having a high risk of divorce if one does marry at all.

3. **How has the globalization of production affected family life in developed and developing countries?** In developed countries such as the United States, the globalization of production has benefited the college-educated, who are adopting a neo-traditional style of family life, while disadvantaging the less educated, for whom marriage is becoming less central to family life. In developing countries, globalization has had positive effects such as increased income and negative effects such as childcare problems, as more women have begun working for pay.

4. **What factors determine the social class position of families?** Sociologists agree that income and wealth are important. In addition, they examine whether the worker belongs to a status group with shared levels of prestige, privilege, and lifestyle. Since many families have more than one earner, the social class position of families can be ambiguous. Therefore, the four social classes that are usually defined— upper, middle, working, and lower—should be considered as hypothetical models (ideal types). Recent trends suggest that

it may be useful to use people's educational levels to define a set of three status groups.

5. **Are there social class differences in kinship?** Poor and near-poor families are distinctive because many of them consist of single-parent units embedded in kin networks although these networks may be less prevalent than in the past. These networks share resources in order to ease the burdens of poverty. Nonpoor families consist mainly of two-parent households that are relatively independent of kin except for vertical ties to grandparents and grandchildren.

6. **Are there differences across classes in how parents raise children?** Poor and working-class parents tend to emphasize obedience and conformity in raising children, whereas middle-class parents are more likely to emphasize independence. As a result, sociologists suggest, poor and working-class children are not as assertive with authority figures such as teachers. They also show less self-direction and independent initiative. Middle-class children develop a sense that they are entitled to a rewarding life. These child-rearing differences tend to steer poor and working-class children toward blue-collar and service work and to steer middle-class children toward professional and managerial work.

Go to the Online Learning Center at www.mhhe.com/cherlin7e to test your knowledge of the chapter concepts and key terms.

Study Questions

1. Why has the globalization of production affected workers without college educations more than the college educated?
2. How has the growth of single-parent families affected the incomes of families with different levels of education?
3. What are the strengths and limitations of the four-class (upper, middle, working, lower) model of social status in the United States?
4. What is a "status group" and how does it relate to the concept of social class?

5. How has the role of education in the marriage market changed over the past several decades?
6. Why might a young woman with little education choose to have a child without marrying?
7. What are the costs and benefits of the sharing networks commonly used by low-income families?
8. What advantages accrue to children with college-educated parents who engaged in "concerted cultivation" of them?

Key Terms

assortative marriage   116
family inequality   111
formal sector   119
ideal type   122
informal sector   119
life chances   120

lower-class families   124
middle-class families   123
neo-traditional   118
polarization
  (of the labor market)   111
social class   120

status group   121
upper-class families   122
women-centered kinship   127
working-class families   123

Thinking about Families

The Public Family	The Private Family
What obligations do you think extended kin like grandparents, uncles, and aunts have to aid parents and children?	How are the relationships between men and women different from social class to social class?

Families on the Internet   www.mhhe.com/cherlin7e

Note: While all the URLs listed were current as of the printing of this book, these sites often change. Please check our Web site (www.mhhe.com/cherlin7e) for updates.

Ten years ago there was little good data on homelessness. Advocates virtually made up numbers that were repeated in the press and in popular debates. That has now changed. The main reason is the reporting system that the U.S. Department of Housing and Urban Development has set up. The Department publishes an annual report to Congress that is based on the information they obtain from this system. To obtain the most recent report, enter this phrase into a search engine: "Annual homelessness assessment report to Congress." You will see a list of the annual reports; choose the most recent one. In the report, you can find the number of people who were homeless on the single night during that year, usually in January, when all of the agencies search for the homeless and report the results to HUD. You can also learn the total number of people who spent at least one night in an emergency shelter during the year. The 2010 report shows a surprising decline, noted in this chapter, in chronic homelessness during the Great Recession. See Exhibit 2-4 in http://www.hudhre.info/documents/2010Hom elessAssessmentReport.pdf

Chapter Five

Race, Ethnicity, and Families

Looking Forward
Racial-Ethnic Groups
Constructing Racial-Ethnic Groups
"Whiteness" as Ethnicity
African American Families
Marriage and Childbearing
Marriage
Childbearing Outside of Marriage
Single-Parent Families
Explaining the Trends
Availability
Culture
Reconciling the Explanations
Gender and Black Families
The Rise of Middle-Class Families
Hispanic Families
Mexican Americans
Puerto Ricans

Cuban Americans
Asian American Families
Social Capital and Immigrant Families
American Indian Families
Racial and Ethnic Intermarriage
Variation in Intermarriage
Intersectionality and Intermarriage
Race, Ethnicity, and Kinship
Looking Back
Study Questions
Key Terms
Thinking about Families
Families on the Internet
Boxed Feature
FAMILIES AND PUBLIC POLICY: *How Should Multiracial Families Be Counted?*

Looking Forward

1. How are racial and ethnic groups constituted?

2. How has African American family life changed over the past several decades?

3. What are the family patterns of the major Hispanic ethnic groups?

4. What are the distinctive characteristics of the family patterns of Asian Americans?

5. How does the concept of "social capital" apply to immigrant families?

6. How is intermarriage affecting racial and ethnic groups?

On January 20, 2009, over a million people crowded the mall in Washington to witness the inauguration of Barack Obama as the 44th president of the United States. Many were African Americans, there to celebrate the election of the nation's first African American president. On that day it was hard to imagine that just two years earlier a debate had raged in the African American community about whether Obama was really an authentic African American. Everyone knew, of course, that President Obama had a white mother from Kansas and a black father from Kenya. Yet the basis of the charge that he was, in the phrase sometimes used, not black enough (Coates, 2007) was not that he had a white mother. Most African Americans have some white ancestry in their backgrounds, due to sexual relationships between slaves and their masters (think of the descendants of Thomas Jefferson's likely liaison with Sally Hemings) and to interracial relationships and sexual violence after emancipation. Moreover, an American with even a trace of African ancestry has traditionally been classified as black according to the so-called one-drop rule of American culture: People are said to be black if they have any "black blood" in their veins. No, Obama's mixed parentage wasn't the heart of the matter.

Rather, the main objection was that he was not descended from African slaves. Critic Stanley Crouch wrote in a column in the *New York Daily News,* "Obama did not—does not—share a heritage with the majority of black Americans, who are descendants of plantation slaves" (Crouch, 2006). In this reading, race depends not just on physical characteristics but also on historical experiences. Obama understood this position but argued subtly that he was an African American because he was treated by whites as if he were one. When asked at a Democratic Presidential Primary debate to respond to charges that he was not authentically black enough, he replied, "You know, when I'm catching a cab in Manhattan . . ."—an allusion to taxi drivers who will not stop to pick up a black man for fear that his destination will be a dangerous neighborhood (*The New York Times,* 2007). Cab drivers, Obama implied, never tell him he's not black enough.

In fact, what turned around black public opinion on the matter of Obama's race was how white America began to treat him and his family—especially when that treatment seemed disparaging. After Obama won the South Carolina primary, Bill Clinton dismissively compared the win to Jesse Jackson's ultimately fruitless victory in South Carolina 20 years earlier. To some ears, Clinton's comment suggested that Obama was just another inconsequential black aspirant whose candidacy would soon fade away. When Michelle Obama said that for the first time in her adult life she was proud of her country, she was accused of being unpatriotic because she had not been proud all along. When clips of the fiery sermons of the Obamas' black minister, Jeremiah Wright, were shown endlessly on television, the Obamas were forced to resign from their church. As these events cumulated, African Americans rallied around Obama and defined him as one of them. By the time of his inauguration, he was universally and triumphantly hailed as the first black president. And he had won 95 percent of the African American vote.

Racial-Ethnic Groups

Obama's swift transition from not being an authentic African American to being a symbol of African American pride suggests that the definition of what constitutes a "race" is fluid. We tend to think of races as if they are natural categories clearly defined by physical characteristics—skin color, hair texture—and unchanging over time. But if that were true, then Obama couldn't have been transformed from a racially ambiguous, mixed-parentage person to an unambiguous African American in two years. Rather, his transformation shows that the racial categories we use are socially constructed. That doesn't make them any less important, just more subject to change and redefinition than is commonly thought (as when Obama's identity changed in the minds of many blacks), more reflective of the beliefs of the dominant group (as when whites began to define Obama as black), and more dependent on a particular time and place. At other times, in other places, race can be defined quite differently than it is in the United States today. In New World countries such as Brazil, there is no sharp division between black and white but rather a continuum of skin color distinctions. As recently as 1910, the U.S. Census included a mixed black and white ancestry category labeled "mulatto." Yet during the twentieth century, the image of two distinct groups, black and white, became fixed in American culture, despite the mixed racial ancestry of many Americans, such as Barack Obama.

Other racial categories remain more flexible, in part because none carries the long history of slavery and racial discrimination faced by African Americans. Consider the individuals in the United States who are descended from the original, indigenous peoples of North America. These peoples include American Indians, the name still often used for Native Americans in the contiguous 48 states, and Alaska natives, such as the Eskimo and Aleut. The 2010 Census questionnaire presented "American Indian or Alaska native" as one of 15 "race"categories. Of the 5.2 million people who chose it, 44 percent chose a second category, most often "white" (U.S. Bureau of the Census, 2011i). Since the 1970 Census, the American Indian population has increased at a far higher rate than counts of births and deaths during the 1970s would suggest (Snipp, 2002). The increases in reporting were greater in California and the East than in traditional American Indian population centers. This pattern suggests that individuals residing in metropolitan areas far from tribal lands and having some Native American ancestry have become more likely to think of themselves as American Indians. Nagel (1995, 1996) wrote of an "ethnic renewal" in which people of mixed heritage have increasingly identified themselves as American Indians due to factors such as American ethnic policies and American Indian political activism.

CONSTRUCTING RACIAL-ETHNIC GROUPS

racial-ethnic group
people who share a common identity and whose members think of themselves as distinct from others by virtue of ancestry, culture, and sometimes physical characteristics

It is even more difficult to define an ethnic group than it is a racial group. Most generally, an ethnic group consists of people who think of themselves as distinct from others by virtue of common ancestry and shared culture—but not necessarily physical characteristics. For example, the skin color and physical features of Mexican Americans range from distinctly European to distinctly Native American, with most people displaying a mixture of the two. Given the ambiguities and overlap between race and ethnicity, let me combine them and define a **racial-ethnic group** as people who share a common identity and whose members think of themselves as distinct from others by virtue of ancestry, culture, and sometimes physical characteristics. Often racial-ethnic group members' shared identity is reinforced by the way they are treated by outsiders. For instance, racial prejudice and, until the 1960s, racially discriminatory legislation have contributed to the sharp distinction between African Americans and whites.

Thus, racial-ethnic groups are social creations, reflecting cultural norms, social inequality, and political power. Consequently, people can redefine these groups or create new ones as circumstances dictate. The clearest recent example of the redefinition of a racial-ethnic group in the United States is the rise of Hispanic ethnicity. In this chapter, the term **Hispanic** refers to persons in the United States who trace their ancestry to Latin America.[1] An alternative term, Latino, is sometimes used instead. A few decades ago, the terms Hispanic and Latino were hardly used; rather, one referred to specific groups such as Puerto Ricans, Mexican Americans, or Cuban Americans. There was no Hispanic category, for example, in the full 1970 Census. During the 1970s, however, political leaders of Latin American ancestry formed alliances based on their shared interest in improving the lives of their disadvantaged constituents. A Hispanic caucus was formed in Congress, the category "Hispanic" was added to the census, and Hispanics came to be seen as a coherent racial-ethnic group. In the 1980 Census, after the individual responding for the household checked boxes indicating which of the so-called races each person in the household belonged to, she or he was asked "Is this person of Spanish/Hispanic origin or descent?" The categories were: (1) No; (2) Yes, Mexican, Mexican American, or Chicano; (3) Yes, Puerto Rican; (4) Yes, Cuban; and (5) Yes, Other Spanish/Hispanic.

Hispanic a person living in the United States who traces his or her ancestry to Latin America

A similar scheme was used in the 2010 Census in which 16.3 percent of the U.S. population chose one of the Hispanic categories. This question was asked separately from the racial question because Hispanics can be of any race. In 2010, 37 percent of people who listed themselves and their household members as Hispanic checked none of the specific racial categories but rather the catch-all racial category "Some other race" (U.S. Bureau of the Census, 2011i). That 37 percent of Hispanics considered themselves to be neither white nor black may reflect both the Latin American tradition of intermediate racial categories and also the sentiment that Hispanics are a separate group from European whites and African blacks.

[1] Strictly speaking, "Hispanic" also includes people who trace their ancestry directly to Spain.

These immigrants, shown taking the oath of U.S. citizenship, are among the large number of Latin Americans and Asians who have immigrated in recent decades.

Similarly, the category **Asian American** has become an umbrella for an extremely diverse group of people who hail from nations as far apart as Japan and Pakistan—people who differ in language, religion, alphabet, and physical features. For instance, South Asians, such as Indians, Pakistanis, and Bengalis, are mostly Hindus or Muslims; and they speak languages belonging to the same Indo-European family from which English evolved. Unlike the category "Hispanic," there was no overall "Asian" category in the 2010 Census but rather a list of many Asian nationalities (e.g., "Chinese," "Asian Indian") in the "race" question. Census tabulations of Asian Americans sometimes include U.S. residents who are Pacific Islanders—people indigenous to Hawaii and to the Pacific islands that are territories of the United States. The number of people choosing one of the Asian categories increased by 43 percent between 2000 and 2010, making it the fastest growing racial-ethnic group (U.S. Bureau of the Census, 2011i).

Marriage patterns are one sign that the umbrella categories of "Asian" and "Hispanic" are beginning to take on a life of their own. In the marriage markets of many metropolitan areas in the United States, the number of marriages in which the bride and groom are both "Asian," meaning any Asian racial category at all, or are both "Hispanic," meaning any of the Hispanic groups, is substantially larger than we would expect by chance (Rosenfeld, 2001). In other words, it's not just that Japanese Americans are more likely to marry each other but also that Japanese Americans are more likely to marry anyone from the many groups that make up the Asian category—and the same holds for Mexican Americans and the Hispanic category. The author of the study suggests that we are seeing the emergence of "pannational" identities in which people identify as "Asian" or "Hispanic."

Nevertheless, for studying family life, the category "Hispanic" or "Latino" is not very useful, and "Asian American" is not much better. As will be

Asian American a person living in the United States who comes from or is descended from people who came from an Asian country

Families and Public Policy

How Should Multiracial Families Be Counted?

How can a child whose parents have different races have only one? Logically impossible, you might think; but until 1997, federal government statistical policy required that individuals check just one race for themselves or their children on official forms such as the Census of Population. People such as Barack Obama had to choose one race prior to 1997 even if they thought of themselves as belonging to more than one. And before 1997, the government recognized four races: (1) white, (2) black, (3) Asian and Pacific Islander, and (4) American Indian and Alaska Native. It also required its agencies, in a separate question, to ask about membership in one ethnic group: Spanish or Hispanic origin.

In 1993, Representative Thomas Sawyer of Ohio, chair of the subcommittee of the House of Representatives that oversees the census and statistical policy, listened to the testimony of Susan Graham, an advocate for multiracial children and a mother of two of them. She told Representative Sawyer:

When I received my 1990 census form, I realized there was no race category for my children. I called the Census Bureau. After checking with supervisors, the Bureau finally gave me their answer, the children should take the race of the mother. When I objected and asked why my children should be classified as their mother's race only, the Census Bureau representative said to me, in a very hushed voice, "Because in cases like these, we always know who the mother is and not the father." (U.S. House of Representatives, Committee on Post Office and Civil Service, Hearings, 1994)

Ms. Graham said her son had been classified as white by the census but black by the school he attended. Her solution: Add a new category, "Multiracial," to the official government list and to the 2000 Census. Yet this seemingly logical step was opposed by many of the political leaders of the minority groups that would be most affected. They opposed a multiracial category because the statistics that agencies collect are used not just to describe the population but also to determine whether federal laws have been carried out. Congress and the courts use the information on race and ethnicity from the census to determine whether congressional districts are providing fair representation to blacks and Hispanics. Agencies that oversee banks use the information to determine whether banks are willing to loan money to members of racial-ethnic groups. Other agencies use the information from employers to determine whether employers are discriminating on the basis of race or ethnicity. Consequently, the political leaders opposed a multiracial category because they feared it would lower the number of blacks, Hispanics, or Asians counted in the census and would therefore dilute the political power that comes with greater numbers (Wright, 1994).

Faced with this dilemma, the government considered what, if anything, to do about Susan Graham's children and the many others like them when it fielded the 2000 Census of Population. In 1997, a government statistical committee decided that the 2000 Census (and all other government surveys) would allow individuals to choose more than one race; but it rejected a separate "multiracial" category. It also decided to place the question about Hispanic ethnicity before the question on race (rather than after it, which was the old policy), a change that probably increased the number of people who said they were "Hispanic."

When Americans filled out the 2010 Census, they saw the ethnic and racial questions shown in the figure. First

discussed, there is nearly as much variation in family patterns among the various subgroups of the Hispanic population as there is between Hispanic families and non-Hispanic families. Indeed, there is substantial variation in family patterns within each of the major racial-ethnic groups. Still, the political discourse on racial-ethnic groups in the United States is increasingly structured around five racial-ethnic groups: African Americans, Hispanics, Asian and Pacific Islanders, Native Americans, and a category we can call **non-Hispanic whites**, meaning people who identify their race as white but do not think of themselves as Hispanic. These categories are still a subject of debate and controversy. (See *Families and Public Policy:* How Should Multiracial Families Be Counted?)

non-Hispanic white people who identify their race as white but do not think of themselves as Hispanic

→ **NOTE: Please answer BOTH Question 8 about Hispanic origin and Question 9 about race. For this census, Hispanic origins are not races.**

8. Is Person 1 Hispanic, Latino, or Spanish origin?

☐ **No**, not Hispanic, Latino, or Spanish origin

☐ Yes, Mexican, Mexican Am., Chicano

☐ Yes, Puerto Rican

☐ Yes, Cuban

☐ Yes, another Hispanic, Latino, Spanish origin — *Print origin, for example, Argentinean, Colombian, Dominican, Nicaraguan, Salvadoran, Spaniard, and so on.* ⤸

9. What is Persons 1's race? *Mark* ☒ *one or more boxes.*

☐ White

☐ Black, African Am., or Negro

☐ American Indian or Alaska Native — *Print name of enrolled or principal tribe.* ⤸

☐ Asian Indian ☐ Japanese ☐ Native Hawaiian
☐ Chinese ☐ Korean ☐ Guamanian or Chamorro
☐ Filipino ☐ Vietnamese ☐ Samoan
☐ Other Asian — *Print race, for example, Hmong, Laotian, Thai, Pakistani, Cambodian, and so on.* ⤸   ☐ Other Pacific Islander — *Print race, for example, Fijian, Tongan, and so on.* ⤸

☐ Some other race — *Print race.* ⤸

Reproduction of the Questions on Hispanic Origin and Race from the 2010 Census

they were asked whether they were "Hispanic, Latino, or Spanish origin," and then they were asked their race. There were 15 choices, and as in 2000, Americans were allowed to check all the categories that applied to them. Overall, only 2.9 percent of the population checked two or more race categories. But 7.4 percent of those who checked "Black, African American, or Negro" also checked another category, as did 15.3 percent of those who checked one of the Asian categories, 43.8 percent who checked "American Indian or Alaska Native," and 55.9 percent who checked "Native Hawaiian" or "Other Pacific Islander" (U.S. Bureau of the Census, 2011i). Clearly, many members of minority groups think of themselves as having more than one race.

Ask Yourself

1. Have you ever been frustrated by questionnaires that require you to select just one racial or ethnic group to describe yourself or a family member? If so, what do you think of the excerpt from the Census 2010 form shown here?

2. Relate the controversy over the wording of the census questions to the concepts of the public and the private family. What was the private family's interest in this matter? The public family's interest?

www.mhhe.com/cherlin7e

"WHITENESS" AS ETHNICITY

Do non-Hispanic whites—the majority group—have an ethnicity? In the past, most scholars wrote as if the concept of ethnicity applied only to minority groups. But of late, many academics have begun to study the social construction of "whiteness" as an ethnicity that ordinarily provides power and privilege (Rasmussen, Klinenberg, Nexica, & Wray, 2001; Twine & Gallagher, 2007). Whiteness is not an inherent characteristic of people; rather, those considered white can differ over time and from place to place (McDermott & Samson, 2005). For example, when European immigrants from Ireland and Italy

Multiracial families constitute a small but growing share of all families.

first began arriving in the United States in the 1800s, they weren't considered white. Only as they moved out of poverty and into the middle class did they acquire "whiteness" and the privileges that go with it.

Since nearly all whites are descended from European immigrants, their family and kinship patterns derive from the European historical experience. In fact, some scholars now prefer the label "European American" to "white," in order to emphasize the origins of white culture. As noted in Chapter 2, the conjugal family of husband, wife, and children dominated the European family. Moreover, European families did not appear to rely on kin for support as much as families in other regions of the world (Goode, 1963). This heritage can still be recognized today. Figure 5.1 shows the differences in children's living arrangements among five racial-ethnic groups. It comprises all children under 18 who were living in households at the time of the 2009 Survey of Income and Program Participation conducted by the Bureau of the Census (a small number were in juvenile institutions, group homes, or the military). As the purple columns show, 86 percent of Asian children and 77 percent of non-Hispanic white children were living with two parents. Hispanic, American Indian and Alaska Native, and African American children were less likely to be living with two parents. As the burnt orange columns show, Asian and

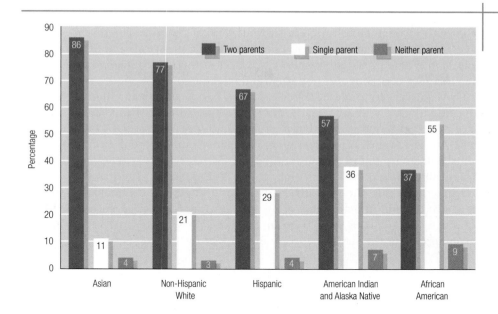

FIGURE 5.1
Percentage of children under 18 living with two parents, a single parent, or neither parent, for all children living in households in 2009, by race and ethnicity. Note: Percentages for American Indians and Alaska Natives are for 2001. (*Source:* U.S. Bureau of the Census, 2011n)

non-Hispanic white children were least likely to be living with neither parent—an arrangement that is much more common among American Indian and African American children. Many of these children were living with grandparents or other relatives. Figure 5.1 suggests, then, that the roles of marriage and of the extended family vary considerably across racial-ethnic groups—an insight we will pursue in the following sections.

Quick Review

- Racial-ethnic groups are socially created and vary from society to society and from time to time.
- Two broad racial-ethnic groups that have emerged recently are "Hispanics" (sometimes called "Latinos") and "Asians."
- Some scholars are now studying the social creation of "whiteness" as an ethnicity that provides power and privilege.
- The roles of marriage and the extended family vary considerably across racial-ethnic groups.

■ African American Families

The economic ups and downs of the second half of the twentieth century had a profound effect on African Americans. In the 1960s, as the economy boomed and the civil rights movement lowered barriers, African Americans made unprecedented gains in employment and income. But the post-1973 economic slowdown hit African Americans hard, especially the men (Levy, 1998), many of whom had moved into industrial jobs in the 1950s and 1960s. In the 1970s, as growth in manufacturing jobs slowed, African American men who did not have a college education watched their economic prospects plummet. African American women had established a position in the growing service sector, so the changing economy did not affect them as much.

These great economic changes, in turn, had a significant impact on less-educated blacks. Without a stable economic base, some African American men were reluctant to marry, for fear they could not provide for their families. And some African American women were reluctant to marry them. In fact, William Julius Wilson argued in two influential books that the drop in semiskilled and skilled blue-collar jobs—their flight to low-wage nations such as China, their disappearance into the circuit boards of computers—is the major reason for the sharp decline in marriage among African Americans (Wilson, 1987, 1996). Yet since the 1960s, a sizable group of more prosperous African Americans has emerged for the first time in American history.

MARRIAGE AND CHILDBEARING

African Americans have long had a greater percentage of single-parent families than have whites as a result of higher death rates among parents and more children born to unmarried mothers. But the differences widened during the twentieth century, peaking around 1970, by which time African American patterns of marriage and childbearing had changed substantially but white patterns had changed much less. Since then, in some ways, racial differences in family patterns have narrowed, as whites—particularly whites without college educations—have altered the ways they go about forming families (Furstenberg, 2009). Here are three measures of family life that provide a window on how African Americans and whites compare. The numbers are summarized in Table 5.1.

Marriage   In the 1950s, nearly nine in ten African Americans married at some point during their adult lives, usually in their late-teenage or early adult years. The 1950s were the high point of marriage for all groups; and 95 percent of whites married. But since then, the likelihood of ever marrying has dropped much more for African Americans than for whites. As Table 5.1 shows, only about two-thirds of African Americans will ever marry at current rates, far fewer than in the 1950s. This sharp decline in marriage did not occur among non-Hispanic whites, for whom the likelihood of marrying has declined a few percentage points but still remains about nine in ten. So over the past half-century, a substantial gap in the marriage rates of whites and blacks has appeared. Marriage may play a lesser role in black family life today than it does among whites.

Childbearing Outside of Marriage   Although African American women are postponing or forgoing marriage, they are not forgoing having children. Fewer and fewer of them are willing to wait until marriage to have their first child. A large majority of all African American children—72 percent, as Table 5.1 shows—are born to unmarried women. In other words, for every 100 African American women giving birth, 72 are unmarried at the time. Young

Table 5.1   Indicators of the Decline of Marriage among African Americans and Whites

INDICATORS OF THE DECLINE OF MARRIAGE	AFRICAN AMERICANS	WHITES
The percentage of young women who will ever marry has fallen more for African Americans than for whites[a]	88% in 1950s → 66% in 2000s	95% in 1950s → 92% in 2000s
The percentage of children born to unmarried mothers has risen for both African Americans and whites[b]	38% in 1970 → 72% in 2007	6% in 1970 → 28% in 2007
The percentage of family households headed by one parent has risen for both African Americans and whites[c]	36% in 1970 → 54% in 2010	10% in 1970 → 19% in 2010

[a]Rodgers & Thornton, 1985; Martin, 2004.
[b]U.S. National Center for Health Statistics, 1995, 2010.
[c]U.S. Bureau of the Census, 2008a, 2010b.

African American women, especially those who are not on track to attend college, look around and see few successful models of the wait-until-marriage style of childbearing. Moreover, they live in a time when the stigma of having a child outside of marriage has declined greatly from the levels of the mid-twentieth century. But in this regard they are similar to other non-college-educated women, all of whom, regardless of race, have become more likely to have a child without marrying. That includes non-college-educated whites, who are much more likely to give birth without marrying than was the case a few decades ago (Furstenberg, 2009). Consequently, the racial gap in nonmarital childbearing, unlike the marriage gap, has actually been narrowing. As Table 5.1 shows, the percentage of births to unmarried women has quadrupled among non-Hispanic whites since 1970 while doubling among blacks.

Single-Parent Families   The high rates of childbearing outside of marriage among African Americans, combined with high levels of divorce and separation (see Chapter 12), combine to create a high level of single-parent families. Currently, as Table 5.1 shows, slightly more than half of all African American family households are headed by a single parent. For non-Hispanic whites, the comparable figure is 19 percent. But note that the white figure has nearly doubled since 1970—a faster rate of change than among African Americans. Overall, the numbers in Table 5.1 suggest these conclusions: (1) African Americans have high levels of childbearing outside of marriage and single-parent families and low levels of marriage; (2) but non-college-educated whites are changing, too; (3) in particular, childbearing outside of marriage has grown at a faster rate among whites in recent decades, leading to a narrowing of this racial difference.

EXPLAINING THE TRENDS

How can we explain the decline in marriage among African Americans and the sharp increase in the proportion to children born to unmarried African American mothers? Studies suggest that both the availability of suitable partners— not incarcerated, steadily employed—and cultural differences play a role.

Availability   As noted earlier, changes in the labor market in the 1970s and 1980s affected all young men without college educations, and they hit African Americans particularly hard. Studies in the 1990s suggested that for every three black unmarried women in their twenties, there was roughly one unmarried black man with earnings above the poverty line (Lichter, McLaughlin, Kephart, & Landry, 1992). The situation is unlikely to be any better today.

In addition to job losses—or perhaps as a result of them—there are other reasons why young black women may face a difficult time finding a suitable spouse. Consider the terrible toll that violence and drugs are taking on young black men. Homicide rates for young African Americans have risen to appalling levels over the past two decades. If the rates in 2007 were to continue, about 1 of every 50 black 15-year-old boys would die violently before reaching age 45.[2] The rates of imprisonment and institutionalization of young black males are also strikingly high. The number of Americans incarcerated—in prison or jail—has soared since the 1980s to levels far above any other country, and black men are eight times more likely to be incarcerated than are white men. Imprisonment is concentrated among the least educated: At current rates, 69 percent of black men without high school degrees are likely to be incarcerated by the time they are in their early thirties. This "mass incarceration" of black males, as some are calling it, removes men from the pool of eligibles while they are in prison and makes it difficult for them to find jobs after they are released (Western & Wildeman, 2009).

What if we could place African Americans in an environment where there is less unemployment and discrimination—would their marriage rates go up? To answer that question, researchers examined the marriage histories of young African Americans in the military, arguing that military life provides a natural experiment of sorts: There is no unemployment, little racial segregation, and less racial discrimination. They found no difference between the marriage rates of black and white soldiers, which suggests that greater unemployment and discrimination in the civilian world may be depressing black marriage rates (Lundquist, 2004; Lundquist & Smith, 2005). Another study found that black men who had served on active duty had higher rates of marriage than black reservists or non-veterans (Teachman, 2007). These findings are an intriguing suggestion that economic conditions and racial discrimination do make a difference in African Americans' propensity to marry.

Is the decline in marriage, then, due to the shortage of men who are available and "marriageable," as Wilson calls them? Overall, the research suggests two conclusions: (1) The employment problems of black men and the high rates of incarceration and homicide are indeed important factors in the decline in marriage, but (2) the racial difference remains substantial even after these problems are taken into account. Several demographic studies have measured the relative numbers of employed black men in the local areas or states where black women live. The authors find that black women are more likely to marry if they live in areas with greater relative numbers of employed black men—thus supporting Wilson's hypothesis. Yet they also find that the drop in the availability of employed men cannot account for all—or even most—of the gap in marriage

---

[2] Author's calculation from homicide rates for black males 15–44 in U.S. National Center for Health Statistics (2011b).

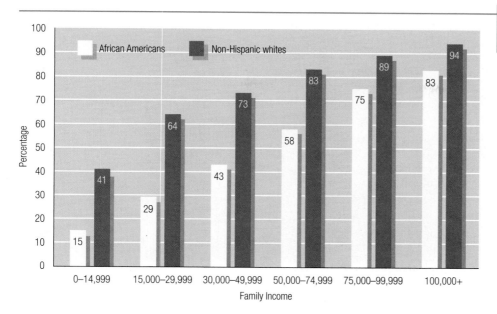

FIGURE 5.2
Percentage of families that were headed by a married couple, by family income, for African Americans and Non-Hispanic whites, 2009. (*Source:* U.S. Bureau of the Census, 2010a)

rates (Mare & Winship, 1991). For instance, a study of Census Bureau data from the 1980s and 1990s reported that African American women were less likely to marry if they lived in states with lower wages and less job growth in the manufacturing sector—a finding that is consistent with the importance of economic restructuring (Lichter, McLaughlin, & Ribar, 2002). However, the study also reported that African American women had substantially lower marriage probabilities than white women even after economic conditions were taken into account. Reviewing the evidence in his more recent book, Wilson (1996, p. 97) acknowledges that "even though the joblessness among black men is a significant factor in their delayed entry into marriage . . . it can account for only a proportion of the decline in marriages in the inner city, including postpartum marriages."

A similar pattern can be seen in a comparison of census data on the percentage of black and white families that are headed by a married couple (as opposed to an unmarried woman or man). Figure 5.2 shows this comparison for families at different income levels. As the reader can see, for both African Americans and non-Hispanic whites, the higher the family's income, the greater is the percentage that are headed by a married couple. Clearly, among both African Americans and non-Hispanic whites, married couples are less commonly found in low-income households. Note also, however, that at each income level, non-Hispanic white families are more likely to be headed by a married couple than black families. Even when there are no income differences between the families being compared, a racial gap still exists, and the gap is particularly pronounced among the poor and near poor. Economics, it seems, is part of the story of racial differences in family structure; but it is not the whole story.

Culture To more fully understand the differences in the family patterns of African Americans and whites, we must turn from economics to culture. There has been a resistance among liberal social scientists and activists to

FIGURE 5.3

Percentages of family households that are extended (contain relatives other than parents and their children), by family income, for African Americans and whites, 2004. (*Source:* Tabulations by Reynolds Farley from 2004 U.S. Bureau of the Census American Community Survey data)

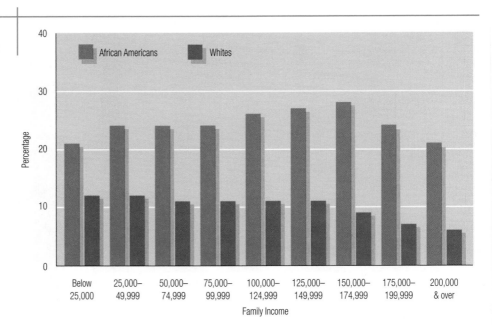

acknowledge the role of culture in shaping African American family patterns. In part, this concern arises from the entirely negative way in which black families are often portrayed: problem-ridden, weak, overwhelmed. The strengths of black families are often overlooked. Figure 5.3 helps to show where these strengths may lie. Graphed across income levels from low to high are the percentage of family households that are "extended"—that is, the percentage that contain relatives other than parents (or stepparents) and their children. Often the additional relatives are grandparents. Note that at all income levels—even among those earning more than $200,000—black family households are much more likely than white households to include a grandparent or other relative. In fact, since about 1970, African Americans have become increasingly more likely to live in an extended family household than whites (Goldscheider & Bures, 2003).

Indeed, grandparents play a stronger role in African American families, on average, than they do among white families. In 1982, just before Frank Furstenberg and I carried out a national survey of grandparents, we visited a group of black grandmothers at a senior citizens' center in Baltimore. The grandmothers told us how involved they were with their grandchildren's upbringing. Most of them had lived at least temporarily with their grandchildren. One woman, for example, said about her grandchildren:

> *I was always named "sergeant"—"Here comes the sergeant." I loved them. I did for them, and gave to them, so that they had an education, so that they had a trade. I went to school regularly to check on them; they didn't know I was coming. (Cherlin & Furstenberg, 1992)*

Very few white grandparents had this kind of hands-on involvement and authority. Our national survey confirmed that black grandparents, on average, were more involved in parentlike activities with their grandchildren than were white grandparents. Moreover, this racial difference still remained when we compared black and white grandparents of similar incomes. Even among more prosperous families, black grandparents seem to play a stronger role than white grandparents.

More generally, in African American families, ties to a network of kin are more important, compared with marital ties, than is the case in white families. When Alice and Peter Rossi measured the strength of people's feelings of obligations toward kin, they found that African Americans felt much stronger obligations to aunts, uncles, nieces, nephews, and cousins than did whites (Rossi & Rossi, 1990). It follows, then, that when African Americans face adversity, they are probably more likely to seek help from kin than are whites. Moreover, African cultural patterns may still be influential: In West Africa marriage is more of a process than an event, with childbearing sometimes occurring before the process is completed.

The chapter on class also discussed the strengths and weaknesses of relying on kin for support. Briefly, membership in a network of kin helps people subsist because it allows them to spread the burdens of poverty by borrowing when they are in need and lending when they are able. It also, however, makes escaping from poverty more difficult because it is difficult and risky for poor people to withdraw from the network. Ever since Stack's (1974) influential account of African American kinship networks in "the Flats," many writers have assumed that black families receive more assistance from their networks than do white families. Several statistical studies, however, have cast doubt on that conclusion (Hofferth, 1984; Roschelle, 1997). It may be that the poor have fewer resources to share now than in the 1970s. We know that the share of income going to families whose heads did not graduate from high school has been declining. Some kin networks, therefore, may be overwhelmed by their members' needs. Or it may be that blacks and whites differ in the kind of support they provide rather than in the quantity of support. According to one study, white women were more likely to give financial support to kin and to receive it (in large part because they had more money to give) than were black women; but black women were more likely to give and receive help with child care, transportation, and housework (Sarkisian & Gerstel, 2004).

Reconciling the Explanations Some observers think the changes in families are entirely due to changes in the economy; others believe that culture may have played a role. I think that both were likely involved. As one sociologist has argued, culture is a sort of "tool kit" (Swidler, 2001). It provides people with a particular set of tools they know how to operate. When faced with difficulties, people tend to reach into their tool kits to fix the problem. For African Americans over the past several decades, the problem has been a very unfavorable economic environment. Not only did they battle discrimination, but as globalization and automation proceeded, they also faced a growing shortage of the kinds of jobs that can sustain families in which the parents do not have college educations. The job situation was worse for black men than for black women because the latter group had attained a foothold in the kinds of service-sector jobs (secretaries, waitresses, health care workers) that grew while blue-collar factory jobs disappeared.

Faced with this problem, African Americans increasingly reached into their tool kits and seized the kind of family support system that their history and culture provided: extended kinship networks rather than married-couple families.

These networks usually relied on women—mothers, sisters, grandmothers—who were able to find jobs or were able to qualify for government assistance to single-parent families. Women-centered kinship was part of the cultural repertoire of African American families. Had it not been, African Americans might not have retreated as much from the marriage-centered kinship patterns of European Americans. Relying on extended kin has risks, but it can allow low-income families to obtain the support they need to make it from day to day.

GENDER AND BLACK FAMILIES

Both black men and black women face discrimination and economic disadvantages. But black feminist writers argue that black women face an additional source of disadvantage because of their gender. For example, unlike black men they may face the earnings gap between jobs primarily held by men and jobs primarily held by women. As women, they are more likely to be victims of domestic violence (see Chapter 11). But their situation also is unlike that of white women; they have always had to work outside the home, so the role of homemaker was rarely available to them. Social scientists with this perspective stress the **intersectionality** of black women's situation: the extent to which their lives are affected by overlapping systems of class, racial, and gender-based disadvantage (Hill, 2005). It is as if black women stand at the intersection of overlapping circles of race, class, and gender. This perspective challenges the idea that there is a universal black experience shared by all African Americans. Instead, it emphasizes the diversity of the black experience, the extent to which it differs for women and men and also for middle-class families and low-income families.

intersectionality (of black women's experience)
the extent to which black women's lives are affected by overlapping systems of class, racial, and gender-based disadvantage

THE RISE OF MIDDLE-CLASS FAMILIES

In fact, a small group of prosperous African Americans has long existed, often through the efforts of two-earner married couples. Landry (2000) presents evidence that in the late nineteenth and early twentieth centuries, more prosperous black women pioneered the ideology that women should combine marriage, careers, and community service. Because black women had been excluded from the "cult of True Womanhood" that enveloped white women in the late 1800s, they were freer to pursue careers. At all times during the twentieth century, the percentage of black women who worked for pay was higher than that of white women. Moreover, the wealthiest black women had the highest rates of paid work, suggesting that better-off black women were working for satisfaction as well as income.

Since the 1960s, the number of relatively prosperous blacks, whom observers tend to call the "black middle class," has expanded substantially. It has been growing long enough that a second generation is moving into higher education. Among black freshmen entering 28 selective colleges in 1999, 60 percent had a father who graduated from college, 25 percent came from families earning over $100,000 per year, and 72 percent said that their parents owned their home (Massey, Charles, Lundy, & Fischer, 2003). Still, middle-class black families tend to have less money in assets (savings, investments, homes, cars) than comparable white middle-class people. In a study of the assets of respondents to the Census Bureau's Survey of Income and Program

Since the 1960s, a sizable middle class has emerged among African Americans. They are often ignored in the public focus on African American poverty.

Participation in 1987 through 1989, Oliver and Shapiro (1995) found much larger differences, on average, in wealth (assets) between blacks and whites than in income. Comparing college-educated blacks with college-educated whites, for instance, they found that whereas the blacks earned 76 cents for each dollar earned by the whites, blacks had assets of just 23 cents for every dollar of white assets. And if homes and cars were excluded from assets (leaving savings accounts, stocks, small businesses), black college graduates had *one cent* of assets for every dollar of white assets. Oliver and Shapiro ascribe the difference to three factors: (1) whites are more likely to inherit some wealth or borrow money for a down payment on a home or car from their parents; (2) whites can more easily obtain home mortgage loans from banks; and (3) homes in predominantly black neighborhoods don't appreciate in value as much as homes in white neighborhoods.

The lower amount of wealth among blacks also affects whether they marry. Wealth ownership is a marker of income security that young adults use to judge whether they and their partners can make a successful marriage. Young men and, to a lesser extent, young women who own a car or have a bank account are more likely to marry, independently of how much money they earn. Since blacks tend to have fewer assets, the wealth differences between whites and blacks account for a portion of the black-white differences in the likelihood of marrying (Schneider, 2011).

Because of residential segregation, middle-class black neighborhoods tend to be closer to poor black neighborhoods, and their neighborhoods usually contain some poor families. Pattillo (2005) writes of the "inbetweenness" of the black middle-class experience. Middle-class blacks tend to live in neighborhoods that have less crime and poverty than the neighborhoods of low-income blacks, but much more crime and poverty than the neighborhoods of middle-class whites. As a result, middle-class African American parents may struggle to shield their children from the lure of street life, with its criminal behavior and drug usage. And middle-class African Americans must coexist with neighbors and relatives in the underground economy in ways most whites need not (Pattillo-McCoy, 1999). Still, the growth of the African American middle class is a success story that is too often lost in the understandable focus on the African American poor.

Black churches have been a great source of social support to African Americans who have newly gained middle-class status. Throughout African American history the church and the family have been the enduring institutions through which black families could gain the strength to resist the oppression of slavery, reconstruction, segregation, and discrimination (Berry & Blassingame, 1982). The church has served as a **mediating structure,** a midlevel social institution (other examples are civic groups, neighborhoods, and families themselves) through which individuals can negotiate with government and resist governmental abuses of power (Berger & Berger, 1983). It has been the greatest source of continuity, outside of the family, in the African American experience. Today the church also serves as a link between the black middle class, many of whom have moved out of inner-city neighborhoods, and the black poor. Often by virtue of sanctuaries that are still in poor neighborhoods, churches provide a direct way for middle-class congregants to provide assistance to the poor (Gilkes, 1995). In some of the poorest black neighborhoods, which have lost both population and organizations over the past few decades (Wilson, 1996), churches are among the few nongovernmental institutions left (McRoberts, 2003).

mediating structures
midlevel social institutions and groupings, such as the church, the neighborhood, the civil organization, and the family

Quick Review

- Marriage has declined among African Americans even more than among whites; childbearing outside of marriage has increased for both groups.
- The impact of economic restructuring—and the employment problems it has caused for African American men—is an important factor in the decline of marriage.
- But cultural differences between African Americans and whites are probably important too.
- In general, African American families rely on ties to extended kin more than white families do.
- African American women's family lives are affected not only by their race and class but also by their gender.
- Over the past several decades, a substantial African American middle class has emerged for the first time.

Hispanic Families

The label "Hispanic" covers groups that are so diverse with respect to family patterns that it makes little sense to combine them, yet that is the direction public discussions have taken. It lumps together recent immigrants with citizens whose families have been in the United States for generations, and lighter-skinned, well-educated political émigrés with darker-skinned, poorly educated laborers looking for work. Americans of Mexican origin are by far the largest group, constituting 63 percent of all Hispanics; Puerto Ricans, all of whom are American citizens, are the second largest group, at 9 percent;

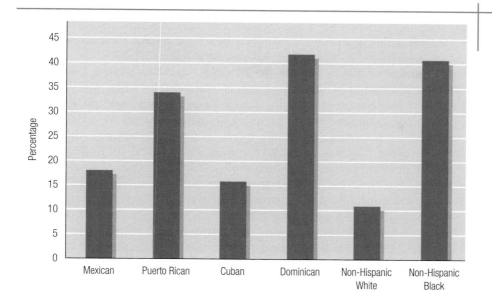

FIGURE 5.4
Percentage of households headed by a woman without a husband or partner present, for Hispanic groups, non-Hispanic whites, and non-Hispanic blacks, 1998–2002. (*Source:* Landale, Oropesa, & Bradatan, 2006)

and Americans of Cuban descent make up 4 percent. Hispanics from El Salvador are the fourth-largest group and those from the Dominican Republic are the fifth largest (U.S. Bureau of the Census, 2011i). Figure 5.4 shows an example of the diversity in Hispanic family patterns. It presents the percentage of households headed by a woman with no husband or cohabiting partner present for four Hispanic groups and, for comparison, non-Hispanic whites and non-Hispanic blacks. At one extreme, Dominicans have levels of households headed by women that are nearly identical to the high levels among non-Hispanic blacks. At the other extreme, Cubans have levels that are not much higher than the low levels among non-Hispanic whites. Consequently, any statement about overall Hispanic levels of households headed by women would mask this great diversity. Any statistic you read about Hispanics as a whole tends to reflect the experience of Mexicans, since they are by far the largest group; but such statistics lump together groups that sharply differ from one another.

MEXICAN AMERICANS

The United States and Mexico share a long history and a long border—the longest border between a developed and a developing country in the world. Some of the estimated 32 million people of Mexican origin in the United States (U.S. Bureau of the Census, 2011i) are the descendants of the early settlers of the Southwest. Others are second- or third-generation Americans, while still others are recent immigrants. In fact, far more immigrants arrive from Mexico than from any other country. In 2009 there were 3.7 million people living in the United States who had arrived since 2000 (Pew Hispanic Center, 2011a). An unknown number migrated illegally; about 6.5 million immigrants from Mexico did not have proper legal documents in 2010 (Pew Hispanic Center, 2011b). In order to understand Mexican American families, one must keep the scale of this immigration in mind.

Americans of Mexican origin have some distinctive family patterns:

- *Marriage.* Mexican Americans marry at a younger age than other Hispanics, non-Hispanic whites, or African Americans. In 2000, for instance, 48 percent of 20- to 24-year-old Mexican American women had already married, compared to 29 percent of comparable white non-Hispanics (Raley, Durden, & Wildsmith, 2004). Even though Mexican Americans are more economically disadvantaged, which should lower their likelihood of marrying, they still marry younger. Moreover, two-parent, single-earner families are more common among Mexican American families than among other Hispanic families (Lichter & Qian, 2004).
- *Number of children.* The Mexican-origin population has a high birthrate by American standards. The **total fertility rate** (TFR) is the average number of births that a woman would have over her lifetime if current birthrates were to remain the same. Mexican American women had a TFR of 3.1 in 2007, by far the highest of any major racial-ethnic group. Other Hispanics have fewer children. Puerto Ricans had a TFR of 2.2, which was nearly the same as the TFR of non-Hispanic blacks, while Cubans had a TFR of 1.6, which was even lower than the TFR for non-Hispanic whites (1.9) (U.S. National Center for Health Statistics, 2010). Births show, once again, the diversity of the Hispanic population.

total fertility rate (TFR)
the average number of children a woman will bear over her lifetime if current birthrates remain the same

What makes the ages at marriage low, and the birthrates so high, among the Mexican-origin population, it turns out, are the family patterns of recent immigrants, rather than of Mexican Americans who were born in the United States. In Mexico the average age at marriage is younger than in the United States (Raley et al., 2004), so immigrants come from a culture where early marriage is more common. Moreover, many Mexican immigrants are already married when they get here. Because most legal immigrants receive visas under a program to reunite them with relatives already living in the United States, many spouses immigrate; in fact, a majority of Mexican women who migrated after age 15 did so after marrying. Moreover, immigrants who arrive in the United States before marrying have an incentive to marry because it will usually allow them to apply for permanent residence. In contrast, Mexican-origin individuals who were born in the United States—who are more distant from Mexican culture and who may have less incentive to marry—marry at similar ages to non-Hispanic whites (Raley et al., 2004). In addition, Mexico had a higher birthrate than the United States until recently. Mexicans who immigrate have grown up in a society that values higher fertility, and they have more children than do non-Hispanic whites. But their children—the second generation—are more influenced by American values and their level of childbearing is not much different from that of non-Hispanic whites.

Yet even with the lower birthrates among those born in America, the massive scale of Mexican immigration is greatly affecting the size of the American population. Between 2000 and 2004, for instance, births to new Hispanic immigrants (a large share of them from Mexico) and births to Hispanics already in the United States accounted for half of the nation's population growth (Haub, 2006). One demographic study predicts that by 2040, Mexican immigrants since the 1980s and their descendants will have produced 36 million additional births (Johnson & Rendall, 2004). Hispanic fertility, with the Mexican-origin Americans in the lead, is an important reason why

Mexican Americans constitute about two-thirds of all Hispanics in the United States.

Americans are much less concerned about population decline than are European nations with less immigration and lower birthrates.

Hispanic households, including Mexican-origin households, also are more likely than non-Hispanic white households to live in extended families rather than conjugal families (Landale, Oropesa, & Bradatan, 2006). A family's household is said to be extended horizontally when a relative in the same generation as the household head—a brother, sister, or cousin—lives there. It is said to be extended vertically when a relative in the generation above the household head—a parent, an uncle, or an aunt—lives there. Mexican-origin households are more likely to be both horizontally and vertically extended than are non-Hispanic white households, in large part due to the migration of relatives (Glick, Bean, & Van Hook, 1997). An extended family can assist newly arrived kin, or older parents can provide child care assistance to their children and grandchildren. Other immigrant groups, particularly Asians, are also more likely to live in extended family households.

PUERTO RICANS

All Puerto Ricans are U.S. citizens because the island of Puerto Rico is a U.S. territory. Consequently, Puerto Ricans, unlike all other major Hispanic groups, are free to move to the mainland if they wish, and many have done so. In 2009, half of all people who identified themselves as Puerto Ricans were residing on the mainland (U.S. Bureau of the Census, 2011b). It is more difficult for individuals from other Hispanic groups to immigrate to the United States; they must either obtain visas, for which there may be a long wait, or find a way to enter and remain illegally. Demographers have long known that when the barriers to immigration are substantial, the people who manage to immigrate tend to have more education and skills than the average person in their home country. Immigration, in other words, is more selective when the barriers are high. People with greater skills are more confident that they can find decent-paying work in the United States, so they are more likely to take the trouble to immigrate. When the barriers are lower, on the other hand, immigration is less selective. We might expect, then, that Puerto Rican immigrants would tend to have less economic success, on average, than other Hispanic immigrants because Puerto Rican migration has been less selective. And that is what the data show: Puerto Ricans have higher unemployment and poverty rates than any other major Hispanic groups (U.S. Bureau of the Census, 2011b).

Consistent with their lower economic standing, Puerto Ricans have a high percentage of children born to unmarried mothers. Yet some of the formally unmarried Puerto Rican mothers are living in a partnership that they consider to be a marriage. In Puerto Rico and other Caribbean islands, a long tradition of **consensual unions** exists. These are cohabiting relationships in which couples consider themselves to be married but have never had religious or civil marriage ceremonies. From the viewpoint of the state and the Church, people in consensual unions are unmarried; but from the viewpoint of the couples and their peers, they are in a marriagelike relationship. Still, Puerto Rican couples who are formally married do exhibit some differences; for instance, married men are more likely to pool their incomes with their partners' incomes (rather than, say, to give their partners an allowance) than are men who are not formally married (Oropesa, Landale, & Kenkre, 2003).

Among Puerto Ricans, then, there are three kinds of socially recognized unions: cohabiting unions, in which the partners do not consider themselves married; consensual unions, in which they have not undergone a marriage ceremony but still consider themselves to be informally married; and formal marriage, in which they have had a marriage ceremony and registered with the state. In a 1985 survey of Puerto Rican women aged 15 to 49 in the New York City area, the participants were asked:

> *As you know, there are various ways in which a man and a woman live in a union. Some couples legally marry, that is, they obtain a license; some couples consider themselves married but without a license; and some couples just live together and do not consider themselves married, legally or informally. I would now like to ask you some questions about your marital history. (Landale & Fennelly, 1992)*

Among all women who had borne a child, 32 percent said they had ever lived in an informal marriage without a license, whereas just 13 percent said they had ever cohabited. The authors of the study report that whether or not a woman has borne a child in a union is a key factor in whether she defines it as an informal marriage or as a cohabitation. The birth of a child seems to change the social meaning of a union, making it more like a marriage (Landale & Fennelly, 1992). Whether consensual unions are still as common as they were in the early 1990s is unknown; little research has been conducted recently.

CUBAN AMERICANS

Most major immigrant groups today in the United States arrived in labor migrations: They came looking for higher-paying jobs. In contrast, the first waves of Cuban Americans came here in a political migration, fleeing the

consensual union a cohabiting relationship in which a couple consider themselves to be married but have never had a religious or civil marriage ceremony

Communist government of Fidel Castro, who had led a successful revolution in 1959. The U.S. government allowed Cuban citizens to enter the country as political refugees. Indeed, the early migrants were drawn from the Cuban upper and middle classes, the elite that Castro's Communist party overthrew. These immigrants arrived with substantial amounts of education, skills, and capital. In addition, they were largely white in racial appearance. The U.S. government, sympathetic to their plight and wishing to isolate and embarrass Castro, welcomed them enthusiastically and provided assistance in retraining (Suarez, 1993).

Despite government efforts at resettlement, most Cuban immigrants chose to settle in the Miami metropolitan area, where 29 percent of Miami-Dade County was of Cuban origin according to the 2000 census (U.S. Bureau of the Census, 2009a). Classic sociological theories of immigration held that immigrants would adjust better and prosper more if they assimilated into the mainstream. (**Assimilation** means the process by which immigrant groups merge their culture and behavior with that of the dominant group in the host country.) In the U.S. context, assimilation implies learning English, sending children to public schools, and dispersing geographically. Many Cuban immigrants chose, instead, to remain clustered in the Cuban neighborhoods of one metropolitan area, to listen to Spanish-language radio stations, to buy their food at markets owned by Cuban Americans, to eat at Cuban restaurants, and to send their children to private Cuban schools. They limited much of their lives to a large, dense, single-ethnic-group, almost self-sufficient community of the type that Kenneth Wilson and Alejandro Portes have called an **immigrant enclave** (Wilson & Portes, 1980).

According to classic immigration theory, then, Cuban immigrants should have suffered. Instead, they prospered. By 1970 the median income of Cuban American families was higher than that of any other Hispanic group or of African Americans, at 80 percent of the median income of non-Hispanic white families; and by 1980 it had reached 88 percent of the median income for non-Hispanic white families (Bean & Tienda, 1987). Portes and other observers claim that Cuban immigrants successfully used the ethnically based connections of the enclave to obtain loans to start businesses when no Anglo bank would lend to them; they also used their connections to find jobs at Cuban enterprises. (See the section, later in this chapter, Social Capital and Immigrant Families.) Portes argues that the enclave strategy is a viable way for an immigrant group to achieve economic success.

Yet it must be remembered that these immigrants started out with a friendly reception from their hosts, arrived with substantial education and skills, received government assistance, and had white skin. These advantages were not shared by those who were part of a later wave of Cuban immigration that began in 1980, when Castro allowed a flotilla of small boats to depart from the port of Mariel. Unlike the first wave of Cuban immigrants, who arrived during an economic boom, the Mariel Cubans arrived at a time of stagnant wages and high unemployment. They were not welcomed enthusiastically or assisted, and they experienced discrimination from the earlier wave of immigrants. By 2001, the median income of Cuban-origin families had slipped to 61 percent of the median for non-Hispanic white families, reflecting the influx of Mariel refugees. Nevertheless, Cuban Americans remained the most prosperous of the major Hispanic groups (U.S. Bureau of the Census, 2011b).

assimilation the process by which immigrant groups merge their culture and their behavior with that of the dominant group in the host country

immigrant enclave a large, dense, single-ethnic-group, almost self-sufficient community

Like the majority of Cuban Americans, these dominoes players in the Little Havana neighborhood chose to settle in the Miami metropolitan area.

The prosperity of Cuban Americans is derived in large part from business ownership. Cuban immigrants have become entrepreneurs, opening new businesses in far greater numbers than other Hispanic immigrants. Many of the businesses were organized on a family basis. As Figure 5.4 showed, Cubans are more likely to form two-parent families than are other Hispanics. Married Cuban men were more likely to be self-employed, even after taking into account differences between married and unmarried men in education, work experience, citizenship, and English proficiency. If the men had children, they were even more likely to be self-employed (Portes & Jensen, 1989). Cuban immigrants appear to have used conjugal families as a means of pooling the labor and accumulating the capital necessary to start a business. Too many adults represented a drain on capital that could be used for the business; too few children or the absence of a spouse, on the other hand, resulted in insufficient labor or outside income (as from a wife's job) for starting a firm.

Quick Review

- Mexican Americans have high birthrates and marry at younger ages, in large part because of the extensive migration from Mexico.
- Mexican immigrants and their descendants are contributing greatly to the American population growth.
- Transnational families, in which members maintain ties with the home country and the United States, are becoming more common.
- Puerto Ricans are the most economically disadvantaged of the major Hispanic groups.
- Puerto Ricans have a tradition of consensual unions, in which couples consider themselves married although their unions have never been formalized.
- Cubans, many of whom settled in immigrant enclaves, are the most prosperous Hispanic group.

Asian American Families

Less has been written about Asian American families than about African American and Hispanic families because of their modest numbers prior to the 1965 immigration act. For example, the Korean population increased from an estimated 69,000 in 1970 to 350,000 in 1980 and to 980,000 in 1998 (Lee, 1998). In the 2010 Census, 14.7 million people checked one of the Asian racial categories (Asian Indian, Chinese, Filipino, Japanese, Korean, Vietnamese, or "other Asian") or wrote in entries such as Pakistani or Thai, a 44 percent increase over the 2000 Asian population of 10.2 million (U.S. Bureau of the Census, 2011a). The family patterns in the many sending nations are diverse, but, in general, Asian cultures emphasize interdependence among kin more, and individualism less, than Western culture (Goode, 1963). Asian families place a greater emphasis on children's loyalty and service to their parents than do Western families. In fact, Asian immigrant parents are more likely to live in households in which their adult children provide most of the income (Glick & Van Hook, 2002).

These Asian ways can conflict with American ways. Two researchers, for instance, read a series of vignettes to a sample of Chinese American immigrants from Taiwan and their parents in Chicago and Los Angeles. Here is one:

> *Wang Hong has to transfer three times on public transportation to get from where he lives to his office. Because of the time and inconvenience of taking public transportation, Wang Hong has tried very hard to save money to buy a car before winter. However, Wang Hong's parents have a need for money and ask Wang Hong to give them the money Wang Hong has saved.*

Both the parents and their adult children were asked to react to this vignette. The authors noted that when a similar vignette had been read to a general U.S. sample of the elderly and their caregivers, about three-fourths of both groups had thought that the child should buy the car. Yet a majority of the Chinese adult children and parents said that Wang Hong should give the money to his parents—placing obligation to one's parents over convenience of transportation (Lin & Liu, 1993).

Immigrants' families frequently pool economic resources to start businesses or to buy homes. Several Asian-origin groups have very high rates of business ownership, often accomplished by borrowing funds from kin and close friends. As for homeownership, shared residence and income pooling often help, as one Vietnamese immigrant told an interviewer:

> *To Vietnamese culture, family is everything. There are aspects which help us readjust to this society. It is easy for us because of [the] tradition of helping in the family.*
>
> *We solve problems because [the] family institution is a bank. If I need money and my brothers and my two sisters are working, I tell them I need to buy a house. I need priority in this case. They say OK, and they give money to me. After only two years, I bought a house.*
>
> *Some Americans ask me, "How come you came here with empty hands and now you have a house?" I told them, it is easy for us because my brother and sister help with the down payment. Now I help them. They live with me and have no rent. (Gold, 1993)*

This is not to say that all Asian immigrants adjust well and prosper. The first wave of Vietnamese immigration occurred in the immediate aftermath of the

Asian immigrants often pool their resources to start family-run small businesses such as this grocery store.

Vietnam War in 1975. Like the initial Cuban influx, it was a political migration of middle-class business and military personnel who were assisted on arrival. They have been successful as a group. Yet like the Mariel immigration, a later, less-educated stream of Vietnamese immigrants escaped in overcrowded boats to refugee camps in Southeast Asia. Those who have emigrated to the United States have fewer skills, have received less assistance, and have encountered a sluggish economy. A 1984 study of some of the later immigrants found that 61 percent had household incomes of less than $9,000 (Gold, 1993). Nevertheless, Asian Americans are a prosperous group overall. In 2009, the median family income for Asians was $75,027, which was 20 percent higher than the median for white families, an impressive achievement for a population that includes so many recent immigrants (U.S. Bureau of the Census, 2011b).

The extent to which Asian-style patterns will survive through the second and third generations of Asian Americans remains to be seen. Among Asian Americans whose families have been in the United States for a few generations, the traditional Asian patterns are less apparent. For instance, the relations between women and men are more egalitarian in third-generation Japanese American families than in the older, immigrant generation (Ishii-Kuntz, 2000). And rates of interracial intermarriages are high among Asians, a topic to which I will turn in a few pages.

Social Capital and Immigrant Families

social capital the resources that a person can access through his or her relationships with other people

The recent literature on immigrants refers often to a concept developed by the French sociologist Pierre Bourdieu (1980) and expanded on by the American sociologist James S. Coleman (1988). **Social capital** is the resources that a person can access through his or her relationships with other people.

To understand this concept, think about the social connections that might allow you to get a ticket to a sold-out concert (because your friend's cousin works in the box office), to be admitted to a competitive college (because your mother is an alumna), or to get your first job after college (because your roommate's father runs the company). In all these cases, the resources you would draw on would not be monetary (which social scientists refer to as "financial capital") or educational (which social scientists call "human capital"), but rather your social links to a network of people who can help you reach a goal you might otherwise fail to achieve.

That is the essence of the concept of social capital. In the literature on immigrants it is sometimes used more broadly to refer to a person's links to an entire immigrant community. The idea is that the community provides members with resources that help them to achieve goals they could not achieve alone, or even as families working together. For example, to explain why the children of Vietnamese immigrants in Versailles Village do better in school than their low social class would predict, Zhou and Bankston (1998) point to the social capital created by the close-knit Vietnamese community. They describe a Vietnamese Catholic church that offers after-school courses, and the Vietnamese Education Association, a community group that holds an annual awards ceremony to honor high-achieving students. Through these institutions, the authors argue, the Vietnamese community in Versailles Village provides social capital that boosts school achievement among Vietnamese students.

As I mentioned earlier, the literature on Cuban immigrants provides another example of the use of social capital. One reason for the growth in the number of Cuban American–owned firms from the late-1960s to the 1980s was that immigrants could use their social standing in the Cuban community in Miami to obtain the initial loans needed to start a business. In the mid-1960s, according to Alejandro Portes and Julia Sensenbrenner, a few small banks owned by South Americans hired Cuban immigrant ex-bankers. The Cubans began to make loans to their fellow immigrants that other financial institutions would have thought risky. As one Cuban banker said:

> *At the start, most Cuban enterprises were gas stations; then came grocery shops and restaurants. No American bank would lend to them. By the mid-sixties we started a policy at our bank of making small loans to Cubans who wanted to start their own business, but did not have the capital. These loans of $10,000 or $15,000 were made because the person was known to us by his reputation and integrity. All of them paid back; there were zero losses. With some exceptions they have continued being clients of the bank. People who used to borrow $15,000 on a one-time basis now take $50,000 in a week. In 1973, the policy was discontinued. The reason was that the new refugees coming at that time were unknown to us. (Portes & Sensenbrenner, 1993)*

Whereas American banks would have required more proof that an applicant would be able to pay back a loan, the Cuban bankers relied solely on the applicant's "reputation and integrity." That reputation was established through a network of ties within the Cuban enclave in Miami. The banker might have known someone who had married the sister of the applicant and could vouch for the applicant's character. To enforce the terms of the loan, the banker relied on the humiliation and, perhaps, ostracism that would befall a person who defaulted. In this way, Cuban immigrants were able to use their ties to a network of relatives and friends to obtain the money they needed to buy a grocery store or restaurant.

American Indian Families

Before the twentieth century, kinship ties provided the basis for governing most American Indian tribes. A person's household was linked to a larger group of relatives who might be a branch of a matrilineal or patrilineal clan that shared power with other clans. Thus, kinship organization was also political organization. Under these circumstances, extended kinship ties reflected power and status to a much greater extent than among other racial-ethnic groups in the United States. American Indian kinship systems allowed individuals to have more relatives, particularly distant relatives, than did Western European kinship systems (Shoemaker, 1991). Even in recent times, extended family ties retained a significance for American Indians that went beyond the sharing of resources that has been noted among other groups (Harjo, 1993). Kinship networks constitute tribal organization; kinship ties confer an identity.

Only one-third of the individuals in the 2000 Census who identified themselves as solely of American Indian origin and who said they were members of a tribe were living in tribal areas (U.S. Bureau of the Census, 2006). By 2000, New York and Los Angeles were the cities with the largest American Indian populations (U.S. Bureau of the Census, 2002). As noted earlier, a substantial share of the growth of the American Indian population in urban areas in the East and on the West Coast reflects a rise in the number of people who considered themselves to be American Indians. In addition, migration from reservations to urban areas may have accounted for some of the drop in the percentage living near tribal lands.

Despite a decline in the power of lineages, extended families remain significant for American Indians.

American Indians remain an economically disadvantaged population. Their median family income is about the same as that of African Americans (U.S. Bureau of the Census, 2011b). Consistent with their high levels of poverty, the percentage of American Indian families headed by an unmarried woman is substantial: As Figure 5.1 showed, 36 percent of American Indian families with children in 2009 were headed by a single parent. Consistent with these figures, 65 percent of American Indian mothers who gave birth in 2006 were unmarried—a percentage exceeded only by African Americans (U.S. National Center for Health Statistics, 2010). The percentage of adults who are divorced is also higher among American Indians than among the U.S. population as a whole (Sandefur & Liebler, 1997).

It's likely that many of the unmarried mothers were enmeshed in kinship networks that provided assistance. Little research, however, has been done on contemporary American Indian family patterns—especially among American Indians outside tribal lands. Beyond these lands, intermarriage and shifting conceptions of American Indian ethnicity make the study of families more complex. It is increasingly difficult to talk of the "American Indian family": There always has been diversity in family patterns among Indian tribes and among persons residing on reservations versus persons not on reservations, and now an American Indian family is often a multiracial family, as the next section discusses.

Quick Review

- Asian family patterns traditionally have placed a greater emphasis on children's loyalty and service to parents than have Western family patterns.
- Ties to family and community can provide social capital to immigrants.
- Kinship networks traditionally provided organization and identity to American Indians.
- The high intermarriage rate and shifting conceptions of identity make American Indian family patterns diverse.

Racial and Ethnic Intermarriage

When Barack Obama was born in Hawaii to an interracial married couple in 1961, at least fifteen states had laws forbidding marriages between whites and nonwhites. Then, in 1967 the Supreme Court, ruling on a case brought against the state of Virginia by a white man, Richard Loving, and his black wife, Mildred Jeter, declared such laws unconstitutional (*Loving* v. *Virginia,* 1967). In 1972, when the General Social Survey started its annual survey of American adults, 39 percent of whites still favored laws against racial intermarriage (Davis & Smith, 2010), and interracial married couples comprised only about 1 percent of all American married couples (Lee & Edmonston, 2005). By the year 2000, just 12 percent of whites favored these laws, and the roughly 3,000,000 interracial married couples comprised 5 percent of all American married couples. By 2008, 7 percent of all married couples were interracial (Lee & Bean, 2010).

VARIATION IN INTERMARRIAGE

The rates at which people of different racial-ethnic groups intermarry vary greatly. There are so many whites in the United States that even though millions of them marry a non-white, the percentage of white people who intermarry remains low. The racial-ethnic group with the next lowest percentage of intermarriage is African Americans: Among all the African Americans who got married in the 12 months prior to the Census Bureau's 2008 American Community Survey 20 percent of men and 11 percent of women married someone other than another African American (all statistics in this paragraph are from Qian and Lichter, 2011). These percentages, though modest, reflect substantial increases over the past few decades. In the 12 months before the 1980 Census, for instance, just 7 percent of men and 2 percent of women married a non-African American. Near the high end are Asian Americans. In 2008, 47 percent of Asian American men and 52 percent of Asian American women who had married in the previous year had non-Asian Americans as spouses. So among young Asian Americans, intermarriage is becoming the norm. The same can be said for American Indians: 57 percent of men and 58 of women had married non-American Indians. Hispanics, although technically an ethnic group rather than a race, also have substantial rates of outmarriage: 58 percent for men and 59 percent for women. Puerto Ricans are the Hispanic group that is most likely to intermarry, whereas Cubans are the least likely (Lee & Edmonston, 2005).

If these rates continue into the future, far more people could identify as "multiracial" when the Census Bureau comes around to ask about race a generation or two from now. For instance, as the children of interracial marriages involving American Indians reach adulthood, the continuing high rates could result in a further decline in the number of people identifying themselves solely as American Indians and a further increase—to a clear majority—in the proportion of people who identify themselves as American Indians and another race. Similarly, a majority of U.S.-born Americans with an Asian American parent could identify themselves as multiracial in a generation. The ultimate number of such people in the United States in the mid–twenty-first century will depend on whether intermarriage increases further and also on two other factors. The first is the level of immigration: Immigrants from Latin America and Asia will replenish the Hispanic and Asian American single-race groups while the U.S. members of these groups continue to marry out. Second, the propensity of people to think of themselves as multiracial could rise. Consider the golfer Tiger Woods, who has become a symbol of twenty-first-century multiracial identity. He describes his race as "Cablinasian": His father was black, Chinese, and American Indian, and his mother is Thai, Chinese, and white. If having a multiracial identity becomes more acceptable, it could provide a further boost to the multiracial numbers that the census will count.

Still, the social distance between African Americans and Americans of other races and of Hispanic ethnicity remains substantial. African Americans are less likely to identify as multiracial and their intermarriage rates remain lower than other nonwhites and Hispanics (Qian & Lichter, 2007). Until recently, the United States had a sharp color line between blacks and whites (Du Bois, 1903; Farley & Allen, 1987). The increasing rates of intermarriage have the potential to finally blur that line. Yet some sociologists note apprehensively that if intermarriages involving African Americans do not increase as fast as other types of intermarriages, then the United States could end up replacing the old color line with a new one, the "black/nonblack divide" (Lee & Bean, 2010). African Americans would be on one side of the line, and the descendants of Asians, Hispanics, American Indians, and non-Hispanic whites would be on the other side. But this result is not foretold. African American intermarriage rates are rising. It is too soon to know how intermarriage will alter racial identity in the next half-century.

INTERSECTIONALITY AND INTERMARRIAGE

The intersectionality perspective has been used to understand the role of marriage in the lives of college-educated black women (Banks, 2011; Clarke, 2011). Between 1970 and 2008, the proportion of young black women (age 25 to 34) with four-year college degrees increased sharply from 6 percent to 22 percent (Autor, 2010). They are more likely to marry than are black women without college degrees; this suggests that their class position, as measured by education, gives them an advantage in the marriage market. However, black women with college degrees are still far less likely to be married than are white women with college degrees (Isen & Stevenson, 2011). So their race puts them at a relative disadvantage compared to white women with the same level of education. In addition, black women are much less likely to marry someone of a different race than are black men. Since more black men are marrying out, the pool of potential spouses for black women is reduced. So the marriage rates of college-educated black women reflect their class position (they marry more often than less-educated black women), their race (they marry less often than white women), and their gender (they outmarry less often than black men). To understand their situation fully, one must consider their class position, race, and gender all at once. This unique intersection of class, race, and gender reduces the marriage rates of college-educated black women below that of comparably-educated white women.

Quick Review

- Racial and ethnic intermarriage has increased greatly over the past few decades.
- Rates vary greatly, with intermarriages of Asians and American Indians at the high end and those of African Americans and non-Hispanic whites (due to their large population size) at the low end.
- Intermarriage has the potential to reshape individual and group identities over the next half-century.

Race, Ethnicity, and Kinship

Family ties have been central to the successes and the struggles of racial-ethnic groups in the United States. All the minority groups that have been discussed in this chapter have relied on their relatives for support—whether that support be food for dinner or money to buy a restaurant. Their reliance on extended kinship contrasts with the nuclear family ideal among non-Hispanic whites. To be sure, there are substantial differences among racial-ethnic groups in the kinds of family lives they tend to lead. Some of these differences reflect economic forces. Put another way, sometimes what we think of as ethnic or racial differences may, in large part, be class differences. For example, to compare Puerto Ricans on the mainland with Cubans on the mainland is to compare an economically disadvantaged group with a more economically privileged one.

Still, in Chapter 4 and this chapter, we have seen similarities across racial-ethnic groups in the ways low-income families organize family and kinship. Among these disadvantaged groups, the strongest family tie is often between a mother and her adult daughter. In what I have called women-centered kin networks, women organize exchanges of support that extend across households, linking networks of people who share their meager resources.

Nevertheless, the precise form of kinship varies from group to group, reflecting, in my opinion, long-standing cultural differences. For example, the distinctive characteristic of Puerto Rican households is the consensual union, although there are also many households headed by women without live-in partners. Single-parent households, or grandmother-daughter-grandchild households, are the common form among African Americans, with young mothers often residing with their own mothers for several years. For all these groups, assistance from family members other than one's spouse or partner is crucial for subsisting from day to day.

Among many immigrant groups, family ties provide critical assistance to individuals who wish to start small businesses. Most banks will not lend money to new immigrants because they are not sure they will be repaid. Immigrants tend not to have homes or other assets that they can use as collateral to secure a bank loan. Sometimes, however, they can obtain start-up loans from members of their kinship and community networks. Those who loan the money rely upon kinship and community ties as a form of moral collateral: A borrower puts his reputation and standing among his peers on the line when he or she obtains a loan. If the borrower were to default, he or she would be dishonored before family and friends. Thus, kinship ties provide a form of social capital that immigrants can use to obtain the financial capital—money, equipment, storefronts—needed to start an enterprise. These same ties also become recruiting networks through which members of the group can find jobs.

The immigrant entrepreneurs utilize what we might call marriage-centered kin networks. These exchanges tend to connect households that are headed by husbands and wives. It is the married couple that starts and maintains the business, although other relatives may work in it. Ties to a wider network of kin provide financial assistance that the married couple is allowed to manage largely for its own benefit. In contrast, women-centered kin networks require that any surplus be shared. In this way, the kin networks of the poor allow the maximum number of people to get the resources they need to avoid becoming destitute. Thus, the two kinds of kinship networks discussed in this chapter and the previous one have different functions: Marriage-centered networks allow for the accumulation of resources by the husband-wife household, whereas women-centered networks allow for the maximum sharing of resources across predominantly single-parent households.

I would suggest that these two forms of kin networks have different strengths and limitations. The women-centered networks are superior for easing the hardships of persistent poverty. They have allowed many poor individuals to subsist from day to day. Yet they make it difficult for network members to accumulate the resources necessary to rise above poverty. The marriage-based networks, on the other hand, are superior for allowing people to be upwardly mobile by accumulating enough resources to start a business or move to a better neighborhood. Yet they make it difficult for network members to provide assistance to all kin who need it. The differences between the two networks suggest, therefore, a tension that many people with low incomes may face: helping all of one's kin who need assistance versus accumulating enough money to better the position of one's own household. Different racial-ethnic groups resolve this tension in different ways.

This is not to suggest that whether a household escapes from poverty is solely, or even primarily, a matter of kinship networks. For instance, education matters. Asian Americans have a higher percentage of college graduates than non-Hispanic whites (U.S. Bureau of the Census, 2011b). A case could be made that, although there has been discrimination against Asian Americans, it has not been as institutionalized and as pervasive as has discrimination against African Americans. Moreover, the restructuring of the economy has had a major effect on the family lives of African Americans. Still, within these constraints, family and kinship patterns appear to make a difference in the life chances of the members of racial-ethnic groups, allowing many to survive and some to prosper.

Looking Back

1. **How are racial and ethnic groups constructed?** Racial and ethnic groups are socially constructed rather than reflecting natural, timeless divisions among people. Beliefs about what constitutes race in the United States have changed over time. Two examples of the changing definitions of race and ethnicity are the categories of "Hispanic" and "Asian." Each was created in the United States and each includes very diverse subgroups from many nations. Even whiteness can be considered as a socially constructed ethnicity.

2. **How has African American family life changed over the past several decades?** African Americans have been adversely affected by economic changes that have reduced the number of semiskilled and skilled blue-collar jobs available to American workers. In part as a result of this economic transformation, the importance of marriage in African American families has declined substantially relative to ties to extended kin such as grandmothers. The link between childbearing and marriage has also weakened; about two-thirds of black children are now born to

unmarried mothers. African Americans have responded to these changes by drawing on the network of kin for mutual support. During the same period, however, a substantial African American middle class has emerged.

3. **What are the family patterns of major Hispanic ethnic groups?** The largest Hispanic group, Mexican Americans, is characterized by early marriage and high birthrates. These reflect the distinctive behavior of recent immigrants; Mexican-origin Americans who were born in the United States, on the other hand, are not as different from other Americans in marriage and childbearing. Among Puerto Ricans, the poorest of the major Hispanic groups, a relatively high number of children are born to unmarried mothers. But some of these mothers live with partners in consensual unions that they consider to be like marriages. Cuban Americans are the most prosperous Hispanic group, although recent immigrants have reduced the group's economic standing. Most Cuban Americans settled in an immigrant enclave in the Miami area and many started family-based businesses.

4. **What are the distinctive characteristics of the family patterns of Asian Americans?** More than in any other group, including non-Hispanic whites, Asian American families are headed by married couples. These families also have comparatively few children born outside of marriage and low divorce rates—characteristics that probably reflect a greater emphasis on the interdependence and mutual obligations of kin. Although some Asian subgroups are poor, Asian American families as a whole have a higher median income than non-Hispanic white families. A majority of young adult Asian Americans now marry non-Asians.

5. **How does the concept of "social capital" apply to immigrant families?** Some Hispanic immigrant groups, most notably the Cubans, and many Asian immigrant groups use ties to others in their ethnic community to achieve certain goals, such as starting a business. This use of social connections to advance oneself is an example of what sociologists call social capital.

6. **How is intermarriage affecting racial and ethnic groups?** Rates of intermarriage have increased greatly in recent decades. For some groups, such as Asians and American Indians, rates are so high that a majority of each group may soon identify as multiracial. Hispanics also have high rates of intermarriage. Rates of intermarriage are lower among African Americans, although they also have increased intermarriage, and may be creating a new black/nonblack color line in America.

Go to the Online Learning Center at www.mhhe.com/cherlin7e to test your knowledge of the chapter concepts and key terms.

Study Questions

1. What are the pros and cons of the use of "umbrella" racial-ethnic group designations such as "Hispanic" and "Asian"?

2. Does it make sense to consider "whites" as a racial-ethnic group?

3. What does research suggest about economic and cultural influences on the decline of marriage among African Americans?

4. Why might middle-class African American families have more difficulty maintaining their status than middle-class white families?

5. Why might Mexican American and Puerto Rican family patterns be different?

6. What are the likely implications of the high rates at which Asian Americans and American Indians marry outside of their racial-ethnic groups?

7. How does the concept of intersectionality help us to understand the marriage rates of college-educated black women?

8. Why might marriage-centered kin networks be advantageous to immigrant entrepreneurs?

Key Terms

Asian American   143
assimilation   161
consensual union   160
Hispanic   142

immigrant enclave   161
intersectionality   154
mediating structures   156
non-Hispanic white   144

racial-ethnic group   142
social capital   164
total fertility rate
   (TFR)   158

Thinking about Families

The Public Family	The Private Family
Should more native-born Americans care for their aging parents the way many immigrant groups do?	Interracial and interethnic marriages are widespread among Asian Americans and American Indians, common among Hispanics, and uncommon but increasing among African Americans. How might intergroup marriage change American families in the early decades of the twenty-first century?

Families on the Internet www.mhhe.com/cherlin7e

Note: While all the URLs listed were current as of the printing of this book, these sites often change. Please check our Web site (www.mhhe.com/cherlin7e) for updates.

The U.S. Bureau of the Census collects detailed statistics through its monthly Current Population Survey, its Decennial Census of Population, and other studies. The information in this chapter on the growth of racial and ethnic minority families, household composition, and interracial families was obtained from the treasure trove of information at the Census Bureau's home page (www.census.gov). For instance, to find out the latest information on Hispanic families, click the "Subjects A to Z" tab, then select "H" on the next screen, then, on the next screen, find "Hispanic Origin" and select the subcategory "Population." You can then select and view the latest data on the Hispanic population in the United States.

The National Academy of Sciences convenes panels of experts to address scientific issues. Many of the panels publish their reports as books through the National Academy Press. The text of hundreds of these reports is available online at its Web site (www.nap.edu). There you can read *America Becoming,* an edited volume on race in American society (Smelser, Wilson, & Mitchell, 2001). The report includes chapters on most major racial-ethnic groups as well as topics such as the changing meaning of race, immigration and race, and racial attitudes. You can also read *Hispanics and the Future of America* (Tienda & Mitchell, 2006).

Part Three

Sexuality, Partnership, and Marriage

In the next three chapters, we move from a focus on the effects of gender, race-ethnicity, and class to a consideration of how intimate relationships are built from the ground up, how they are structured as partnerships and marriages, and how family members care for each other. These chapters examine the challenges that people experience as they come to love someone and to form partnerships and marriages. • Chapter 6 discusses the emergence of the modern concept of sexuality. It traces the great changes in sexual attitudes and practices over the past few decades and examines the living arrangements that these changes have produced. It also covers childbearing outside of marriage, which is a consequence of changing sexual practices. Attention then shifts in • Chapter 7 to marriage and cohabitation. We will first study courtship, dating, and the recent phenomenon of hooking up. We will then review how marriage changed to a companionship in the early 1900s and how it recently has changed again to a more individualized kind of partnership. We will examine cohabitation and the vision of the "pure relationship." • Chapter 8 will examine the complex connections between work and families. We will first examine the growth in dual-earner couples as married women have entered the paid labor force. We will also examine the important, largely unpaid, caring work that family members, most of them women, do for their partners, children, parents, and kin. We will also consider changes in who does the housework and the child care in dual-earner families. Finally, we'll look at how the workplace can become more family friendly.

Chapter Six

Sexualities

Looking Forward

Sexual Identities

The Emergence of Sexual Identities

Sexual Acts versus Sexual Identities

The Emergence of "Heterosexuality" and "Homosexuality"

The Determinants of Sexual Identities

The Social Constructionist Perspective

The Integrative Perspective

Points of Agreement and Disagreement

Questioning Sexual Identities

Queer Theory

Strengths and Limitations

New Families and Beyond?

Beyond the Family?

Networks of Friends

Living Apart Together

Blurred Boundaries

Marital and Nonmarital Sexuality

Nonmarital Sexual Activity

Marital and Extramarital Sex

Adolescent Sexuality and Pregnancy

Changes in Sexual Behavior

The Teenage Pregnancy "Problem"

The Consequences for Teenage Mothers

Sexuality and Family Life

Looking Back

Study Questions

Key Terms

Thinking about Families

Families on the Internet

Boxed Features

HOW DO SOCIOLOGISTS KNOW WHAT THEY KNOW?: *Asking about Sensitive Behavior*

FAMILIES AND PUBLIC POLICY: *The Rise and Fall of the Teenage Pregnancy Problem*

Looking Forward

1. When did the idea of a sexual identity develop?

2. What determines people's sexual identities?

3. Is "sexual identity" a useful way to think about people's sexuality?

4. Are people's living arrangements going beyond the boundaries of the family?

5. What is the nature of the teenage pregnancy "problem"?

In April 1779, Alexander Hamilton wrote to John Laurens, with whom he had served in the American Revolution:

Cold in my professions, warm in [my] friendships, I wish, my Dear Laurens, it m[ight] be in my power, by action rather than words, [to] convince you that I love you. I shall only tell you that 'till you bade us Adieu, I hardly knew the value you had taught my heart to set upon you.

In September, after almost giving up hope of receiving a letter from Laurens, Hamilton wrote of his joy at finally receiving one:

But like a jealous lover, when I thought you slighted my caresses, my affection was alarmed and my vanity piqued. I had almost resolved to lavish no more of them upon you and to reject you as an inconstant and an ungrateful—. But you have now disarmed my resentment and by a single mark of attention made up the quarrel. (Katz, 1976)

Nor were famous American men the only ones who wrote intimate letters to other men. Karen Hansen tells the story of Brigham Nims, who lived for most of his life on his family's farm in New Hampshire, married, and had three children. In the 1830s, prior to marrying, Nims worked in a box factory in Boston for two years, where he struck up a close friendship with J. Foster Beal. They corresponded for a few years afterward. In one passage, Beal writes:

can not forget those happy hours [th]at we spent at G. Newcombs and the evening walks; but we are deprived of that privilege now we are separated for a time we cannot tell how long perhaps before our eyes behold each other in this world.

In a later letter, Beal reminds Nims of the time Beal nursed him through an illness:

I guess you have forgot all about you being at Boston last Sept. when you was so sick, and I took care of you, doctored you up, even took you in bed with myself; you will not do as much, as, to write me. (Hansen, 1989)

Upon discovering these accounts, it is the instinct of the contemporary reader to immediately consider whether the relationships were homosexual. Yet historians argue that such a question represents the myopia of a person steeped in contemporary culture peering back at another time. The categories of homosexual and heterosexual did not yet exist, and therefore eighteenth- and early-nineteenth century people did not need to fit into them. Whether or not Hamilton's intimate friendship ever involved a sexual act was not its defining

Alexander Hamilton was one of many eighteenth- and nineteenth-century Americans who wrote intimate letters to other men.

feature. As historian Jonathan Katz notes, even if many of the phrases in these letters were merely rhetorical flourishes, it is striking how easy it was for men to use language that today would be seen as indicating a sexual relationship.

In fact, what seems so different about these relationships is the seeming ease with which two same-sex individuals could engage in intimacies, such as sharing a bed or declaring their love for each other, without these acts marking the relationship as sexual or asexual. (Indeed, Hansen tells us that sharing a bed was not uncommon among the working class in nineteenth-century Boston because of the lack of space.) A broad range of public affection and intimacy was open to same-sex friendships in a way that, for most men at least, it is not today (Adam, 2004).

The best-known study of same-sex intimacy in the late eighteenth and nineteenth centuries is Carroll Smith-Rosenberg's "The Female World of Love and Ritual" (Smith-Rosenberg, 1975). Smith-Rosenberg explored the "separate sphere" of middle-class women and found that they often formed deep emotional bonds of friendship with other women. Immersed in a network of female kin and friends, women helped one another in crises such as childbirth, helped to prepare one another for weddings, and spent long hours together talking. Some of their correspondence seems, by today's standards at least, to have a romantic and even erotic tone. Smith-Rosenberg writes of Sarah Butler Wister and Jeannie Field Musgrove, who first met as teenagers during a summer vacation, attended boarding school together for two years, and formed a lifelong intimate friendship. At age 29, Sarah, married and a mother, wrote to Jeannie, "I shall be entirely alone [this coming week]. I can give you no idea how desperately I shall want you." Jeannie ended one letter "Goodbye my dearest, dearest lover" and another "I will go to bed . . . [though] I could write all night—A thousand kisses—I love you with my whole soul."

The point of studying exchanges such as these, as Smith-Rosenberg herself argued, "is not whether these women had genital contact and can therefore be defined as heterosexual or homosexual." Rather, the point is that these women lived in a social context that allowed them the freedom to form a friendship that was quite intimate without the friendship's being labeled as anything more than that. Middle-class women's bonds could be loving and sensual without necessarily being sexual; it is likely that even if they were, the sexual acts would not be seen as the defining characteristic of the relationship. The social context allowed women more flexibility in creating intense emotional ties than is the case today, when we tend to think that close, sensual same-sex relationships must be "homosexual."

Smith-Rosenberg believes that the creation of a separate sphere for middle-class women established the conditions that allowed such close friendships to flourish. But the correspondence between Nims and Beal suggests that some men may also have established intimate friendships. How unusual Nims was we cannot know. Other than the two years he spent in Boston, he worked on the farm. Hansen argues that rural men, who did not leave home to work in a factory every day, did not experience as strict a split between the worlds of women and men. Perhaps, she suggests, they had a more fluid conception of gender that allowed them to be intimate friends with other men.

But in the late-nineteenth and twentieth centuries, these more fluid conceptions congealed into two master categories that people saw as central to their senses of themselves—two sexual identities, heterosexual and homosexual. Most people think of them as "natural," but they are modern creations. Moreover, there are intellectuals and researchers today who argue that these identities are becoming more fluid again, and some who argue against even using the concept of a sexual identity. Some of these same writers, who include sociologists, claim that people who do not follow the dominant heterosexual model are creating new modes of living that challenge the usefulness of the concept of "the family" or even of diverse "families" to describe personal life in the twenty-first century. In this chapter we will examine the rise, and perhaps the beginning of the fall, of sexual identities and the implications for studying family life. We will then turn to the topics of sexual behavior in and outside of marriage and among unmarried adolescents.

Sexual Identities

Of course, there is nothing new about sex, or about people having sexual preferences and attractions. What's new—or at least no more than 150 years old—is the way that sexual acts and preferences are currently socially organized. Other societies have organized sexuality somewhat differently: Think of the two-spirits, the in-between-gender individuals found among many American Indian tribes. What's also new is the important role this organization of sexuality has played in social life—how one's sexual preferences and behaviors have become a central way of defining who one is. They were not as central to Alexander Hamilton or Brigham Nims.

THE EMERGENCE OF SEXUAL IDENTITIES

Although sex isn't new, sexual identities are. By a **sexual identity,** I mean a set of sexual practices and attitudes that lead to the formation in a person's mind of an identity as heterosexual, homosexual, or bisexual. Most people in our society today could give a clear and immediate answer to the question "Are you heterosexual or homosexual?" Our sexual identity, in turn, becomes an important part of our sense of who we are. Furthermore, we see this as "natural"—everyone, we assume, has a sexual identity.

sexual identity a set of sexual practices and attitudes that lead to the formation in a person's mind of an identity as heterosexual, homosexual, or bisexual

Sexual Acts versus Sexual Identities   Yet the question "Are you heterosexual or homosexual?" would have stumped Americans until the nineteenth century. Not only the terms "homosexual" and "heterosexual" but also the idea of "being" homosexual or heterosexual had not yet been invented. There were only two categories of sexual activities: the socially approved (sexual intercourse within marriage, in moderation, and undertaken mainly to have children) and the socially disapproved (all other activities, including acts between persons of the same sex, masturbation, oral sex regardless of the genders of the partners, and so forth). To perform any of the latter was sinful, but such behavior did not define a person as having a particular sexual identity. Then, during the nineteenth century the concept of an orientation toward the same sex began to emerge. Men and women were recognized and sometimes punished and persecuted for their same-sex attraction, and some participated in clandestine social clubs and searched for persons of similar orientations. Yet the nature of one's sexual orientation was not as central in defining one's sense of self as it would become in the late-nineteenth and twentieth centuries (Robb, 2003). The concept of a sexual identity requires a self-consciousness and self-examination that was not prominent until the late nineteenth century.

The Emergence of "Heterosexuality" and "Homosexuality"   Americans defined the categories they use today in part by mounting a public campaign against homosexuality beginning in the late nineteenth century. At that time, an influential body of medical literature began to describe not merely homosexual acts but homosexual persons—distinctive individuals who were seen as suffering from a psychological illness that altered their sexual preferences. Their supposedly unnatural condition was labeled "homosexuality," and it was said to pervade their personalities. They were no longer just men or women who engaged in sexual acts with a same-sex partner; they were homosexuals—seriously ill people (Foucault, 1980). In contrast to them, the same writers defined a "normal" sexual preference for the opposite sex as "heterosexuality." Heterosexuals were seen as mentally healthy as opposed to sick. This was the way sexuality entered our everyday language and our consciousness: as a means of organizing people into two contrasting sexual identities, one viewed as normal and one disparaged as diseased.

The medical model remained dominant until 1973, when the American Psychiatric Association removed homosexuality from its list of mental disorders (Silverstein, 1991). The medical model stigmatized homosexual people and served as a basis for prejudice and discrimination. But the very force of the critique also created a group identity for individuals who had previously had none. Much as the ideology of separate spheres created conditions that allowed for social and political action by women's groups, so the discourse on homosexuality as an illness created conditions that ultimately provoked social and political actions by homosexual persons. "Homosexuality began to speak in its own behalf," wrote Michel Foucault, "to demand that its legitimacy or 'naturality' be acknowledged, often in the same vocabulary, using the same categories by which it was medically disqualified" (Foucault, 1980).

Quick Review

- The idea that people have a sexual identity did not arise until the late nineteenth century.
- Homosexuality was initially defined as a "psychological illness," whereas heterosexuality was seen as "normal."

THE DETERMINANTS OF SEXUAL IDENTITIES

Given this history, and given the variety of ways in which societies have organized sexual life, some sociologists and like-minded scholars take the position that sexual identities are completely determined by society. Others take the position that biological influences may also play a significant role in determining people's sexual identities. Here is the case for each of these viewpoints.

social constructionist perspective (on sexuality) the belief that human sexual identities are entirely socially constructed

The Social Constructionist Perspective   What we might call the **social constructionist perspective** on human sexual identities is that sexual identities are *entirely* socially created (Seidman, 2003). Advocates of this perspective point to many kinds of evidence. They note the unclear boundaries of the two-gender, heterosexually dominant model. For instance, they might cite the between-man-and-woman genders such as the two-spirits. They might remind us of the deep friendships of women such as Sarah Butler Wister and Jeannie Field Musgrove. They would note that in much of ancient Greece and Rome, men were allowed, even expected, to desire sex with other men or boys as well as with women (Ariès, 1985b). The Greek biographer and historian Plutarch wrote:

> *The noble lover of beauty engages in love wherever he sees excellence and splendid natural endowment without regard for any difference in physiological detail. The lover of human beauty [will] be fairly and equally disposed toward both sexes, instead of supposing that males and females are as different in the matter of love as they are in their clothes.*[1]

Yet although the Greeks had words for specific sexual tastes, they had no general term comparable to "homosexuality" (Weinrich & Williams, 1991).

The social constructionists would also argue that even today sexual identities vary from culture to culture. For example, in Brazil and some other Latin American countries, a man who always takes the active, penetrating role in sex with other men would not necessarily be thought of as a "homosexual," whereas a man who always takes the passive role would (Rebhun, 1999). In other words, a man's sexuality depends on whether he plays the "masculine" role in sex, in which case he may be considered heterosexual even if he

[1] Quoted in Boswell (1982).

Sex researcher Alfred Kinsey sits at his desk at Indiana University surrounded by his co-authors and associates (left to right) Wardell B. Pomeroy, Paul H. Gebhard, and Dr. Clyde E. Martin.

sometimes has sex with other men. Cultural and historical variations such as these lead sociologists to argue that the sexual categories we use are defined by the society we live in.

No one did more to demonstrate that the boundaries between heterosexuality and homosexuality are unclear in American society than Alfred Kinsey, a zoology professor at the University of Indiana. In 1948 he published the results of thousands of interviews with men about their sexual behavior. Kinsey's dry, statistical book with 173 figures and 162 tables, often referred to as the **Kinsey Report,** became an immediate best seller. His findings on homosexuality shocked the country: Half of all men in his sample, he reported, acknowledged having had erotic feelings toward other men; one-third had had at least one sexual experience with another man; one out of eight had had sexual experiences predominantly with other men for at least three years; and 4 percent had had sexual experiences exclusively with other men (Kinsey, Pomeroy, & Martin, 1948). Kinsey concluded from his study that sexual orientation was a continuum running from exclusively heterosexual behavior to a mixture of heterosexual and homosexual behavior to exclusively homosexual behavior. Thus the book contained two far-reaching conclusions. First, the proportion of men whose experiences were predominantly homosexual was higher than most had imagined. Although Kinsey gave a range of figures, the one that came to dominate public discussion was that 10 percent of males were "more or less exclusively homosexual" for at least three years between the ages of 16 and 55 (Kinsey et al., 1948). Second, an even larger number of men had had some homosexual experience or feelings.

Although Kinsey's general conclusions still stand, his figures are not representative of the U.S. population now and probably were not then either. His study was based entirely on interviews with volunteers, the vast majority of them white, well educated, young, and from the Midwest and Northeast. Recently, a U.S. government agency asked detailed questions about sexual life in a random-sample survey of Americans ages 15 to 44, the National Survey of Family Growth (or NSFG), which was conducted from 2006 through 2008. (Although the researchers strongly defend their methods, some observers have expressed skepticism about the possibility of doing a survey on

Kinsey Report a 1948 book by Alfred Kinsey detailing the results of thousands of interviews with men about their sexual behavior

How Do Sociologists Know What They Know? — Asking about Sensitive Behavior

How do sociologists collect information on people's behaviors and attitudes? For the most part, they ask them. The most common way of doing so is through the random sample survey. Typically, a survey research organization will be hired to randomly select households and to ask the occupants a list of questions. In 1992, the National Opinion Research Center, one of the leading academic survey research organizations, asked a random sample of 3,432 adults detailed questions about their sexual activities and preferences. Researchers from the University of Chicago, who had written the questions, tabulated the results and published *The Social Organization of Sexuality* (Laumann et al., 1994). In 2006 through 2008, the U.S. National Center for Health Statistics used similar questions in a national survey. Some of the results are presented in Figures 6.1 and 6.2 (on pages 185 and 196).

But can those findings be trusted? After all, the interviewers were inquiring about some of the most private and sensitive aspects of behavior. Biologist Richard Lewontin, writing in the *New York Review of Books* (Lewontin, 1995a), ridiculed the Chicago sociologists for believing the responses of their subjects. His scathing critique, and the subsequent exchange of letters between social scientists and him, addressed the limits of survey-based sociological research.

Lewontin's main objection is that sociologists can't be sure that people tell the truth when asked about their behavior, especially when the topic is as sensitive as sexuality. Some people may lie, while others may not even admit the truth to themselves. Lewontin also pointed to a discrepancy in the data: Men reported 75 percent more sexual partners in the previous five years than did women. A few complexities aside, the average number of sexual partners of men and women should be almost the same. The authors examine this discrepancy and conclude that the most likely cause is that men exaggerate or women understate the number of partners when asked. Writes Lewontin: "If one takes the authors at their word, it would seem futile to take seriously the other results of the study" (1995a, p. 29).

The authors responded that although they "readily admit that we were not always successful in securing full disclosure," they "spent a great deal of time worrying about how we could check the reliability and honesty of our respondents' answers" (Laumann et al., 1995, p. 43). They used techniques such as asking similar questions at different points in the interview to see if a person's responses were consistent. For some sensitive questions, the respondents were given a form to fill out that they could return in a sealed envelope.

Lewontin was not appeased. For him, the sex survey is an example of sociology reaching for knowledge that is beyond its grasp. When they accept self-reports of sensitive behaviors and statistically analyze them, he argues, sociologists are trying too hard to imitate the natural sciences. Without adequate ways to measure information such as sexual behavior, and above all without the possibility of performing experiments, he maintains, sociology is limited:

> [Sociologists] are asking about the most complex and difficult phenomena

sexual behavior. See *How Do Sociologists Know What They Know?:* Asking about Sensitive Behavior.)

The NSFG measured sexual orientation in several ways, four of which are shown in Figure 6.1 (on page 185). Each person was asked whether he or she had had any same-sex sexual contact in their lifetime; the set of two bars on the left shows that 12.5 percent of women and 5.2 percent of men said yes. The second set of bars shows the percentage with same-sex contact during the previous 12 months; women also reported more contact than men. The questions were worded differently for women and men, however, so these percentages are not directly comparable. Women were asked broadly about "sexual experience of any kind with a female," whereas men were asked only about specific acts of oral and anal sex. The third set of bars reports responses to a question, "People are different in their sexual attraction to other people. Which best describes your feelings?" Then a range of responses was presented, from "only attracted" to the opposite sex to "mostly" to "equally attracted to males and females" to "mostly" and "only" attracted to the same sex. The bars show

in the most complex and recalcitrant organisms, without that liberty to manipulate their objects of study which is enjoyed by natural scientists. In comparison, the task of the molecular biologist is trivial. . . . Like it or not, there are a lot of questions that cannot be answered, and even more that cannot be answered exactly. There is nothing shameful in that admission. (Lewontin, 1995b, p. 44)

Lewontin's argument must be taken seriously by sociologists. There are indeed limits on how much sociologists can learn about human behavior, and random sample surveys and statistical analyses can't surmount these limits. For some problems, sociologists might be better off abandoning surveys and turning to the kind of intensive, long-term field observations that anthropologists and some sociologists do—even though the findings from field studies aren't necessarily representative of the population under study.

Does it follow that we should reject all findings from the study of sexual behavior because it is likely that men exaggerated, or women understated, their number of partners? This is a matter of judgment. My answer would be no. For one thing, comparisons among different groups represented in the 1992 and 2006–2008 samples are likely to be valid even if the individual responses aren't entirely accurate.

In addition, survey researchers have developed a better technique for asking about sensitive topics—the audio computer-assisted self-interview. Interviewees are given a laptop and provided with earphones. They see and hear questions that no one else in the room can see or hear. They respond merely by pressing number keys on the laptop, as instructed by the program. Studies have shown that this technique raises substantially the reported rates of injection drug usage, violent behavior, risky sex, and abortion (Turner, Forsyth et al., 1998; Turner, Ku et al., 1998). This technique was used in the 2006–2008 national survey. It is an improvement, but its very success confirms that older surveys probably did underestimate sensitive behavior.

We should be wary of pushing survey research techniques beyond the limit of their usefulness. The sex surveys press on that limit. The more sensitive the material and the more subjective the questions, the more skeptical readers should be. Nevertheless, we needn't dismiss the contributions of survey research to understanding sensitive issues. We should seek to supplement surveys with other, more intensive forms of data gathering. And we should recognize that there may be some questions about society that are beyond the capability of sociology to answer.

Ask Yourself

1. If you were asked to participate in a study of college students' sexual behavior, would you answer all the questions truthfully? Would you participate in the study?

2. Why is knowing about people's sexual behavior and attitudes important? Give a specific example.

www.mhhe.com/cherlin7e

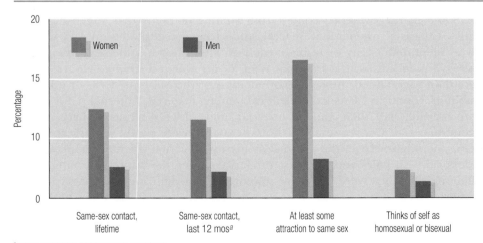

Percentage

Same-sex contact, lifetime
Same-sex contact, last 12 mos[a]
At least some attraction to same sex
Thinks of self as homosexual or bisexual

[a] 2002 and 2006–2008 surveys combined

FIGURE 6.1
Prevalence of four measures of same-sex sexual activity, women and men, aged 15 to 44 (sexual contact) and 18 to 44 (sexual orientation and attraction), in the United States, 2006–2008. (*Source:* U.S. National Center for Health Statistics, 2011c)

that 16.7 percent of women reported at least some attraction to the same sex (in other words, they did *not* choose "only attracted to males"), compared to 6.5 percent of men. The last set of bars shows responses to a question on sexual identity: "Do you think of yourself as . . . Heterosexual, Homosexual, Bisexual, or Something else?" Among women 4.6 percent chose homosexual or bisexual, and among men 3.8 percent did. Women were more likely to choose bisexual (2.8 percent) than homosexual, while men were more likely to choose homosexual (1.7 percent) than bisexual.

The NSFG survey, therefore, shows that the percentage of Americans who think of themselves as homosexual or bisexual is lower than the percentages who have ever had a same-sex sexual experience or who find same-sex activity at least somewhat appealing. Its findings confirm Kinsey's claim that sexual orientation is multidimensional and that no single number can adequately represent its prevalence. (Nevertheless, all the relevant percentages in the NSFG survey are considerably lower than comparable percentages reported by Kinsey in 1948.) This conclusion suggests that there is no clear dividing line between heterosexuality and homosexuality and that the distinction is at least in part socially created. In addition, the NSFG suggests that women's sexual identities may be more fluid than men's: More women find same-sex experiences at least somewhat attractive and more describe themselves as bisexual than homosexual.

The Integrative Perspective   Does biology also play a role in people's sexual identities? Almost no sociologists take the position that human sexuality is entirely driven by genes and hormones. However, some sociologists (I am one of them) take what Schwartz and Rutter (1998) call the **integrative perspective** on human sexuality: They argue that it is influenced by both social and biological factors. They would claim that while the social construction of sexual identities is very important, people may also be born with a sexual nature—a tendency to be attracted to partners of the opposite or the same gender. These sociologists reject the argument that genes and hormones have no influence on sexuality just because some societies have in-between genders and because the boundaries between the orientations are unclear. They note the evidence of biological influences on heterosexual and homosexual orientation.

Some of the evidence comes from studies of twins that suggest genetic links to sexual orientation. Several studies have recruited men and women who identified as gay or lesbian, each of whom had a same-sex sibling who was an identical twin, a fraternal twin, or an adopted sibling. The researchers then ascertained the sexual orientation of the subjects' twin or adoptive siblings. Identical twins have identical genetic material; fraternal twins share, on average, half their genetic material; and adopted siblings share no genetic material. Consequently, if homosexuality were partly biological in origin, one might expect the greatest similarity of sexual orientation among the identical-twin pairs and the least similarity among the adoptive-sibling pairs. If homosexuality were not at all biological in origin, one might expect no difference in the similarity of sexual orientation among the three groups of siblings, since both siblings in every pair had been raised in the same home by the same parents. In one such study, the authors found that, among the men, 52 percent of the identical twins, 22 percent of the fraternal twins, and 11 percent of the adoptive brothers were homosexual, which supports the

integrative perspective (on sexuality) the belief that human sexual identities are determined by both social and biological factors

Like this crowd dancing at a gay pride celebration, more men and women are living an openly gay or lesbian lifestyle today than a half-century ago.

biological model (Bailey & Pillard, 1991). Similarly, among the women, 48 percent of the identical twins, 16 percent of the fraternal twins, and 6 percent of the adoptive sisters were homosexual (Bailey, Pillard, Neal, & Agyei, 1993). A review of these sibling studies concluded that there are "almost certainly" genetic influences on sexual orientation for men, although it is "somewhat less certainly so" for women (Bailey & Dawood, 1998).

These studies, however, also show that sexual orientation is *not* completely genetically determined. After all, about half the identical twin pairs—who shared the same genetic material—had different sexual orientations in the studies cited above. Something about the twins' environments may influence them differently. As is the case with gender differences, any biological effects probably operate not by determining a person's sexual orientation but rather by creating predispositions toward one orientation or the other. Social and cultural factors then further influence sexual orientation. But unlike gender differences—where substantial evidence exists of the different treatment boys and girls receive from parents, peers, schools, and the like—there is little evidence that parents or peers treat children who will grow up to be gay or lesbian differently than they do other children. Moreover, the general failure of psychiatrists and psychologists to change the sexual orientation of gay and lesbian clients who wish to do so has undermined the credibility of the psychoanalytic explanation for homosexuality, which emphasizes unresolved issues of identification with one's parents (Haldeman, 1991). Nor is there much evidence that children and adolescents learn homosexual behavior from adults. So, although social and cultural factors quite likely play a role in sexual orientation, no satisfactory theories have been advanced to explain their role.

The biological studies have been controversial, in large part because of their political implications. Some observers argue that if homosexuality is not a lifestyle choice but rather an inherent, immutable part of an individual's personality, there is little justification for restricting the legal rights of gay men and lesbians. Other gay advocates argue that the studies are less consequential because civil rights should not depend on whether a person's style of life is cultural or biological in origin. And some opponents of legal rights for homosexuals, noting that there is evidence of biological influences on behaviors such as alcoholism, argue that a person needn't give in to biological predispositions if they are undesirable or objectionable to others. The issue of whether homosexuality is at least partly based in biology has resurfaced in current debates about same-sex marriage. People who think that sexual orientation has a biological basis and is not a matter of personal choice are more likely to support same-sex marriage. In a 2003 national survey, 55 percent of those who agreed that homosexuality is something people are born with favored same-sex marriage, compared to 21 percent of those who think it is just the way some people prefer to live (Pew Forum on Religion and Public Life, 2003).

To be sure, research into the biological origins of sexual orientation need not have political significance. Rather, its purpose could be the same as that of most of the research discussed in this book—to increase our understanding of why people behave as they do in their family and personal lives. The great variation from society to society in the ways that sexual orientation is structured—the two-spirit tradition, the acceptance of homosexual relations among the ancient Greeks and Romans, the mental illness model of the United States in the first half of the twentieth century, the recent emergence of an open lesbian and gay subculture—shows that social forces are an important part of the explanation for the behaviors and attitudes that emerge. But it seems likely that biological forces are also part of the story.

Points of Agreement and Disagreement   In sum, almost all sociologists agree that the type of society a person lives in influences such characteristics as whether individuals become exclusively heterosexual or homosexual, what social groups they draw their partners from, and what range of sexual acts they undertake. The main disagreement, then, between partisans of the social constructionist and integrative perspectives is whether society *completely* determines sexual identities. The former group would say that the influence of biology is minimal, whereas the latter group would say that both society and biology matter.

Quick Review

- Some sociologists believe that sexual identity is entirely socially created; they cite variations over time and from society to society.
- Surveys suggest that a substantial number of people have some homoerotic feelings but a smaller percentage are exclusively homosexual.
- Other sociologists believe that both biological and social factors determine sexual identities; they point to studies of twins, ordinary siblings, and adopted siblings.

QUESTIONING SEXUAL IDENTITIES

Over the past decade or so, a newer perspective has emerged which questions the whole idea of fixed, stable sexual identities. Whereas the older literature focused on questions such as the extent to which a person's gay or lesbian identity is socially constructed, the newer literature focuses on whether it is meaningful to speak of a gay, lesbian, or heterosexual identity at all. In reality, the newer perspective says, such identities are always shifting, unstable, and arbitrary. There are many kinds of "gay identities," the writers argue, including the resident in a "gay" neighborhood who openly lives with a partner; the business executive who restricts his social life to weekends; and the married suburbanite who occasionally and furtively has sex with men. Because of this diversity, it is argued, you cannot simply label someone as gay (or straight). To use these labels is to buy into a system in which heterosexuals regulate everyone's sexual behavior along rigid and constraining lines. Instead, sociologists are urged to examine the entire system by which we classify people's sexual lives in a way that privileges the people we call heterosexual and puts the rest at a disadvantage.

Queer Theory   The name that the advocates of this point of view, who span cultural studies, comparative literature, history, sociology, and other disciplines, have chosen for their perspective is "queer theory" (Seidman, 1996; Gamson & Moon, 2004). By deliberately choosing a term that until recently, at least, was offensive and derogatory, the writers suggest a challenge to the conventional understanding of sexuality. **Queer theory** is not a formal, scientific theory but rather a critical standpoint (Green, 2002). Its essence is the view that sexual life is artificially organized into categories that reflect the power of heterosexual norms. These norms restrict the possibilities for a more fluid, changing sexual identity in order to protect the dominance of heterosexuality as it is currently organized. Queer theorists reject a sharp split of sexual activity into either a heterosexual or homosexual way of life. Some of them even reject the subdiscipline of gay and lesbian studies, arguing that to accept these categories as the starting point is to accept what must be questioned: the restrictive organization of sexuality (Gamson, 1996).

queer theory the view that sexual life is artificially organized into categories that reflect the power of heterosexual norms

The queer theorists suggest studying how this organization came about and how it is maintained. They reject the view that there are any biological influences on the organization of sexuality. Rather, scholars (e.g., Butler, 1990) argue that we unconsciously re-create heterosexual "masculinity" and "femininity" in everyday interactions. In other words, we "do sexuality" in a way that is similar to how the interactionists say we "do gender." Without this daily reinforcement, it is said, our sexual categories would be less rigid and more subject to change. Just as some feminist theorists say that gender distinctions are problematic, so do queer theorists say that distinctions on the basis of sexuality are problematic.

Strengths and Limitations   One does not have to agree with all the claims of queer theory to appreciate the point that the labels we attach to people—she's a lesbian, he's straight—are complex social constructions that give social advantages to the straights and create disadvantages for the lesbians and gay men. For instance, straights can marry and receive many legal protections and rights that gays cannot obtain. Queer theorists and many other Americans believe these inequalities to be oppressive; other Americans believe they are morally justified. But what this perspective reminds us is that these inequalities, whether justifiable or not, were consciously created rather than being "natural." Americans had to create a body of family law, for example, that allows a man with the legal status of "married" to visit his dying wife in the hospital but may prevent a gay man with the legal status of "single" from visiting his dying partner.

One must also agree that the boundaries of sexual identities are more fluid than people ordinarily think. Queer theory contributes the insight that a rigid split between heterosexual and homosexual is not "natural" but rather reflects prevailing heterosexual norms in our society. Nevertheless, many observers (I am one) think that in its rejection of the concept of sexual identity, queer theory goes too far. Because the boundaries of concepts are unclear doesn't mean that the concepts are invalid. After all, the boundaries of "class," "gender," and "race" are all unclear, yet rare is the sociologist who doesn't use any of these concepts.

Moreover, in rejecting the utility of studying gays and lesbians as such, queer theory restricts our ability to understand important aspects of American society. Topics such as whether and how a gay person can be a parent, whether marriage ought to be extended to same-sex couples, how gays and lesbians create networks of friends and relatives they call family, and so forth, should be studied because they represent issues with real consequences for the lives of Americans today. Perhaps these topics reflect an unequal distribution of power, but they are no less consequential because of it. To be sure, the identities of gay and lesbian are socially constructed at least in part; but, as a critic of queer theory writes, these constructions still "may exhibit an extraordinary capacity to shape identities, sexual interactions, social movements, and political histories as a whole" (Green, 2002, p. 528). Consequently, I will use the categories of heterosexual, gay, and lesbian in this book.

Quick Review

- Queer theorists claim that sexual identities are always unstable and arbitrary.
- They argue that we should reject the concept of sexual identities as meaningful, fixed categories.
- They urge instead that we study the ways in which conventional sexual identities are organized according to norms that privilege heterosexuals.
- Their rejection of sexual identities, however, makes it difficult to study important social issues involving gay men and lesbians.

New Families and Beyond?

Americans are becoming more accepting of families formed by same-sex partners and their children. In a 2010 national survey of adults who were asked whether various living arrangements constituted families, 64 percent responded that a "same-sex couple with children" was a family. When they were asked about a same-sex couple without children, just 44 percent said that the couple was a family; but then again only 43 percent said that a *heterosexual* couple without children was a family (Pew Research Center, 2011b). The general principle that seems to be emerging is that either marriage or the presence of children qualifies a couple to count as a family, regardless of the sexual orientation of the couple. Not everyone takes this position, but even the opinions of Americans who exclude same-sex couples seem to be in transition. In a similar survey done in the mid-2000s, for instance, many of the respondents who said that same-sex couples with children were not a family expressed ambivalence about their opinions. One woman said, "I don't know. I'm still working on this for myself, and I still don't have one answer . . . We're not adamant against it [same-sex couples], but like I said, I mean, process is changing. If you call me next year, I might change my mind" (Powell, Bolzendahl, Geist, & Steelman, 2010, p. 207).

BEYOND THE FAMILY?

But some sociologists are urging that we adopt an even broader view of what constitutes a family. In fact, some are questioning the usefulness of the very concept of family itself, even if it is used in the plural form "families" to acknowledge diversity. They argue that emerging forms of sexual and other close relationships stretch the boundaries of "families" so far that the concept becomes inadequate for understanding them (Budgeon & Roseneil, 2004; Roseneil & Budgeon, 2004). They advocate more inclusive terms such as "personal communities" (Pahl & Spencer, 2004) or "personal life" (Smart, 2007). For example, an unmarried, childless individual may maintain a personal community of close friends, brothers and sisters, and co-workers who provide her with support and comfort. This personal community, it is argued, should not be any less privileged in our values and laws than more conventional marriage-and-partnership-based families. To be sure, these claims would push most Americans well beyond their comfort zone in thinking about families. They certainly push beyond my definition of the private family in Chapter 1, which included the requirements that family members usually live in the same household and pool their incomes and household labor. Yet the idea of supportive, unconventional communities is not that far from some of the support networks of low-income single mothers in poor neighborhoods.

Let's examine two types of personal communities that extend over more than one household. One type is the network of friends and relatives that gay men and lesbians sometimes construct for intimacy and care. Another is the living arrangements of couples who have the kinds of committed, intimate relationships that cohabiting or married couples have but who choose, or are forced, to live in different households.

NETWORKS OF FRIENDS

Some lesbians and gay men use the term "family" to describe their close relationships, but they mean something different from the standard, marriage-based family. Rather, they often refer to what sociologists have called a **family of choice:** one that is formed largely though voluntary ties among individuals who are not biologically or legally related (Weston, 1991; Weeks et al., 2001). That is to say, lesbians and gay men, who cannot marry in most jurisdictions and who may have little contact with parents or siblings who do not accept their sexuality, must actively construct their families. Networks of friends and cohabiting partnerships are central to these constructed families. In fact, friends may be more central to your family than a partner because of the high likelihood that you and your partner will eventually dissolve your union. The families that Weston (1991) studied consisted fundamentally of networks of friends and lovers who provided social and emotional support for one another. Similarly, Weeks et al. (2001), in a study of the intimate lives of 96 lesbian and gay individuals in Britain, noted the frequent use of the term "family" to refer to a more or less stable group of people who served as a support network for one another.

family of choice a family formed through voluntary ties among individuals who are not biologically or legally related

In some respects, these families of choice are similar to the kin networks found among the poor or to the complex families formed after divorce and remarriage (as we will see in Chapters 12 and 13). Yet the largely friendship-based family networks may be even more important to lesbians and gay men than to heterosexuals because lesbians and gay men often cannot rely on their biological and legal relatives to the extent that heterosexuals can. What gay people must do is create a family from the relationships they can retain with biological kin, the close friends they have, and their partners. One person told Weston, "Gay people really have to work to make family" (Weston, 1991). The families woven together by lesbians and gay men are another example of created kinship—the kind of kinship that people must work to construct. In practice, these families of choice are often complex and frequently do involve relatives as well as friends. But even the ties with relatives are in some sense created, as gays and lesbians include only those family members with whom they feel comfortable and enjoy spending time. In this way, the families of choice blur the boundaries between relatives and friends, as relatives become more like friends to the person at the center of the network, while close friends become more like relatives (Pahl & Spencer, 2004).

Most research on lesbians' and gay men's personal communities is based on studies of white, prosperous individuals in major urban areas. Carrington (1999) studied both "upper-middle-class" and "lower-middle-class" gay and lesbian couples and found that extensive, friendship-based families of choice were more common among the upper-middle-class couples. The reason is that maintaining large friendship-based families takes time and money. Couples with better-paying, more flexible jobs could more easily arrange social events and spend more on entertaining, travel, long-distance calls, and presents. Carrington found, in contrast, that less affluent couples often described themselves as isolated. In addition, African American, Latino, and Asian couples had less extensive friendship networks and were more likely to rely on biological kin. This study suggests that substantial class and racial-ethnic variation exists in the ways that lesbians and gay men organize their personal communities.

LIVING APART TOGETHER

The second challenge to the household-based idea of family comes from heterosexual and gay couples who are carrying on cohabitation or marriagelike relationships, who define themselves as couples, but who live in separate households. The phenomenon was first noted in Europe and became known as **living apart together,** or LAT (Levin, 2004; Castro-Martin, Domínguez-Folgueras, & Martín-García, 2008). Reports from national statistical agencies in Britain and Canada suggest that LAT relationships are relatively common, but they also suggest how difficult it is to conceptualize and measure the phenomenon. In 1996 and 1998, the General Social Survey asked a sample of Americans this question if they were not married: "Do you have a main romantic involvement—a (man/woman) you think of as a steady, a lover, a partner, or whatever?" And if they said yes, they were asked if they lived with that partner. Seven percent of women and six percent of men aged 23 to 70 said that they had a heterosexual partner but did not live with that person (Strohm et al., 2008). The Canadian statistical agency

living apart together
a relationship in which two people define themselves as a couple but do not live together

asked a briefer question, "Are you in an intimate relationship with someone who lives in a separate household?" and reported that 8 percent of Canadians 20 and over, and 56 percent of Canadians in their twenties, said yes (Milan & Peters, 2003). Yet both of these questions may be so broad that they capture conventional steady relationships as well as mature separate-residence unions.

There are two types of LAT relationships, those in which the partners live apart because of a constraint and those in which they live apart by choice (Levin, 2004). One of the constraints is children from previous relationships; researchers have uncovered many LAT couples in which one or both is raising children from a previous relationship and prefers not to alter the household. A divorced mother who cares for her children during the week may prefer to live apart from her partner and then spend time with him when her ex-husband has the children on the weekends. In the Canadian survey, 23 percent of the women in LAT relationships were living with children (Milan & Peters, 2003). Another constraint occurs when the couple would prefer to live together but each partner has a good job which he or she does not wish to give up, even though the jobs are in different cities.

Other LAT couples may live apart by choice because they prefer to be more independent of each other. One Swedish couple with two children saw their relationship deteriorating but still loved each other. They sold their house and bought two apartments a few minutes' walk from one another. The children stayed with the mother but spent time at their father's apartment, and he spent a good deal of time at the mother's apartment. They viewed this move as saving their relationship (Levin, 2004). Other individuals in LAT relationships include people who have previously divorced and are hesitant to move in with a partner for fear of experiencing a second disruption.

To some extent, an LAT relationship may be a stage in an individual's life course. In both the Canadian and British studies, LAT relationships were more common among people in their twenties than among older people. One's twenties is the period of "early adulthood," the emerging life stage in which some individuals are not fully taking on adult roles. As people age out of that stage, the chances may increase that they will live with their partners. During their twenties, early adults may be obtaining advanced education or working long hours at entry-level positions such as an associate at a law firm—situations they may see as incompatible with a living-together relationship. About half of the Canadians in LAT relationships expected to live with their partners at a future time (Milan & Peters, 2003), suggesting that some individuals will transition out of an LAT relationship and into a living-together one.

In fact, the line between living apart and living together may be so fuzzy that the partners themselves may not be sure whether they are living together. In a study of moderate-income early adults in the Toledo, Ohio, area who had cohabited, two sociologists found that it was not always easy to determine when a cohabiting relationship began (Manning & Smock, 2005). For half the individuals, living together was not a deliberate decision but more of a "slide" into cohabitation: "Respondents say, 'it wasn't planned,' 'it just snuck up on me,' or 'it just happened'" (p. 996). People with separate residences may gradually spend more and more time together, and they may keep their residences for a while even after they are cohabiting full-time.

BLURRED BOUNDARIES

As all of these studies suggest, the personal communities being constructed today often blur the boundaries between relatives and friends, between living together and living apart, and between being part of a family and not being part of one. Moreover, these personal communities are fluid, with people moving into and out of various relationships over the life course. The flexibility of these new arrangements allows people to construct ways of obtaining intimacy and of giving and receiving care that fit their particular preferences and constraints at a particular point in their lives. These arrangements can be used by gay men and lesbians whose options for building a conventional family are limited. They can be used by heterosexuals who, due to either constraints or preferences, would like intimacy and care without coresidence.

Because these arrangements are based on voluntary participation, however, they are also less stable than institutionalized family forms such as marriage. A person can withdraw from a network of close friends or an LAT relationship at any time. To some, this easy exit may be a further advantage of the new arrangements. But instability can undermine the hard work of building a personal community or investing in a shared partnership. "There's a way of doing it gay," another person remarked to Weston about building familylike ties, "but it's a whole lot harder, and it's less secure" (Weston, 1991). Moreover, instability can be a problem for children, who, as we will see in Chapter 12, may be at higher risk for developmental problems if they live in unstable families. For that reason, flexible networks may better suit the needs of adults than the needs of children. In fact, the focus of the literature that questions the idea of family is almost entirely on adult relationships. Two such theorists, for example, criticize the sociologies of family and gender for being "overwhelmingly focused" on relationships "which have produced children, and on changes within these relationships" (Roseneil & Budgeon, 2004). But there is a reason for that focus: Children are a public good. How they are being raised is an important public issue that the queer theorists and personal communities literatures avoid (but gay and lesbian studies address, as we will see when we consider gay parenthood in Chapter 9).

Do couples in LAT relationships or networks of friends constitute families? The LAT couples are at the margin of the private family as I defined it in Chapter 1, where I said that such families "usually" live in the same household; LAT families don't. The network-based families of choice do not fit my definition of the private family. Of course, if either form includes adults who are actively raising children together, they fit the definition of the public family. But in any case, the main lesson of these new arrangements is that the boundaries of the category "families" are becoming fluid and blurred, much as the boundaries between sexual identities are becoming blurred. And many people move across the boundaries at various points in their lives. This does not imply that family is a "zombie category"—a walking corpse—as two theorists of postmodernity have alleged (Beck & Beck-Gernsheim, 2002). But it does suggest that the category has limitations and needs to be supplemented with other perspectives as new forms of sexual relationships and caring arrangements are formed.

Quick Review

- New living arrangements are challenging the conventional definitions of what constitutes a family.
- Lesbians and gay men construct families of choice from partners, friends, and some relatives.
- Some partners view themselves as a couple and yet live apart in what is called living-apart-together (LAT) relationships.
- These arrangements blur the boundaries between family living and nonfamily living.

■ Marital and Nonmarital Sexuality

Neither LAT relationships nor same-sex or opposite-sex cohabiting partner-ships would be so common without the increasing acceptability of sexual activity outside of marriage in the United States. To understand that story, we need to step back a bit. There have been three eras in the attitudes toward sexuality and love in the United States. Before about 1890, sexual attraction and romantic love were thought to be inappropriate bases for choosing a spouse. Rather, one chose a spouse for practical reasons such as the abil-ity to manage a farm or run a household. Moreover, even within marriage, sexual expression was thought to be an activity best done in moderation. From about 1890 to about 1960, in contrast, sexual attraction and romantic love were increasingly viewed as not only appropriate but, in fact, crucial criteria. Within marriage, people increasingly valued the emotional fulfillment they could obtain through sex and romantic love. The idea of a sexual iden-tity, based on one's attitudes and practices, passed into common usage. Still, sexual expression outside marriage continued to be seen as illicit.

Since the 1960s, the positive value given to sexual expression and grati-fication has continued and even increased. In addition, sexual activity has become defined even more as a private matter. In 1965, for example, the Supreme Court ruled that a state law prohibiting the use of contraceptives violated marital privacy by allowing police to search the "sacred precincts of marital bedrooms" (*Griswold* v. *Connecticut,* 1965). In 1972, the Court, using similar reasoning, overturned laws prohibiting the sale of contraceptives to unmarried persons (*Eisenstadt* v. *Baird,* 1972). The rationale for these laws had been that sexual activity was carried out in order to have children and that the state had an interest in seeing that married couples did, in fact, have children and that unmarried persons did not. In this way, the state could pro-mote and control the reproduction of the population. By the time of these court decisions, however, sex had become primarily a means of individual fulfillment. Therefore, the rationale for state intervention had weakened.

This changing view of sexual activity is part of the broader growth of indi-vidualism during the twentieth century. In the post-1960 era, cultural changes were spurred, in part, by the increasing economic independence of women, which made it possible for young adult women to postpone marriage without postponing intimate sexual relationships. In turn, young men were able to ini-tiate sexual relationships with women without making a commitment to sup-port them. (Women's economic independence will be discussed in more detail in Chapter 8.) The changes in sexual behavior were also guided greatly by the availability of more effective means of contraception, notably the birth control pill.

NONMARITAL SEXUAL ACTIVITY

Within marriage, the changes have increased the possibility of mutually and personally fulfilling sexual relations. Yet as the idea of sex for personal pleasure spread during the twentieth century, the rationale for restricting sex to married couples weakened. Through the 1950s, moralists were successful in limiting sexual intercourse to engaged or married persons, especially among middle-class women. But beginning in the late 1960s, sexual activity prior to marriage rose to unprecedented levels. Moreover, in the 1970s, unmarried, middle-class young adults began to live together openly, a previously unheard-of arrangement except among the poor. Rates of cohabitation rose so high that more than half of young adults today are likely to live with a partner before marrying.[2]

Among women who had entered adulthood in the 1950s, two-thirds had had only one partner. Clearly, having sex just with one's husband was the norm. Only a daring few had many sex partners: 3 percent reported five or more (Laumann et al., 1994). In fact, although there are few numbers in the historical record, virtually every historical study suggests that through the 1950s, a majority of American women had their first intercourse only after they were engaged to be married (Rothman, 1984). Women's sexual needs still were thought to be less than men's, and women were still seen as the guardians of virtue—which in this case meant abstinence until marriage. Yet among women who entered adulthood in the 1960s, just 46 percent reported only one partner by age 30; and 18 percent reported five or more. The proportion reporting only one partner by age 30 fell further to 36 percent among women who entered adulthood in the 1970s, whereas the proportion reporting five or more rose to 22 percent.

The changes over time have been less dramatic for men, for whom the sexual double standard always allowed more nonmarital sexual activity than it allowed women. Still, the double standard has now disappeared. Figure 6.2 shows the number of opposite-sex sexual partners in the past 12 months

FIGURE 6.2

Number of opposite-sex sexual partners in the past 12 months, for never-married, noncohabiting women and men, ages 15 to 44, in the United States, 2002 and 2006–2008. (*Source:* U.S. National Center for Health Statistics, 2011c)

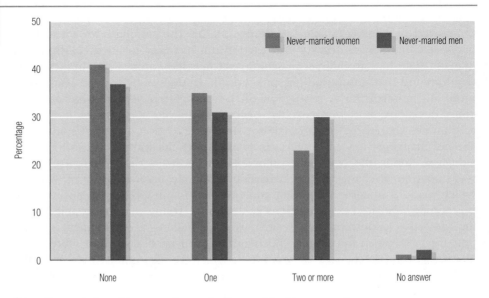

[2] See Chapter 7 for evidence on the trends discussed in this paragraph.

Sexual activity prior to marriage rose greatly in the late 1960s and the 1970s.

reported by never-married, noncohabiting women and men in the 2002 and 2006–2008 NSFG surveys. Under the old double standard, we would expect that far more women than men would report having had no sex partners; but the percentage reporting no partners is only slightly higher for women than for men (although men were more likely to report having had two or more partners).

MARITAL AND EXTRAMARITAL SEX

Given the increases in sexual activity outside marriage, you might expect that married persons would be increasingly likely to have **extramarital sex.** Indeed, some authors have suggested that marital relationships could coexist with, and perhaps even be enriched by, extramarital affairs (Kipnis, 2003). Yet **sexual monogamy**—having just one sex partner—is still the rule rather than the exception among married persons. Consider trends in public opinion. There is no doubt that the American public has become more tolerant of sexual activity among persons who have not yet (and may never be) married. Almost every year since 1972, the General Social Survey, or GSS, an annual or biennial national survey of American adults, has asked people their opinions about both premarital and extramarital sex. Between 1972 and 2008, the proportion who agreed that *premarital* sex was "always wrong" or "almost always wrong" declined from 48 percent to 33 percent. During the same period, however, the proportion agreeing that *extramarital* sex was "always wrong" or "almost always wrong" increased from 84 to 93 percent.[3] Moreover, according to the NSFG 2002 and 2006–2008 surveys, 94 percent of currently married men and

extramarital sex sexual activity by a married person with someone other than his or her spouse

sexual monogamy the state of having just one sex partner

---

[3] The question on extramarital sex was first asked in 1973; for both questions I have excluded "Don't know" and "No answer" responses (Davis & Smith, 2010).

97 percent of currently married women said that they had had no sex partners other than their spouses during the previous 12 months (U.S. National Center for Health Statistics, 2011x). Clearly, most married couples adhere to the norm of monogamy almost all the time.

Adolescent Sexuality and Pregnancy

One consequence of the cultural changes in sexuality is the rise in childbearing outside of marriage. Starting in the mid-1960s, young adults' sexual lives changed in two ways. First, having sexual intercourse prior to marriage, often many years before, became common. Figure 6.3 displays the findings of a series of national surveys of unmarried adolescent girls, aged 15 to 19, since 1971 and of boys the same ages since 1988. The percentage who had ever had sexual intercourse rose sharply during the 1970s and then peaked in the late 1980s. Second, in the half-century between the mid-1950s and the mid-2000s, the age at which half of all first marriages occurred rose by nearly five years for men and women (U.S. Bureau of the Census, 2008s). Consequently, far more young women and men remain single throughout late adolescence and early adulthood. The combination of earlier sexual activity and later marriage has lengthened the stage of life when young adults can have a child outside of marriage.

CHANGES IN SEXUAL BEHAVIOR

Adolescent sexual activity, however, declined sharply in the 1990s and 2000s, particularly for boys, as shown in Figure 6.3. In 1988 never-married adolescent boys were more likely to have had sexual intercourse (60 percent) than were comparable girls (51 percent), reflecting a long-standing pattern (Darling, Kallen, & VanDusen, 1984). But by the 2006–2010 period, there was virtually no difference between boys (42 percent) and girls (43 percent). Class and racial differences in premarital sexual activity were also smaller at the end

FIGURE 6.3
Number of 15- to 19-year-olds who have ever had sexual intercourse, 1971–2010 for girls, 1988–2010 for boys, in the United States. (*Sources:* U.S. National Research Council, 1987; and U.S. National Center for Health Statistics, 2011d . For 1971–1982, percentages are for girls residing in metropolitan areas only. However, the 1982 percentage, which is available for both the U.S. and metropolitan areas, is nearly identical.)

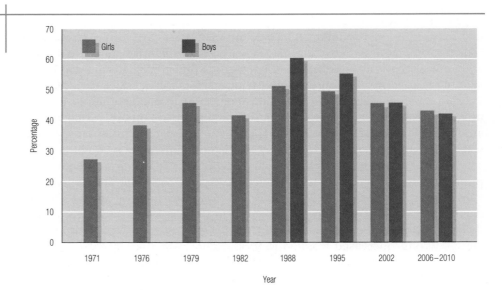

of the century because the rise in adolescent sexual activity had been greater among the middle class than among the poor, more noticeably among whites than among blacks (Forrest & Singh, 1990).

Summing up these trends:

- Adolescent sexual activity is more common today than it was in the middle of the twentieth century, although it declined in the 1990s and 2000s.
- The historical difference in the sexual activity of adolescent boys and girls has disappeared.
- The increases in adolescent sexual activity have been greater for the middle class and whites than for other groups, although sexual activity is still more common among the poor and African Americans.

Yet even with the declines that have occurred since the 1990s, adolescent sexual activity still was much more widespread than it had been at midcentury, especially for girls. Coupled with a rising age at marriage, this increase in sexual activity among adolescents led to a greater proportion of teenage pregnancies and births outside marriage.

THE TEENAGE PREGNANCY "PROBLEM"

Most people have read or heard something about the teenage pregnancy "problem," but few people have a good understanding of exactly what the problem is. About 750,000 15- to 19-year-old women in the United States become pregnant each year. About 40 percent of these pregnancies are ended by an abortion or a miscarriage, leaving about 450,000 births (Alan Guttmacher Institute, 2011). Despite widespread talk about an "epidemic" of teenage childbearing, this is a lower number of births than was the case 10 or 20 years ago. In fact, the birthrate for teenage girls is at an all-time low (Child Trends, 2011). That is to say, the probability that a teenage girl will have a baby in a given year is lower than at any time since the federal government began to keep statistics in the 1940s.

Then what is the problem? Marriage, or rather the lack of it. Marriage among teenagers has decreased faster than birthrates have. A pregnant 18- or 19-year-old who got married in 1960 would have had plenty of company—31 percent of all 18- to 19-year-old women were married. But to marry at those ages today is to stand out: Just 4 percent of 18- to 19-year-old women were married in 2010 (U.S. Bureau of the Census, 2011b). As sexual activity among unmarried teenagers increased and as the proportion of teenagers of all races who were unmarried rose, the consequence was a sharp rise in the proportion who were risking a pregnancy outside marriage. Teenagers can lower that risk by using contraceptives more effectively; and, as noted, contraceptive usage has indeed increased among teenagers. But over the long run, the increased use of contraceptives has merely kept pace with the increasing numbers of unmarried teenagers who are sexually active. Consequently, the **nonmarital birth ratio**—the proportion of all births that occur to unmarried women—has increased sharply for teenagers, even though the *birthrate*—the probability that a teenager (married or not) will have a birth—has declined. For example, in 1970 the nonmarital birth ratio for 15- to 19-year-olds was less than one out of three; by 2002 it had risen to

nonmarital birth ratio
the proportion of all births that occur to unmarried women

The teenage birthrate has been declining, but the proportion of teenage mothers who are unmarried has been increasing.

more than five out of six (U.S. National Center for Health Statistics, 2009). The increased ratio is the source of public concern.

THE CONSEQUENCES FOR TEENAGE MOTHERS

Despite support from their parents and other kin, adolescents who bear children appear worse off later in life, on average, than adolescents who wait until their twenties to begin having children. Teenage mothers complete fewer years of schooling, have jobs that pay less, are more likely to be dependent on public assistance payments, and are less likely to have stable marriages. The more difficult issue to resolve is whether these differences are due to having a child as a teenager per se or to the kinds of impoverished backgrounds common among teenage mothers. It may be that having a baby as a teenager poses few penalties for young women who are already poor, because they are likely to remain poor regardless of whether they bear children or not. This latter point is an example of a **selection effect,** the principle that whenever individuals sort, or "select," themselves into groups nonrandomly, some of

selection effect
the principle that whenever individuals sort, or "select," themselves into groups nonrandomly, some of the differences among the groups reflect preexisting differences among the individuals

the differences among the groups reflect preexisting differences among the individuals. Selection effects frequently complicate the interpretation of data that sociologists collect.

For example, suppose we want to know whether teenage mothers grow up to be poor at a higher rate because of the effects of (1) having a child as a teenager or (2) coming from low-income families. To truly settle this issue, a truth-seeking but cold-blooded social scientist would want to conduct the following experiment: Obtain a list of all families with teenage girls in the United States and then assign at random some of the girls to have children and others to remain childless until their twenties. Because of the random assignment, teenage childbearing would be about as likely to occur in middle-class families as in poor families. In this way, the social scientist could eliminate family background as a cause of any differences that emerge between teenage mothers and nonmothers.

In the real world, of course, teenage pregnancies don't occur randomly; rather, they are more likely to occur in families that were poor before the teenager gave birth. The teenage childbearers are self-selected, in a sense, from less-fortunate families. It is very difficult to separate out the selection effect of family background from the true effect of having the baby per se. Recent studies suggest that some of the apparent effect of teenage childbearing is indeed a selection effect—in other words, teenage mothers probably would grow up to have somewhat lower incomes even if they had waited until after age 19 to have children (Geronimus, 1991; Geronimus & Korenman, 1992; Hotz, McElroy, & Sanders, 1996). But some studies still suggest that the economic circumstances of teenage mothers remain worse after the selection effect is accounted for. For example, these young women may be less likely to graduate from high school and more likely to have reduced annual incomes as young adults (Fletcher & Wolfe, 2009). (See *Families and Public Policy:* The Rise and Fall of the Teenage Pregnancy Problem.)

Moreover, the life course of teenage mothers varies substantially. Some of those who drop out of school later return to school and obtain a high school diploma or its equivalent. In 1995 and 1996, Frank Furstenberg located and reinterviewed about 200 women who had been in a study of teenage mothers he had conducted 30 years earlier (Furstenberg, 1976). Only 51 percent of these women had graduated from high school by the time they were age 21, and few of the dropouts were in school. But by the 30-year reinterview, 80 percent had obtained a high school degree or its equivalent by taking classes as adults. Two-thirds were working full-time, and a majority were earning enough to be classified as working-class or middle-class (Furstenberg, 2007). They were not a prosperous group, but they were far better off than one would have predicted when they were teenage mothers. Furstenberg suggests that they might not be much better off today even if they had not given birth as teenagers.

To sum up what we know about teenage mothers:

- They are disadvantaged in education, income, and employment.
- Some, although probably not all, of their disadvantages are due to other factors in their lives, such as growing up in low-income families.
- There is much variation in the way their lives turn out.

Families and Public Policy

The Rise and Fall of the Teenage Pregnancy Problem

Teenage pregnancy returned to the news in 2008 when the public learned that Bristol Palin, the unmarried 17-year-old daughter of Republican Vice Presidential nominee Sarah Palin, was pregnant. After Bristol's baby Tripp was born in late December, the family released a statement welcoming the grandson but cautioning teenagers to avoid pregnancy. "Teenagers need to prevent pregnancy to begin with—this isn't ideal," the statement quoted Bristol as saying, "but I'm fortunate to have a supportive family which is dealing with this together." In the years since then, Bristol has become, through numerous speaking engagements and interviews, a well-known advocate for preventing teenage pregnancy.

In fact, family planning experts have been issuing warnings about teenage pregnancy for four decades. In the late 1960s, alarmed by the initial signs of a sharp rise in births to unmarried teenagers, government demographer Arthur Campbell famously warned:

The girl who has an illegitimate child at the age of 16 suddenly has 90 percent of her life's script written for her. She will probably drop out of school . . . she will probably not be able to find a steady job that pays enough to provide for her and her child. . . . Her life choices are few, and most of them are bad. (quoted in Ericksen & Steffen, 1999, p. 88)

What has happened to the teenage pregnancy problem, however, must have surprised Campbell. At first, as birthrates rose, and as surveys during the 1970s showed a worrisome rise in teenage sexual activity, the public became alarmed. Teenage pregnancy became a major social issue. Advocacy groups urged better contraception or less sexual activity, or both. But then came research suggesting that some of the problems faced by teenage mothers were really problems of poverty, not early motherhood, and might have occurred even if they had postponed childbearing until the teenage years were over. This is the so-called selectivity argument for why teenage mothers have difficulties, which I have discussed elsewhere in this section. A study that followed a group of teenage mothers for 30 years found some of them doing better than expected (Furstenberg, 2007). Perhaps not all of them had 90 percent of their life's scripts written.

As the controversy raged over whether teenage pregnancy was the root cause of young mothers' difficulties, another trend, unnoticed at first, got underway: The birthrates of teenage mothers began to decrease. In the 1990s and the 2000s, levels of sexual activity among teens

Quick Review

- Sexual activity among teenagers is much more common than it was prior to the 1970s.
- Both the birthrate and the marriage rate have been declining among teenagers.
- The proportion of teenage births that are to unmarried girls and women has increased.
- Some of the problems shown by teenage mothers reflect disadvantages they had prior to becoming pregnant.

Sexuality and Family Life

As recently as the 1950s, heterosexual marriage was the only morally-approved venue for sexual activity; and the only approved purpose of marital sex was to have children. Recall that prior to a 1965 Supreme Court ruling, a state could ban the sale of contraceptives entirely; and prior to a 1972 ruling, sales could be limited to married couples. Many individuals who would today come out as gay or lesbian entered into heterosexual marriages and had children in the mid-twentieth century because that was the only respectable way to have a family life. Living with a sexual partner, even of the opposite sex, without marrying was seen as shameful. Contraception was unreliable—the birth control pill was not widely used until the 1960s. The Kinsey Report

declined and the use of contraceptives increased. By the end of the 2000s, teenage birthrates had dropped to levels not seen in two decades (Child Trends, 2011). In contrast, births to unmarried women in their twenties rose sharply because women were postponing marriage but not postponing having children as much. Whereas in 1970 teenagers accounted for 50 percent of all nonmarital births, by 1999 they accounted for only 29 percent (U.S. National Center for Health Statistics, 2000). Some of the births to unmarried twenty-somethings were planned; in fact, an increasing share of them were to cohabiting couples, but a goodly number were unplanned or mistimed (Child Trends, 2001).

By the mid-2000s, the birthrates for unmarried women in their twenties far exceeded the birthrates for unmarried teens (U.S. National Center for Health Statistics, 2009). Organizations took note, and some began to reorient their activities. For instance, the National Campaign to Prevent Teen Pregnancy, which was founded in 1996 to work exclusively on decreasing teenage pregnancy, expanded its mission a decade later to include unwanted pregnancies among women in their twenties. Its leaders argued that teenage pregnancy was still a cause for concern, but that teenagers had made more progress in reducing unwanted pregnancies than had older women. They changed the name of the organization to the National Campaign to Prevent Teen and Unplanned Pregnancy.

In noting the decline in teenage births and the large share of nonmarital births to women in their twenties today, I do not mean to suggest that teenage pregnancy is benign or that we should ignore it. As Bristol Palin said, it is not ideal. Teenage birthrates are still higher in the United States than in nearly all other Western countries (Singh & Darroch, 2000). And teenage motherhood may somewhat lower the chances of graduating from high school and college and reduce economic well-being later in life. Teenagers would be better off if the rate fell further. Nevertheless, we can now see that teenage pregnancy is part of a larger problem of nonmarital, and sometimes unwanted, pregnancies among women and their partners, especially among low- and moderate-income families. It is this larger problem that more and more advocacy groups and researchers are now focusing on.

Ask Yourself

1. Do you know anyone who has given birth as a teenager? If so, how has her life turned out?

2. Does it make sense to broaden the focus of pregnancy prevention programs to include women in their twenties?

www.mhhe.com/cherlin7e

---

shocked Americans in 1948 because it suggested the unthinkable—that the expression of sexuality was more varied than the focus on heterosexual marriage suggested.

Over the past half century, the domain of sexuality—sexual activity, attraction, and orientation—has expanded far beyond heterosexual marriage. Sexual expression is much broader than in the past, and the variety of acceptable family living arrangements has greatly increased. Today, much that was shocking in the 1950s is commonplace: premarital sex, opposite-sex and same-sex cohabiting relationships, unmarried teenagers having children, single parenthood, gay and lesbian public identities, and so forth. This transformation is a mark of how diverse both sexual expression and family life have become. In fact, sexual activity outside of any family context (for example, sex between two non-partnered individuals) is now routine. And conversely, the idea that people can create a family without sexual relationships (for example, a personal community centered on close friends and siblings) is now being proposed. Still, sexuality remains a central focus of any analysis of what family life is like today.

As we come to terms with the great changes in sexuality and family life in the past half-century, social theorists are pushing us to consider new frontiers. The personal community theorists challenge us to broaden the scope of family ties beyond biology and marriage. Queer theorists challenge us to forgo the heterosexual and homosexual identities that define our sense of ourselves as sexual beings and our roles in families. These new ideas may seem strange to most of us; but then again, the idea that marriage could be just one of several outlets for sexual expression would have seemed strange to most Americans in the mid-twentieth century. Informed by a broader understanding of sexuality, we will now turn to a consideration of the great changes that have occurred in marriage and cohabitation.

Looking Back

1. **When did the idea of a sexual identity develop?** The idea that individuals have a coherent sexual identity involving a preference for either opposite-sex or same-sex partners did not exist until the nineteenth century. Before then, though religious doctrine and civil law forbade numerous sexual practices, a person who broke those laws was not thought to have a different personality from people who displayed conventional sexual behavior.

2. **What determines people's sexual identities?** Social constructionists believe that sexual identities, such as "heterosexual" and "gay," are entirely created by the way society is organized—the dominant norms and values, the legal privileges and restrictions, and so forth. They note the different ways in which sexual identities have been expressed in other societies cross-culturally and historically. They cite surveys which suggest a continuum, rather than a sharp line, between heterosexuality and homosexuality. Other social scientists think that there is a biological component to sexual identities. They cite evidence from behavioral genetic studies.

3. **Is "sexual identity" a useful way to think about people's sexuality?** A group of cultural theorists questions whether stable, fixed sexual identities really exist and whether they are useful concepts for understanding social change. They point to the multiple forms that each "identity" takes. They charge that current social norms restrict sexual behavior and force people into arbitrary categories. Those who disagree say that the categories we commonly use have important consequences for the lives of Americans and should be used to study topics such as parenthood, marriage, and other contested issues.

4. **Are people's living arrangements going beyond the boundaries of the family?** People whose sexual activity is outside of marriage and cohabitation are creating living arrangements that do not clearly fit into the conventional definition of a family. Two examples are, first, the personal networks of friends and relatives that many gay men and lesbians create as an alternative form of family and, second, the living-apart-together relationships of people in committed partnerships who choose to, or are compelled to, live apart. Personal communities such as these are blurring the boundary between family and nonfamily life. They are valuable to the individuals who use them, but are probably less stable than conventional arrangements.

5. **What is the nature of the teenage pregnancy "problem"?** Over the past few decades, the proportion of teenage births that occur outside of marriage has risen sharply because of a decline in marriage among teenagers. Bearing a child as a teenager somewhat reduces a woman's chances of leading an economically successful adult life. Yet some of the disadvantages observed in these cases occur because teenage mothers tend to come from disadvantaged families, not solely because they had a child at a young age.

Go to the Online Learning Center at www.mhhe.com/cherlin7e to test your knowledge of the chapter concepts and key terms.

Study Questions

1. What cultural features of American society influence people's senses of their sexual identity?
2. Does it make a difference whether there is a biological component to sexual identities? If so, why?
3. What is the case for discarding the concept of a sexual identity?
4. How far can the definition of a "family" be stretched before the concept loses its value?
5. Compare trends in attitudes toward premarital sex with trends in attitudes toward extramarital sex.
6. Why has concern about teenage pregnancy grown if the likelihood that a teenager will give birth has been declining?
7. Explain what a "selection effect" is.
8. What was the social significance of the Kinsey Report?

Key Terms

extramarital sex   197
family of choice   191
integrative perspective
   (on sexuality)   186
Kinsey Report   183

living apart together (LAT)   192
nonmarital birth ratio   199
queer theory   189
selection effect   200
sexual identity   181

sexual monogamy   197
social constructionist perspective
   (on sexuality)   182

Thinking about Families

The Private Family	The Public Family
Has the contemporary American culture gone too far in accepting sex without romantic love?	Should the government be involved in discouraging teenage pregnancy?

Families on the Internet   www.mhhe.com/cherlin7e

Note: While all the URLs listed were current as of the printing of this book, these sites often change. Please check our Web site (www.mhhe.com/cherlin7e) for updates.

The Sexuality Information and Education Council of the United States (www.siecus.org), an organization that favors the dissemination of information about sexuality and sex education through the schools, maintains a Web site with a great deal of information about sexuality and sex education in schools. A search on the topic "homosexuality," for example, will return links to a number of fact sheets and articles.

The Alan Guttmacher Institute, a research center devoted to family planning issues, offers much relevant information about adolescent pregnancy and childbearing, birth control, and abortion at its Web site (www.guttmacher.org). Click on "sex and relationships" to reveal information, including highlighted research and policy articles.

The Web site of the National Campaign to Prevent Teen and Unplanned Pregnancy, mentioned in the *Families and Public Policy* essay, is www.thenationalcampaign.org.

Chapter Seven

Cohabitation and Marriage

Looking Forward

Forming a Union

American Courtship

The Rise and Fall of Dating

Hooking Up

Independent Living

Cohabitation

Cohabitation and Class

College-Educated Cohabitants

Moderately-Educated Cohabitants

The Least-Educated Cohabitants

Summing Up

Cohabitation among Lesbians
and Gay Men

Marriage

From Institution to Companionship

The Institutional Marriage

The Companionate Marriage

From Companionship
to Individualization

Toward the Individualistic Marriage

The Influence of Economic Change

The Globalization of Love

The Current Context of Marriage

Why Do People Still Marry?

Marriage as the Capstone Experience

The Wedding as Status Symbol

Marriage and Religion

Is Marriage Good for You?

The Marriage Market

The Specialization Model

The Income-Pooling Model

Social Change and Intimate Unions

Changes in Union Formation

Marriage as an Ongoing Project

Looking Back

Study Questions

Key Terms

Thinking about Families

Families on the Internet

Boxed Features

FAMILIES AND PUBLIC POLICY: *Domestic
Partnerships*

FAMILIES AND THE GREAT RECESSION: *Putting
Plans on Hold*

Looking Forward

1. What is the history of courtship and dating?

2. What is the role of cohabitation in the American family system?

3. How has marriage changed over the past century?

4. What is marriage like today?

5. How does the marriage market work?

Between 1882 and 1884, Isabella Maud Rittenhouse was courted by several suitors. Maud's diary, discussed by Steven Seidman, reveals that two stood out (Seidman, 1991). The first was Robert Witherspoon, a handsome, charming, educated, and cultivated man, to whom Maud was powerfully attracted. The other was Elmer Comings, a rather plain-looking and socially awkward man who was, nevertheless, hardworking, reliable, and responsible. Today, the choice between them would be easy: 9 out of 10 Mauds would pick Robert, the object of romantic love, over unexciting Elmer. The real Maud, however, chose Elmer. Her reasoning shows how different the relationship among sex, love, and marriage was in the Victorian era than it is now.

To Maud and to most other nineteenth-century women and men, marrying someone because of strong romantic feelings was considered risky. Passionate, romantic love was thought to be a base emotion that faded away quickly, leaving little support for the couple. Far longer lasting was a spiritual love in which the partners joined together in a moral, uplifting marriage. The spiritual relationship rested upon a deep knowledge of each other and a sense of mutual obligation. Spiritual love was "true love," a union not only of the heart but also of the soul and the mind. Strong sexual attraction was equated with "romantic love," a dangerous emotional state that was hard to control. True love was much to be preferred.

There were practical reasons rooted in the structure of nineteenth-century society why people thought this way. The general standard of living was far lower than it is today, and most married women did not work outside the home. In order to have a comfortable life, it was crucial for a woman to marry an economically reliable, hardworking man. Correspondingly, a man needed to marry a woman who would raise children and manage a home competently. Feelings of romantic love could tempt a person to choose passion over partnership. Indulging in passion was a luxury most nineteenth-century people could not afford.

Maud decided that her romantic love for Robert was immature and that she could not overlook some lapses of character. She wrote that he had "beauty of feature and charm of tongue with little regard for truth and high moral worth"; whereas Elmer, "though not graceful . . . and handsome . . . [had an] inward nobility in him." Maud was well aware that she was rejecting romance when she rejected Robert: "If I do marry [Elmer] it will be with a respectful affection and not with a passionate *lover* love."[1] Moreover, Maud knew that, unlike Robert, Elmer did not share her knowledge of and interest in the arts and literature: "All the time I am planning to bring him up to a standard where I *can* love him." Thus, she girded for the task of marrying Elmer. Fortunately for

---

[1] All quotations are from Seidman (1991).

her—although not for Elmer—she broke off the courtship when Elmer entered into some suspicious business dealings that cast doubt on his character. But even in ending the courtship, Maud relied on practical and ethical considerations rather than on her feelings.

This separation between romantic love and sex, on the one hand, and marriage, on the other hand, was typical of the cultural tradition of the Western nation-states prior to the twentieth century. One historian studied the detailed writings on marital sexual activity by 25 medieval theologians and found that only 2 of them ever addressed the subject of love (Flandrin, 1985). Sexual relations that were too passionate were thought to be immoral and to compete with a person's worship of God. Sensual pleasures were for the love affairs a person had outside of his or her marriage—never sanctioned by theologians but tolerated, in practice, for men only. St. Jerome, quoting the Roman philosopher Seneca, wrote:

> *A prudent man should love his wife with discretion, and so control his desire and not be led into copulation. Nothing is more impure than to love one's wife as if she were a mistress . . . Men should appear before their wives not as lovers but as husbands. (Ariès, 1985a)*

This separation between erotic love and marriage evaporated during the twentieth century. Both Seneca and Maud would be surprised to read the 1987 treatise *Super Marital Sex: Loving for Life*, the author of which states, "Super marital sex is the most erotic, intense, fulfilling experience any human being can have" (Pearsall, 1987). They would also be surprised by an article in a social science journal which reported that men and women who were married, or who expected their current relationships to last a lifetime, reported greater pleasure from their sex lives than men and women with short-term partners (Waite & Joyner, 2001). More surprising still would be the increase in sexual activity outside the context of any kind of long-term relationship, the increase in childbearing outside of marriage, and the emergence of gay and lesbian subcultures. All these changes, to which we have become accustomed, were nearly unthinkable until the twentieth century.

Since Maud's time, then, expectations about marriage have changed dramatically. Most people view romantic love, compatibility, and companionship as essential to a good marriage. In this chapter we will examine the expectations people have today about their marriage partners and, more generally, about the meaning of their unions. I define a **union** as a stable, intimate relationship between two people who live in the same household, but may or may not be married. Increasingly, people's expectations are played out first in a cohabiting union and then in marriage. Consequently, we need to study the growth of cohabitation over the past few decades. Then we will turn to the changing nature of marriage.

union a stable, intimate relationship between two people who live in the same household but may or may not be married

Forming a Union

Maud's deliberate decision-making process shows that the choice of a husband was largely hers to make. Parental influence was more direct in most societies historically, and it is still more direct in some developing nations today. For instance, in rural villages throughout the developing world, parents who have land or wealth to pass on to their children are especially likely to have a voice. In many Asian nations, it is still common for parents, even prosperous city dwellers, to play an important role in the choice of their children's spouses.

AMERICAN COURTSHIP

But by the 1800s most young adults in the United States at least shared with their parents the responsibility for choosing a spouse. Indeed, young adults from the lower economic classes probably had substantial autonomy because there was little property for parents to worry about. (Among the upper classes, parents undoubtedly retained a stronger role.) Young people went about finding a spouse through courtship, a process that had been developed in Europe. **Courtship** is a publicly visible process with rules and restrictions through which young men and women find a partner to marry. The words *publicly visible* emphasize the important role of the community—and, in particular, parents—in watching over, and participating in, the courting a young adult does. For instance, in early modern Britain, the first stages of courtship occurred mainly outdoors, in plain view of peers and kin (Gillis, 1985). By and large, it was acceptable for casually acquainted young men and young women to be seen together only at public events such as festivals, games, or dances, and even then only in groups. At dances young people changed partners so frequently that no couple spent too much time together.

This centuries-old system of courtship met its demise after 1900. Its decline in the United States was linked to great social and economic changes: migration from rural areas (and from overseas) to cities, the rise of industrial capitalism, higher standards of living, and the lengthening of adolescence. As more and more people moved to cities and worked in factories and offices, the number of potential partners and the places where they could meet grew. Consequently, it became harder for parents to monitor and oversee the process. And as standards of living rose, it became possible for young adults to keep some of their earnings or to receive allowances from their parents. Thus, young people began to accumulate a key resource: spending money. The city provided plenty of places to spend it, most notably the movie theater and the dance hall. Rising standards of living also allowed many families to buy an automobile. This marvel of technology let young couples wander far from home; it also gave them a private place for necking (kissing) and petting (touching below the neck). As a result, courtship, in the words of historian Beth Bailey, went from "front porch to back seat" (Bailey, 1988).

In addition, a new view of the teenage years arose: They were seen as a time during which teens needed to develop their personalities and capabilities free of the pressures of the adult world (Kett, 2003). In an influential 1904 book, psychologist G. Stanley Hall popularized the term "adolescence" for this newly recognized stage of life (Hall, 1904). Attention to adolescence emerged as child labor laws restricted how much younger teenagers could work and as more prosperous middle-class families no longer needed their children to work. Moreover, it arose as changes in the economy made it clear to parents that children needed at least a high school education in order to obtain better-paying jobs. Consequently, adolescence was embodied most clearly in the high school, which removed teenagers from the world of adults. Not until the early decades of the twentieth century did a majority of teenagers enroll in high school. College enrollments also increased early in the century and then skyrocketed after World War II. The high school and college years gave adolescents a protected time in which they could create and participate in their own subculture, relatively free of parental involvement.

courtship a publicly visible process with rules and restrictions through which young men and women find a partner to marry

THE RISE AND FALL OF DATING

What evolved, then, after the turn of the twentieth century was a new system of courtship based on dating. Although some might think that dating has been around for a long time, it was rare until 1900 or so, and the term was not even used until then. The spirit of the change was captured in a 1924 short story in *Harper's* magazine. A man comes calling at the home of a young woman, expecting to spend the evening in her parlor. But when she opens the door, she has her hat on—a clear sign that she expects to go out.[2] As the story suggests, suddenly a young man was expected to take a young woman somewhere on a date—which meant he had to spend money. A firm rule of the dating system was that the young man paid the expenses. In return, he enjoyed the company of the young woman. Dating placed courtship on an economic basis. Young men provided goods such as movie tickets or restaurant meals in exchange for companionship and, often, necking and petting. Through these rules, argues Bailey, dating shifted the balance of power in courtship from women to men (Bailey, 1988). Under the old system, women received men in their own homes, at times they chose, and usually with their parents nearby. (During a girl's first season of receiving callers, her mother might initially invite the young men.) Now the evening was initiated and controlled by males, and it depended on cash earnings, which favored men over women.

Dating also shifted power from parents to teenagers and young adults. The movement of activity away from public gatherings and the home made it much harder for parents to influence the process. Rather, adolescents became oriented toward the dating system of their peer group—the other adolescents in the local school or neighborhood. With the triumph of dating, courtship moved from a parent- and other-adult-run system to a peer-run system where the participants made the rules and punished the offenders.

The dating system probably had its heyday in the 20-year period—1945 to 1965—after World War II. Throughout the period, college enrollments rose sharply and most young adults at least completed high school. Postwar parents had grown up in the dating system, and so there was less parent-child disagreement about it than had been the case in the 1920s and 1930s. At the same time, young people in the 1950s may have started to date earlier than their parents.[3] In a national survey of high school students conducted in 1960, about two-thirds of all boys and three-fourths of all girls stated that they had begun to date by grade 9; virtually all had dated by grade 12 (Modell, 1989).[4]

But as age at marriage began to rise in the 1960s and 1970s, the dating system became less closely connected to marriage. Steady dating in high school seemed more and more remote from serious attempts to find a spouse. What's more, cohabitation, perhaps a new stage of courtship, became a common event in young adults' lives prior to marriage. Also, the sharp rise in premarital

---

[2] This story is cited in both Rothman (1984) and Bailey (1988). It is cited by Bailey as Black (1924).

[3] Both Bailey and Rothman suggest that adolescents began to date at younger ages in the 1950s. But when a random sample of Detroit-area women in 1984 was asked to recall when they had begun to date, there was little difference in the responses of those who had married before the war versus after the war; see Whyte (1990).

[4] The data came from the Project Talent survey of 4,000 high school students nationwide.

intercourse for teenage boys and girls demonstrated that the dating system was increasingly ineffective in holding sexual activity to petting. Adolescents began to socialize more often in larger, mixed-sex groups (Modell, 1989).

Recently the Internet has emerged as an important way in which individuals find partners. Its use has grown dramatically since it became available in the mid-1990s, relative to traditional face-to-face ways of meeting, such as through friends, family, and co-workers. In a national survey, 22 percent of heterosexual women and men reported that they used the Internet to meet their partners—a larger percentage than for any other method, except friends. The same survey showed that the Internet is particularly important for people who are looking for partners with characteristics that are relatively uncommon because it is harder to find these partners through traditional means. More than 60 percent of gay men and lesbians, for example, reported meeting their partners through the Internet, making it by far the most widespread way of finding partners (Rosenfeld & Thomas, 2012).

HOOKING UP

Dating has declined so much that, in a 2000 national survey of women undergraduates at four-year colleges, a third of the seniors reported having at most two dates; and only half reported having six or more (Glenn & Marquardt, 2001). Young women and men reported that they mainly "hang out" in groups. When they do pair off, it is likely to be in the form of a "hookup," a phenomenon that seems to have begun in the 1980s and become common in the 2000s (Stepp, 2007; Bogle, 2008; England, Armstrong, & Fogarty, 2012). **Hooking up** is a sexual encounter with no expectation of further involvement. Unlike dating, it is not necessary, or even desirable, that either of the individuals have a romantic attraction to the other. Hookups commonly occur at parties or other group settings and often involve alcohol, which serves to loosen inhibitions and provide a rationale for acting in a sexually forward manner (Bogle, 2008). In a survey of Stanford undergraduates, men said they had consumed an average of five drinks, and women said three drinks, before hooking up (England & Thomas, 2007). In an online survey of over 14,000 students at 21 colleges and universities, 69 percent of women reported at least one hookup by senior year (England, Armstrong, & Fogarty 2012). A hookup does not necessarily imply sexual intercourse. About one-third of students in the online survey of undergraduates at several universities reported only kissing and nongenital touching; about one-third reported genital touching or oral sex; and a little more than one-third reported intercourse (England, Shafer, & Fogarty, 2008). The increased popularity of the hookup, however, does not mean that college students are not having relationships. In the online survey, 73 percent of women reported being in a relationship of six months or more while in college (England, Armstrong, & Fogarty, 2012).

The hookup culture can be seen in a positive or negative light. On the positive side, hooking up may be a rational response to the increasingly long stage of life between sexual maturity and the older ages at marriage we see today. It may be especially attractive to students who wish to postpone marrying and having children until after they have obtained a college degree and established their careers. During this long transition to adulthood, they may seek sexual pleasure but not serious relationships that could distract them from their goals (Hamilton & Armstrong, 2009). Hooking up seems to be more common among white students from economically privileged backgrounds—the kinds of students who are most likely to adopt a strategy of postponing marriage and

hooking up a sexual encounter with no expectation of further involvement

childbearing—than among non-whites or those from moderate- to low-income backgrounds (Hamilton & Armstrong, 2009; Owen, Rhoades, Stanley, & Fincham, 2010). Less privileged college students, who are more likely to make a quicker transition to family formation, may be more uncomfortable with sex outside of relationships. In addition, hooking up may be shifting the balance of power in relationships back toward women, since they can initiate hookups more easily than women in the twentieth century could initiate dates.

On the negative side, the hookup culture, first of all, seems to retain the sexual double standard that often favors men over women. The ambiguity of the hookup—neither partner knows whether the other has any romantic interest—places a person who would like to have a romantic relationship at a disadvantage. Young women, according to studies of hooking up, tend to be more troubled by this lack of commitment than young men (Bogle, 2008). Even the nature of the sexual activity seems to favor men; in the online sample of several universities, men were far more likely to report having an orgasm during a hook up than were women (England, Shafer, & Fogarty, 2008). Moreover, women who engaged in multiple hook ups were more likely to be stigmatized as sexually loose than were similar men. Second, critics of the hookup also question whether, later in adulthood, these women and men will be skilled enough interpersonally to form committed relationships that can be sustained for the remainder of their adult lives (Stepp, 2007). In other words, they suggest that dating in the past, conducted with the guidance and supervision of parents, was valuable as emotional practice for marriage, and that its absence may be a disadvantage. Both the positive and negative views of hookups, of course, could be valid.

INDEPENDENT LIVING

Once out of college, many young adults live on their own, rather than with their parents. Many non-college-graduates live on their own, too. This is a recent phenomenon. Figure 7.1 shows the percentage of unmarried women and men in their twenties who headed their own households from

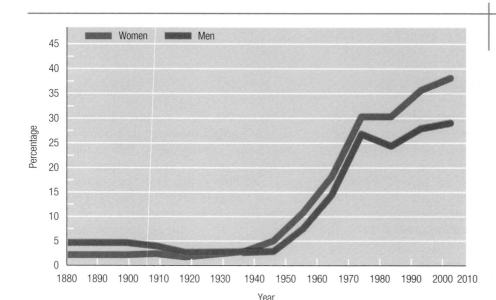

FIGURE 7.1
Percentage of unmarried men and women aged 20–29 who headed their own household, 1880 to 2005. (*Source:* Rosenfeld, 2007, Figure 3.3)

1880 to 2005, according to historical census data tabulated by Rosenfeld (2007).[5] You can see how uncommon heading one's household was in the late-nineteenth and early-twentieth centuries. Standards of living were lower, more people lived in rural areas, there was less housing, and women's lives were more constrained. Most unmarried young adults helped support their families by turning over their wages to their parents. But in the second half of the century, the percentage living on their own rose sharply. Standards of living increased, and it became common—even expected—for young adults to keep their wages. Women became more independent as they obtained college degrees and worked outside of the home. In addition, the rise in independent living was consistent with the broader growth of expressive individualism, which uncoupled sexual activity from marriage (with help from the introduction of the birth control pill in the 1960s).

As the typical age at marriage rose in the late twentieth century, it became common for young adults to set up an independent household years before they married. These independent living arrangements reduced the control that parents had over their children's choice of spouse. Some of these independent young adults were cohabiting with a partner, while others lived alone. Observers have been concerned that the rise in young adults living alone has increased the degree of isolation and loneliness in American society. But adults who are living alone are more socially active than are married couples (and probably cohabiting couples, too): They are more likely to visit friends, stay in contact electronically or by telephone, or join a social group. "Living alone and being alone," writes Eric Klinenberg (2012, p. 19), "are hardly the same."

Quick Review

- In the 1800s, young adults found spouses through the publicly visible process of courtship.
- The rise of dating in the twentieth century shifted much of the control over meeting partners from adults to their children and their children's peer group.
- Dating declined late in the twentieth century.
- Spending time in groups and hooking up have become more common.
- Single young adults are much more likely to live separately from parents than was the case a century ago.

■ Cohabitation

cohabitation the sharing of a household by unmarried persons who have a sexual relationship

By **cohabitation,** commonly called "living together," I mean a living arrangement in which two adults who are not married to each other but who have a sexual relationship share the same house or apartment. Before the 1960s, cohabitation was common mainly among the poor and near poor. With little in the way of resources to share and little prospect of leaving money or possessions to their children, the poor had less reason to marry. For many, cohabitation had served as an acceptable substitute for legal marriage. But beginning around 1970, the proportion of all young adults who lived with

[5] I thank Michael Rosenfeld for adding a 2005 data point to the published version of Table 3.3 in his book.

Domestic Partnerships

Getting married is not only a way for couples to express their love and commitment to each other but also a way for them to obtain important practical and financial advantages not available to couples who cohabit or live apart. In most nations the law has long recognized marriage as a privileged relationship in which the spouses have special rights and responsibilities. Here is a partial list of rights and responsibilities that married couples have but cohabiting couples, in most jurisdictions in the United States, do not have:

- They can include each other as beneficiaries on pension and annuity plans offered by their employers, and they can purchase health insurance for each other through their employers.
- They can file a joint income tax return, which may reduce their tax liability.
- They can receive Social Security survivors' benefits if their spouse dies, and they can inherit from each other even when there is no will.
- They are jointly responsible for their children, and each can give legal permission to schools, doctors, and the like, for trips, operations, and so forth.
- They can adopt children together.
- In the event of a divorce, they are both normally entitled to either custody or visitation rights.

This list reflects the view, virtually unchallenged until a few decades ago, that marriage constitutes the only legitimate context for the raising of children. It also reflects the ideal, prominent in the first half of the twentieth century, that families should have one wage earner (the husband), who should be able to provide health insurance, survivors' benefits, and so on, to his wife.

Yet social changes have made the granting of rights solely to married couples debatable. For instance, nearly 20 percent of all births in the United States occur to women who are cohabiting with the fathers of their children, as I note elsewhere in this chapter. Cohabitation itself is so common that some observers question the rationale for denying cohabiting couples similar rights to those married couples have. They argue that there is little difference between a cohabiting couple raising children and a married couple raising children—and that the former ought to have the same rights and receive the same benefits as the latter. Others favor retaining the privileged place of marriage for any of several reasons: because of a moral or religious belief that heterosexual marriage is the only proper setting for having and raising children; because of a pragmatic belief that marriage provides a more stable two-parent setting than cohabitation; or because of a wish to avoid further spending by government or business that would be triggered by treating cohabitors like spouses.

In the United States, states and municipalities are moving toward granting cohabiting couples some of the rights and responsibilities that married couples have. Canada has gone further: Under the Modernization of Benefits and Obligations Act of 2000, legal distinctions between married and unmarried same-sex and opposite-sex couples were eliminated for couples who have lived together for at least a year.

In France, where almost 9 out of 10 unions begin outside of marriage, opposite-sex and same-sex cohabiting couples may enter into Civil Solidarity Pacts, which give them most but not all of the rights and responsibilities of married couples after the pact has existed for three years (Martin & Théry, 2001). Some Scandinavian countries also have registered partnerships for opposite-sex couples (Lyall, 2004). Others, such as the United Kingdom, have domestic partnerships exclusively for same-sex couples.

The issue of whether the state should recognize same-sex partnerships or allow same-sex marriage is contentious in the United States, as we will see in Chapter 14. But even giving opposite-sex cohabiting couples a legal status is controversial. Several states have passed laws banning not only same-sex marriage but also domestic partnerships. Their rationale is that domestic partnerships are just another form of same-sex marriage. The debate reflects the weakening role of marriage in the institution of the family. Although still dominant, heterosexual marriage is no longer the only acceptable way for couples to live together. Rather, heterosexual cohabitation is broadly tolerated. This toleration is so recent, however, that there is little consensus on the rights and responsibilities heterosexual partners should have toward each other and toward the children in their households.

Ask Yourself

1. Are any of the couples you know cohabiting? If so, have their relationships reached the point at which legal considerations would be meaningful to them?

2. Should couples who are cohabiting have the same legal rights as married couples? Why or why not?

www.mhhe.com/cherlin7e

A majority of first marriages are preceded by cohabitation.

someone prior to marrying increased sharply. By the early 2000s, about 60 percent of women in their thirties had cohabited, and 62 percent of marriages were preceded by a period of cohabitation (Kennedy & Bumpass, 2008). As cohabitation has become more common, its role in the family system has increased. States and localities have been implementing legal changes that give cohabiting couples rights that once were reserved for married couples. (See *Families and Public Policy:* Domestic Partnerships.)

In 2011, the Census Bureau estimated that there were about 7.6 million households in the United States maintained by two opposite-sex persons who said they were unmarried partners (U.S. Bureau of the Census, 2011y). These couples are more diverse than many people realize. Although the common image is one of a childless couple, many cohabiting couples have children in their households: In 2011, 40 percent of unmarried couples had the children of one or both partners present, including 62 percent of Hispanics, 51 percent of African Americans, and 32 percent of non-Hispanic whites (U.S. Bureau of the Census, 2011z). In fact, about half of the births listed in official statistics as occurring outside of marriage are in reality births to cohabiting couples rather than to single mothers living without partners (Kennedy & Bumpass, 2008). (Cohabiting mothers are counted simply as "unmarried" because birth certificates, on which these statistics are based, ask whether the mother is married but not whether she is living with a partner.) Over the past decade or two, most of the rise in childbearing outside of marriage has been the result of births to cohabiting couples, not births to women living alone (Kennedy & Bumpass, 2008).

Cohabitation has been increasing among individuals of all social classes. Figure 7.2 shows the percentage of women aged 19 to 44 who had ever cohabited in 1995 and in the more recent period of 2006 to 2008, separated according to how much education they had. The percentage rose over time for all educational groups. In some Western countries, young adults are entering into long-term unions that are similar to marriage but do not involve a legal commitment.

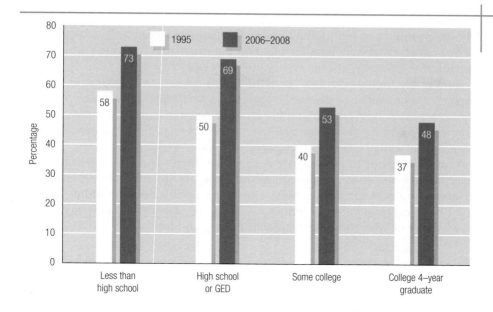

FIGURE 7.2
Percentage of women aged 19 to 44 who had ever cohabited: 1995 and 2006–8. (*Sources:* For 1995, Kennedy and Bumpass, 2008. For 2006–8, authors' calculations.)

In France, for example, about one-fourth of all children in the mid-1990s were living with cohabiting parents in families that typically lasted 9 or 10 years (Heuveline & Timberlake, 2004). In Sweden, cohabitation is becoming almost indistinguishable from marriage (Kiernan, 2002). But cohabitating relationships in the United States are shorter, on average, than in most other Western countries (Cherlin, 2009). Within two years, half of all cohabiting relationships have ended either by marriage or dissolutions (Kennedy & Bumpass, 2008).

COHABITATION AND CLASS

Yet although cohabitation has increased across the board, it differs by social class (Sassler & Miller, 2011). Figure 7.2 shows that the more education a woman has, the less likely she was to have ever cohabited in either period, 1995 or 2006–2008. In the later period, about half of college-educated women under age 45 had ever cohabited, compare to about three-fourths among women who had not graduated from high school. So although college-educated young adults are sometimes thought of as a cultural vanguard, they are the least likely to live with a partner before marrying. In addition, the increase in cohabitation from 1995 to 2006–2008 was smallest among college graduates, as the figure shows; consequently the gap between them and the non-college-graduates has widened over time.

The meaning of cohabitation—what individuals who are living together think that their relationship signifies—also varies by social class, although there is substantial variation and overlap. Let us examine these meanings.

College-Educated Cohabitants College-educated young adults, as Chapter 4 demonstrated, are much more likely to wait until after marriage to have their first child than are less-educated young adults. As a result, they do not have children while cohabiting as often as people with less education. Twenty-three percent of college-educated cohabiting women had a child (of either partner) in their households in 2011, compared to 44 percent of cohabiting women who graduated from high school but did not have a 4-year college degree, and 59 percent of cohabiting women who had not graduated from high school (U.S. Bureau of the Census, 2011z).

Among the highly-educated, cohabitation is often a testing ground for marriage. Childless college-educated couples may live together as a way of determining whether they are compatible enough to get married. They may cohabit after college while pursuing graduate school or starting careers. Some of them may already be formally engaged and have wedding dates set. Few will have children prior to making the decision to marry, and few will cohabit for more than two or three years without marrying or breaking up. By and large, college-educated adults use cohabitation as a step in a family-building process that I have called neo-traditional (see Chapter 4): Most eventually marry, and they wait until after they marry to start having children.

Moderately-Educated Cohabitants

Cohabitation among moderately-educated young adults—those who have graduated from high school but do not have a four-year college degree—is less closely tied to marriage. These individuals may wish to eventually marry, but they do not think it is possible, or even desirable, at the moment. Marriage may not be foremost in their mind when they begin to live together. In a study of young adults in the Toledo, Ohio, area, who typically had graduated from high school and perhaps had some college courses, the authors (as noted in Chapter 6) reported that many childless cohabiting adults seemed to drift into living together without much thought as to what the relationship might become in the long run and sometimes even without a deliberate decision to cohabit. In fact, none of the 115 cohabiting young adults in this study said that he or she was deciding between marriage and cohabitation at the start of the union (Manning & Smock, 2005). The process of moving in may occur rather quickly for moderately-educated couples, often within the first six months of their relationships (Sassler & Miller, 2011).

For moderately-educated cohabiting adults who already have children together, the experience may have unfolded differently. Rather than first living together and then having a child, it is common for unmarried couples to begin living together *after* the woman becomes pregnant, whether or not the pregnancy was planned (Reed, 2006). Rather than drifting into cohabitation, they decide to live together as a response to the impending birth. They do often think about marriage as a long-term goal. But few think that just because they have a child, they should marry.

Whether or not children are present, most moderately-educated cohabitants eventually think about the issue of marriage. Few will remain together for long without marrying (Sassler & Miller, 2011). But their standards for marriage are high. In the Toledo study, many did not want to marry until they had a financial package in place that often included homeownership, being out of debt, and having a stable, adequate income. A 25-year-old woman told the authors that she and her partner were interested in getting married, but they had a lot to accomplish beforehand:

> *Um, we have certain things that we want to do before we get married. We both want very good jobs, and we both want a house, we both want reliable transportation. I'm about to start taking cake decorating classes, and so I can have*

Children are present in the household of two out of five cohabiting couples.

me some good income, and he—he's trying his best you know? He's been looking out for jobs everywhere, and we—we're trying. We just want to have—we gotta have everything we need before we say, "Let's get married." (Smock, Manning, & Porter, 2005)

If they fail to acquire everything they need, couples such as this one are likely to dissolve their unions within a few years.

The Least-Educated Cohabitants
Cohabitants who did not graduate from high school, most of whom have low-incomes, can be even further removed from considering marriage. Some low-income women see no prospect of finding a man who is suitable for marriage. They may live instead in **serial cohabitation** with two or more live-in partners with little or no thought of marriage, interspersed with romantic relationships that do not involve living together.

serial cohabitation living with a series of partners without marrying them

They may enter into cohabiting relationships because of pregnancy, as is the case with the moderately-educated; and these relationships are rarely stable. In a study of the parents of nearly 5,000 babies born in urban hospitals, about half of the fathers who were living with the mothers at the birth of their child were no longer romantically involved with the mother five years later (Bendheim-Thoman Center for Child Wellbeing, 2007). Low-income mothers may also enter into cohabiting relationships because of dire financial need. In these instances, the mothers expect that their partners will provide financial support while they are co-residing. In a small number of cases, women may even allow destitute former partners to live with them without restarting sexual relationships (Cross-Barnet, Cherlin, & Burton, 2011). In all, marriage is uncommon among low-income cohabitants: Only about one-fourth of poor cohabiting couples marry their partners within five years, compared to about two-thirds of non-poor cohabiting couples (Lichter, Turner, & Sassler, 2010). For these individuals, a mixture of cohabiting and non-cohabiting romantic relationships is often a long-term substitute to marriage.

Yet these low-income individuals mostly say they would like to marry. But like the moderately-educated, they will do so only when they are sure they can do it successfully: when their partner has demonstrated the ability to hold a decent job and treat them fairly and without abuse, and when they have a security deposit or a down payment for a decent apartment or home.

In a study of low-income families in three United States cities that I helped to conduct (Cherlin et al., 2004), one woman, who was already living with the man she was engaged to and had children with, told an ethnographer she was not yet ready to marry him:

> But I'm not ready to do that yet. I told him, we're not financially ready yet. He knows that. I told him by the end of this year, maybe. I told him that last year. Plus, we both need to learn to control our tempers, you could say. He doesn't understand that bills and kids and [our relationship] come first, not [his] going out and getting new clothes or [his] doing this and that. It's the kids, then us. He gets paid good, about five hundred dollars a week. How hard is it to give me money and help with the bills?

Note that for this woman, more is required of a man than a steady job before his is marriageable. He has to learn to turn over most of his paycheck to his family rather than spending it on his friends and himself. He must put his relationship with his partner ahead of running with his single male friends, a way of saying that a husband must place a priority on providing companionship and intimacy to his wife and on being sexually faithful. And he and his partner have to learn to control their tempers, a vague referent to the possibility that physical abuse exists in the relationship. In sum, the demands low-income women place on men include not just a reliable income, as important as that is, but also a commitment to put family first, provide companionship, be faithful, and avoid abusive behavior—similar standards to those better-off women have.

Summing Up   While there is much variation in the complex and growing phenomenon of cohabitation, an overall pattern is apparent: The more education that cohabitants have, the more closely their relationships are linked to marriage. Among college graduates, cohabiting relationships are for the most part a stage in the marriage process. As well-educated young adults postpone marriage and invest in careers, they choose to live with partners whom they may wish to marry and someday—after marrying—have children with. Cohabitation is for many a testing ground for marriage. The couple may even be engaged to wed. Among the moderately educated, cohabitation is more often a short term alternative to marriage. It is a living arrangement that provides intimacy, financial savings, and sometimes co-parenting for couples who do not have the resources that they think are necessary for marriage. Most moderately-educated individuals will eventually marry, although not necessarily with the person they first lived with. And among the least educated, cohabitation is an alternative to marriage that may be long-term. But rather than having one long-term cohabiting relationship, it is common for the least-educated to have a series of relationships, some involving cohabiting and some not.

COHABITATION AMONG LESBIANS AND GAY MEN

For lesbians and gay men, cohabitation remains the only form of partnership available except in the modest number of states where same-sex marriage has been legalized. Several surveys were conducted in the 2000s in California during which people were asked their sexual orientation, unlike Census Bureau surveys, which do not ask. The California surveys show that depending on the survey, 37 to 46 percent of gay men were cohabiting with a partner, as were 51 to 62 percent of lesbians (Carpenter & Gates, 2008). By comparison, 62 percent of heterosexuals of comparable ages were either cohabiting or married. So nearly as many lesbians in California were partnered as were heterosexual women. Cohabitation was common among gay men, but they were less likely to be partnered than were heterosexual men. Partnered lesbians were also more likely to have children present in their household (14 to 31 percent, depending on the survey) than were partnered gay men (3 to 5 percent).

Studies that have compared gay, lesbian, and heterosexual couples find no significant differences in love or relationship satisfaction (Savin-Williams & Esterberg, 2000). When a sample of homosexual and heterosexual couples was asked what were the "best things" and "worst things" about their relationships, a panel of raters who were given the written comments could not tell which comments came from which group of couples (Peplau, 1991). Weston (1991), who studied lesbian and gay couples in San Francisco in the 1980s, reported a concern about excessive "merging." Subsequent research suggests the issue is more relevant for lesbian partnerships than for gay male partnerships (Savin-Williams & Esterberg, 2000). The problem, Weston wrote, is to avoid becoming so united with and dependent on your partner that you lose your independence and can't develop as an individual. This language recalls the way that many married heterosexual persons talk about the need to maintain a growing, independent self.

Among lesbian and gay couples, both partners tend to work for pay; and they seem to split the domestic chores more equitably and flexibly than the typical heterosexual couple (Seidman, 1991; Weeks, Heaphy, & Donovan, 2001). However, Carrington (1999) observed the daily home lives of 52 gay and lesbian couples and found that a majority of them did not divide the homework equally—even though most said they did. In homes where one partner worked longer hours and earned substantially more than did the other partner, the one with the less demanding, lower-paying job did more housework or more of the work of keeping in touch with family and friends. Carrington suggests that holding a demanding professional or managerial job may make it difficult for a person to invest fully in sharing the work at home, regardless of gender or sexuality.

Quick Review

- Cohabitation is a rapidly growing and diverse living arrangement.
- For most couples, it is a short-term partnership that ends in either a marriage or a dissolution within a few years.
- It is more common among the less-educated.
- The more education that cohabitants have, the more closely their relationships are linked to marriage.
- Studies that have compared gay, lesbian, and heterosexual couples have found no significant differences in love or relationship satisfaction.

Marriage

Even though many adults will live in cohabiting unions, about 9 out of 10 whites and 2 out of 3 African Americans are projected to marry eventually (see Table 5.1). Their expectations, the kinds of marriages they form, and the way their social and economic environment affects their chances of forming and maintaining a marriage have been the topics of much social scientific research and theory. (The recent economic downturn may have delayed the marriage and childbearing plans of young adults. See *Families and the Great Recession:* Putting Plans on Hold.) The literature suggests two great changes in the meaning of marriage during the twentieth and early twenty-first centuries.

FROM INSTITUTION TO COMPANIONSHIP

Family life in preindustrial Western nations was guided more by law and custom than by affection and emotional stimulation. The local government in Plymouth Colony, you will recall, kept a close watch over the conduct of family members. Parents played a greater role in selecting a spouse for their children than was the case in later centuries. In general, husbands and fathers had greater authority than they do today: Religion and law certified the father as head of the family, with broad powers over his wife (whose property he could sell) and his children (who remained with him in the event of a divorce). In addition, the marginal existence of poor farm families and the modest standard of living of most urban families made the family's subsistence a higher priority than the personal development of the parents and children.

institutional marriage a marriage in which the emphasis is on male authority, duty, and conformity to social norms

The Institutional Marriage   We might call this pre-twentieth-century form of marriage the **institutional marriage.** A social institution, you will remember, consists of a set of rules and roles that define a social unit of importance to society. Marriage prior to the twentieth century fit this description. It was held together by clear rules and roles: The husband was expected to be the head of the household, the wife was to be dutiful and submissive, and the children obedient. Although the husband and wife may have been fond of each other, romantic love wasn't necessary or even desirable—which is why Maud Rittenhouse chose Elmer over Robert. Rather, spouses were expected

Families and the Great Recession

Putting Plans on Hold

Between 2009 and 2010, according to the Bureau of the Census, the number of opposite-sex couples who were cohabiting jumped by 868,000, or 13 percent (Kreider, 2010). Why did that happen during an economic downturn? It seems unlikely that tough economic times would somehow increase the number of young adults who liked their boyfriends or girlfriends so much that they decided to move in together. No, that's not it. It's much more likely that young couples who were already in serious relationships decided not to make long-term commitments until the job market improved and therefore decided to live together rather than to marry; or couples who were already cohabiting decided to delay their weddings until recession was over.

If this is the explanation, then we might expect that newly-formed cohabiting unions in 2009 would have involved more individuals who were unemployed than longer-term cohabiting unions (because the older unions were formed before people were as worried about jobs). That is, in fact, what the Census Bureau found: Newly-formed cohabiting couples had a lower proportion with both partners employed (39 percent) than did couples who were already together (50 percent).

The Great Recession also put on hold some people's plans to have children. Between 2008 and 2010 the birth rate fell 7 percent to 13.0 births for every 1,000 people in the nation, the lowest figure on record (U.S. National Center for Health Statistics, 2011a). Children are a major investment of time and money, and it stands to reason that couples would hesitate to have them until the job market improves. Fourteen percent of adults under 35 in a 2009 national survey said that they had postponed having a baby because of the recession (Pew Research Center, 2009b).

We can expect that some of the couples who were postponing births during the recession will have children once the economy recovers. But the experience of the Great Depression suggests that not all couples catch up. Some never marry, and they choose not to have a child outside of marriage. Some experience fertility problems as they age. Although births rose as the Depression faded, women whose prime childbearing years occurred during the Depression had the highest risk of never having children of any generation in the twentieth century. Among women born between 1905 and 1914, for instance, nearly one-fourth never had children (Rowland, 2007). It is unlikely that rates of lifetime childlessness will be that high among young adult women today; but the proportion could reach as high as one-fifth.

What economic downturns do is make people more uncertain about big decisions in their personal lives, such as whether to marry, whether to have another child, or whether to buy a home. So they are more cautious and take longer to make decisions. Recessions, in other words, slow down the course of people's lives. And as people slow down, their actions further slow the economic recovery: With fewer children born, fewer baby clothes are sold; with more families staying in their current abodes, fewer new homes are built. In fact, by reducing the demand for goods and services, the recession-induced slowdown in personal life has the unintended effect of extending the time until the economy is strong enough for people to get their lives back on track.

to work together under the husband's authority to manage the farm, raise children, and keep food on the table. The local community, the church, and the law all supported the rules and roles of the institutional marriage.

But in the early twentieth century, companionship and sexual fulfillment became more important to a successful marriage. Prior to that time, as noted in the previous chapter, sexual relations in marriage (and there was relatively little sexual activity outside marriage) were seen more as a means of producing children than as a means of emotional fulfillment. But after the turn of the twentieth century, progressive writers argued that an active sex life was central to a happy marriage. In the 1920s, Robert and Helen Lynd conducted a famous study of life in Muncie, Indiana, which they selected as a typical American town and called "Middletown" (Lynd & Lynd, 1929). The Lynds reported that, compared with the 1890s, young adults were more likely to view romantic love as the only valid basis for marriage. In this new romantic

The single-earner families of the 1950s exemplified the companionate marriage.

climate, they wrote, women were more concerned with "youthful beauty." Throughout the country, mass production and rising incomes made fashionable clothing affordable. Advice columnist Dorothy Dix told her readers that "good looks are a girl's trump card." And she counseled, "Dress well and thereby appear fifty percent better looking than you are. . . . Make yourself charming" (May, 1980).

The Companionate Marriage

In a 1945 textbook, Ernest Burgess, the leading family sociologist of the first half of the twentieth century, famously described this transition in the meaning of marriage:

> *The central thesis of this volume is that the family in historical times has been, and at present is, in transition from an institution to a companionship. In the past the important factors unifying the family have been external, formal, and authoritarian, as the law, the mores, public opinion, tradition, the authority of the family head, rigid discipline, and elaborate ritual. At present, in the new emerging form of the companionship family, its unity inheres less and less in community pressures and more and more in such interpersonal relations as the mutual affection, the sympathetic understanding, and the comradeship of its members. (Burgess & Locke, 1945)*

Burgess meant the family-as-institution and the family-as-companionship to be seen as ideal types. Thus, he cautioned that purely institutional or purely companionship families exist "nowhere in time or space." In the spirit of the ideal type, we can call the kind of marriage that was emerging in the 1940s the **companionate marriage.** It emphasized affection, friendship, and sexual gratification. Keep in mind, however, that the style of marriage Burgess saw emerging was the single-earner, breadwinner–homemaker marriage that flourished

companionate marriage
a marriage in which the emphasis is on affection, friendship, and sexual gratification

in the 1950s—not the dual-earner family that emerged only in the second half of the twentieth century. The husband and wife in the companionate marriage ideally adhered to a sharp division of labor (he worked outside the home, she worked inside the home). Nevertheless, they were supposed to be each other's companions—friends, lovers—to an extent not imagined by the spouses in the institutional marriages a generation or two earlier. Husbands' authority, although still substantial, was less than in the institutional marriage. Young women were increasingly seen as needing higher education, not so they could establish careers but rather so they could be stimulating conversationalists and efficient homemakers. By midcentury, large state universities enrolled hundreds of thousands of bright young women who majored in home economics or consumer science and joked that what they really hoped to get at college was an "MRS." degree.

FROM COMPANIONSHIP TO INDIVIDUALIZATION

The companionate marriage reached its peak at midcentury. The spouses who married at young ages and in record numbers in the late 1940s and the 1950s were its exemplars. Most wives, except among the poor, did not work outside the home. Instead, they focused on creating an emotionally satisfying home life centered on affectionate relations between spouses and on child rearing—these were, after all, the parents who produced the baby boom. They found meaning in the successful performance of their social roles: the homemaker who raised children well and was a pleasant companion and friend to her husband; the man who supported his family through steady employment, enjoyed the company of his wife, and was a loving, if sometimes distant, father.

By the mid-1960s, however, the breadwinner–homemaker companionate marriage was losing ground as both a cultural ideal and a demographic reality. It was gradually overtaken by family forms that Burgess had not foreseen, particularly marriages in which both the husband and the wife worked outside the home. Although women continued to do most of the housework and child care, the roles of wives and husbands became more flexible and open to negotiation. Moreover, an even more individualistic perspective on the rewards of marriage took root. When people evaluated how satisfied they were with their marriages, they thought more in terms of individual satisfaction with how their own lives were developing than in terms of satisfaction gained through building a family.

Toward the Individualistic Marriage In other words, it mattered less how well they were performing the roles society expected of them, such as earning money, raising children, or working hard on the job. It mattered more how much they enjoyed their jobs, how much emotional gratification they were getting from their marriages, how gratifying their sex lives were, and how pleased they were with the ways their lives were changing and developing. Being a good citizen or a responsible parent was less important; being emotionally satisfied was more important. Feeling that you were meeting your obligations to others was less central; feeling that you had opportunities to grow as a person was more central. Starting in the 1960s popular magazine

Growing financial pressures on working-class families may have limited the focus on personal development.

articles offering marital advice emphasized three themes that characterized beliefs about the post-1960-style marriage. The first was "self-development," the belief that each person should develop a fulfilling, independent self instead of merely sacrificing oneself to one's partner. Second, roles within marriage should be flexible and negotiable; and, third, communication and openness in confronting problems are essential (Cancian, 1987). Assuming the content of these magazines reflects cultural beliefs about love and marriage, they support the idea of a shift toward a more individualized conception of marriage.

This shift produced the second great change in the meaning of marriage during the twentieth century. Given its emphasis on self-development, flexible roles, and open communication, we might call the form that emerged after 1960 the **individualistic marriage.** It, too, is something of an ideal type: Even people who evaluate their satisfaction in very individualistic terms may also take pride in being a good parent. But its general form represents an important break with the meaning of marriage in the past. The change in meaning that accompanied the transition to the individualized marriage has been called a shift "from role to self" (Cancian, 1987).

individualistic marriage
a marriage in which the emphasis is on self-development, flexible roles, and open communication

The Influence of Economic Change   In addition, both transitions—from the institutional marriage to the companionate marriage, and from the companionate marriage to the individualistic marriage—had economic roots. First, both are related to changes in the nature of work. The transition from institution to companionship occurred as the United States was becoming increasingly industrialized and urbanized. Husbands (although not wives at first) took jobs that paid wages. Farm families needed to function as production units—as small-scale firms if you will—in order to be successful. In most agricultural societies, older men retained substantial authority to run these production units. Wage work, in contrast, provided young adults with some independence from their parents: They could move away to jobs in the city. Their parents had less control over whom they married. Moreover, men's authority was reduced in urban marriages because of the demise of the family as production unit. Later, the transition from companionship to individualistic marriage occurred as married women took paid jobs in large numbers. In doing so, they gained greater independence from men and were exposed to new ideas beyond the home. Women as well as men could now think in terms of their own individual development through adulthood. These circumstances supported the emergence of a more individualistic perspective on the rewards of marriage.

Second, both transitions are related to increases in families' standards of living. When most people's living standards were so low that they had difficulty earning enough money for food and shelter, few had time for personal fulfillment. People needed to pool earnings and housework with spouses and children in order to subsist, and marriage was therefore more of an economic partnership. The rising standard of living during the twentieth century gave more people the luxury of focusing on their own feelings of satisfaction. They did so first in the context of the companionate marriage in which a higher standard of living allowed many wives to stay home rather than work for pay. But increasingly high standards of living meant that people could live alone if their marriages were not personally fulfilling, and this development accelerated the transition from companionate marriage to individualistic marriage.

Quick Review

- In the institutional marriage, wives' and husbands' behavior is governed by strong social norms, tradition, and law. Men have substantial authority.
- In the companionate marriage, the spouses expect affection, friendship, and sexual gratification and find satisfaction in being good parents and spouses.
- In the individualistic marriage, each spouse expects self-fulfillment, intimacy, and continuing personal growth.
- Industrialization and urbanization hastened the transition to the companionate marriage.
- The increase in married women working for wages, as well as rising standards of living, underlay the transition to the individualistic marriage.

THE GLOBALIZATION OF LOVE

Marriage is being transformed in much of the developing world as well. Anthropologists in many developing countries have noticed the spread of a more emotionally based style of relations between women and men that emphasizes romantic love, sexual fulfillment, communication, and companionship (Padilla et al., 2007). What seems to be happening is the globalization of the Western pattern of companionate marriage, or even individualistic marriage, to much of the rest of the world. Not all societies react the same ways to this development, but the commonalities are notable. In Hong Kong and Singapore, young wives melt down traditional jewelry passed to them at marriage and buy diamond rings or even computers (Chan, 2006). In Papua New Guinea young married couples build "family houses" to live in rather than following the traditional custom of separate men's, women's, and bachelors' houses (Wardlow, 2006).

Older women in a Mexican village say that what was most important when they married was that a husband "respected you." They described how the ideal of marriage has changed over a generation from *respeto* (respect) to *confianza* (trust, intimacy). Among the older generation, if a husband showed respect to his wife, his sexual infidelity was not seen as a failing serious enough to warrant a separation or divorce. But among the younger generation, a woman expects her husband to be an intimate companion and would view his infidelity as a serious threat to a marriage (Hirsch, 2003).

There are a number of forces pushing marriage in this direction:

1. *Urbanization and the shift to wage labor.* Women and men, once bound to the authority of parents in the villages, can escape that authority in the cities. The anonymity of city life—in contrast to the web of kinship and friendship ties in a typical village—allows for more privacy in the development of a marital relationship. And when women and men both earn wages, they become co-partners in a way that suggests a more egalitarian relationship. Anthropologist L. A. Rebhun (1999, 2007) argues that in impoverished Northeast Brazil, migration to the cities and a shift to a cash economy have increased the salience of romantic love in marriages.

2. *Exposure to modern media.* Seeing movies and television programs can alter people's views of marriage. An anthropologist noted the huge popularity of a romantic Turkish movie among Papua New Guinean women. In part, their fascination arose from the lives of the film's protagonists, who wear modern clothes, live in a modern house, and are shown eating together, walking hand-in-hand, and laughing at each other's jokes (Wardlow, 2006). In one region of Nepal, the first movie theater was built in 1969 and television first appeared in the late 1980s. In that region, younger adults were more likely to have participated in the choice of their spouse than were older adults, most of whom had no influence in their parents' choice of whom they would marry. Researchers found that adults who had listened to radio, seen a movie, and watched television were particularly likely to have taken part in the choice of their spouses. These media outlets provided messages from the Western countries that, in the words of the authors, "include the information that those who are the very richest in today's world choose their own spouse and do not necessarily marry a person of their parents' choosing" (Ghimire, Axinn, Yabiku, & Thornton, 2006).

   In Brazil, researchers have traced changes in family patterns that occurred as television was first introduced, area by area, between 1970, when only 8 percent of the country received a television signal, and 1991, when 81 percent received a signal. They focused on the popular soap operas that dominated Brazilian television programming. These *novelas*, as they are called, filled the small screen with images of emancipated and empowered women, working outside the home, living in small, urban middle-class families, and pursuing pleasure and love. The soap operas were so popular that after television was introduced into an area, parents were more likely to give their children names used by the main characters. And after the introduction of television into an area, birth rates dropped and divorce rates rose (La Ferrara, Chong, & Duryea, 2008; Chong & La Ferrara, 2009). These findings are consistent with the changes that have occurred in the United States during the last half of the twentieth century, when the companionate style of marriage was widespread and the individualistic style of marriage was on the rise.

It's not just the media that spread Western values. In Papua New Guinea, Christian missionaries encourage young couples to live in family houses, and they created spaces where young women and men could meet, such as coed youth groups, which had never been allowed in the past (Wardlow, 2006).

3. *Migration flows.* Direct contact with the developed world also influences the nature of marriage. In Mexico, many families include women and men who have spent time in the United States as migrants. When they return to Mexico, they carry with them not only money and new possessions but also new values.

4. *Demographic change.* Birthrates have fallen sharply in many developing countries, reducing family size. And medical and public health advances have increased adult life expectancy. As a result, married couples have more time together without young children at home—time they can devote to their relationship.

All this has spread two ideas about family life (Wardlow & Hirsch, 2006): First, a person should think more individualistically about the kind of marital relationship she or he wants. Second, they should see their marriage as a project to be worked on and maintained, rather than as an institution whose rules are unchanging and taken for granted. These are modern ideas: You must construct your family life in ways that are satisfying to you personally. They are analogous to the expressive individualism that arose in the West and altered American family life in the twentieth century.

These developments also suggest that the process of globalization is not limited to the flow of goods and money around the world. Rather, globalization can also occur on the level of ideas and values. As new ways of thinking about family and personal life diffuse through developing countries by way of modern technologies such as television and film, people may begin to make different decisions than their parents made about marriage, divorce, and childbearing. The effects are particularly powerful on women because their lives have typically been constrained more than men's lives.

There are still many ways that family lives of married couples in developing countries reflect their own history and culture rather than Western ideals. Nevertheless, studies suggest striking change—as when the Northeast Brazilians watch Portuguese-language soap operas in which characters declare meaningfully to each other, in borrowed English, *Ai lóvi iú* ("I love you") (Rebhun, 1999, p. 184). An anthropologist who studied social change in a Spanish village aptly summed up the change in marriage as a shift "from duty to desire" (Collier, 1997).

The Current Context of Marriage[6]

Overall, research and writing on the changing meaning of marriage suggest that it is now situated in a very different context than in the past. This is true in at least two senses. First, individuals now have a great deal of choice in how they live their personal lives. More forms of marriage and more alternatives to marriage are socially acceptable. You may fit marriage into your life in many ways: You may first live with a partner, or sequentially with several partners, without thinking about whether the arrangement will lead to marriage. You may have children with your eventual spouse or with someone else before marrying. You may, in Connecticut, Iowa, Massachusetts, New Hampshire, New York, Vermont, Washington, DC, and Canada, marry someone of the same gender and build a shared marital world with few guidelines to rely on. Moreover, you can have partnerships and children without ever marrying at all. Within marriages and cohabiting unions, roles are more flexible and negotiable, although women still do more than their share of the household work and child rearing (as we will see in the next chapter).

The second difference is in the nature of the rewards that people seek through marriage and other close relationships. People want the individualistic rewards of what's often called personal growth or self-development—a sense that your inner life is changing and developing in a way that gives you great satisfaction—and deeper intimacy. People try to attain these rewards through more open communication and mutually shared disclosures about feelings with their partners. To attain personal growth, they may feel justified in insisting on changes in a relationship that no longer allows them to grow in the directions they wish. In contrast, they are less likely than in the past to focus on the rewards to be found in fulfilling socially valued roles such as the good parent or the loyal and supportive spouse. The result of these changing contexts is that social norms about family and personal life count for less than they did during the heyday of the companionate marriage, and far less than during the period of the institutional marriage. Instead, personal choice and self-development loom large in people's construction of their marital careers.

WHY DO PEOPLE STILL MARRY?

There is, however, a puzzle within the story of the changes in marriage that needs solving: Why do most people still want to marry? After all, with the many choices adults have, it's not necessary, strictly speaking, to marry anymore. To be sure, fewer Americans are marrying than during the peak years of marriage in the mid-twentieth century, but at least 84 percent, according to the best estimate—will eventually marry (U.S. National Center for Health Statistics, 2012). A survey of high school seniors conducted annually since 1976 shows no decline in the importance they attach to marriage. The percentage who respond that "having a good marriage and family life" is extremely important has remained constant, at about 80 percent for young women and 70 percent for young men. And when asked in 2010, "If it were just up to you, what would be the ideal time for you to get married?" only 6 percent of men

---

[6] This section draws upon Cherlin (2009), which provides a fuller discussion of the current context of marriage.

and 5 percent of women chose the response "I don't want to marry" (Johnston, O'Malley, Bachman, & Schulenberg, 2011). Clearly, marriage remains important to many people in the United States. Consequently, I think the interesting question is not why so few people are marrying, but rather, why so many people are marrying, or planning to marry, or hoping to marry, when cohabitation and single parenthood are widely acceptable options.

The dominant theoretical perspectives on marriage in the twentieth century do not provide much guidance on the question of why marriage remains so popular. The functionalist sociologists of the mid-twentieth century, such as Talcott Parsons, argued that the breadwinner–homemaker family was best suited to the demands of the modern world (Parsons & Bales, 1955), but tens of millions of married women have entered the workforce since then. Economist Gary Becker (1965, 1991) and others developed a similar model of the utility of "specialization" by husbands as wage earners and wives as caring for children and the home, but it too seems less applicable now, as I will argue later in this chapter when we examine the marriage market.

MARRIAGE AS THE CAPSTONE EXPERIENCE

Rather, what has happened, I would argue, is that although the practical importance of being married has declined, its symbolic importance has increased. Marriage is less dominant than it was—you don't have to marry anymore. But it is also more distinctive than it was—precisely because it is optional, it causes married couples to stand out from others. It has evolved from a marker of conformity (doing what every adult was virtually required to do) to a marker of prestige (attaining a special status). Today, marriage is a status young couples build up to, often by living with a partner beforehand, by gaining steady employment or starting a career, by putting away some savings, and even by having children. A half-century ago, marriage's place in the life course used to come before those investments were made, but now it often comes afterward. It used to be the foundation of adult personal life; now it is sometimes the capstone—the last brick put in place when the structure is finally complete.

This new meaning of marriage is not limited to the college-educated. We saw it earlier in the chapter in the attitudes of cohabitants without college degrees, who will not marry until all the bricks are in place. Edin and Kefalas (2005), who studied childbearing and intimate relationships among mothers in low- and moderate-income Philadelphia neighborhoods, wrote,

> *In some sense, marriage is a form of social bragging about the quality of the couple's relationship, a powerfully symbolic way of elevating one's relationship above others in the community, particularly in a community where marriage is rare.*

Two generations ago, young adults got married *before* they had everything they needed. But cohabiting was not an option back then, so they faced the choice of marrying or not living together. Today, with cohabitation as an acceptable option, many young adults are postponing marriage until they pass the milestones that used to occur early in marriage.

Consider a nationally representative survey of 1,003 adults, ages 20–29, conducted in 2001 on attitudes toward marriage (Whitehead & Popenoe, 2001). A majority responded in ways suggestive of the view that marriage is a status that one builds up to. Sixty-two percent agreed with the statement "Living together with someone before marriage is a good way to avoid an eventual divorce," and 82 percent agreed that "It is extremely important to you to be economically set before you get married." Moreover, most indicated a view of marriage as centered on intimacy and love more than on practical matters such as finances and children. Ninety-four percent of those who had never married agreed that "when you marry, you want your spouse to be your soul mate, first and foremost." In contrast, only 16 percent agreed that "the main purpose of marriage these days is to have children." And over 80 percent of the women agreed that it is more important "to have a husband who can communicate about his deepest feelings than to have a husband who makes a good living." Being a soul mate, communicating deep feelings: These are hallmarks of the individualistic marriage.

THE WEDDING AS A STATUS SYMBOL

Even the wedding has become an individual achievement. In the distant past, a wedding was an event at which two kinship groups formed an alliance. More recently, it has been an event organized and paid for by parents, at which they display their approval and support for their child's marriage. In both cases, it has been the ritual that provides legal and social approval for having children. But in keeping with the individualistic marriage, it is now becoming an event centered on and often controlled by the couple themselves, having less to do with family approval or having children than in the past.

You might think, then, that weddings would become smaller and that many couples would forgo a public wedding altogether. But that does not appear to have happened for most couples. The wedding, it seems, has become an important symbol of the partners' personal achievements and a stage to display their self-development. Studies suggest that the percentage of weddings held in a religious institution, the percentage with receptions, and the percentage followed by a honeymoon have increased (Whyte, 1990). In recent decades, then, when partners decide that their relationship has finally reached the stage where they can marry, they generally want a ritual-filled wedding to celebrate it (Boden, 2003; Bulcroft, Bulcroft, Bradley, & Simpson, 2000; Bulcroft, Bulcroft, Smeins, & Cranage, 1997; Ingraham, 1999; Mead, 2007).

Even low- and moderate-income couples who have limited funds and who may already have children and may be living together seem to view a substantial wedding as a requirement for marriage. Some of the young adults in the Toledo study said that merely going "downtown" for a civil ceremony at a courthouse or a justice of the peace's office did not constitute an acceptable wedding. A home health care aide said she was waiting for her boyfriend to change his mind about a church wedding because, "until he does, we just won't get married. I'm not going downtown. . . . I say, you don't want a big wedding, we're not going to get married" (Smock, Manning, & Porter, 2005). The authors of the Philadelphia study write, "Having the wherewithal to throw a 'big' wedding is a vivid display that the couple has achieved enough financial security to do more than live from paycheck to paycheck" (Edin & Kefalas, 2005). The couples in these studies wanted to make a statement through their weddings, a statement both to themselves and to their friends and family that they had passed a milestone in their personal development.

Big weddings are popular as a symbol of a successful personal life.

Through wedding ceremonies, the purchase of a home, and the acquisition of other accoutrements of married life, individuals hoped to display their attainment of a prestigious, comfortable, stable style of life. People marry now not only for the social benefits that marriage provides but also for the personal achievement—the capstone experience—it represents.

Quick Review

- People have more choices today about how to live their personal lives.
- The rewards that people seek in marriages and other close relationships center on personal growth and deeper intimacy.
- Marriage still provides partners greater trust that both will honor their commitment, although less so than in the past.
- Marriage is still important as a symbol of status and prestige.
- Increasingly, young adults are delaying marriage until they have accomplished other goals such as obtaining steady employment or buying a home.

MARRIAGE AND RELIGION

Organized religion in the United States has always supported marriage, and it has continued to do so throughout the transitions to the companionate and independent marriages. The United States is probably the most religious nation in the Western world. A comparable set of surveys conducted in more than 60 nations between 1999 and 2001 shows that Americans go to church more often than do people in every other Western nation except Ireland and that they think of themselves as "religious persons" more than in any Western nation except Italy. Moreover, they tend to believe that what they learn from

Studies show that married men and women tend to live longer than divorced or never-married men and women.

religion is relevant to their family lives. When asked, "Generally speaking, do you think that the churches in your country are giving adequate answers to . . . the problems of family life?" more Americans (61 percent) said yes than did people in any other Western country (Inglehart et al., 2004).

Conservative (or evangelical) Protestant and Mormon young adults, particularly those who attend church regularly and say that religion is important, tend to marry at earlier ages than other young adults (Lehrer, 2004; Xu, Hudspeth, & Bartkowski, 2005; Eggebeen & Dew, 2009). Among married persons, those who are active religiously describe themselves as somewhat happier with their marriages (Booth, Johnson, Branaman, & Sica, 1995); and they also tend to report better mental health (Waite & Lehrer, 2003). Couples who attend religious services frequently have a lower risk of divorce than do those who attend less often (Bramlett & Mosher, 2002). (I will have more to say about divorce risks in Chapter 12.) It is not clear, however, whether religious activity causes these differences or whether other, unmeasured factors cause both greater well-being and more religious activity.

In recent years, churches have been an expanding base for counseling, educational programs, and other attempts at "marriage strengthening." For example, churches have participated in the development of programs to teach communication skills to engaged or recently married couples so that they will be better equipped to discuss and resolve problems that may arise (Markman et al., 2004). The main exception to the emphasis on marriage among religious groups is among African American churches. Although these churches are strong supporters of African American families, they emphasize marriage relatively less and extended family ties relatively more than do predominantly white churches (Gilkes, 1995).

IS MARRIAGE GOOD FOR YOU?

Do individuals benefit from being married? A substantial body of literature shows that married men appear advantaged compared with unmarried men in many ways and that, to a lesser extent, married women seem advantaged as well. But it is difficult to know whether marriage *causes* these differences. For example, married men and women live longer, on average, than do unmarried men and women. One study estimated that unmarried men have a 33 percent higher risk of dying than do married men; and unmarried women have a 14 percent higher risk of dying than do married women (Rendall, Weden, Favreault, & Waldron, 2011). A number of studies have found evidence that married men and women have substantially better health than unmarried men and women, in terms of general life satisfaction, depression and anxiety, and treatment for psychiatric difficulties (Simon, 2002; Waite & Lehrer, 2003).

There are two possible reasons for these findings:

1. *Being married actually causes people to feel better and live longer.* Waite (1995) suggests two ways that marriage might be good for one's physical and mental health. First, it may deter people from undertaking risky behavior. Married men and women are less likely to drink and drive, abuse alcohol or drugs, and get into serious arguments (Umberson, 1987). Marriage may provide people with a sense of responsibility to children and spouses that leads them to take fewer risks. In addition, marriage may provide a partner who monitors a person's health closely and urges a healthier lifestyle. Second, married people have higher incomes and more wealth (Smith, 1994), in part because of economies of scale (two people can share a home or a car). A higher standard of living eases stress and makes people less likely to abuse alcohol or drugs.

2. *Mentally and physically healthier people are more likely to get married and to stay married.* As women and men choose partners, we would expect them to favor the healthy and the happy over the troubled and the ill. So there should be *positive selection into* marriage: People with positive qualities are more likely to enter into it. Recall the discussion of the selection effect on teenage childbearing: Young women who have children as adolescents are not a random sample of all adolescents. Similarly, people who marry are not a random sample of all adults; rather, they represent the most attractive 90 percent of the population in the marriage market. Moreover, people with poorer mental health have marriages that are more troubled and are therefore more likely to divorce. So as couples age, there is *negative selection out of* marriage: People with negative characteristics are more likely to leave it. Because of selection into and out of marriage, we would expect currently married individuals to be physically and mentally healthier even if what goes on in a marriage has nothing to do with it.

Because sociologists cannot randomly assign some people to marry and others to stay single and then study them, we cannot say definitively whether being married actually causes people's health and mood to improve or whether we are merely witnessing a selection effect. But the findings for men, at least, are so strong and consistent across a number of studies of different domains of life as to suggest that some of the advantages shown by married men are caused by the marriage relationship itself. And it is likely that there are benefits for women as well. If the effects of marriage were purely due to selection, we would expect that as people get older, the difference between the married and unmarried would increase—because the unmarried group would be composed more and more of unhealthy individuals who never married or who divorced. But data on death rates and treatment for mental illness do not show a gap between the married and the unmarried that increases with age (Rendall et al., 2011). Marriage might benefit men more than women because unmarried men have fewer social resources to draw on. As Chapter 10 will show, women are enmeshed in support networks with other women—mothers, sisters, grandmothers—much more than men are. In contrast, men tend to rely heavily on their wives for social support; and they therefore have more to gain from marrying.

Quick Review

- People who are actively religious marry earlier and have somewhat happier marriages.
- The advantages married people show may be partly due to selection and partly to marriage itself.

THE MARRIAGE MARKET

Despite the rise of cohabitation, most Americans eventually marry. When sociologists and economists study who marries whom, they often make an analogy to the labor market, in which people seeking employment look for employers who will hire them at an acceptable wage. In the **marriage market,** unmarried individuals (or their parents) search for others who will marry them (or their children). Instead of an acceptable wage, the searchers require that a partner have an acceptable set of desired characteristics, such as a college education, good looks, a pleasant disposition, and so forth.

marriage market an analogy to the labor market in which single individuals (or their parents) search for others who will marry them (or their children)

There are three components to this market model of marriage. The first component is simply a group of people who are actively looking for a spouse at the same place at the same time. They constitute the *supply* of men and women who are in the marriage market. The second component is *preferences.* Each person has an idea of his or her own preferred characteristics in a spouse. Some people may care more about good looks, others more about personality or earning potential. A person will try to find a mate who ranks as high as possible on the characteristics she or he prefers. And that same person will probably have a minimum set of characteristics that she or he will accept. The third component is *resources.* These are the characteristics a person possesses that are attractive to others. In a sense resources are the flip side of preferences: Resources are what I have that a partner might want; preferences are what I want a partner to have.

So people who are looking for spouses, who have preferences about the qualities they want, and who have resources to offer create a marriage market. To be sure, it is difficult in real life to decide just who is looking for a spouse and who isn't. The growth of cohabitation makes this problem even more difficult. Moreover, this depiction of searchers as rational, calculating individuals who tote up the pluses and minuses of prospects is at odds with the popular image of people falling in love with each other. Clearly, the market metaphor can't explain everything about who marries whom. Nevertheless, in the aggregate, the behavior of unmarried persons resembles that of job searchers enough that the metaphor is useful.[7]

Sometimes preferences and resources are so incompatible that the market can't provide acceptable spouses for all who are looking. One explanation for the drop in the African American marriage rate is that decent-paying industrial jobs—making steel or cars or television sets—have moved to firms in developing countries, so that men without college educations (and African American men are less likely to have attended college) have a harder time finding a job that can support a family. Therefore African American women, so this argument goes, can't find enough employed African American men to marry (Wilson, 1987). Recent studies have indeed found that women's marriage rates are lower in areas where more men were unemployed, although the effect has not been large enough to fully explain racial differences in marriage patterns. High levels of homicide, imprisonment, and drug use also remove some black men from the marriage market.

The Specialization Model   In the predominant marriage bargain of the mid-twentieth century, men placed a greater emphasis on the homemaking skills of their wives; conversely, women placed a greater emphasis on the earning potential of their spouses. This, as I noted earlier in the chapter, is the bargain hailed in the writings of Talcott Parsons and his associates in the 1950s. It is also the bargain implied by the theory of the division of labor advanced by economist Gary Becker, whose theoretical work since the 1960s pioneered the economic approach to studying the family (1991).

Becker drew his model from the theory of international trade, under which each country is said to have a "comparative advantage" in producing particular goods relative to other countries. For example, a poor, underdeveloped country with land and farmers but few schools and factories might be able to produce grain more "efficiently" than tractors. In contrast, a developed country such as the United States, with its assembly-line factories and skilled workers, may be able to produce tractors (and other manufactured goods) more efficiently than grain. If so, according to the theory, each country will benefit if the underdeveloped country specializes in producing grain, some of which it can trade for tractors, and the developed country specializes in producing tractors, some of which it can trade for grain. Becker's application of this model to the family is straightforward: If women are more "efficient" at housework and child care relative to earning money—either because they are better at caring for children or because they tend to be paid less than men—and men are more efficient at earning money rather than at housework and child care, both will benefit if the wife specializes in housework and child care and the husband specializes in paid work outside the home. Consequently, the model predicts that in the marriage market women will search for good providers and men will search for good homemakers. We might call this the **specialization model** of the marriage market.

specialization model a model of the marriage market in which women specialize in housework and child care and men specialize in paid work outside the home

---

[7] The job search analogy has been carried furthest by Oppenheimer (1988).

Table 7.1   Changes in the Importance College Students Attach to Characteristics of Potential Marriage Partners, 1939–1996

CHARACTERISTICS THAT HAVE INCREASED IN VALUE (1996 RANKING IN PARENTHESES)

FOR MEN	FOR WOMEN
Love (1)	Love (1)
Education (5)	Education (5)
Sociability (7)	Sociability (8)
Good looks (8)	Good looks (13)
Similar educational background (12)	
Good financial prospects (13)	

CHARACTERISTICS THAT HAVE DECREASED IN VALUE (1996 RANKINGS IN PARENTHESES)

FOR MEN	FOR WOMEN
Desire for home and children (9)	Ambition, industriousness (7)
Refinement, neatness (11)	Good health (9)
Good cook, homemaker (14)	Refinement, neatness (7)
Chastity (16)	Chastity (17)

Source: Buss, Shackelford, Kirkpatrick, & Larsen, 2001.

The Income-Pooling Model   But the specialization model no longer fits the marriage market well. Consider a set of 18 characteristics of potential marriage partners that was presented to a sample of college students in 1939 and then again to college samples in 1956, 1967, 1977, 1984/1985, and 1996 (Buss, Shackelford, Kirkpatrick, & Larsen, 2001). The students were asked to rank the characteristics in order of importance to them. Several of the most highly valued characteristics hardly changed their rankings: Dependable character, emotional stability and maturity, and pleasing disposition were among the top five at all times. What's of interest are the characteristics that increased or decreased in the rankings over the decades. Table 7.1 shows, for men and women, characteristics that increased in value (defined as increasing by at least three ranks) or decreased in value (decreasing at least three ranks), along with their final, 1996 rank.

It's clear from Table 7.1 that characteristics associated with intimacy and companionship, such as love, sociability, and good looks (the last of which is ranked higher by men than by women), have increased in value for both men and women. But notice, in addition, that good financial prospects increased in importance for men, which suggests that men increasingly value the earnings prospects of potential wives. Moreover, education, which can connote both shared cultural values and better earnings prospects, increased for both men and women. The bottom half of the table shows that characteristics associated with domesticity, such as caring about home and children, being a good cook, and being refined and neat, have declined in value for men. For women, characteristics associated with being a good provider, such as good health, ambition, and industriousness, have declined in value. For both men and women, the value of chastity declined in importance, reflecting the greater acceptance of premarital sexual activity.

Overall, the changes in the rankings are consistent with a newer marriage bargain in which, relative to the twentieth century, the following conditions hold: (1) Both men and women place more importance on companionship and intimacy, (2) men place more importance on a woman's earning power, (3) men place less importance on a woman's domestic skills, and (4) women place less importance on signs that the man is a good provider. The changes suggest that the breadwinning-for-homemaking bargain was less salient to young adults at the end of the century. Of course, these studies only included college students, but other more representative surveys suggest similar conclusions (South, 1991).

In general, the specialization model of the marriage market predicted that women with less education and lower earnings would be *more* likely to marry than better-educated, higher-earning women. The former group, it was said, has more to gain by marrying a man who will earn money while they specialize in housework and child care. But the newer bargain suggests an **income-pooling model** of the marriage market, in which both spouses work for pay and pool their incomes. Under this model, a woman with greater earning potential should be more likely to marry because she is more attractive to men seeking to pool incomes. This now seems to be the case: Men with higher earning potential are more likely to marry women with higher earning potential than they were a generation or two ago—suggesting a shift from a specialization model to an income-pooling model. The change may have occurred in the 1980s. Sweeney (2002) and Sweeney and Cancian (2004) compared data for young adults in the 1970s, on the one hand, and the 1980s and early 1990s; they found that the tendency for men and women with higher earning potential to marry each other strengthened over that period. This development probably means that young men are paying more attention to young women's earning potential when they choose a wife because women tend to earn more than they used to.

Comparisons across countries also support this shift in the marriage market. Ono (2003) found that in Japan, where few women work and the specialization model would seem to apply, women with more income are less likely to marry, whereas in Sweden and the United States, where many women work and the income-pooling model is gaining strength, women with more income are more likely to marry. Several other studies of the United States also show that women with greater earning potential have higher rates of marriage (Lichter, McLaughlin, Kephart, & Landry, 1992; Qian & Preston, 1993; Oppenheimer, Blossfeld, & Wackerow, 1995; Oppenheimer & Lew, 1995; McLaughlin & Lichter, 1997), although one study found that women's earning potential was unrelated to the likelihood of marriage (Xie, Raymo, Goyette, & Thornton, 2003).

It appears, then, that the marriage bargain now includes the preference, for most couples, that both spouses will contribute to the family's income. Why has this change occurred? In part, it reflects the greater acceptance of married women's work outside the home. In addition, it reflects the prolonged stagnation of men's wages since the early 1970s. Valerie Oppenheimer (2003) finds that young men with a recent history of unstable employment are less likely to marry than are men with stable employment; but they are *more* likely to cohabit—as if cohabiting is a fallback position for young men whose employment situations are not adequate for marrying. Her article implies that the declining employment prospects of less-educated young men may be a factor in the increase in cohabitation and the later age at first marriage.

income-pooling model a model of the marriage market in which both spouses work for pay and pool their incomes

Quick Review

- A specialization model of the marriage market, in which men traded earning potential for women's housework and childbearing efforts, predominated in the mid-twentieth century.
- An income-pooling model, in which women and men both offer earning potential, arose over the past few decades.
- The greater acceptance of married women's work outside the home and the declining earning power of men without college educations underlie this transition.

Social Change and Intimate Unions

Prior to about 1960, marriage was the only acceptable way for adults to have intimate partnerships and to raise children. So dominant was marriage that people who never married were viewed as having incomplete lives and as being perhaps defective in some way. Never-married older women were derided as "spinsters" or "old maids." A historian labeled the period from 1850 to 1960 in Britain, which had similar trends, "the age of mandatory marriage" (Gillis, 1985). During this age a strict division of labor arose, in which husbands were to work outside the home and wives were to manage the home and care for children. But great changes have occurred since the mid-twentieth century.

CHANGES IN UNION FORMATION

union formation the process of beginning to live with a partner through cohabitation or marriage

Table 7.2 summarizes the changes since the 1950s in **union formation,** the process of beginning to live with a partner through cohabitation or marriage. In the 1950s, most young women and many young men did not have sex until they were engaged or married. If a premarital pregnancy occurred, the mother and father usually married quickly to avoid the stigma of an "illegitimate" birth. Cohabitation was scandalous and virtually unknown among the middle class; and even among the poor it was less common than today. Nearly everyone married, and they did so at younger ages than before or since. The birthrate rose to a twentieth-century high. Women expected to stay at home after marrying, and men expected to be the family's sole earner—the so-called good provider (Bernard, 1981). Husbands and wives expected to be loving companions and friends and to derive great pleasure from being successful spouses and parents.

In the early twenty-first century, nearly all these conditions have changed. Most young adults begin to have sex many years before they marry, and better birth control technology and legalized abortion make it easier for them to do so. The typical age at marriage is much higher than at midcentury, and the proportion of people who never marry has grown. Unmarried women can give birth to children outside of marriage with little stigma, although many cohabiting couples who conceive marry before the child is born. More than half of all young adults cohabit prior to marrying. For some, cohabitation is an alternative to marriage, whereas for others, it is a way to see whether they and their partners are compatible enough to marry.

Table 7.2   Changes in Union Formation Since the Mid-Twentieth Century

	1950s	1990s
When do sexual relations begin?	For a majority of women and many men, sexual relations began only after engagement or marriage.	Sexual relations typically begin many years before a union is formed.
What happens when premarital pregnancies occur?	Usually led to a hasty marriage because childbearing outside of marriage was highly stigmatized.	Much less likely to lead to marriage because childbearing outside of marriage is more acceptable. Still, many cohabiting couples marry when a pregnancy occurs.
Who cohabits?	Cohabitation is common only among the poor; it is not considered respectable among the nonpoor.	More than half of all young adults will cohabit before they marry. It has become an important part of the process of finding a marital partner.
Who marries and when?	About 95 percent of whites and almost 90 percent of blacks married; average age at marriage was younger than in any other decade.	About 90 percent of whites will marry, and about two-thirds of blacks will marry. Typical ages at marriage are several years older than in the 1950s.
What is the economic bargain?	Men typically exchanged their earning power for women's housework and child-rearing effort. Middle-class and working-class married women rarely worked outside the home.	Men and women typically pool their earnings and achieve economies of scale (i.e., only one mortgage to pay for). Women with higher earning potential are more likely to marry.
What is the cultural expectation?	Companionship and satisfaction through playing the roles of spouse and parent.	Ongoing self-development, intimacy, and communication.

The marital bargain has also changed. It is based more on a pooling of joint earnings than on an exchange of men's earnings for women's housework and child care. Men are still required to be good, steady earners in order to be acceptable as husbands; but increasingly women are expected to be good earners as well. Although women still provide more of the housework and child care, the marital bargain typically calls for men to do more work at home than was the case at midcentury. Women with higher earning potential may be using their economic attractiveness to strike a bargain that results in a more equitable distribution of work in the home. On an emotional level, wives and husbands are increasingly concerned with self-development, intimacy, and communicating their feelings and desires. In addition, more lesbian and gay couples are living openly in same-sex cohabiting relationships and, in at least five states, marriages. Like heterosexual couples, many are concerned with self-development, intimacy, and communication.

Many of the changes since the mid-twentieth century have weakened the role of marriage in personal life. In fact, given the greater acceptability of alternative living arrangements, one might ask why so many people still marry. One reason is that marriage still allows a partner to have greater trust in the commitment the other partner has to the relationship. Marriage requires a commitment to a long-term, possibly lifelong, relationship, although that advantage is weaker than it used to be.

The marital bargain is increasingly based on pooling the earnings of wives and husbands.

In addition, marriage is still a marker of prestige and distinction. In fact, as fewer people marry and young adults take longer to do it, the prestige that marriage confers may be growing. Marriage is now, in part, a step people take to distinguish themselves from others. Some cohabiting couples are postponing marriage until after they have achieved job stability, have amassed enough savings to buy a home, and in some cases have had children together. Marriage used to be the foundation of adult personal life; now it is sometimes the crowning achievement. Church ceremonies and wedding parties seem to be popular, even among people who aren't particularly religious, in part because they demonstrate commitment, but also because they show family and friends that one's personal life is a success. Nevertheless, despite these advantages, it is clear that marriage does not hold as privileged a position in our family system as it did in the mid-twentieth century. The gains to marriage, relative to alternatives, are perceived to be lower on average today than they were 50 or 60 years ago.

MARRIAGE AS AN ONGOING PROJECT

Perhaps the most fundamental change in marriage is this one: Whereas in earlier times what mattered most in a marriage was how well you and your spouse carried out your duties, now what matters most is whether the marriage helps you to achieve a more fulfilling sense of self, to grow as an individual, or to experience a greater level of personal satisfaction. Intimacy and love are now a quest for fulfillment and identity (Swidler, 2001). Unlike in the past, the quest doesn't end when you find a marriage partner; on the contrary, it involves a continuing effort to find a better personal life through an evolving relationship. It also implies a new model of adulthood. In the old model, you developed an identity in young adulthood, found a partner compatible with that identity, got married, and then further personality development stopped. Now there is a cultural imperative to keep changing and developing your identity throughout adulthood in order to maintain, or better yet, increase your personal fulfillment.

Developing a satisfying sense of self through love and sexual expression, then, becomes an ongoing project throughout adulthood. To carry out this project, a married person must be able to communicate openly and honestly with his or her spouse about thoughts and feelings. Consequently, communication and understanding become highly valued qualities. But suppose one partner isn't satisfied with his or her self-development in the relationship. Or suppose one partner feels he or she has gotten all the personal benefits out of the relationship that are possible. Then, given the new emphasis on self-development as the standards by which to judge intimate relationships, there is little reason for the unsatisfied partner to stay in the relationship. On the contrary, the emphasis on self-development encourages this partner to leave.

In this way, the emphasis on self-development devalues qualities such as commitment, trust, and permanence (Swidler, 2001). The cultural changes surrounding love and marriage have made it more acceptable for a person to leave a relationship if he or she feels personally dissatisfied. One is no longer expected to keep a marriage together for the sake of the children. This emphasis on self-fulfillment and development in marriage has placed high expectations on the relationship. Only in the twentieth and early twenty-first centuries has marriage had to bear such a heavy responsibility for personal happiness, and the institution may not be able to match the expectations spouses now have. To be sure, there are other important causes of the post-1960 rise in divorce, foremost among them the increasing economic independence of women and the declining economic prospects for men without college degrees. (This topic will be examined in detail in Chapter 12.) Nevertheless, the cultural changes in the way people evaluate love and marriage have certainly played a significant role.

The increased emphasis on self-development in marriage has been criticized as creating shallow, potentially exploitative relationships in which each partner seeks what's best for his or her own development—but not what's best for the marriage and for their children. Yet there is also a positive side to this form of marriage. Communication and negotiation may allow couples to attain greater intimacy than if they were forced to retain their initial way of relating. Although it is easy to criticize the excesses of the search for a more fulfilling personal life, the ability of couples to increase their satisfaction through communication and openness may revitalize some marriages. The independence of the partners may also create a more democratic marriage in which husbands and wives are equals.

The egalitarianism of late-modern marriage has also relieved men of the obligation to be the sole supporters of their families. Its flexible roles have provided men with the opportunity to be more involved in their children's roles. In these ways, the individualistic marriage holds out the possibility of a fuller life, and a more equal partnership for both spouses. Whether the emergence of the individualized marriage is favorable for children is another issue, which will be examined in Chapter 9. Moreover, even for the spouses, the possibilities are not always realized: Only a minority of fathers share the child care and housework equally, and power imbalances remain a feature of many marriages, as the next chapter will show.

Looking Back

1. **What is the history of courtship and dating?** In the United States and other Western nations, for centuries young adults went about finding a spouse through the publicly visible process of courtship. The practice declined in the United States after 1900 due to migration to large cities, growing affluence, and the emergence of adolescence as a protected time between childhood and adulthood. The rise of dating after 1900 placed courtship on an economic basis and transferred power from young women (and their parents) to young men. The heyday of dating was probably 1945 to 1965; toward the end of the century, it declined. In recent decades, spending time in groups and relationship-free sexual encounters (hook ups) has increased.

2. **How has marriage changed over the past century?** The institutional marriage was held together by community pressure and the authority of the family head. But by the mid-twentieth century, it had been eclipsed by the companionship marriage, which was held together more by mutual affection and intimacy. The ideal type of companionate marriage was the single-earner breadwinner–homemaker family that flourished in the 1950s. Beginning in the late 1960s, this model was overtaken by the individualistic marriage, in which both spouses were increasingly concerned with personal growth and self-fulfillment. In the individualistic marriage, the relationship between spouses tends to be seen as an ongoing project that is open to negotiation and change.

3. **What is marriage like today?** Although Americans now have more choices about their personal lives, most still marry. Marriage still provides some benefits that cohabitation does not, such as greater trust in one's partner's commitment. However, people also see marriage as a symbol of achieving a successful adult life. They build up to marriage, postponing it until they have all of the prerequisites in place. They use religious wedding ceremonies (rather than courthouse weddings) to display their personal achievements to friends and relatives.

4. **What is the role of cohabitation in the American family system?** Prior to 1970, cohabitation was found largely among the poor. Since then the practice has expanded greatly at all income levels. In the United States today, a majority of marriages are now preceded by a period of cohabitation. These unions tend to lead within a few years to either marriage or a breakup. Cohabitation is a diverse phenomenon that includes not only childless young adults, but also couples with children. A substantial share of the children who are officially born outside of marriage are actually born to two cohabiting parents. The nature of cohabitation varies by social class. For college-educated young adults, cohabitation is often a stage in the marriage process. For the non-college-education, cohabitation is not as closely linked to marriage.

5. **How does the marriage market work?** The marriage market—a model that is widely used by social scientists—consists of individuals who are searching for a spouse in a particular geographic area, who have a set of preferences concerning the type of person they wish to find and a set of resources to offer in return. The predominant marriage bargain at mid-twentieth century, based on the specialization model of marriage, involved a husband who traded his earnings in return for child care and housework by his wife. This model of marriage no longer fits the present-day marriage market. In particular, evidence suggests that both men and women now prefer partners with good earnings potential.

Go to the Online Learning Center at www.mhhe.com/cherlin7e
to test your knowledge of the chapter concepts and key terms.

Study Questions

1. What are the differences between nineteenth-century courtship and twentieth-century dating?
2. How do the cohabiting relationships of college-educated young adults differ from the cohabiting relationships of less-educated, lower-income young adults?
3. What did Burgess mean when he wrote that marriage was "in transition from an institution to a companionship"?
4. What distinguishes the individualistic marriage from the companionate marriage?
5. What does it mean to say that marriage has become a "capstone" experience?
6. Why is it difficult to tell whether marriage improves the well-being of women and men?
7. What characteristics of women and men have become more highly valued on the marriage market in recent decades, and why?
8. Is marriage so weakened as an institution that it is likely to become just one of many possible adult lifestyles?

Key Terms

cohabitation   214
companionate marriage   224
courtship   210
hooking up   212
income-pooling model   239

individualistic
   marriage   226
institutional marriage   222
marriage market   236
serial cohabitation   219

specialization model   237
union   209
union formation   240

Thinking about Families

The Private Family	The Public Family
Do people expect too much emotional satisfaction from a cohabiting partner or spouse?	Should the public be concerned about the rise of cohabitation and childbearing outside marriage?

Families on the Internet   www.mhhe.com/cherlin7e

Note: While all the URLs listed were current as of the printing of this book, these sites often change. Please check our Web site (www.mhhe.com/cherlin7e) for updates.

Believe it or not, a thriving market exists for men who want to import brides from other countries, much as the pioneers of the old West imported "mail order brides." Only now the Internet is central. For example, to investigate the market in Russian women who are willing to marry American men, enter "Russian brides" into a search engine. It will return the Web addresses of numerous matchmaking agencies. For information on the modern mail-order bride industry, go to www.bridesbymail.com, which includes an online resource library. It lists numerous Web sites offering introductions to women from Russia and many other countries around the world.

In recent years, a loosely knit "marriage movement" has arisen to promote marriage. Visit the Web site of the Coalition for Marriage, Family, and Couples Education (www.smartmarriages.com) to obtain information. What is the case this group is making for marriage?

Chapter Eight

Work and Families

Looking Forward

From Single-Earner to Dual-Earner Marriages

Behind the Rise

A Profound Change

The Current Situation

The Division of Labor in Marriages

Rethinking Caring Work

Breaking the Work/Family Boundary

Care Work as a Public Responsibility

Valuing Caring Labor

Toward an Ethic of Care

Who's Doing the Care Work?

Wives' Earnings and Domestic Work

The Current State of Sharing

Work-Family Balance

Overworked and Underworked Americans

When Work Interferes with Family Life

Task Size

Job Stress

Nonstandard Work Hours

Toward a Responsive Workplace?

Looking Back

Study Questions

Key Terms

Thinking about Families

Families on the Internet

Boxed Features

FAMILIES AND THE GREAT RECESSION: *What Long-Term Unemployment Does to Marriage*

FAMILIES AND PUBLIC POLICY: *Paid Parental Leave*

Looking Forward

1. How has married women's work changed over the past half-century?

2. How does our society treat the labor of caring for others?

3. How has the division of labor in marriages changed?

4. What are some of the strains working parents can experience?

5. How is the workplace responding to the needs of working parents?

"Women call the shots at home," was the title of the press release that a reporter read to me over the phone. She was referring to a national telephone survey of married or cohabiting women and men that was conducted by the Pew Research Center (Morin & Cohn, 2008). Their interviewers asked people whether they or their partners had the final say in making four decisions: choosing shared weekend activities, buying major things for the home, deciding what to watch on television, and managing the household finances. In 43 percent of the cases, the person being interviewed (who could be a woman or a man) indicated that the woman in the relationship made more of these decisions than the man, compared to 26 percent who said that the man made more. What did I think of that, she asked? Well, first of all, I said, these percentages would change if other kinds of decisions were included (like what car to buy). But I was most interested in a third category: 31 percent said that the couple shares these decisions equally. The interviewers, it turns out, had not explicitly asked the respondents whether they shared each of these decisions; rather, they had just asked for a choice between the woman and the man. In these kinds of surveys, it's rare for people on the other end of the telephone line to volunteer a choice that was not read to them, yet that's just what many did. Forty-six percent, for example, volunteered that they decide together with their partners about buying major things for the home; and 46 percent said they decide together about weekend activities. The real news, I said, was not whether women or men call the shots. It was the rise of shared decision making.

Indeed, other surveys have demonstrated this rise. In 1980 and 2000, random samples of married persons were asked who has the final word most often in decision making. The results showed a clear movement toward more equal decisions. Husbands who reported that the decision making was equal rose from 51 percent in 1980 to 63 percent in 2000, and wives' reports rose from 47 percent to 64 percent. Nearly two-thirds, then, reported equality in the more recent survey (Amato, Booth, Johnson, & Rogers, 2007). The increase in shared decision making, which probably began well before 1980, occurred at the same time that the proportion of housework and child care that husbands do was increasing (although wives still do more of it than their husbands). Both changes in married life were probably linked to the growing number of married women who were working outside the home during the second half of the twentieth century. As women began to do more paid work, they brought in more of the family's income, which may have given them a greater say in making decisions that involve money and which restricted the amount of time they could spend on housework. In other words, changes in the work that family members were doing outside the household influenced the work that family members were doing inside the household, as well as how household decisions were made. The important link between market work and family work is the topic of this chapter.

From Single-Earner to Dual-Earner Marriages

Figure 8.1 shows the low levels of married women's work outside the home at the middle of the twentieth century and the great changes since then. The two lines show the percentage of married women with children who were in the labor force for every year between 1948 and 2007. Government statistical agencies consider the **labor force** to be all people who are either working outside the home or looking for such work. In 1948, only about one-fourth of married women whose youngest children were at least six years old (and therefore in school) were in the labor force, as were only about one-tenth of married women with children under age six.

> **labor force** all people who are either working outside the home or looking for work

The rates rose sharply through the 1990s, leveled off around 2000, and have declined slightly since then. For the moment, at least, the historic rise in married women's labor force participation rates seems to have peaked. In 2010, 77 percent of all married women with school-aged children, and 64 percent of those with pre-school-aged children, were in the labor force, although a majority were working part-time (U.S. Bureau of Labor Statistics, 2011e).

BEHIND THE RISE

Several factors contributed to the increase in married women's labor force participation. During the twentieth century, the service sector of the economy expanded greatly. The **service sector** consists of the workers who provide personal services such as education, health care, communication, restaurant meals, legal representation, entertainment, and so forth. Many of the jobs in the service sector had come to be stereotyped as women's work; these jobs usually required some education but paid less than men's work. Examples include secretary, nurse, and elementary school teacher. As the demand for these kinds of jobs increased, wages increased (although they remained lower than men's wages) and more married women were drawn into the labor force (Oppenheimer, 1970).

> **service sector** workers who provide personal services such as education, health care, communication, restaurant meals, legal representation, entertainment, and so forth

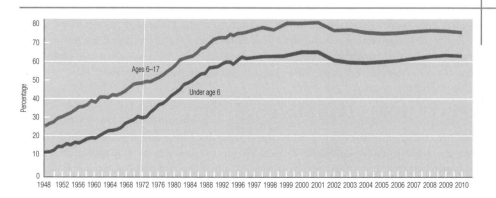

FIGURE 8.1
Labor force participation rates of married women with children under age 18, by age of youngest child, 1948–2010. (*Sources:* U.S. Bureau of Labor Statistics [1988] and U.S. Bureau of the Census, Statistical Abstract of the United States, various years)

The movement of married women into the paid work force is one of the most important changes in family life.

In addition, as the population shifted from farms to cities, each generation (except for the parents of the baby boomers) had fewer children. There was no longer a need for lots of child labor to help on the farm; moreover, the rising wages of women in the labor force meant that women who stayed home were passing up more and more income. As a result, parents' preferred strategy was to have fewer children and to invest more resources in each—to pay for college education or job training courses, for example. This strategy reduced the number of years in which young children would be present in the home and therefore freed married women sooner from child care, the major responsibility that had kept them out of the labor force. Moreover, the decline in the wages of men without college educations since the early 1970s has motivated many wives to take paying jobs. Finally, the high divorce rate of the past several decades made it increasingly risky for married women to leave the labor force and let their job skills deteriorate. Given the low amount of child support payments that most divorced women receive (see Chapter 12), they need to be able to rely on their earning power.

A PROFOUND CHANGE

This great movement of married women into the labor force is one of the most important changes in American family life in the past century. It has profoundly altered women's and men's lives. It has affected the balance of power between women and men. It has been instrumental in the shift from the companionship marriage to the independent marriage, as described in the previous chapter. It has provided the backdrop for debates on issues such as abortion, about which women whose identity is bound up in home and child rearing tend to disagree with women who value working outside the home (see Chapter 14). To be sure, the change has been less pronounced for women from poor or minority backgrounds, who have always had a greater need to work. For example, census statistics show that in 1975, when only 35 percent of white married women with pre-school-aged children were in the labor force, 55 percent of comparable African American women were. Still, labor force participation has increased among African American women as well: By 2007, 69 percent of married African American women with pre-school-aged children were in the labor force (compared with 61 percent of whites) (U.S. Bureau of the Census, 2011v).

THE CURRENT SITUATION

In the early twenty-first century, it is common for married women to remain at work outside the home from young adulthood to retirement. Still, some observers have noted the slight decline in labor force participation rates since 2000 and have speculated that we may be seeing a reversal of the long-term rise. Stories in the media have suggested that well-educated, professional women are "opting out" of the labor force—quitting their jobs to care full-time for their children (Belkin, 2003). But there is little evidence of anything more than a very small decline in the number of professional women who are employed; more than 90 percent are either working or in school (Percheski, 2008). Married women's employment remains at a high level, even if the growth has stopped.

Because of the rise in married women's employment, dual-earner married couples are the rule rather than the exception: Both spouses worked outside the home in 60 percent of all marriages in 2009. And wives' earnings are becoming a more important component of the family's income. In 2009, the median employed wife contributed 37 percent of her family's income (meaning that half provided more than that, and half less than that), up from 27 percent in 1970. It is even becoming common for wives to out-earn their husbands. Thirty-eight percent of employed wives earned more than their husbands in 2009 (U.S. Bureau of Labor Statistics, 2011v). Still, husbands are the main earners in a majority of married-couple households. The rising unemployment rate of the Great Recession hit them harder than it hit their employed wives. (See: *Families and the Great Recession:* What Long-Term Unemployment Does to Marriage.)

Quick Review

- The percentage of married women who work outside the home increased greatly during the second half of the twentieth century.
- The expansion of the service sector of the economy and the drop in the number of children per family contributed to the increase.
- In the 2000s, married women's rates of labor force participation remained high, although with a slight decline.
- Both spouses are employed in a majority of married couples, and it is becoming more common for wives to out-earn their husbands.

Families and the Great Recession

What Long-Term Unemployment Does to Marriage

What happens to marriages when the main earner becomes unemployed? That's an important question for the millions of married couples whose top earners lost their jobs during the Great Recession. Husbands are usually the top earners in a marriage, since not all wives work, and even when they do, their husbands tend to earn more than they do. Men have lost more jobs during the recession than have women because the losses have been greater in the kinds of occupations that tend to hire men, such as factory work and construction. Not that the recession has been easy for women: This is the first recession where they, too, have suffered job losses. For instance, as the recession wore on, hard-pressed state and local governments began to lay off clerical and administrative workers, who were disproportionately women (Boushey, 2011a).

Does a wife who had been caring for children and the home full-time look for paying work when her husband loses his job? If she was working part-time, does she try to get full-time work? Entering the work force is a big step, and in prosperous times, a wife who is devoted to child care and housework won't usually try to find a paying job because she assumes that her husband will quickly find another one. The couple may just dip into their savings, get help from relatives, or cut back on expenses until the husband finds another position.

But during sharp downturns such as the Great Recession, it takes longer for an unemployed breadwinner to find another job. In fact, the Great Recession is causing much more long-term unemployment than any other recession. By the end of 2009, four out of ten unemployed individuals had been out of work for at least one-half of a year, by far the highest level of long-term unemployment in the past half-century (U.S. Bureau of Labor Statistics, 2010). Under these circumstances, the other member of the couple might be compelled to find a job. That's what seems to be happening: In the years before the Great Recession, few wives entered the labor force because their husbands lost jobs; but between 2008 and 2009, many more of them did (Mattingly & Smith, 2010).

The problem can be worse for older couples, who have been more likely to experience unemployment during the Great Recession than have younger couples (Boushey, 2011b). When older adults lose their jobs, it takes them longer to find an employer who will hire them. And it can be especially hard for an older woman who has been out of the labor market for decades to re-enter it because she would typically lack the experience and skills necessary to compete for a job. Long-term unemployment in later life, a feature of the recession, can make it difficult for couples to save for retirement and make them more dependent on Social Security benefits when they do retire.

Moreover, the entrance of wives into the work force can affect relationships within the family. Early on in an economic downturn, families tend to pull together and morale can be high, as the Great Depression teaches us, but the esprit de corps is often temporary. As the downturn continues, tensions surface. During the Depression, some of the men who were unemployed for years eventually lost the respect of their families—and their self-respect—because they could not fulfill the breadwinner role (Komarovsky, 1940). The norm of the male breadwinner is still with us, although it's now acceptable, even preferable, for both spouses to work. Husbands who are out of the work force for several years may still lose the respect of wives and children.

In addition, some wives may not wish to take jobs. Studies tell us that, in general, wives who are employed because they choose to and who gain satisfaction from their work are happy with their choice, whereas wives who say they are working mainly because they need the money are not as happy to be working (Amato, Booth, Johnson, & Rogers, 2007). Many of the latter group say they would prefer to stay home. Wives who are reluctant breadwinners may become dissatisfied with their new roles, especially if their husbands do not reciprocate by doing more around the house. Long-term unemployment, then, can erode the quality of family relationships in a way that a short-term spell out of work does not. And in the Great Recession, long-term unemployment has been stunningly common.

The Division of Labor in Marriages

We have seen that the role of women in the paid labor market has changed dramatically over the past half-century. Great changes have also occurred in the roles of women and men in the home. In addition, how sociologists think about housework and child care has evolved, as a new perspective—care work studies—has arisen in response to the trends.

RETHINKING CARING WORK

It's clear that society can no longer rely on the unpaid labor of stay-at-home wives and mothers to provide the care that family members need. In this sense, the movement of women into the labor force has created a "crisis in care" (Glenn, 2000a). The crisis has also spawned a growing body of social research, theory, and advocacy on the topic of caring. In this new literature, "care work" has emerged as the central concept—one might even speak of a care work movement (Stone, 2000). Some authors conceive of care work very broadly, but I will propose a narrower definition consistent with this book's focus on families. Let us define **care work** as activity in which one person meets the needs of spouses, partners, children, parents, or others who cannot fully care for themselves. The person who does the care work is the caregiver, and the person who gets the care is the care-receiver. Within families, children, the frail elderly, and the ill or disabled are the obvious care receivers. But wives and husbands also perform care work by providing emotional support and household goods and services to each other.

care work activity in which one person meets the needs of spouses, partners, children, parents, or others who cannot fully care for themselves

Breaking the Work/Family Boundary The writers in the care work movement put forth at least four principles. First, they argue that the separation between what goes on in families and what goes on in the world of work is artificial and should be abolished. As the suffix "work" in care work suggests, these authors maintain that what caregivers do should be thought of as work. This seems obvious when one thinks about workers in child care centers. The care work movement suggests that we view caring labor not just through the lens of the private family but also through the lens of the public family. To be sure, care work provides private, emotional satisfaction for family members, but it also provides a publicly useful service.

Valuing Caring Labor Third, caring labor, the writers maintain, is often underpaid, undervalued, and even demeaned relative to other kinds of work (Tronto, 1993). Care is often considered "women's work," a phrase that often implies unpaid or low-paid work of marginal importance. Women constitute the vast majority of paid caregivers: 95 percent of child care workers and 88 percent of health aides, for example (U.S. Bureau of the Census, 2011b). Moreover, they are disproportionately drawn from the less advantaged racial-ethnic groups—such as immigrant Hispanic and Asian women.

People who perform paid care work earn less than people who do comparable work that does not involve care. Three researchers estimated the "wage penalty" that women who are employed at child care centers or as nannies pay for doing care work: Even taking into account the skills required

American society has relied on stay-at-home wives to perform much of the care of infirm elderly parents.

for the job, the education needed, and the prior work experience they tend to have, women who are employed as child care workers earn 26 percent less then women who work at comparable noncaring jobs (England, Budig, & Folbre, 2002). Other statistics tell the same story of low pay for child care work: A government earnings survey in 2004 reported that full-time child care workers had average hourly earnings of $9.42, which was two cents less than the average hourly earnings of garage and gas station workers (U.S. Bureau of Labor Statistics, 2005).

Paula England (2005) presents three possible reasons why care work does not pay as much as noncaring work:

- As noted above, people tend to devalue and even demean labor that is thought of as "women's work," which care work historically has been. Employers either underestimate the value of the work women do or are culturally biased against paying women as much as they pay men for comparable work. For example, they may still believe it's more important to pay men well because they should be the breadwinners for their families—a common position a half-century ago.

- Labor that creates public goods, such as children who will grow up to be responsible members of society, tends to be underpaid. The reason is that it is difficult to stop people from "free-riding," obtaining the benefits of the public goods without having to pay for them. I don't have to pay child care workers to benefit from the next generation of responsible workers because I will receive a Social Security check based on the taxes they will pay whether or not I have children.

- Many people find satisfaction in caring for others. In other words, they may find caring work intrinsically fulfilling and be willing to accept lower pay for a caring job than for a noncaring job. Child care workers may enjoy caring for children and accept low pay to enter the field, or they may get attached to the children they are caring for and not leave the job for a higher paying one. Employers of child care workers may, in a sense, take advantage of people's desire to help others by offering low wages.

The care work movement urges that caregivers such as child care workers and nursing home aides receive higher pay and greater respect.

Toward an Ethic of Care   Fourth, some writers urge the development of an "ethic of care" (Tronto, 1993) in American society. They argue that Americans overvalue individualism and autonomy and undervalue interdependence and caring (Fineman, 2004; Eichner, 2005). Americans are not just autonomous, they contend, but also interdependent. Therefore, everyone needs care on some level (Glenn, 2000a). As the old morality in which housewives were the guardians of caring has faded, the writers maintain, a newer morality of interdependence and mutual caring must replace it. Currently, women and economically disadvantaged individuals seem to value an ethic of care more than other Americans. For example, Michèle Lamont (2000) interviewed both white and African American working-class men. The white men, she wrote, evinced a "disciplined self," in which hard work and responsibility—showing up at work each day to earn a paycheck for one's family—are of paramount importance. In contrast, many of the African American men evinced more of a "caring self," in which solidarity with the less fortunate and generosity to those in need are central. An ethic of care would seek to balance these orientations to the world—to temper autonomy with interdependence, to augment personal responsibility with care for others. It is an attractive vision, but it isn't clear that it can successfully take root in late modern culture.

Quick Review

- The movement of wives into the paid workforce limits their ability to provide unpaid caring work in the home.
- The resulting "crisis in care" has focused attention on care work, the face-to-face caregiving that used to be done in families by wives who weren't working for wages.
- From the care-work perspective, the caring that goes on in families should be considered as "work" whether or not the caregivers are paid.
- Caring labor is often undervalued; it is also done disproportionately by women and members of minority racial-ethnic groups.

WHO'S DOING THE CARE WORK?

Do young adults want to share the care work as well as the paid work? Most of the New York-area young adults in a recent study said that they hoped to create marriages or committed partnerships that would be egalitarian (Gerson, 2010) in sharing both kinds of work. Young men were looking for a partner to share not only the child care but also the responsibility of earning enough to support a family. Young women were looking for a partner who would not just earn a good living but also participate fully in life at home.

FIGURE 8.2
Minutes per day spent in unpaid domestic work, Americans aged 19 to 64, 1965–2003.
(*Source:* Fisher, Egerton, Gershuny, & Robinson, 2007)

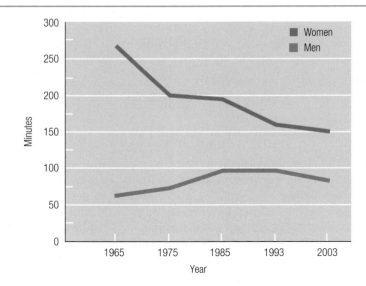

The term "egalitarian" didn't necessarily mean a strict 50/50 division of paid work and home work; it connoted a major investment by each partner in both employment and family life. It meant being flexible in the tasks each partner performed and mutually supportive of the other's roles. The wish for egalitarian partnerships was so widespread that it was even expressed by most of the young adults who had grown up in homes where mothers and fathers played traditional roles.

The changes that have occurred in marriage over the past few decades make it more likely that young adults will be successful in starting egalitarian partnerships, although barriers still exist. We have already seen how much more involved wives are in the world of paid work. There has also been great change in the involvement of husbands in caring work at home. We can see change through the results of the similar national telephone surveys of married persons, mentioned earlier, that were conducted in 1980 and 2000 (Amato et al., 2007; a different sample was interviewed in each survey). In the earlier survey, 29 percent of wives said their husbands did no housework at all; but by the later survey, just 16 percent said that. Meanwhile, the percentage of wives who said their husbands did 50 percent or more of the housework increased from 22 percent to 32 percent. Nearly a third of all wives in 2000, then, told an interviewer that they had an equal division of the housework with their husbands.

time-diary studies
surveys in which people are asked to keep a record of what they were doing every minute during a time period

Or consider almost 40 years of information from **time-diary studies,** in which a random sample of people were asked to keep a record of what they were doing for every minute of a single day. The results of comparable time-diary studies conducted from 1965 to 2003 are shown in Figure 8.2, which displays the number of minutes women and men spent in unpaid domestic work (cooking, cleaning, laundry, shopping, and other unpaid work) but not including child care. In 1965 the average woman spent about five times as many minutes on domestic work as did the average man. By 2003 the gap narrowed to about two to one. Women still do more, but a substantial convergence has occurred, not just in the amount of time spent but also in the attitudes and expectations of women and men about domestic work (Sullivan, 2004).

The trend in who does the child care is similar. According to the time-diary studies, women spent four times as many minutes as did men caring for children in 1965, a gap that narrowed to two times as many minutes in 2003.

WIVES' EARNINGS AND DOMESTIC WORK

How does the amount of work that wives and husbands do outside the home relate to the amount of work they do inside the home? This is an important everyday issue for tens of millions of dual-earner couples. Social exchange theory predicts that if wives' earnings increase relative to their husbands' earnings, they should become less dependent and their household power should increase. They should be able to use that power to get their husbands to do more child care and housework.

But time-diary studies show that, contrary to expectations, husbands do not increase the total amount of time they spend with their children when their wives are employed. They do, however, change what they are doing during the time spent with their children. In particular, they take more responsibility for routine care such as feeding them or dressing them. In nationally-representative time-diary surveys conducted in 2003 through 2007, fathers whose wives were employed reported being alone with their children for three to six hours more than men with non-employed wives (Raley, Bianchi, & Wang, 2012). During this alone time, they can't rely on their wife's presence to help them out. These shifts suggest that employed wives are able to negotiate for their husbands to be more involved in physical caregiving, consistent with the exchange perspective.

In addition, as the mother's income rises, the couple is likely to purchase more outside care for children, such as use of a day care center (Brandon, 1999). The same goes for housework: Another look at Figure 8.2 shows that the total time that men and women spent in domestic work declined between 1965 and 2003 because the time women spent decreased more than the time men spent rose. Married couples today are more likely to purchase services to replace some of the housework that wives used to perform, such as cooking and cleaning. Daily lives depend not only on the couples' labor but also on cleaning services and fast food restaurants. Married couples may also have become accustomed to slightly less clean homes and more wrinkled clothing than in the past.

THE CURRENT STATE OF SHARING

What, then, should we conclude about the current division of labor between husbands and wives in dual-earner families? Figure 8.3 shows the total hours per week that mothers and fathers spend in paid work, child care, and other unpaid family work (such as housework and shopping), based on time-use surveys from 2003 through 2005 (Milkie, Raley, & Bianchi, 2009). There are bars for mothers employed full-time and part-time and for fathers whose wives are employed full-time and part-time. The height of each bar is the sum of the time spent in all three activities per week. You can see that wives employed full-time spent 73 total hours in all three kinds of work, compared to 68 hours for fathers whose wives worked full-time. The fathers tended to work longer hours for pay (see the blue sections of the bars). They did less childcare (see the red sections) and housework (see the green sections)—about

FIGURE 8.3
Hours per week in work activities among married parents, wives employed full- or part-time, with preschool-aged children, 2003–2005. (*Source:* Milkie, Raley, & Bianchi, 2009)

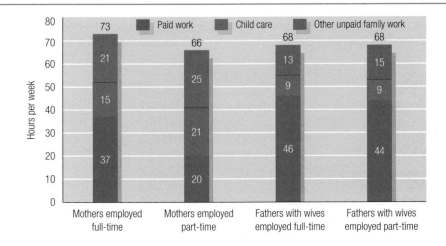

40 percent of it. This 40/60 split of the child care and housework is more equitable than would have been the case a few decades ago; moreover, we have seen that fathers are taking on more responsibility in caring for their children while their wives work. Nevertheless, 40/60 isn't 50/50, and wives do spend a total of five more hours per week (73 minus 68) on all three tasks than do husbands.

Wives also have less leisure; elsewhere in the survey they report spending less time with just adults and less time watching TV than do fathers—a total of seven fewer hours of leisure per week. That's about two weeks less leisure time over the course of a year of 24 hour days. In her classic 1980s study of the "second shift" that employed mothers worked when they came home, Arlie Hochschild estimated that they had about four weeks less leisure time per year. "So twenty-five years didn't rid women of an extra shift," she wrote in the afterword to a recent, revised edition. "But it did cut the length of it in half" (Hochschild, 2012).

When wives work part-time, according to Figure 8.3, they do more child care and housework than do wives who work full-time, not surprisingly. But fathers with wives employed part-time are hardly any different from fathers whose wives work full-time. Fathers don't seem to adjust their time allocation to the amount of time their wives work. (Fathers whose wives don't work at all have very similar time use patterns.) It's wives, not husbands, who seem to make most of the adjustments. The more money the wife makes, the more the family spends on substitutes for housework (restaurant meals) or child care (day care centers). But families do not seem to spend the husband's income on substitutes (Gupta, 2007), just as they don't seem to adjust the father's time in housework and child care when wives increase time spent in paid work. It is as if husbands are entitled to work outside the home regardless of what their wives are doing, and their income goes for housing, utilities, and other day-to-day expenses. The tacit agreement is that the wife will do more of the housework in return. If a job reduces her ability to do household work, then the family may set aside some of her earnings—but not the husband's earnings—to pay others to do what she cannot. It is a reminder that couples still do not see women's and men's earnings as fully equivalent, despite the great increases in wives' earnings over the past several decades.

Overall, we see a mixture of persistence and change in the division of labor between employed wives and husbands. Fathers do more in the home than they used to. Yet although it's more acceptable for husbands to do half the housework and the childcare, only a minority does. Fathers take more responsibility when their wives work for pay, but wives feel more pressure. If young adults consider a 40/60 split to be equitable, then many of the women and men in the New York City study mentioned earlier should be able to establish marriages that meet their hopes. If young adults consider only a 50/50 split to be equitable, then fewer will find the kinds of marriages they are looking for unless changes in husbands' and wives' roles continue.

Whether the changes to date in the division of labor have led to an improvement in people's sense of satisfaction about their marriages is an open question. There was no overall change in the amount of marital happiness that wives and husbands reported in the 1980 and 2000 surveys. When men do more housework and child care, they report lower satisfaction with their marriages, but their wives report greater satisfaction, leading some observers to suggest that sharing the housework leads to the best balance (Amato et al., 2007). Moreover, class differences exist in how wives feel about working for pay. College-educated wives are more likely to report that they are working in part for fulfillment, rather than just for the money, and their marital satisfaction is higher if they are working for pay. In contrast, non-college-educated wives are more likely to report working mainly for the money. They say they receive less help from their husbands; they are more likely to say they would like to work part-time or not at all, and they report lower marital quality than comparably educated wives who do not work for pay (Amato et al., 2007). Not everyone feels the same way about work, and not everyone aims for a fifty-fifty split of both inside- and outside-the-home work (Wilcox & Nock, 2006). The conditions of paid work, the rewards it brings, and the ability to get assistance from spouses can all affect wives' assessment of the quality of their marriages.

Quick Review

- Over the past few decades, the share of housework and child care done by husbands has increased, although they still do less, on average, than their wives.
- The total time spent doing housework has declined, and couples are purchasing more services.
- Husbands in dual-earner marriages take more responsibility of caring for children by themselves.
- Wives feel more pressure and do more multitasking.
- College-educated women report higher marital satisfaction if they are working for pay, whereas less-educated women report lower marital satisfaction if they are working for pay.

■ Work-Family Balance

Ultimately, the division of labor at home contributes to the larger issues of whether it's easy or difficult to combine paid work with unpaid family work; whether stress from work corrodes the daily interactions of spouses, parents, and children; whether, in the opposite direction, stress from family life reduces performance at work; and whether the joint demands of work and family are

Historically, African American married women have worked outside the home more than white married women, but the percentage who work has increased in recent decades.

so consuming as to leave no time for relaxation and recreation. These larger questions are ways of asking whether the activities in one's life are in balance. Of course, whether life is balanced is a subjective judgment—the combination of work and family activities that I find most satisfying may not satisfy you. But for all of us, the way that paid employment is organized—who does it, when they do it, where they do it, what the job conditions are like, and so forth—greatly affects our ability to achieve the balance we seek. So an examination of how well work fits with family life these days is important.

OVERWORKED AND UNDERWORKED AMERICANS

Some observers have suggested that balancing work and family has become more difficult for Americans because they are working longer hours. Yet a closer look reveals that while some Americans are overworked, others are underworked. Jerry A. Jacobs and Kathleen Gerson (2004) compared census data from 1970 and 2000 and found two very different trends. People with professional and managerial jobs were indeed working longer hours in 2000 than in 1970. Most of these people received weekly salaries that remained the same no matter how many hours they worked. Consequently, employers had an incentive to pressure them to work longer hours, especially given the downsizing of the workforce in many firms. In contrast, people in other occupations were working fewer hours in 2000 than in 1970. These workers tended to receive hourly wages, which meant their employers had to pay them more for every extra hour worked. Instead of encouraging these sales and these service workers to work longer hours, employers have tended to hire more part-time workers. Often part-time workers are not eligible for fringe benefits such as health insurance, which provides further savings to employers. In sum, the labor market seems to be moving in opposite directions at the top and bottom, toward longer hours among the college educated and shorter hours among the less well educated.

The stresses of work can spill over to the home lives of married couples.

Overall, however, the percentage of Americans who work very long weeks (50 hours or more) is higher than in Canada and eight European countries, including the United Kingdom, France, and Germany (Jacobs & Gerson, 2004). And dual-earner couples in the United States work a higher number of total hours than do couples in these countries. Yet despite the number of parents working long hours, fewer preschool children are in publicly financed child care in the United States than in most of these countries. So although more parents work long hours in the United States, public support for child care is relatively low.

WHEN WORK INTERFERES WITH FAMILY LIFE

A pair of surveys conducted 25 years apart show how feelings of conflict between work and family have increased. In 1977, 34 percent of workers said they felt "some" or "a lot" of interference between their jobs and their family lives, while 45 percent gave that response in 2002 (Families and Work Institute, 2002; see also Nomaguchi, 2009). In the General Social Surveys of 2002, 2006, and 2010, employed adults were asked about interference in both directions (Davis & Smith, 2010). When asked "How often do the demands of your job interfere with your family life?" Fifty-three percent of people who were married with children at home said "often" or "sometimes." A smaller number, 28 percent, gave those responses when asked "How often do the demands of your family interfere with your work on the job?" Nor was work interference limited to married couples. Forty-six percent of single parents and even 37 percent of single adults not living with children said that their jobs interfered with their family lives often or sometimes. Interference flows from work to home more often than from home to work because the workplace is less flexible and gives workers little control over factors such as where and when to work. In contrast, workers can adjust their family lives more easily (as by arranging for child care) in order to reduce the extent to which home life affects one's mood at work (Roehling, Moen, & Batt, 2003).

Task Size   There are two senses in which work could interfere with family life. The first is what we might call task size: the sheer size and scope of the demands of the job. Task size is mainly a problem for professional and managerial employees who work long hours. Their jobs often place unlimited demands on their time and energy and become all-consuming, almost like religious callings. And yet family life also demands an unlimited commitment, so that work and family become "competing devotions" (Blair-Loy, 2003) that are very difficult to reconcile. Individuals are caught between trying to fulfill the cultural ideals of what it means to be a good worker and a good parent. The tools of modern communication—the smart phone, the laptop, scanners, fax machines—allow professionals and managers to do some of their work at home, which can help ease the strain but which also can make it worse by making the workplace always accessible.

Task Stress   The second sense in which work could interfere is to increase emotional stress. Task stress is not necessarily correlated with task size. Many professionals who work long hours find their jobs rewarding and not unduly stressful. Rather, task stress is more likely to be found among less-educated Americans, who perform physically difficult or dangerous work, or who have little job security and could be laid off at any time, or who work under close supervision without the ability to check on their children by calling home. They may bring that stress home with them in what researchers call **spillover,** the transfer of mood or behavior between work and home.

spillover the transfer of mood or behavior between work and home

Psychologists Nicole A. Roberts and Robert W. Levenson (2001) studied the effects of work-to-home spillover on the marriages of 19 male police officers who, at the end of each workday for a month, completed questionnaires about their level of job stress. Once per week the officers and their wives came to a university laboratory, where they were wired to machines that monitored their physiological responses. They were then told to discuss the day's activities. On days when the police officers reported more job stress, they showed heightened arousal in their autonomic nervous system—the "fight or flight" response that people may feel if surprised by something unpleasant. They also displayed less positive emotion and more negative emotion in their conversations with their wives. These reactions—the arousal, the greater negative emotion in conversations—have been shown to be correlated with marital distress and divorce in other studies conducted by the authors and their collaborators.

NONSTANDARD WORK HOURS

Balancing work and family can also be challenging for parents who do not work a standard daytime, Monday through Friday, schedule. Eighteen percent of all workers had evening, night, or rotating (sometimes day, sometime evenings, sometimes night) schedules, according to a 2004 government survey; and 17 percent said that they usually worked either Saturday or Sunday or both (McMenamin, 2007). Nonstandard work has increased as the service

Most Western European governments provide parental leave with partial pay to care for newborn or seriously ill children. In all U.S. states except California and Washington, only unpaid leave is offered.

sector of the economy has grown. Evenings and weekends are when people eat at restaurants and do their shopping. The growing health care industry must care for patients around the clock. But child care providers mostly work a standard schedule; few day care centers, for instance, are open evenings, nights, or weekends. So parents working these nonstandard shifts must find other means of obtaining child care.

One way in which dual-earner couples manage nonstandard work hours is to work different shifts. Perhaps one-third of all dual-earner couples with pre-school-aged children have at least one spouse working an evening, night, or rotating shift (Presser, 1999); and many of these couples are sharing the child care. It is an arrangement that can provide good care, but couples working different shifts may have little time for each other and their relationships may suffer. For instance, when wives work a fixed night schedule, their risk of divorce increases (Presser, 2000; Kalil, Ziol-Guest, & Epstein, 2010). Single parents working nonstandard hours face an even more difficult situation because they don't have a spouse they can rely on for assistance. Overall, the children of parents who work nonstandard hours may be at risk of poorer academic or emotional development (Han & Waldfogel, 2007; Joshi & Bogen, 2007; Han & Fox, 2011).

TOWARD A RESPONSIVE WORKPLACE?

The concerns of workers, and increasingly of the corporate managers who employ them, about easing the conflicting demands of work and family have led to a movement toward what is called the **responsive workplace**—meaning a work

responsive workplace
a work setting in which job conditions are designed to allow employees to meet their family responsibilities more easily

setting in which job conditions are designed to allow employees to meet their family responsibilities more easily. Advocates argue that it will be beneficial not only to employees but also to employers (Levin-Epstein, 2007). Fewer workers, it is said, will quit work because of family responsibilities, which will save employers the costs of recruiting and training replacements. Workers will be less stressed, it is claimed, which will increase productivity. Employers have, in fact, become more responsive to employees' family concerns, if only out of self-interest. The Census Bureau projects that 48 percent of the growth of the labor force between 2010 and 2018 will be due to women workers, many of whom will have family responsibilities (U.S. Bureau of the Census, 2011b). Employers who wish to recruit and retain good workers realize that they must make their jobs attractive to people who are caring for children—and to the growing number who are caring for elderly parents.

Although some small employers and many mid-size employers offer family-friendly policies, large firms tend to offer the most extensive policies, such as child care assistance and some form of paid maternity leave (Families and Work Institute, 2008). Large firms invest more money in training new workers, so they have more to lose if an employee quits due to family constraints. Because of higher sales revenues, large firms can more easily pass along the costs of policies. Since large firms tend to have better-paying, steadier jobs and better-educated workforces, a two-tiered class system is developing in which well-educated managers and professionals and better-paid blue-collar factory workers tend to be offered more assistance than are less-advantaged workers.

flextime a policy that allows employees to choose, within limits, when they will begin and end their working hours

The most common, and most widely used, employee benefit is **flextime,** a policy that allows employees to choose, within limits, when they will begin and end their working hours. For example, a company might allow its employees to begin work anytime between 7:00 and 9:00 A.M. and to leave anytime from 3:00 to 5:00 P.M., as long as they work eight hours. In 2004, 30 percent of wage and salary workers could vary the start and end of their work days to some degree, a sharp rise from 14 percent in 1987 (McMenamin, 2007). Again, college-educated employees benefit more than high-school-educated employees: The more prestigious the occupational category, the more likely workers are to have flextime. Employed parents use flextime to match their work schedules to the school or day care schedules of their children. Flextime doesn't necessarily increase the amount of time parents can spend with their children, but it does allow them to avoid stressful conflicts between childcare and job responsibilities.

parental leave time off from work to care for a child

To be able to spend more time with their children, especially when they are infants or when they are sick, employed parents need other options. One of these is **parental leave,** time off from work to care for a child, with a guarantee that the employee can have her or his job back when she or he returns. Most wealthy nations require employers to grant parental leave with at least partial pay, yet in this regard, as in many family policies, the United States lags behind. Canada, for instance, provides one year of leave at 55 percent of the worker's wage (Clearinghouse on International Developments in Child, Youth, and Family Policies, 2011). In the United States in 1993, Congress passed the Family and Medical Leave Act, which requires companies with 50 or more employees to provide 12 weeks of unpaid leave

Paid Parental Leave

A half-century ago, women workers who became pregnant were expected to give up their jobs and stay home to raise the child. In fact, teachers in some school systems were required to leave their jobs if they gave birth. Today those norms are long gone. Mothers tend to return to the workforce quickly, their incomes needed to pay the mortgage or their career ladder in jeopardy. More than half of all married mothers with children under one were working for pay in 2011 (U.S. Bureau of the Census, 2011x). Some of these mothers (and some of their husbands) would prefer to stay home with a new baby for several months or perhaps a year, but few employers allow it and few parents can afford it. In response, the federal government passed the Family and Medical Leave Act in 1993, which requires firms with 50 or more employees to allow new mothers up to 12 weeks of unpaid leave. Yet because the leave is unpaid, many parents cannot afford to take it.

Some workers can cobble together a sort-of paid leave by combining sick leave, pregnancy disability leave, and vacation days. But only about half of employers allow that route (Families and Work Institute, 2008). And some employers—typically large ones that can better afford it—offer some paid leave (U.S. Joint Economic Committee, 2008). Even when it is offered, however, the culture of some firms discourages employees from taking it out of fear that they will not be perceived as fully committed employees worthy of good assignments and promotions (Blair-Loy, 2003).

Most other countries provide parental leave with pay. The standard in the nations of the European Union is 14 weeks with pay equal to what a worker would receive if on sick leave, and many nations provide longer leaves. The United States lags behind for two reasons. First, the American government provides fewer protections against loss of earnings in general than do other nations. American workers are at the mercy of the labor market more than workers in most other nations. Second, European nations have been concerned for decades, and in some cases for centuries, with encouraging births. These modest-sized nations, surrounded by others, have long been anxious about keeping the size of their populations up to a level where they could field an army capable of defending the country. Americans have not worried about birthrates. We have an ocean separating us from potential adversaries, and we have a tradition of expanding the size of the nation through immigration. So the American government has not felt the need to subsidize births by providing paid leave.

Now, however, with so many dual-earner couples and employed single mothers, support is growing for paid parental leave in the United States. Two states, California and New Jersey, require employers to offer parental leave with partial pay for six weeks. The State of Washington passed a paid leave bill in 2009 but delayed its start date for budgetary reasons. Supporters in Congress have unsuccessfully introduced legislation to provide paid leave for federal workers. Opponents have criticized the cost of the measure, while supporters have argued that it would increase the retention of federal employees who give birth and assist the recruitment of prospective employees.

Even if parental leave for federal workers is enacted, no national parental leave law for all workers is likely to be passed any time soon. The more likely scenario is that more states will enact the law. Yet given the Great Recession and its effect on state budgets, state-by-state expansion is likely to be slow and the issue is likely to remain contested for years.

Ask Yourself

1. Do you know any couples who are trying to raise a family while both of them work full-time? If so, what is their major problem? Could a change in public policy help to solve it?

2. Should American workers receive paid parental leaves, like workers in some European countries?

www.mhhe.com/cherlin7e

---

for birth, adoption, foster care, or personal or family illness. Employers must allow employees to return to their jobs at the end of the leave. The issue of paid parental leave remains contentious. (See *Families and Public Policy: Paid Parental Leave.*)

The spread of computers, smart phones, and fax machines allows employees to work at home, or indeed anywhere. Experts in work and family policies touted the growth in **telecommuting**—doing work from home using

telecommuting doing work from home using electronic communication electronic communication—as a new way to allow workers to combine work and caregiving. In the mid-2000s, 10 percent of wage and salary workers worked at home on an average day (U.S. Bureau of Labor Statistics, 2009). But telecommuting has been a mixed blessing. While it does allow workers to be home with a child, parents report difficulty in actually caring for a child while attempting to focus on work (Chesley, Moen, & Shore, 2003). Having electronic access helps employees manage their work but it also makes it difficult for them to leave work behind, so the anxieties of the workplace are more likely to invade the home. In fact, people who work long hours report *more* work-to-family interference when they control their own schedules than when they don't—quite possibly because it's more difficult for them to separate their work from their home life (Schieman, Milkie, & Glavin, 2009).

Although the spread of family-friendly policies such as flexible schedules and caregiving leaves is necessary to create a responsive workplace, they will be insufficient unless workers use them. That depends on the culture of the workplace which, Joan Williams (2010) argues, is still shaped by the masculine norms of the mid-twentieth century, when men were expected to focus completely on work and to rely on their wives to take care of home and family. Men still don't like to admit to their supervisors that they need to go home for family emergencies, Williams writes, because it would show insufficient commitment to their jobs. In some firms, employees fear that they will be shunted aside and denied promotions if they take advantage of flexible schedules or caregiving leaves. Looking at what has happened to work-family balance over the past few decades, one gets the sense that the conditions of family life have changed more than the conditions of work. Egalitarian norms that encourage sharing the housework and child care are stronger than in the past, and husbands contribute more than they used to. But at least in the United States, the norm of the fully-committed worker with no family responsibilities is still present. Thus, individuals are caught between trying to fulfill the cultural ideals of what it means to be a good worker and a good parent. To solve this dilemma requires a "culture of flexibility" (Families and Work Institute, 2011), an atmosphere in which supervisors who are knowledgeable about family-friendly benefits encourage employees to use the benefits and do not penalize them for doing so. More broadly, it requires a culture in which being a good worker and a good parent are not defined as mutually exclusive.

Quick Review

- In spite of some concerns, having multiple roles (parent, spouse, paid employee) does not seem to reduce mental health.
- A greater percentage of American workers, and American dual-earner couples, put in very long work weeks than do workers in most other developed nations.
- The stress of one's paid job can spill over into one's family life and cause family conflict.
- Workers in large firms receive more benefits to help them balance their family and paid work lives.

Looking Back

1. **How has married women's work changed over the past half-century?** In the second half of the twentieth century, married women entered the labor force in large numbers. A majority of married women with young children are now employed outside the home. The rise of the service sector and the long-term decline in fertility are two important reasons for women's increase in labor force participation. In the 2000s, married women's labor force participation declined slightly but remains at a high level.

2. **How does our society treat the labor of caring for others?** Much of the caring labor in families was provided by wives in the home. It was not considered "work" because it was unpaid and consisted of caring for people. As women have moved into the paid labor force, the value of the caring they provided has become evident and has proven difficult to replace. Some authors suggest that we must place a higher value on caring labor—paid and unpaid.

3. **How has the division of labor in marriages changed?** Wives have greatly reduced the amount of housework they do, while husbands have increased theirs. As a result, the relative amount of housework done by husbands and wives has become less unequal. Husbands take more responsibility for the routine care of their children when their wives work. Wives, however, feel more pressure and do more multitasking. Overall, the total amount of housework being done has declined; couples are buying more services, such as restaurant meals, than they used to.

4. **What are some of the strains working parents can experience?** Work can interfere with family life through the amount of work to be done, which may intrude into family time, or from the stress of the workplace. One increasingly common way for dual-earner couples to manage child care is to work split shifts, a practice that provides children with parental care but can strain a marriage to the point of divorce.

5. **How is the workplace responding to the needs of working parents?** Workers are concerned about meshing their jobs with their family responsibilities, and corporations and government are responding. Large corporations are increasingly providing assistance such as caregiving leave and flexible hours. So far, these and other reforms have benefited college-educated workers and employees of large corporations more than high-school-educated workers and employees of small corporations. To be effective, family-friendly reforms will require a more flexible culture in the workplace.

 Go to the Online Learning Center at www.mhhe.com/cherlin7e to test your knowledge of the chapter concepts and key terms.

Study Questions

1. How has the life of the typical married woman changed since the middle of the twentieth century?

2. How has the life of the typical married man changed?

3. How have the changes in work outside and inside the home changed the quality of marriages?

4. What does an "ethic of care" mean?

5. Why do some Americans feel overworked while others feel underworked?

6. Does work interfere with family life the same way for a professional as it does for a factory worker or service provider?

7. Why do well-paid workers typically receive more family-related benefits than workers who earn less?

8. How do the cultural expectations of being a good worker and a good parent clash?

Key Terms

care work 255	parental leave 266	spillover 264
flextime 266	responsive workplace 265	telecommuting 267
labor force 251	service sector 251	time-diary studies 258

Thinking about Families

The Public Family	The Private Family
Are benefits such as family leave or tax credits for child care unfair to workers without children?	Might couples' feelings toward each other be different if they shared the housework and child care equally?

Families on the Internet www.mhhe.com/cherlin7e

Note: While all the URLs listed were current as of the printing of this book, these sites often change. Please check our Web site (www.mhhe.com/cherlin7e) for updates.

There are many sources of good information on work-family issues on the Internet. The Families and Work Institute, established in 1989, is one of the oldest non-profit groups dedicated to achieving better work-family balance. It promotes workplace flexibility and works with many corporations. Its website, www.familiesandwork.org includes a research and publications page that has reports available for downloading. A more practical site oriented toward giving parents and other family caregivers advice on work-life balance is Work and Family Life, www.workandfamilylife.com. It also offers a monthly newsletter.

On the academic side, the Work and Family Researchers Network, based at the University of Pennsylvania, is a clearinghouse for research; it seeks to promote knowledge and understanding of work and family issues: http://workfamily.sas.upenn.edu. It is creating the "Work and Family Commons," an open access online repository of research articles.

Part Four

Links across the Generations

I n this part, we shift from same-generational relations of spouses and partners to intergenerational relations between parents and children. How adequately parents are meeting their overall responsibilities for raising children is a topic of much discussion and concern. In addition, working-age adults bear most of the responsibility for supporting and taking care of the elderly. The increasing number of elderly persons raises the question of whether family care will continue to be adequate. In the terms of this book, the issue is whether the public family is meeting its caretaking responsibilities for children and the elderly. • Chapter 9 examines the care of children by their parents. No public issue involving the family has received more attention in recent years than the well-being of children. The chapter begins by asking two questions: What are parents supposed to do for children? And what might prevent parents from doing what they are supposed to do? It then evaluates the complex question of whether children's well-being has declined. In • Chapter 10 the focus shifts from the young to the old. The chapter first reviews the substantial changes that occurred in the lives of the elderly during the twentieth century. It subsequently examines the assistance provided to, and provided by, the elderly, as well as levels of contact and affection between the elderly and their adult children and grandchildren.

Chapter Nine

Children and Parents

Looking Forward

What Are Parents Supposed to Do for Children?

Socialization as Support and Control

Socialization and Ethnicity

Socialization and Social Class

Socialization and Gender

Religion and Socialization

What's Important?

What Difference Do Fathers Make?

Adoption

Domestic Adoption

Transnational Adoption

Lesbian and Gay Parenthood

What Might Prevent Parents from Doing What They Are Supposed to Do?

Unemployment and Poverty

Unemployment

Poverty

Family Instability

Different Kinds of Households

Multiple Transitions

Family Complexity

Mass Incarceration

Time Apart

How Parents Compensate for Time Apart

The Consequences of Nonparental Care

Transnational Families

Immigrant Caregivers

The Effects on Children

The Well-Being of American Children

Which Children?

Diverging Destinies

Poor and Wealthy Children

Children in the Middle

Looking Back

Study Questions

Key Terms

Thinking about Families

Families on the Internet

Boxed Features

HOW DO SOCIOLOGISTS KNOW WHAT THEY KNOW?: *Measuring the Well-Being of Children*

FAMILIES AND PUBLIC POLICY: *Do Children Have Rights?*

Looking Forward

1. What are the main goals in socializing children, and how do parents differ in the way they fulfill their role?

2. How does the socialization of children vary by ethnicity, class, gender, and the sexual orientation of parents?

3. What barriers must parents overcome in socializing their children?

4. How much time do parents and children spend together?

5. How is the growth of transnational families affecting parents and children?

6. How has the well-being of American children changed over time?

In 2011 the proportion of American families that had children under 18 fell to a modern-day low of 44 percent (U.S. Bureau of the Census, 2011s). The high point was reached in the early 1960s, at the end of the baby boom, when the proportion was 57 percent. It fell below 50 percent in 1985 and has continued to drop ever since. The main and most obvious reason for the decline is that people are having fewer children than they were during the baby boom. Even among families that had children under 18 in 2008, the most common number of children was one, and few had more than two. Children, as I argued in Chapter 1, are a public good. With their numbers relatively low, our nation will need all of them to lead productive adult lives in the coming decades. So it is important that we raise them well. In part, that is a collective responsibility: Our schools and our health system must not fail them. But for the most part, the responsibility for raising today's children falls on their parents. We need them to succeed in raising them well. This raises two questions that will be the subject of this chapter: What are parents supposed to do for children? And what might prevent them from doing what they are supposed to do?

What Are Parents Supposed to Do for Children?

For the first several years of life, at least, families provide the main setting in which children's fundamental needs are met. In the United States, parents are given broad powers to shape their children's lives. What are the lessons children need to learn from their families, and how are those lessons shaped by social forces such as ethnicity, class, and gender? What behaviors by parents provide the best foundation for children's development?

First and foremost, parents, and sometimes other adult relatives, supply most of the love, nurturing, and care that children need in order to develop a basic sense of trust in other human beings. They also train young children in the skills they need to become more autonomous, such as dressing and feeding themselves. Later they provide the guidance, support, and discipline children need in order to become competent members of their society. In other words, family members socialize their children. Indeed, families are the major source of primary socialization—the settings for the first lessons children learn about their society.

SOCIALIZATION AS SUPPORT AND CONTROL

As parents socialize their children, they act in two broad ways. First, they provide emotional support—love, affection, warmth, nurturing, or acceptance. Emotional support shows children that parents care about their actions. It makes children feel more positively about themselves. Because children want to continue receiving such support, they try to act in ways they think will please their parents. Second, parents exercise control—they seek to limit or change children's behavior. Sometimes parental control is coercive, consisting of the use or threat of punishment or force. But control also may be inductive—that is, based on setting consistent limits, explaining the reasons for these limits to the child, requesting that the child comply, and praising her or his compliance. Parents may also exercise control by threatening to withdraw their love if the child does not behave well.

Numerous studies have examined the ways in which parents combine various aspects of support and control. In what is probably the most influential analysis, psychologist Diana Baumrind distinguished among three styles of parental behavior (Baumrind, 1971). In the **authoritative style,** parents combine high levels of emotional support with consistent, moderate control. Children are provided with warmth and affection and with firm, consistent discipline. But the discipline is moderate and is based on requests and explanations rather than on the use of force or punishment. Baumrind and others claim that authoritative parenting produces children who are more socially competent—meaning that they have higher self-esteem, cooperate better with others, develop a better moral sense, and are more independent. The two other styles of behavior, it is claimed, produce children who are less competent and who may show more behavior problems, anxiety, or depression. In the **permissive style,** parents provide support but exercise little control over their children by any means. And in the **authoritarian style,** parents combine low support with coercive attempts at control. The implication of this research tradition is that children are socialized best when parents set clear standards, enforce them consistently but without harsh punishment, and provide substantial emotional support. One can spare the rod without spoiling the child, it seems, but setting no limits on children's behavior is virtually as bad as relying solely on the stick.

authoritative style (of parenting) a parenting style in which parents combine high levels of emotional support with consistent, moderate control of their children

permissive style (of parenting) a parenting style in which parents provide emotional support but exercise little control over their children

authoritarian style (of parenting) a parenting style in which parents combine low levels of emotional support with coercive attempts at control of their children

SOCIALIZATION AND ETHNICITY

The three-category classification of parenting styles is still widely cited, and the authoritative style is generally seen as more effective than the authoritarian style. Yet recently, some scholars have questioned whether the model can be applied to racial and ethnic minority families. African American parents, for instance, are somewhat more likely than white parents to use physical punishment; and Asian American parents are more likely than white parents to insist on discipline and obedience (McLoyd, Cauce, Takeuchi, & Wilson, 2000). Within African American or Asian American culture, according to critics, these actions may not have the negative meaning that whites, especially middle-class whites, attach to them (Chao, 1994; McLoyd, Kaplan, Hardaway, & Wood, 2007). In fact, one study found that parents' physical discipline—mostly spanking or slapping—in the first five years of a child's life and during early adolescence was associated with more behavior problems among eleventh-grade European American children but fewer behavior problems among eleventh-grade African American children (Lansford, Deater-Deckard, Dodge, Bates, & Pettit, 2004). Another study found that white early adolescents (with an average age of 12) perceived their mothers as less warm if their mothers used harsh parenting methods such as spanking them with their hands when they had done something wrong, but African American early adolescents did not see mothers who spanked them as less warm. White early adolescents also perceived their mothers as less warm if their mothers did not explain to them why they were being punished, but African American early adolescents did not. The authors suggest that when physical discipline is more commonly accepted, children may interpret this style of parenting as expressing warmth and love, especially in low-income African American families, for whom their findings were strongest (Jackson-Newsom, Buchanan, & McDonald, 2008). These studies suggest that researchers must be cautious in applying Baumrind's classification scheme to racial and ethnic minority parents.

One of the primary tasks in socialization, in fact, is to familiarize children with the culture in which they are growing up. Consider the acquisition of language. Learning to talk not only allows children to communicate with others, but also carries important lessons about their society. A French child learns two words for *you:* Siblings and friends are called *tu,* and parents and other adults are called *vous.* Thus the child learns which relationships are characterized by equality and intimacy and which are characterized by respect and social distance. A Japanese girl learns to show deference to men by addressing them differently than she does women. At a conference I attended in Tokyo, a female Japanese professor was criticized by a male colleague—in Japanese. She replied to him in English. When asked later why she responded in English, she said that, had she chosen Japanese, she would have had to use the "respect language" a polite woman must employ when addressing a man. In English, she could respond as a linguistic equal.

norm a widely accepted rule about how people should behave

value a goal or principle that is held in high esteem by a society

Socialization also involves teaching children norms and values. **Norms** are widely accepted rules about how people should behave. **Values** are goals and principles that are held in high esteem by a society. The norms and values may be those of the dominant culture in the society, of a subculture, or of both. Families begin this process; schools, churches, peer groups, and even the media carry it on. For example, Japanese children learn to place a higher value on loyalty to the group in situations where an American child would learn to value independent action. When asked about desirable characteristics for children, Japanese mothers are more likely than American mothers to mention interdependence: fitting in with the group, getting along with others (Rothbaum, Kakinuma, Nagaoka, & Azuma, 2007).

SOCIALIZATION AND SOCIAL CLASS

In Chapter 4 we reviewed studies showing that middle-class parents tend to socialize their children somewhat differently than working-class and low-income parents. These differences can be overstated; there are many commonalities,

Japanese children are taught to be loyal to the group, whereas American children are taught to be more independent.

such as a consumer culture that drives lower-income and higher-income parents alike to purchase expensive sneakers and personal electronic devices for their children (Pugh, 2009). Still, the class differences seem important. To review, middle-class parents tend to emphasize autonomy and self-direction. They seek actively to enhance their children's talents and opinions, in a style that Lareau (2011) called "concerted cultivation." Others have called it "intensive mothering" (Hays, 1996). Working-class and lower-income parents, on the other hand, are more likely to emphasize obedience and conformity. They seek to provide a safe, loving environment in which children can grow on their own—in Lareau's terms, they aim for "the accomplishment of natural growth." Kohn (1969; Kohn & Schooler, 1978) claimed that the differing parenting styles derive from the occupational conditions of the parents. Middle-class parents whose jobs provide autonomy and self-direction are more likely to emphasize those values with their children. Thus, middle-class parents socialize their children, in effect, to grow up and take middle-class jobs. Working-class parents, with their emphasis on obedience and conformity, socialize their children for the kinds of blue- and pink-collar jobs the parents have held.

SOCIALIZATION AND GENDER

Chapter 3 presented evidence that parents socialize their daughters differently than their sons; here that discussion will be briefly summarized. Researchers now think of socialization as a two-way process in which children and parents influence each other. Because of their predispositions or because of other factors that may make them behave differently, children can influence how parents treat them. Parents then make decisions that reinforce these differences, such as buying stereotypically female toys for girls and stereotypically male toys for boys. The distinctions parents make may reflect, in part, biologically based differences between girls and boys (Painter-Brick, 1998); yet parents' actions

also tend to magnify and exaggerate gender differences. The emphasis in sociological studies of this process has been on the conscious social learning children
do as they are rewarded for some behaviors and punished for others—and as
they watch and imitate adults of the same gender. Schools, peer groups, and
the media further exaggerate gender differences, so that adult gender roles are
far more distinctive than any inherent differences might warrant.

RELIGION AND SOCIALIZATION

Do religious denominations differ in what they say parents are supposed to
do for their children? Are some religious beliefs more consistent with authoritarian than authoritative parenting? Some social scientists have suggested that
conservative Protestantism leads fathers to be more authoritarian with their
children. The argument is that conservative Protestantism—the denominations
and independent churches sometimes called evangelical or fundamentalist,
such as the Southern Baptist Convention, the United Pentecostal Church, and
the Assemblies of God—teaches that men are the head of the family and therefore encourages a strict, discipline-oriented, distant style of fathering (Gottman,
1998). But national surveys that ask parents about their religious activities and
their relationships with their children suggest that the story is not that simple
(Wilcox, 2004). Yes, conservative Protestant men are more likely to believe in
traditional gender roles: It's better if the husband is the earner and the wife
stays home to raise the family, the wife should do more of the housework,
and so forth. But they are also more likely to combine discipline with what
sociologists call "emotion work" (Hochschild, 1979), the act of influencing and
managing the emotions of others—in this case their wives and children.

W. Bradford Wilcox (1998, 2004) reports that conservative Protestant
fathers who frequently attend church spank their children more often, which
fits the authoritarian style, but in other ways they are quite authoritative: They
hug and praise their children more than other fathers, yell at them less, and
spend more time in leisure activities like playing together or having private
talks. Wilcox argues that conservative Protestant churches teach that being
the household head means, in part, being an involved father. The churches
urge fathers not just to be disciplinarians but also to be emotionally expressive toward their children and to spend time with them. As a result, Wilcox
argues, fathers become "soft patriarchs" who combine strict discipline with
warmth and involvement in a style that blends the authoritarian with the
authoritative. Religious fathers from "mainline" Protestant groups, such as the
Episcopal, Lutheran, Presbyterian, Lutheran, and Methodist churches, are less
authoritarian—they spank their children less—but they aren't as involved in
activities with them and are less likely to set rules for television viewing or to
know where their children are when they're not at home.

WHAT'S IMPORTANT?

Social class and gender differences do exist, then, in how children are socialized. Nevertheless, it is possible to make some general statements about what
parents are supposed to do. First, they should provide support to their children. This includes material support such as food, clothes, and shelter, as well
as emotional support such as love and nurturing. The need for the former is
obvious: Without material support, the child is in physical danger. Yet without

emotional support, she or he is likely to grow up without a sense of security or a capability for trusting and loving other people. Second, parents should provide control. They must supervise and monitor their children's behavior not only to help them avoid physical harm but also to teach children the limits of acceptable behavior.

One could supplement this basic list according to one's values. Some might stress the importance of religious and ethical training—an upbringing that teaches children about the spiritual and moral side of life. Those who believe that people of both genders should undertake a wide range of behaviors that are now stereotyped as masculine or feminine—who believe, for example, that men should provide more care for children and women should have better opportunities for careers—might add that parents should encourage more **androgynous behavior** (i.e., behavior that has the characteristics of both genders) in their children. From this perspective, boys should be encouraged to be more nurturing and girls more aggressive. Similarly, those who believe that the values passed along to working-class children limit their occupational achievements might add that parents of all classes ought to encourage autonomous behavior in their children.

androgynous behavior
behavior that has the characteristics of both genders

Quick Review

- Parents socialize their children by providing emotional support and control and by teaching them about norms and values.
- Authoritative parenting—combining warmth with consistent, moderate discipline—is thought to be most beneficial, but this conclusion may not apply to racial-ethnic minority groups.
- Middle-class parents tend to emphasize autonomy and self-direction, while working-class and lower-income parents tend to emphasize obedience and conformity.
- Parents tend to socialize their daughters differently than their sons, creating or magnifying gender differences.
- Conservative Protestant men tend to combine strict discipline with an involved style of fatherhood.

WHAT DIFFERENCE DO FATHERS MAKE?

Most of the literature on parenting focuses on mothers rather than fathers—an understandable emphasis, since mothers do more child rearing than fathers in nearly all societies. But over the past few decades, scholars conducted a great deal of research on the role of fathers in child rearing. Most studies were conducted in the context of families with two heterosexual parents and in which the mother is the primary caregiver. This is the most typical scenario, but others do exist—such as single heterosexual fathers or single or coupled gay men. These studies suggest that fathers do make a difference in their children's lives (Marsiglio, Amato, Day, & Lamb, 2000; Pleck, 2007). For example, adolescents in two-parent families who reported a more positive relationship with their fathers (for instance, by agreeing with the statement "I really enjoy spending time with him" or reporting that he often helped the adolescent do important things) were subsequently less likely to engage in delinquent acts (such as damaging or destroying property or stealing something) than were adolescents with a less positive relationship, even after taking into account

The amount of time fathers spend with their children is less important than how actively engaged they are.

how positive the relationship between the adolescent and the mother was (Bronte-Tinkew, Moore, & Carrano, 2006).

Fathers have both direct and indirect effects on their children's development. They influence children directly by interacting with them: talking to them, playing with them, asserting authority, and so forth. For instance, toddlers whose fathers provide more supportive behavior to them (for instance, by encouraging and assisting them during play sessions) show greater vocabulary and cognitive gains, whether or not their mothers are supportive (Tamis-LeMonda, Shannon, Cabrera, & Lamb, 2004). Fathers can influence children indirectly in two ways. First, they can provide financially for the family, which is the traditional role of the father. Having a steady, adequate income benefits everyone in the family by ensuring that basic needs will be met. Second, they can be supportive of the mother—cooperating with her in child rearing, responding positively to the parenting she does. Children whose fathers support them in these indirect ways are better adjusted at home and at school (Cabrera, Tamis-LeMonda, Bradley, Hofferth, & Lamb, 2000).

A large proportion of children experience their parents' divorce or are born to single mothers (see Chapter 12). Most of these children live with their mothers. One might think that the more time these children spend with their fathers, the better their development would be, but a majority of studies on this topic do not show a strong link between the frequency by itself of a father's visits and child development (Marsiglio et al., 2000; Sobolewski & King, 2005). (Although a father who rarely sees his children has little influence on them.) What studies do show is that children whose nonresident fathers have an authoritative parenting style (for example, who encourage their children and discuss their problems) tend to develop better than children whose visits with their fathers are purely recreational (Amato & Gilbreth, 1999). Within limits, then, the way nonresidential fathers behave as parents seems to make more of a difference than how often they see their children. Even among fathers who live with their children, the simple amount of time they spend together is less important than how actively engaged they are and how much responsibility they take for the children's care (Palkovitz, 2002).

ADOPTION

Adoptive families are usually successful, and most adopted children exhibit normal emotional development. A minority of adopted children, however, do show elevated levels of emotional or behavioral difficulties (Brodzinsky, Schechter, & Marantz, 1992). These difficulties may stem from events prior to the adoption, such as maternal substance abuse during pregnancy, time spent in multiple foster homes, or neglect in an overseas orphanage. But despite the successes of the majority, adoption may still be, in the words of one observer, "a devalued status" (Fisher, 2003). Most people may admire it in the abstract, but many seemingly good candidates for adoptive parenthood, such as middle-class couples who are unsuccessful in efforts to conceive a child, avoid it in practice, either out of a strong preference for biological children or a fear that an adoption will not work out.

In 2007, according to a national survey of adoptive parents, 2.4 percent of all children under age 18 in the United States were adopted (Vandivere, Malm, and Radel, 2009). The nature of adoption has been changing over the past few decades. A half-century ago, the typical adoption used to involve an unmarried, white mother placing an infant for adoption with an unrelated married couple. But after the introduction of the birth control pill in the 1960s and the legalization of abortion in the 1970s, the number of unplanned births declined sharply. Moreover, the stigma of raising children outside of marriage decreased. As a result, the proportion of white, unmarried mothers who gave up their newborns for adoption declined from almost 20 percent in the early 1970s to 2 percent in the first half of the 1990s (U.S. National Center for Health Statistics, 1999). (The proportion of African American mothers who give up their newborns for adoption has always been lower and is estimated at about 2 percent.) But other forms of adoption have become more common.

Domestic Adoption   Of all children who are adopted from within the United States, about half are adopted through private agencies and about half are adopted through the foster care system (Vandivere, Malm, & Radel, 2009). Children adopted through the foster care system tend to be more disadvantaged. About two-thirds of them are from racial-ethnic minority groups (National Center for Family and Marriage Research, 2011a). More than half have special health needs such as learning disabilities (Vandivere, Malm, & Radel, 2009). Most parents adopting from foster care said they did so because they wanted to provide a permanent home for a child (Vandivere, Malm, & Radel, 2009). Children who have been placed in foster care and whose parents' rights to them have been terminated due to neglect or abuse are sometimes adopted by their foster parents or by kin such as aunts or grandparents. (See Chapter 11, *Families and Public Policy:* The Swinging Pendulum of Foster Care Policy.)

Americans are adopting children from developing countries whose parents are too poor to care for them.

Transnational Adoption   One-fourth of all adopted children in the United States were born in other countries (Vandivere, Malm, & Radel, 2009). In 2010, Americans adopted 11,100 foreign children (U.S. Office of Immigration Statistics, 2011). The rise of transnational adoptions in the United States is a reaction to the declining number of American children who are placed for adoption at birth. But it also reflects other factors, among them geopolitics, population policies, and the globalization of the adoption market.

As for geopolitics, the receiving countries tend to be wealthy and the sending countries less so. The United States is by far the leading receiving country (Riley & Van Vleet, 2012). For instance, Ethiopia sent the second largest number of transnationally-adopted children to the United States in 2010. Struggling with war and disease, Ethiopia had difficulty caring for five million orphans. Its government decided to encourage foreign adoption to ease the situation (Riley & Van Vleet, 2012).

China, the largest sender of children for years, has been responding to a different sort of problem. The Chinese government, concerned that birthrates were too high, instituted a policy whereby most families were limited to having a single child. Given the traditional preference of Chinese parents for sons, the one-child policy led to a flood of abandoned girl babies in Chinese orphanages. While discouraging Chinese families from adopting these girls, the government created an agency to work with international organizations that found willing adoptive parents in the West.

Transnational adoption could not occur without modern means of communication and transportation. Adopting a child internationally is a long and complex process for the prospective parents. Typically, two government agencies, one in the sending and one in the receiving country, are involved, along with a nonprofit social service agency with representatives in both countries. Paperwork, interviews, and permits are required. As a last step, the adopting parents must travel to the sending country to obtain final approvals and to return with a child. It is an option that barely existed a half-century ago. Now it is one of the leading edges of the globalization of family life.

LESBIAN AND GAY PARENTHOOD

It is only since the 1960s that circumstances have allowed children to live with an openly lesbian or gay parent and, often, that parent's partner. Those circumstances, which are discussed elsewhere in this book, include the following: the sharp, post-1960 rise in divorce, which encouraged more homosexual men and women who were in heterosexual marriages (often with children) to end their marriages; the emergence of an openly gay subculture in large cities, which provided a supportive environment for lesbian and gay couples; the greater tolerance of childbearing outside marriage and single parenting in general; and the development of reproductive technologies that make conception possible without heterosexual intercourse. There are three main types of gay and lesbian families with children (Patterson, 2000). In the first type, the children were born to a married parent who later came out as lesbian or gay, obtained a divorce, and retained custody of the children. Because women retain custody of children much more often than men after a divorce, most of these families include a lesbian mother, her children, and often her new partner. Children in this type of family have experienced the transitions and difficulties associated with a parental divorce (see Chapter 12). This type of family is declining in numbers as the recent, more open climate leads fewer lesbian and gay individuals to enter into heterosexual marriages. The second type of gay and lesbian family consists of the growing number of couples who have either adopted a child or conceived one through **donor insemination**—the insertion of donated semen into the uterus of an ovulating woman. The third type is the emerging number of gay male fathers who have children through arrangements such as hiring a surrogate mother to carry fetuses inseminated with their (or their partner's) sperm or through adoption, often of children from the foster care system (Stacey, 2011). In 2010, children were present in 115,000 same-sex partner households; an unknown number of children were being raised by single lesbian or gay male parents (U.S. Bureau of the Census, 2011m).

Many studies have attempted to compare children living with lesbian parents and children living with heterosexual single or married parents (Tasker, 2005). Most of the early studies were of lesbian or gay families of the first type: children born to mothers who were married and who subsequently divorced and began living openly lesbian lives. Studies of the well-being of these children cannot easily distinguish between the effects of parental divorce and of living with lesbian parents (Regnerus, 2012). More recently,

donor insemination a procedure in which semen is inserted into the uterus of an ovulating woman

The 2000 Census counted over 336,000 same-sex partner households with children.

several studies have been published of lesbian families of the second type, those with planned births, usually by donor insemination. Virtually all of the lesbian mothers have been white and well-educated, typically with managerial or professional occupations. Moreover, almost all the studies have been based on modest-sized, nonrandom samples, which means that the subjects either volunteered to be studied or were recruited through acquaintances or organizations known to the authors. They may not, therefore, be representative of lesbian mothers in general.

The results of these studies consistently show that children raised by two lesbian parents are very similar to children raised by two heterosexual parents (Patterson, 2000; Stacey & Biblarz, 2001; Tasker, 2005; Bos, van Balen, & van dem Boom, 2007; Telingator & Patterson, 2008; Biblarz & Stacey, 2010). They have similar levels of behavior problems and perform similarly in school. They seem to be as well-adjusted emotionally. Consider a British study that followed 25 lesbian families that had planned the birth of their child, along with 38 single heterosexual mothers and 38 two-parent heterosexual families, from the birth of their children until the children were twelve years old (MacCallum & Golombok, 2004). The three groups of children did not differ significantly in school adjustment, peer relationships, and self-esteem. When asked a set of questions about characteristics typically associated with masculinity and femininity, boys in lesbian homes and heterosexual single-mother homes showed higher scores on "femininity" (being loyal, affectionate, and sympathetic), but their scores on "masculinity" (being self-reliant, ambitious, assertive) were just as high as those of boys living with two heterosexual parents. These results suggest that boys living without fathers, regardless of their mothers' sexual orientation, may display a more androgynous character; but they do not suggest that boys from lesbian homes are otherwise any different from boys from heterosexual two-parent homes.

Researchers have also attempted to study the sexual orientation of adults who were raised in lesbian mother households with those raised in heterosexual households. If sexual orientation is at least partially socially constructed, we might expect differences between children raised in lesbian and heterosexual households (Bailey & Dawood, 1998). If lesbian parents provide children with fewer opportunities to interact with a heterosexual father, it is possible that the children's sexual orientation as adults could be affected. One research group followed 46 children until they were 23.5 years old, on average (Tasker & Golombok, 1995). They found that the children who had grown up in lesbian families were more open to the possibility of same-gender sexual relationships. The greater openness was observable in two ways: First, 6 of 25 children from lesbian families reported at least one same-gender relationship, ranging from a kiss to cohabitation; but none of the 21 children from heterosexual families reported a same gender relationship. Second, 14 children from lesbian families said they had considered the possibility of a same-gender relationship, compared with 3 of the children from heterosexual families. Nevertheless, only two of the children from lesbian families were currently in a same-gender relationship and identified as lesbian (both were women). In other words, growing up in a lesbian family seems to have made the children more open to same-gender sexual relationships, but most still identified as heterosexual.

Quick Review

- Fathers influence their children's development directly through interacting with them.
- Fathers influence their children's development indirectly by providing financial support and by supporting the parenting behaviors of mothers.
- Children adopted from foster care tend to be more disadvantaged and have more health problems than children adopted through private agencies.
- Children adopted transnationally move largely from poorer countries to wealthier countries.
- Children raised by two lesbian parents from birth appear to be as well-adjusted as children raised by two heterosexual parents.

What Might Prevent Parents from Doing What They Are Supposed to Do?

Yet even parents with the best intentions sometimes cannot care for their children and socialize them as well as they would like to. The larger society sometimes interferes, as when a parent loses a job or a family cannot climb out of poverty. The transformation of the U.S. economy over the past few decades has hurt many parents and made child rearing more difficult. Social change also may interfere: Some observers have argued that recent changes in the organization of families make successful parenting more difficult. Among the changes causing these alleged difficulties are the great increase in the proportion of children who are cared for by someone other than a parent because their parents work for pay, the sharp increase in the divorce rate since the 1960s, and the increasing proportion of children born outside marriage. Newer arrangements, such as children who live with lesbian or gay parents, have also generated interest and concern. In this section, the effects of these developments on the quality of parenting will be examined.

UNEMPLOYMENT AND POVERTY

On the most basic level, low income means fewer clothes and less food. It can mean being evicted from your apartment. It can mean that your children's bedroom has peeling, lead-filled paint. The effects of poverty on children can start before they are born. Pregnant, poor women are more likely to receive inadequate prenatal care and to engage in behaviors harmful to the fetus—such as smoking and using drugs, which reduce birth weight (Aber, Jones, & Cohen, 2000).

In addition, the consequences of unemployment and poverty can be more subtle. They can change the ways parents act toward each other, and they can also change the way parents and children interact. Consider the declining fortunes of agricultural communities in the American Midwest in the late twentieth century. In 1987, sociologist Glen Elder, psychologist Rand Conger, and several collaborators studied 76 families in a rural Iowa county (Elder, Conger, Foster, & Ardelt, 1992). All were white, a majority were middle class, and each consisted of a married couple and at least two children, one of whom was in seventh grade. After obtaining background information from the family members, the research team set up a video camera. While the tape rolled, they asked the parents to spend 30 minutes reviewing the history and present status of their marriage. Then they taped a 15-minute discussion in which the parents attempted to solve a problem in their marriage. They then taped one of the parents and the seventh-grader in two discussions: talking about a family activity and talking about a family problem such as doing chores or getting along with a younger sibling. Finally, they taped the other parent and the seventh-grader in the same two discussions. Over the next several months, trained raters viewed and reviewed the videotapes, coding the kinds of behaviors each person displayed, such as warmth, affection, or anger.

Unemployment   Nineteen of the fathers had lost their jobs, had had their hours cut back, or had been demoted in the preceding year. Other families had experienced a drop in income or very little growth. The researchers combined these events into a measure of how much "economic pressure" each family was facing. (Even though most of the mothers were employed outside the home, the researchers focused on fathers, who were still the main earners in nearly all the families.) Studies of families during the Great Depression had shown that men who had lost their jobs were tense and irritable in their relations with wives and explosive and punishing in their relations with their children (Liker & Elder, 1983). The tapes showed similar behavior: Fathers in families under economic pressure were more irritable and hostile toward their wives and children. Their wives often replied in kind. One daughter said that at dinnertime "we are kinda cautious, like walking on hot ground or something" (Elder et al., 1992). The interviews revealed that fathers under economic pressure tended to be depressed, lacking energy and interest—more so than their wives. One father said, "There would be some good days, but there would be more bad ones than good ones. Kind of lethargic. Oh, I know it's gotta be done, but I'll do it tomorrow. We kind of floated." Moreover, during the taped discussions, children whose fathers were more hostile and irritable were themselves more sullen, angry, and abrasive. In their interviews, these children admitted to more symptoms of depression (e.g., feeling lonely, hopeless, no interest) and aggressiveness (e.g., I am tempted to break a rule if I don't like it; I do the opposite of what a bossy person says; I yell back if I'm yelled at).

The study suggests a chain of events running from economic difficulties to children's behavior problems. The loss of a job or a drop in income causes psychological distress for the husband, who is still expected to be the family's main earner. The distress in turn leads to depression and to angry, explosive exchanges with his wife and children. And the children then become more depressed, hostile, and aggressive. It is possible, however, that causation could run the opposite way: Men who are depressed and hostile may be more likely to lose their jobs and to have children with similar characteristics. Still, the sequence proposed by the Iowa researchers is plausible and is supported by other studies (Price, Choi, & Vinokur, 2002).

Poverty   Studies of poor urban families show similar dynamics (Edin & Kissane, 2010). A parent in poverty may be depressed about job prospects, anxious about paying the bills, or angry about crime and drugs in the neighborhood. Such a parent has few psychological resources left to devote to her or his children. Instead of reasoning with the child or explaining why a certain behavior is good or bad, a depressed and anxious parent may respond to perceived misbehavior simply by threatening harsh punishment—but may then give in if the child refuses to obey. Thus, the child obtains little emotional support and receives discipline that is inconsistent, harsh, and punitive. As noted earlier, this style of parenting has been associated with diminished social competence among children, although some scholars question its application to racial-ethnic minority groups. There are many other potential pathways in which poverty could affect children's well-being. For instance, children in poverty tend to have parents who have less education and who may provide less cognitive stimulation, such as reading less to the child. They tend to live in neighborhoods where schools are of lower quality. The continual stress produced by their environment could lead to higher overall levels of stress hormones in their bodies, which in turn could affect brain development and lead to behavior problems (Evans, Chen, Miller, & Seeman, 2012). One set of studies suggests that low income has more of an effect on children's school achievement than it does on their behavior; moreover, low income seems to be more detrimental to younger children than to adolescents (Duncan & Brooks-Gunn, 1997).

FAMILY INSTABILITY

Given the increase over the past half century of divorce, cohabiting relationships, and single parenthood, another factor that might prevent parents from doing what they are supposed to do is the growing instability of family life. Children today experience more changes in the composition of the households they live in. Moreover, American children experience more changes than do children in any other Western country. Figure 9.1 compares the percentage of children living with their mothers, who experience three or more of their mothers' partnerships by age 15, in 12 countries. For example, consider a child whose mother is married when the child is born; the mother later separates

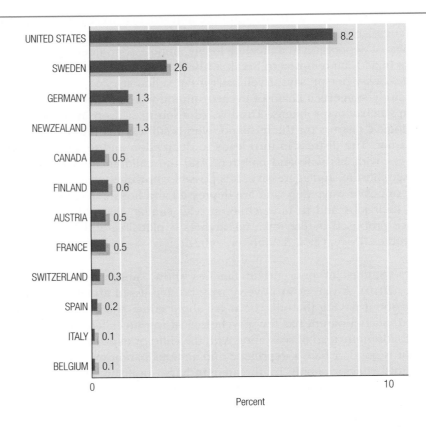

from her husband and lives for a time as a single parent, then cohabits with a man and then ends that relationship, and then lives with another man, all before the child turns 16. That child will have experienced three maternal partnerships—three men living in his or her house. Figure 9.1 shows that in some countries such as Belgium and Italy, 0.1 percent, or one in a thousand, children experience this much turnover. In Sweden, 2.6 percent of children experience this much turnover, the highest rate in Western Europe. But in the United States, 8.2 percent of children experience this much turnover, triple the rate in Sweden. Instability is much higher in the United States because Americans have high rates of marrying, divorcing, and remarrying, and they start and end cohabiting relationships more quickly (Cherlin, 2009).

Different Kinds of Households   There are two ways in which this high level of instability could affect children negatively. First, it exposes them to several kinds of households, each of which could be problematic:

- A divorcing household. Chapters 12 and 13 will examine the effects of divorce and remarriage in detail. To summarize, experiencing one's parents' divorce raises the risk of experiencing outcomes such as dropping out of school, having a child as a teenager, or receiving public assistance. Still, most children do not experience these undesirable outcomes despite the increased risk.

- A single-parent household. Stable single-parent families can be good environments for children, and any difficulties they have may stem more from having low incomes than from not having a second parent present.

Even so, living with one parent can sometimes be a handicap for children, even after low income is taken into account. Other potential difficulties include higher rates of depression (Carlson & Corcoran, 2001) and less effective monitoring and supervision (Astone & McLanahan, 1991). As with parenting styles, racial and ethnic differences may be important: The association between having a single parent and child outcomes such as delinquency may be weaker among African Americans than among whites (Dunifon & Kowaleski-Jones, 2002).

- A household with a parent and her or his cohabiting partner. A biological parent might be willing to live with a partner she or he would not be willing to marry; and these partners may devote less time and energy to child rearing than would a married parent. In any case, in one large, national study, children living with a biological parent who was cohabiting (for example, a mother and her boyfriend) were less engaged with school (skipped school more often, had trouble getting homework done) than children in most other kinds of families (Brown, 2006). In another study, children living with a biological parent who was cohabiting were less likely to graduate from high school than were children in a two-biological-parent family, or children living with a remarried parent, or children living with a divorced parent who had never re-partnered (Raley, Frisco, & Wildsmith, 2005). Families in which a biological parent is cohabiting with a partner may be particularly unfavorable environments for children.

Multiple Transitions   The second way in which a high level of instability could affect children negatively is through the sheer number of transitions to which the child has to adjust, regardless of the type of family that is formed. Repeated movements of parents' partners in and out of the home could produce disruptions in the child's family system that could undermine her or his sense of security and trust. Researchers report that the number of transitions that children experience is associated with undesirable outcomes such as behavior problems at home and in school (Cavanagh & Huston, 2006; Fomby & Cherlin, 2007; Osborne & McLanahan, 2007; Cavanagh & Huston, 2008). It is not clear, however, whether this is a cause-and-effect association (a greater number of transitions cause more problems) or whether it reflects underlying, unmeasured factors that cause both the parents to have more partners and their children to have more problems. And if it is causal, the precise mechanisms are not well understood. The researchers typically suggest that frequent transitions cause greater family stress, which affects children.

FAMILY COMPLEXITY

Because of the increasing number of partners that adults have during their lifetimes, it's becoming more common to have children with more than one partner—what demographers are calling **multiple-partner fertility** (hereafter MPF). This phenomenon is leading to complex family households in which different children have different sets of parents, and in which half-siblings (who share one parent) and step-siblings (who are from parents' previous relationships) are common. Some MPF has long existed: A man or woman whose spouse dies might remarry and have more children, or a divorced woman or man might remarry and have more children.

multiple-partner fertility
having children with more than one partner during one's lifetime

FIGURE 9.2
Percentage of urban births to couples in which fathers or mothers had previous children by other partners, 1998–2000, by marital status. (*Source:* Carlson & Furstenberg, 2006, Table 2)

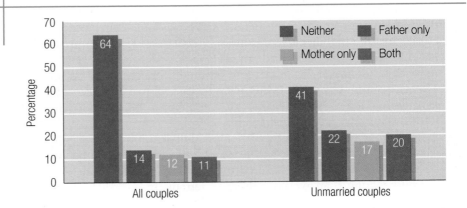

But cohabiting relationships have accelerated the process because they are much less stable than marriages. After cohabiting relationships end, parents may go on to have children with other partners. A second, important source of the rise of MPF is the considerable amount of childbearing outside of any kind of partnership. In 1950, only 4 percent of all children were born to unpartnered parents; but by the mid-2000s 20 percent were[1]. Parents who give birth to a child without a partner are much more likely to subsequently have children with another partner.

We do not have good statistics on the percentage of Americans who have had children with more than one partner. But Figure 9.2 (Carlson & Furstenberg, 2006, Table 2) shows the percentage of births to couples in 20 large cities between 1998 and 2000 that would fit the definition of MPF. In each set of four bars, the left-most bar shows the percentage of new babies whose mothers and fathers did *not* already have a child by another partner; the other three bars show the percentage of babies whose mothers or fathers, or both, already had a child. For instance, among all couples (married or cohabiting), the baby's mother already had a child by a previous partner in 14 percent of the cases; the baby's father had one in 12 percent; and they both had one in 11 percent. In sum, 37 percent (14 + 12 + 11) of urban births to couples met the definition of MPF. If we consider only births to unmarried couples (the second set of bars), 59 percent fit the MPF definition. Clearly, MPF is widespread in urban America among couples having a child together.

MPF is more common among mothers who had their first children at an early age, who were African American, and who attended religious services less often (Carlson & Furstenberg, 2006; Guzzo & Furstenberg, 2007a, 2007b). Having a child by more than one partner is not necessarily a problem, but it complicates child rearing, to say the least. Women who had children with multiple partners were less likely, according to one study, to say that they had family or friends they could count on for social support, such as a small loan or a place to stay—although whether the lack of support is a cause or an

---

[1] My estimate. In 2007, 39.7 percent of births were to unmarried women (U.S. National Center for Health Statistics, 2010). But about half these women were likely to have been cohabiting with a partner at the time of the birth (Kennedy & Bumpass, 2008), leaving about 20 percent truly unpartnered. In 1950, when cohabitation was much less common, nearly all nonmarital births were to unpartnered women.

effect of MPF is unclear (Harknett & Knab, 2007). According to a study in Wisconsin, a majority of mothers receiving Temporary Assistance for Needy Families, the main cash welfare program, had children with more than one father (Meyer, Cancian, & Cook, 2005). Beyond these rudimentary demographic differences, however, we as yet have little understanding of how the complexity that MPF introduces into family life plays out in the daily lives of the parents and children who are involved.

MASS INCARCERATION

Another development over the past quarter-century, sadly, also prevents parents from doing what they are supposed to do: **mass incarceration,** the term sociologists use for the extremely high rates of imprisonment today, particularly of African American males. The percentage of Americans imprisoned or jailed has grown enormously since about 1980. A major factor in its growth has been an increase in arrests for nonviolent drug-related crimes and increases in the sentences that the violators receive—including laws that limit a judge's discretion by requiring mandatory minimum sentences. African American men have been at the center of this increase; by 2004 one-third of young African American men without high school degrees were in prison on any given day (Western, 2006). Many of these men are parents. In fact, in 2002, 1.1 million parents with 2.4 million children were in state and federal prisons (Bendheim-Thoman Center for Research on Child Wellbeing, 2008).

Mass incarceration has made imprisonment something close to a life-cycle stage for African American children and their fathers. Among black children in the early 2000s whose parents did not graduate from high school, about half saw a parent sent to prison (Western & Wildeman, 2009). The imprisonment of fathers leaves mothers to cope with raising children on their own. It leaves children with fathers who are not in their daily lives but not completely gone, either—fathers who can be visited, who make collect telephone calls home, and who write letters, but who cannot be counted on for support. The anxiety-producing state of having a parent who is not present but not totally absent is an example of what is called "ambiguous loss" (Voss, 1999). Children may grieve the loss of their fathers, but that loss cannot be fully resolved because the fathers remain a shadow presence in their lives. Young boys whose fathers are incarcerated tend to show more physically aggressive behavior (Wildeman, 2010). Mass incarceration also affects children because when their fathers are released from prison, they often have a difficult time finding employment.

mass incarceration extremely high rates of imprisonment, particularly of African American males

Quick Review

- Unemployment and poverty can change the way parents act toward each other and the way they interact with their children.
- American children experience more instability in parents' spouses and partners entering and exiting their households than do children in other Western countries.
- Family instability could affect children by exposing them to kinds of households that may increase the risk of negative outcomes such as behavior problems.
- Family instability could also affect children because of the difficulties of adjusting to the frequent movements of parents and parents' partners into and out of the household.
- Mass incarceration is leaving many children with imprisoned parents.

TIME APART

Because of the great increase in the proportion of mothers who work outside the home, more children face daily periods of separation from their parents. Neither parent may be available to care for a preschool child or to be home when an older child returns from school. The issue is usually framed in terms of "working mothers" even though fathers are working outside the home and could provide care when they are home. This development raises two questions: How much less time do children spend with their parents? and What are the consequences of spending more time apart?

How Parents Compensate for Time Apart   You would think children must be spending much less time with their parents now than in the past. But recent studies suggest that the increase in time apart has been smaller than one would expect (Bianchi, Robinson, & Milkie, 2006). Employed parents seem to be compensating during nonemployed hours for some of the time they spend away from their children. Booth, Clarke-Stewart, Vandell, McCartney, and Owen (2002) compared the time spent with parents by two groups of infants in a national study: those who were in child care 30 hours or more per week and those who were not in child care at all. ("Child care" is the term commonly used for nonparental care provided to children while their parents work.) Although the mothers of the first group could potentially have spent 30 fewer hours with their infants, they spent only 12 fewer hours with them, on average. Thus, they had compensated for more than half the hours their children were in child care settings.

How are they doing it? First, they are cutting back on housework. Second, they have less leisure time. Married women, for instance, spend less time reading, visiting people, and participating in clubs or other organizations. All parents are spending less time eating, suggesting quicker meals. Third, they are combining activities much more—working or trying to relax while taking care of their children at the same time, for example (Bianchi et al., 2006). Fourth, in the time that they have with their children, parents are making a priority of intensive activities with children, such as playing or reading to them, rather than just monitoring them (Bittman, Craig, & Folbre, 2004). Overall, family life would seem to be a bit more hectic for parents, with less time for leisure and household tasks. But as a result, children's time apart from parents has not increased as much as labor force trends would lead one to expect.

The Consequences of Nonparental Care   More than 60 percent of all pre-school-aged children today spend some time each week in child care (U.S. Bureau of the Census, 2011p). Some observers worry that nonparental child care is inferior to the care parents can provide. The best evidence comes from a research network organized by the National Institute of Child Health and Human Development (NICHD). Researchers studied over 1,000 infants in eight states, visiting the children's families and child care settings repeatedly from birth through age five; and they have continued to monitor their development. When the children were age 15, they found a small positive effect of child care quality on academic achievement (higher quality care predicted higher cognitive test scores) and a small negative effect of spending more time in child care on impulsive and risk-taking behavior (Vandell et al., 2010).

So the long-term effects appear to be modest, with negative effects noticeable mainly among children who had lower-quality care (for example, fewer care givers per child) when they were young.

■ Transnational Families

Finally, there is a factor that we don't think about unless we raise our gaze beyond the borders of the United States, but which could prevent parents from doing what they are supposed to do. It is distance—often thousands of miles of distance. It involves a new type of immigrant and the family she leaves behind. Immigrants to the United States have long sent part of their earnings back to family members in their country of origin; indeed, that was the main reason why many people migrated in the past. Until recently, however, nearly all of the people who migrated to wealthy countries to send money back home were men. Many of them were fathers who had left their children, and often their wives, in the home country. Since the gendered expectation is that a father's main task is to provide economically for his children, researchers paid little attention to the consequences of this separation for the well-being of the children left behind. But more recently, the number of women migrating to the wealthy countries in order to send money back has increased sharply, although figures are hard to come by. Some of these women have left their children at home. Since the gendered expectation—and the reality—is that mothers are the main caregivers, many observers have expressed concern about the consequences for children and for the distant caregivers themselves.

IMMIGRANT CAREGIVERS

There are at least two sources of the growing migration of immigrant caregivers. The first is the growth in wealthy countries of the kind of low-wage service jobs that women have traditionally done. For instance, because more middle-class mothers in the United States now work outside the home, the demand has risen for nannies to care for their children while they work. It is common for dual-earner American families to hire caregivers from countries such as Mexico and the Philippines, many of whom have left their own children in the care of others in their home countries, and who are willing to work for low wages (Ehrenreich and Hochschild, 2003). The second factor is the development of inexpensive means of computer-based communication across long distances: e-mail, text messages, video services such as Skype, long-distance calling cards, and so forth. Better means of communication allows immigrant mothers to stay in touch with their children.

In the past, immigrants had little contact with their families. A European immigrant to the United States in 1900 could only send letters that might take a month or two to be delivered, and he could only travel home by boat. Today, a caregiver in the United States can remain a part of her children's lives: She can call them weekly, keep track of how they are doing in school, and return home for a major family event. As a result the families of today's immigrants transcend national boundaries. Many families have begun to think of themselves as living in two (or more) countries at once. They are **transnational families:** families that maintain continual contact between members in the sending and receiving countries.

transnational families
families that maintain continual contact between members in the sending and receiving countries

More than half of all preschool children now spend some time each week in nonparental care.

THE EFFECTS ON CHILDREN

Mothers (and fathers) who migrate do not make the decision lightly. They do it to provide their children with financial support for what they think will be a better life. Even a restaurant worker in the United States can make as much as a well-educated professional in some developing countries. Still, being separated from their children can be difficult for transnational mothers (Dreby, 2010). Mothers who migrate tend to reunite sooner with their children—either by returning home or bringing them to the United States—than do fathers who migrate (Suárez-Orazco, Todorova, & Louie, 2002). Typically, mothers leave their children in the care of a maternal grandmother or other relatives; and they do it in societies in which kin such as grandparents traditionally play a larger role in family life than is the case in the United States. The money that parents send home can pay for a better diet, clothes for school, or medical treatment—basic expenditures that an American family would take for granted. The money that a mother sends home also can help the grandmother, too—perhaps paying for a better roof or an additional room for her house. In these ways, the children left behind and their caregivers can benefit from the sacrifices that the mothers make.

Yet the question still remains of the effect of mothers' migration on the well-being of the children left behind. Over time, parents and children may move further apart. Children may resent the mother's absence, or may simply be lonely; and they may withdraw emotionally from their parents in phone calls and messages. The transnational family can become complex if, for instance, a divorced mother finds a new partner in the United States and has a child with him (Dreby, 2010). As they reach the teenage years, children in the home country may be more difficult for a grandmother to control. The separation can be trying for all three generations involved.

Nevertheless, family bonds remain. In one Mexican town, when children were asked to draw a picture of their family, 70 percent those with migrant parents included them in the picture. Just 38 percent of those with divorced parents, in contrast, included them in the picture (Dreby, 2010). In nations in which the migration of mothers is very common, the family and community may adapt. For instance, in the Philippines, where women outnumber men among international migrant workers, children with a parent overseas showed a level of psychological well-being no different from children whose parents had not migrated (Graham & Jordan, 2011).

It is difficult, consequently, to make an overall judgment of the effects of transnationalism on the lives of children in the sending countries (Mazzucato & Schans, 2011). Any attempt to do so is fraught with difficult questions that depend upon one's values more than on hard data. These questions include the importance of economic advancement versus the emotional loss of separation; the extent to which the increasing ease of electronic communication can compensate for distance; the proper role of parents versus other kin such as grandmothers in raising children; and whether Western ideals of the independent conjugal family should apply. The issue is complex, and no simple answer is satisfactory.

Quick Review

- Working parents spend nearly as much time with their children as do non-employed parents by cutting back on other uses of their time such as housework and leisure.
- The long-term effects of child care during the preschool years are a small positive effect on academic achievement (if the quality of care was good) and a small negative effect on impulsive and risk-taking behavior.
- An increase in mothers who immigrate to wealthy countries such as the United States without their children has led to a growth in transnational families.
- Transnational families can strain the ties between mothers and children, but the funds sent home also provide benefits to the children and their caretakers.

■ The Well-Being of American Children

Now that we have studied what parents should do for their children and how social changes may have aided or hindered parents' tasks, we are ready to confront what is probably the most critical question to be asked about the public family: Has the well-being of children declined? This is a question that, in recent years, has often been posed and answered affirmatively by national commissions, politicians, and editorial writers. Yet the American public believes that children's well-being is worse than it actually is. Half or more of participants in national surveys in 2002 and 2003 estimated that at least 30 percent of children live in poverty (almost twice the true figure at the time), that about 20 percent have no health insurance (the true figure was about 12 percent), and that the number of children on welfare has increased or stayed the same since the welfare laws were changed in 1996 (the true number has dropped sharply) (Guzman, Lippman, Moore, & O'Hare, 2003). (We should also examine how children's well-being is studied by sociologists and other participants in this debate: See *How Do Sociologists Know What They Know?: Measuring the Well-Being of Children.*) The answer to the question of how children are doing depends on which children you are talking about.

How Do Sociologists Know What They Know?
Measuring the Well-Being of Children

Concern about the well-being of American children has created a demand by policymakers, journalists, and other observers for better information about the well-being of children. Until the 1980s, the federal government collected relatively little information about children. Family sociologists were focused on the conjugal family of husband, wife, and children—but paid little attention to the children themselves. The rise in divorce and in childbearing outside of marriage in the 1960s and 1970s increased the demand for better knowledge about the consequences for children, and academic researchers and government agencies began to respond.

The first questions they had to consider were the following: How do you measure children's well-being in the large-scale surveys that the federal government tends to fund and that sociologists study? And what aspects of children's lives are important for well-being? The most obvious areas are basic needs such as a child's standard of living and health. The Bureau of the Census gathers information annually about income levels and poverty of households with children. In 1981, the government fielded the first child health supplement to the National Health Interview Survey, a large, ongoing survey of Americans' health. The data from these and other government surveys are made available (with names and addresses deleted to ensure confidentiality) to sociologists who wish to analyze them.

But these indicators tell only part of the story. Sociologists and psychologists are interested in two other important domains: *cognitive* indicators of what children are

learning and *socioemotional* indicators of how they are feeling and behaving. Cognitive indicators are relatively straightforward; sociologists studying random samples of children and their families can ask permission to talk to children's teachers and to obtain test scores from their schools. For pre-school-aged children, of course, there are no test scores to obtain. As a result, survey researchers interested in young children sometimes administer short tests directly to them. For example, a child might be shown a progressively more difficult series of pictures and asked to identify each one.

More difficult to measure are the socioemotional aspects of well-being. For younger children, the best strategy for survey researchers is to ask parents questions about their children's behavior. Older children can be asked directly about problematic behavior.

For instance, since 1991 a federally funded national study, Monitoring the Future, has annually asked nationwide samples of 8th-, 10th-, and 12th-graders about drug use. To be sure, we cannot determine whether students are being fully truthful in their responses. (See *How Do Sociologists Know What They Know? Asking about Sensitive Behavior,* page 184) But even so, changes in their responses from year to year are likely to represent real increases or decreases. For example, the surveys showed that between 1991 and 2011, the percentage of twelfth graders who said they had ever used marijuana or hashish rose from 37 to 46 percent (Johnston, O'Malley, Bachman, & Schulenberg, 2011).

Demographer Kenneth Land and his colleagues have developed an "index of

child well-being," a number they have calculated for each year from 1975 to the present. They combine 28 statistical indicators in domains such as health, economic well-being, safety/behavioral concerns, and emotional/spiritual well-being. They state that their index declined through 1993 but has increased slightly since then and is 3 percent higher than in 1975, suggesting very modest progress (Land, 2011). But not everyone agrees that it's possible to derive a single number that adequately reflects a condition as complex as children's well-being.

Overall, far more information on children's well-being is available from survey research today, compared with two decades ago. In recent years, interest in indicators of children's well-being has been so high that federal government agencies have coordinated their data gathering. Their annual compendium, "America's Children: Key National Indicators of Well-Being," provides very useful information for sociologists and for students writing papers on the well-being of children and is available on the Internet. (See "Families on the Internet" at the end of this chapter.)

Ask Yourself

1. Have you ever responded to a survey of children's well-being? If so, were you truthful in your responses?

2. Which measures of children's well-being—income and health, cognitive achievement, or socioemotional status—do you think are most critical? Explain your viewpoint.

www.mhhe.com/cherlin7e

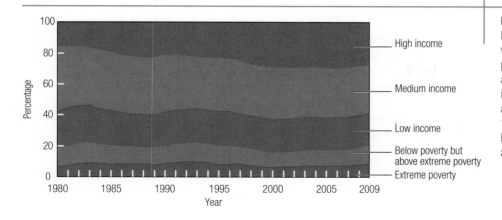

FIGURE 9.3
Percentage of U.S. children who were living in "extreme poverty," "below poverty but above extreme poverty," "low income," "medium income," and "high income" families, 1980–2009. (*Source:* Federal Interagency Forum and Child and Family Statistics, 2011)

WHICH CHILDREN?

Over the past few decades, the fortunes of children have diverged, with some doing better while some are doing worse. Since the 1970s, the incomes of the families of the college educated have been rising the fastest. Figure 9.3 shows what this trend has meant for children over the period from 1980 to 2009. It divides all children into five groups, depending on how their family's income compares to the federal poverty line (which was $22,050 for a family of four in 2009):

Extreme poverty: Less than 50 percent of the poverty line.

Below poverty, but above extreme poverty: Between 50 and 99 percent of the poverty line.

Low income: Between 100 and 199 percent of the poverty line.

Medium income: Between 200 and 399 percent of the poverty line.

High income: 400 percent or more of the poverty line.

The chart stacks these five groups of families one on top of the other like a five-layer cake so that the height equals 100 percent of all families in every year. What changes from year to year is the thickness of each layer of the cake, which represents the proportion of children in each group.

You can see that the proportion of children in the high-income group grew markedly. In 1980, 17 percent of children lived in high-income families, and by 2009 that proportion had grown to 28 percent. What this means is that an increasing share of all children were living in families that were prospering economically, which is good news. But a further look at the chart shows that the medium-income group of children contracted sharply: whereas it included 41 percent of all children in 1980, it included 31 percent in 2009. The low-income group also contracted. In contrast, the size of the below poverty group remained the same, while the size of the extreme poverty group *increased* from 7 to 9 percent—which is bad news. In sum, during this 29-year period, the proportion of well-off children increased while children in low-to-middle-income families were squeezed, and the proportion of children in poverty or extreme poverty increased.

DIVERGING DESTINIES

Like the diverging demographics of families in different status groups that were described in Chapter 4, the trends in well-being we have reviewed suggest what one observer called "diverging destinies" for America's children (McLanahan, 2004). In the first half of the twentieth century, most children, rich or poor, white or black, lived in two-parent families (Tolnay, 2004). But since then, as divorce and childbearing outside of marriage increased, the living arrangements of children have diverged by income. Most of the decline in two-parent families took place among people with less education and lower incomes. In 1960 about one-fourth of all poor families were headed by single mothers; but by the 2000s about half were headed by single mothers. In addition, by the end of the century, more than half of the wealthier families had two earners, reflecting the movement of married women into the workforce (Levy, 1998).

Poor and Wealthy Children   As a result of these trends, you can tell more about a child's standard of living by the type of family he or she is living in than was the case a half-century ago. Children whose families are prosperous—those who are in the top layer of Figure 9.3—usually live with two parents, both of whom work outside the home—in fact, these have been the only kinds of families whose incomes have grown significantly (U.S. Bureau of the Census, 2011u). Children who are poor—those in the bottom two layers—are more likely to live with one parent. To the extent that living in a single-parent family makes it more difficult to escape from poverty, poor children may be experiencing hardships for a longer period of their lives. Moreover, there are strong racial and ethnic differences in whether children are well-off or not. Hispanic and African American children are underrepresented in the top, "high income" layer of Figure 9.3; and as one moves downs the layers, the percentages of Hispanics and African Americans generally rise.

Children in the Middle   It is among children from families in the narrowing middle of Figure 9.3, neither poor nor affluent, many of which have been hard-pressed to maintain their standard of living, that a judgment about trends in well-being is most difficult. My own sense is that, on average, the children in the middle have experienced a moderate downward drift in well-being. They are less likely to live with two parents than in the past, and their families have become less stable and more complex. They have grown up during a period of economic belt tightening by the working and middle classes. Even a moderate deterioration in well-being among children in the middle is cause for concern to those who believe in the idea of progress—the idea that our society ought to be improving the lives of its citizens rather than backsliding. It also raises the question of whether children have a basic right to an upbringing that meets high standards. (See *Families and Public Policy: Do Children Have Rights?*) I think that changes in the family contributed to this deterioration, but I'm not convinced the family was the major actor. The family itself was acted upon by larger forces such as the globalization of the economy and a cultural shift toward ever-greater individualism. Yet parents are not merely passively acted on by social forces; they must be assigned some responsibility for the consequences of their actions, such as getting divorced and having children in short-term cohabiting unions.

Families and Public Policy · Do Children Have Rights?

In 1989, the United Nations established the Convention on the Rights of the Child, an international treaty designed to protect children and ensure their basic needs (UNICEF, 2011). The treaty requires states to take steps to protect the economic, social, and cultural rights of children. Only two countries in the world have not ratified the treaty: Somalia and the United States. In the Walden University Presidential Youth Debate during the Presidential campaign of 2008, Barack Obama said, "It's embarrassing to be found in the company of Somalia, a lawless land. I will review this and other treaties and ensure that the United States resumes its global leadership in human rights."[1] As of 2012, the United States still had not ratified it.

According to the Constitution, international treaties must be approved by a two-thirds majority of the United States Senate, and opposition in the Senate has been strong enough to prevent the Convention from being approved. Some Americans believe that the treaty undermines the authority of parents over their children, which they see as a basic, non-negotiable principle. The Convention does say that all nations "shall respect the responsibilities, rights and duties of parents . . . to provide, in a manner consistent with the evolving capacities of the child, appropriate direction and guidance." But it's that clause, "in a manner consistent with the evolving capacities of the child," that makes opponents uneasy. It seems to suggest that there are limits on parental authority, especially among pre-teens and adolescents.

In a report critical of the Convention (Marshall & Smith, 2006), the conservative Heritage Foundation cited Article 13 as an example of how it infringes on parental rights and authority:

> The child shall have the right to freedom of expression; this right shall include freedom to seek, receive and impart information and ideas of all kinds, regardless of frontiers, either orally, in writing or in print, in the form of art, or through any other media of the child's choice.

Critics would argue that parents should have the authority to monitor and restrict the information that their children, even their teenagers, receive. For instance, parents may block certain television channels from being viewed in their homes. Supporters of the treaty would argue that it does not prevent parents from making restrictions that are in the broad interests of their children, such as blocking sexually explicit cable channels or pornographic Web sites. Yet the wording of the Article suggests to some that children may surf the Internet as they please.

The fact is that nations and groups differ on what restrictions should be placed on children. For example, some poor nations would disagree with the American law that children have the right to go to school to age 16. Even within a particular society there are disagreements. In the United States, for instance, many schools distribute contraceptives to students without their parents' consent, much to the dismay of some parents. More controversially, a pregnant teenager may obtain an abortion without her parents' permission in most of the nation. Many parents approve of these measures, but a minority do not.

Some advocates for children's rights argue that children should have the right not only to have their interests protected (adequate food, shelter, education, etc.) but also to voice opinions over how they are treated. Article 12 says:

> States Parties shall assure to the child who is capable of forming his or her own views the right to express those views freely in all matters affecting the child, the views of the child being given due weight in accordance with the age and maturity of the child.

Some international agencies have added children's empowerment and participation to their goals for assisting families. These goals are generally not considered by American organizations. Nevertheless, older children in the United States are often allowed to testify in contested divorce cases as to which parent they wish to reside with. Exactly how old the children have to be in order that their opinions count is a matter of debate.

The United Nations subsequently added two optional protocols to the Convention, covering matters that are almost universally condemned: conscripting children into the military and trafficking in child prostitution and child pornography. The United States did sign on to these addenda. But opposition to the main body of the treaty remains strong.

Ask Yourself

1. What restrictions did you have on your rights growing up?
2. At what age should children be granted a say in matters such as which parent they would prefer to reside with after a divorce?

[1]Retrieved February 27, 2009, from http://debate .waldenu.edu/video/question-12/#content

www.mhhe.com/cherlin7e

And although I am skeptical of those who claim that there is a pervasive crisis in the well-being of American children, I do think that a real crisis is occurring among children at the bottom of the income distribution. Their share of the population has not decreased significantly in decades. An increasing number live in what Figure 9.3 labeled as "extreme poverty" (family incomes of less than half the poverty line). They are the most likely group to have unstable and complex families and to have parents who did not graduate from high school. They also have a higher concentration of Hispanics and African Americans. The families of children such as these are continually struggling to keep their heads above water. Moreover, the economic crisis of the late 2000s hit them hard, further undermining the supports for poor children.

Quick Review

- Over the past few decades, the proportion of children in economically prosperous families has increased.
- Over the same period, the proportion just below the poverty line has remained the same while the proportion in extreme poverty has increased.
- Children at the top are probably doing better than in the recent past; children at the bottom are doing worse.
- Trends in the well-being of children in the middle are harder to assess; they may have experienced a moderate decline in well-being.

Looking Back

1. **What are the main goals in socializing children and how do parents differ in the way they fulfill their role?** By socializing their children, parents equip them to function well in society. Among other things, parents teach children norms (widely accepted rules about how to behave) and values (goals and principles that are held in high esteem in a society). Parents provide both material and emotional support to their children and exercise control over them. A combination of high levels of emotional support and consistent, moderate discipline, called an authoritative parenting style, seems to produce children who are most socially competent, at least among white families.

2. **How does the socialization of children vary by ethnicity, class, gender, and the sexual orientation of parents?** In racial and ethnic groups such as African Americans and Asian Americans, parents rely more on strong discipline than white parents. Working-class parents stress obedience and conformity more than middle-class parents; conversely, middle-class parents stress autonomy and self-direction more than working-class parents. Members of each social class emphasize values that are consistent with the kinds of jobs they perform. Parents also socialize boys and girls differently, so that any pre-existing differences are exaggerated in childhood and adult behavior. Evidence on children who grow up with lesbian parents from birth suggests that they do not differ much from children with heterosexual parents, although they may be more open to the possibility of same-sex relationships.

3. **What barriers must parents overcome in socializing their children?** Unemployment and poverty can affect the way parents act toward each other and toward their children. Job loss or low earnings can cause a parent to become depressed and angry; fathers in these situations are likely to have angry, explosive exchanges with their wives and children. Family instability could affect

children because of exposure to types of household that may increase negative outcomes such as behavior problems or by exposure to the difficulties of adjusting to the frequent movements of parents and parents' partners into and out of the home. Mass incarceration is affecting parenting among African Americans. There is evidence of small long-term effects of nonparental child care.

4.   **How much time do parents and children spend together?** While it seems as though parents should be spending less time with their children because so many mothers have entered the paid workforce over the past half-century, parents are spending as much time with children as they did several decades ago. They accomplish this feat in several ways including doing less housework and cutting back on leisure time.

5.   **How is the growth of transnational families affecting parents and children?** The demand for household workers in wealthy countries and improvements in communication have led to an increase in mothers from developing countries who immigrate to countries such as the United States without their children. They send money home and keep in touch with the children and their caregivers (often grandmothers) regularly, creating transnational families that retain contact across national borders. These families can strain the ties between mothers and children, but the funds sent home also provide benefits to the children and their caregivers.

6.   **How has the well-being of American children changed over time?** Comparisons between the "average" child today and the "average" child a few decades ago can be misleading. Economic inequality has increased since the early 1970s: The percentage of children at both the bottom and the top of the income ladder has risen, whereas the middle group has decreased in size. The growing proportion of children who live in relatively wealthy settings tends to be doing well. At the other extreme, the growing proportion of children in the poorest families are doing worse. Children in the shrinking middle group may have suffered a moderate reduction in well-being over the past few decades.

Go to the Online Learning Center at www.mhhe.com/cherlin7e to test your knowledge of the chapter concepts and key terms.

Study Questions

1.   Why might authoritative parenting be more effective in some social settings than in others?
2.   Why might adoption be a "devalued status"?
3.   In what ways might we expect children in lesbian families to be similar to children in heterosexual families? In what ways might we expect them to be different?
4.   How does a father's unemployment change the relationships among parents and children in a household?
5.   How might experiencing several parents and parents' partners enter and exit the home affect children?
6.   How does having a father in prison affect family life?
7.   Can a family extend successfully across national boundaries?
8.   Why is it too simplistic to conclude, as some observers have, that children's well-being has declined among all social classes and races/ethnicities in recent decades?

Key Terms

androgynous behavior   279
authoritarian style
  (of parenting)   275
authoritative style
  (of parenting)   275

donor insemination   283
mass incarceration   291
multiple-partner
  fertility   289
norm   276

permissive style
  (of parenting)   275
transnational families   293
value   276

Thinking about Families

The Public Family	The Private Family
What are the crucial duties society expects of parents in raising their children?	**What kind of satisfaction do parents get from raising children?**

Families on the Internet   www.mhhe.com/cherlin7e

Note: While all the URLs listed were current as of the printing of this book, these sites often change. Please check our Web site (www.mhhe.com/cherlin7e) for updates.

A great deal of information on children is available on the Internet. Several federal statistical agencies jointly maintain the site www.childstats.gov. From there, click on "Publications" to access the latest edition of "America's Children: Key National Indicators of Well-Being," an annual compendium of statistical trends. It includes graphs and charts on topics such as family composition, poverty, health, education, and substance abuse. Other resources include the National Center for Children in Poverty (www.nccp.org), which maintains a Web site with several well-done reports about child poverty. For example, click on "Publications," and then "Fact Sheets" to obtain summaries on various topics.

Monitoring the Future (www.monitoringthe-future.org) is an annual survey of 8th-, 10th-, and 12th-grade students, undertaken by the University of Michigan's Institute for Social Research. The survey includes information about drug and alcohol usage and cigarette smoking (click on "Tables and Figures") as well as many publications that can be downloaded.

Chapter Ten

Older People and Their Families

Looking Forward

The Modernization of Old Age

Mortality Decline

The Statistics

The Social Consequences

Fertility Decline

Rising Standard of Living

Variations by Age, Race, and Gender

Social Consequences

Separate Living Arrangements

Contact

Intergenerational Support

Mutual Assistance

Altruism

Exchange

Moving In with Grandparents

Multigenerational Households

Skipped-Generation Households

Rewards and Costs

The Return of the Extended Family?

Care of Older Persons with Disabilities

The Rewards and Costs of Caregiving

The Quality of Intergenerational Ties

Intergenerational Solidarity

Intergenerational Conflict
and Ambivalence

The Effects of Divorce and Remarriage

The Family National Guard

Looking Back

Study Questions

Key Terms

Thinking about Families

Families on the Internet

Boxed Features

FAMILIES AND PUBLIC POLICY: *Financing Social
Security and Medicare*

FAMILIES AND THE GREAT RECESSION: *Still, or
Once Again, Living at Home*

Looking Forward

1. How has grandparenthood changed over the past century?

2. How much support do older adults provide to, and receive from, their kin?

3. Who cares for the frail aged?

4. Are older adults isolated from their kin?

5. What sources of tension exist in intergenerational relations?

In early 2005 a reporter for the *New York Times* called me to say that she was working on a story about grandparents and grandchildren in an age of high divorce and remarriage rates. Some grandchildren, she said, had more than four grandparents because one or more grandparents had divorced and remarried, bringing a stepgrandparent into the family. Did I know anything about this? Yes, I replied, not only because I study families, but also because I was one of eight grandparents of two young children. All four of their biological grandparents had divorced and remarried before they were born. Their maternal grandmother had married me. I was technically one of their stepgrandparents, but that sociological distinction was lost on them. They eagerly accepted the attention and affection of all eight: Grandma Peach, Grandma Linda, Oma (German for granny) Gerda, Nanny, Papa Andy (me), Papa Jay, Papa David, and Papa Dude. "The upside of all this is that children can have more grandparents who love them," the reporter quoted me as saying. "What message it will give them about marriage, I'm not quite sure" (Harmon, 2005).

In fact, the more-than-four grandparents phenomenon is so new that no one is sure what influence it may have on family life. For one thing, the divorce rate reached its current peak in 1980, so that the adults who drove its rise are only now aging into later life. (We will discuss divorce and remarriage in Chapters 12 and 13.) For another, people are living longer than they used to, making it possible for so many grandchildren to have so many grandparents. Until the last few generations, it was far less common for children to have four (let alone eight) living grandparents (Uhlenberg, 2004). Now grandparents are a dime a dozen, it seems, and many are active and independent.

This is not to say that all older adults are healthy and active. As the older population has expanded, so has the number of frail persons in need of care. The cost of the technology-driven health care provided to the increasing numbers of frail older adults has risen dramatically in recent years and has become a major problem for the nation. In addition, a disproportionately large part of the older population sits precariously just above the poverty line—not poor, but not by much.[1] The incidence of poverty is greater for older women than for men, as we shall see.

This chapter will focus on the family lives of older adults—their interactions with spouses, children, grandchildren, and other relatives. As birthrates and death rates both decline, there are relatively more older people and relatively fewer younger people in the population. Whether society will

---

[1] Figures will be given later in this chapter.

Adults live much longer, healthier lives than a century ago.

be able to adequately meet the needs of the older population is an issue of great importance from the perspective of the public family. Spouses and relatives, as will be demonstrated, provide most of the assistance to older adults. Providing adequate assistance is likely to be more difficult when the huge baby boom generation begins to retire. Other changes in family life, such as the increase in women's work outside the home and the rise in divorce, may also affect the task of caring for the older population.

But it would be a mistake to think of older adults only as *recipients* of assistance because they are also important *providers* of assistance to children and grandchildren. Much of that assistance is provided on an as-needed basis: help with a down payment for a house, help when employed parents need child care, help when a daughter separates from her husband. In fact, over the past few decades, the percentage of grandchildren who are living in their grandparents' homes—sometimes without either parent present—has been increasing. We will examine more closely the assistance that older adults give to their families.

Although recent trends in the well-being of children are mixed, as noted in the previous chapter, recent trends in the well-being of the older population deserve at least two cheers. Programs for older people have been the one indisputable success of U.S. social welfare policy since the Great Depression. In fact, so successful have the programs been, and so far have both death rates and birthrates fallen, that most people fail to realize how new is the kind of life most older Americans are leading today—a longer, healthier life in which they provide substantial assistance to their family members. In order to understand what has happened, we need to begin by looking back in history.

The Modernization of Old Age

We tend to associate grandparents with old-fashioned families—the large, rural, three-generation kind. We have a nostalgic image of Grandma, Grandpa, Aunt Bess, Mom, Dad, and the kids sitting around the hearth, baking bread and telling stories. Correspondingly, many observers think that the role of older people in families has become less important since the farm gave way to the factory. According to this view, industrialization meant that older people could no longer teach their children and grandchildren the skills needed to make a living. Moreover, older people no longer controlled the resources—such as farmland—that gave them influence over the lives of the young. There is some truth to this perspective. But the historical facts suggest that grandparenthood—as a distinct and nearly universal stage of life—is a post–World War II phenomenon. To be sure, there have always been grandparents around, but never this many and never with so few of their own children left to raise.

MORTALITY DECLINE

The Statistics   First of all, a century ago—even 50 years ago—far fewer people lived long enough to become grandparents. Much of the decline in adult **mortality** (the demographers' term for deaths in a population) from preindustrial levels occurred in the twentieth century. Only about 37 percent of all women born in 1870 survived to age 65; in contrast, about 77 percent of women born in 1930 reached age 65 (Uhlenberg, 1979, 1980). The number of years that the average 40-year-old woman could expect to live increased by 12 between 1900 and 2000, and for men it increased by 9. The trends for whites and nonwhites are similar, but in every decade the life expectancy of nonwhites has been lower than that of whites. In 2007, white babies had a life expectancy of 78 years, compared with 74 years for black babies (U.S. National Center for Health Statistics, 2011e).

A more difficult question is whether the gains in life expectancy that have been occurring recently have added healthy years or infirm years at the end of life. Have modern medicine and improved standards of living allowed older adults more years of activity or merely more years in which they are ill or disabled? **Active life expectancy** is the term for the number of years a person can expect to live without a disability. A series of national surveys shows that rates of chronic disability among older Americans declined from 1982 to 2004, with the rate of decline increasing in the more recent years (Manton, Gu, & Lowrimore, 2008). The roughly 7-month increase in life expectancy that Americans 70 years old and older gained between 1984 and 1994 was completely in disability-free life (Crimmins et al., 2009). The older population seems to be gaining not just longer lives but also healthier years of life.

The Social Consequences   The decline in mortality during the twentieth century has had two consequences. First, both women and men can expect to live much longer lives than was the case several decades ago. Second, women tend to outlive men. In 2007, the average female baby could expect to live 80 years, the average male baby 75 years (U.S. National Center for Health Statistics, 2011e). A century ago the sex difference was much smaller because many

mortality the number of deaths in a population

active life expectancy the number of years a person can expect to live without a disability

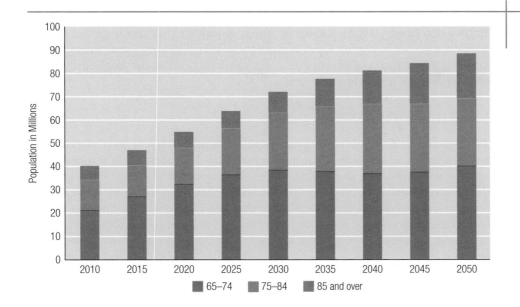

FIGURE 10.1
Projected population 65 years old and over in the United States: 2010–2050. (*Source:* U.S. Bureau of the Census, 2008x)

more women died in childbirth. So it is the case today that (1) there are many more older people in the population than there used to be, and (2) 57 percent of older people are women. Figure 10.1 shows the projected growth of the U.S. population aged 65 and over from 2010 to 2050. Under the usual convention, which I will follow, the **older population** is defined as all persons aged 65 and over. This is an arbitrary cutoff point that is used because 65 has been the age at which a person could retire and receive full Social Security benefits. Most 65-year-old persons are healthy and active, however, and a recent law will gradually raise the retirement age to 67. Figure 10.1 shows that the older population is projected to more than double by 2050 to about 89 million, compared to about 40 million today. By 2030, when today's college students will be middle-aged, about one in five Americans will be age 65 or over.

Moreover, the greatest growth will occur among the age 75 to 84 population (the middle section of each bar) and the 85 and over population (the top section). In other words, not only will the older population increase but it will itself become older and older, increasingly top-heavy with those in their seventies, eighties, and nineties. As the older population has expanded, **gerontologists** (social and biological scientists who specialize in the study of aging) invented the following terms to differentiate among the aged: **young-old** for those 65 to 74, **old-old** for those 75 to 84, and **oldest-old** for those 85 and over. Now they are talking about **centenarians**—people who are at least 100 years old. In 2010, there were about 50,000 centenarians, more than 80 percent of them women (U.S. Bureau of the Census, 2011o).

The sharp decline in mortality has caused a profound change in the relationship between older persons and their children and grandchildren. For the first time in history, as I noted at the beginning of this chapter, most adults live long enough to get to know most of their grandchildren, and most children have the opportunity to know most of their grandparents. The chances were only 50–50 that a child born at the beginning of the twentieth century would still have two living grandparents when he or she reached the age of 15.

older population the group of people aged 65 years and over

gerontologist a social/biological scientist who specializes in the study of aging

young-old the group of older people 65 to 74 years of age

old-old the group of older people 75 to 84 years of age

oldest-old the group of older people 85 years of age and over

centenarian a person who is 100 years old or older

In contrast, the comparable chances rose to 9 in 10 for a 15-year-old in the 1970s (Uhlenberg, 1980). Currently, then, nearly all children have the opportunity to get to know at least two of their grandparents—and many get to know three or four (or even eight). But children born at the beginning of the century were not nearly as fortunate.

FERTILITY DECLINE

The decline in **fertility** (the demographer's term for births in a population) is the second reason why grandparenthood on a large scale is a recent phenomenon. As recently as the late 1800s, American women gave birth to more than four children, on average (Ryder, 1980). Many parents still were raising their younger children after their older children left home and married. Under these conditions, being a grandparent took a backseat to the day-to-day tasks of raising the children who were still at home. Today, in contrast, the birthrate is much lower, and parents are much more likely to be finished raising their children before any of their grandchildren are born. When a person becomes a grandparent now, there are fewer family roles competing for her or his time and attention. Grandparenthood is more of a separate stage of family life, unfettered by child care obligations—one that carries its own distinct identity. It was not always so.

The combination of falling mortality and fertility rates has also altered the bonds of kinship that people have. Because birthrates have fallen, younger people tend to have fewer brothers and sisters than their parents and grandparents. So the horizontal bonds of kinship—those to relatives in the same generation as you—have tended to shrink. In contrast, lower mortality means that you have a much greater chance of having living parents well into your middle years than your parents or grandparents had. Vertical kinship ties—those to relatives in preceding or following generations—have tended to grow. The result is a kinship structure with growing links up and down the generations and withering links across them sometimes referred to as the "beanpole family" (Bengtson, 2001). A number of gerontologists have argued that lowered mortality rates are making the four- and five-generation family (e.g., my grandparents, my parents, me, my children, and my grandchildren) common. Yet although there are more of these linkages than there used to be, they are still the exception rather than the rule. A survey in the Boston area showed that at no stage of the adult life course up through age 70 did more than 20 percent of the respondents belong to more than a three-generation linkage of kin. And the number in five-generation linkages never topped 2 percent. At all ages, the most common generational depth was three. In young adulthood, the three generations were typically my grandparents, my parents, and me; in middle age the three were my parents, me, and my children; and at older ages they were me, my children, and my grandchildren.

The authors of the Boston study, Alice and Peter Rossi, conclude:

> *The truly remarkable demographic change over the twentieth century is the impact of increased longevity on the number of years when the majority of the population may still have at least one living parent. (Rossi & Rossi, 1990)*

The watershed age, they argue, is 50. Prior to age 50, there is little drop-off in the percentage of adults who have at least one living parent; at about age 50 the percentage declines sharply. (And at about the same age, the percentage who have grandchildren increases sharply.) Thus, the lives of most parents and children now overlap by about 50 years. These long, potentially rich cobiographies are the product of lower mortality.

RISING STANDARD OF LIVING

Older people also have more money, on average, than they did a few decades ago. As recently as 1960, older Americans were an economically deprived group: 35 percent had incomes below the poverty line, compared with 22 percent of the total population. Now they have caught up: Their poverty rate of 9.0 percent in 2010 was lower than the rate for non-older adults (U.S. Bureau of the Census, 2011f). The main reason they are no longer disadvantaged is Social Security, the federal government program that provides retirement benefits to persons aged 62 and over. Beginning in the 1950s and 1960s, Congress expanded Social Security coverage, so that nearly all workers, except some who are employed by government, are now covered. And since the 1960s, Congress has increased Social Security benefits far faster than the increase in the cost of living. As a result, the average monthly benefit has doubled in purchasing power since 1960, even after taking inflation into account. Today's older adults benefited from the societywide rise in economic welfare in the 1950s and 1960s, when they were working; then, as they reached retirement, they benefited from the increase in Social Security benefits.

Variations by Age, Race, and Gender   Still, there are sharp variations by age, race, and gender in the proportion of the older population who are poor. Overall, the old-old are more likely to be poor than those who are younger, older women are more likely to be poor than men, and African Americans and Hispanics are more likely to be poor than whites. For example, in 2010, 8.1 percent of persons aged 65 to 74 were poor, compared with 10.0 percent of those aged 75 and over. Only 6.7 percent of older men were poor, compared with 10.7 percent of women. And 6.8 percent of the non-Hispanic white aged were poor, compared with 18.0 percent of blacks and 18.0 percent of Hispanics (U.S. Bureau of the Census, 2011j).

Moreover, as I said earlier, a larger percentage of the older population have incomes that place them just above the poverty level. In 2010, 13 percent had incomes between 100 and 150 percent of the poverty level, compared with 9 percent of all adults under the age of 65 (U.S. Bureau of the Census, 2011j). This nearly poor group is in some ways more vulnerable to economic and health crises than the poor older population because they fall between the poor, who can qualify for additional public assistance, and the middle class, who can supplement their Social Security checks with savings and pensions. Although nearly all older persons are covered by **Medicare,** the government program of health insurance for the older population, Medicare pays for less than half of their health expenditures. Moreover, it pays nothing for nursing home care. Persons with incomes below the poverty line are also eligible for **Medicaid,** the government health insurance program for the poor of all ages, which does pay for nursing home costs. Middle-class older persons can afford to purchase private health insurance to pay the bills Medicare doesn't cover. But those with incomes that are just above the poverty line typically have too much income to qualify for Medicaid and too little to buy private insurance.

Medicare the government program of health insurance for all older people

Medicaid the government program of health insurance for people with incomes below the poverty line

Families and Public Policy | Financing Social Security and Medicare

Until the recent debates about how to finance Social Security, many people believed in a myth: The government saved the Social Security taxes they paid—as if the money were put in a drawer with their name on it—and paid it back to them when they retired. In fact, Social Security is a pay-as-you-go system in which the taxes workers pay today are mostly given to today's older recipients. But as the proportion of the population that is older rises, the tax burden on the younger, working-age population becomes greater. The problem could become severe in the near future as the large baby boom generation begins to retire.

Even today, the expenditures are huge: Social Security benefits accounted for 20 percent of the federal budget in 2007—$13 billion more than all expenditures on national defense. Benefits under Medicare, the government health insurance program for the aged, constituted another 13 percent (U.S. Bureau of the Census, 2011b). In other words, one-third of the federal budget was spent on benefits for the older population.

In 2005, President George W. Bush proposed to partially replace Social Security with a new system based on investing some of people's Social Security taxes in the stock and bond markets (Kosterlitz, 2005). Under this plan, part of the taxes workers pay would indeed be saved under their names, just as the myth suggested, only instead of keeping the money in a drawer the government would invest it. Partial privatization, as the plan is called, would eventually save federal money, since the government would reduce the benefits it pays to retired workers and substitute the proceeds of their personal accounts. Supporters of the plan touted it as a way to reduce the growth of Social Security spending while relying on private investments. Critics of the plan, however, opposed investing people's tax dollars in the markets because the returns are not guaranteed. Although in the past the returns from stocks and bonds have been substantial, no one can be certain what future returns will be, as the Great Recession has showed. President Bush was unable to get the plan through Congress.

Although the public pays more attention to the cost of Social Security than to the cost of Medicare, Social Security is actually in better shape. In 1983, Congress passed legislation that greatly strengthened the long-term financial status of the system. Among other things, the legislation increased the payroll taxes that workers and their employers pay into the government's Social Security trust fund. The legislation also raised the age at which people can retire and receive full benefits from 65 to 67 in 2027. (Although a two-year increase may seem modest, it will save money because 3 to 4 percent of 65-year-olds die within two years, and others will keep working and paying taxes.) Due to the increased payroll taxes, the Social Security trust fund is collecting large surpluses that theoretically should be saved to pay for future costs. Unfortunately, politicians are finding it difficult to resist the temptation to use the surpluses to reduce the federal budget deficit today rather than to save them for the future. Consequently, the surpluses may not provide as much help as they should.

It is also uncertain whether the Social Security and Medicare systems will provide the olders of the future with the same level of benefits that today's olders receive. Low birthrates today mean that there will be fewer workers in a decade or two to pay Social Security taxes for the growing number of older people. In 2000 there were five people of working age (20 to 64) for every older person; by 2030, according to current estimates, there will be only three people of working age for every older person (U.S. Bureau of the Census, 2008c). In addition, the increases in the number of old-old and oldest-old may strain the already costly Medicare system. (See *Families and Public Policy:* Financing Social Security and Medicare.)

Social Consequences Nevertheless, because of the general rise in their standard of living, older parents and their adult children are less dependent on one another economically. Family life in the early decades of the twentieth century was precarious; lower wages, the absence of social welfare programs,

Little has been done, however, to control the spiraling growth of Medicare payments. Three factors are contributing to the growth: the increase in the older population, the growing share of the older population that is in the old-old and oldest-old categories (and therefore at greatest risk of serious illness and disability), and the increasing cost of health care. The Patient Protection and Affordable Care Act, the major health care reform law enacted in 2010, includes provisions that are designed to reduce spending on Medicare. For instance, it would reduce the growth in payment rates to doctors who treat Medicare patients. It would increase the premiums that higher-income beneficiaries must pay for supplementary coverage. If the Act's provisions are successful, which is not yet clear, it would reduce the rate of growth of Medicare expenditures. But it would not solve the problem (Kaiser Family Foundation, 2011b).

Further steps may be needed. The government could raise the payroll tax that pays for Medicare, as has been done with the Social Security payroll tax. Workers

Older Americans, their numbers expanding, have become an important political interest group.

see one combined deduction on their paychecks for Social Security and Medicare; given the recent increases in this deduction, there could be opposition to further hikes. The government could also raise the age of eligibility for Medicare and cover the youngest of the older population through national health insurance. In addition, older people who are better off economically could be charged larger deductibles (the amount an individual must pay for a service before Medicare pays anything) or larger copayments (the percentage of the cost of a service that the individual, not Medicare, must pay after the deductible is met). But it

is very difficult to make major changes in popular programs for the older population.

Ask Yourself

1. Do you have older relatives who receive Medicare benefits? If so, how important is government health insurance to them? If the government did not offer Medicare benefits, would your relatives, or their children, be able to afford their medical care?

2. Should Medicare beneficiaries be charged according to their ability to pay? Explain your reasoning.

www.mhhe.com/cherlin7e

and crises of unemployment, illness, and death forced people to rely on their kin for support to a much greater extent than is true today. There were no such things as unemployment compensation, welfare checks, food stamps, Medicare, Social Security benefits, or government loans to students. Often there was only your family. Some older people provided assistance to their kin, such as finding a job for a relative, caring for the sick, or minding the grandchildren while the parents worked. Sometimes grandparents, their children, and their grandchildren pooled their resources into a common family fund so that all could subsist. When older parents became frail, their children cared for them at home. Historical accounts suggest that intensive intergenerational cooperation was more common than it is today because it was needed more.[2]

[2] See, for example, Anderson (1971); Hareven (1982).

Although Social Security income helps the older population greatly, a substantial number have incomes just above the poverty line.

SEPARATE LIVING ARRANGEMENTS

But since the mid-twentieth century, the percentage of older women who live alone has increased greatly. To a lesser extent, so has the percentage of older men. Figure 10.2 displays trends in living arrangements between 1940 and 1980 for persons aged 60 and over, and it also displays living arrangements in 2000 and 2008 for persons aged 65 and over.[3] Living arrangements are grouped into four categories: (1) living alone, (2) living with their spouse, (3) living without a spouse but with other relatives, or (4) living with nonrelatives only. The upper panel is for women, the lower for men. Among women, there was a sharp increase in the percentage who were living alone—as you can see from the increasing size of the uppermost section of each bar, moving from left to right. Conversely, there was a sharp fall in the percentage who were living without a spouse but with other relatives (such as a daughter or son). By 2008 it was nearly as common for an older woman to live alone as to live with a husband.

[3] Figure 10.2 excludes older people who were living in nursing homes. Data for 2000 and 2008 are taken from a published report from the Census Bureau's Current Population Survey, which presented information for people aged 65 and over.

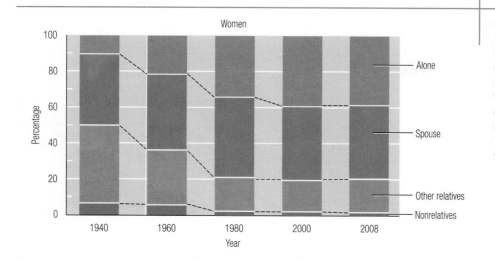

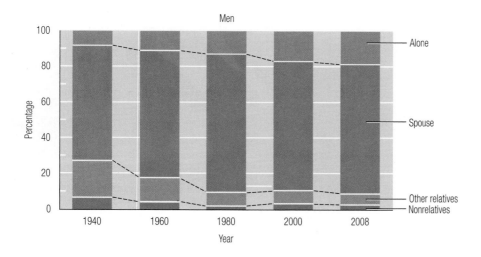

FIGURE 10.2
Living arrangements of women and men 60 years old and over in the United States, 1940 to 1980, and for women and men 65 years old and over, 2000 and 2008. (*Sources:* Sweet & Bumpass, 1987; U.S. Bureau of the Census, 2001, 2009b)

This shift toward older women's living alone has occurred for three reasons. First, women have been outliving men by a greater and greater margin each decade, so that the number of older widows has grown much larger, and fewer widows remarry because of the imbalance between the sexes. In 2008 there were four times as many unmarried widowed older women than there were unmarried widowed older men (U.S. Bureau of the Census, 2009b). Second, it is less common now for a child to remain at home with his or her parents after reaching adulthood than in the past (although there has been some reversal of this pattern in recent years, as we will see). It used to be common for a child to remain with a farm family and to take over the farm when the older generation retired, but far fewer farm families exist today. With the decline of farming and the rise of wage labor, children have better economic opportunities outside of their parents' home than in the past (Ruggles, 2007). Third, older Americans tend to prefer to live near their children but not with them—a cultural preference that has been labeled "intimacy at a distance"

Older widowers often find it difficult to manage the daily household tasks their wives did.

(Rosenmayr & Kockeis, 1965). They want to see their children and grandchildren but maintain their independent residences. As the incomes of the older population have increased, they have been able to fulfill this preference by renting or owning their own housing units.

Nevertheless, Figure 10.2 shows a very different pattern for older men than for older women. To be sure, the percentage living alone has increased, as indicated by the top section of the bars, but the increase has been modest. At all times since 1940, the vast majority of older men have been married and sharing a household with their wives. Moreover, the proportion who were married *increased* between 1940 and 2008—as you can see by the increasing size of the next-to-the-top section of each bar. This marriage bonanza for older men was the flip side of the spouse drought for older women. Men had a higher risk of dying than women, but if they managed to live longer than their wives, their remarriage prospects were better than were older women's. The current generation of older men has been cared for by women throughout their lives—by their mothers when they were growing up and by their wives (many of whom did not work outside the home after marriage) in middle age. They continue to be cared for by women in old age. Most older widows, on the other hand, must continue to care for themselves or to rely on relatives living mostly in other households.

And so the older years have taken on an increasingly different character for women than for men—women more likely to be living apart from kin, men more likely to be living with their wives. (The rise in divorce in early and mid-adulthood has also separated the worlds of men and women; more on that in a few pages.)

CONTACT

Given the rise in independent living among the older population, you might think that grandparents must be isolated from their children and grandchildren. But that is not the case. About 75 to 80 percent of older people live within an hour's drive of at least one of their children (Agree & Glaser, 2009). Moreover, grandparents typically see at least some of their grandchildren regularly. In a 1992–1993 national survey, 39 percent of grandparents reported that at least one set of grandchildren lived less than 10 miles from them; and a majority reported that they saw at least one grandchild every week (Uhlenberg & Hammill, 1998).

Many studies have shown that the strongest predictor of how often grandparents see their grandchildren is how far apart they live (Cherlin & Furstenberg, 1992; Uhlenberg & Hammill, 1998). The dominance of distance illustrates both the strength and the vulnerability of the grandparent-parent-grandchild relationship. As for its strength: When grandchildren live close by, grandparents see them regularly, except under unusual circumstances. Parents and children, with few exceptions, make sure they visit the grandparents. The pull grandparents exert when they live nearby shows how strong is the sense of obligation among adult children to keep in touch with their parents and their in-laws. This sense of obligation is usually overlaid with love, concern, and assistance, but even when it is unsupported by these props, it is often still honored. The uniformly high frequency of visiting among nearby kin suggests that the bond among grandparents, their adult children, and their grandchildren is still strong.

On the other hand, when adult children move away, grandparents' access to their grandchildren drops dramatically. To be sure, adult children who have weaker ties to their parents may be the ones who tend to move from their hometowns. Job possibilities, marriage, and many other events also enter into the decision to move. Still, from the grandparents' point of view, whether or not adult children live close by involves a large element of luck. When a son takes a job in another state or a daughter-in-law moves away after a divorce, the grandparent is rarely able to overcome this impediment to regular contact.

In addition to living close by, grandparents see their grandchildren more frequently if they have a close relationship with the mother of the grandchild—their daughter or daughter-in-law. Middle-aged women do the work of "kin keeping" more often than middle-aged men, and studies show that their ties with older and younger generations are stronger and more consistent, on average, than men's (Rossi & Rossi, 1990). In general, grandmothers see their grandchildren more than grandfathers do, and grandmothers on the mother's side see even more of them than grandmothers on the father's side (Uhlenberg & Hammill, 1998).

Quick Review

- Because of dramatic declines in mortality, grandparents' and grandchildren's lives overlap much more than in the past. Also, women tend to live longer than men.
- Because of declines in fertility, most grandparents are no longer raising children, which makes grandparenthood a more distinct stage of life.
- A rising standard of living, due in large part to Social Security, has made the older people less dependent on their children.
- Older women are much more likely to be living alone than in the past, and older men are more likely to be married than in the past.
- Although most grandparents live apart from their grandchildren, they tend to see at least some of them often.

Intergenerational Support

In middle and old age, as in childhood, most people in need of assistance turn to their kin. The majority of help that the older population and their adult children receive comes from one another. And because of lengthening life expectancy, this stage of mutual assistance lasts longer than ever before. At current rates of fertility and mortality, according to one demographic estimate, the average person can expect his or her life to overlap slightly longer with a parent over the age of 65 than with children under the age of 18 (Watkins, Menken, & Bongaarts, 1987). But although adult children will provide assistance during the years when they have aging parents, most of them also will *receive* substantial help from their aging parents as well. Until their last years, most aging parents are relatively healthy and economically independent.

In fact, the role of older parents as providers of support to their children has increased over the past generation. The employment struggles of young adults have led more of them to live in their parents' homes well into their twenties or early thirties; and their numbers have increased sharply since the start of the Great Recession. (See *Families and the Great Recession:* "Still, or Once Again, Living at Home.") The struggles of low-income parents to support their children has led to a growth in the percentage of grandchildren who live with their grandparents, sometimes without the parent generation present. Overall, the extended family has been making something of a comeback lately, with older parents in the role of householders and providers assisting their children and grandchildren rather than in the historical role of dependents who are being cared for by their children and grandchildren.

MUTUAL ASSISTANCE

Why do older persons and their adult children provide so much assistance to each other? While it may seem natural that they do, there are patterns to this behavior that need explanation, such as these: Until they are very old or very ill, older persons typically give more assistance to their adult children than the children give to them (Agree & Glaser, 2009). They tend to give more assistance to adult children with greater needs and to adult children who have provided them with more assistance (Suitor, Sechrist, & Pillemer, 2007). Adult children who earn higher wages spend less time caring for their parents (Bianchi, Hotz, McGarry, & Seltzer, 2008). People give more assistance to biological parents and children than to stepparents and stepchildren (Cox, 2008). Two perspectives have been proposed to explain these patterns, and both probably influence intergenerational assistance.

Altruism   The first is altruism—caring about others, wanting to make their lives easier and better. People behave more altruistically toward close relatives than toward others. They tend to feel most obligated to help their children, second most to help their grandchildren, and then their parents and grandparents (Nock, Kingston, & Holian, 2008). Sociologists would say that these altruistic sentiments reflect strong social norms about how to live one's family life. We are taught that a good person cares for her or his children and gives time and effort generously to them. American law reinforces that norm: It is a crime to grossly mistreat one's children or to abandon them. And although it is not a crime to abandon one's older parents when they are in need, most people would be ashamed to do so. These norms about family life, however, have limits. For instance, they say little about whether a person has an obligation to help a step-relative, perhaps accounting for the lower level of assistance that studies show.

Evolutionary theorists would add that stepparents may provide less assistance to stepchildren (and vice versa) because they are not genetically related. More generally, evolutionary theorists would argue that much of our altruistic family behavior reflects our biologically based drive to reproduce our genes, so when assisting a family member aids that goal, we are more likely to do it (Cox, 2008). That is why, so the theory goes, more assistance flows down the generations from parents to children than flows upward from children to parents until the parents are old and frail: Older parents have a continuing, genetic interest in ensuring the survival and well-being of their children and grandchildren. In practice it's very difficult to sort out the influence of social norms from the influence of evolutionary pressures. The altruistic behavior we witness probably reflects a mixture of the two. In fact, one reason social norms about family life are so strong may be that they often reinforce our evolutionary interests.

Exchange   The second perspective on intergenerational assistance is exchange theory, which we have seen before in this book. It suggests that in deciding whether to assist family members, individuals consider the benefits that they would receive and the costs that they would incur; and if the benefits exceed the costs, they act. No one suggests that most people make decisions about intergenerational caregiving in a cold, hard-hearted way. Nevertheless, people do seem to weigh the pluses and minuses. For instance, a high-earning adult child with an ailing mother may make the following calculation: My time is worth a lot of money, so I will gain more and lose less if, instead of taking time from work to care for my mother, I hire someone to care for her. A low-earning child, faced with the same trade-off, might decide to provide care herself.

Families and the Great Recession

Still, or Once Again, Living at Home

When a recession hits and getting a job is tough, what's a young adult to do? The answer for some is to move back home—or to never move out. That's what the behavior of young adults during the Great Recession shows. Consider men age 25 to 34. The green line in the accompanying figure shows the percentage of men in that age range who were living in their parents' homes for each year between 1995 and 2010. The red line shows the unemployment rate for 25- to 34-year-old men in each year. The two lines largely move in parallel. The late 1990s were a time of rising prosperity, and as unemployment dropped, so did the percentage that were living at home. The bump upward in unemployment in the early 2000s reversed the trend and produced a modest increase in living at home. Then the sharp spike in unemployment between 2007 and 2009, and the continued high unemployment of 2010 produced a steady upward drift in the percentage living at home that by 2010 had eclipsed the previous high point in 1995.

In fact, in a 2009 national survey, 10 percent of people aged 18 to 34 said that they had moved in with their parents because of the recession (Pew Research Center, 2009b). Their reasoning is easy to understand: The U.S. Bureau of Labor Statistics reported that since the recession began, the percentage of young adults who were employed has dropped to the lowest level since the Bureau began measuring it in 1948 (U.S. Bureau of Labor Statistics, 2011d). Meanwhile, college enrollments soared, particularly at community colleges, because many young adults decided that with jobs in short supply, the time was ripe to improve their education and skills (Pew Research Center, 2009a).

For young adults, living at home can be an enormous help while they search for jobs or continue their education. They may have the confidence to turn down an undesirable job offer and search for a better one because their expenses are low. They may be able to afford to enroll in a degree program only because they don't have to pay rent. Parents' homes can be temporary homeless shelters for adult children's families when unemployment strikes. For older parents, having an adult child at home can prolong, or rekindle, close family bonds.

That's the upside. But there's also a sense in American culture that young adults are supposed to be successfully launched by their late twenties or early thirties. Americans value autonomy and personal responsibility, which encourages them to establish independent households. There's also a sense that older parents, having raised their children to adulthood, deserve to turn their lives toward their own personal interests and to build savings for their retirement. As much as they love their children, they also value autonomy.

Countries around the world vary in how they balance the positives and negatives of remaining at home. Italians tend to routinely remain at home in their twenties and to marry at older ages than do young adults in almost any other country. A shortage of available housing and a dearth of good job opportunities in Italy contribute to the phenomenon. By most reports, Italians embrace the prolonged parent-child households that result. Parents say that they enjoy having their children live with them through their twenties. They do not define staying at home as a problem. In Japan, too, a housing and job market crunch leads to young adults remaining in their parents' homes longer. But the reception isn't as positive as in Italy, especially for those who are employed but still at home: They are sometimes criticized as "parasite singles" who receive free room and board and spend freely on personal pleasures such as clothes and eating out (Newman, 2012).

Nothing comparable to the parasite singles label has emerged in the United States. And no one would look askance at children who move back home because they have lost their jobs. Moreover, in some immigrant families, such as the intergenerational

generalized exchange the provision of assistance to one member of a family with the expectation that someone in the family will reciprocate at a later time

Sometimes these calculations of the benefits and costs of providing assistance take a subtler form called **generalized exchange.** In this situation I help an individual in my family with the expectation that at a later time I will be able to request assistance from anyone in the family—not necessarily the individual I helped (Takahashi, 2000). It's the same principle that might lead you to stop your car to help someone who is changing a flat tire, not because you expect that person to ever help you but rather because you expect that if you have a flat tire, *someone* will help you. As long as enough people behave as you do, you will be right. Similarly, I may choose to help one of

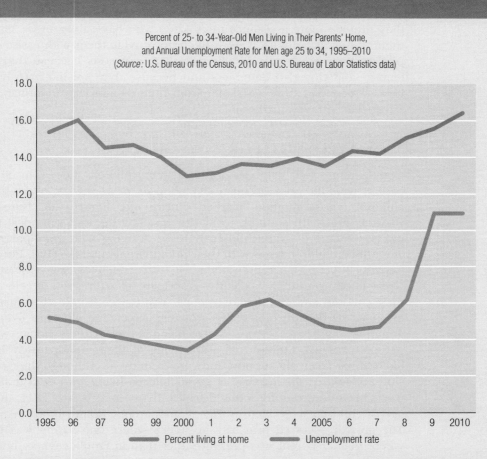

Percent of 25- to 34-Year-Old Men Living in Their Parents' Home, and Annual Unemployment Rate for Men age 25 to 34, 1995–2010 (*Source:* U.S. Bureau of the Census, 2010 and U.S. Bureau of Labor Statistics data)

Asian-American families mentioned in Chapter 5, older parents and adult children may be pooling their funds into a common pot as a strategy to get ahead. Still, the phenomenon of prolonged residence in one's parents' home leaves some adult children and older parents ambivalent. The situation was parodied in the 2006 film *Failure to Launch*, in which a thirty-something slacker living at home falls in love with a woman and begins to suspect that his parents hired her to lure him out of their house. The film grossed almost $90 million. Only a year later, the Great Recession forced many more young adults to live at home; and no one was laughing about it.

my children with the down payment on a house today, and two years later I may help the other child with school fees for a grandchild, with the expectation that if I need assistance later in life, someone in my little family system will reciprocate. In this way, my assistance creates a generalized obligation, an indirect IOU of sorts, that I can carry in my pocket and, in time of need, present to either child. As long as our family has built up relations of trust and reciprocity, I will be likely to collect.

In practice, the mutual assistance between older parents and their adult children represents a mixture of altruism and exchange. Adult children and older parents provide assistance up and down the generations of their families both because they have strong emotional bonds and because they think that they will receive help in return when they need it. Altruism (and its cousins, emotional closeness and love) helps to explain why older parents provide more assistance to children who need it more. Exchange helps to explain why they provide more assistance to children who have given more assistance to them. When asked who is most likely to provide them with assistance, older parents tend to choose daughters rather than sons because they may feel emotionally closer to daughters and because they are likely to have a history of receiving more assistance from their daughters (Fingerman, Pillemer, Silverstein, & Suitor, 2012).

MOVING IN WITH GRANDPARENTS

Grandparents often help care for their grandchildren. Indeed, in 2010, grandparents were the primary source of child care for 21 percent of pre-school-aged children whose mothers worked outside the home (U.S. Bureau of the Census, 2011l). In addition, over the past few decades a modest but growing percentage of grandchildren have been living with grandparents. In all, 7.6 million children lived with their grandparents in 2011 (U.S. Bureau of the Census, 2011r). That represents a 23 percent increase since the start of the Great Recession in 2007. Clearly, grandparents are playing a role in helping their children and grandchildren cope with the economic downturn. Observers have particularly noted the growing percentage who are living in their grandparents' homes (as opposed to living in their parents' homes with grandparents present). Children who are living in their grandparents' homes are likely to be receiving support and care from them. Although the Great Recession accelerated the increase in grandchildren living with their grandparents, it has been occurring for a few decades. Between 1970 and 2011, the percentage of children who lived in their grandparents' homes more than doubled. The growth occurred primarily in homes where one parent was present or where neither parent was present rather than in families where both parents were present.

Multigenerational Households   Households in which grandparents, grandchildren, and one parent are present usually are formed after either of two events: The parent gives birth to a child while neither married nor cohabiting, or the parent separates from a spouse or partner after the birth of the children. In these **multigenerational households,** as we will call households in which at least three generations of family members reside, grandparents can provide important child-rearing assistance. For instance, in one national survey it was found that teenagers who lived with at least one grandparent in a multigenerational household were just as likely to graduate from high school and no more likely to smoke or drink than were children who lived with two married parents (DeLeire & Kalil, 2002). The number of multigenerational households increased from about three million in 1990 to about four million in 2000 and about five million in 2010. The continuing immigration from Latin America and Asia may have played a role because in these cultures multigenerational living is more common. Only 2.7 percent of non-Hispanic white households

multigenerational households households in which at least three generations of family members reside

were multigenerational in 2010, compared to 7.4 percent of African American households, 8.1 percent of Asian households, and 9.8 percent of Hispanic households (U.S. Bureau of the Census, 2012b).

Skipped-Generation Households   Researchers sometimes refer to households with grandparents and grandchildren but neither parent present as **skipped-generation households.** More than one-third of all grandparents who say they are responsible for most of the basic needs of a grandchild are in skipped-generation households—meaning that neither of the grandchild's parents were in the home (U.S. Bureau of the Census, 2012a). Skipped-generation households tend to form when parents are unable to care for their children. The parents may have had their children removed from them and placed with a grandparent due to child abuse or neglect; the parents may have been incapacitated by drug abuse or illness; or they may have been incarcerated. Skipped-generation households are the most disadvantaged of all the kinds of grandparent–grandchild households: They have higher poverty rates, greater usage of public assistance, and less health insurance coverage (Silverstein & Giarrusso, 2010).

skipped-generation households households containing grandparents and grandchildren without either parent present

Rewards and Costs   Overall, the movement of more grandchildren into their grandparents' homes seems to represent a response to family crises rather than a greater preference for intergenerational living. Although some middle-class mothers have moved in with their parents after a separation or divorce, most of the families involved in this trend tend to be poor or near-poor. So while the typical middle-class grandparent attains "intimacy at a distance," a growing share of poor and near-poor grandparents are directly involved in raising their grandchildren. This is particularly true among African American grandparents, 30 percent of whom, in one national survey, reported having the primary responsibility for raising a grandchild for at least six months at some point in their lives (Fuller-Thomson & Minkler, 2000). Grandparents tend to find caring for their grandchildren rewarding, but it can also occur at times in their lives when they would prefer not to be caring for children anymore. It is a situation that can produce ambivalent feelings—a point to which I will return shortly.

THE RETURN OF THE EXTENDED FAMILY?

So far we have discussed three kinds of households in which older parents are living with their adult children, their grandchildren, or both. There are households in which adult children in their twenties and early thirties are living at home, perhaps unable to find employment in a tough economy. There are multigenerational households in which grandparents, adult children, and grandchildren co-reside, sometimes as a way of coping with low incomes. And there are skipped-generation households in which grandparents care for their grandchildren with the middle generation present. I will refer to these three family forms for simplicity as extended-family households. All three have grown recently, and as they grow, they challenge the idea that the simple household consisting only of parents and their non-adult children has become the dominant living arrangement. Are we seeing a large-scale return of the extended

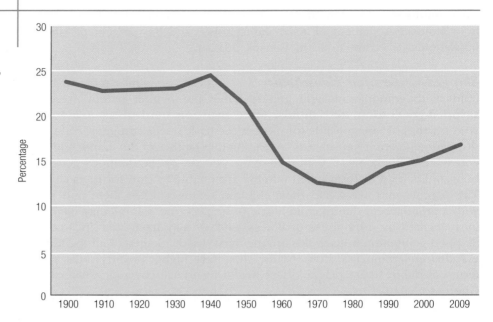

family household? How do recent changes compare with long-term trends in intergenerational co-residence? Figure 10.3 provides some answers to those questions. In compiling it, the Pew Research Center (2010, 2011a) combined the three kinds of households we are focusing on: (1) older parents who are co-residing with adult children age 25 and older; (2) multigenerational households in which three or more generations of family members live together; and (3) skipped generation households. The figure shows the percentage of all households that met one of these criteria from 1900 to 2009.

The figure demonstrates, first, that the increase in recent decades has been substantial but that the percentage of extended-family households today is still far below the levels of the first half of the twentieth century. As you can see, the percentage of extended-family households was much higher in the period from 1900 to 1940 than in subsequent years. During this period, as noted earlier, family life was more precarious, and young adults married at later ages and often remained at home until marriage. Second, the figure shows a sharp decline from 1940 to 1980. This was a period of growing prosperity, increasing government support for the older population, and the lowest marriage ages of the century. Third, the figure demonstrates that the more recent increase in extended-family households began in the 1980s, decades before the current economic downturn. Consequently, although the Great Recession undoubtedly accelerated the increase after 2007, it cannot be the main cause. Rather, the rise after 1980 reflects long-term causes such as older ages at marriage and later exits of young adults from home; increases in divorce and childbearing outside of marriage that led many single parents to live with their older parents at least temporarily; and the growth of immigrant populations with stronger cultural traditions of multigenerational living.

Extended-family households are clearly playing a greater role in American family than was the case twenty or thirty years ago. Will the share of extended-family households ever reach early twentieth-century levels? It is always difficult to predict the demographic future. As late as the 1970s, for instance, no sociologist predicted that the percentage of extended-family households would soon begin to increase. Nevertheless, I think there are several factors which make reaching early twentieth-century levels unlikely. Standards of living are higher than a century ago, which encourages independent living. Government support for the older population encourages them to live in separate households, and better health allows them to be independent longer into old age. It is commonplace for young adults to cohabit with partners prior to marrying, so that the effect of later marriage on household composition is reduced. As immigrants adapt to American culture, it is likely that fewer of them will live in extended-family households. In any case, at current rates of increase, it would take decades more for extended-family households to reach early twentieth-century levels.

Quick Review

- Until they are very old or ill, older people provide more assistance to their children and grandchildren than they receive.
- Both altruism and social exchange underlie this assistance.
- A growing number of young adults are remaining in their parents' homes.
- More grandparents are caring for their grandchildren, sometimes in skipped-generation households in which no parent is present.
- The increase in extended-family households since 1980 has been substantial, but levels remain lower than in the early twentieth century.

CARE OF OLDER PERSONS WITH DISABILITIES

You might think that most seriously impaired older persons are cared for in nursing homes, but that is not so. More are living in the community (that is, in private homes or apartments, not institutions) than in nursing homes. In order to measure physical impairment, gerontologists have developed standard questions about the activities a person needs help with. The most common set, **activities of daily living,** or ADLs, refers to personal care, including bathing, dressing, eating, getting into and out of bed, walking indoors, and using the toilet. Among all older persons with limitations in one or more ADLs in 1994, two-thirds were living in the community. Even among those with limitations in three or more ADLs, nearly half were living in the community (Liu, Manton, & Aragon, 2000).

> **activities of daily living (ADLs)** personal care activities, including bathing, dressing, getting into or out of bed, walking indoors, and using the toilet

Much of the care of disabled older people who live in the community is provided by relatives. According to a 1999 national survey of dependent older persons, 80 percent of their primary caregivers were spouses and children and an additional 10 percent or so were other family members (Wolff & Kasper, 2006). Moreover, women do more of the care of the older population than do men. Two-thirds of the caregivers identified in the survey of the dependent older persons were women (Wolff & Kasper, 2006). And there is a rough hierarchy of caregivers. If the older person's spouse is alive and reasonably healthy, she or he will normally become the primary caregiver; if the spouse is not alive, an adult daughter is usually next in line; and if there is no daughter who can manage the care, another relative, such as a son or a sister, may be called upon (Gatz, Bengtson, & Blum, 1990). Since a majority of older women survive their husbands, this hierarchy means, in practice, that older women are likely to be cared for eventually by their daughters, although sons do contribute.

These mostly female caregivers not only assist their relatives but also perform a critical public service. Without the care that they provide, our already expensive government health care programs would be much more costly. Since Medicare does not pay for nursing home care, individuals must pay nursing home costs by spending their own money first. Only when individuals have spent most of their savings—and therefore meet the government requirements for being poor—are they eligible for Medicaid, which will then step in and pay the bills. Typically, persons of modest means who enter nursing homes—the costs of which average more than $40,000 per year—"spend down" their assets in several months and then turn to Medicaid. Medicaid and Medicare spending for nursing home care totaled about $73 billion in 2009. Individuals in care spent another $40 billion out of their own pockets. Insurers paid another $9 billion (U.S. Bureau of the Census, 2011b).

About 4 percent of the older people in the United States resided in nursing homes in 2009 (U.S. Bureau of the Census, 2011b). As was noted in the discussion of Figure 10.1, the oldest-old, those aged 85 and over, are the fastest-growing segment. Perhaps 60 percent of them, at current rates, will reside in a nursing home at some point during their last years. From the public standpoint, it is crucial to hold down the number of persons who will need institutionalized care.

THE REWARDS AND COSTS OF CAREGIVING

The informal care system has depended on the availability and goodwill of middle-aged women. A few decades ago, most married women were not employed outside the home; presumably, they had more time to devote to caring for an aging parent. But a majority of married women now work outside the home. As family caregivers increasingly combine working outside the home with caregiving for an older spouse or parent, one might imagine that their levels of stress would increase. Yet having other roles to play (employee, wife) may lower the stress that caregivers of the older people feel. Having a job you like, for instance, may take your mind off your caregiving responsibilities, making it easier to provide care. Some studies have noted this "buffering" effect: Success or social support in one role may compensate for the stress provoked by another. From this perspective, the stress caregivers feel largely derives from the care they give, not from an overload of responsibilities.

Moreover, adult children with disabled parents may find the situation stressful even if they are not the main caregivers. According to one national survey of adults in their fifties, those who had a parent who needed extensive care were, in some circumstances, more depressed if they were *not* the main caregiver than if they were (Amirkhanyan & Wolf, 2003). The authors suggest that caregivers feel the stress of having a disabled parent but also reap the rewards of providing care, whereas their husbands, wives, or siblings feel the stress but get none of the rewards. And the rewards can be substantial: becoming closer to a parent, making a difference in his or her daily life, gaining a greater sense of the meaning of life. Caregiving to an older parent is not simply a burden, as difficult as it may be. It can also give people a sense of connectedness and satisfaction.

Quick Review

- Family members provide more of the care of frail older persons than do nursing homes.
- Caring for older people can be both rewarding and stressful.

■ The Quality of Intergenerational Ties

Beyond giving and receiving care when needed, what can be said about the quality of the relationships between older people and their kin today? What social forces strengthen intergenerational kinship bonds and sustain close emotional relationships? What social forces act to undermine these bonds and undercut emotional closeness? In addressing these questions, sociologists have used the concepts of intergenerational solidarity and intergenerational conflict to help us to understand what brings the generations together or pushes them apart. A newer concept, intergenerational ambivalence, allows us to examine the role of mixed feelings across the generations.

INTERGENERATIONAL SOLIDARITY

The concept of solidarity is a broad one, and, fittingly, *solidarity* is a word with many connotations. When asked, a word processor pops up the following synonyms: cooperation, fellowship, harmony, unity, stability, and reliability. An unabridged dictionary defines solidarity as "an entire union of interests and responsibilities in a group," and it quotes a phrase from Joseph Conrad: "Solidarity that knits together innumerable hearts" (*Webster's Third New International Dictionary,* electronic version). We might say, after Conrad, that **intergenerational solidarity** refers to the characteristics of family relationships that knit the generations together.

> **intergenerational solidarity** the characteristics of family relationships that knit the generations together

With respect to the older parents and their adult children, three broad characteristics of intergenerational solidarity have received the most attention from social scientists (Silverstein & Bengtson, 1997):

- *Contact:* How frequently parents and children see each other and are in touch electronically through telephone calls or e-mail messages.
- *Assistance:* The amount of assistance, in either time, goods, or money, that parents and children provide to each other.
- *Affinity:* How emotionally close parents and children feel and how much they agree on values, attitudes, and beliefs.

We have already discussed contact and assistance. Let us focus on affinity. It is relevant for judging whether the older population obtains the closeness and emotional support they wish—and whether they provide closeness and emotional support to their children and grandchildren. It is the kind of question included under the umbrella of the private family.

The ties between grandparents and grandchildren are increasingly based on love and affection, rather than authority and discipline.

Hand in hand with the demographic and economic changes in the lives of the older population have come great changes in the emotional content of their relationships with their children and grandchildren. During the twentieth century, there appears to have been an increasing emphasis on bonds of sentiment: love, affection, and companionship. There is no evidence that the emotional ties between parents and children have grown weaker. As part of the research for a book we wrote about grandparents (Cherlin & Furstenberg, 1992) Frank Furstenberg and I talked with many grandparents at senior citizens' centers. When we asked grandparents whether grandparenthood had changed since they were grandchildren, we heard stories of their childhood that differed from our idyllic image of the past. Their grandparents, we were told, were respected, admired figures who often assisted other family members. But again and again, we heard them talk about the emotional distance between themselves and their grandparents:

The only grandmother I remember is my father's mother, and she lived with us.

INTERVIEWER: What was it like, having your grandmother live with you?

Terrible [laughter]! She was old, she was strict. . . . We weren't allowed to sass her, I guess that was the whole trouble. No matter what she did to you, you had to take it. . . . She was good, though. . . . She used to do all the patching of the pants, and she was helpful. But, oh, she was strict. You weren't allowed to do anything, she'd tell on you right away.

INTERVIEWER: So what difference do you think there is between being a grandparent when you were a grandchild and being a grandparent now?

It's different. My grandma never gave us any love.

INTERVIEWER: No?

Nooo. My goodness, no, no. No, never took us anyplace, just sat there and yelled at you all the time.

INTERVIEWER: Did you have a lot of respect for your grandmother?

Oh, we had to whether we wanted to or not, we had to.

Grandma may have helped out, and she certainly was respected, even loved, but she was often an emotionally distant figure. This is not to say that affection was absent from the relations between young and old. But there has been a shift in the balance between respect and affection.

Granted, it is hard to judge the accuracy of these recollections of two generations ago. But the story that the grandparents consistently told us fits with the demographic and economic developments that have been discussed. It is easier for today's grandparents to have a pleasurable, emotion-laden relationship with their grandchildren because they are more likely to live long enough to develop the relationship, because they are not still busy raising their own children, because they can travel long distances more easily and communicate over the telephone and via e-mail, and because they have fewer grandchildren and more economic resources to devote to them. Earlier in the nation's history, the generations were often bound up in economic cooperation that took precedence over affection and companionship. In fact, there may be a trade-off between bonds of obligation and authority, on the one hand, and bonds of sentiment. Historian David Hackett Fischer, in his book on the history of aging in America, noted the following differences between the nation's early and later years:

> *Even as most (though not all) elderly people were apt to hold more power than they would possess in a later period, they were also apt to receive less affection, less love, less sympathy from those younger than themselves. The elderly were kept at an emotional distance by the young. (Fischer, 1978)*

Conversely, in modern America:

> *As elders lost their authority within the society, they gained something in return. Within the sphere of an individual family, ties of affection may have grown stronger as ties of family obligation grew weak. (Fischer, 1978)*

This increasing emphasis on affection appears to be continuing among older Americans and their children and grandchildren today. Nearly all studies report a high level of warmth and emotional closeness among the different generations in a family (Silverstein & Bengtson, 1997; Bengtson, 2001).

Quick Review

- Intergenerational solidarity depends on frequent contact, emotional closeness, and mutual support.
- Sentiment and affection have become increasingly central to intergenerational relations, whereas the authority of older people may have declined.

Adult children may have conflicting feelings about caring for aging parents.

INTERGENERATIONAL CONFLICT AND AMBIVALENCE

Yet intergenerational relations aren't always warm, and older parents and adult children don't always get along. Tensions, criticisms, and arguments occur, not just among family members who are alienated from each other but also among family members who generally get along well. **Intergenerational conflict** refers to discord among family members that pulls the generations apart. In its mild forms, it can intrude from time to time into the relationships of emotionally close kin. In its more virulent forms, it can underlie a hostile relationship. Intergenerational conflict commonly occurs over communication and interaction styles (such as being overly critical, dominating, or treating family members in ways that are perceived as unfair) and habits and lifestyles (such as using alcohol or drugs, adopting a particular style of dress, or engaging in types of recreation that some find objectionable) (Clark, Preston, Raksin, & Bengtson, 1999). Together, the concepts of solidarity and conflict define a wide range of intergenerational behaviors and attitudes.

Scholars have suggested, however, that another middle-ground concept is necessary to fully understand intergenerational relations today: intergenerational ambivalence (Lüscher & Pillemer, 1998; Connidis & McMullin, 2002; Pillemer & Lüscher, 2003). It refers to the contradictory emotions or mixed feelings that family members may hold toward each other.

For instance, adult children may have conflicting feelings about caring for ailing parents. On the one hand, they may find caring for parents deeply fulfilling and meaningful. On the other hand, they may feel resentful of the demands that caring makes on their time and energy. Even in the mind of a dedicated, loving caregiver, these contradictory feelings may coexist. In one national study, women who began to care for an older parent reported

intergenerational conflict discord among family members that pulls the generations apart

both an increase in depression and a greater sense of purpose in life (Marks, Lambert, & Choi, 2002). The older parent may also feel ambivalent toward the adult child—at once understanding that children have independent lives to lead and yet desiring care from them.

Ambivalence is a broad concept, applicable to many situations in which a person can have conflicting feelings. Sociologists focus on situations in which ambivalence is socially structured, meaning that it reflects authority, power, or strong social norms. Let us define **intergenerational ambivalence** as socially structured contradictory emotions in an intergenerational relationship. The conditions of contemporary life probably make ambivalence more common now than in the past (Connidis & McMullin, 2002). As noted earlier, more grandparents are being called upon to care for their grandchildren in circumstances that can lead to ambivalent feelings. Or consider gender differences in social norms about caregiving. Women are still expected to do more of the care of older parents; and they, in fact, do provide the bulk of care (Agree & Glaser, 2009). More middle-aged children have living parents today than in the past because of increases in life expectancy. Yet women also have greater opportunities to work outside the home than in the past. Adult daughters' greater responsibilities for providing care, combined with greater opportunities for self-advancement in the workplace, can create ambivalence. Middle-aged sons may also feel ambivalence about caregiving, but because they aren't expected to be the primary caregivers, they may more easily resolve their feelings by hiring a caregiver. Middle-aged daughters, in contrast, may be more likely to provide the care themselves because that's what they are expected to do—and leave their ambivalent feelings intact.

> **intergenerational ambivalence** socially structured contradictory emotions in an intergenerational relationship

The results of two studies confirm the prediction that women feel more ambivalence than men in their relations with older parents: In one study, older women reported more ambivalent feelings toward their daughters than toward their sons, as indicated by their greater agreement with statements such as mother and daughter "get on each other's nerves but nevertheless we feel very close" (Pillemer & Suiter, 2002). Another study of rural Iowa families found that women who were caring for parents reported more ambivalence than men who were caring for parents: The women were more likely to agree with both positive statements (e.g., feeling appreciated and loved) and negative statements (feelings of conflict, tension, or disagreement) about their relationship to their parent (Willson, Shuey, & Elder, 2003). These ambivalent feelings do not necessarily prevent caregiving, but they suggest that caregiving often creates simultaneous positive and negative feelings for the provider and the recipient of care.

Ambivalence may be a property not just of the relationship between two family members but also of relationships within the larger family group. For instance, an older adult with more than one child may be grateful for the care provided by some of her children but disappointed by the lack of care from others. If we just look at her feelings about each child separately, we may not see any ambivalence: She either feels positively or negatively toward each child. But when we consider her feelings toward her children as a group, we see ambivalent feelings. This group level process consisting of mixed feelings across multiple children has been called **collective ambivalence** (Silverstein & Giarrusso, 2010). For instance in a national survey, the happiness of older parents was associated with not only their positive

> **collective ambivalence** mixed feelings across multiple children

relationships with the adult children they felt closer to but also their less positive relations with the adult children they felt least close to (Ward, 2008). Their happiness, in other words, corresponded to their feelings about their children collectively.

THE EFFECTS OF DIVORCE AND REMARRIAGE

Other studies also show that older divorced fathers and their children, on average, have relationships that are less close than the relationships of fathers and children from families with no divorce (Agree & Glaser, 2009). In the study of rural Iowa families previously mentioned, grandfathers who were divorced reported less contact and closeness with their grandchildren, in part because they lived farther away and in part because they were less close to the middle generation—their adult children (King, 2003). A 1992–1993 national survey showed that grandfathers who were separated, divorced, or remarried were very unlikely to see their grandchildren from their previous marriage frequently (Uhlenberg & Hammill, 1998).

Older parents who have remarried during midlife will often have stepchildren as part of their families. But research suggests that adult stepchildren provide much less assistance to older stepparents than biological children provide to their older parents. According to one study of adults age 70 or over with disabilities and their biological and stepchildren, the biological children were three to four times more likely to spend time caring for the older parent or to provide financial support to her or him than were the stepchildren (Pezzin, Pollak, & Schone, 2008). Another study suggested that if the marriage between the natural parent and the stepparent had ended, either because of a divorce or because the natural parent had died, the ties between an adult stepchild and stepparent often ended as well: 57 percent of the adult stepchildren in stepfamilies ended by divorce never saw their stepparent, and 46 percent of adult stepchildren in stepfamilies ended by death never saw their stepparent (White, 1994). Thus, the relationship between adult stepchildren and stepparents, which in any case seems less close than between adult biological children and parents, may not even survive a divorce or death.

It seems doubtful, then, that the daughters and, secondarily, sons who provide so much of the care for the frail older population will provide as much care for noncustodial fathers, never-married fathers, or stepfathers as for biological fathers they lived with continuously while growing up. As Chapter 12 will note, the divorce rate doubled in the 1960s and 1970s, and the proportion of children born outside marriage rose during (and after) those decades as well. The men who reach the age of 65 after the year 2000 will be part of the first generation to have lived most of their adult lives in the high divorce era. Many of them will have divorced decades before reaching age 65 and will have had little contact with their adult children. Moreover, divorce is increasing in later life. The annual rate of divorce for adults age 50 and over doubled between 1980 and 2008. About one in four divorces in 2008 occurred to people age 50 and over. All told, there are far more divorced older persons than in the past. In fact, the percentage of 65- to 69-year-old women who are divorced is a large as the percentage that are widowed, which is a historical first for older Americans (Brown & Lin, 2011).

Many fathers have little contact with their children decades after a divorce or a separation from the children's mother. How will these men find care when they need it? Anthropologist Katherine Newman (2003) noticed two strategies in her study of middle-aged and older adults in a low-income community in New York, where childbearing outside of marriage is common. First, men sometimes reappeared unexpectedly at the homes of their former partners and their adult children. After long periods of separation, they attempted to reenter the family systems they had largely abandoned, with varying success. The second strategy was to marry a woman their age. As greater mortality among men reduced their supply, the surviving men found that the demography of the older cohabitation and marriage market favored them.

It is possible, however, that the strategy of finding a wife to care for you doesn't work as well as it used to. Some of the low- and moderate-income single mothers in Newman's study told her that they had no intention of having a serious romantic partner again. Moreover, the women now reaching old age belong to the first generation to have extensive employment histories throughout adulthood. They may be more independent financially when they retire, and they may not find it attractive to remarry an older man. If divorced men aren't remarried in old age, and if they can't rely on their children, they may have no one to help them in their last, frail years. In fact, the percentage of older men who live with their wives, after increasing from 1940 to 1980 (see Figure 10.2), has now leveled off. Research on divorce, wrote one observer, "has focused on women and children as the 'victims'" because of the loss of the father's income. Yet in old age, when kinship ties matter, "it is males who are at risk" (Goldscheider, 1990).

Older gay men and lesbians may also face challenges in obtaining support in old age. Their ability to call on others for assistance will depend on how well they have been able to construct a network of friends, partners, and biological relatives. The effectiveness of these networks is likely to vary widely. In addition, many of their ties are likely to be with people in the same generation; consequently, their access to younger adults who could provide help may be limited.

The Family National Guard

In all, how important a part of the American family system are intergenerational relations? Gerontologist Vern L. Bengtson is the leading advocate of the view that intergenerational relations are very important. In fact, Bengtson (2001; see also Bengtson, Biblarz, & Roberts, 2002) suggests that with the decline of the two-parent nuclear family, intergenerational relations are becoming more important than nuclear family ties to many Americans—and will continue to be important in the twenty-first century. Bengtson argues that the increasing longevity and better health of the older population mean that adult children are fortunate enough to have parents available to them well into midlife. He would note how commonly parents take in daughters and grandchildren after a divorce or care for grandchildren when parents are unable to do so. He contrasts the durability and longevity of parent-child-grandchild bonds with the increasing fragility of marriage bonds.

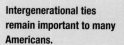

There is much to be said for this argument, but it does have limitations. Among the nonpoor, grandparents tend to leave the child rearing to parents, live independently, and seek "intimacy at a distance." Relations between many divorced older men and their adult children are strained, and it's not clear how much mutual support stepparents and stepchildren will provide to each other over the life course. Some skeptics believe that there has been a loss of family feeling since the time when most older people were living with their children. They charge that modern grandparents, in their rush to retire in the Sun Belt, have abandoned their bonds to their grandchildren.

Perhaps the best way to balance these views is to think of grandparents as the family national guard (Hagestad, 1985). In the middle classes, at least, the guard is usually on inactive reserve—keeping in contact with children and grandchildren, having pleasant relations, but providing (and receiving) little assistance. When a crisis occurs in an adult child's or a grandchild's life—a divorce, a birth outside of marriage, a sudden illness—the family national guard is called up. The key questions are how often the guard shows up for duty when called and how long they stay active. Because older Americans lead longer, healthier lives than in the past, more of them are available. Because most feel emotionally close to their children and grandchildren, they are motivated to help. So in most circumstances, grandparents willingly provide substantial assistance. But active duty has its costs, and, like the national guard, most grandparents prefer to return to inactive duty—to resume their independent lives. And not many may show up to help a divorced relative who has wandered away from the kin, only to show up later, hat in hand.

When Furstenberg and I were writing our book, we visited a senior citizens' center in a Jewish neighborhood in Baltimore. There we talked with a group of grandparents who told us that the new development in the neighborhood was the immigration of many families from Russia. With some envy, they described to us the relationships the Russian grandparents had with their grandchildren: "The grandparents live with their children and grandchildren." "They go on vacation together." "They go out to eat together." "They are very involved in the care of their grandchildren." After listening to these remarks, one of us asked whether anyone in the group would trade places with the immigrant grandparents in order to have their type of relationship. The question was met with immediate cries of "No way!" "No" and "I'm satisfied." The questioner pursued the point further: "Why wouldn't you trade places? There are all these strong family ties?" A woman replied, "I don't think I could live with my children," and a chorus of "No" and "No way" followed.

One grandmother said, simply, "It's too late." What she meant was that, given the opportunity for independence, most American grandparents had already seized it and couldn't give it up. To live with their children, they would have to adjust their daily schedules to fit their children's busy lives. It's easy to look at current living arrangements and criticize the older population for emphasizing autonomy and personal satisfaction in their daily lives. But they are merely engulfed in the same flood of self-fulfillment that has washed over their children and grandchildren. To ask grandparents to lead a retreat to a family system that emphasizes cooperation over companionship, obligations over independence, duty over love, is perhaps unfair. This is the first generation in which most older Americans have had a choice in these matters; should they be criticized for making the same choices as everyone else?

Quick Review

- The older population and their children may have ambivalent feelings toward each other that are socially structured.
- Social changes such as more women working outside the home may have increased intergenerational ambivalence.
- Men who have separated from the mothers of their children may not be able to rely on kin for support in old age. Stepparents may not receive support from stepchildren.
- Some observers argue that social change is making intergenerational relations a more important part of family life.

Looking Back

1. **How has grandparenthood changed over the past century?** Today most adults live long enough to get to know their grandchildren because adult life expectancy has lengthened substantially, particularly for women. And because birthrates are lower, and most adults have finished raising their children by the time they become grandparents, grandparenthood is now a more distinct stage of life. Declining births mean that the average person has fewer links to kin in the same generation; but because of declining mortality the average person has more links to kin in preceding or succeeding generations. Moreover, over the past half-century the incomes of older people have risen dramatically, thanks to the expansion of the Social Security rolls, increases in Social Security benefits, and the growth of private pension programs.

2. **How much support do the older people provide to, and receive from, their kin?** Most of the help that the older people and their adult children receive is mutual. The principles of altruism and exchange underlie this assistance. Except when they are ill, the olders provide more help than they receive. Among those who need care, most older men get it from their wives, while most older women must rely on daughters and other relatives. A modest but increasing percentage of grandparents are caring for the grandchildren in their own homes. These grandparents tend to have lower incomes and poorer health, and their caregiving is usually in response to a crisis in their adult children's lives.

3. **Who cares for the frail aged?** The majority of seriously disabled older persons are cared for in their homes by family members, rather than in a hospital or nursing home. The most common family caregiver other than a spouse is an adult daughter. In the future, fewer adult daughters will be available as caregivers, both because more of them will be employed and because the older generation will have fewer adult children. Caring for an aging family member can be both rewarding and stressful. Higher rates of divorce and remarriage among older Americans may reduce the number of caregivers available to them.

4. **Are the olders isolated from their kin?** The olders value both their independence and contact with their kin. Most have frequent contact with at least one child, especially with those who live nearby. There is a greater emphasis on affection and companionship, and a lesser emphasis on economic cooperation, in intergenerational relations now. Some observers suggest that the quality of intergenerational relations has declined, but others counter that older people and their children have chosen a style of relating to one another—that is, separate residences and fairly frequent contact—that suits them both.

5. **What sources of tension exist in intergenerational relations?** Despite the generally positive feelings the older people and their children have for each other, ambivalent feelings do exist. Those who are giving or receiving substantial care may find it both rewarding and tension-producing. Women experience ambivalence more than men because they are expected to provide care. In addition, older men who have separated from the mothers of their children may be unable, later in life, to rely on their adult children for support.

 Go to the Online Learning Center at www.mhhe.com/cherlin7e to test your knowledge of the chapter concepts and key terms.

Study Questions

1. How have the great declines in adult mortality and fertility altered old age?
2. Should the trend toward the olders living apart from their children be viewed as a positive or negative development for family relations?
3. How do the lives of older women differ from the lives of older men?
4. How do the lives of older non-Hispanic whites differ from the lives of older African Americans and Hispanics?
5. In what ways are women the family caregivers and kin-keepers?
6. Under what kinds of circumstances would intergenerational ambivalence be high in a family?
7. What is the evidence that intergenerational relations, as some suggest, are becoming a more important part of American family life?
8. How do childbearing outside of marriage, divorce, and remarriage affect the likelihood that men will receive the support they need late in life?

Key Terms

active life expectancy   308
activities of daily living
  (ADLs)   325
collective ambivalence   331
centenarian   309
fertility   310
generalized exchange   320
gerontologist   309

intergenerational
  ambivalence   331
intergenerational conflict   330
intergenerational
  solidarity   327
Medicaid   311
Medicare   311
mortality   308

multigenerational
  households   322
old-old   309
older population   309
oldest-old   309
skipped-generation
  households   323
young-old   309

Thinking about Families

The Private Family	The Public Family
Should we be surprised that American grandparents want to live near their grandchildren but not with them?	Together, the federal and state governments spend twice as much money on Social Security and Medicare as the federal government spends on the entire defense budget. Is government spending too much money on the older generation?

Families on the Internet   www.mhhe.com/cherlin7e

Note: While all the URLs listed were current as of the printing of this book, these sites often change. Please check our Web site (www.mhhe.com/cherlin7e) for updates.

The Population Reference Bureau (www.prb.org) has many good reports on aging. Enter "aging" into the search line and several interesting reports will come up. "Rethinking Age and Aging" argues that in light of gains in life expectancy, we should rethink what we mean by middle age and old age.

GrandFamilies of America (www.grandfamilies ofamerica.org) is an organization formed to support grandparents who are taking care of their grandchildren because the parents—the middle generation—cannot. Many of the grandchildren have been placed with their grandchildren by child welfare agencies. The Web site provides information and resources to these grandparent caregivers.

The U.S. Bureau of the Census (www.census.gov) maintains many data-oriented publications about the older population. Go to the Census Web site, click on "Subjects A to Z," select "A," then "age," and then "Elderly (65+) / Older (55+) Population." A chart book of population aging throughout North, Central, and South America is available at http://www.census.gov/population/international/files/ageame.pdf.

Part Five

Conflict, Disruption, and Reconstitution

Conflict between women and men has a public significance beyond the immediate family context. It spans both the private family, where it affects the quality of emotional support, intimacy, and cooperation, and the public family, where its social consequences are played out on a larger scale. Conflict between adults can also lead to separation, divorce, and remarriage. • Chapter 11 considers violence and abuse between spouses and partners and by parents against children. After a brief review of the history of domestic violence, the chapter summarizes current knowledge. The most important theories of domestic violence are presented, followed by an examination of sexual aggression and violence in dating relationships and a discussion of public policies. Marital conflict, these days, often leads to divorce. Nearly one in every two marriages in the United States at current rates would end in divorce. • Chapter 12 probes the causes and consequences of this high level of marital dissolution. It examines the process that divorcing couples experience and the consequences for both children and adults. A majority of divorced persons remarry. Yet remarriage, as • Chapter 13 shows, can bring difficulties for adults and children. The chapter describes the new kinds of family relationships and kinship networks that form after remarriages or after parents cohabit with a new partner. Then it discusses why children living with a parent and the parent's new partner seem to fare no better than children in single-parent families.

No. _____

SUMMONS
DOMESTIC RELATIONS

Chapter Eleven

Domestic Violence

Looking Forward

Domestic Violence in Historical Perspective

Early History

The Twentieth Century

The Political Model of Domestic Violence

The Medical Model of Domestic Violence

Intimate Partner Violence

Two Kinds of Violence?

Prevalence and Trends in Intimate Partner Violence

Prevalence

Intimate Partner Rape

Trends

Which Partnerships Are at Risk?

Marital Status

Social Class

Child Abuse

Incidence

Sexual Abuse and Its Consequences

Physical Abuse and Its Consequences

Poly-victimization

Poverty or Abuse?

Elder Abuse

Sexual Aggression and Violence in Young Adult Relationships

Prevalence

The Intimate Setting

Explanations

Social Learning Perspective

Frustration–Aggression Perspective

Social Exchange Perspective

Domestic Violence and Public Policy

Diminished Policy Debates

Social Programs

Looking Back

Study Questions

Key Terms

Thinking about Families

Families on the Internet

Boxed Features

HOW DO SOCIOLOGISTS KNOW WHAT THEY KNOW?: *Advocates and Estimates: How Large (or Small) Are Social Problems?*

FAMILIES AND PUBLIC POLICY: *The Swinging Pendulum of Foster Care Policy*

Looking Forward

1. When did domestic violence become a social issue?

2. What do we know about violence between intimate partners?

3. What is the extent of child abuse?

4. What do we know about sexual aggression by dates or acquaintances?

5. Why does domestic violence occur?

6. What are the public policy debates concerning domestic violence?

In October 2003, a churchgoing New Jersey couple was arrested after a neighbor saw one of their children looking for food at 2:30 A.M. in the neighbor's garbage cans. Although the boy rummaging through the trash was 19 years old, he stood 4 feet tall and weighed 45 pounds. The parents had adopted him from the New Jersey foster care system. The authorities charged that, along with three other boys they had also adopted, he had been locked out of the kitchen and fed a diet of pancake batter, peanut butter, and breakfast cereal. The boys were so chronically hungry, it was said, that they ate wallboard and insulation. Meanwhile, five other children in the household—biological, foster, and adopted—were well fed. The parents denied the charges. The public uproar about the case grew when it was reported that a caseworker from the state Division of Child and Family Services had visited the home 38 times in the previous two years without noticing that anything was wrong. Nine child welfare service workers were fired as a result of the arrest. The family was receiving about $30,000 in stipends from the state for caring for the adopted and foster children (Peterson, 2003; Polgreen & Worth, 2003).

Cases such as this one—and the death in 1995 of six-year-old Elizabeth Izquierdo, who was beaten to death by her mother after several visits by caseworkers—often lead to demands that child welfare service workers be more aggressive in removing children from potentially abusive parents. Yet removing children from their homes has its own risks, as when children separated from their families drift through the foster care system.

The problem is that the public hears about child abuse or intimate partner violence mainly through sensational cases, such as the New Jersey boys' malnourishment, Elizabeth's death, or former football star O.J. Simpson's trial for the murder of his former wife. A few decades ago, even social scientists ignored **domestic violence,** which will be defined in this chapter as violent acts between family members or between women and men in intimate or dating relationships. Not a single article on the topic appeared in *Journal of Marriage and the Family,* the major scholarly journal in the field, between its founding in 1939 and 1969 (O'Brien, 1971). Now, however, hardly an issue appears without one. In fact, the increase in research has been so sudden and so massive that it requires an explanation. It wasn't spurred by an increase in domestic violence, because there isn't convincing evidence of an increase, as will be noted later. Rather, its rise reflects the increased political power of the feminist movement, which views domestic violence as an important barrier to women's equality, and the increasing cultural emphasis on individualism in

domestic violence violent acts between family members or between women and men in intimate or dating relationships

marriage and family life. To appreciate what has occurred, it is necessary first to examine the history of domestic violence as a social problem.

Domestic Violence in Historical Perspective

The recent attention to highly publicized cases of child abuse and wife battering is not the first outpouring of public concern about domestic violence. Rather, the history of domestic violence in the United States shows short periods of public attention separated by longer periods of neglect. The periods of attention have had less to do with the prevalence of violence than with the power of various political and social groups (Pleck, 1987).

EARLY HISTORY

In the New England colonies, the Puritans believed that it was the responsibility of the government to enforce moral behavior, even if that meant intervening in the affairs of the family. And moral behavior excluded violent acts by husbands against their wives. The well-known minister Cotton Mather told his congregants that for "a man to Beat his Wife was as bad as any Sacriledge" and that "any such a Rascal were better buried alive, than show his Head among his Neighbours any more" (Pleck, 1987). Friends, neighbors, and fellow churchgoers watched over a family's conduct in ways we would view today as nosy, if not meddlesome. In 1641, the Massachusetts Bay Colony enacted the first law against wife beating in the Western world, according to historian Elizabeth Pleck; it also prohibited parents from exercising "any unnatural severitie" with their children (Pleck, 1987).

How strictly this law was enforced, however, is unclear because the number of persons actually charged with wife beating was small. The Puritans must have felt the tension between respecting the integrity of the family and intervening to protect women and children from abuse. After the Puritans, government officials in most eras were even more reluctant to intervene. Indeed, the history of the issue of domestic violence is, in large part, a story of conflict between the goals of preserving the family unit and of protecting women and children. When intervention was seen as shoring up the family (as among the Puritans), it received broader support; when it was perceived as undermining men's authority and contributing to divorce, it received less.[1]

A peak of concern occurred in the late 1800s, when the child protection movement arose. In 1874 the first society for the prevention of cruelty to children was founded; 40 years later there were 494 of them. Pleck argues that the growth of these societies, usually started by leaders of the local social elite, reflected a desire to control the behavior of the unruly, growing immigrant and working-class populations. In addition, I think, the growth came at a time when attitudes toward children were evolving from seeing them as economic assets to seeing them as emotionally rewarding beings to be nurtured (Zelizer, 1985). Still, leaders of the movement were careful to reassure parents

---

[1] This paragraph, and the next several, draw heavily from Pleck (1987).

that their authority to discipline their children, even by occasional physical punishment, was not in question. The founder of the New York Society for the Prevention of Cruelty to Children assured nervous supporters that he favored "a good wholesome flogging for disobedient children," although he wished to protect children from "undue parental severity" (Pleck, 1987). And the few organizations that sought to help battered wives had to fight suspicion that they were encouraging the breakup of the family.

THE TWENTIETH CENTURY

The Political Model of Domestic Violence   During the twentieth century, two ways of thinking about domestic violence emerged. The first is what might be called the *political model* of domestic violence—political not in the sense of Democrats and Republicans but rather in the sense of the relations of power and authority between men and women. Historian Linda Gordon has argued that domestic violence has been a politically constructed problem in two senses:

> *First, the very definition of what constitutes unacceptable domestic violence, and appropriate responses to it, developed and then varied according to political moods and the force of certain political movements. Second, violence among family members . . . usually arises out of power struggles in which individuals are contesting real resources and benefits. These contests arise not only from personal aspirations but also from changing social norms and conditions. (Gordon, 1988)*

The struggles are usually about men's power to control the behavior of women. Resorting to force is a way for a husband to compel his wife to behave as the husband wishes. Traditionally, social structure has supported men's control over women through law and social custom. Laws that allowed husbands to use physical force against their wives are an example: The term "rule of thumb," for instance, comes from a rule in old English law that a husband was allowed to hit his wife with a stick no thicker than his thumb (Gelles & Cornell, 1990). The political model implies that domestic violence is deeply rooted in laws and customs that reinforce male dominance and is unlikely to be ended without political action by women's groups and their allies.

The Medical Model of Domestic Violence   The second way of thinking is the *medical model,* under which domestic violence is seen as an illness and a source of injuries. In contrast to the political model, the main concern is not with relations of power but rather with illness and well-being. Health and social welfare professionals who have campaigned against child abuse, for example, have focused attention on the physical and mental harm that children suffer from physical and sexual violence. Some have argued that both the victims and the perpetrators of violence suffer from various "syndromes," illnesslike complexes of symptoms, injuries, and attitudes, that need to be treated. The professionals point to links between being violent and such personal problems as a history of abuse as a child, alcoholism, or mental illness. The medical model therefore conceives of the problem as though it can be solved by the intervention of health and social welfare professionals, much as they might attack schizophrenia or tuberculosis.

The first two decades of the twentieth century were a time when domestic relations courts, which treated family disputes more as social welfare cases than as criminal cases, were established throughout the states. But the issue of domestic violence was relatively quiescent until 1962, when pediatrician C. Henry Kempe and his colleagues, troubled by X-ray pictures of broken bones in children and reports of maltreatment, published an article titled "The Battered Child Syndrome" (Kempe, Silverman, Steele, Droegemuller, & Silver, 1962). Kempe and his colleagues brought the medical model of domestic violence to the public's attention. In their view, child abuse was centered on a "syndrome" of repeated violence and inadequate parenting. This perspective created sympathetic concern not only for the blameless victims but also for the abusers, who seemed to be fighting a mental illness that needed treatment. In these ways the "syndrome" attracted broad public interest; within five years, every state had enacted laws that required medical personnel to report suspected cases of child abuse.

Still, there was little attention paid to wife beating until the mid-1970s, when feminist groups succeeded in making violence against women into a political problem. A decade earlier, the feminist movement had undergone a major revival, boosted by the parallel growth of the civil rights movement. Some feminist groups focused on combating rape. Part of their strategy was the formation of services for rape victims, such as hot lines, crisis centers, and legal support. The issue of rape led organizers to the issue of sexual and physical violence directed toward married women. The movement's fundamental goal was not to treat the injuries of the victims or ease the personal problems of the perpetrators—valuable as those steps might be—but rather to remove the social supports for male violence, such as a reluctance to prosecute alleged offenders. Consequently, activists worked for changes in the law, funds for crisis centers and shelters for battered women, and the rejection of social norms that tolerated violence directed at women. With feminist influence at a high point in the 1970s, political pressure for action grew. By the end of the 1970s, nearly every state had enacted laws to protect women from violence through a mixture of support services, requirements that physicians report suspected cases, and tougher criminal procedures.

Quick Review

- The New England colonies passed the first laws against wife beating in the Western world.
- The issue of domestic violence historically has reflected a conflict between the goals of preserving the family unit and protecting women and children.
- A political model of domestic violence, reflecting relations of power and authority, arose in the twentieth century.
- A medical model of domestic violence, which views it as an illness and a source of injury, also developed in the twentieth century.

Intimate Partner Violence

The beatings that many women in shelters have endured from husbands and live-in boyfriends would fit anyone's definition of family violence. But how far in the other direction should the concept of domestic violence go? Is a slap in the face domestic violence, or should the term be reserved for more serious acts of aggression? There is disagreement among the public and academic researchers about exactly what constitutes domestic violence. It's not even clear how to define the term "domestic." Most early studies of adult domestic violence focused on married and cohabiting couples, but many recent studies have focused on the broader concept of "intimate partners," or boyfriends and girlfriends.

TWO KINDS OF VIOLENCE?

Some researchers recommend that we distinguish between two types of violent behavior among intimate partners. This view emerged after sociologists began to study the extent of violent acts among intimate partners in random-sample surveys of the general population. They asked people whether, and how often, in the previous year they had engaged in behaviors against their spouses or cohabiting partners that ranged from the less serious (e.g., grabbing, pushing, or slapping) to the more serious (e.g., hitting with a fist) to the very serious (e.g., threatening or using a knife or gun) (Straus, 1979; Straus et al., 1996). Surprisingly, men and women in 1975 and 1985 national surveys were about equally likely to report engaging in these acts in the previous year, although most acts were of the less serious kind (Straus & Gelles, 1986). This pattern has been confirmed in more recent surveys (Fergusson, Horwood, & Ridder, 2005). In other words, surveys suggest that both women and men at times initiate violence against their intimate partners. In contrast to the picture of battered women and violent men that the shelter and social services studies show, surveys paint pictures of violent couples in which both partners engage in aggression.

To reconcile this seeming contradiction, some researchers argue that there are two distinct types of intimate partner violence. Michael Johnson calls the first kind **situational couple violence** (Johnson, 2008). It is the more common kind of conflict; and it usually involves the less serious kinds of aggression. It typically occurs, the authors say, when a specific dispute leads one partner to get angry and to lash out at the other, and it rarely escalates into serious violence or injury. That is, it arises from a particular situation rather than from a larger, long-term pattern of violence. Moreover, men and women are about equally likely to initiate it. Most of the violent acts reported in surveys are of this type.

Johnson claims that a second, more serious kind of violence exists, which he labels **intimate terrorism** (Johnson, 2008). I think the use of the word "terrorism," with its connotation of suicide bombers and September 11, is unfortunate. Two psychologists (Emery & Laumann-Billings, 1998) suggest instead that we distinguish between "maltreatment" (less serious) and "family violence" (more serious), but the label "intimate terrorism" has been adopted in the literature. This is the type of violence, Johnson argues, that researchers who study shelters or the legal system see. While it affects a much smaller share of the national population than does situational couple violence, its consequences are more dire. It involves a pattern of violence such as repeatedly beating one's partner; it is therefore more likely to cause injuries; and unlike situational violence, it is almost entirely perpetrated by men. Johnson argues that the heart of the distinction between these two types is that the men who engage in intimate terrorism are trying to control women's behavior: whom they see, whom they talk to, when they leave the house, where they go, and so forth. These men may also seek to dominate their wives or girlfriends by keeping them economically dependent and by instilling fear of the consequences of disobeying them. The key difference is motivation: control rather than mere anger. Table 11.1 compares these two hypothetical kinds of domestic violence.

Without doubt, far more seriously injured and abused women than men show up at shelters or hospital emergency rooms or testify at the trials of abusive partners who have been arrested. Even among studies of the general population, women are more likely to be reported engaging in the less serious acts such as slapping or kicking, whereas men are more likely to be reported

situational couple violence violence that arises from a specific situation in which one or both partners act aggressively in anger

intimate terrorism a pattern in which a man seeks to control the behavior of his partner through repeated, serious, violent acts

Table 11.1	Characteristics of Situational Couple Violence and Intimate Terrorism	
	SITUATIONAL COUPLE VIOLENCE	**INTIMATE TERRORISM**
Prevalence	Common	Less common
Type of aggression	Less serious (e.g., slapping)	More serious (e.g., beating up)
Gender of perpetrators	Both men and women	Almost entirely men
Motivation	Anger	Control

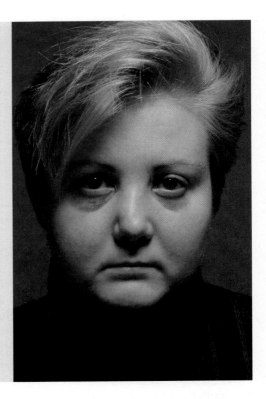

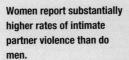

Women report substantially higher rates of intimate partner violence than do men.

engaging in serious acts such as beating up or choking; and women are more likely to report being injured than are men (Archer, 2000, 2002). So while a majority of violent incidents involving couples may involve minor acts of aggression by both spouses, it seems clear that a minority of incidents do involve serious aggressions by men which cause injuries in women.

The research and debate about distinguishing types of intimate partner aggression can be seen as an extension into the twenty-first century of the tensions between the political and medical models of domestic violence. The idea of situational couple violence fits the medical model; however, in this case the doctor is not a pediatrician like C. Henry Kempe but rather a clinical psychologist or a psychiatrist. The problem is framed as a dysfunctional couple who cannot resolve conflicts peacefully. This framing suggests remedies such as family psychotherapy or marital counseling. In contrast, the idea of intimate terrorism fits the political model. Here the problem is framed as a controlling male who dominates his wife or girlfriend in part by inflicting serious and even life-threatening violence. The remedy is to remove the violent man from the household and prevent him from having contact with the woman. This remedy suggests not psychotherapy but rather legal action: an arrest, a restraining order, or incarceration. Researchers and advocates for battered women were incensed by the findings from sociological surveys that women seemed to engage in partner violence as often as men because they saw no battered men at their shelters, only women who had been the victims of severe violence at the hands of controlling men. Johnson (1995) first proposed his distinction in order to show that both models of intimate partner violence had their place. In a sense, he and his colleagues are arguing that the medical model may be more appropriate for the majority of incidents, but that the political model may still be valid for the minority of incidents that cause serious injury and trauma.

Nevertheless, it's still debatable whether two distinct, easily identifiable kinds of intimate partner violence exist (Anderson, 2010). Alternatively, we could think of them as the two end points of a continuum on which we could place individuals according to factors such as severity and frequency of violence and levels of psychopathology. Some couples progress from mild to extreme violence while others do not, for reasons that are not well understood (Holtzworth-Monroe, 2005). We do not know how many of the serious incidents involve men who are engaging in a pattern of controlling women through violence and how many are merely expressing anger and hostility. Clinicians have found that some couples exhibit symptoms of both kinds in intimate partner violence (Capaldi & Kim, 2007). Consequently, it is best to see Johnson's two kinds of violence as ideal types—conceptual models that help us to understand sociologically the motivations and forces behind the intimate partner violence we see, rather than as guidelines for clinical diagnosis of a violent individual undergoing treatment.

PREVALENCE AND TRENDS IN INTIMATE PARTNER VIOLENCE

In this mixture of concern and debate, one important question often gets lost: How much intimate partner violence is there? We know little about how much violence there was in the past. The official records of court proceedings can tell us only about the rare instances when abuse came to the attention of the legal system. Consequently, it's impossible to know whether domestic violence has increased, decreased, fluctuated, or stayed the same over the past 100 years—or even over the past 50 years. Most likely, what has changed the most over time is not the prevalence of intimate partner violence but the amount of attention we have paid to it. (See *How Do Sociologists Know What They Know?:* Advocates and Estimates: How Large [or Small] Are Social Problems?) Nevertheless, we do have information on current rates and on trends in the last few decades.

Prevalence   Women are much more likely to report being victimized by an intimate partner than are men. In 2010, for example, 22 percent of all the violent victimizations experienced by women were committed by an intimate partner, whereas among men just 5 percent were committed by an intimate partner (U.S. Bureau of Justice Statistics, 2011a). Among women who experienced violence by an intimate partner between 2001 and 2005, 27 percent of women reported that the offender threatened to kill them, compared to 15 percent of men (U.S. Bureau of Justice Statistics, 2007). Less serious threats, however, were more symmetrical; for instance, 14 percent of women and 13 percent of men tried to hit, slap, or knock down the victim. These findings probably reflect situational couple violence more than intimate terrorism, as is typical in large-scale, random surveys. The gender difference even carried over into same-sex couples. Men who had lived with male partners were more likely to have experienced violence than men who had lived only with women, while women who had lived with female partners were less likely to have experienced violence than were women who had lived only with men

Advocates and Estimates: How Large (or Small) Are Social Problems?

The government announced in 2006 that between 1979 and 2004 the number of rapes per 1,000 people in the United States dropped by 85 percent, according to the National Crime Victimization Survey. (The figure is for all rapes, not just the rapes by intimate partners that are discussed in this chapter.) This was good news, except to some advocates for victims of rape and sexual abuse. "When the conversation gets bogged down around, 'How prevalent is this problem?' you can't even get to the next steps, of 'Now, what are we going to do about it?'" Jennifer Pollitt Hill, executive director of the Maryland Coalition Against Sexual Assault, told the *Washington Post* (Fahrenthold, 2006). In other words, Hill was suggesting that stories reporting a decline in rape are unhelpful because they make it more difficult for advocacy groups to win support for services and laws that

could help rape victims. It would be better not to talk about it. Dean Kilpatrick, director of the National Crime Victims Research and Treatment Center in Charleston, South Carolina, told the *Post,* "If there's been a change, it's been a very small change." He said that high-profile rape cases may have persuaded more rape victims to stay silent so that their personal lives would not be publicly scrutinized. But it is hard to see how that factor could explain a drastic fifteen-year drop.

Pollitt and Kilpatrick were responding no differently than many advocates for (and against) social causes when they describe the scope of the problem they care about. When it would benefit their perspective for the problem to be defined broadly, they tend to describe it as large (e.g., the rate of rape has not really declined; let's stop talking about how it has declined). Consider

homelessness. In the 1980s, advocates for the homeless repeated an estimate by activist Mitch Snyder that two to three million people were homeless. Although observers who argued that Synder's estimate was too large were criticized by some advocates, Synder later admitted that his estimate was based on little more than guesswork. No one really knew how many homeless persons there were.

When it is beneficial to advocates' perspectives to define a problem as modest, they tend to describe it as small. Robert Rector of the conservative Heritage Foundation believes that the problem of poverty in the United States has been exaggerated and that government programs to assist the poor are ineffective and too costly. He therefore argues that many of the families whose incomes fall below the official poverty line are not really poor. The living standards

(U.S. National Institute of Justice, 2000). Moreover, women who had been victimized by intimates were more likely to have been injured than were men who were victimized. For instance, 9 percent of women who had been victimized by intimate partners reported receiving medical or hospital care, compared with 3 percent of men (U.S. Bureau of Justice Statistics, 2012). The statistics paint a picture in which women face a higher risk of being injured by someone they know well than men.

Intimate Partner Rape   Of all the individuals who were raped or sexually assaulted in 2008, 46 percent said the assailant was well-known to them (U.S. Bureau of Justice Statistics, 2011b). The typical partner rape does not take place in a happy home, in which an otherwise nonviolent man forces his partner to have sex. Rather, it appears to take place in a troubled, violent home. Thirty-six percent of the women who reported being raped by an intimate in the 1995–1996 National Violence Against Women Survey also reported being injured in the most recent rape. Although most of the injuries were minor, one out of six injured women reported lacerations or knife wounds (U.S. National Institute of Justice, 1998).

Attention to rape by intimates—especially by husbands—is fairly new. Until recently, laws against rape have specifically excluded sexual relations

of the officially poor, he notes, are higher today than in the past: nearly three-fourths own a car; 97 percent have a color television, 78 percent have a VCR or DVD player, 89 percent have microwave ovens, a third have a dishwasher. "Most of America's 'poor' live in material conditions that would be judged as comfortable or well-off just a few generations ago," he wrote in a background paper (Rector, 2007). But liberal poverty analysts counter that although the standard of living of the poor has increased, the standard of living of the non-poor has increased much more. As a result, the gap between the poor and the non-poor is wider than in the past. "In the early 1960s," wrote Rebecca M. Blank and Mark H. Greenberg, "the poverty line was just under 50 percent of median income for a family of four. By 2007, it was at 28 percent of the median" (Blank & Greenberg, 2008).

This is not to say that any of the advocates described here are distorting the data or lying. There is more than one way of defining most social problems. It is probably true, for example, that rape and sexual assaults are still underreported in government surveys, as advocates would claim. So the problem is larger than official statistics show. It is difficult to find all of the homeless, who hide themselves in the abandoned buildings and alleyways of low-income neighborhoods. And it is true that the absolute level of living has probably risen for most of the poor compared to the mid-twentieth century.

My point is only that, as a consumer of social statistics, you should always ask yourself what the biases are of the people who are presenting you with the numbers. If they have a strong stake in convincing you that the problem is large in scope, they will probably choose an expansive definition of it. If they want to convince you the problem is not serious, they'll usually choose a much narrower definition. Evaluate not only their numbers but also their social and political arguments with this tendency in mind.

Ask Yourself

1. In doing student research or observing local politics, have you noticed dramatic differences in the statistics people quote to support their positions? If so, give an example. Did you understand the reason for the discrepancy?

2. What other reasons besides bias might help to explain conflicting statistics on social problems?

www.mhhe.com/cherlin7e

between husband and wife. The long-accepted legal principle was that by marrying, wives give their consent to sexual intercourse, so their husbands may demand it, by force if necessary. Some advocates of family privacy and the traditional authority of the husband still agree with that position. But as attitudes toward physical violence in marriage changed, forced sexual acts among married couples increasingly came into question. By the mid-1990s, almost every state had fully or partially repealed the exemption of spouses from rape statutes (Bennice & Resick, 2003).

A New Definition of Rape   In 2012, the Department of Justice changed the definition of forcible rape that will be used in the annual Uniform Crime Report issued by the Federal Bureau of Investigation. The old definition, "the carnal knowledge of a female, forcibly and against her will," applied only to women and to vaginal intercourse. The new definition is gender neutral and applies to a broader range of sex acts: "The penetration, no matter how slight, of the vagina or anus with any body part or object, or oral penetration by a sex organ of another person, without the consent of the victim." It is likely that this change will produce an increase in the number of rapes reported by the FBI. It may also encourage more men to report being raped (U.S. Department of Justice, 2012).

Trends   Over the past two decades or so, intimate partner violence appears to have declined substantially in the United States. The U.S. Bureau of Justice Statistics conducts an annual National Crime Victimization Survey of about 75,000 people. Between 1993, when the survey was redesigned, and 2005, the percentage of people who reported a rape or a sexual assault by an intimate partner declined by more than half, and the percentage who reported a nonsexual assault by an intimate partner dropped by about two-thirds. Over the same period, the number of women who were killed by an intimate partner dropped by half (U.S. Bureau of Justice Statistics, 2012). Two national surveys of married couples conducted in 1980 and 2000 produced similar findings. The proportion who said that violence (slapping, hitting, kicking, or throwing things) had occurred in their marriages in the three years before the survey dropped from 12 percent in 1980 to 6 percent in 2000 (Amato, Booth, Johnson, & Rogers, 2007). It is unlikely that these reductions in violence merely represent changes in what people are likely to report to survey interviewers in the two surveys or in the National Crime Victimization Surveys. There was no reduction, for instance, in the percentage of couples reporting serious quarrels between 1980 and 2000—just in violent incidents. If anything, the changing climate concerning domestic violence should have made people *more* likely to report violence in recent surveys, but instead they reported less. It seems reasonable to conclude that the prevalence of intimate partner violence has dropped in recent years.

WHICH PARTNERSHIPS ARE AT RISK?

Some intimate partnerships are more likely to lead to violence than others. Whether the couple is married seems to matter, as does their social class.

Marital Status   The National Crime Victimization Surveys show that married women reported the lowest levels of intimate partner violence and that women who were separated but not divorced reported by far the highest levels (U.S. Bureau of Justice Statistics, 2012). These surveys did not ask about cohabitation, but other studies suggest that married women have a substantially lower rate of intimate partner violence than do cohabiting women (U.S. National Institute of Justice, 2000). There are several possible explanations for these findings. Women who have separated but not divorced are more likely to have recently ended their relationships because they were violent; consequently, violent incidents may have caused the separations. The lower risk for married women than for cohabiting women could be a selection effect: Women may refuse to marry cohabiting partners who seem violent (Repetti, 2001; Kenney & McLanahan, 2006). It is also possible that cohabiting women are more likely to have been abused as children, which is associated with greater subsequent abuse as an adult (Cherlin, Burton, Hurt, & Purvin, 2004). Finally, it could be that marriage transforms the relationships of the partners in ways that reduce the likelihood of violence through, for instance, greater commitment or a greater propensity to forgive partners for transgressions (Fincham, Stanley, & Beach, 2007).

Social Class   Although domestic violence affects all social classes, several studies report substantially higher rates of domestic violence among low-income than among middle-income couples (U.S. Bureau of Justice Statistics, 1995;

Sorenson, Upchurch, & Shen, 1996). Part of this difference may reflect a greater reluctance of middle-income individuals to admit to violence or a greater vigilance toward poor families by social welfare agencies. Still it appears that there is at least a modest association between lower social class and violence against spouses and partners. Johnson (2008) found that having less education is strongly associated with being a controlling "intimate terrorist." But these findings do not necessarily mean that less-educated or low-income couples are inherently more violent; rather, they may be responding to factors such as frustration over lack of resources or social isolation. A study of the 1987–1988 National Survey of Families and Households found that employment instability and financial strain increased the likelihood of intimate violence against women, as did living in a neighborhood of concentrated poverty and disadvantage (Benson, Fox, DeMaris, & Van Wyk, 2003). So both a couple's own economic difficulties and the difficulties of their neighborhood can influence the level of intimate violence.

In fact, there are theoretical reasons to expect these associations: Several decades ago, William Goode suggested that men with more income and education have additional resources besides force that they can use to control the behavior of their wives (Goode, 1971). This relationship between social class and violence against wives also holds in developing countries: A Bangkok, Thailand, survey found that men with more income, education, and prestigious occupations were less likely to have hit, slapped, or kicked their wives (Hoffman, Demo, & Edwards, 1994). Married women in an Egyptian national survey who had a higher household standard of living were less likely to report that their husbands had acted violently toward them (Yount & Li, 2010). In general, when wives and husbands have more resources available to them, husbands tend to be less violent.

Quick Review

- Most incidents of intimate partner violence involve minor acts of aggression that usually do not lead to injuries and that are initiated by both men and women.
- A minority of incidents involve serious acts of aggression that more often lead to injuries and are initiated by men in order to control their partners.
- Married couples have lower rates of violence than other couples.
- Violence against spouses and romantic partners occurs in all social classes but is more common in less-educated, lower income families.

CHILD ABUSE

Hitting children is the most tolerated form of family violence. Indeed, nearly all parents spank or slap their children at some point (Straus & Stewart, 1999). Although it is difficult to make historical comparisons, the use of physical force against children may have been more prevalent in colonial times than ever since. The Puritans believed children were born tainted with sin and expressed their diabolical nature through stubbornness, willfulness, and disobedience. Consequently, good parents had a moral duty to defeat such expressions of sin. When two- and three-year-olds first began to act contrary, the task of the father was to "break the child's will" and instill obedience through stern discipline. Even a century ago, physical force was probably more common than it

Although there is wide-spread support for parents' right to spank or slap children, most people probably view beating or punching as child abuse.

child abuse serious physical harm (trauma, sexual abuse with injury, or willful malnutrition) of a child by an adult, with intent to injure

is now. No one today could imagine the head of a children's welfare organization announcing his or her support for flogging.

Even if we grant parents the right to spank or slap, at some point physical force shades into physical abuse. As with violence between spouses and partners, there is no single definition of exactly what constitutes **child abuse.** The definition that earns the greatest consensus among child welfare professionals is serious physical harm (trauma, sexual abuse with injury, or willful malnutrition) with intent to injure—although it is difficult to determine whether there has been intent to injure. There is less consensus about other possible forms of abuse, many of which adults would find disturbing, such as sexual abuse without injury or various forms of neglect (e.g., leaving young children home by themselves all day). A frequently cited 1985 national survey of married or cohabiting adults with children found that 2 percent had kicked, bitten, punched, or beaten up their children during the previous year. (This percentage excludes parents who had hit their children with an object such as a stick or a belt.) I think that most people would view repeated kicking, punching, and beating as child abuse (Straus & Gelles, 1986).

Incidence   More recent information on the incidence of child abuse comes from the National Incidence Study of Child Abuse and Neglect (NIS), a series of national surveys of child welfare professionals, conducted in 1980, 1986, 1993, and 2005–2006. The NIS obtained information from a broad range of professionals who serve children; they were asked to report on any children they had seen who appeared to be abused or neglected (Sedlak et al., 2010). Although this survey misses children who did not come to the attention of community professionals, it still provides some of the best recent information. Figure 11.1 shows the rate of abuse and neglect per 1,000 children in the 1993 and the 2005–2006 surveys.[2] The first two bars are for all forms of maltreatment combined. They show that the overall rate of child maltreatment cases declined from

[2] The Figure displays rates according to the "harm standard," which requires a judgment that actual harm had occurred to the child, rather than the more lenient "endangerment standard," which only requires a judgment that the child is at risk of harm (Sedlak et al., 2010).

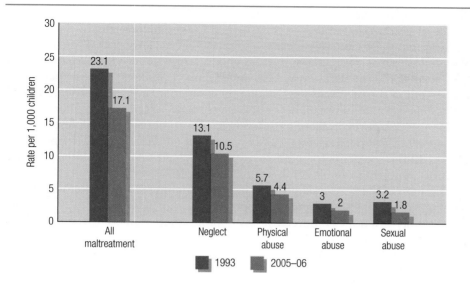

FIGURE 11.1
Rates of maltreatment
per 1,000 children, 1993
and 2005–2006. (*Source:*
Sedlak et al., 2010)

about 23 out of every 1,000 children in 1993 to about 17 out of every 1,000 children in 2005–2006. The other pairs of bars show the trends between 1993 and
2005–2006 for specific kinds of maltreatment. All of them show declines. Thus,
child abuse and neglect appear to have declined during this period.

Note that the rates were higher (and therefore the bars in Figure 11.1
are higher) for neglect than for the abuse categories. In fact, 60 percent of
the cases were reported for neglect rather than for abuse. More than half
of the neglect cases referred to educational neglect, which typically means
that the children weren't attending school regularly and that their parents
were not making much effort to have them attend. The remainder of the
cases of neglect referred to physical neglect, which usually means that
children were left unattended or poorly supervised by their parents, and
emotional neglect, which includes situations such as inadequate nurturance
or exposure to bad behaviors and environments. Only about one-third of
all the reported cases of maltreatment were for physical abuse or sexual
abuse, the kinds of child-related domestic violence that are of greatest public concern.

The NIS also suggests that child maltreatment was not equally likely in
all families. Children whose parents had incomes of below $15,000 per
year or who had not graduated from high school or who participated in
a poverty program had rates of maltreatment that were five times higher
than children whose parents had none of these characteristics. Children
whose parents were unemployed had twice the rate of maltreatment as
children whose parents were employed (Sedlak et al., 2010). As was true
for intimate partner violence, there is good theoretical reason to think that
the hardships of poverty and unemployment might lead distressed parents
to have less patience with their children or at least to be more neglectful.
In fact, family disadvantage is more closely associated with neglect than it
is with abuse in the NIS. It is poor families that are more often forced to
leave a child unattended while adults work, or that have little faith in the
present system of education and therefore don't make sure their children
attend school.

Sexual Abuse and Its Consequences   The NIS indicates a relatively low incidence of chid sexual abuse—1.8 cases per 1,000 children. But social surveys suggest that the problem is more common. In a 1992 survey of sexual activity, the adult subjects were asked, "Before you [reached puberty] did anyone touch you sexually?" (Laumann et al., 1994). Seventeen percent of the women and 12 percent of the men said yes. Among the women, nearly all the touching had been done by men (63 percent) or adolescent boys (28 percent) rather than by women. Men, however, were most likely to report touching by adolescent girls (45 percent), followed by men (23 percent) and adolescent boys (15 percent). Nearly all the incidents for both sexes had involved touching genitals, with a minority reporting vaginal, oral, or anal sex.

The interviewers also asked who did the touching (Laumann et al., 1994). Among women, the most common responses were an older relative (29 percent) or a family friend (29 percent); even more men named a family friend (40 percent). As for cases of sexual abuse that would fit the usual legal definition of **incest**—sexual relations between a child and her or his parent, brother, or sister—16 percent of women who had been touched named a father or brother. Thus, our best estimate is that, overall, about 3 percent of adult American women (that is, 16 percent of the 17 percent who reported touching by anyone) had experienced incest as children. The percentage of women whose experiences fit the definition of incest may be even lower today, given the apparent decline in the rate of child sexual abuse. As for abuse at preschools or schools, only 3 percent of the women who were touched and 4 percent of the men reported that a teacher had done the touching. Despite attention in the media to alleged incidents of sexual abuse of children in day care centers, less than 1 percent of all substantiated cases of child abuse in 1992 occurred in day care or foster care settings (McCurdy & Daro, 1994).

A large research literature suggests that having been sexually abused as a child can have profound long-term consequences for an adult's sexual behavior and intimate relationships (Loeb et al., 2002). The seriousness of the consequences is associated with factors such as the number of incidents, the severity and duration of the incidents, and the age of the child during the incidents. Traumatic sexual experiences can produce inappropriate sexual behavior and feelings of betrayal, lack of trust, and powerlessness (Kendall-Tackett, Williams, & Finkelhor, 1993). They can produce later-life consequences such as poor self-image, depression, and lack of a clear sense of boundaries between oneself and others (Briere & Elliott, 1994). In adolescence and adulthood, these conditions can lead to early onset of sexual activity, riskier sexual activity, and multiple partners (Fergusson, Horwood, & Lynskey, 1997; Thompson, Potter, Sanderson, & Maibach, 1997). As adults, women who were sexually abused as children may have more frequent sexual encounters and relationships from which they derive less pleasure than other women. The 1992 national survey of sexual activity found that women who said they had been touched sexually as children by older persons were, as adults, more likely to experience forced sex, to have multiple sex partners, to engage in riskier sexual behavior, and to experience difficulties such as greater anxiety about sex and less pleasurable sex (Laumann et al., 1994). One-fourth of about 2,000 low-income women in Boston, Chicago, and San Antonio reported that they had been sexually

incest sexual relations with one's child, brother, or sister

Physical or sexual abuse of children can lead to emotional problems such as depression.

abused as children; and these women were more likely to have had a series of short-term intimate relationships, many of them violent, in adulthood (Cherlin, Burton, Hurt, & Purvin, 2004).

Physical Abuse and Its Consequences   Physical abuse can lead to some of the same consequences as sexual abuse, such as lower self-esteem, lack of trust, and depression. In addition, physical abuse can lead to brain injuries and growth retardation (English, 1998). Young children are at the greatest risk of dying from physical abuse: Of the roughly 1,100 fatalities in 1999 from child abuse, 86 percent involved children under six and almost half involved children under one (Chalk, Gibbons, & Scarupa, 2002). Physical abuse is also associated with behavior problems such as aggression and increased risk of arrest for violence (English, 1998; English, Widom, & Brandford, 2001). Some children, however, do not show lasting consequences of physical abuse; these children tend to have been abused fewer times and to have had a supportive adult available to them.

Poly-victimization   Three-fourths of the low-income women in the study of Boston, Chicago, and San Antonio who reported experiencing sexual abuse also reported experiencing physical abuse (Cherlin et al., 2004). This overlap raises the question of what it means to experience more than one type of abuse. Researchers have studied this question by obtaining information on all of the types of maltreatment children have experienced, including not only sexual and physical abuse but also being victimized by theft or other violent crimes, by witnessing violent crime or abuse, and by bullying. They define **poly-victimization** as experiencing multiple types of child maltreatment (Anderson, 2010). It is not uncommon: 22 percent of the children in a

poly-victimization experiencing multiple types of child maltreatment

The Swinging Pendulum of Foster Care Policy

Foster care—the removal of children from their parental home and their placement in another home—is a program with few admirers and many critics. It involves a difficult choice between two worthy goals: protecting the integrity of the family unit and protecting children from physical and mental harm. In most circumstances, the children are removed without their parents' permission after a child protective worker investigates a report of abuse or neglect. Consequently, foster care embodies the most severe form of state interference between parents and children—seizing the children against the parents' will. Because child protective workers tend to be middle class and the affected children tend to be poor, it is sometimes criticized as a class-based intrusion into family life. Because it substitutes state-directed care for parental care, it is sometimes criticized as antifamily. Because it fails to return many children to their families in a timely manner, it is criticized for warehousing children from problem families, rather than helping the parents provide better care. Yet few would disagree that children should be protected from some parents—the drug-addicted, the physically or sexually abusive, for instance—who are not fit to raise them.

In the late 1970s, when about 500,000 children were living in foster care, a policy consensus formed: Alarmed by the numbers of children in care, both conservatives and liberals agreed that child protective workers should place a higher priority on helping troubled parents keep their children and care better for them. If a foster care placement was needed, greater efforts should be made to return the children to a permanent home—either by sending them back to their parents or, if absolutely necessary, by putting them up for adoption. Congress codified this consensus in the Adoption Assistance and Child Welfare Act of 1980.[1]

The new consensus worked as intended for several years. As the pendulum swung toward keeping children with their parents, the number of children in foster care declined to about 275,000 in 1983 through 1985. Then, suddenly, it rose sharply to 340,000 in 1988 and to 442,000 in 1992 (Toshio, 1993). By 1999, it was back over the 500,000 mark, where it remained through the mid-2000s (U.S. Administration for Children and Families, 2011b). The new law, it appears, was overwhelmed by a huge, unexpected wave of children at risk of harm. The wave was greatest in large cities such as New York and Chicago, and the

largest percentage increases in foster care occurred among newborns and infants, many of whom were low birth-weight or otherwise impaired babies born to mothers who had had little or no prenatal care.

Many observers speculated that at least some of this rise was the result of the rapid spread of crack cocaine usage during the same period. Women in poor neighborhoods used crack more than they had used earlier addictive drugs such as heroin. An increase in mothers who were incarcerated or who died due to AIDS may also have contributed. A rise in homelessness among families also occurred during the late 1980s and early 1990s. Consequently, some parents were not able to provide basic shelter and security to their children, and child protective workers are more likely to remove a child from a homeless family than from one in a home.

The surge in abandoned and drug-impaired infants led some experts to call for seizing more at-risk children from parents. More important, highly publicized cases such as the starving boys in New Jersey, in 2003, described at the beginning of the chapter, caused a public outcry against child protective workers who were seen as too slow to remove children from potentially abusive

national sample had experienced four or more types of victimization during the previous year; and these children were reported to be more anxious, depressed, and aggressive (Finkelhor, Ormrod, & Turner, 2007). The claim is that experiencing several types of maltreatment has a cumulative effect, even after considering the effects of each type of maltreatment separately, as if poly-victimization were to overload the brain's capacity to cope with traumatic events. That claim may be true, but it is also possible that the seeming effects of poly-victimization may reflect other causes of distress such as pre-existing psychological problems or living in a disadvantaged neighborhood.

Poverty or Abuse? More generally, some of the problems that physically or sexually abused children display, such as depression or aggressive behavior, may be related to growing up in low-income families and disadvantaged families. Thus, the pendulum of professional and public opinion swung back to the 1970s, before the movement toward keeping families intact reached its peak.

Yet neither option—vigilance and early removal of children perceived to be in danger, or increased efforts to help troubled parents so that they can keep their children—has worked well. The foster care system was designed on the basis of assumptions about families that no longer hold. It assumed that the family problems leading to foster care were temporary—as when a mother became ill with a disease such as tuberculosis and needed six months or a year to recuperate. It assumed that large numbers of mothers who did not work outside the home could be found to care temporarily for children whose parents couldn't care for them. It didn't anticipate the shortages, now occurring, of suitable and willing foster parents (Cameron, 2003). It didn't foresee families sleeping in homeless shelters and drug-addicted newborns abandoned in nurseries. In addition, it probably ignored levels of child abuse that today would be unacceptable.

The heart of the problem is that there still are no good alternatives to parental care for children. Long-term foster care,

with children frequently shuttled from family to family, is problematic. Yet abusive or neglectful parents also harm children. One recent innovation is to place children in the homes of relatives and pay them. In 2010, 26 percent of foster children were placed in relatives' foster homes (U.S. Administration for Children and Families, 2011a). This so-called kinship care option preserves some of the child's family bonds and seems preferable to care by non-relatives, but it is not without problems. Relatives may have more difficulty than strangers in restricting visits by abusive parents. Moreover, they tend to keep children for a longer period of time than other foster parents; yet they are sometimes reluctant to adopt the children for fear of angering the parents. Thus, kinship care can conflict with the goal of finding a permanent home for foster children. In addition, foster parents typically receive substantially more money per child than parents do under Temporary Assistance to Needy Families (the cash welfare program), creating a possible incentive for families receiving TANF to place the children in kinship foster care.

In the 2000s, the foster care pendulum swung back again. Congress passed laws in 1997 and 2008 designed to move children

out of foster-home placements into adoptive homes more quickly (DeVooght, Malm, Vandivere, & McCoy-Roth, 2011).[2] By 2010, the number of children in foster care was down to 408,000 (U.S. Department of Health and Human Services, 2011a).

The only real, long-term hope of stopping the swings of the foster care pendulum is to prevent more children from being abused and neglected in the first place. That would require an assault on poverty, unemployment, and family breakups. Meanwhile, the quandary of what to do about abusive and neglectful parents and their children continues.

Ask Yourself

1. Do you know anyone with experience as a foster parent? If so, what was that person's opinion of the foster care system?
2. Which do you think is more important, protecting a family's integrity or protecting children from abuse?

[1] Public Law 96–272.
[2] Public Laws 105–89 and 110–351.

www.mhhe.com/cherlin7e

---

neighborhoods, rather than resulting from the abuse itself. Consequently, some of the problems that abused children show would probably have occurred even if they hadn't been abused. In fact, Douglas Besharov, the first director of the National Center on Child Abuse and Neglect, argues that child protective workers sometimes overreact to families in which the real problem is poverty, not maltreatment. When they remove a child from his or her parents in cases of neglect without physical or sexual abuse, Besharov maintains, workers often make his or her problems worse. Such children are usually sent into the foster-care system, which has its own problems and is not a clear improvement over living at home. (See *Families and Public Policy:* The Swinging Pendulum of Foster Care Policy, on pp. 358–359.) Besharov and Lisa Laumann advocate, instead, that more social services be focused on assisting the parents of these children (Besharov & Laumann, 1997).

ELDER ABUSE

elder abuse physical abuse or neglect of an elderly person by a caregiver

Another kind of domestic violence that has drawn public attention is **elder abuse,** which we might define as physical abuse or neglect of an elderly person by a caregiver. Yet relatively few elderly are abused in this sense: A National Academy of Sciences report estimates that perhaps one to two million elderly Americans have been "injured, exploited, or otherwise mistreated" by a caregiver (Bonnie & Wallace, 2003). That would be 3 to 6 percent of all elderly persons; and if we restricted the definition to just physical abuse the percentages would be even lower. Figure 11.2 shows the types of elder abuse, according to substantiated cases in a 2004 national report.[3] Physical and sexual abuse account for about one-fourth of the cases. The most common type is neglect by a caregiver, such as leaving unattended an older person who cannot feed herself or get out of bed by herself. Most incidents of elder abuse occur in the home, and the victim usually has a personal relationship with, and is often dependent upon, the perpetrator. In fact, the perpetrators were adult children in 33 percent of the cases in the 2004 report, the older person's spouse in 11 percent, and other family members in another 22 percent (U.S. National Center on Elder Abuse, 2006). Even though only a few percent of the older population are mistreated in these ways, the existence of the problem is troubling. Researchers think that elderly persons have a higher risk of maltreatment if they and their caregivers are isolated from family and friends, if they have dementia, if the caregiver has mental health problems, and if the caregiver is financially dependent on the abused (Lachs & Pillemer, 2004).

Much of the abuse of older people is neglect or financial exploitation, such as these victims of a scam experienced.

[3] I have excluded two types of abuse that are included in the total number of cases in the report: "self-abuse," which accounts for 37 percent, and "financial exploitation," which accounts for 14 percent. These types do not fit my definition of elder abuse.

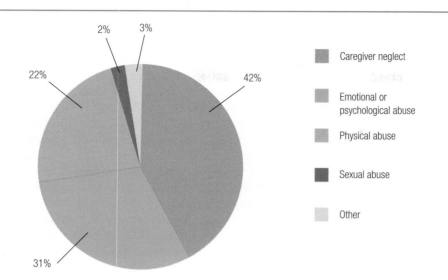

2%   3%

22%

42%

31%

Caregiver neglect

Emotional or
psychological abuse

Physical abuse

Sexual abuse

Other

FIGURE 11.2
Type of elder abuse in
substantiated cases in 2004.
(*Source:* U.S. National Center
on Elder Abuse, 2006)

Quick Review

- Definitions of child abuse range from a narrow focus on serious physical harm to an inclusion of sexual abuse without injury and various forms of neglect.
- More than half of official reports of child abuse are for neglect.
- Like adult domestic violence, child abuse occurs in all social classes but is more common in lower-income families.
- Childhood sexual abuse can have long-term negative consequences for sexual behavior and intimate relationships in adulthood.
- Some older persons are abused or neglected by their caregivers.

Sexual Aggression and Violence in Young Adult Relationships

Partner, child, and elder abuse are not the only aspects of violence between men and women that have received attention of late. As courtship and dating have changed, so have attitudes toward the use of coercion to obtain sexual intercourse. Since the 1980s, researchers and clinicians have been studying sexual aggression by men against women whom they were dating and against acquaintances, as well as physical assaults by acquaintances.

There are at least two reasons for the lack of attention to this problem before 1980. First, the rates of sexual activity among unmarried young persons were substantially lower prior to the 1970s; consequently, the incidence of acquaintance rape was probably lower also (although there are no satisfactory data). Second, young women tended to be blamed for their dates' improper sexual advances. As the practice of blaming the victim began to weaken and as rates of sexual activity increased, researchers brought forth study after study showing significant amounts of sexual coercion, including forcible rapes that were rarely reported to the police.

PREVALENCE

In a 2010 national telephone survey conducted by the National Center for Injury Prevention and Control (Black et al., 2011), 18 percent of women responded that during their lifetimes they had been subjected to completed or attempted unwanted vaginal, oral, or anal penetration, which was the study's definition of rape. Of those women, 33 percent said they had been victimized by an acquaintance, defined as friends, neighbors, family friends, first date, someone briefly known, and people not known well. Overall, then, we can estimate that about 6 percent of all adult women (that is, 33 percent of the 18 percent who reported being raped) have experienced forced sex by an acquaintance. Other studies of sexual aggression by acquaintances have focused on college students. For example, in the spring semester of 1997, interviewers contacted by telephone a random sample of 4,446 women in two- and four-year colleges (U.S. National Institute of Justice, 2000). They asked detailed screening questions about types of sexual victimization the women might have experienced in the seven months, on average, "since school began in fall, 1996." As Figure 11.3 shows, 1.7 percent reported a "completed rape," which the study defined as sexual penetration of various kinds by force or the threat of force; and 1.1 percent reported, by this definition, an attempted rape. If these numbers seem low, remember that they are only for a seven month period, on average, not for a woman's entire college career.

Most sexual assaults on college campuses are committed by someone the victim knows. Only about half of the women categorized as experiencing a completed rape answered "yes" when asked, "Do you consider this incident to be rape?" Does this mean the study, with its graphic questions, overestimates the prevalence of rape? Not necessarily. Some women may be reluctant to define an incident as rape because of embarrassment or because they don't want to define themselves as victimized. Some may not know that the legal definition of rape in most jurisdictions includes not only vaginal intercourse but also forced sexual penetration of other kinds.

In addition, as Figure 11.3 shows, 1.7 percent reported a completed incident, and 1.3 percent an attempted incident, of "sexual coercion," defined as unwanted sexual penetration with the threat of nonphysical punishment, promise of reward, or pestering or verbal pressure. So about as many women

FIGURE 11.3
Percentage of college women reporting completed or attempted rape or sexual coercion in seven months, on average, "since school began in fall, 1996." (*Source:* U.S. National Institute of Justice, 2000)

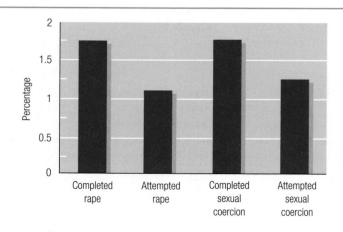

Awareness of sexual aggression in intimate settings is much greater on college campuses than a generation ago.

experience sexual coercion as experience rape under these definitions. Slightly higher percentages reported unwanted "sexual contact" such as touching or fondling of breasts or kissing by force or the threat of force. Overall, women who reported frequently drinking enough to get drunk, who were unmarried, and who had been a victim of sexual assault before the current school year were more likely to have been victimized.

Young men who commit sexual aggression against acquaintances are more likely to show hostility toward women and to believe that men are supposed to be more dominant and women more subordinate (Abbey & McAuslan, 2004). The men also show greater physiological arousal when presented with rape scenarios in psychology experiments, are more likely to consider violence against women acceptable, and are more sexually active than men who don't commit sexual aggression. In contrast, there are relatively few differences between women who have been victims of sexual aggression and those who haven't (Cate & Lloyd, 1992).

THE INTIMATE SETTING

Much of the research on sexual aggression and physical violence among young adults stems from a time when dating was the predominant setting in which college students were sexually intimate. Studies have suggested that the prevalence of physical violence in college students' dating relationships may be as high as 20 to 33 percent (Fincham, Cui, Braithwaite, & Pasley, 2008). Dating couples appear to be more violent than married couples but less violent than cohabiting couples (Magdol, Moffitt, Caspi, & Silva, 1998). But with the demise of dating and the rise of the hook-up culture, it is not clear how relevant these past studies are to current patterns of intimacy among high school and college students. We know very little about physical violence and sexual aggression among students who are hooking up. Observers have noted some students' discomfort with sexual encounters in which both partners have been drinking heavily, some level of sexual activity is begun, but the level progresses further than one partner wanted (Stepp, 2007). The potential for abuse and aggression is high in these incidents.

Quick Review

- Sexual aggression and violence in dating relationships have received considerable attention since about 1980.
- In several surveys, women have reported the prevalence of forced and coercive sex with intimate partners.
- Young men who commit sexual aggression against acquaintances are more likely to show hostility to women and to believe that men should be dominant.
- Sexual assaults also occur in dating relationships, and we know little about assaults in hook-up relationships.

■ Explanations

Why do people abuse their spouses, partners, or children? According to the political model of domestic violence, assaults against spouses and partners arise, in part, from power struggles between men and women. Men have an advantage in these struggles because of their greater physical strength, on average, and because of a social system that often reinforces male dominance. During the many thousands of years humans spent as hunter-gatherers, male strength was central to the life of bands. Men defended the band's territory against intrusions by other bands, and men armed with spears hunted animals. It is likely that men used their strength to compete for women and to dominate them. Later, in larger social groups, men were often able to shape laws and norms—such as the belief that the husband should be the head of the household—to their advantage so that they didn't need to use force to achieve their ends. The system of male dominance that still appears to some extent in virtually every society today is based in part upon the use of, or the threat of the use of, force against women.

But most men, despite their advantage in strength and despite cultural beliefs, don't hit their wives. In addition, both men and women sometimes abuse their children. Consequently, the general notion of male dominance isn't useful in explaining why some husbands are violent and others are not or why parents abuse their children. Many other explanations have been proposed, most of which have some plausibility. These explanations are often referred to as "theories" of domestic violence, although most of them are just collections of related propositions. Some of these perspectives emphasize psychological factors, whereas others emphasize social structural factors. At the present time, we don't know enough to tie them together into a single, coherent explanation. Let's focus on the ones I think are the most important.

SOCIAL LEARNING PERSPECTIVE

The explanation that is probably cited the most draws upon the **social learning perspective** developed by social psychologists. According to this perspective, individuals learn behavior they will later exhibit by observing what others do and seeing the consequences of these actions. Thus, children from violent homes are said to learn by observation and personal experience that aggressive or violent behavior is an acceptable and often successful way of controlling others and getting what you want (Bandura, 1973). In fact, a number of studies do show that children who grow up in homes characterized by domestic violence are more likely, as adults, to act violently toward their spouses and children. (All children may, to some extent, learn that violent behavior is acceptable through watching the pervasive violence in television programs and films.)

> **social learning perspective** the theory that individuals learn behavior they will later exhibit by observing what others do and seeing the consequences of these actions

For example, in 1999 researchers mailed a questionnaire to several hundred people in upstate New York who, 25 years earlier, had been randomly selected for a psychological study. In the questionnaire, the subjects were asked whether they had seen or heard as a child physical fights between their parents or between a parent and the parent's partner; 26 percent responded that they had, and 14 percent said they had seen two or more incidents. They were also asked a series of questions about whether their current relationships were violent: were they ever physically threatened by their partner and did *they* threaten their partner; were they ever kicked, bitten, or hit with a fist by their partner, or did *they* ever kick, bite, or hit their partner with a fist; and so forth. Even after taking into account the extensive information they had on file about these individuals since childhood, they found that individuals who had seen two or more violent incidents as children were more than twice as likely to have acted violently toward their own current partners or to have been on the receiving end of violent acts by their current partners (Ehrensaft et al., 2003).

This pattern of findings can be interpreted in two ways. The glass-half-empty interpretation is that people are far more likely to assault their partners if they have witnessed hitting or been hit by their parents. This interpretation shows why the social learning perspective does help us to understand why some people are violent. The glass-half-full interpretation is that the vast majority of people who have witnessed hitting or been hit by their parents do *not* beat their spouses. This second interpretation shows the limitations of the social learning perspective as an explanation for violent behavior: It doesn't explain why most people who have been exposed to violence are not themselves violent.

FRUSTRATION–AGGRESSION PERSPECTIVE

An alternative explanation is derived from the **frustration–aggression perspective.** Here the central idea is that aggressive behavior occurs when a person is blocked from achieving a goal, such as when economic inequalities cause men and women to work for low wages, high unemployment rates make it hard to find a job, or racial discrimination limits the opportunities of people from racial-ethnic groups. When these conditions occur, it is said, the person may displace his or her frustration and anger onto a safer target—such

> **frustration–aggression perspective** the theory that aggressive behavior occurs when a person is blocked from achieving a goal

as his or her spouse or children. These targets are safer than employers or strangers because there is less chance of being arrested, being hit hard in return, or losing one's job. In contrast to the social learning approach, violent behavior is not viewed as directed toward a specific end, such as dominating a wife. Rather, violence is seen as an emotional outburst of displaced anger, usually by a man. So this perspective suggests that, regardless of what people have learned about violence as children, they will be more likely to act violently if they are frustrated by forces they feel are blocking their ability to get a job, move out of a dangerous neighborhood, or attain other important goals. Consequently, the frustration–aggression approach helps us to understand why domestic violence is somewhat more common among the lower social classes, whose members are more likely to be blocked from attaining their goals (but who may also be more likely to have grown up in violent homes).

The frustration–aggression approach raises the question of where a person's basic tendency to act violently (when blocked or frustrated) comes from, other than social learning. A national study of armed services veterans found that husbands who had higher levels of testosterone—the male sex hormone—were more likely to have hit or thrown things at their wives (Booth & Dabbs, 1993). The possibility of biological influences is not presented here to excuse the behavior of violent men. Most people can (and do) control their urges and predispositions. Even in the testosterone study, 71 percent of men in the group that had the highest levels of the hormone did *not* hit or throw things at their wives—just as most men who come from violent homes do not beat their wives. Still, men with a greater biological predisposition toward aggression might be more likely than others to beat their wives and their children if they are frustrated and angry about events occurring outside the home.

SOCIAL EXCHANGE PERSPECTIVE

social exchange perspective the theory that people calculate whether to engage in a particular behavior by considering the rewards and costs of that behavior and the rewards of alternatives to it

A third explanation draws upon the **social exchange perspective.** This explanation proposes that people calculate whether to engage in a particular behavior by considering the rewards and costs of that behavior and the rewards of alternatives to it. The model here is that of the rational actor. It suggests that a man may decide whether to beat his wife by considering the rewards (he can control her; he can let out his anger and frustration at the rest of the world) against the costs of violence (she might seek a divorce) and the rewards of not being violent (she will continue to do much of the child care and contribute the paycheck from her job). This approach helps to explain why wives are more likely to be the victims of violence if they don't work for wages; in that case, the costs of violence to the husband (she might seek a divorce) are lower and the rewards of not being violent (she will contribute earnings) are lower because the wife is not employed. The social exchange perspective also helps to explain the greater violence against women among the lower social classes. Men with more income can influence their wives' actions by exchanging money for the desired behavior. With money they can get the same rewards poorer men must use force to obtain, but without incurring the high costs of force—such as the possibility that the wife will seek a divorce.

Quick Review

- The social learning perspective emphasizes that people learn through observation and experience that violent behavior against intimates is acceptable.
- The frustration–aggression perspective emphasizes that violent behavior results when a person is blocked from achieving a goal.
- The social exchange perspective suggests that people engage in violent behavior against intimates when the rewards exceed the costs.

■ Domestic Violence and Public Policy

In the epilogue to her book on U.S. social policy against domestic violence since the Puritans, Pleck wrote:

> *The history of social policy against domestic violence has been one of persistent, even inherent conflict between protecting the victim and preserving the family, and the gradual development of alternatives within and outside the family for victims of abuse. (Pleck, 1987)*

In the mid-1970s this often dormant conflict surfaced again, as the feminist movement raised the issue. There is a subtext to the protect-the-victim versus preserve-the-family discourse. Public policies that protect the victim restrict men's use of their superior physical force and therefore decrease the power of men over women. That is why feminist groups worked so hard to bring the problems of battered women to the public's attention, to create crisis centers, shelters, and support services, and to modify the law in nearly all states. Wrote Gordon (1988), "Defining wife-beating as a social problem . . . was one of the great achievements of feminism."

DIMINISHED POLICY DEBATES

Today, several decades after domestic violence reemerged as an issue, the political landscape has been transformed. To a large extent, the liberal-feminist view has carried the day. Consequently, the differences between conservatives and liberals on domestic violence are much smaller than when feminists first raised the issue. A half century ago, one could still find principled conservative defenders of the idea that a husband could, within limits, hit his wife as a corrective action. Today one would be hard pressed to find more than a handful of defenders of physical violence against wives, husbands, or intimate partners in any circumstances. While conservatives may still favor the two-married-parent family with the husband as the head, they tend to endorse the role of the husband as a "soft patriarch" (Wilcox, 2004) who is affectionate and appreciative toward his wife and who spend lots of time in joint activities with his children. The soft patriarch may still spank his kids, but he would not approve of any greater physical discipline than that and would not strike his wife. In fact, Evangelical Protestant husbands who attend church regularly have lower rates of domestic violence than do most other kinds of fathers (Wilcox, 2004). So while conservatives may still object to expansive definitions of domestic violence that would, for instance, ban all forms of corporal

Many jurisdictions make an arrest mandatory when police are called to a domestic violence dispute.

punishment, and while they may oppose new government programs, the issue is much further down their priority list than are same-sex marriage, abortion, or nonmarital childbearing.

SOCIAL PROGRAMS

Moreover, advocates have found it challenging to translate protect-the-victim policy into effective programs. Consider the spread since the early 1980s of mandatory arrest policies in domestic violence complaints. This approach was influenced by an experiment conducted by the Minneapolis police force in 1981 and 1982. When responding to domestic violence complaints, the police randomly assigned the offender to one of three treatments: arresting him, ordering him to leave the home for eight hours, or trying to mediate the dispute. The results, based on subsequent arrest records and interviews with the victims, showed that arresting the suspect resulted in the lowest level of repeat violence (Sherman & Berk, 1984).

Intrigued officials at the Department of Justice decided to support replications of the experiment in other cities. But many state governments—eager to take action against the problem—legislated mandatory arrest policies without waiting for the results of the replications. The results of the experiments in other localities suggest, in the words of one review article, a "modest preventative effect" of mandatory arrest policies (Maxwell, Garner, & Fagan, 2002). The authors suggested that while these policies may be helpful in reducing intimate partner violence, they are far from a cure-all. Moreover, they note that prosecuting offenders rather than merely arresting them does not further reduce the chances of subsequent violence. In order to make greater progress in reducing intimate partner violence, organizations will need to identify men at higher risk of repeat offenses—due to factors such as alcohol abuse, prior arrest records, and unemployment—and treat them or restrict their actions. But our knowledge of how to go about this larger task is incomplete (Leisenring, 2008).

Altogether, these results illustrate the difficulty of designing programs to address spouse abuse. Still, in the current period of high divorce rates, greater gender equality, and rising individualism, the image of the bruised and battered woman has led most Americans to approve of government efforts to help her escape her husband. It is hard to imagine returning to a time when men could hit their wives with impunity or parents could boast of giving their children a good wholesome flogging.

Quick Review

- Public policy discussions about domestic violence often have a preserve-the-family versus protect-the-victim theme.
- Starting in the 1970s, feminists succeeded in moving social norms and policies toward protecting the victims.
- Policy disagreements between conservatives and liberals still exist but are smaller than in the past.
- Still, it is difficult to design programs that effectively protect victims of domestic violence.

Looking Back

1. **When did domestic violence become a social issue?** Domestic violence has been a social issue at various points throughout U.S. history. The Puritans, who took a strong stand against wife beating, passed the first laws against it. A period of renewed interest occurred in the late 1800s, and another in the 1960s. Two theoretical models, a medical model and a political model, have been applied to this social problem. The current interest and activity are largely a result of political and social action by feminist groups and by health and social welfare professionals.

2. **What do we know about violence between intimate partners?** The more common kind is situational incidents in which spouses become angry and engage in minor violent acts. Women seem as likely to initiate these incidents as men. The less common but more serious kind is a pattern of serious violent acts carried out by a man against a woman. In many of these cases, the man is seeking to control his partner's behavior. Women are more likely to be the victims of aggressive acts over their lifetimes than are men. Domestic violence is more common among cohabiting couples than among married couples, and more common among low-income families than higher-income families. Over the past two decades or so, intimate partner violence appears to have declined substantially.

3. **What is the extent of child abuse?** Though the physical abuse of children has probably decreased over the long term, surveys continue to show disturbing levels of child abuse by parents. More than half the reported cases refer to educational or physical neglect; less than one-third, to physical or sexual abuse. Child neglect and, to a lesser extent, physical abuse are somewhat more common among low-income families than others. Some cases of neglect may reflect the constraints of poverty more than abuse by parents. Childhood sexual and physical abuse can have long-term undesirable consequences. Children who are victimized by several different types of maltreatment are at greater risk of emotional and behavioral difficulties. Severely neglected or abused children are sometimes placed in foster care. In the late 1980s and 1990s, the number of children in foster care rose dramatically. There is a continuing debate about whether government social programs should emphasize the preservation of families or the protection of children.

4. **What do we know about sexual aggression by dates or acquaintances?** Although adequate data does not exist, studies suggest that men commit substantial amounts of sexual aggression and violence against women they are dating and other female acquaintances. According to one national survey, about 4 percent of adult women in the United States have been forced into sex by an acquaintance. Men who commit sexual aggression are more likely than others to show hostility to women, to be easily aroused by rape scenarios, to be sexually active, and to belong to sexually aggressive peer groups. People who try to control the other partner's behavior or are less able than others to imagine another person's point of view are more likely than others to be physically abusive. Physical assault may be most common among cohabiting partners, less common among couples who are dating, and least common among married couples.

5. **Why does domestic violence occur?** Assaults against spouses and partners arise in part from power struggles between men and women. Men have an advantage in these struggles because of their greater physical strength, and because of a social system that often reinforces male dominance. But most men do not hit their wives, so other explanations are needed for domestic violence. According to the social learning approach, children from violent homes will learn that violent behavior is an acceptable and often successful means of controlling others; consequently, they will be more likely as adults to use violence against spouse and children. The frustration–aggression approach emphasizes that individuals who are blocked from attaining a goal may displace their frustration and anger onto their spouses and children. The social exchange approach suggests that people calculate the rewards and costs of violent behavior and the alternatives to it. According to this approach, women who have some economic resources are less likely than others to be victimized, as cross-cultural studies show.

6. **What are the public policy debates concerning domestic violence?** The long-term fundamental tension has been between preserving the family and protecting the victim. Feminists raised the issue of domestic violence in the 1970s and have largely succeeded in moving social norms and public policy toward protecting the victims. Conservatives may still favor the husband-headed family, but they advocate no physical violence other than perhaps spanking children. Crafting successful policies to protect victim of domestic violence has been challenging.

 Go to the Online Learning Center at www.mhhe.com/cherlin7e to test your knowledge of the chapter concepts and key terms.

Study Questions

1. How would the political and medical models of domestic violence differ in the way that the perpetrators of violence are viewed?

2. How narrowly or broadly should domestic violence be defined?

3. What are some likely explanations for why domestic violence against women appears to be more common among lower-income families?

4. Much of the data on the number of new cases of child abuse come from reports by state child welfare agencies. What are the likely biases of this way of collecting information?

5. What are some of the long-term consequences of childhood sexual and physical abuse?

6. How does the trade-off between family reunification and child protection affect the foster care system?

7. Why are so many cases of rape and sexual assault carried out by acquaintences of the victims?

8. What patterns of domestic violence does the social learning perspective explain well? What patterns doesn't it explain well?

Key Terms

child abuse   354
domestic violence   342
elder abuse   360
frustration–aggression
   perspective   365

incest   356
intimate terrorism   347
poly-victimization   357
situational couple
   violence   347

social exchange
   perspective   366
social learning
   perspective   365

Thinking about Families

The Public Family	The Private Family
Should child protective workers leave children with parents who have not been violent, but who seem likely to be violent in the future, or should they take children away from potentially violent parents?	Is rape a concept that should be applied to married couples?

Families on the Internet   www.mhhe.com/cherlin7e

Note: While all the URLs listed were current as of the printing of this book, these sites often change. Please check our Web site (www.mhhe.com/cherlin7e) for updates.

Several sites offer information and links on the topic of child abuse. The U.S. Administration for Children and Families runs a "Child Welfare Information Gateway" site with a useful child abuse and neglect page (www.childwelfare.gov/can). The organization Prevent Child Abuse America (www.prevent childabuse.org) offers information on steps people can take to prevent child abuse. Several fact sheets are available under "research."

Futures without Violence (www.futureswith outviolence.org) also maintains a website with news briefs and recent developments. The Minnesota Center Against Violence and Abuse (www.mincava.umn.edu) maintains a site that has links to thousands of documents and hundreds of organizations and research centers.

Chapter Twelve

Divorce

Looking Forward

Three Eras of Divorce

The Era of Restricted Divorce

The Era of Divorce Tolerance

The Era of Unrestricted Divorce

Diverging Divorce Rates in the United States

Factors Associated with Divorce

Societal Risk Factors

No-Fault Divorce Legislation

Cultural Change

Men's Employment

Women's Employment

Summing up

Individual Risk Factors

Age at Marriage

Race and Ethnicity

Premarital Cohabitation

Parental Divorce

Spouse's Similarity

How Divorce Affects Children

Child Custody

Contact and Co-parenting

Economic Support

Single-Father Families

Psychosocial Effects

Parental Conflict

Multiple Transitions

After the Crisis Period

Long-Term Adjustment

Glass Half-Empty/Half-Full

Genetically Informed Studies

In Sum

Looking Back

Study Questions

Key Terms

Thinking about Families

Families on the Internet

Boxed Features

How Do Sociologists Know What They Know?: *Measuring the Divorce Rate*

Families and Public Policy: *Enforcing Child Support Obligations*

Looking Forward

1. What is the history of divorce in the United States and other Western nations?

2. What accounts for the trends in divorce over the past half-century?

3. What happens to children during the divorce process?

4. What are the short-term effects of divorce on children?

5. What are the long-term effects of divorce on children?

What if you and your spouse-to-be had to sign a pledge, enforceable in court, to undergo marriage counseling before you wed and to undergo more counseling if you ever wanted a divorce? And what if you waived the right to divorce without your spouse's consent, except after a 24-month waiting period? Would that lower the chances that you would ever divorce? The Louisiana legislature hoped that it might. In 1997, legislators passed a bill creating a new, optional form of marriage called "covenant marriage." When applying for a marriage license, couples who chose covenant marriage would sign a document in which they pledged to follow these restrictive rules. Arizona and Arkansas have since enacted similar legislation.

Covenant marriage hasn't been the success its supporters hoped it would be. About 2 percent of couples who have married in Louisiana, and even fewer in Arizona and Arkansas, have chosen covenant marriage. One study suggests that the court clerks who issue marriage licenses sometimes fail to tell couples about the option, which requires more work on their part than a standard marriage license. But even when couples do learn about covenant marriage most opt for a standard marriage license. The few couples who have chosen it tend to be much more religious and a bit more politically conservative than others (Baker, Sanchez, Nock, & Wright, 2009; Nock, Wright, & Sanchez, 1999).

Still, covenant marriage stands as a symbol of public concern about the high levels of divorce in the United States. It represents a reaction to the introduction in every state of "no fault" divorce laws, which allow one partner to obtain a divorce after a short period, even if the other partner doesn't want one. But, as will be noted below, it's not clear whether the liberalized divorce laws helped cause the high level of divorce or whether the laws were a reaction to it. What is clear is that the United States has the highest rate of divorce of any developed country. The probability of a marriage ending in divorce doubled between the early 1960s and late 1970s. At current rates, perhaps 45 percent of all American marriages begun since the late 1970s would end in divorce or a permanent separation (Schoen & Canudas-Romo, 2006). (See *How Do Sociologists Know What They Know?:* Measuring the Divorce Rate.)

About one-fourth of all children born to married parents are likely to experience the breakup of their parents' marriage by age 12 (Kennedy & Bumpass, 2008);[1] and if we add the experiences of children born to two unmarried parents

---

[1] The estimate that one-fourth of all children will experience divorce by age 12 differs from the estimate that nearly half of all marriages will end in divorce because not all married couples have children under 12 (or at all) when their marriages end in divorce.

How Do Sociologists Know What They Know?

Measuring the Divorce Rate

A newspaper reporter calls a sociologist who does research on divorce and asks, "What's the most recent statistic for the divorce rate in the United States?" "In 2009," the sociologist replies, "about 20 out of every 1,000 married women divorced." "Twenty out of a thousand," she responds, "No way! That's tiny. The divorce rate has got to be much higher than that."

"Well," says the sociologist, "another way of saying it is that nearly half of all marriages would end in divorce at current rates." "Great," the reporter replies, "and what year is that for?" "It's not for a year," the sociologist tries to explain, "it's a projection based on this year's rates . . ." But he can tell that the reporter is losing patience fast. She wants a figure and a year, not a lecture in demography, and she's writing a story on a deadline.

In fact, it's hard to answer the question, "what's the current divorce rate?" in a way that is both precise and meaningful. The difficulty is that the most meaningful statistic describes the proportion of all current marriages that will end in divorce, but it's impossible to know that proportion until everyone who is now married has grown old and died. So sociologists try to estimate this lifetime figure, but their estimates are just educated guesses. The precise statistic is based on the number of divorces in the most recent year for which data are available, but it doesn't tell us much about people's experience with divorce.

The 20-out-of-1,000 rate is the precise statistic; it represents the number of divorces in the United States in 2009 divided by the number of married women (and then multiplied by 1,000) (U.S. Bureau of the Census, 2011h). It includes women who have been married for many years as well as those who married only recently. It gives the probability that a married woman would have

become divorced in 2009: 20 ÷ 1,000, or 2 percent. So in 2009, 2 percent of married women obtained divorces.

This does indeed sound like a very low figure, given all of the public concern about divorce. No wonder reporters are unhappy with it. It is a *cross-sectional rate,* meaning a rate at one point in time. It provides a snapshot of the experiences of married American women during a single year. In the following year, 2010, the 980 of every 1,000 women who did *not* divorce in 2009 were still at risk of divorcing, and another 20 or so probably did. In 2011, yet another 20 or so would obtain divorces, and so on, year after year, into the future. Consequently, although the average woman married in 2009 had a 2 percent chance of becoming divorced *in 2009,* she had a far higher chance of becoming divorced *over the rest of her married life.*

Just how high her lifetime chances are, we cannot know with certainty. But let us conduct the following thought experiment: Suppose the risks of divorce were to stay the same, at every duration of marriage, in the future as they are today. That is to say, suppose that in the future, a woman who has been married for 10 years would have the same risk of divorce as a woman today who has been married for 10 years. And suppose similarly that in the future, a woman who has been married for 20 years would have the same risk of divorce as does a woman today who has been married for 20 years, and so on for marriages of 30 years and 40 years. Now think of a hypothetical woman whose wedding is today. We could fast-forward her through time and calculate her risk of divorce at every duration of her marriage—because we are assuming that her risks will remain the same as those observed this year. Then we could sum these risks. The result would be a measure of her lifetime probability of divorce.

When sociologists do this calculation, based on current rates, they find that the lifetime probability of divorce for a young woman marrying today is close to 50 percent (U.S. National Center for Health Statistics, 2012). I write "close to" because the exact answer depends on some of the technical assumptions in the calculations, and different sociologists make different assumptions. It's important to recognize that this figure is just a projection of current risks into the future. In fact, it is unlikely that divorce risks will stay the same for the next few decades. As Figure 12.1 (on p. 379) suggests, the risks of divorce have been changing since the Civil War. They could change again tomorrow.

The utility of the lifetime estimate, then, is not that it will prove accurate 40 years from now—it may not—but rather that it indicates the underlying force of divorce that is implied by the behavior of married people today. The lifetime estimate, in other words, answers an important *what if* question: What if the risks of divorce at each duration of marriage stayed the same as they are now; what lifetime level of divorce would these current risks imply? This is the question most newspaper readers want an answer to, even if the answer is necessarily uncertain.

Ask Yourself

1. How many couples in your family have divorced in the past year? In the past 10 years? The past 20? Is your family's divorce rate similar to the divorce rate for the country as a whole?

2. In general, do news reporters do a good enough job of explaining the significance of social statistics such as the divorce rate? What are the dangers of misreporting such statistics?

www.mhhe.com/cherlin7e

who are cohabiting, it is likely that about one-third of all children born to two parents will experience a breakup by age 12—a higher figure than in nearly all other Western nations (Andersson & Philipov, 2002). When two childless adults end their union, the breakup, although emotionally painful, is straightforward. If they were cohabiting, they basically walk away. If they were married, they conclude their legal business and often do not see each other again. When children are involved, however, a clean break is not possible. Even though the ties between the parents are severed, the breakup does not sever the ties between each parent and the children. In the majority of cases, the mother keeps custody of the children, forming a single-parent family that may endure for years. The father's relationship—typically reduced to regular visits, or less—is problematic. Indeed, many fathers fade from their children's lives. Nevertheless, a modest but growing number of fathers are obtaining custody of their children, either by themselves or jointly with their wives.

Moreover, for many adults and children, a breakup does not signal the end of the changes in their family lives. Most parents will form another partnership, usually by cohabiting with the new partner and then marrying him or her if the relationship lasts. In some cases, this second partnership will fail and a parent may move on to a third one. Repartnering further complicates adults' and children's lives. It introduces a stepparent into the child's family but doesn't subtract a biological parent—unlike remarriage after a parental death. It can bring a bewildering network of quasi-relatives that extends over several households. In short, it necessitates another major adjustment for adults and children who may have struggled to adjust to single-parent life.

These developments have greatly altered American family life. They have also been a source of concern. What do we know about the causes and consequences of divorce? About the effects of repartnering and remarriage on stepparents and stepchildren? How are divorce, remarriage, and the breakups and repartnering of cohabiting parents altering the nature of the family? These are the questions to be pursued in this chapter on divorce and in the next chapter on repartnering and remarriage.

Three Eras of Divorce

We know the name of the first person to obtain a divorce in England: John Manners, also known as Lord Roos. We know it because the only way for someone to obtain a divorce in England prior to 1858 was to ask Parliament to pass an act granting him one. (Few women were granted divorces.) Lord Roos, whose wife had given birth to a child fathered by another man, introduced a bill in the House of Lords in 1669 that dissolved his marriage and left him free to marry again. From that time until 1858, a grand total of 325 divorces were granted by Parliament (Phillips, 1991). All were granted to wealthy persons, because a common person could not hope to get his or her case taken up by Parliament. Today, far from requiring an act of Parliament or permission from a state legislature, divorce is now easy to obtain in most Western nations. It was not always so. The law and public opinion have changed dramatically over the past two centuries, greatly altering the way in which marriage is viewed. It is useful to think of three historical eras of divorce.

THE ERA OF RESTRICTED DIVORCE

England's law before 1858 was one approach to divorce taken during what I will call the **era of restricted divorce,** which characterized the Western nations until the middle of the nineteenth century. In nearly all the countries, according to historian Roderick Phillips (1991), it was very difficult to obtain a divorce.[2] Still, the European countries differed from one another in how restrictive their divorce laws were according to what religion was most prominent in each country. Catholic countries, such as France, followed the Catholic Church's position that divorce was forbidden. Only if Church officials granted an **annulment**—a ruling that a marriage had never been properly formed in the first place—could a couple dissolve their marriage. Annulments could be granted only in situations such as a marriage between relatives of too close a degree or one in which the spouses had never had sexual intercourse. Protestant countries (except for England) were more liberal, typically granting divorces in cases of adultery or desertion. Several of the American colonies were more liberal still. Most of the colonies recognized the grounds of adultery and desertion; some also allowed divorces on the ground of extreme violence by a husband.

Nevertheless, divorce remained rare everywhere. Its rarity, in large part, reflected the strong male dominance in marriage. Most divorces were granted on grounds of the wife's adultery, but very few wives were granted divorces on grounds of the husband's adultery. In fact, as mentioned earlier, few divorces were granted to women at all. Adultery was the main ground used by men for divorce not just because of sexual jealousy but also because of men's concern about who would farm their land and inherit their property. If, for example, a farmer's wife gave birth to a child fathered by another man, the child might have a claim on the farmer's land—especially if the farmer was unaware that he was not the father. Thus, divorce in this era was very difficult to obtain and, when obtained, was usually invoked because a man wished to ensure that his wife would not bear a child by another man. Marriage, for both men and women, was primarily an economic partnership—a means of pooling labor in order to grow enough food, or to make enough money, to subsist. Its romantic aspects were decidedly secondary, if only because making a living took so much effort. One reason why wives were valuable to husbands was that they could bear children, who were a major source of labor. In fact, fathers took custody of children after divorces in colonial America.

It is inconceivable, however, that marital breakups in this era were as rare as the low frequency of divorce implies. Although divorce was usually unavailable to the landless and the poor, separation without divorce must have been commonplace. Contemporary studies of families around the world demonstrate that the legalities of coupling and uncoupling—obtaining a legal marriage or a legal divorce—are less important in the poorer classes, where little money or property is involved (Therborn, 2004). Cohabitation without marriage and separation without divorce are much more common. Moreover, the African slaves in the American colonies, as noted in previous chapters,

era of restricted divorce the time of a restrictive approach toward divorce, until about the middle of the nineteenth century; divorces were usually granted only on the grounds of adultery or desertion, and generally only to men

annulment a ruling that a marriage was never properly formed

---

[2] The historical material in the next few paragraphs draws upon Phillips (1991). The eras and their titles are mine.

were denied access to legal marriage or divorce. Thus, a considerable amount of separation and desertion must lie hidden beneath the history of formal divorce in the era of restricted divorce as well.

THE ERA OF DIVORCE TOLERANCE

era of divorce tolerance
the time of a tolerant approach toward divorce, from the middle of the nineteenth century until, in the United States, 1970; the grounds for divorce were widened, and divorce was made more accessible to women

The middle of the nineteenth century marked the beginning of the **era of divorce tolerance**, which lasted in the United States until 1970. During this period, it gradually became easier to obtain a divorce. As the doctrine of separate spheres, with its emphasis on domesticity for women, became more widespread, legislatures and courts grew more sympathetic to cases in which husbands' conduct toward their wives was reprehensible. Most jurisdictions in the United States added as grounds for divorce behaviors such as habitual drunkenness or failure to provide for one's wife. In the twentieth century, legislatures added less specific offenses such as "mental cruelty." These new grounds made divorce more accessible to mistreated wives.

Just as the doctrine of separate spheres was important to changes in divorce laws, so too was the shift in how marriage was viewed. Marriage in the nineteenth and twentieth centuries underwent a gradual change from an economic partnership first and foremost to an emotional partnership based on love and companionship—from an institution to a companionship, in Burgess's memorable phrase. As this transition was made, the failure of a marriage to involve love and companionship came to be seen as a valid reason for divorce. Figure 12.1 shows the annual divorce rate for the United States from 1867 (the earliest year for which statistics exist) until 2009. It shows, for example, that less than 1 of every 1,000 people in 1867 obtained a divorce that year, whereas 5 of every 1,000 people obtained a divorce in 2009. (These numbers may seem small, but they compare the number of divorces with the total population, including children and unmarried adults.)

The divorce rate rose substantially in the late 1800s and early 1900s. According to demographic estimates of lifetime divorce experience, 8 percent of all marriages begun in 1880 eventually ended in a divorce, compared with 12 percent of marriages begun in 1900 and 18 percent of marriages begun in 1920 (Preston & McDonald, 1979). Divorce was transformed from a rare privilege granted mainly to wealthy men in the previous era, to a common, if still frowned upon, occurrence increasingly available to women. In fact, Phillips reports that more than two-thirds of divorces in the United States between 1880 and World War I were granted to women. During the same period, divorce caused great concern among social reformers in the United States—not unlike the concern expressed today (O'Neill, 1967). Organizations such as the National Divorce Reform League encouraged legislatures to make divorce laws more restrictive.

Still, the annual rate of divorce kept rising, as can be seen in Figure 12.1. The steady rise through the first half of the twentieth century was broken only by two spikes in the years after World Wars I and II and a dip during the Great Depression years. The spikes were caused by the disruption and pent-up demand for divorce that had built up during each war. The dip occurred not because marriages were happier during the depths of the Depression but rather because many unhappy couples couldn't afford to get divorced. After World War II the annual rate of divorce fell somewhat, reflecting the

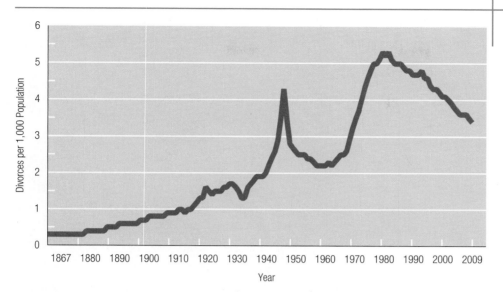

FIGURE 12.1
Divorces per 1,000 Population, United States, 1867–2009. (*Sources:* 1867–1945, Historical Statistics of the United States; 1946–1990, Monthly Vital Statistics Report, vol. 43, no. 9, Supplement; 1991–2009, Statistical Abstract of the United States.)

home- and family-oriented ethos of the 1950s baby boom years. Then, in the early 1960s, a sharp rise began. It soon led to the end of an era when divorce was merely tolerated and to the start of a new era in which divorce was widely acceptable and unrestricted.

THE ERA OF UNRESTRICTED DIVORCE

As recently as the 1960s, in order to obtain a divorce, a person had to prove that her or his spouse had done something wrong—and not just anything wrong, but rather one of a short list of specific wrongs: adultery, desertion, nonsupport, mental cruelty, and so forth. In truth, however, an increasing number of people were seeking divorces not because the other spouse had committed a terrible act but rather because the divorce seeker was unfulfilled by the marriage, unsatisfied emotionally, and trapped in a relationship that no longer seemed worth maintaining. Often, the other partner, feeling angry and alienated, consented to the divorce. Self-fulfillment, as has been discussed in earlier chapters, has become a dominant, perhaps *the* dominant, criterion for evaluating marriages. As a result, a divorce hearing was often a sham, in which one partner would "prove," with the tacit cooperation of his or her spouse, that some nonexistent or overblown wrong had occurred. In reaction to this situation, sentiment grew for eliminating altogether the idea that one spouse had to be at fault for a divorce to be granted.

The first major laws to eliminate fault were implemented in the United States in 1970, ushering in the **era of unrestricted divorce,** in which a divorce has been available virtually without restriction, except for a waiting period, to any married person who wants one. In that year California became the first jurisdiction anywhere in the Western world to eliminate fault grounds for divorce and to replace them with **no-fault divorce,** the granting of divorce simply for marriage breakdown due to "irreconcilable differences" (Glendon, 1987). Coming several years after rising divorce rates had begun to clog the courts, no-fault divorce was hailed as the way to bring the law into line with changes in societal attitudes toward divorce. It reflected the belief that a person should

era of unrestricted divorce the time of a virtually unrestricted access to divorce, from, in the United States, 1970 to the present; divorces are usually granted without restriction to any married person who wants one

no-fault divorce the granting of a divorce simply on the basis of marriage breakdown due to "irreconcilable differences"

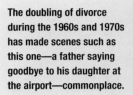

The doubling of divorce during the 1960s and 1970s has made scenes such as this one—a father saying goodbye to his daughter at the airport—commonplace.

not be forced to continue in a marriage that she or he found to be personally unacceptable. Such an individualistic view of the marriage bond would have outraged the American colonists and their Western European contemporaries; yet in 1970 it carried the day. It was consistent with the shift from the companionate marriage to the individualized marriage. England, where a century earlier only Parliament could authorize the end of a marriage, also added no-fault grounds to its divorce law in 1969. By the end of the 1980s, virtually every Western nation and every state in the American union had adopted some form of no-fault legislation. England, France, Germany, and other countries required that if only one partner wanted the divorce, and children were involved, he or she had to wait several years before it was granted. In contrast, the typical U.S. state required a waiting period of one year or less (American Bar Association, 2003). Divorce had changed from a way for wealthy men to protect their property from heirs fathered by other men to a way for the average person to improve her or his own sense of well-being. In the most liberal no-fault states and nations, it had become something close to an individual right. As Figure 12.1 shows, the American divorce rate rose sharply through the 1970s and peaked about 1980.

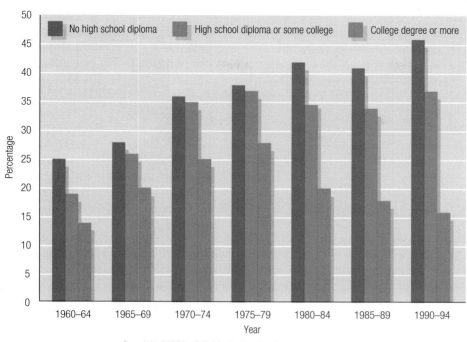

FIGURE 12.2
Percentage of Women with a Permanent Separation or Divorce Within Ten Years of a First Marriage. (*Source:* Martin, 2006)

DIVERGING DIVORCE RATES IN THE UNITED STATES

Since 1980, as Figure 12.1 shows, the divorce rate of the population as a whole has declined. But the decline has not been uniform. Rather, divorce has declined more for married people with four-year college degrees than for married people with less education. As was discussed in Chapter 4, the divergence in divorce is one of the manifestations of the growing social class gap in family life. Figure 12.2 illustrates what has happened. Steven Martin (2006) calculated the percentage of women who were divorced or permanently separated within ten years of marrying, for five-year periods from 1960–1964 to 1990–1994. He used data from the Survey of Income and Program Participation. Look first at the blue bars, which show the trend in divorce for women who did not have a high school degree; you will see that the percentages increased throughout the 30 year period. So divorce risks rose steadily for women with the least education. Now look at the red bars, and you will see that the percentages rose through 1975–79 and but then stabilized for women with a high school degree but no college degree. Finally, the green bars show that for women with a college degree, the percentages rose through 1975–1979 and then *fell* sharply. By the early 1990s, the percentage of the well-educated women who were divorcing within ten years was not much different from the percentages 30 years earlier. A large social class difference in divorce has emerged. More recent data confirm that the difference remained as large in the late 2000s (U.S. National Center for Health Statistics, 2012).

Quick Review

- In the era of restricted divorce, divorces were usually granted only on grounds of adultery or desertion, and generally only to men.
- In the era of divorce tolerance, grounds for divorce were widened, and divorce was made more accessible to women.
- In the era of unrestricted divorce, divorces are usually granted without restriction, except for a waiting period, to anyone who wants one.
- Since about 1980, divorce rates have diverged by social class.

■ Factors Associated with Divorce ■

How can we explain these trends in divorce—the sharp rise for everyone in the 1960s and 1970s and the divergence since then? Let us examine the social factors that may influence the risk of divorce on both a societal and an individual level. Table 12.1 provides a summary of these factors.

Table 12.1 Factors Associated with Divorce	
SOCIETYWIDE FACTORS	
No-fault divorce legislation	State no-fault divorce laws produced an initial surge of divorce in the 1970s, but it is unclear whether no-fault laws have had a lasting effect.
Cultural change	A greater emphasis on personal fulfillment made divorce a more acceptable option for people who felt unfulfilled by their marriages.
Men's employment opportunities	As young men's economic opportunities decreased since the early 1970s, their reduced earning potential may have caused stress in marriages.
Women's employment opportunities	Women's growing employment opportunities led to a rise in the number of wives working outside the home. Under the specialization model of marriage, employment raised the risk of divorce, but under the income-pooling model, employment seems to lower it.
INDIVIDUAL FACTORS	
Age at marriage	People who marry as teenagers have a higher rate of divorce. They may not choose partners as well as those who marry later.
Race and ethnicity	African Americans have higher rates of separation and divorce than most other groups. Low income and unemployment, a lesser emphasis on marriage in African American kinship, and discrimination in job and housing markets may contribute.
Premarital cohabitation	People who cohabit prior to their marriage have a higher rate of divorce. They may have a weaker commitment to marriage than do people who marry without cohabiting first.
Parental divorce	People whose parents divorced are more likely to end their own marriages in divorce. They may model their behavior on their parents' marriages, or they may have a genetic tendency toward having problems in intimate relationships.
Spouse's similarity	People who marry people who are similar to them in characteristics such as religion have a lower rate of divorce. Such couples may be more compatible in their values and interests.

SOCIETAL RISK FACTORS

There have been some broad changes in American society that are likely to have influenced levels of divorce, most of which I have discussed in previous chapters. Here is a brief discussion of each:

No-Fault Divorce Legislation   The introduction of a no-fault divorce law seems to have caused a surge of divorces in the first few years after a state enacted it, perhaps reflecting a "backlog effect" of couples in unhappy marriages who were quick to take advantage of it (Nakonezny, Shull, & Rodgers, 1995; Rodgers, Nakonezny, & Shull, 1997). But it is not clear whether the no-fault laws have had a lasting effect on divorce rates. Some studies in the United States and Britain suggest that they have done so, but another study suggests that their effects faded within a decade (Wolfers, 2006). In any event, no-fault divorce laws may have had other effects, such as allowing women in violent marriages to end them or, because they could more credibly threaten to leave violent marriages, discouraging husbands in intact marriages from being abusive (Stevenson & Wolfers, 2006). It's also likely that the enactment of no-fault legislation itself reflected widespread changes in behavior and values, such as those discussed in the next few subsections.

Cultural Change   Previous chapters have examined the growing place of individualism and personal fulfillment in marriage, and an extensive discussion will not be presented here. Cultural critics claim that this emphasis erodes bonds of obligation and trust. As a framework for thinking about relationships, it is alleged, the emphasis on personal fulfillment results in a vocabulary that is rich in ways of thinking about individual well-being but impoverished in ways of thinking about commitment (Bellah, Madsen, Sullivan, Swidler, & Tipton, 1985). For instance, numerous books, articles, lecture series, courses, and support groups exist on self-actualization or self-development or human potential, but much less intellectual activity is centered on maintaining personal responsibilities and obligations to others. Put another way, a focus on personal fulfillment represents a shift toward the concerns of the private family as against the concerns of the public family. Under these circumstances, divorce becomes a more acceptable option for people who feel personally unfulfilled; indeed, *not* divorcing in the face of personal dissatisfaction comes to need justifying.

The growing emphasis on personal fulfillment probably was a major contributor to the rise in divorce prior to 1980, but it does not help us explain the diverging trends since then. For example, college-educated women, who had the most permissive attitudes toward divorce laws in the 1970s, now favor restrictions on the availability of divorce more than do non-college-educated women (Martin & Parashar, 2006). This change is inconsistent with rising individualism, so there must be other reasons for it, such as increasing gains to marriage.

Men's Employment   Men are still culturally expected to work steadily in order to be seen as good husbands. In the older, specialization model of the marriage market, men traded their wages for women's housework and child care services. In the newer, income-pooling model of the marriage market, men and women combine their incomes. But even in the income-pooling model, the expectation is that men will contribute financially. While it may now be *desirable* for a wife to work steadily outside of the home, it remains almost *mandatory* that the husband work steadily. If he does not provide a steady income, the chances that his marriage will end in divorce increase, many studies show (Burstein, 2007). Since the 1970s, the employment opportunities for men without college educations have been declining because of the globalization and automation of production. Their growing problems in the job market are a likely cause of the increase in divorce among less-educated couples. Conversely, the transformed economy has increased opportunities for college-educated managers and professionals. The strong job market they enjoy may explain why divorce has declined among college-educated couples.

Women's Employment   While the effect of men's employment on divorce is straightforward, the effect of women's employment is complex. Wives' employment theoretically could have contrasting effects:

- *Independence effect.* Employment could raise the likelihood of divorce by providing an opportunity for the wife to support herself independently of her husband. This opportunity would make divorce a more attractive option for wives who were unhappy with their marriages (Schoen et al., 2002).
- *Income effect.* On the other hand, employment could lower the likelihood of divorce because the increase in the family's income could relieve financial pressures and thereby reduce tensions in the marriage.

Which effect predominates seems to depend on which cultural model of marriage is dominant. In the specialization model of marriage that was dominant in the mid-twentieth century, wives were not supposed to work outside the home. They were highly dependent on their husbands' earnings. When they did work, their employment undermined the breadwinner–homemaker bargain that was the heart of the specialization model. Studies from this period suggest that wives' employment, on balance, increased the risk of divorce (Becker, Landes, & Michael, 1977). In other words, the independence effect of women's earnings predominated several decades ago. With the rise of the income-pooling model of marriage, however, both spouses are supposed to work for pay. Wives' earnings are an acceptable way for a family to increase its income. Wives' earnings also can bring them more bargaining leverage on issues such as how much housework and child care each spouse does. Newer studies suggest that wives' incomes may now lower the risk of divorce for most couples—especially when they are married to men who also have substantial earnings (Sayer & Bianchi, 2000; Burstein, 2007). The income effect is becoming more important today.

Summing Up   Said otherwise, what matters for marriage and divorce is not just whether a particular man or woman is employed but also how the larger society views men's and women's employment in general. Does the employment of women clash with the norm that women should stay home and be housewives? If so, it is likely to be disruptive. Or is women's employment seen as complementary to men's employment, providing the family with needed income and providing women with opportunities for a fulfilling life in the world of work? If so, it may reduce the risk of divorce. Consider a study that compared national surveys of families in Germany, a country with a stronger male-breadwinner (specialization) model of marriage, and the United States, where the male-breadwinner model is now weaker (Cooke, 2006). The earnings of German wives seem to destabilize marriage and increase the risk of divorce. But the earnings of American wives seem to reduce the risk of divorce for most couples, particularly when the couples also shared the household tasks. So the consequences of wives' employment depended on the kind of culture in which it was embedded, a national culture which can change, as has occurred in the United States.

The change from wives' income being destabilizing to stabilizing seems to have begun at some point in the last quarter of the twentieth century and is still in progress (Sweeney, 2002; Sweeney & Cancian, 2004). It is consistent with the greater emphasis on individualism and personal fulfillment because it allows both women and men to participate in the labor market. Along with the trend toward a more egalitarian division of housework and child care, the spread of the income-pooling model appears to reflect the emergence of a new cultural climate in which greater equality in men's and women's roles inside and outside the home, rather than a sharp division of labor, leads to greater stability in marriage. This change helps to explain why the divorce rate has been declining recently among college-educated married couples, in which both the husband and the wife typically have stable, substantial earnings.

INDIVIDUAL RISK FACTORS

In addition, there are many other social and economic factors that seem to increase or decrease an *individual's* likelihood of ever experiencing a divorce but have not contributed to the recent, *societywide* increase. Consider teenage marriage: As will be noted below, people who marry as teenagers have a greater likelihood of divorce than those who postpone marriage. Yet the societywide average age at marriage has been increasing since the 1960s. Consequently, we can rule out teenage marriage as a cause of the societywide rise in divorce. The list of individual risk factors includes the following.

Age at Marriage Teenagers probably cannot choose partners as well as older persons can. In part, they are not mature enough. Compared with people in their twenties, teenagers may not know as well what kinds of persons they will be as adults and what their needs in a partner will be. Even if they do have a good sense of their emerging selves, they will have a more difficult time picking an appropriate partner because it is hard to know what kind of spouse an 18-year-old will prove to be over the long run. Moreover, teenage marriages are sometimes precipitated by an accidental pregnancy, and it is known that a premarital birth raises the likelihood of divorce. It does so partly because it brings together a couple who might not otherwise have chosen to marry each other. It also may be more difficult, on a practical level, for a couple to make a marriage work if a young child is present from day one. About half of all marriages of teenagers end in divorce within 15 years, compared to about one-third of marriages of people who marry in their mid-to-late twenties and about one-fourth of marriages of people who are age 30 or older (Raley & Bumpass, 2003). Still, earlier marriage cannot be an explanation for the post-1960 rise in divorce because age at marriage increased after 1960.

Race and Ethnicity   African Americans have substantially higher rates of marital separation and divorce than most other racial-ethnic groups; about one-half of the marriages of black women end within 15 years compared to about one-third of white women's marriages (Raley & Bumpass, 2003). Although lower income, unemployment, and lower educational level are important sources of this racial difference, these factors alone cannot account for it. It is possible that the lesser emphasis in African American culture on marriage, relative to extended kinship ties, also plays a role. African Americans, who can rely more heavily on mothers, grandmothers, and other kin, have less need to stay married; they also have an alternative source of support if a marriage ends (Orbuch, Veroff, & Hunter, 1999).

In addition, black women who separate from their husbands are considerably less likely to obtain a legal divorce, and again the differences are not due solely to economics or education. Within three years of separating, 57 percent of black women had obtained a divorce, according to a survey, compared with 66 percent of Hispanic women and 91 percent of non-Hispanic white women (Bramlett & Mosher, 2002). What these statistics imply is that black women have a higher likelihood of separating from husbands, but they turn these separations into divorces at a much slower pace. Perhaps their lower expectations of remarrying, which will be discussed in the next chapter, provide less motivation to obtain a legal divorce.

Nevertheless, discrimination and unequal access to jobs and income may still play a role in the marriage differential between African Americans and whites. As noted in a discussion of racially based differences in marriage in Chapter 5, the military provides something of a natural experiment with regard to family life: it is an institution with less discrimination than in civilian life and in which blacks receive similar salaries and benefits (such as health insurance) as do whites. This is particularly true in the Army, which has the highest proportion of blacks of all branches of the armed services and has substantial numbers of blacks in supervisory positions. Teachman and Tedrow (2008) compared the risk of divorce for married black soldiers on active duty to married blacks who were in the reserves. Both active-duty and reserve-duty soldiers must meet the same entrance requirements to join the service (for instance, being a high school graduate), but reservists experience the potential discrimination of the civilian labor and housing markets, whereas soldiers on active duty do not. They found that black soldiers while on active duty had a much lower risk of divorce than did black reservists; in fact, their risk of divorce was comparable to that of white civilians. The implication is that the discrimination and unequal treatment of civilian life may be a reason for the higher divorce rates of African Americans.

Premarital Cohabitation   Since married couples who live together prior to marriage have already had, in a sense, a trial run at marriage, we might expect that they would have a lower divorce rate than couples who did not live together before marrying. Just the opposite has been true, at least until recently: couples who cohabit before marriage have higher divorce rates than do couples who marry directly without cohabiting first (Smock & Gupta, 2002). Researchers have suggested that the reason is the selectivity of the people who are willing to cohabit: they may have more unconventional attitudes toward marriage, they may be less committed to marriage, or they may have personality characteristics that make it difficult for them to have a stable marriage. All this may be true, but just as the effects of wives' employment on divorce depends upon the cultural context (specialization versus income-pooling models of marriage), so does the effect of premarital cohabitation. When it is more common and more accepted than currently in the United States, it may be more compatible with stable marriage. Already, in the province of Quebec, where premarital cohabitation is more common than anywhere else in North America, the divorce differential shows signs of narrowing (Le Bourdais & Juby, 2002). In Europe, premarital cohabitation has little effect on divorce in countries where about half of all couples live together before marrying, so that neither cohabitors nor non-cohabitors is a small, select group (Liefbroer & Dourleijn, 2006). And in Australia, premarital cohabitation, which was associated with higher divorce risks among people who married before 1988, is associated with lower divorce risks since then (Hewitt & de Vaus, 2009). It may be that future studies in the United States, where roughly half of married couples live together first, will begin to show that premarital cohabitation makes less difference.

Parental Divorce   A number of studies show that persons whose parents divorced while they were growing up are more likely than others to become divorced themselves (Amato, 1996; Dronkers & Härkönen, 2008; Li & Wu, 2008; White, 1990). Yet persons who lost a parent through death while they were growing up are *not* more likely than others to become divorced (Diekmann & Engelhardt, 1999). These contrasting findings suggest that more than a parent's absence must be involved, because otherwise the effect of a parental death would be the same as the effect of a parental divorce. Rather, something about growing up in a divorced family must be associated with a higher risk of divorce as an adult. One possibility is that living through a parental divorce somehow diminishes a person's ability to sustain a successful marriage. For example, children of divorce may witness more parental conflict than other children and may adopt a conflict-laden style of relating in their own marriages. A second possibility is that children in divorced families may share characteristics inherited from their parents (such as a tendency to become seriously depressed) that make a lasting marriage difficult for both generations (McGue & Lykken, 1992). But even if there were a genetic mechanism, it could not account for the nineteenth- and twentieth-century increases in the nation's divorce rate because, as noted in earlier chapters, evolutionary genetic changes occur far more slowly.

Spouse's Similarity   Finally, people who marry people who are similar to them are, in general, less likely to divorce, probably because the couples are more compatible in their values and interests. For example, Catholics married to Catholics and Protestants married to Protestants are both less likely to divorce than Catholics married to Protestants (Lehrer & Chiswick, 1993). People who marry someone of a different race have a higher probability of divorce (Better & King, 2008), perhaps because they receive less social support. People who are far apart in age also have higher divorce probabilities than people who are closer in age, particularly if it is the wife who is much

People who marry others similar to them are less likely to divorce.

older (Hall & Zhao, 1995). We don't know exactly why; it may be that a large age difference, especially if the wife is much older (which goes against the social norm), indicates that one or both of the partners had personal characteristics that made them less desirable on the marriage market.

How Divorce Affects Children

At least one partner chooses to divorce in every case of marital disruption. Presumably, then, at least one partner's well-being is enhanced by the divorce. But children do not choose that their parents divorce. While the end of a violent, dysfunctional marriage might benefit the children involved, it isn't true in general that children's well-being is enhanced by their parents' divorce. In fact, there are good reasons to think that their well-being should be, in many cases, diminished. They lose the benefits of having both of their parents living in the same household with them. They must go through an emotionally difficult process of adjusting to the breakup. Sometimes they must cope with continuing, bitter conflict between their parents. Nevertheless, most of them manage to cope with divorce without major long-term problems. Here are the important aspects of their experiences.

CHILD CUSTODY

There is first the matter of custody: Who will have responsibility for the children, and where will they live? **Legal custody** refers to having the right to make important decisions about the children and to having legal responsibility for them. **Physical custody** refers to where they actually live. In the United States in the past, the two kinds of custody were usually merged; the father typically had custody in both senses prior to the mid-nineteenth century, the mother, after that. Family law throughout much of the twentieth century was based on a presumption that maternal custody was better for young children; indeed, custody was awarded to the mother in about 85 percent of the cases (Weitzman, 1985). In most states, however, that presumption has been replaced with the rule that the court should decide according to the "best interests of the child"—a standard that formally favors neither parent. Nevertheless, it is still the case today that in the majority of divorces, mothers have physical custody. (It is also the case that in a majority of divorces, fathers do not want physical custody.)

Some states are moving toward a presumption in favor of **joint legal custody,** which means that both parents retain an equal right to make important decisions concerning the children (as opposed to sole legal custody, in which one spouse can make the decisions without consulting the other) (Bartlett, 1999). A decree of joint legal custody is essentially a decree that the parents' responsibilities toward their children have not changed; despite the divorce, they both remain responsible. In California, which has led the move toward this kind of custody, a majority of cases now end in joint legal custody (Kelly, 2007). In practice, however, joint legal custody has little impact because the parent with physical custody makes most of the daily decisions. Joint legal custody may be valuable mainly as a symbol of the father's continuing responsibility for his children (Maccoby & Mnookin, 1992).

In a growing but still small number of cases, divorcing couples are agreeing to **joint physical custody,** under which the children spend substantial time in each household—perhaps alternating on a weekly basis. Joint physical custody, however, requires a great deal of cooperation between the ex-spouses, who must transport children back and forth, share clothing, coordinate schedules, and so forth. Many—perhaps most—divorcing couples cannot manage this much cooperation. To jump ahead briefly to the psychosocial effects on children, a California study shows that joint physical custody can work very well for the children when the parents voluntarily choose it and can cooperate. But if the parents are still angry and warring with each other, the children tend to feel caught in the middle. For example, a parent may attempt to extract information about the private life of the ex-spouse from the children, which often causes stress and anxiety. The researchers urge judges not to impose joint physical custody on parents who don't want to undertake it (Buchanan, Maccoby, & Dornbusch, 1996).

CONTACT AND CO-PARENTING

Regardless of state laws, the reality is still that most children remain in the care of their mothers most of the time. This imbalance persists because it carries forward the typical child care situation in two-parent families—namely,

legal custody (of children after a divorce) the right to make important decisions about the children and the obligation to have legal responsibility for them

physical custody (of children after a divorce) the right of a divorced spouse to have one's children live with one

joint legal custody (of children after a divorce) the retaining by both parents of an equal right to make important decisions concerning their children

joint physical custody (of children after a divorce) an arrangement whereby the children of divorced parents spend substantial time in the household of each parent

FIGURE 12.3
Involvement of nonresident
fathers with their children,
1976 and 2002. (*Source:*
Amato, Meyers, & Emery,
2009)

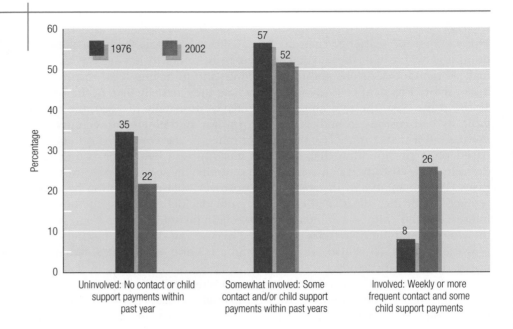

FIGURE 12.3
Involvement of nonresident fathers with their children, 1976 and 2002. (*Source:* Amato, Meyers, & Emery, 2009)

the wife does more of the care than the husband does. It can be difficult to get fathers involved in care after the divorce because some of them were not intensively involved before. Nevertheless, nonresident fathers—men whose children live primarily with the children's mother—have increased the amount of involvement they have with their children. Figure 12.3 shows the change in involvement for all nonresident fathers, whether they had been married to the mother at the time of the child's birth or not. The authors of the study on which the graph is based (Amato, Meyers, & Emery, 2009) divided nonresident fathers into three groups: *uninvolved fathers,* who had neither seen their child nor paid any child support in the past year; *involved fathers,* who had seen their child weekly or more often in the past year and had also paid some child support; and a middle group I will call *somewhat involved fathers,* who had seen their child in the past year but less frequently than weekly, and/or had paid some child support in the past year. These are crude categories, to be sure, but national surveys in 1976 and 2002 can be used to see how the proportions have changed over time. The results show that the percentage of "involved" fathers has increased sharply from 8 to 26 percent, whereas the percentage of "uninvolved" fathers has decreased from 35 to 22 percent. The uninvolved fathers represent a mixture of fathers whose involvement with their children started at a high level but declined over time and fathers who had little contact with their children starting at the first year after the separation. The former group was more likely to have had their children while married to the mother, whereas the latter group was more likely to have had their children at a younger age and outside of marriage (Cheadle, Amato, & King, 2010). The authors of the study suggest that the increase in "involved" fathers may reflect a growing cultural norm that nonresident fathers should remain in their children's lives. The spread of this norm would be beneficial to children: research shows that children's adjustment to divorce is better when

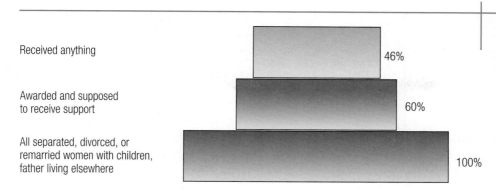

Received anything — 46%

Awarded and supposed to receive support — 60%

All separated, divorced, or remarried women with children, father living elsewhere — 100%

FIGURE 12.4
The child support pyramid: award and receipt of child support payments to women with children under the age of 21 living in their households who have fathers living elsewhere, 2009. (*Source:* U.S. Bureau of the Census, 2011c)

they have regular contact with their fathers, except in the small number of cases in which fathers have serious problems such as substance abuse or violent behavior (Kelly, 2007).

Conflict between divorced parents tends to diminish over time. Still, the parents don't necessarily cooperate in rearing the children. Advocates of joint legal custody had hoped it would encourage more ex-spouses to practice **cooperative parenting,** in which the divorced parents coordinate their activities and cooperate with each other in raising the children. Cooperative parenting does occur, but more commonly the parents gravitate toward a more detached style: They talk as little as possible, avoid meeting each other, send messages through their children, rendezvous at restaurant parking lots to exchange them, and go about their parenting business separately. Rather than cooperative parenting, this dominant style might be called **parallel parenting,** in recognition of the separate tracks the two parents follow in their dealings with the children. More than half of divorced parents follow this style (Kelly, 2007).

ECONOMIC SUPPORT

Many fathers seem to fade from their children's lives in part because they will not or cannot contribute to their children's support. Figure 12.4 displays the child support pyramid. The figures are from a Bureau of the Census study of the 7.0 million separated, divorced, or remarried mothers who in 2005 had children under the age of 21 who were living with them and whose fathers were absent from the household. The base of the pyramid represents all these women. Moving up the pyramid, we can see that only 60 percent had been awarded child support payments and were supposed to receive them in 2009. (Most of the rest had not been awarded child support payments for various reasons, such as inability to find the father.) Only 46 percent had actually received any child support money in 2009 (U.S. Bureau of the Census, 2011c). (The situation was worse for the 4.1 million mothers who had never married the fathers of their children; just 25 percent had received any child support payments in 2009.) Custodial parents received less child support in 2009 than they did earlier in the decade, probably because the Great Recession reduced fathers' ability to pay.

Many mothers, therefore, are hit with a financial double whammy when they divorce. First, they lose their husbands' income, which typically exceeds theirs by a substantial margin. Second, just half receive any money in child support payments.

cooperative parenting an arrangement whereby divorced parents coordinate their activities and cooperate with each other in raising their children

parallel parenting an arrangement whereby divorced parents gravitate toward a more detached style, going about their parenting business separately

Families and Public Policy

Enforcing Child Support Obligations

Children in single-parent families would benefit if every absent parent knew he or she would have to pay child support. This has been the goal of several new laws that were enacted in the 1980s and 1990s. Since 1994, for example, all parents who have been ordered by the courts to pay child support have had their payments deducted automatically from their paychecks. Moreover, states are now required to adopt guidelines for the amount of child support a parent should pay, according to income and number of children; judges must follow these guidelines or state in writing why they didn't.

The 1996 welfare reform act contained a number of additional measures to strengthen the system. For instance, it provided more support for programs to establish paternity in hospitals at the birth of the children, and it penalized welfare recipients who failed to cooperate. It required employers to send the names of newly hired employees to state and federal agencies that will match the names against lists of parents who have not paid child support obligations. It allowed states to deny occupational and driver's license renewals to parents who fail to pay (U.S. Administration for Children and Families, 1996). In fact, toughening child support enforcement has been one of the most popular family policies among both conservatives and liberals. Conservatives

favor tougher enforcement because making fathers pay is consistent with their belief that parents should take responsibility for the well-being of their children. (Although the law applies equally to absent mothers who owe child support payments, in practice the vast majority of payments are collected from fathers and distributed to mothers.) The new measures send a message to fathers that they can leave their marriages, but they can't leave their children. Conservatives hope that the measures will deter men from fathering children they can't, or don't intend to, support. Liberals favor tougher measures because increased collection of child support payments will provide more economic support to children in low-income single-parent families.

There is evidence that these measures are producing results. Between 1993 and 2007, the proportion of custodial mothers who had active child support awards and who reported receiving the full amount of child support they were supposed to receive increased from 37 to 47 percent in 2007, before falling to 42 percent in 2009, as the Great Recession impeded fathers' ability to pay (U.S. Bureau of the Census, 2011c). However, most of the measures help middle-class single parents more than poor single parents and their children. Most middle-class fathers are employed and can make some child support payments.

Many poor fathers are not working steadily and may not be able to make the child support payments a court has ordered. As they fall behind, they build up an "arrearage" of back payments they owe the mothers of their children. In many states, the arrearage continues to accumulate even if they are in prison. It may get so high that it discourages fathers from working because so much of their income would go toward paying down the arrearage. Consequently, some experts warn that child support programs that rely solely on enforcement of child support orders will not work for poor families. Rather, these experts advocate programs to increase the earnings capacity of single fathers, so that they can afford to pay the child support they owe (Mincy, Klempin, & Schmidt, 2011).

Ask Yourself

1. Do you know anyone who has had difficulty collecting court-ordered child support payments? If so, was the problem caused by the absent parent's inability to pay or simply an unwillingness to pay?

2. Besides the measures described here, what other steps could government take to improve the economic well-being of children in single-parent families?

www.mhhe.com/cherlin7e

As a result, the average mother's standard of living is reduced by about one-third in the first year after she separates from her husband. In contrast, the average father's standard of living increases somewhat, particularly if he earned most of the family income before the separation (Bianchi, Subaiya, & Kahn, 1999; McManus & DiPrete, 2001). Because of this situation, there have been several attempts to increase the amount of child support fathers pay. (See *Families and Public Policy: Enforcing Child Support Obligations.*)

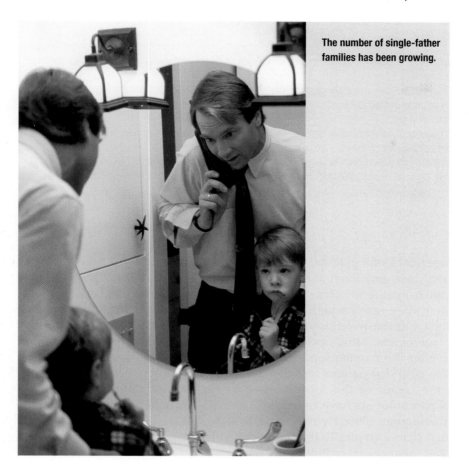

The number of single-father families has been growing.

Single-Father Families   Although most single-parent families are headed by mothers, the number of single-father families has been growing rapidly. Between 1980 and 2008, the number of single fathers living with their own children under 18 increased from 690,000 to 1.7 million. These families now constitute 15 percent of all single-parent families with children (U.S. Bureau of the Census, 2011x). In addition, there are hundreds of thousands of custodial fathers who have remarried and therefore are not counted in the single-father total. Single fathers tend to have higher incomes than single mothers because men's wages are typically higher than women's. However, single fathers tend to have lower incomes and less education than married fathers. Nineteen percent had incomes below the government poverty line in 2011 (U.S. Bureau of the Census, 2011w). Yet few single fathers are granted child support awards, since most have higher incomes than their ex-wives. Nevertheless, some single fathers with low incomes may need assistance from their former wives. Our mental image of the single-father family is the divorced dad living alone with his children. However, less than half of single-father families consist of divorced men living alone with their children. Of the rest, most are sharing their households with mothers, sisters, or new girlfriends, who may be doing much of the child care (Eggebeen, Snyder, & Manning, 1996). Yet the census counts them as "single-father families" as long as the mother of the child is not in the household.

Quick Review

- Joint legal custody is now common after divorce, and joint physical custody is still less common but growing.
- Most children live with their mothers after a divorce. Nonresident fathers are more likely to be involved in their children's lives than in the past, but a minority do not see their children or support them.
- A majority of parents evolve into a style of parallel parenting after a divorce in which each of them goes about parenting with little contact, cooperation, or conflict with the other one.
- Mothers and the children in their custody tend to experience a decline in their standard of living; less than half of custodial mothers receive child support payments from the fathers.

PSYCHOSOCIAL EFFECTS

The experience of a parental divorce could potentially affect the well-being of children: their emotional and behavioral development, their school achievement, their long-term mental health, or the work and family lives they seek out when they reach adulthood. A great deal has been written about what we might call the psychosocial effects of divorce, and not all of the writers are in agreement. Most observers, however, would agree that the first year or two after the parents separate is a time of dramatic change during which both the custodial parents and the children—most whom are intensely upset when they learn of the separation—often experience difficulties. Developmental psychologists have called this time the **crisis period** (Chase-Lansdale & Hetherington, 1990; Hetherington & Kelly, 2002). After the breakup, the custodial parent (typically the mother) is often angry, upset, and depressed. One consequence, according to observers, is the "diminished parenting" that often occurs during the crisis period (Wallerstein & Kelly, 1980; Wallerstein, Lewis, & Blakeslee, 2000). Distracted, distressed parents may have difficulties providing the daily mixture of emotional support and moderate, consistent discipline that psychologists called "authoritative parenting." Instead, parents seem to be emotionally distant and preoccupied, prone to ignore misbehavior or to lash out with harsh discipline. For example, a child misbehaves, prompting the harried, depressed parent to respond angrily. Her response can set off more negative behavior: A toy is thrown on the floor or a bowl of cereal is knocked off the table. The parent responds even more angrily, further provoking the child.

In this way, the parent and child are drawn into what Hetherington and others call "coercive cycles," in which the parent's and child's responses aggravate the situation. Hetherington found that acting-out behavior and coercive cycles are more common among boys than girls (girls show fewer outward problems, although they may be holding in feelings that will erupt years later). After a year or two, however, many custodial parents have reorganized their lives and begun to manage their anger and depression enough to provide a more supportive and structured routine for their children (Hetherington & Kelly, 2002).

Parental Conflict Most divorcing parents are able to greatly reduce their conflict with each other by two or three years after they break up (Kelly, 2007), but for a minority the disputes and difficulties continue. A continuing

crisis period a period during the first year or two after parents separate when both the custodial parent and the children experience difficulties in dealing with the situation

high level of conflict is probably the most widely cited factor in harming children's adjustment after a divorce. When parents fight, children tend to become fearful and distressed—whether the parents are married or divorced. After the breakup, children have fewer problems if their parents can cooperate or at least engage in parallel parenting (Buchanan, Maccoby, & Dornbusch, 1996; Hetherington & Kelly, 2002).

It's important to recognize that the conflict that harms children can begin before the breakup. Divorce is not just an event that happens the day a parent moves out; rather, it is a process that typically begins much earlier. In a research project that I carried out with several collaborators, we examined the records of thousands of British and American children who had been followed from age 7 to age 11 (Cherlin et al., 1991). We focused on children whose parents had been married at the beginning of the study and watched as they split over time into two groups: those whose parents divorced and those whose parents stayed together. Not surprisingly, the children whose parents divorced were showing more behavior problems and were doing worse in school. But then we looked back to the start of the study, before anyone's parents had been divorced. We discovered that children whose parents would later divorce were *already* showing more behavior problems and doing worse in school than children whose parents would remain together. This finding suggests that some of the trauma of divorce begins before the separation, as unhappy parents begin to move apart. In addition, it suggests that the problems that children exhibit after a divorce might have occurred to some extent even if their conflicted parents had remained together.

Multiple Transitions   Apart from exposure to the parents' distress and conflict, the breakup forces children to adjust to jarring transitions. The first, of course, is the departure of a parent from the home. This is not necessarily the last transition, however. The financial settlement between the parents frequently requires that the family's house be sold. As a result, children must often move to a new neighborhood, begin classes at a new school, and make new friends. Some divorced mothers move in with their parents temporarily while they make the transition to single parenting. Other adults will probably move in and out of the child's household. A majority of single parents remarry, and, as will be discussed in Chapter 13, many remarriages are preceded by a period of cohabitation. More will be said about remarriage shortly; for now I will suggest that the cumulative stress of these multiple transitions may cause difficulties, as was discussed in Chapter 9. The idea is that the number of transitions in family living arrangements that a child makes—how many times parents or parent-figures move in and out of the household—may cause more adjustment problems than living in any particular kind of family. (Amato, 2010).

AFTER THE CRISIS PERIOD

After the crisis period, the majority of children resume normal development (Emery, 1999). Still, a study by Hetherington and W. Glenn Clingempeel found that, six years after the disruption, 20 to 25 percent of young adolescents were displaying serious behavior problems, as opposed to 10 percent of young adolescents who were still living with both parents (Hetherington & Clingempeel, 1992; Hetherington & Kelly, 2002).[3] The researchers found that the problems of some boys in the crisis period had persisted; in addition, girls were now displaying as many problems as boys. Early adolescence is a time when tension between parents and children can increase as the children try to become more independent. It is possible that this task is more difficult for children whose parents have divorced. According to the Hetherington and Clingempeel study, single mothers monitored their children's behavior less closely and engaged in more arguments with them than did married mothers. Moreover, the researchers speculated that children who are just coming to terms with their own burgeoning sexuality may have a more difficult adjustment when they must confront intimate relationships between a parent and that parent's new boy- or girlfriend or spouse.

Long-Term Adjustment   How do children of divorced parents fare over the long term? The psychologist Judith Wallerstein followed a group of such children for 25 years. Her books about their well-being after 10 years (Wallerstein & Blakeslee, 1989) and 25 years (Wallerstein, Lewis, & Blakeslee, 2000) report widespread, lasting difficulties in personal relationships. At the 25-year mark, a minority had managed to establish successful personal lives, but only with great effort. The legacy of divorce, Wallerstein claims, doesn't fade away:

> *Contrary to what we have long thought, the major impact of divorce does not occur during childhood or adolescence. Rather, it rises in adulthood as serious romantic relationships move center stage. When it comes time to choose a life mate and build a family, the effects of divorce crescendo.*

[3] By "serious" behavior problems, I mean scores on a checklist of behavior problems that were high enough to indicate that some clinical help might be needed. See the commentary by Maccoby (1992).

Because these young adults didn't have the chance to observe successful marriages, Wallerstein maintains, they didn't learn how to create one. Faced with the choice of a partner or a spouse, their anxiety rises; they fear repeating their parents' mistakes. Lacking a good model to follow, they are more likely to make bad choices. Overall, Wallerstein states, only about half the women and one-third of the men in the group were able to establish successful personal lives by the 25-year mark.

Yet Wallerstein's study is based on just 60 families who voluntarily came to her clinic for counseling and therapy soon after a divorce. Although she screened out children who had seen a mental health professional, many of the parents had extensive psychiatric histories.[4] Troubled families can produce troubled children, whether or not the parents divorce, so blaming the divorce and its aftermath for nearly all the problems Wallerstein saw among the children over 25 years may be an overstatement. Still, I suggest that Wallerstein's study is a valuable description of the lives of children from *troubled* divorced families, one that reveals what can happen to children when conflict or mental health problems accompany a divorce. And many divorcing parents do face the kinds of difficulties Wallerstein saw in her study. Moreover, her basic point that the effects of divorce can sometimes last into adulthood, or even peak in adulthood, is valid. Wallerstein was the first person to write about children who seemed fine in the short term, but experienced emotional difficulties later, in adolescence or young adulthood. In her book on the 10-year follow-up (Wallerstein & Blakeslee, 1989), she called this delayed reaction the "sleeper effect."

But the negative effects of divorce probably are not as widespread as Wallerstein claims. Some portion of what she labels as the effects of divorce on children probably weren't connected to the divorce. And the typical family that experiences divorce won't have as tough a time as Wallerstein's families did. Parents with better mental health than those in her sample can more easily avoid the worst of the anger, anxiety, and depression that comes with divorce. They are better able to maintain the children's daily routines at home or in school. And their children can more easily avoid the extremes of anxiety and self-doubt that plagued the children in Wallerstein's study.

Glass Half-Empty/Half-Full   Rather than solely reflecting Wallerstein's pessimistic picture, the long-term view seems to encompass both a glass-half-full and a glass-half-empty perspective. When parents divorce, or when single parents raise children outside marriage, their children run a higher risk of experiencing undesirable events (such as dropping out of school) in young adulthood and beyond. Nevertheless, most children from single-parent families will not, as a consequence, experience such problems. Hetherington reported that in her 20-year study, 80 percent of the children were eventually able to adapt and become "reasonably well adjusted" (Hetherington & Kelly, 2002). This is not to say that parental divorce has no lasting effect whatsoever on most children. Even young adults who are happy and successful—college graduates with good jobs and good marriages—may nevertheless feel a sense

---

[4] See the appendix to Wallerstein and Kelly (1980).

of loss over or painful memories of childhoods spent coping with parents' divorces (Marquardt, 2005). In the terms of two psychologists, they may show "distress" but not "disorder" (Laumann-Billings & Emery, 2000).

It is possible that some of these long-term difficulties are due to the poor quality of the parents' marriages, rather than to the divorces themselves. A study by Paul R. Amato and Alan Booth (1997) attempted to disentangle these two possibilities. The study began as telephone interviews with a nationally representative sample of married couples in 1980. The interviewers asked their respondents multiple questions on marital quality, including marital happiness, marital interaction (e.g., "How often do you eat your main meals together?"), marital conflict ("How many serious quarrels have you had in the past two months?"), and divorce proneness (e.g., "Has the thought of getting a divorce or separation crossed your mind in the last three years?"). The researchers divided all of the families into two groups, low conflict and high conflict, using all of the information. Then in 1992 all of the children who had lived with their parents in 1980 and who were now age 19 or older were interviewed.

The investigators report that offspring who experienced high marital conflict in 1980 were doing *better* in 1992 if their parents had divorced than if they had stayed together; on the other hand, offspring from low-conflict families were doing worse if their parents had divorced. This finding confirms the oft-stated but rarely substantiated belief that if family conflict is severe, children may benefit from a divorce. But the researchers caution that only a minority of the divorces that occurred were in high-conflict marriages (such as marriages with physical abuse or frequent serious quarrels). For that minority, the consequences of experiencing continuing conflict between their parents probably would have been worse than the consequences of the divorce. But the majority of offspring who experienced parental divorce probably would have been better off if their parents had stayed together.

Genetically-Informed Studies   It is possible that divorce itself is just a marker for other, less observable factors that are the real causes of the seeming effects of divorce on children. One alternative explanation is that parents and children in divorced families share genetic tendencies that make it more likely that the parents will divorce *and* that the children will show behavior problems. If so, then the naïve social scientist, seeing a correlation between parental divorce and children's problems, mistakenly assumes that divorce causes the problems when, in fact, both the divorce and the children's problems are the result of a genetic tendency toward, say, antisocial behavior or depression. If that's the case, we ought to see differences in the responses to divorce between people who share inherited genes and those who do not.

Researchers in the field of behavioral genetics study people of varying degrees of genetic relatedness to see whether evidence exists of possible genetic causes of behavior. One study, for example, compared the academic achievement and behavior problems of children after a divorce in two types of families (O'Connor, Caspi, DeFries, & Plomin, 2000). In the first type, the children were adopted and therefore they shared no genes with their parents. In the second type, the children were the biological offspring of the parents. If the apparent "effects" of divorce are really the effects of common genetically based tendencies, the researchers reasoned, then the adopted children should show fewer difficulties after the divorce because they have not inherited any problematic tendencies from their adoptive parents, whereas the biological children may have. But that is not what they found. Rather, the adopted children showed as many problems as the biological children. This finding, the researchers argued, suggests that divorce may truly have effects on children's behavior since the difficulties the adopted children showed cannot be due to genetic inheritance. Another behavioral genetic study with a different design also suggests that divorce may truly have effects on substance abuse and behavior problems (D'Onofrio et al., 2005). These researchers located pairs of twins in Australia in which one of the twins had divorced and one had not. They then compared the behavior problems of the children of the divorced twin with the problems of their cousins, the children of the nondivorced twin. If problems are driven by genes rather than divorce, they would have expected to find similarities among the cousins because they had genes in common, even though some of them had experienced a divorce and some had not. But they found that divorce made about as much difference in behavior problems among these cousins as it did among unrelated children in the same sample. So the differences among the cousins seem to have been due to something about the divorce rather than to their relatedness.

Some children may have genetic tendencies that make them more sensitive to the effects of living with two biological parents or not. Recent studies are taking advantage of technologies that can analyze a person's genes from DNA that is extracted from a blood sample or a cheek swab. In one study, for instance, the researchers classified adolescents by whether or not they had variant forms of genes that had been associated with antisocial behavior. They then found that adolescents with the variant form of one gene were more likely to engage in serious delinquent behavior (for instance, selling drugs or using a weapon to get something from someone) than were other adolescents if they were living with a single parent or with stepparents. But they were *not* more likely to engage in serious delinquent behavior than were other adolescents if they were living with their two biological parents (Guo, Roettger, & Cai, 2008). This study suggests that it is the interaction of genetic tendencies (whether a child has a predisposition toward greater antisocial behavior) and the family environment (whether a child is living with two biological parents or not) that determines whether children and adolescents exhibit behavior problems such as serious delinquent behavior.

In Sum   Overall, the research literature on the effects of divorce on children suggests the following conclusions:

- Almost all children experience an initial period of intense emotional upset after their parents separate.
- Most resume normal development without serious problems within about two years after the separation.
- A minority of children experience some long-term problems as a result of the breakup that may persist into adulthood.

From the glass-half-empty perspective, we can conclude that divorce may cause a substantial percentage increase in the number of individuals who may need the help of a mental health professional or who may not obtain as much education as they should or who may be unemployed more often than they should. As a society, we should be troubled by this development. From the glass-half-full perspective, however, it seems that most individuals do not suffer serious long-term harm as a result of their parents' divorce. We need to keep both perspectives in mind when considering the effects of divorce.

As noted, a divorce is not the end of the changes faced by many single parents and their children. A majority of the parents will either live with another partner, marry one, or do both. The next chapter explores the determinants and consequences of remarriage. I will postpone an overall discussion of the effects of divorce until the end of that chapter.

Quick Review

- Nearly all children and parents are upset and distressed during the first year or two after the separation, sometimes called the "crisis period."
- The loss of a parent from the home, continuing parental conflict, and multiple transitions are factors that often cause difficulties for children during the crisis period.
- After the crisis period, a majority of children resume normal development, but a minority do experience continuing difficulties.
- For some children, the effects of divorce may last into or even peak in adulthood.
- The difficulties children show after divorce do not merely reflect inherited genetic tendencies.

Looking Back

1. **What is the history of divorce in the United States and other Western nations?** There have been three eras in the history of divorce in modern Western nations. During the first era, which lasted until the middle of the nineteenth century, divorce was very difficult to obtain. It was granted mainly to wealthy men who owned land, usually to ensure that an adulterous wife would not bear a child who would have a claim on the man's property. During the second era, divorce became increasingly available in cases of reprehensible conduct, but was still frowned upon. The third era began in 1970, when the state of California eliminated the need to prove a spouse was at fault to obtain a divorce. Divorce became available on demand, with few restrictions other than a waiting period.

2. **What accounts for the trends in divorce over the past half-century?** Divorce rates rose sharply in the 1960s and 1970s. Since then the overall rate has declined, but most of the decline has occurred among the college educated. This has widened the social class gap in the risk of divorce. Factors contributing to the rise in the 1960s and 1970s include changes in divorce laws, the increased emphasis on self-fulfillment as the central criterion for judging marriages, and the growing economic independence of women. The diverging trends since then may reflect the labor market advantage of college graduates and disadvantage of those without college educations. Wives' employment now seems to reduce the risk of divorce.

3. **What happens to children during the divorce process?** Legally, couples must agree on custody arrangements for their children, if any. States have been moving toward joint legal custody of children; in a small but growing number of cases, parents also share physical custody. Nonresident fathers are more likely to be involved in their children's lives

than a few decades ago. In families in which the father does remain involved, the dominant style of parenting is a detached, low-conflict, low-cooperation mode that can be described as parallel parenting. Economically, the income of mother and children usually falls after a divorce, both because of the mother's lower wages and because many men pay little in child support.

4.   What are the short-term effects of divorce on children?
Divorce has several effects on children. First, one parent, usually the father, leaves the household, depriving the remaining parent of a source of support and help in monitoring and supervising the children's behavior. Second, during the crisis period following the separation, the custodial parent is often upset and angry; consequently, maintaining the children's daily routine and providing emotional support and consistent, moderate discipline can be difficult. In addition, the custodial parent must often cope with a substantial drop in family income.

Third, the child may suffer if he or she is caught up in continuing conflict between the two parents, though the conflict and its negative effects may have preceded the separation. Finally, the sheer number of transitions involved, each requiring adjustment on the children's part, may overwhelm their ability to cope.

5.   What are the long-term effects of divorce on children?
Long-term studies suggest that parental divorce raises the risk of undesirable outcomes in their children, such as dropping out of high school, bearing a child before marrying, or suffering from mental health problems as an adult. But some of the problems that children from divorced families show probably preceded the divorce, and might have occurred even if the parents had not separated. Studies suggest that a majority of children whose parents divorce will not experience serious long-term problems. Genetic studies show that the effects of divorce are not just due to inherited tendencies.

 Go to the Online Learning Center at www.mhhe.com/cherlin7e to test your knowledge of the chapter concepts and key terms.

Study Questions

1. In the era of restricted divorce, how did the rules for granting divorce reinforce male dominance?
2. How is the current era of unrestricted divorce consistent with our more individualistic approach to marriage?
3. What societywide factors were influential in the great rise in divorce rates in the 1960s and 1970s?
4. Why might wives' paid employment outside the home have two—offsetting—effects on the likelihood of divorce?
5. Why is it that couples who cohabit before marrying have a higher divorce rate than couples who marry directly?
6. Do fathers stay in touch with their children after a divorce?
7. What is the evidence that the effects of divorce on children are not simply due to genetic inheritance?
8. Why might the "glass-half-empty/half-full" metaphor fit the effects of divorce on children?

Key Terms

annulment 377	era of restricted divorce 377	legal custody 389
cooperative parenting 391	era of unrestricted divorce 379	no-fault divorce 379
crisis period 394	joint legal custody 389	parallel parenting 391
era of divorce tolerance 378	joint physical custody 389	physical custody 389

Thinking about Families

The Public Family	The Private Family
Should parents in unhappy marriages stay together for the sake of their children?	Why is it emotionally difficult for ex-spouses to establish cooperative parenting relationships after a divorce?

Families on the Internet   www.mhhe.com/cherlin7e

Note: While all the URLs listed were current as of the printing of this book, these sites often change. Please check our Web site (www.mhhe.com/cherlin7e) for updates.

There are numerous Web sites about divorce, most devoted to practical information for people who are about to divorce, in the process of obtaining a divorce, or dealing with postdivorce issues, such as modifying the legal agreement. Balanced overviews are hard to find. In addition to dispensing practical advice, www.divorceonline.com reprints many articles on divorce-related topics.

See also www.divorcesupport.about.com for a sense of the issues of greatest concern to people going through a divorce.

Robert Emery, a professor of psychology at the University of Virginia and an expert on divorce mediation, maintains a useful website with information on divorce and children at www.emeryondivorce.com/.

Chapter Thirteen

Stepfamilies

Looking Forward

An Incomplete Institution?

What Is a Stepfamily?

Stepfamily Diversity

Doing the Work of Kinship

Stepfamilies in Later Life

The Demography of Stepfamilies
and Remarriages

Who Remarries?

Divorce Rates among the Remarried

Building Stepfamilies

The Transitional Period

The Stepparent as Affinity-Seeker

The Stepparent as Polite Outsider

Adjustment of the Stepchildren

Drawing Boundaries

The Stabilization Period

Differences Between the Roles
of Stepmother and Stepfather

**The Effects of Stepfamily Life
on Children**

Cohabiting v. Married Stepfamilies

Age at Leaving Home

**Divorce, Remarriage, and
Stepfamilies: Some Lessons**

The Primacy of the Private Family

New Kinship Ties

The Impact on Children

Looking Back

Study Questions

Key Terms

Thinking about Families

Families on the Internet

FAMILIES AND PUBLIC POLICY: *The Rights
and Responsibilities of Stepparents*

The Origins of the Wicked Stepmother

Looking Forward

1. What is the place of stepfamilies in custom and law?

2. What are the forms of stepfamily life?

3. How do stepparents, parents, and children go about building a stepfamily?

4. How does the well-being of children in stepfamilies compare to the well-being of children in other kinds of families?

5. How have increases in divorce, remarriage, and related trends altered family life?

In 1979, when Danny Henrikson was a year old, his parents divorced. What happened next resulted in a court case that still influences judges today. Danny's mother, Nancy, was awarded custody of his eight-year-old brother, Jay; his three-year-old sister, Joie; and him. Nancy soon married James Gable, and then in 1982 she died. The children's father, Gene Henrikson, agreed that Gable would retain custody of the children. Henrikson moved from Michigan to New York and rarely visited or called his children. Gable, on the other hand, was a devoted stepfather who worked continually with Danny to overcome a learning disorder. In 1983, Jay, who was then 12, visited his father in New York. Upon his return, Jay told Gable that he wanted to live with his father. Gable consented and transferred custody of Jay to Henrikson in New York. Then, at the end of 1985, Henrikson filed a court action seeking custody of Danny and Joie.

At this point, Danny was seven and had lived in Michigan with Gable since he was one. Gable fought the transfer, arguing that it was in Danny and Joie's best interests to remain in the home where they had been, by all accounts, raised well. The trial judge ruled in Gable's favor, writing, "the length of time the children have lived in a stable, satisfactory environment and [the] desirability of maintaining continuity . . . is weighed very strongly on behalf of the Gables." Henrikson, however, appealed to a higher court. In 1987, the Michigan Court of Appeals reversed the decision and awarded custody to Henrikson. Yes, the appeals court judges wrote, an established custody arrangement shouldn't be changed unless doing so is in the best interests of the child. However, another presumption also applied:

> *When the dispute is between the parent or parents and . . . a third person, it is presumed that the best interests of the child are served by awarding custody to the parent or parents. (Henrikson v. Gable, 1987)*

After seven years of being Danny's dad, James Gable was not a parent, in the eyes of the court; rather, he was a "third person." Gene Henrikson, who had moved to New York and had hardly stayed in contact with Danny, was the parent. The appeals court clearly felt that the biological parents remain the legal parents, even if they have little to do with their children; whereas stepparents, even if they have raised the children since infancy, are still the legal outsiders.

■ An Incomplete Institution?

Today, stepparents are still third parties—their rights and responsibilities continue to be limited (Ganong & Coleman, 2004). The law still gives little standing to the relationship between stepparents and stepchildren. In most states, the stepparent has no legal obligation to contribute to the support of the stepchildren, even if he has lived with them for years and the nonresident biological parent has paid nothing. And if the stepparent and the custodial parent end their relationship, the stepparent has no further obligation to support the stepchildren, even if he had been supporting them informally for years. When judges must choose between stepparents and biological parents, observes Chambers, their decisions vary widely from case to case and jurisdiction to jurisdiction. (See *Families and Public Policy:* The Rights and Responsibilities of Stepparents, on page 408.)

The conflict and lack of resolution are even broader. Three decades ago, I published an article titled "Remarriage as an Incomplete Institution" (Cherlin, 1978). Curious about the complex families formed when divorced people remarry, I had reviewed the research literature and interviewed a number of remarried couples in Maryland. In all of them, at least one spouse had children from a previous marriage living in the household. Sometimes both did, but more often the father's children, if any, lived with his former wife. Some of the families also had a mutual child from the new marriage. What I found were people who were working hard to create a coherent family life. Every day they faced issues and problems that people in first marriages never dream of, such as, Does a stepfather have the authority to discipline his stepchild if the child does something wrong? What should a child call the woman his father married after he divorced the child's mother? Where is the "home" of a child who spends four days a week living with his father and three days living with his mother?

These daily problems often cut to the heart of more fundamental questions: What is a family, and what are its boundaries? Who is a relative and who is not? What obligations do adults and children sharing the same household owe to one another? People in first marriages rarely think about these questions because our culture provides us with a set of social roles (patterns of behavior associated with positions in society—in this case, parent, spouse, and child) and social norms (widely accepted rules about how people should behave) that address them. These roles are so ingrained that we take them for granted—we know, for example, who our relatives are; we know what a parent is. The widely accepted, taken-for-granted character of the roles and rules of family life is what makes the family a social institution. Recall that a social institution is a set of roles and rules that define a social unit of importance to society.

But stepfamilies create situations in which the taken-for-granted rules and the well-established roles don't apply. Consequently, stepfamilies must create their own rules, their own shared meanings, through a long and sometimes difficult process of discussion, negotiation, and trial and error. In other words, as I argued in my article, life in stepfamilies is incompletely institutionalized in our society.

As I reflect on this article more than three decades later, I see that stepfamilies are no longer the only "incompletely institutionalized" family form. Cohabiting couples, it has been suggested, have a similar task in creating

The Rights and Responsibilities of Stepparents

Until recently, the legal rights and responsibilities of stepparents with regard to their stepchildren in American and English law could be summed up easily: There weren't any. Even if stepparents had resided with their stepchildren for many years, they had no obligation to support them or to care for them in any way. And even if a stepparent had provided most of the care of the stepchildren for years, the biological parent would still retain custody of the children if the marriage ended. The lowly status of the stepparent extends back hundreds of years in English common law. Under common law, a remarriage did not create any legal link between the stepchildren and their stepparent. "It was as if," British legal scholar Stephen Cretney writes, "the remarriage had never happened" (Cretney, 1993).

Today, 9 in 10 remarriages are formed as a result of divorce rather than widowhood. Children typically reside with a custodial parent, usually their mother, and a stepparent, while a second biological parent resides elsewhere. Consequently, the traditional body of law gives the biological parent who resides outside the home legal priority over the stepparent who lives with the children. So sweeping is this priority that the judge in the Henrikson case was only following standard legal precedent when he gave Danny's biological father in New York custody over the objections of a stepfather who had lived with Danny for years.

The judge's decision stems from a time in which the custody of children was treated fundamentally as a matter of the ownership of property. For children were indeed seen as property a few centuries ago—not because they were unloved but rather because they were valuable sources of labor for a family. A man who remarried after his wife died wanted to protect his children from the claims of his new wife's family. His children

were an important asset. Today, however, our conception of children has changed, and we view them primarily in terms of the emotional and financial investments parents make in them and the emotional gratification parents receive. When courts consider custody and support cases, they usually base their decisions on the standard of what is in the best interests of the child. And it is not clearly in the best interests of children to be removed from homes in which they have been given good care, even if the caregiver was not a biological parent. This is why many people find judges' decisions in cases such as *Henrikson v. Gable* troubling.

Slowly, the law concerning stepparents is changing. In England, the Children's Act of 1989 allows stepparents to assume some responsibilities and gives them the right to petition the court under a number of circumstances (Cretney, 1993). Although the stepparent does not have legal responsibility for the child, if he or she is caring for the child, he or she may do what is reasonable to promote the child's well-being. If the marriage between the parent and the stepparent ends, the stepparent may request that the children live with him or her. (The judge, of course, need not grant this request.) Should the biological parent die, the surviving biological parent has the right to take the children, as happened in the Henrikson case, but the stepparent may ask the court to let the children remain with him or her. Still, the stepparent has no recognized legal status.

In the United States, the practices of the courts seem to be evolving slowly in the direction of recognizing some rights and responsibilities for stepparents. With respect to custody, all states give biological parents priority, but about 60 percent of the states give stepparents the right to ask the court for custody (Hans, 2002). In one Ohio case, the children had been living with their

biological father and their stepmother. After the father died, the court awarded custody to the stepmother, over the objections of the biological mother, ruling that the children viewed their stepmother as their mother figure and that relocating them would have "devastating" and "detrimental" effects on them (*In re Dunn,* 1992). But in general, biological parents are given custody unless there are unusual circumstances. The Montana Supreme Court, in fact, overturned a decision giving custody to a stepparent because, it said, the lower court did not have the "authority to deprive a natural parent of his or her constitutionally protected rights absent a finding of abuse and neglect or dependency" (*In re A.R.A.,* 1996).

I think it is likely that this slow evolution will continue, as parenthood comes to be defined partly in terms of what parents actually do for children, not just whether they are biologically related. This is not to say that the claims of resident stepparents should always win over the claims of biological parents living elsewhere. Yet, given the number of stepparents who are caring for children, it seems time to recognize the importance of their contribution and to provide them with some of the rights and responsibilities that until now have been reserved for biological mothers and fathers.

Ask Yourself

1. Do you know anyone who has been involved in a child custody dispute between a biological parent and a stepparent? If so, in whose favor was the dispute resolved, and on what grounds?

2. Should stepparents be given more rights and responsibilities? What might be the consequences of such a change for stepchildren? For biological parents? For society as a whole?

www.mhhe.com/cherlin7e

meanings and rules for themselves (Nock, 1995). So must gay and lesbian couples; even in states where same-sex marriage is allowed, couples have to develop the kinds of marital relationships make sense for them. Even couples in first marriages have had to negotiate new roles at work and in the home as the old breadwinner-homemaker norms for husbands and wives have become dated. When I wrote the article, I expected that over time remarriage would become more like first marriage—a widely-accepted set of norms and expectations would emerge. Instead, first marriage has become more like remarriage, as first-married couples work to establish marital relationships that are relevant in the twenty-first century. So in some sense, what has happened is not the institutionalization of remarriage and stepfamily life that I expected but rather the *de*institutionalization of life in first marriages (Cherlin, 2004).

Nevertheless, the problem still exists for stepfamilies. Stepparents still have few rights and obligations involving stepchildren. In many states, they still cannot sign a stepchild's field trip permission form. Should a remarriage end in divorce, the stepparent still has no responsibility to provide child support (Mason, Harrison-Jay, Svare, & Wolfinger, 2002). In a book about stepfathers, Marsiglio (2004) writes, "considerable confusion still exists about what norms should guide stepfamily life." The lack of shared meanings can create problems for parents, stepparents, and children. Negotiation and bargaining take time and effort and can cause bruised feelings. To be sure, stepfamilies offer the possibility of creating useful new roles that have no counterparts in first marriages (such as the trusted "intimate-outsider" roles discussed later in this chapter that some stepparents play). Still, institution building is difficult work and takes its toll on stepfamilies.

There are other reasons why we might expect the tasks of family life to be more difficult for stepfamilies than for families formed by first marriages (White, 1994). In terms of social networks, individuals in stepfamilies have ties to different sets of individuals, such as biological parents living elsewhere or children living with another parent. The pull that these networks exert can undermine attempts to strengthen the unity of the stepfamily. In addition, stepparents who join families well after the stepchildren were born do not have the investment of time and effort that the parent already has made; therefore, the role of stepparent may be less central to their identities. Finally, evolutionary psychologists would note that parents pass on their genes to children, whereas stepparents do not pass on genes to stepchildren (Popenoe, 1994). Therefore, they would predict that stepparents would express less warmth and support toward stepchildren, on average, than biological parents, as research on stepfamilies confirms (Hetherington & Jodl, 1994). Despite these limitations, many stepfamilies are successful. How parents and stepparents put their families together, what these families look like, and how they are changing the very nature of family and kinship are the subject of this chapter.

What Is a Stepfamily?

But first, let's think about what constitutes a stepfamily these days. The Henrikson-Gable household, until Nancy Henrikson died, was recognizable as a typical American stepfamily: a mother (Nancy Henrikson), her biological children (Jay, Joie, and Danny), and a husband who was not biologically related to her children (James Gable). It was formed after a divorce, rather than after the death of a biological parent, as are most remarriages today. In 1979, it *was* typical of what we might label the twentieth-century American stepfamily. But because of the great changes in family life since then, the twenty-first-century American stepfamily is more diverse (Stewart, 2007). To be sure, there still are many families that have the same form as the Henrikson-Gable family did. But we now need to expand the concept to other forms: households in which the partners are cohabiting rather than married; households in which the children come not from a previous marriage but from nonmarital relationships; families in which physical custody of the children is shared across two households; and other kinds of families.

STEPFAMILY DIVERSITY

Consider cohabitation. It's even more common for couples to live together prior to a remarriage than it is prior to a first marriage. By some estimates, two-thirds of remarriages are preceded by a period of living together. Moreover, many additional cohabiting unions fit the stepfamily form but never result in marriage, either because the couple breaks up (most commonly) or because they remain together for a long period of time without ever formalizing their relationship through a marriage (less common in the United States than in some European countries). Some of the new partners in these cohabiting families invest enough time and effort into being a presence in the daily lives of their partner's biological children to be considered stepparents by any standard except remarriage. Others, however, remain in the home briefly and never play a role in the children's lives.

Or consider the families that form when a woman who has had a child in a previous relationship but never married the father subsequently marries another man. She and her husband may be in their first marriages, rather than in remarriages, and yet her new family takes on the structure of a stepfamily. In some cases, her previous partner, the father of her child, may continue to be part of the child's life, and the stepfamily will function much the way a remarriage following a divorce often does. In other cases, however, the mother may have had only a casual relationship with the father and he may never have been a part of the child's life. In this case, the family may function more like a conventional first-marriage family. In yet other cases, the mother and the father may have had children with several other partners in a pattern I described earlier as multiple-partner fertility, creating multiple links with previous partners and biological children living elsewhere.

So let me define a **stepfamily** in a broader way than we conventionally have thought of one. It is a household in which

1. Two adults are married or cohabiting, and
2. At least one adult has a child present from a previous marriage or relationship.

This definition does not require that the adults be married. Indeed, under this broad definition, at least one-fourth of stepfamilies involve cohabiting couples rather than married couples, according to national figures. Almost two-thirds of children first enter stepfamily life through cohabitation rather than marriage; in many instances, the cohabiting partners subsequently marry (Bumpass, Raley, & Sweet, 1995). I will use the term **cohabiting stepfamily** to mean only the kind of stepfamily in which the partners are cohabiting; I will use the parallel term **married stepfamily** to mean only those in which the partners are married.

stepfamily a household in which two adults are married or cohabiting and at least one has a child present from a previous marriage or relationship

cohabiting stepfamily a stepfamily in which the partners are cohabiting without marrying

married stepfamily a stepfamily in which the partners are married

Our definition also does not require that the biological parent in the stepfamily was previously married to, and then divorced, the biological father of her children. Rather, it allows for previous relationships to have been outside of marriage. This path is particularly common among African Americans: About two-thirds of African American stepfamilies, under this definition, were preceded by a nonmarital birth rather than a divorce (Bumpass et al., 1995).

This way of conceptualizing stepfamilies is becoming more common in the research literature (Stewart, 2007). But most of the research on stepfamilies has been conducted within the framework of divorce and remarriage because cohabitation did not play a major role until the last few decades. Consequently, much of the research evidence I will present in this chapter will be based on studies of married stepfamilies. This restricted definition, focused on divorce and remarriage, has made it easy for researchers to determine whether a stepfamily actually exists: In addition to the presence of stepchildren, the partners must be married. Under our broader definition of stepfamilies, it may be unclear whether a stepfamily exists. Recall the discussion in Chapter 1 of boundary ambiguity, the state in which family members are uncertain about who is in or out of the family. Only one-half of teenagers who were in cohabiting stepfamilies according to their mothers' reports, you may remember, considered the cohabiting partners to be part of their families, as if their mothers were single parents in the other half. Some of the men in these households may have been more tenuously attached to the family than the mother reported, perhaps not sleeping there some nights; and some of the teenagers may have had distant relationships with men who were present and did not think of them as parent-like figures.

DOING THE WORK OF KINSHIP

If parents and children cannot agree sometimes on whether they are in a stepfamily, how are sociologists to decide? I would suggest that in potentially ambiguous settings, what determines whether a stepfamily exists is not just who is present in the household but also who is investing time and effort into building and maintaining a stepfamily. Stepfamily ties are another example of created kinship, the kind of family tie that individuals must construct actively, rather than relying on legal and socially recognized bonds of "blood" or marriage. **Blood relatives** are people who share common ancestors: parents and children, uncles and aunts, nephews and nieces, grandparents and grandchildren. In theory, this network of blood relatives spreads out to an almost limitless number of people: second cousins (two people whose parents were first cousins), third cousins, and so forth. It spreads out on both the maternal and paternal sides, which is why anthropologists classify the Western countries as having **bilateral kinship,** a system in which descent is reckoned through both the mother's and father's lines (as opposed to kinship systems in which relatives are counted only on the mother's side or only on the father's side). Yet if I were to draw my family tree, I would include very few second cousins and no third or higher-order cousins because I don't know them. A friend of mine whose mother was estranged from her family never saw many of her maternal kin; her family tree includes many more relatives on her father's side than on her mother's side.

As these examples suggest, the mere existence of a blood tie does not make a relative. In American kinship, people must establish a relationship to consider each other kin. Having a relationship means seeing each other

blood relatives people who share common ancestors: parents and children, uncles and aunts, nephews and nieces, grandparents and grandchildren

bilateral kinship a system in which descent is reckoned through both the mother's and father's lines

regularly, corresponding, and/or giving or receiving help—somehow making repeated connections. If there is no relationship, even a blood relative may not be counted as kin. Now, it's true that almost everyone considers their parents and their children to be relatives even if they haven't seen them in a long time. But you would understand what someone meant if she said, "My father left home when I was three and I never saw him again; I don't consider him part of my family." And you might not consider a cousin whom you last met when you were a child to be a relative.

To be a relative, then, you must do the work of creating and maintaining kinship. Among biological parents and children, this happens almost automatically—so much so that we rarely think about it. But among stepparents, it does not happen automatically. For one thing, a stepparent in a remarriage or cohabiting union that has followed a divorce or a nonmarital birth does not replace the stepchild's nonresident parent, as was the case when most remarriages followed a death. Rather, the stepparent adds to the stepchild's stock of potential kin. If both biological parents are still involved in the stepchild's life, it's not clear what role the stepparent is supposed to play.

Still, if the mother and stepfather are married, the chances are good that their union will be recognized by everyone as a stepfamily. But if they are cohabiting, the question of whether a potential stepfather is viewed by those around him as a true stepfather depends almost entirely on how he does the work of creating kinship. A cohabiting father may need to work harder than a married stepfather at developing a relationship with a skeptical teenager. He may have a greater need to go to teacher conferences at the stepchildren's school so that teachers consider him part of the family. Or he may make a special effort to bring the stepchildren back and forth on visits to the biological father and his new family so that they will consider him a stepparent. If instead he is passive or distant, he may never become a stepparent in a meaningful sense. Researchers can still try to identify stepfamilies according to their structure—who is in the household, who has ties to children or parents in other households—and they will be correct in most cases; but at the fuzzy boundaries of stepfamily life, their counts will be approximate. Only direct observations of daily life in the families on the boundary would yield a reliable decision on whether a stepfamily exists. This blurred boundary is one of the consequences of the complexity of early twenty-first century family life.

STEPFAMILIES IN LATER LIFE

People think stepparents and stepchildren are more obligated to help each other the longer the relationship has lasted and the closer they feel emotionally (Ganong & Coleman, 1999). So if stepfamilies break up quickly while children are still young, an ex-stepfather isn't expected to provide support to the stepchildren. (And when the ex-stepfather is older, the now adult stepchildren aren't expected to provide support to him.) Where a stepfamily has existed for a long time—let's say long enough for the stepchildren to grow into young adulthood, and where the stepfather has had a close relationship with them, both are expected to continue to support each other.

Yet it is unclear what happens to most stepfamilies after the children are adults and long out of the home. Do the bonds continue, or does the stepparent-stepchild tie fade away? This is an important question not just in the private-family sense of enduring family bonds but also in the public-family sense of who will care for older Americans. If an older man has seen little of his biological children since his divorce decades ago, he probably cannot rely on them; and he may not be able to count on support from his stepchildren. In general, the relationships between older stepparents and their adult stepchildren are of lower quality than the relationships between older biological parents and their adult biological children (Ward, Spitze, & Deane, 2009). Several factors make a difference, according to a study of adults who, earlier in life, had lived with a stepparent. They were asked to what extent they still considered that person a parent and a member of their family. The adults were much less likely to consider a stepparent a parent and a family member if his or her relationship with their biological parent had ended; 64 percent of those whose parents had ended the relationships did not consider the stepparent a member of their family and 80 percent did not consider the stepparent to be a parent (Schmeeckle, Giarusso, Feng, & Bengtson, 2006). So the stepparent-stepchild bond may not survive the end of the stepparent's relationship with the biological parent; this kinship tie may need continual reinforcement through communication and shared activities. The same study also found that stepparents were more likely to be considered parents and family members if they had married the biological parent and if the stepchild had lived with the stepparent. So a stepparent who comes into a stepchild's life after the stepchild is out of the home, or who never marries the stepmother, often does not establish bonds that could be relied upon for support. The long-term continuation of stepparent-stepchild bonds seems problematic in many cases.

There is also greater variability in how older stepkin relate to stepgrandchildren. When Frank Furstenberg and I carried out a national study of grandparents, we asked them about relationships with stepgrandchildren. The younger the children had been when the grandparents had acquired them by virtue of an adult child's remarriage, the more the grandparents reported feeling that the children were like biological grandchildren. One stepgrandmother, who had not acquired her stepgrandchildren until they were teenagers, was asked what they called her:

> *Harriett. I insisted on that. They started by calling me Mrs. Scott. . . . But from the beginning, you realize, these children were in their teens, and it was hard to accept somebody from an entirely different family, and they didn't know me from Adam. . . . Now if they were smaller—you know, younger—it would have made a difference. (Cherlin & Furstenberg, 1992)*

It also made a big difference whether the stepgrandchildren were living with the grandparents' adult children (as when a son married a woman who had custody of children from a previous marriage) or were living most of the time in another household (as when a daughter married a man whose children lived with his former wife except for every other weekend and a month in the summer). Within these constraints, the closeness of the relationship depended on how much effort the stepgrandparents and their adult children put into creating the relationship. Being a steprelative depends on doing the work of kinship.

THE DEMOGRAPHY OF STEPFAMILIES AND REMARRIAGES

In 2009, 4.8 million children were living with a biological parent and a stepparent who were married. Another 0.5 million were living with a biological parent and a stepparent who were cohabiting. In addition, another large group

Remarriage rates are higher among non-Hispanic whites than among African Americans and Hispanics.

of children, about 4.3 million, were living with both biological parents but had a half-sibling or stepsibling in the household. For example, a child may have been born to married biological parents in a household that included her mother's children from a previous marriage. If we sum up all of these living arrangements, we find that about 9.6 million children were living in households that fit our definition of a stepfamily.[1] That is about 1 out of 8 children in the nation. From a parent's perspective, 11 percent of all fathers of children under 18 were living with at least one stepchild, compared to 3 percent of all mothers—a difference that reflects the tendency for children to remain with their mothers when marriages and cohabiting relationships end.

Who Remarries? We know more about the demography of remarriages (forgetting for the moment whether they comprise stepfamilies). At current rates, about two-thirds of all divorced women will ever remarry (Bramlett & Mosher, 2002). (And recall that about two-thirds of the ones who remarry will cohabit first.) Some divorced persons are more likely to remarry than others. For instance, women who divorce at a younger age are more likely to remarry than those who divorce at an older age (Bramlett & Mosher, 2002). Given the norm that wives should be younger than their husbands, older women face a shrinking marriage market. They are expected to marry from the diminishing pool of older single men, whereas men can choose from the expanding pool of younger women. What is more, the greater financial independence of some older divorced women, who may be more established in their jobs, may make them less interested in remarrying.

In addition, remarriage is more likely among non-Hispanic whites than among Hispanics or African Americans. According to one estimate, 58 percent of

---

[1] Author's estimate from U.S. Bureau of the Census (2011g) and 2011x (2011n).

all divorced non-Hispanic white women will remarry within five years of their separation, compared with 44 percent of Hispanic women and 32 percent of African American women (Bramlett & Mosher, 2002). These differences occur, in part, because remarriage rates are lower for the poor than for the nonpoor. With few assets or little property to pass on to children, people with low incomes have less need for the legal protection marriage brings. Yet lower incomes don't account for the entire difference. The low remarriage rates for African Americans are also consistent with the lesser place of marriage in the African American family. Recall that fewer African Americans ever enter a first marriage and that they take longer to do so than whites. This explanation doesn't apply to Hispanics, whose rates of first marriage are more similar to those of non-Hispanic whites. It is likely that the Catholic Church's opposition to remarriage influences the behavior of this heavily Catholic group. Little good demographic information is available on cohabiting stepfamilies. But we do know that among all previously married adults (whether they have children present from a previous marriage or relationship or not), those who are in cohabiting relationships are less advantaged than those who are in remarriages. They are less likely to have attended college, more likely to have a household income below the poverty level, more likely to be unemployed, and more likely to receive public assistance (Elliott & Lewis, 2010). So it is likely that cohabiting stepfamilies are less advantaged than married stepfamilies.

Divorce Rates among the Remarried Remarriages are somewhat more likely to end in divorce than first marriages. Among women, about 39 percent of remarriages dissolve within 10 years, compared to 33 percent of first marriages (Bramlett & Mosher, 2002). Studies suggest that remarried people tend to express more criticism of spouses and to have more disagreements (Coleman, Ganong, & Fine, 2000). It may be that remarried people, all of whom have already divorced once, are more willing to resort to divorce when their marriages are unsatisfactory than are people in first marriages, or it may be that remarried people, on average, are less skilled in choosing a compatible partner or holding a marriage together. These explanations are another example of a selection effect, the idea that two groups differ because certain kinds of people select (or are selected into) one group more than the other. Alternatively, the greater complexity of remarriages may contribute to the higher risk of divorce. Consistent with this argument, remarriages in which the wife's stepchildren are present have a higher probability of ending in divorce than do remarriages without the wife's stepchildren present (Teachman, 2008).

Despite the prevalence of divorce and remarriage in the United States, as well as the higher divorce rates among the remarried, relatively few people have more than two marriages during their lifetimes. In 2008, just 5 percent of all ever-married people were in a third or higher-order marriage (Elliott & Lewis, 2010). Getting to a third marriage takes time and many life transitions. Typically, a person might live with a partner, marry, divorce, live with one or two partners, remarry, divorce again, live with another partner, and only then remarry for a third time. Some twice-married individuals may be hesitant to attempt marriage again. And people in third (and higher order) marriages are largely white (88 percent in 2008), reflecting higher marriage rates among whites than among minority groups.

Quick Review

- Adults and children in stepfamilies often lack established norms about how to act toward each other.
- Stepfamilies are formed by both cohabitation and marriage. Those formed by cohabitation are less economically advantaged.
- In American kinship, people must do the work of establishing and maintaining a relationship to be considered kin.
- Remarriages are somewhat more likely to end in divorce than are first marriages.

■ Building Stepfamilies

After a divorce or the breakup of a long-term cohabiting relationship, single parents and their children establish, often with some difficulty, agreed-upon roles and new daily schedules. They work out ways of relating to each other that may differ from those of earlier days. A daughter may become a special confidante to her mother; a son may assume new responsibilities, such as taking out the garbage, washing the car, and performing other tasks his father used to do. Put another way, single parents and children create a new family system. Then, into that system, with its shared history, intensive relationships, and agreed-upon roles, walks a stepparent. No wonder members of the stepfamily may have difficulty adjusting to his or her presence.

Table 13.1 summarizes some general ways in which stepparents and stepchildren tend to interact during the life course of a typical stepfamily.

American kinship ties spread out to a potentially large number of people through both one's mother's and one's father's sides.

	STEPPARENT	STEPCHILDREN
Table 13.1 Relations between Stepparents and Stepchildren		
Transitional period (first 2 to 4 years)	Goes from "affinity-seeker" or "polite outsider" to "warm friend"	Young children: Accepting of stepparent Early adolescents: May be distancing and resistant
Stabilization period (subsequent years)	Continued warmth Supportive of biological parent Avoids discipline	Accepting of stepparent (but some long-term problems with late adolescents)

I have labeled the first two to four years as the "transitional period," during which stepfamily members must adjust to the new family system (Bray, 1999). This is a time when parents are trying to build the stepfamily. I have labeled the subsequent years as the "stabilization period," when the new family system is firmly in place in most stepfamilies. These periods are approximate; a given stepfamily might have a shorter or longer transitional period, and some stepfamilies never stabilize.

THE TRANSITIONAL PERIOD

At the start, the stepparent is an outsider, almost an intruder into the system. At first, in what Papernow (1998) calls the "fantasy stage," the stepparent may view himself or herself naively as a healer who will nurse the wounded family back to health. But these initial efforts to help out may backfire. A stepdaughter may resent the intimacy and support a new stepfather provides to her mother; a son may not wish to relinquish certain responsibilities, such as washing the car, to a well-meaning stepfather who thinks fathers are supposed to do those chores. As Furstenberg and I wrote, "Stepparents quickly discover that they have been issued only a limited license to parent." The wiser ones among them accept the limits of their job description and bide their time (Furstenberg & Cherlin, 1991, p. 85). Stepparents who first have this fantasy soon discover that they cannot quickly become full parents to their stepchildren.

The Stepparent as Affinity-Seeker   Instead, most stepparents try to establish a more limited role. Many avoid disciplining their stepchildren and focus on being warm and friendly so that they can induce their stepchildren to begin to like them. In doing so, they become what some observers of stepfamily-building call "affinity-seekers" (Ganong & Coleman, 2004). This strategy—seeking warm, congenial relations with stepchildren—may be the best way for stepparents to establish themselves in the stepfamily. They pay attention to their stepchildren's needs and interests, endeavor to be helpful, and try to do joint activities together. At this early stage, assuming the role of disciplinarian seems to get in the way of establishing warm relationships.

The Stepparent as Polite Outsider   Other stepparents may take on the role of "polite outsider" during the early months of the stepfamily's existence (Hetherington & Stanley-Hagan, 2000). Not only do they avoid discipline but they also make fewer efforts to be friends. Rather, they adopt a more disengaged style and interact with the child less than the biological parent does (Coleman, Ganong, & Fine, 2000). They may even tone down displays of affection and support to the children. But as the family begins to adjust, the stepparent may display more warmth and support, and more actively back up the biological parent in efforts to supervise and discipline the children.

Until recently, there was no agreed-upon word by which a stepchild could call his or her stepparent. But in recent years, the use of the stepparent's first name has become increasingly common. If this usage becomes widespread, it will institutionalize the stepparent's role as neither parent nor stranger, but someone in between. That is, a child doesn't (usually) call a parent by his or her first name, nor use the first name of a stranger. Rather, the first-name usage suggests a role that is akin to that of a kindly uncle or aunt—a relative whom the child likes and can turn to for support, but not someone who has the authority to discipline the child.

Adjustment of the Stepchildren   As for the stepchildren, some show increased behavior problems in the early stage of a stepfamily (Bray, 1999). Some stepchildren also display resistance or hostility toward the stepparent, who may be surprised that his or her overtures are rejected. A key factor in how stepchildren respond is their age when the stepparent joins the household (Coleman, Ganong, & Fine, 2000). Very young children are much more likely to consider a new stepparent a "real" parent (Marsiglio, 1992). While the evidence isn't precise enough to establish an age cutoff, I would speculate that if the stepparent arrives during the preschool years, a parentlike relationship is possible; but if the stepparent arrives in later years, that kind of relationship is much harder to establish. Still, if the stepparent arrives during the stepchild's elementary school years, the stepchild will probably accept the stepparent after an initial adjustment period. The outlook is especially favorable if the stepparent is a man (which is usually the case) and the stepchild a boy (Hetherington & Stanley-Hagan, 2000), because young boys seem to accept stepfathers more easily than young girls do.

Research suggests that the most difficult time to start a stepfamily is when the children are in early adolescence (about ages 11 to 14). For both girls and boys, the transition to adolescence is a difficult time in which to adjust to a remarriage (Hetherington & Jodl, 1994). This is a time when children must come to terms with their own burgeoning sexuality. Having a parent's adult sexual partner move into the house—especially one for whom the traditional incest taboos do not hold—may be disconcerting.

Drawing Boundaries   Beyond establishing stepparent-stepchild relationships, the task of the remarried couple is to create a shared conception of who is in their family and how their family is to go about its daily business. They cannot rely on generally accepted norms, as adults in first marriages do, because few norms exist. Yet it is difficult for the couple to draw a boundary around their family because of continuing ties between stepchildren and the biological parents they don't live with, which can create ambiguity. Is a stepchild who lives with you every other weekend part of your family? In fact, the remarried couple may not even agree on who lives in their household and who lives elsewhere: In one national survey in which both spouses were asked about children of theirs or their partners living in their homes or elsewhere, one-fourth of the couples with stepchildren gave different answers (Stewart, 2005).

Children making the transition to adolescence sometimes have a difficult time adjusting to a remarriage.

THE STABILIZATION PERIOD

Most stepfamilies come through the transition period successfully and form lasting bonds. As children emerge from early adolescence, relations with their stepparents generally improve. Even in stable stepfamilies, however, few stepparents take on a fully parentlike role. Instead, they perform a stepparent role that includes (1) warmth toward, and support of, the stepchildren; (2) little disciplining of the stepchildren; and (3) support for the biological parent's child-rearing style (Hetherington & Stanley-Hagan, 2000).

In sum, those stepparents who manage to integrate into the stepfamily successfully often play a valued role that is somewhere between that of parent and trusted friend—what one family therapist calls an **intimate outsider** role (Papernow, 1998). Teenage stepchildren, for example, may feel close enough to their stepparents to discuss with them issues that are too highly charged to discuss with their biological parents, such as sex, drugs, or their feelings about their parents' divorces. As one stepmother told Papernow:

> *Mary calls me her "motherly friend." Sometimes I think of myself as her mentor. I'm the one who helped her decide she could be an architect.*
> *She confides deeply in me, and it is such an honor and a pleasure to be so intimately involved in guiding her life, and yet to be seen as someone with enough distance that she can trust me not to take what she says personally. It is worth all the struggle to have this relationship with her. (Papernow, 1988)*

Stepparents can also influence their children indirectly. In a study of 36 actively involved stepfathers in Florida, Marsiglio (2004) focuses on what he calls overlooked aspects of stepfathering. He argues that stepfathers help to build up stepchildren's "social capital"—their connections to the outside world and the resources they can draw upon. A stepfather, for example, may take the lead in talking with teachers and guidance counselors about a child's problem in school.

intimate outsider a person, such as a stepparent, who plays a role in a family that is somewhere between that of a parent and that of a trusted friend

The Origins of the Wicked Stepmother

"It is, perhaps, too much to expect that the second wife of a working man should have the same affection toward her husband's children by a former wife as towards her own," wrote Dr. Barnardo, a nineteenth-century English philanthropist and child welfare advocate. "But case after case has come before us in which the jealousy of a stepmother has led to the most cruel treatment of the little folks committed to her charge."[1] The good doctor was repeating a charge against stepmothers that is hundreds, if not thousands, of years old. For further confirmation, just ask Cinderella or Snow White. Where did this view of stepmothers come from, and how does it relate to stepmothers today?

The prefix "step" in Old English signified a family relationship caused by death. In fact, "stepchild" originally meant "orphan," and "stepmother" can be rendered as "one who becomes a mother to an orphan." The common meaning of stepmother, however, was a woman who married a man whose wife had died. The term has long had the connotations of cruelty, neglect, and jealousy. Pliny the Elder wrote in the first century A.D., "It is

far from easy to determine whether she [Nature] has proved to man a kind parent or a merciless stepmother." Leonardo da Vinci, perhaps cribbing from Pliny, asked of Nature, "wherefore art thou thus partial, becoming to some of thy children a tender and benignant mother, to others a most cruel and ruthless stepmother?" Shakespeare had the Queen say in *Cymbeline* that "you shall not find me, daughter, after the slander of most stepmothers, evil-eyed unto you."[2] Numerous fairy tales contrast the wicked, jealous stepmother to the kindly but unfortunately deceased mother.

These connotations are rooted in the reality of stepfamilies in preindustrial societies. Because of the amount of labor it took to provide food, clothes, and shelter and to raise children, a family needed two parents in order to subsist. Yet it was common for a parent to die before her or his children reached adulthood. In particular, women faced a substantial risk of dying in childbirth. If a mother of small children died, her husband had no choice but to remarry quickly. Alone, he simply could not farm the land, perform household tasks, and care for his children. If he attempted to do so, he might

be risking his children's lives. Moreover, the strong patriarchal norms of preindustrial Western society discouraged him from even trying. Rather, economic necessity and social norms led him to remarry after a short period of mourning—often within several months (Mitterauer & Sieder, 1982).

Under these circumstances, the husband's remarriage choices were often limited. It was common for a second or third wife to be considerably younger than the husband—indeed, sometimes decades younger. These large age differences and the patriarchal norms sometimes led the husband to treat his second wife as if she were a child rather than a spouse (Mitterauer & Sieder, 1982). The young stepmother was relatively powerless before the older husband. In addition, she had little authority over the older children in the household, who could be roughly her age.

The stepmother's best strategy for gaining some power within the household was to bear and raise her own children. They would at least be bound to her by the typical emotional bonds between mother and child. As her biological children grew, she would be able to

Marsiglio also found that stepfathers sometimes become allies of the biological father in ways that help stepchildren, such as by discouraging the mother from saying negative things about the biological father in front of the children, encouraging the children to communicate with their father, and even suggesting directly to the father that he ought to keep in touch more often. Active stepfathers such as these often find that their involvement with stepchildren alters their sense of themselves, such as by deepening their sense of purpose and responsibility. They are, however, a minority. Stepfathers in general tend to invest less time and effort in their stepchildren's lives than do biological fathers. They may be focused on their marital or cohabiting relationship; they may find it difficult to find a place in the mother-child family system; or they may feel less interest in stepchildren than biological children because they are not genetically related to them (Coleman, Ganong, & Fine, 2000).

One leading researcher cautions, however, that a minority of stepchildren may be well-behaved until late adolescence or young adulthood, when they begin to show more stress and behavior problems (Bray, 1999). This phenomenon is

The wicked stepmother is a staple of fairy tales such as Hansel and Gretel.

influence their actions; and in her old age, they would be more likely to provide for her.

One could therefore imagine a stepmother's desire to advance her biological children's interests within the household and her jealousy over the advancement of her stepchildren. One could also imagine that her stepchildren would be angry at her

and resent her biological children. And one could imagine the appeal of a story in which the stepmother wants her biological daughters, not her stepdaughter, to meet the prince at the ball. From household dynamics such as these, the malevolent image of the stepmother may have been formed.

Today, as noted earlier, the vast majority of remarriages are formed as a result of divorce rather than widowhood. If there are stepchildren, they probably live for most of the week with their biological mother, who, unlike the situation in the past, is still alive. The age difference between spouses in remarriages, although greater, on average, than in first marriages, is probably smaller than in the preindustrial past. Husbands and wives relate to each other as emotional equals more than in the past. The most direct route for wives to gain power in the household is not to raise loyal children but rather to work for pay outside the home. In all these ways, stepmothers today face a situation so different from the past that perhaps we shouldn't even use the same term. In fact, Hallmark has stopped publishing greeting cards that use the word "step" (Morello, 2011). The French have dropped the old,

pejorative term for stepmother, *marâtre,* and replaced it with *belle-mére,* literally "fine" or "beautiful" mother, a term which also means "mother-in-law." French scholars of the family lament the absence of a prefix, such as "step," with which to precisely label relationships brought about by remarriage. But the *belles-méres* of France may be fortunate that, unlike their Anglo American counterparts, they no longer have to bear the stigma of an outmoded, archaic term.

Ask Yourself

1. Do you know anyone who fits the description of a wicked stepmother? Do you know anyone who might be described as a *belle-mére?*

2. If folktales like *Cinderella* and *Snow White* were based on real problems of the past, what kind of conflict would a modern-day children's tale describe?

[1] *Day and Night,* May 1885, p. 74. Cited in Cretney (1993).
[2] The quotations from Pliny the Elder and da Vinci are cited in Bartlett's Familiar Quotations. The quotation from Shakespeare is cited in Cretney (1993).

www.mhhe.com/cherlin7e

similar to the "sleeper effect" Wallerstein (Wallerstein, Lewis, & Blakeslee, 2000) and others have noted. It occurs at a time when children begin to establish their own identity and independence, which may require some distancing from their parents. Bray (1999) speculates that older adolescents may once again be coming to terms with their parents' divorces. Unfortunately, stepparents may react with dismay and disengage even more from their stepchildren.

DIFFERENCES BETWEEN THE ROLES OF STEPMOTHER AND STEPFATHER

During this process, being a stepmother can be harder than being a stepfather. Prior to the twentieth century, most stepmothers moved into a household in which the children's mother had died—an event for which they were sometimes blamed. (See The Origins of the Wicked Stepmother.) In the typical stepfamily system today, the children live with their biological mother and a stepfather; they visit their biological father and his new partner, their stepmother. Consequently, the typical stepmother does not live with her stepchildren; rather, she must establish a relationship during the visits. She is usually dealing with children whose primary tie is to their biological mother, with whom she must compete. Stepmothers who do not live with their stepchildren are less likely to take on a parental role and more likely to see themselves as friends or extended family member of the stepchildren; and they tend to find stepmothering more stressful than do stepmothers who live with their stepchildren (Stewart, 2007).

In contrast, stepfathers compete with noncustodial fathers, some of whom, as has been discussed, see little of their children. Stepfathers, in other words, can often fill a vacuum left by the departed biological father, whereas stepmothers must crowd into the space already occupied by the biological mother. Studies suggest that many children are able to accept two father figures (e.g., a biological father and a stepfather) (White & Gilbreth, 2001), but it may be more difficult for them to accept two mother figures. Moreover, stepmothers may judge themselves according to the culturally dominant view that a mother should play the major role in rearing children; if so, they may fall short of these high standards. Stepfathers, in contrast, may hold themselves to the lower standard that a father is supposed to provide support to the mother but let her do most of the hands-on child rearing. If so, they may feel satisfied with their role performance, even if they are doing less than many dissatisfied stepmothers (Ganong & Coleman, 2004).

Quick Review

- Parents and children build a stepfamily during a transitional period of two to four years.
- Relationships solidify during a stabilization period.
- Stepmothers often face different tasks than stepfathers do.

The Effects of Stepfamily Life on Children

You might think that the addition of a stepparent would improve the overall well-being of children whose parents had divorced. For one thing, when a single mother finds a new partner, her household income usually rises dramatically because men's wages are so much higher, on average, than women's wages. Consequently, if a decline in the standard of living hurts the well-being of children in single-parent families, an increase after the mother starts a new partnership should improve it. In addition, the stepparent adds a second adult to the home. He or she can provide support to the custodial parent and back up the custodial parent's monitoring and control of the children's behavior. A stepparent can also provide an adult role model for a child of the same gender.

Despite these advantages, children in stepfamilies show lower levels of well-being than children in two-biological-parent families (Sweeney, 2010). In fact, some studies find no difference between children in stepfamilies and children in single-parent families (Ganong & Coleman, 2004). To be sure, most children in stepfamilies do not demonstrate serious problems (Hetherington & Jodl, 1994). But the risk of having problems is higher in stepfamilies. For instance, psychologists studied 100 stepfamilies and 100 first-marriage families, then followed most of them for three to four years (Bray, 1999). The project included extensive interviews, psychological assessments, and videotapes of family interactions. The authors reported that 20 percent of the children in step-families had clinically significant behavior problems, compared to 10 percent of the children in first-marriage families—results similar to those of the Hetherington and Clingempeel study.

In addition, the sheer number of family transitions might impair the adjust-ment of children in stepfamilies (Coleman, Ganong, & Fine, 2000). Having coped with a divorce, and possibly with the introduction of a live-in part-ner, these children must now cope with another major change in their family system. Some studies, as noted previously, have found a relationship between the number of family transitions a child has experienced, on the one hand, and behavior problems and subsequently bearing a child before marrying. Finally, children and parents with certain unknown personal characteristics that impair family cohesion could be self-selecting into the population of divorced and remarried families.

COHABITING V. MARRIED STEPFAMILIES

Moreover, the well-being of children in cohabiting stepfamilies may be lower than that of children in married stepfamilies (Sweeney, 2010). For instance, adolescents in cohabiting stepfamilies are more likely to drink or smoke (Brown & Rinelli, 2010). A study showed that they were more likely to engage in antisocial behavior such as stealing, getting suspended from school, or run-ning away from home (Apel & Kaukinen, 2008). Not all studies show differ-ences, but enough evidence exists to question whether children benefit from the addition of a cohabiting stepparent to their households.

There are plausible reasons why cohabiting stepparents may be problem-atic for children. First, a wide variation exists in the level of commitment and involvement among cohabiting stepparents. They have no clearly defined obligations—their role is even less institutionalized than is the role of the mar-ried stepparent. There is no wedding ceremony, no public acknowledgment of a cohabiting stepparent's entry into the household. Some cohabiting step-parents may be very engaged with the children whereas others have little to do with them. Second, many cohabiting partnerships are short-term; cohabit-ing stepparents may have recently arrived and may soon be gone. They may not see themselves as stepparents, and the stepchildren may not see them as such—as was the case in the survey of mothers and their adolescent chil-dren who differed in their reports on whether a stepfather was present in the household, as discussed in Chapter 1 (Brown & Manning, 2009). This bound-ary ambiguity probably reflects men who have an intimate relationship with the mother, spend most nights in the household, but do not engage the chil-dren. It is these kinds of cohabiting stepparents who are of little benefit to the children. Other stepparents, in contrast, may involve themselves in children's lives and become valued members of the family.

AGE AT LEAVING HOME

One finding about the long-term effects on children of having lived in a step-family is well established. Children in stepfamilies—particularly girls—leave their households at an earlier age than children in single-parent households or two-parent households (Coleman, Ganong, & Fine, 2000). They leave earlier either to marry or to establish independent households prior to marrying. An analysis of a large, six-year national study of high school students showed this pattern for girls (Goldscheider & Goldscheider, 1993). In a British study, 23-year-olds who had left their parental homes were asked the main reason why they had left. Demographer Kathleen Kiernan reported that those who had lived in stepfamilies were substantially more likely to have said that they had left due to "friction at home" than those who had not lived in stepfamilies (Kiernan, 1992). Again, the differences were greater for girls. An analysis of the National Survey of Families and Households found that girls who had lived in a stepfamily were more likely to have left home by age 19 to marry or to live independently than girls who had lived with a single parent or with two parents; the differences were much weaker for boys. If a girl had also lived with stepsiblings, her likelihood of leaving home by age 19 was even higher (Aquilino, 1991). The "friction" in the household may be due to the disruption of the mother–daughter bond or to the presence of the mother's male sexual partner, whose relationship to the daughter is ambiguous.

Quick Review

- The well-being of children in stepfamilies is lower than that of children in two-biological-parent families and roughly equivalent to that of children in single-parent families.
- The number of transitions children have experienced may impair their adjustment to stepfamilies.
- Children in stepfamilies leave home at an earlier age than children in two-biological-parent or single-parent households.
- Children in cohabiting stepfamilies seem to fare worse than children in married stepfamilies.

Divorce, Remarriage, and Stepfamilies: Some Lessons

What can be learned from these two chapters on divorce, remarriage, and stepfamilies? The evidence we have reviewed suggests three themes. First, the emphasis on personal fulfillment, the growth of women's economic independence, and the worsening economic prospects for young men since 1973 have made marriage more fragile than a half-century ago. There is simply less glue holding couples together. This is particularly true for young adults without college educations, who have been hit the hardest by the globalization and automation of production. Second, divorce, remarriage, nonmarital childbearing, and cohabitation are increasing the frequency with which people create their own kinship ties out of the many possibilities available to them—rather than accepting the set of relatives that automatically come with first marriages. These efforts, like the efforts of poor people in creating sharing networks and of gay men and lesbians in constructing families of choice, are changing the nature of kinship. Third, the increases in single-parent families and stepfamilies have altered many children's lives, causing short-term distress, increasing the risk of long-term harm, but leaving the majority relatively unscathed. Let us consider the implications of the developments.

THE PRIMACY OF THE PRIVATE FAMILY

The first theme, it seems to me, is this: The transformation of divorce from a highly restricted device used by wealthy men to protect against unwanted heirs, to a frowned-upon but tolerated option for disastrous marriages, and finally to an individual right for anyone whose marriage isn't personally fulfilling, represents a triumph of the private family. The changes in divorce law mirror changes in the way marriage has been viewed. Once it was an economic partnership in which sentiment was secondary and men were the masters of their homes. The public functions of marriage were dominant: reproducing the population (which wasn't an easy task given widespread disease and poverty), educating children, preparing them for their adult roles, and caring for the ill and the elderly. This is not to say that people didn't find their marriages satisfying, but satisfaction was likely to come primarily from keeping a family alive and fed, from passing one's craft on to one's children, or from marrying a daughter into a good family.

Those days are gone. With the rise of the private family in the twentieth century, marriage is now primarily an instrument of individual fulfillment, a means of personal growth, an expression of romantic love. As such, it is much more fragile, more vulnerable to crises, than ever before (Coontz, 2005). When men and women each specialized in certain tasks and pooled their labor, their economic partnership tied them together. Now that the division of labor is less pronounced and men and women are more economically independent of each other, marriage is held together mainly by the bonds of sentiment.

It is easy to criticize the narcissistic excesses of the search for personal fulfillment in marriage. But the expansion of private life has been a great social advance. It is an advance that the standard of living of most people in our society is high enough that they need not concern themselves daily with sustenance. It is an advance that they no longer need to labor 12 hours a day on the farm or in the factory. It is an advance that they have the time to pursue gratifying intimate relationships and that they have the luxury of marrying purely for love.

The changing nature of marriage has also been an advance for women. Once unable to sever a marriage unless they were subject to terrible cruelty, women (and men) now have the ability to divorce unilaterally. This option must provide them with greater leverage against the worst excesses of husband dominance. Nor do they need to marry as much as their ancestors did. Yet the gains for women have come at a price. A half-century ago, when divorce was more difficult to obtain and stigmatizing to live with, wives who specialized in rearing children could be reasonably sure that their husbands would not abandon them. It was safe for them to withdraw from the labor market and let their earning power atrophy because their husbands, according to the bargain, would have to provide for them. Today they no longer have that protection. Choosing to be a homemaker is far riskier than it was in the 1950s. Just ask any of the older, divorced women who lived up to their part of the breadwinner–homemaker bargain only to see their husbands leave them.

A central contradiction of the current era of divorce, then, is that the law assumes that husbands and wives are economic equals, when in fact they still are not. To be sure, women's wages have increased enough that life as a single parent is much more feasible than it was a few decades ago. Still, if a woman chooses to end her marriage, she must often accept a steep drop in her standard of living, like a nun taking a vow of poverty before entering an order. And if a woman chooses to stay home and raise children, she cannot count on the lifetime support of her husband.

Men, however, are not the winners in every divorce. They, too, pay a cost under the new regime. The men who have gained the most are those who care the least about their children. Divorce law allows these men to walk away from their wives and children for a modest monthly fee; sadly, many do. The men who pay the highest price are those who care the most about being a daily part of their children's lives—for they no longer have the guarantee that if they fulfill their husbandly responsibilities, their wives will remain with them. On the contrary, if their wives initiate a divorce, they know they are likely to lose custody of their children, or at best to share it.

What, then, would we expect prudent women and men to do to protect themselves in the current system of unilateral divorce? A woman would be wise to develop good labor market skills in young adulthood and to maintain a connection to the labor market throughout her child-rearing years. In fact, the trends in married women's employment are consistent with this strategy. A man who cares about living with his children would be wise to spend a substantial amount of time on child rearing throughout his marriage. That way, his claims to his children will be far stronger in a custody dispute, should one arise. And men are indeed doing more child rearing than their fathers did. Given the rewards and costs of the new system, we are likely to see continued investment by married women in developing job skills and careers and increased investment by men in caring for their children.

NEW KINSHIP TIES

Divorce, nonmarital childbearing, cohabitation, and remarriage are altering kinship in two fundamental ways that aren't yet fully appreciated. First, they are breaking the correspondence between family and household. Until recently, the unchallenged family unit in Western nations was the conjugal family of husband, wife, and children residing in the same household. At some points in the life cycle of the family they might have welcomed elderly parents, or young servants and apprentices, into their household. They also had many relatives living in other households. There was, however, a clear demarcation between the members of one's own household, who were the core of the family system, and those beyond the household's boundaries, who were the periphery. The correspondence between family and household is so deeply ingrained that we take it for granted. For example, our entire government apparatus for collecting statistics on "families" actually surveys households. The official Bureau of the Census definition of a family is two or more people living in the same household and related by blood, marriage, or adoption. It is not clear how long this definition will survive. Statistically, we may have to give up the idea that we can count families simply by knocking on doors. We may have to accept that a family can be defined only in reference to a person, not a household.

Stepfamilies are increasing the importance of created kinship ties that people such as these stepsiblings have to actively construct.

Second, the rise in divorce, nonmarital childbearing, cohabitation, and remarriage is increasing the importance of what I have called created kinship, the ties that people have to actively construct, as opposed to assigned kinship, the ties that people automatically acquire at birth or through first marriage. In this regard, kinship after relationship dissolution and repartnering is similar to the extended kin networks among low-income and racial-ethnic populations and to the efforts of gay men and lesbians to form alternative families. In all these situations, individuals find it in their interest to build their own family ties and to create families of choice. Being a father or a mother was once a status assigned to a person automatically at the birth of his or her child. To be sure, people have children through their own efforts; nevertheless, one does not have to do anything else to be a parent, nor can one easily resign from the post. Being a grandparent was ascribed similarly. All that is still the case when children are born to, and raised by, two married parents.

The creation of stepfamilies, though, adds a number of other potential kinship positions. Whether these positions are filled depends on the actions of the individuals involved. The most obvious positions are stepfather and stepmother. This chapter has described the wide variation in the roles step-parents play. Some are parentlike figures who are intensely involved with their stepchildren. Many others are more like friends or uncles and aunts. Others, particularly stepparents who don't live with their stepchildren every day, are more distant. In all cases, how much like a family member a stepparent becomes depends in large part on the effort he or she puts into developing a close relationship with stepchildren and also on the stepchild's actions. Intergenerational ties to stepgrandparents are even more dependent on individual action; they range from no contact to a kinlike role, depending in large part on the investment the stepgrandparents make.

Yet the challenge of created kinship is as follows: Kinship ties that can be created by people's actions can also be ended by lack of action. In contrast, it is much harder to end assigned kinship ties. Therefore, created kinship ties are more likely to change over the course of one's life than assigned kinship ties. Created ties may even change from year to year, as a stepparent moves into or out of the household or as contact diminishes with a stepgranddaughter who moves out of state. Just as containment within one household made families easy to spot, so, too, assignment at birth and first marriage made kinship easy to track. Now, family and kinship require new mental maps that can change from year to year. We are just beginning to draw them.

THE IMPACT ON CHILDREN

There is, finally, the important question of the effects of divorce and stepfamily life on children. I would argue that the effects are neither minor nor massive. On the one hand, the evidence suggests that most children who experience these events do not have serious, long-lasting problems because of them. On the other hand, it is clear that a minority of children do experience lasting problems that appear to be caused by divorce and remarriage. Some of these problems might have occurred even if the children's families had remained intact. Other problems, though, seem clearly linked to the disruption and its aftermath.

Let us suppose, for the sake of argument, that 10 percent of children from two-parent families will grow up to have serious mental health problems as adults. Further, let us suppose that the prevalence of serious mental health problems is twice as high—20 percent—among children in single-parent families and stepfamilies. A little algebra will show that if 4 in 10 children experience single-parent and stepfamily life (as current levels imply), the overall rate of serious mental health problems in the population would rise to 14 percent when this generation reaches adulthood.[2] An overall rise from an expected 10 percent (if there were no breakups in the population) to 14 percent may not seem like much. But it would require a 40 percent expansion of mental health facilities around the country and the training of 40 percent more mental health professionals. At current population levels, it would alter the lives of an additional three million people in each generation. It would mean that about 1 in 7, rather than 1 in 10, adults might need clinical help. In sum, it would mean a significant decline in mental health.

Consequently, even if only a minority of children will experience long-term problems, we should be troubled by this possibility. Some people might wish to work toward reducing the divorce rate, and it has declined for the better educated. But we might also wish to assist divorcing parents and children. We might promote conflict-resolution strategies for divorcing couples, urge that children be kept out of conflict, and provide guidelines on how to minimize the impact of divorce. We might wish to encourage support groups and services in schools. In sum, we might take whatever steps we can to reduce the negative effects of divorce, remarriage, and stepfamily life on children.

[2] $(.40 \times .20) + (.60 \times .10) = .14$, or 14 percent.

Quick Review

- The growing emphasis on personal fulfillment has made marriage more fragile.
- Newer living arrangements are increasing the frequency with which people are creating their own kinship ties.
- The changes in single-parent families have altered children's lives.

Looking Back

1. **What is the place of stepfamilies in custom and law?** Stepfamilies do not have a clear place in our laws or in our customs and norms. In many respects, a stepparent remains "a legal stranger" to his or her stepchildren. Courts give stepparents few rights and few responsibilities. In American society there is little agreement about how the members of a stepfamily should customarily behave toward each other. Consequently, stepfamily members must establish ways of behaving without much guidance from social norms and customs. This process can be long and difficult.

2. **What are the forms of stepfamily life?** Stepfamilies take many forms. Some display the remarriage-after-divorce-based form that was dominant in the twentieth century: two married parents, at least one of them in second marriage, and at least one stepchild. But a majority of all stepfamilies today begin with a cohabiting couple and stepchildren. These cohabiting stepfamilies tend to either formalize their ties by marrying at some point or they break up. Some stepfamilies are formed after a mother has a child outside of marriage as a single parent and then begins a relationship with a new partner. A broad definition of stepfamilies is needed to encompass these and other forms.

3. **How do stepparents, parents, and children go about building a stepfamily?** During the transitional period, which can last two to four years or even longer, stepparents and stepchildren adjust to each other's presence. Successful stepparents often play the roles of "affinity-seekers" or "polite outsiders." With time they often become a "warm friend" to stepchildren, a trusted and liked figure who does not discipline them or wield authority. Stepchildren need time to adjust to a remarriage and sometimes show increased behavior problems. Young children are more likely to accept a stepparent quickly; children in early adolescence, who are dealing with the changes of puberty, can be resistant to a new stepparent. In the long run, most stepchildren do adapt successfully to the addition of a stepparent to the family.

4. **How does the well-being of children in stepfamilies compare to the well-being of children in other kinds of families?** Many studies show that the well-being of children in stepfamilies is no better, on average, than the well-being of children in divorced, single-parent households. Both groups show lower levels of well-being than children in biological two-parent families. Several studies show that children in stepfamilies, especially girls, leave home earlier than children in other families. Children in cohabiting stepfamilies appear to fare worse than children in married stepfamilies.

5. **How have increases in divorce, remarriage, and related trends altered family life?** Divorce, nonmarital childbearing, cohabitation after divorce, and remarriage have altered family life in important ways. Because of the emphasis on personal fulfillment and the economic independence of women and men, marriages are now more fragile and vulnerable to crises. The nature of kinship has been altered, and the correspondence between household and family is breaking down. People are constructing new kinship ties to fit the new stepfamilies they have formed. While these new family forms cause short-term distress for many children and increase the risk of long-term harm to them, the majority of stepchildren grow up without serious long-term problems.

Go to the Online Learning Center at www.mhhe.com/cherlin7e to test your knowledge of the chapter concepts and key terms.

Study Questions

1. In what sense is remarriage an "incomplete institution"?
2. What are the different forms that stepfamilies can take on?
3. What happens to stepfamilies in later life when stepparents and stepchildren are older?
4. How do stepparents and stepchildren decide who is related to them and who isn't?
5. What challenges do stepparents and stepchildren face in the first few years as they attempt to build a stepfamily?
6. What kind of role do stepparents settle into after the stepfamily has existed for several years?
7. What is the origin of the myth of the wicked stepmother?
8. Why isn't the well-being of children in stepfamilies better than that of children in single-parent families?
9. How concerned should we, as a society, be about the effects of divorce and remarriage on children?

Key Terms

bilateral kinship   411
blood relatives   411
cohabiting stepfamily   410
intimate outsider   419
married stepfamily   410
stepfamily   410

Thinking about Families

The Public Family	The Private Family
By and large, do stepfamilies do a good enough job of raising the next generation?	What are the sources of the tension that sometimes exists between stepparents and stepchildren?

Families on the Internet   www.mhhe.com/cherlin7e

Note: While all the URLs listed were current as of the printing of this book, these sites often change. Please check our Web site (www.mhhe.com/cherlin7e) for updates.

There are few sources of information on the number and composition of stepfamilies. The best demographic information comes from the U.S. government's Survey of Income and Program Participation, which collects information on how each person in the household is related to all the others. Its most recent portrait of stepchildren—in both cohabiting stepfamilies and married stepfamilies—is available as a report, "Living Arrangements of Children, 2009." See http://www.census.gov/prod/2011pubs/p70-126.pdf.

There are many organizations devoted to assisting stepparents and stepchildren. These include the Stepfamily Foundation, http://www.stepfamily.org, and the National Stepfamily Resource Center, http://www.stepfamilies.info. Visit their web sites for information, reports, articles, and advice about stepfamily life.

Part Six

Family and Society

Where do all the great social changes of the twentieth century leave the institution of the family? • Chapter 14 examines government policy toward families. We begin by studying the relationship in the past and present between the family and the state. An understanding of conservative and liberal interpretations of this relationship helps one better comprehend current political debates. We then turn to some important issues affecting families, such as "welfare reform." Next, we turn to two contemporary family issues. First, work–family balance: how to help employed parents manage the demands of their work and family lives. Second, marriage: whether to promote marriage and how to respond to court decisions favorable to same-sex marriage.

Chapter Fourteen

The Family, the State, and Social Policy

Looking Forward
The Development of the Welfare State
The Welfare State
The Rise and Fall of the Family Wage System
Family Policy Debates
The Conservative Viewpoint
The Liberal Viewpoint
Which Families Are Poor?
Practical Compromises
The Earned Income Tax Credit
The 1996 Welfare Reform Law
Reasons for the Policy Reversal
The Effects of Welfare Reform
Current Debates
Marriage Promotion
Same-Sex Marriage

Nonmarital Childbearing
Single-Parent Families
National Health Insurance
Responsible Fatherhood
Work–Family Balance
Family Policy in the 2010s
Looking Back
Study Questions
Key Terms
Thinking about Families
Families on the Internet
Boxed Features
FAMILIES AND PUBLIC POLICY: *The Abortion Dilemma*
FAMILIES AND THE GREAT RECESSION: *"The Safety Net"*

Looking Forward

1. What is the "welfare state"?

2. What are the themes that conservatives and liberals stress in debating family policies?

3. Why was the 1996 welfare reform law a sharp break from earlier government policies toward low-income families?

4. What should be the government's stance toward marriage?

5. How much should the government assist low-income families and middle-class working parents?

Consider two hypothetical families. In family A, a poor single mother struggles to raise two children. She receives cash assistance and food stamps from the government. When she or her children are sick, they visit the emergency room at the local hospital, where their care is paid for through Medicaid, the federal program of health insurance for the poor. She lives on the 15th floor of a publicly owned housing project that charges less for rent than she would pay if she rented an apartment privately. Her four-year-old goes to government-funded Head Start classes to learn skills that will be useful for school. It is obvious that family A receives a great deal of assistance from the government.

In family B, two employed, college-educated parents are raising two children. They are not receiving welfare, and they own their own home. It may seem as though they receive no assistance from the government, but they do. Their elderly parents in Miami Beach and Sun City receive Social Security checks, relieving family B of having to support them. Moreover, the couple deduct the interest payments for their home mortgage from their taxable income, which makes it easier for them to own a home. They receive an income tax credit for having children. They take an additional income tax credit for part of the cost of the day care center their four-year-old attends, which makes it easier for both of them to hold jobs outside the home. In addition, when Mr. B was laid off from his job as a computer programmer for three months this past year, he collected federally funded unemployment compensation.

In truth, most American families, including most middle-class families, receive substantial government assistance. It has not always been the case that most families receive assistance. In the colonial era, almost no economic assistance was provided; rather, the family was viewed as an independent entity that ought not to be interfered with—a "little commonwealth" in Demos's phrase (Demos, 1970). In fact, there was relatively little government financial assistance to families throughout the nineteenth century. In the early decades of the twentieth century, however, labor unions gained enough strength to demand higher pay, shorter hours, old-age pensions, and unemployment compensation. Moreover, civic groups led by middle-class women pressed for programs, such as pensions for widows, to assist mothers and children in poverty (Skocpol, 1992).

Then, in 1929 came the economic collapse of the Great Depression. The masses of unemployed workers looked to the government for assistance. Herbert Hoover, a Republican president who opposed most government involvement in the economy, was defeated in the 1932 election by Franklin Delano Roosevelt. Under Roosevelt, the federal government developed a number of programs to assist unemployed workers and their families. Among them was the **Social Security Act of 1935,** which created, among other provisions, Social Security (the system of pensions for the elderly), unemployment compensation (payments to workers who lose their jobs), and aid to mothers with dependent children. The latter program was subsequently renamed Aid to Families with Dependent Children. It was the program of financial assistance to low-income, single-parent families that became commonly known as "welfare." Beginning in the 1960s, government programs to assist families expanded greatly.

Today, government assistance to low-income families such as family A takes many forms, as the following examples from 2008 reveal:

- 3.8 million adults and children received assistance through Temporary Assistance for Needy Families, the program that replaced Aid for Families with Dependent Children in 1996, at a cost to the federal government of $22 billion.
- 27.6 million people received food stamps (now called the Supplemental Nutrition Assistance Program), which allowed them to avoid hunger, at a cost of $39.3 billion.
- 463,000 children were living in foster care, most having been removed from their homes by state and local caseworkers.
- 907,000 three-to-five-year-old poor children were enrolled in Head Start, a program that provides early readiness for school.

But programs to assist moderate- and middle-income families such as family B are even more extensive—and expensive. Consider these examples from 2008:

- 32.4 million retired workers received Social Security payments, which eased their children's burden of support, at a cost of $506 billion.
- 8.0 million workers who had been laid off from their jobs received unemployment compensation, cash payments that partially offset their lost wages, at a cost of $45 billion (which rose to $160 billion in 2010 during the Great Recession).
- 6.6 million parents at all income levels deducted part of the cost of out-of-home child care from their income taxes, a subsidy that made it easier for them to work outside the home and that cost the federal government $3.5 billion in lost tax revenue.
- 38.7 million federal income filers included deductions for the interest paid on home mortgage loans, a subsidy to homeowners that cost the federal government $94.8 billion in lost tax revenue.[1]

Social Security Act of 1935 the federal act that created, among other provisions, Social Security, unemployment compensation, and aid to mothers with dependent children (later renamed Aid to Families with Dependent Children)

---

[1] These figures were taken from the annual volumes of the Statistical Abstract of the United States for the years 2009 through 2012.

The Head Start Program, which helps young children from low-income families develop the skills they will need in school, is politically popular.

This list, which could be expanded, demonstrates that the government is far more involved in supporting families economically than was the case in earlier times. Extensive federal economic support began in the twentieth century. Most government involvement is based on a concern about the well-being of children (as in the cash assistance or foster home programs) or of the elderly (as in Social Security). In other words, most government programs that affect families do so out of concern about the proper caretaking and support of dependents—people too young or too old or too ill to care for themselves. Most, therefore, reflect the perspective of the public family. The great attention government pays to these issues of caretaking and dependency shows that the family is still viewed as an important source of care.

Yet many of these measures were conceived at a time when the family was different than it is today—a time when there were far fewer divorces, births outside marriage, married women working outside the home, and unmarried couples living together; a time before birth control pills allowed better control of pregnancy, before medical technology allowed fertilized eggs to be implanted in a woman's uterus, and before large numbers of gay and lesbian couples, some with children, were living openly and some were marrying. For example, the Social Security Act's program of aid to mothers with dependent children (the forerunner of the "welfare" program) was originally designed to help widowed women support their children. Its designers never dreamed that, a few decades later, most of its recipients would be never-married or divorced parents.

In the wake of these changes, public support rose in the 1980s and 1990s for new laws and government policies that would assist families. **Family policy,** which I will define as political beliefs about how the government should assist families in caring for dependents, had become a major political issue. Much of the debate centered on two sets of issues: (1) how to respond to

family policy political beliefs about how the government should assist families in caring for dependents childhood poverty and the related increases in nonmarital childbearing and single-parent families, such as by reforming welfare or by enforcing the child support obligations of absent fathers; and (2) whether, and how, to assist parents employed outside the home, such as by providing child care subsidies or work leave to care for infants or seriously ill relatives. In all recent presidential campaigns, family issues have been prominent themes.

This chapter will probe these policy debates for what they reveal about the underlying themes in public discussions on the family. It will focus on the increasing public concern during the twentieth and early twenty-first centuries about the family's ability to care for dependents—and on the public laws and programs that have been enacted to assist it. In order to do so, however, it is necessary first to examine more generally the often thorny relationship between the family and the state. The current debates are rooted in long-standing questions about how involved in people's family lives the government should be. More specifically, how actively should the government, through law and social policy, regulate and support the family in its care and nurturing of children, the frail elderly, and the chronically ill? And how is the government to decide what kinds of interventions are best to provide? Issues of gender roles have nearly always been central to these debates; often issues of class and race have also been important. The answers to these questions depend, in part, on ethics and morality—subjects beyond the bounds of sociology. Yet the answers also depend on social structure and social change, subjects to which a sociological inquiry can contribute.

Quick Review

- Both low-income and middle-income families receive substantial assistance from the government.
- Federal government programs of income assistance began with the Social Security Act of 1935.
- Family issues have been part of the political debates during all recent presidential campaigns.

The Development of the Welfare State

I will use the term **state** to mean a government that claims the right to rule a given territory and its population and to have a monopoly of force in that territory. I will use the term **nation** to refer above all to a people with shared economic and cultural interests—people who have a sense of belonging, a common bond. The countries of the world today are most accurately described by the term **nation–state,** which combines the governmental and cultural connotations of the two words it comprises. Yet most people use the simpler term "nation" rather than "nation–state" to refer to countries, and I will sometimes follow this simpler usage. The emergence of nation–states has been the central political development in the world since the late 1400s, when monarchs consolidated territories in England, France, and Spain, breaking the power of medieval lords over their lands. Today, the nation–state system, as embodied in the United Nations, is firmly entrenched throughout most of the world.

state a government that claims the right to rule a given territory and its population and to have a monopoly on force in that territory

nation a people with shared economic and cultural interests

nation–state a term that combines the governmental and cultural connotations of the two words it comprises

THE WELFARE STATE

The economic system in the Western nation–states and in most others is capitalism. It is an economic system in which goods and services are privately produced and sold on a market for profit. Workers offer their labor to the owners of the means of production, such as factories, and accept the highest offer of wages they receive. The owners then try to sell their products at a price high enough to yield a profit after they subtract the wages, rents, and other expenses they have paid. In its purest form, the ideology of capitalism argues that there should be no interference by government in the labor market or in the market for products. Beginning with Adam Smith, capitalist economic theorists have argued that the forces of the market—the interplay of the demand for and supply of goods—produce a socially optimal distribution of wages and prices. The market, in Smith's famous phrase, acts as an "invisible hand" that guides the economy toward an outcome that is the best for all (Smith, 1776).

It is but a short extension to argue that, according to capitalist economic theory, the government should not intervene in family affairs. To intervene is to disturb the workings of the invisible hand and therefore to risk doing more harm than good. For example, some critics of cash assistance to poor families argue that it discourages them from taking jobs, thereby reducing their standard of living in the long run. Yet not to intervene is to do nothing to help people in need or assist groups that might be unjustly disadvantaged in the labor market.

As noted earlier, the view that the government should not intervene in family affairs prevailed in the United States until the hardships of the Depression. Since then, the U.S. Congress has passed substantial legislation to protect workers and their families from the most harmful consequences of the labor market. In the social scientific literature on these laws and programs, authors refer to them as "social welfare" measures, and they write of the **welfare state,** by which they mean a capitalist government that has enacted numerous measures—such as Social Security, unemployment compensation, and a minimum wage—to protect workers and their families from the harshness of the capitalist system and to raise their standard of living above what wages paid in the labor market alone would do. Here the term "welfare" is used not in its common meaning of cash assistance to the poor but rather in the broader sense of the well-being of members of society. These social welfare measures expanded greatly in the 1950s and 1960s, as labor and minority groups pushed for them and as growing affluence allowed the government to raise taxes to support them.

welfare state a capitalist government that has enacted numerous measures to protect workers and their families from the harshness of the capitalist system

THE RISE AND FALL OF THE FAMILY WAGE SYSTEM

The welfare state has treated husbands and fathers differently from wives and mothers. In the terms of feminist theory, the development of the welfare state has been "gendered" (Orloff, 1993; Borchorst, 2000). Beginning around the turn of the twentieth century, reformers campaigned, without much success initially, for laws that would require employers to pay male workers enough so they could support their families without wives (and children) having to work for wages. During the same period, women's organizations

Franklin D. Roosevelt signed the landmark Social Security Act of 1935, which created the Social Security System, unemployment compensation, and aid to mothers with dependent children.

and labor unions campaigned, with more success, for protective legislation: laws to limit the number of hours women could work for wages to "protect" them from having to work too long and hard outside the home (Skocpol, 1992). Together, these different objectives for women and men supported the **family wage system,** a division of labor in which the husband earns enough money to support his family and the wife remains home to do housework and child care. This system is now in decline, but an examination of its development is useful for understanding the family policy debates occurring today.

The moral vision behind campaigns for the family wage system specified that the family works best when men and women inhabit separate spheres: his, paid work outside the home; hers, unpaid homemaking and child rearing inside the home. This view, as has been discussed, gained in popularity in the nineteenth-century United States as industrialization moved the workplace out of the home. The family wage system was never a reality for many working-class and minority families, whose men could not earn enough to support a family. Nevertheless, it remained the dominant cultural view of the family throughout the first half of the twentieth century.

The Social Security Act of 1935 followed the division of labor implicit in the family wage system. It provided old-age pensions only to persons who "earned" them by working a certain number of years in the paid labor force; originally only industrial and commercial workers were covered. The clear expectation was that these covered workers would overwhelmingly be men. The act therefore ignored the value of the care work done by women at home. In 1939, Congress passed an extension of the act that allowed widows of Social Security recipients to receive continued benefits after their husbands died. Women whose husbands were absent for other reasons, and who were still raising children, were eligible for the Aid to Dependent Children program—but only

family wage system a division of labor in which the husband earns enough money to support his family and the wife remains home to do housework and child care

if their income was below a certain level. Congress did not anticipate that large numbers of women raising children might need assistance because they were divorced from their husbands or had never had a husband. It did not anticipate that large numbers of women would qualify for Social Security benefits themselves by working outside the home. The system presumed that, until the death of one spouse, families would consist of a husband who would *provide* for the family and a wife who would *care* for the family.

Throughout the 1950s, the prosperous decade in which the breadwinner–homemaker family was much celebrated, the family wage system remained the cultural ideal. Beginning in the 1960s, however, it began to weaken; and by the end of the twentieth century, it had faded away. To be sure, husbands still worked for wages and wives still did the housework and child care in a minority of marriages, but the prestige and popularity of this type of marriage had greatly declined. The factor most responsible for its downfall was the enormous increase in wives working outside the home. Women worked before having children and withdrew only temporarily from the workforce when their children were young. Women who gave up paid work also risked financial hardship if their marriages ended in divorce, as more and more were doing. The rise of cohabitation and childbearing outside of marriage further challenged the dominance of the family wage system. By the 1990s, as the system lay in tatters, the family policies of both conservatives—who had strongly supported it—and of liberals had evolved beyond it. That evolution and the legislation and controversy it has engendered are the story of the rest of this chapter.

Family Policy Debates

In the aftermath of the family wage system, no dominant vision of the family has emerged. Instead, family policy remains a highly contentious topic. In order to understand what these issues symbolize, it helps to study the kinds of positions that conservative and liberal policymakers have taken in the recent past.

THE CONSERVATIVE VIEWPOINT

Conservatives have sought to defend and encourage heterosexual, marriage-based families (Wilson, 2002). In the past, they have championed the breadwinner–homemaker marriage that fits the family wage system; but many conservatives now accept the fact that most married women will work outside the home. From the conservative viewpoint, the declining role of marriage in American family life is due to a change in American culture: an erosion of traditional norms and values that supported marriage. These values included strong community disapproval of couples living together, which was seen as shameful prior to the 1960s. They also included the stigma associated with having children outside of marriage, which used to be called "illegitimacy," a word which implies that children born outside marriage are not legitimate members of society. Conservatives tend to minimize the role of the economy in producing family change. For instance, in a widely-cited conservative lament over the decline of work and marriage among white Americans without college degrees, Charles Murray (2012, p. 181) addressed the declining employment and income of young men in this fashion:

> *There is no evidence that men without jobs in the 2000s before the 2008 recession were trying hard to find work but failing. . . . The simpler explanation is that white males of the 2000s were less industrious than they had been twenty, thirty, or fifty years ago, and that decay in industriousness occurred overwhelmingly in [working-class communities].*

In other words, until the Great Recession, changes in the job market had nothing to do with the lower rate of employment among young men, according to Murray; rather it was caused by the decline of the traditional value of "industriousness," meaning a willingness to work hard and to strive to get ahead.

As the earlier discussion of the Social Security Act has shown, the U.S. welfare state was constructed to support the breadwinner–homemaker family. To a large extent, its programs encouraged women to marry and men to be the main providers. For example, programs such as Social Security and unemployment compensation were designed with male recipients in mind. Full-time homemakers can accrue eligibility for Social Security only through marriage, and they cannot receive unemployment benefits. The income tax system also encouraged the formation of breadwinner–homemaker marriages and discouraged the formation of two-earner marriages. Until recently, if a man earned $50,000 and a woman earned nothing, they paid less in taxes if they married than if they stayed single. On the other hand, if a man and a woman each earned $25,000, they paid more in taxes if they married than if they stayed single.

Conservatives generally favor a modest role for government in supporting families. They are skeptical of proposals for expensive new social welfare programs. They are concerned that if social benefit levels are raised, the beneficiaries will have less incentive to work. Yet their support for the Social Security and tax policies described above shows that they are not opposed to all government interventions into family life. Rather, conservatives have defended a particular set of interventions that supported the family wage system. The Depression-era and 1950s roots of these programs lie so far in the past that government's role can seem almost invisible. It's understandable, then, that a politician might mistakenly believe that the government has had no role in shaping the contemporary family.

In fact, conservative groups have long advocated government intervention when court rulings and legislation have undermined their vision of the family. After *Roe v. Wade,* the 1973 Supreme Court decision legalizing abortion, grass-roots conservative organizations joined with religious groups to campaign for restrictive state laws and for a constitutional amendment banning abortion. The anti-abortion forces succeeded in passing legislation that prohibited the use of federal funds for performing abortions, thus restricting poor women's ability to obtain them (Tribe, 1990). In 2003, conservatives were able to win passage of a law banning a late-term procedure opponents called a "partial-birth abortion," and the constitutionality of the law was affirmed by the Supreme Court in 2007. Abortion remains one of the most divisive issues pertaining to families. (See *Families and Public Policy: The Abortion Dilemma.*)

Families and Public Policy

The Abortion Dilemma

Abortion has been one of the most bitterly contested and divisive of issues in our society. It starkly contrasts two visions of women's roles: one that emphasizes childbearing and mothering versus one that emphasizes autonomy and employment.

From the late 1800s to the early 1970s, access to abortion was restricted in the United States, generally available only when physicians certified that it was necessary to save the life of the mother. In the 1960s, feminist groups began to demand access to abortion as a woman's right—thereby making abortion a political issue. With the fertility rate falling to about two births per woman, on average, and with life expectancy lengthening, childbearing no longer lasted most of a woman's adult life. Pro-abortion-rights activists, who prefer to be called "pro-choice," sought to control the timing and numbers of the children they bore. They did so, in part, on behalf of poor women who simply wanted to limit how many children they would have. Yet the pro-choice advocates, as Kristin Luker (1984) has written, also shared a "worldview" in which women and men are equal and deserve equal opportunity to work outside the home. Legal abortions, by helping women to plan when to have children, would help them obtain equal opportunity.

Their cause was aided immensely by a 1973 Supreme Court decision, *Roe v. Wade* (1973). In this case, the Court ruled that women had the constitutional right to terminate a pregnancy by abortion during the first trimester and that in the second trimester the state may regulate access to abortion only for reasons reasonably related to the mother's health. *Roe* made abortions legal, but it also spurred the formation of a strong, national movement against abortion. The "pro-life" forces, as the anti-abortion

Americans continue to be divided on the topic of abortion.

movement came to be known, view human life as beginning at conception and therefore oppose abortion except to save the life of the mother. According to Luker (1984), they share a worldview in which women and men are fundamentally different and women's primary role is to raise children.

Abortion rights also vary by class, because the biggest victory for the pro-life forces was the passage of legislation in 1976 that prohibited the use of government funds to pay for abortions. Since most poor women receive medical care through the government program Medicaid, the law makes it difficult for them to obtain an abortion. Supporters argue that the ban on the use of public funds is morally justified because abortion is repugnant to many taxpayers. Nevertheless, the ban made abortion a class-related issue because middle-class women have an

easier time finding the funds to pay for an abortion than do poor women. In a 1989 case, *Webster v. Reproductive Health Services* (1989), a divided Court upheld some restrictions on abortion in a Missouri law. More important, the Court nearly overturned *Roe,* with four members clearly leaning in that direction.

Public opinion remains divided. In 2010, 37 years after *Roe v. Wade,* a national sample of adults was asked, "Please tell me whether or not you think it should be possible for a pregnant woman to obtain a legal abortion if she is married and does not want any more children." Fifty-two percent said no, and 48 percent responded yes (Davis & Smith, 2010). In the early years of the twenty-first century, abortion is still an issue that deeply divides Americans in ways that reflect different views of women's lives.

THE LIBERAL VIEWPOINT

Liberals have accepted, and even defended, the diverse forms of family life we see today, including single-parent families and cohabiting families. Whereas conservatives believe that cultural change has driven the transformation of family life, liberals tend to believe that economic change, such as the globalization and automation of production, has been more important. They argue that government has a responsibility to assist all kinds of families, and they generally support expansions of existing programs and propose new ones. For instance, Katherine S. Newman (2012, p. 202), in a book on the growing number of adult children who are living with their parents rather than moving out and starting their own families, sees the globalized economy and government policies as the keys to whether they can succeed:

> *What becomes of them is as much a matter of what the economy provides in the way of opportunity and what we decide we owe them as citizens, future parents and providers. These are not simply natural outcomes. They are expressions of social solidarity, given shape by the governments we elect and the policies they enact.*

In other words, young adults' prospects of moving out are constrained by the globalized economy, rather than by a lack of industriousness; and government should adopt policies to help them find their way out of the house and into stable jobs.

The kinds of measures advanced by liberals tend to help married couples in which wives are employed outside the home and single parents more than they help breadwinner–homemaker couples. Liberals have consistently advocated more support for employed parents. For example, the child care programs and child tax credits that liberals favor make it less difficult for mothers to participate in the work force. Only in the mid-1990s, when welfare reform (see below) mandated that low-income single mothers find employment, did liberals begin to defend the right of mothers to stay home and care for their children. By and large, liberals, a political category in which there is a large overlap with feminists, believe that the breadwinner–homemaker family is at best no better than other family forms or at worst a form that unjustifiably restricts the autonomy of women.

Debates over whether and how government should help families arose in the 1960s, as social change began to undermine the breadwinner–homemaker family that was so prominent in the 1950s. At first, these divisions led to a policy stalemate. For example, in 1971, a Democratic-controlled Congress passed a comprehensive child development bill that would have established a national system of preschools for children ages three to five. But President Richard M. Nixon vetoed the legislation on the grounds that it "would commit the vast moral authority of the national government to the side of communal approaches to child rearing over against the family-centered approach"—in other words, government support for child care would undermine the independent, breadwinner–homemaker family.[2]

---

[2] *Congressional Record,* December 10, 1971, pp. 46057–59. (Text of President Nixon's veto message of the Child Development Act of 1971.)

WHICH FAMILIES ARE POOR?

poverty line a federally
defined income limit defined
as the cost of an "economy"
diet for a family, multiplied
by three

But let us suspend this story for a moment to ask how the government determines which families are economically deprived and in need of assistance. Each year the U.S. government calculates an official **poverty line** and publishes statistics on the number of families with incomes below the line.

The poverty line is a strange concoction that no one likes but no analyst can do without. It was established in the mid-1960s when federal officials figured out how much it would cost to buy enough food to meet the Agriculture Department's standard for an "economy" diet—and then, on the assumption that families spend one-third of their income on food, simply multiplied by three (Katz, 1989). To account for inflation, this standard (which is adjusted for the number of people in the family) is multiplied every year by the increase in the cost of living. Advocates for the poor claim it is too low and therefore underestimates the low-income population; many conservatives claim it is too high. Its main virtue is that it can be used to examine changes over time in the percentage of families that fall above or below it. In 2011, the line stood at $22,811 for a family of two adults and two children under 18 and at $18,123 for a family of one adult and two children (U.S. Bureau of the Census, 2011k).

Figure 14.1 shows the percentage of families with children under 18 that fell below the poverty line in each year from 1959 to 2010. Information on African American families is available only from 1967 onward, and for Hispanic families (which may be of any race) from 1972 onward. Poverty rates for families tend to fluctuate with the state of the economy. When the economy was strong in the mid to late 1990s, poverty levels fell. They rose sharply during the late 2000s as the Great Recession took hold. In 2010, 15.6 percent of white families with children under 18 were poor, according to the official definition, as were 30.6 percent of Hispanic families and 34.0 percent of African American families (U.S. Bureau of the Census, 2011q). So African American and Hispanic families remain much more likely to be poor than white families, although African American poverty, as Figure 14.1 shows, is well below its historic highs. And even among whites, about one in six families with children was poor during the economic dark days of 2010.

FIGURE 14.1

Percent of families with children under 18 that had incomes below the poverty line, for whites, blacks, and Hispanics, 1959–2010. (*Source:* U.S. Bureau of the Census, 2011q)

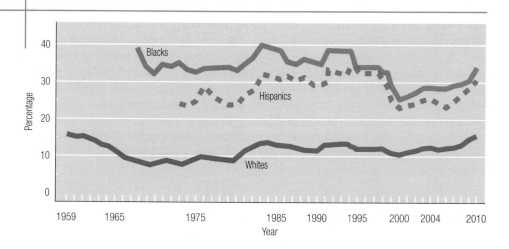

Quick Review

- The welfare state emerged in the twentieth century.
- At first, the welfare state supported a family wage system in which fathers were treated differently from mothers.
- Conservatives favor a modest role for government in supporting families and are skeptical of new programs.
- Liberals believe that government has a responsibility to assist all families; they favor expanding government programs.
- The government calculates an official poverty line and determines how many families have incomes that fall below it.

Practical Compromises

Despite their differences, conservatives and liberals have sometimes reached a pragmatic consensus that has led to new or expanded programs. The consensus is far from complete: Important differences still exist, as I will note below. But several important programs have been launched or strengthened.

THE EARNED INCOME TAX CREDIT

Perhaps the foremost example of the consensus is the expansion of the **Earned Income Tax Credit (EITC).** Introduced in 1975 but still little known except among low-income families, it cost $55 billion in 2010, which was more than double the cost of the main "welfare" program (U.S. Bureau of the Census, 2011b). The EITC provides a refundable tax credit to low-income families with children in which at least one parent is employed. Even if the family earns so little that its members owe no taxes, they still receive a check for the value of the credit from the government if they file their tax returns. Essentially, the EITC is an income subsidy for parents who earn low wages. It has become one of the main anti-poverty programs. Conservatives like it for two reasons. First, it goes only to families in which a parent is employed; in the policy jargon, it targets the "working poor," those who earn barely enough (or not enough) to stay above the poverty line. (For a family of four, benefits begin to phase out at incomes in the low $20,000s.) An unemployed single parent is not eligible. Therefore, the EITC reinforces the obligation to work. Second, it applies not only to dual-earner, two-parent families but also to breadwinner–homemaker families because a family qualifies even if only one parent works outside the home. It therefore appears neutral toward wives working outside the home.

Liberals, on their part, like the EITC because it provides income assistance to many low-income families. Liberals also realize that there are relatively few breadwinner–homemaker families among the working poor (who can't afford a stay-at-home parent), so that, in reality, most of the money goes to two-earner families and to employed single parents. Finally, liberal members of Congress in this era realized that a program of tax credits for the working poor went as far as they could convince conservatives to move with regard to

Earned Income Tax Credit (EITC) a refundable tax credit to low-income families with children in which at least one parent is employed

Government assistance with child care costs increased in the 1990s and early 2000s.

income assistance. The EITC was increased several times and provides a maximum benefit of about $5,000 to a family with two children and an income of about $12,000 to $16,000.

THE 1996 WELFARE REFORM LAW

One piece of legislation enacted in 1996, which has become known as "welfare reform," is particularly important for the evolution of conservative and liberal views of family policy. As discussed earlier, Aid to Families with Dependent Children (AFDC) was originally designed to support widows and their children, as part of the Social Security Act. Both AFDC and Social Security were created as entitlement programs by Congress. If a government program is an **entitlement,** the government is obligated to provide benefits to anyone who qualifies, regardless of the total cost of the program. For example, if I reach the official retirement age, walk into my local Social Security office, and ask to sign up for benefits, they cannot say to me, "We're sorry, but we don't have any more money left this year. Come back next year." They *must* pay me the benefits I am entitled to. Not all government programs for low-income families are entitlements; housing subsidies, for instance, are limited: Only 19 percent of families receiving welfare benefits also receive subsidies (or live in publicly owned housing) (U.S. Administration for Children and Families, 2009). But starting in the 1930s, the government pledged to provide assistance through the AFDC program to any

entitlement a program in which the government is obligated to provide benefits to anyone who qualifies, regardless of the total cost of the program

Table 14.1   Main Differences between AFDC and TANF

	AFDC	TANF
Limit on government expenditures	Government expenditures are unlimited because AFDC was an *entitlement:* The government had to provide benefits to all who qualified, regardless of the cost. The federal government and the state governments each provided about half the funds.	Federal government expenses are limited because each state receives a fixed amount of funds, called a *block grant.* States may add more of their own funds to the program, but the federal government will not provide more.
Time limit on families' receipt of assistance	Families can receive benefits for an unlimited time, as long as they continue to qualify for the program.	States can use federal funds to pay for only five years of benefits for a family. States may enforce a shorter time limit if they wish. If states want to pay for more than five years of benefits, they may do so if they use only their own state funds.
Work requirements	Twenty percent of recipients were supposed to be working (usually part-time) by 1995.	Adults are required to work within 24 months after they receive assistance.

family that qualified (usually by having a low income, just one parent, and children under 18).

In 1950, Congress increased the AFDC benefit level in the hope that poor mothers would be able to stay home and care for their children. Starting about 1970, however, Congress passed a series of laws that encouraged, and later required, mothers receiving AFDC to take jobs and leave their children in the care of others. Yet "welfare" remained unpopular with the public. In a 1990 national survey, 70 percent of adults favored "reducing welfare benefits to make working for a living more attractive" (Davis & Smith, 2010). Bill Clinton, running against President George H. W. Bush in the 1992 election campaign, seized upon this unpopularity by promising to "end welfare as we know it." In 1996, after negotiations between President Clinton and the Republican-controlled Congress, the President signed a bill that in many ways did end welfare as we knew it. (See Table 14.1.) "Welfare reform," as it came to be known, was a stunning rollback of policies toward poor families that had stood since 1935. First, it ended the entitlement to welfare benefits. States would be given a fixed amount of money each year—a so-called **block grant**—which they would have to match with state funds. If a state exhausted its block grant and matching funds, it could choose to turn away new applicants until the next year. (But no state has yet turned anyone away.) No longer would the government guarantee to assist every poor single-parent family in need.

block grant a fixed amount of money that the federal government gives each state to spend on a set of programs

Second, the bill set a five-year time limit on cash assistance. People still on the rolls after five years would be cut off. States were free to set an even shorter time limit (and about 20 subsequently did). Recipients also had to accept work within two years of being on the rolls or their families would lose their benefits.

No longer could poor mothers stay home full-time to care for their children. The emphasis was on temporary assistance and on getting a job, any

Temporary Assistance for Needy Families (TANF) a federal program of financial assistance to low-income families that began in 1996, following passage of new welfare legislation (see Aid to Families with Dependent Children)

job. The legislation scrapped the title AFDC and renamed the time-limited cash assistance program **Temporary Assistance for Needy Families,** or **TANF.**

Reasons for the Policy Reversal   What caused such a sweeping reversal of six decades of social policy toward poor families? Three differences between the 1930s and the 1990s stand out:

1. *Attitudes toward women's roles* First, attitudes toward women's roles had changed greatly. By the 1990s, a majority of mothers were working outside the home. It seemed less punitive to require that poor, single mothers attempt to find jobs when the majority of middle-class mothers were employed as well. Encouraging self-reliance and independence among poor mothers seemed consistent with emerging values for non-poor women.

2. *Characteristics of the recipients* Second, the characteristics of welfare recipients had also changed. No longer are most widowed; rather, the vast majority are separated, divorced, or never married. About 200 years ago, a distinction emerged in both American and British society between the "deserving" and "undeserving" poor (Katz, 1989). There was, and there remains, substantial public sympathy for the deserving poor, those whose poverty is seen as beyond their control. There has been much less sympathy for the undeserving poor, those whose poverty is perceived, whether fairly or not, as somehow their "fault" because they have failed to behave as society expects. Widows, as victims of their husbands' deaths, fall among the deserving poor—their poverty is not their "fault." The situation of separated, divorced, and never-married mothers is less clear. Some observers view the mothers—and perhaps even more so, the fathers of their children—as having chosen, in some sense, an irresponsible path to parenthood. Whether fairly or not, many Americans believe that people should refrain from having children until they can provide for them and are not willing to exempt the poor.

   Moreover, there is another troubling subtext to the discourse about "deservingness." Not only the marital status but also the racial composition of the AFDC population has changed since the early days of the program. African American single-parent families are heavily overrepresented among the persistently poor and, therefore, among TANF recipients. In 2010 African Americans, who constituted 32 percent of the TANF rolls, were overrepresented, compared with their percentage of the total U.S. population and even compared with their percentage of the total population with incomes below the poverty line (U.S. Bureau of the Census, 2011b). Observers of the welfare debate have suggested that racial animosity may underlie some of the public opposition to welfare spending (Grubb & Lazerson, 1988; Quadagno, 1994). Both Heclo and Katz argue that whites in the 1960s came to identify antipoverty policy with African Americans because of the civil rights movement, the activities of welfare rights organizations, the black urban riots in Watts and northern cities, and the largely black bureaucracy that arose to administer the antipoverty programs (Heclo, 1986).

3. *Concern about "dependency"* The third reason for the policy reversal is the spread of the idea that the welfare-receiving poor had become too dependent upon public assistance. According to this line of reasoning, usually advanced by conservatives, people who receive public assistance for years and years often lose their initiative to find jobs. It is rational, they argue, for welfare recipients to stay on the rolls: If they were to take a job, they would not only lose their benefits but also incur child care, transportation, and clothing costs. Their new jobs probably wouldn't pay well and might not include health insurance (whereas TANF recipients are covered by Medicaid). We have built a system, so this argument goes, that discourages people from moving from welfare to work (Mead, 1992).

Some liberal defenders of time-unlimited welfare contested the dependency perspective. Adults on welfare don't lack initiative, the defenders said; rather, they lack the opportunity to find steady jobs paying wages that can sustain a family (Handler, 1995). Ending cash assistance after five years, they argued, is a cruel step that will further impoverish many poor children and their parents. Despite these different points of view, a Democratic president and many Democratic members of Congress joined with Republicans to enact the welfare reform law. By 1996, many liberal members of Congress had joined a new consensus that endorsed work outside the home with social support, rather than continued dependence on cash assistance, as the preferable goal for poor mothers.

The Effects of Welfare Reform   Welfare reform has coincided with dramatic declines in the TANF caseload and substantial increases in the employment of low-income single mothers. Between 1996 and 2010, the number of families receiving TANF declined by almost two-thirds (U.S. Administration for Children and Families, 2011). Most of the decline, however, occurred between 1996 and the early 2000s, a period of economic prosperity. Indeed, welfare reform had the good fortune to be launched during the strongest economic boom in decades. The proportion of single mothers in the paid workforce also increased during the boom. The drop in the TANF caseload appears to have been caused by a combination of the new rules of welfare reform, the strong economy, and wage supports such as the EITC (Schoeni & Blank, 2000; Grogger & Karoly, 2005). Nevertheless, the decline continued at a slower pace through 2010, despite the onset of the Great Recession, suggesting that potential recipients were avoiding TANF, perhaps because they are saving their last years of eligibility or they find the work requirements onerous. In fact, some of the drop in the TANF rolls occurred not because more people left but because fewer people were entering than before welfare reform (Grogger, Haider, & Klerman, 2003). One might have expected a program that provides "temporary assistance for needy families" to have expanded during a severe recession, when temporary needs are greatest. That it contracted instead suggests that the government "safety net" for the needy may have some holes. (For a broader look at how the American safety net was functioning during the recession, see *Families and the Great Recession: "The Safety Net."*)

What has happened to the families that have left TANF? The picture is mixed (Danziger, 2010). According to a study of African American and Hispanic families in three cities, neither the dire consequences that critics of the legislation

How well did the safety net of the American welfare state do in catching families whose economic fortunes fell during the Great Recession? There were, in effect, two safety nets. The first net consisted of existing government programs to aid the jobless and the less fortunate. These included Unemployment Insurance, the Supplemental Nutrition Assistance Program (SNAP, which used to be known as Food Stamps), the Earned Income Tax Credit (EITC), and Temporary Assistance for Needy Families (TANF). These programs were already available when the recession started. The second net consisted of several bills passed by Congress that provided tax cuts and incentives to individuals and businesses, increases in income support, assistance to state and local governments, and infrastructure spending. They are collectively known as the "stimulus" programs. Although much maligned by the public as ineffective, they made a big difference in the ability of government to cushion the effects of the recession.

The front-line program in the first net is Unemployment Insurance, a state and federal program that provides cash benefits for a limited period of time after a worker becomes unemployed. But not everyone qualifies: workers must have lost jobs through no fault of their own (if you quit voluntarily you are not eligible), must be ready to take another job, and must have earned a certain amount of money in the previous year or so. The last criterion excludes many young jobless men,

who tend to have limited work histories. In fact, less than half of unemployed workers receive Unemployment Insurance benefits except during recessions. The benefits replace, on average, about half of a worker's lost income (Center on Budget and Policy Priorities, 2010). The basic benefit lasts for 26 weeks, paid for by state taxes on employers. But as part of the stimulus package, the federal government extended the benefits to a total of 99 weeks in states hard hit by the recession, providing substantial relief to the unemployed—at least for those who qualified. The stimulus package also provided funds to help laid off workers buy health insurance coverage, which was important because most non-poor Americans receive health insurance through their jobs.

As the recession continued, the number of long-term unemployed individuals rose. By 2010, 9 percent of the unemployed had been jobless for 99 weeks or more (U.S. Bureau of Labor Statistics, 2011c). That's well over one million people, all of whom had exhausted their eligibility for benefits. There were reports, hard to verify, that some employers preferred to hire workers who had been unemployed for a shorter time, perhaps on the theory that the long-term unemployed were less desirable workers. If these reports were true, then the 99ers were doubly-disadvantaged—passed over by employers and no longer receiving Unemployment Insurance.

Temporary Assistance for Needy Families (TANF), which provides cash assistance

and child care subsidies to low-income single parents was another existing component of the first safety net. Its very title, which dates to the 1996 welfare reform law, suggests that its purpose is to offer temporary help to families in need. It would seem reasonable for the number of families receiving TANF benefits to have risen during the recession. But the accompanying figure shows that there was surprisingly little increase in recipients through 2010.

Perhaps some potential recipients stayed away because of the job search rules that required recipients to look for employment, even though little was available. Perhaps some families had reached their five-year lifetime benefit limit or were saving their remaining years of eligibility until other means of support were exhausted. In any case, a program designed to provide temporary assistance during tough times was not serving many new families during the toughest time since the Great Depression, a situation that anti-poverty advocates found troubling.

In contrast, enrollment soared in the SNAP program, which provides funds—formerly as food stamps and now mostly as electronic debit cards—for people to purchase food. The top line in the figure shows that by 2010, a stunning 40 million Americans were receiving SNAP benefits, more than twice the number that received benefits a decade earlier. That's about one out of every eight Americans, and one out of every four children (Smeeding & Carlson, 2011). Receiving food assistance is much

have warned of nor the substantial benefits that some supporters had hoped for have yet occurred. Overall, families that left TANF between 1999 and 2005 showed a slight drop in the percentage living in poverty. Mothers who had not only left the rolls and also were employed in 2005—about half—tended to be doing better when they were receiving TANF, but the other half, who were neither working nor receiving TANF, were struggling, and many were worse off than in 1999 (Cherlin, Frogner, Ribar, & Moffitt, 2009). The study ended in 2005;

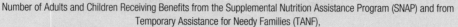
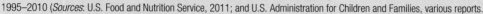

Number of Adults and Children Receiving Benefits from the Supplemental Nutrition Assistance Program (SNAP) and from Temporary Assistance for Needy Families (TANF), 1995–2010 (*Sources*: U.S. Food and Nutrition Service, 2011; and U.S. Administration for Children and Families, various reports.

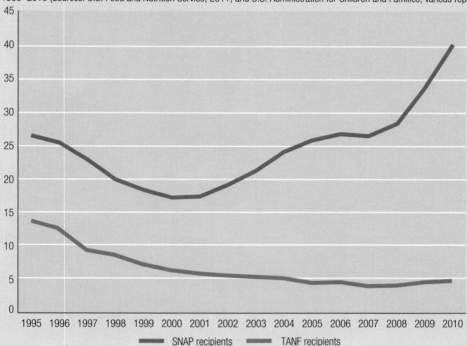

less stigmatizing than receiving TANF, especially now that recipients don't have to pull out their books of stamps at supermarket checkout counters. SNAP had become, along with extended unemployment benefits, one of the strongest components of the safety net.

Other provisions in the federal government's stimulus bills provided tax credits to families with children, reduced the payroll tax that is withheld from workers' paychecks, increased the value of the EITC, and increased tax credits for post-secondary school tuition. These changes in taxes increased the incomes of vulnerable families.

In fact, according to one analysis, the two safety nets kept Americans' disposable incomes—the amount they have available for spending after paying taxes—roughly the same as prior to the recession, on average, despite the millions of people who lost their jobs and earnings (Burtless & Gordon, 2011). If this is true, it was a remarkable achievement. Had there been no second net—no stimulus programs—the first net would still have helped, but the total amount of assistance would have been substantially less. The stimulus programs were, by design, temporary; and they began to fade away in 2011 and 2012. What's left to catch fallings families is the pre-recession safety net, some parts of which were responsive to tough economic times (SNAP) and other parts hardly responsive at all (TANF).

the situations of these families probably worsened when the Great Recession arrived. Other studies show a troublesome nationwide rise in the number of "disconnected" single mothers who are not working, not receiving TANF benefits, and who do not have adults in their households who are earning money. Among all single mothers who are not living with other earners, the percentage who were disconnected from both welfare and work doubled to 25 percent between the enactment of welfare reform and 2008 (Danziger, 2010).

Many former welfare recipients have taken low- and moderate-wage jobs since the welfare system was changed in 1996.

As for the impact on children in low-income families, the picture is similarly better than the welfare-reform skeptics thought, although not as good as the supporters had hoped. Studies that have followed survey samples of low-income families have found that young children's well-being does not seem to have changed much when their mothers begin paid work or stop receiving TANF (Chase-Lansdale et al., 2003; Kalil & Dunifon, 2007). However, experimental studies of changes in welfare policy suggest that welfare reform could cause some declines in teenagers' well-being (Gennetian et al., 2002).

Quick Review

- Beginning in the 1980s, conservatives and liberals were often able to reach practical compromises that led to new legislation.
- The Earned Income Tax Credit is a program that is popular with liberals and conservatives.
- The 1996 "welfare reform" bill that ended entitlements and established time limits and work requirements marked a major change in welfare policy.
- Changes in women's roles, the characteristics of recipients, and policymakers' view of "dependency" underlaid the passage of welfare reform.
- The effects of welfare reform on parents and children appear to be mixed.

■ Current Debates

Although liberals and conservatives have been able to agree on some programs, sharp divisions still exist on a number of issues. In general, liberals are inclined to accept the great changes in family life, such as the increase in single-parent families and in women's work outside the home. They advocate for programs that improve conditions for these families, such as income and employment support for the poor and child care and parental leave assistance for working parents. Conservatives tend to advocate for programs that strengthen traditional family arrangements. They wish to promote heterosexual marriage, discourage nonmarital births, and ensure that fathers help support their children. Let's examine some of the key family policy issues of the 2010s from these two perspectives—the liberal viewpoint of accepting the changing family and assisting parents and children versus the conservative viewpoint of strengthening family ties by supporting marriage and parental responsibility (Smeeding & Carlson, 2011).

MARRIAGE PROMOTION

In 2006, Congress passed and President George W. Bush signed a bill extending the welfare reform legislation. This bill included a much debated program, the Healthy Marriage Initiative, that provided the states with up to $100 million per year from 2006 to 2010 to promote heterosexual marriage and $50 million per year to support "responsible fatherhood" (Center for Law and Social Policy, 2006). Supporters, who were mainly conservative, had argued that the government should encourage low-income women and men to marry in order to ease the hardships of poverty for their children and themselves. Opponents, who were mainly liberal, argued that the government should not be promoting one kind of family over another and that, furthermore, the funds could be better spent on other needs such as providing more child care assistance or discouraging teenage pregnancy.

The debate is not just about research questions—Is it better for children to be raised with two married parents? Can single parents do as good a job if they receive more support?—but also about political and moral issues. These include the autonomy of women, the authority of men, and the wisdom of imposing a particular moral view of family life on those who choose other lifestyles. As we have seen, until the mid–twentieth century, marriage was so central to family life that its dominance was taken for granted. It was an institution in which men held considerable power, in part because of their typically greater earnings and in part because of social norms. Since the 1950s, a number of options have made it possible for women to live full lives outside of marriage. Gains in the labor market provide the opportunity for an independent income, and the availability of welfare provides an income floor (although welfare reform now limits reliance on that floor to five years). The birth control pill allows for sexual activity without unwanted pregnancies, and the greater acceptability of raising a child outside of marriage allows single women to have the children they want. At the same time, the economic fortunes of men without college educations have diminished, reducing the economic benefits of marriage to women. All told, paths to parenthood and child rearing other than long-term marriage are now more feasible and more attractive.

The supporters of marriage promotion, however, contend that marriage provides a superior setting for raising children. They acknowledge that many single mothers and fathers are good parents, but they read the evidence as showing that for the most part, one parent can't provide care and supervision as well as two. From this point of view, the key objective of family policy should be to promote marriage in order to reduce the number of children born to unmarried women and their partners.

Yet it is not clear that we know how to promote marriage effectively. Most of the existing, relationship-skills training courses have been focused on middle-class couples. They may not work well with couples who have less-developed reading skills and who come from different cultural backgrounds. The centerpieces of the Healthy Marriage Initiative were two large, random-assignment studies of marriage- and relationship-enhancement programs for low-income couples with children (or who were expecting a birth) in multiple sites across the country. The cores of these programs were curricula that teach better communications skills and conflict management. At all sites, couples were randomly allocated to a "treatment" group that was enrolled in the curriculum and a "control" group that was not.

The studies will not be completed until 2013. But preliminary reports on the first year or so have been released. In the study that focused almost entirely on unmarried couples, called "Building Strong Families" (Wood, McConnell, Moore, Clarkwest, & Hsueh, 2010), 17 percent of the treatment group had married over the 15-month period and 18 percent of the control group had married. The most reasonable conclusion is that, so far, the program has had no effect on marriage. In the study that focused on already-married low-income couples who would like to strengthen their relationships, called "Supporting Healthy Marriage," the treatment group showed small gains in marital happiness, greater warmth and support, positive communication, and other similar characteristics, compared to the control group (Hsueh, Alderson, Lundquist, Michalopoulos, Gubits, Fein, & Knox, 2012). But there was no difference in the proportion that stayed married. Perhaps the planned three-year follow-up will provide a different view.

SAME-SEX MARRIAGE

While conservatives have urged support for heterosexual marriage, they have by and large opposed efforts to extend marriage, or domestic partnerships legally similar to marriage, to same-sex couples. It has become one of the more divisive family issues of our time, with rapidly shifting laws and referenda continually changing the states where it is legal, and with signs of recent changes in public opinion. In 2000 in Vermont, the legislature, under pressure from the state courts, enacted a law establishing "civil unions," a type of domestic partnership that gives the partners most of the legal rights the state gives to married couples. Then in 2003, the Massachusetts Supreme Court ruled that the state law restricting marriage to opposite-sex couples was unconstitutional because it denied same-sex couples a status that is "specially recognized in society and has significant social and other advantages" (*Goodrich v. Department of Public Health*, 2003). Only legalizing same-sex marriage would suffice because anything else, the Court wrote, would create "second-class citizens." In England and France, however, civil unions aren't necessarily seen as second-class citizenship. Both countries have passed domestic partnership laws but neither has had much of a debate about same-sex marriage, in large part because fewer gay and lesbian activists view marriage as a status worth achieving. Only in the United States has the right to control the boundaries of marriage produced so much controversy.

In 2004 same-sex marriage became legal in Massachusetts. In 2005 it became legal throughout Canada. State courts subsequently ruled in favor of same-sex marriage in California, Connecticut, and Iowa. Several state legislatures have voted to legalize same-sex marriage since then. These developments have also spurred strong opposition. Voters have overturned the legalization through referenda held in states such as California and Maine. A drive to amend the federal constitution to ban same-sex marriage has been unsuccessful; but state constitutions have been amended to ban it in about half of the states. Until recently, a majority of Americans opposed same-sex marriage, but that may no longer be the case. The Pew Research center has conducted annual surveys that ask respondents whether they favor or oppose "allowing gays and lesbians to marry." In 2011, 45 percent favored it, up from 39 percent in 2008. The percent who opposed it in 2011 was 46 percent, down from 51 percent in 2008 (Pew Research Center, 2011c).

Some opponents of gay marriage state that it violates their religious teaching about marriage, and others express discomfort about homosexual sexual activity. Nevertheless, same-sex marriage is a logical consequence of the increasingly individualized meaning of marriage. In the past, most people viewed marriage primarily as an arrangement for having children. Since same-sex partners cannot have biological children together, same-sex marriage was not considered. But by the end of the twentieth century, this view had faded. In 1994 the General Social Survey asked a national sample of adults whether they agreed or disagreed with the statement "The main purpose of marriage these days is to have children." Only 13 percent agreed (Davis & Smith, 2010). Instead, marriage is viewed by most people now as primarily a setting for love and intimacy. Given this changed meaning, the rationale for excluding same-sex partnerships is much weaker. Moreover, many lesbian and gay couples are raising children together, through adoption or donor insemination. When courts examine the issue, they look at the meaning heterosexuals give to marriage, and they often can find no compelling reason to uphold laws that restrict marriage to opposite-sex partners. Those who view marriage more traditionally oppose this stance.

NONMARITAL CHILDBEARING

The objective of reducing nonmarital childbearing is less controversial. Teenage childbearing, in particular, produces a consensus: Most people agree that it ought to be discouraged, although they don't agree on how. Some religious, community, and school groups are attempting to discourage adolescent sex by urging abstinence. Other groups accept the current level of sexual activity and urge teenagers to use contraceptives. In fact, as noted in Chapter 6, adolescent sexual activity did decline in the 1990s and 2000s, especially among boys, while contraceptive usage went up—pleasing both the abstinence and contraception camps. Moreover, teenage birthrates declined to all-time lows. Some research suggests that teenage childbearing may be more a reflection of a young woman's disadvantaged background than a cause of future problems. If so, then discouraging teenage childbearing without addressing the underlying disadvantages might not make much difference to a young woman's life chances.

Moreover, as noted in Chapter 6, the nonmarital childbearing problem is no longer just a teenage childbearing problem. In 2010 only 20 percent of all nonmarital births occurred to teenagers. Sixty percent occurred to women in their twenties (U.S. National Center for Health Statistics, 2011a). It is true that teenagers account for a large share of all *first* nonmarital births; but programs that focus solely on teenagers will miss the much larger number of older unmarried women who give birth. Many of them are in cohabiting relationships with the fathers of their children—relationships with a high risk of breaking up. And a breakup may be followed by having a child with another partner, leading to the problem of multiple-partner fertility, discussed in Chapter 9. But designing programs that discourage adult women from having children outside of marriage is more difficult. In addition, the case for doing so is more controversial: Many of these births represent childbearing decisions by adults, not adolescents. Some liberals would argue that government should respect their choices, rather than try to discourage them.

SINGLE-PARENT FAMILIES

In fact, many liberals argue that the proper response to family change is to provide greater support to single parents. Advocates of this approach believe that increases in the number of single-parent families result from broad economic and cultural trends that are not easily reversed by government programs. The pertinent economic trends are the movement of women into the workforce and the decline in the earning potential of non-college-educated young men. Women's labor force participation increases their economic independence, reducing the necessity of their being married. Few people today would favor policies that restrict women's economic opportunities. The decline in poorly educated young men's job prospects has made them less attractive as marriage partners and may thus have increased the likelihood that teenagers and young adults would bear children outside of marriage. The cultural trend behind the increase in single-parent families is increasing individualism, which has been rising in the United States at least since de Tocqueville noticed it in the 1830s but which appeared to take another quantum leap in the latter half of the twentieth century. During the 1960s and 1970s, in particular, a turbulent time of political and social protest, the divorce rate doubled, cohabitation emerged among the middle class, and sexual activity outside marriage became more acceptable.

This analysis of social trends leads to a pragmatic argument for assisting low-income single-parent families. Like it or not, its advocates say, they are here to stay in large numbers, and withholding aid from them would hurt their children. Some writers offer a more positive view: They maintain that marriage-based families are not necessarily better for children, and that the diversity of family forms may be beneficial (Stacey, 2011). Either position translates into advocacy for increased support to single parents. This has not been a politically popular position in recent years. The thrust of the welfare reform legislation has been to restrict aid to single parents in order to encourage marriage and discourage nonmarital childbearing. This policy is consistent with the view of conservatives.

NATIONAL HEALTH INSURANCE

A potentially more popular alternative is to assist families through benefits that are universal rather than means-tested (for example, available to all parents rather than only to parents with incomes below a certain level). In other words, provide the same benefit to *all* families with children, whether headed by two parents or one parent, whether the mother is working outside the home or not. Many European countries, for example, provide universal child allowances—a fixed annual payment per child that the government pays to all parents, regardless of their incomes. The argument is that universal benefits acquire broad political support among families of all incomes. Some students of public policy have argued that only universal social programs, such as Social Security, gather enough political strength to retain adequate funding over the long run (Skocpol, 1991). The Achilles heel of universal programs, however, is that because of their universal coverage they are very expensive. Programs targeted on the poor are cheaper but command less political support.

The U.S. Congress did recently enact an important universal program of assistance to families. It is the Affordable Care Act, otherwise known as national health insurance. It is scheduled to go into effect fully in 2014. Implementing national health insurance would be very positive from the standpoint of liberal family policy because it would extend coverage to most of the 19 percent of single-parent family households and 12 percent of two-parent family households who do not currently have health insurance coverage (Kaiser Family Foundation, 2011). In addition, the lack of health insurance benefits in many part-time and low-wage jobs creates a perverse incentive for parents to apply for, or remain on, the public assistance rolls. This is because parents and children receiving public assistance also receive health insurance through the Medicaid program for the poor. When a parent gives up public assistance to take a job, she may find that she loses all her medical coverage, and she may decide that having protection from large medical bills dictates that she quit her job. The problem has been eased by recent expansions of Medicaid to some children in nonwelfare, low-income families, but the parents of these children are still at high risk of not having health insurance.

The future of the Affordable Care Act was tied to the 2012 Presidential election. The act was strongly supported by President Obama, who viewed it as one of the most significant achievements of his presidency. But it was opposed by conservatives, who pledged to repeal it. They argued that such a massive expansion of government, including a requirement that everyone purchase health insurance, was a threat to personal freedom. If, by the time you read this, President Obama has won reelection, the Act will likely go forward; if not, its future will be uncertain.

RESPONSIBLE FATHERHOOD

As with reducing teenage childbearing, the goal of encouraging fathers to take more responsibility for their children is noncontroversial—but surprisingly complex. Policy-makers have focused on fathers who do not live with their children; and in the 1980s and 1990s, they had in mind divorced fathers, many of them middle class, and most of them employed. As part of their divorce decrees, judges often ordered them to pay their former wives a set amount of funds per month in support of their children. To increase the number of fathers who fully met their child support obligations, lawmakers passed a series of bills that enforced this obligation. For example, employers can be required to withhold part of the pay of their workers and to send those funds to the child-support system. These measures did increase compliance with court orders.

But recent attention has shifted to a more difficult problem: how to increase the involvement of low-income fathers who have never married the mothers of their children. And nearly all of the concern has been about child support payments rather than about paternal involvement with their children in a wider sense. State agencies now routinely try to identify the fathers of children whose mothers are receiving public assistance, order them to pay child support, and attempt to collect. But many of these men work in intermittent, low-wage jobs and do not have steady earnings. Moreover, they face a substantial likelihood of spending time in prison, as noted in Chapter 9. All too often, these men pile up "arrears," or unpaid child support amounts, that increase every month, whether they have a job or not and whether they are incarcerated or not. These large arrears can discourage them from working and encourage them to engage in under-the-table arrangements with the mothers.

In addition, given high rates of multiple-partner fertility, low-income fathers often have children by more than one mother; consequently, they may live with some of their children but not others. How they should divide their income and their time among these children and their mothers isn't clear (Cancian, Meyer, & Han, 2011). Moreover, although low-income men may value the role of fatherhood and wish to succeed in it, they may have had no good role models when they were children. In any case, problems such as lack of employment, incarceration, and gender distrust between women and men often make it difficult to succeed (Tach & Edin, 2011). Many low-income fathers view themselves as doing the best they can, given their limited resources: supporting themselves, providing financial assistance to the partner and children they are living with, and helping out the mothers of their past children if anything is left over (Nelson & Edin, 2013).

This complex situation suggests to many liberals and some conservatives that government agencies may have gone as far as they can go with policies that only focus on collecting money from fathers. Observers argue that what's needed is to also improve low-income men's position in the labor market so that they can become steady earners. For this reason, it is said, encouraging young adults to stay in school longer, along with providing better job training, would be important (Smeeding & Carlson, 2011). So would discouraging early unplanned pregnancies (Furstenberg, 2011). It's clear that the current policies, designed for a world of middle-class divorced dads, aren't working well among the low-income population; and it will be a challenge to develop better ones.

WORK–FAMILY BALANCE

Chapter 8 presented information about the potential conflicts employed parents feel between their work and family responsibilities: work overload, spillover, and the difficulty some parents face in finding adequate child care.

How much to increase government support for employed parents is a current political issue.

It discussed the movement to create a "responsive workplace" that allows workers to fulfill their family responsibilities more easily. Although most conservatives agree that government should provide support to employed parents, liberals want a much broader and more costly set of supports than conservatives. Consider parental leave. In 1993, as noted in Chapter 8, Congress enacted a law requiring large employers to provide their employees with 12 weeks of unpaid leave to care for newborns or deal with other family medical emergencies. Opponents claimed it would place an unfair burden on employers, who would be required to hold open employees' jobs until they returned from parental and medical leaves. Advocates of parental leave, on the other hand, were disappointed that the leave would be unpaid. They argued that low- and moderate-income workers would not be able to afford to take an unpaid leave. The advocates noted that many European countries provide a longer leave with at least partial pay. In fact, European nations provide substantially more support to employed parents than does the United States.

More generally, liberal advocates maintain that the rise of the dual-earner couple has created a harried lifestyle that should be eased for the sake of parents and children. One book laid out an ambitious agenda that includes paid parental leave, responsive workplaces, a higher minimum wage, increased tax relief for parents, higher quality and more affordable child care, after-school programs, and more (Hewlett & West, 1998). Conservatives counter that the past few decades have seen large increases in government support for working parents, such as the expansion of the EITC, and significant increases in child care funds, much of it targeted to mothers receiving TANF, who must make a transition from welfare to paid employment (Haskins, 2001). In fact, between 1997 and 2006, government funding for child care subsidies more than doubled to $9 billion (Danziger, 2010). Conservatives would prefer tax credits that would assist all families with at least one worker, including married couples in which the wife is not employed. It is a debate that is likely to remain at the forefront of the family policy agenda in the near future.

Quick Review

- Conservatives favor government programs to support heterosexual marriage and oppose the recognition of same-sex marriage, while liberals take the opposite view.
- Conservatives and liberals both support reducing nonmarital childbearing. Conservatives favor programs that advocate abstinence, whereas liberals prefer sex education and more access to contraception.
- Liberals favor accepting family diversity and support policies that would expand aid to single parents and their children, while Conservatives prefer to emphasize work obligations.
- Liberals support the Affordable Care Act, which creates government-regulated health insurance with near-universal coverage; Conservatives believe the Act represents an unwarranted extension of government into family life.
- Liberals propose an expanded governmental role in helping parents manage work and family responsibilities, whereas conservatives prefer programs that don't aid employed mothers more than mothers who aren't employed.

Family Policy in the 2010s

These are the kinds of issue that are being discussed and debated in the 2010s. Table 14.2 summarizes the liberal and conservative positions on each of them. Opinions are not quite as polarized as the table suggests. There is some conservative support for same-sex marriage, on the principle that marriage is a source of stability and security in personal life that should be extended to same-sex couples (Sullivan, 1996; Olson, 2010). There is some liberal support for marriage promotion, on the principle that marriage provides an excellent environment for children and that couples who wish to marry should be supported (Ooms, 2004). Nevertheless, the political divisions are apparent:

- Liberals, by and large, believe that the growth of diverse forms of family life should be accepted and even welcomed. They oppose programs that promote heterosexual marriage over other family forms, and they approve of same-sex marriage. They favor policies that provide direct assistance to employed parents, single-parent families, and low-income fathers. They support national health insurance.
- Conservatives, in general, believe that heterosexual marriage is the superior setting for raising children and favor programs that promote it; they oppose same-sex marriage. They are neutral at best on the issue of married

Table 14.2   Liberal and Conservative Positions on Family Issues

ISSUE	LIBERAL POSITION	CONSERVATIVE POSITION
Marriage promotion	Do not promote one type of family over other kinds.	Promote marriage by enhancing communication skills among young adults.
Same-sex marriage	Legalize it.	Prohibit it, and perhaps prohibit civil unions, too.
Nonmarital childbearing	Increase sex education and availability of contraception.	Encourage sexual abstinence. Don't support nonmarital births to mothers receiving TANF.
Single-parent families	Provide greater cash assistance and child care subsidies.	Enforce work obligations as a condition of assistance.
National Health Insurance	Achieve universal coverage through government regulations, mandates, and financial assistance.	Rely on the private system of obtaining insurance through employment for most of the non-poor.
Responsible fatherhood	Support more education and job training for non-resident fathers.	Maintain strong child support enforcement system.
Work–family balance	Implement paid parental leave and more child care assistance for working parents.	Assist all marriage-based families, regardless of whether both spouses work.

women working outside the home. They wish to discourage nonmarital childbearing. They approve of programs that enforce the obligations of welfare recipients to search for work and of non-resident fathers to pay child support. They oppose national health insurance.

While one could favor elements of both viewpoints, there are important trade-offs between them. Measures that provide assistance to unmarried parents, favored by liberals, may weaken the incentive to marry, which is important to conservatives. Programs that are restricted to two-parent families, favored by conservatives, risk excluding some of the neediest families. And universal programs, favored by liberals, help all parents and children but are costly and expand the role of government. In a world of limited government budgets, allocating funds to programs that support one worldview sometimes precludes expenditures that support the other worldview. At a time of recovery from a historic recession, options are limited. How best to support families in this challenging environment remains a critical and contentious issue.

Looking Back

1. **What is the "welfare state"?** In the twentieth century, the United States and other Western nation–states enacted numerous social programs to provide support to workers and their families. These "welfare state" measures softened the hardships of the labor market. In the United States, the programs were initially designed under the assumption that husbands would work full-time for wages, and wives would do full-time domestic work in the household. Congress did not anticipate that large numbers of wives would work outside the home or that divorce and childbearing outside of marriage would become more common.

2. **What are the themes that conservatives and liberals stress in debating family policies?** Conservatives believe that heterosexual marriage-based families are the best family form and provide an optimal environment for raising children. They tend to believe that the upheaval in family life over the past half-century has been a result of cultural change: a deterioration in the values that supported marriage. They also believe in a modest role for government programs in support of family life. Liberals accept and defend the emergence of family diversity. They see family change as rooted in changes in the economy; and they favor more assistance for low-income families and working parents.

3. **Why was the 1996 welfare reform law a sharp break from earlier government policies toward low-income families?** The 1996 welfare reform law authorized states to set a time limit of five years or less on the receipt of cash assistance in the new TANF program. The law also strengthened work requirements and ended the entitlement to cash assistance for low-income single-parent families. Supporters of the bill argued that dependence on public benefits was detrimental to low-income families; liberals countered that dependence was a symptom of the deeper problem of poverty.

4. **What should be the government's stance toward marriage?** Conservatives favor programs to promote heterosexual marriage such as the Healthy Marriage Initiative. They mostly oppose same-sex marriage and support laws and constitutional amendments banning it. Liberals oppose marriage promotion programs and the idea that government should favor one kind of family over another. They favor allowing same-sex marriage.

5. **How much should the government assist low-income families and middle-class working parents?** Liberals favor further assistance to low-income families, such as increased child care subsidies and a larger Earned Income Tax Credit. They also favor easing the time crunch on middle-class working parents through measures such as paid parental leave and child care assistance. Conservatives favor tying benefits to the poor with strong obligations to find jobs. They do not favor further assistance to middle-class working parents.

 Go to the Online Learning Center at www.mhhe.com/cherlin7e to test your knowledge of the chapter concepts and key terms.

Study Questions

1. What kinds of assistance does the government provide to middle-class families?
2. Describe the rise and fall of the family wage system.
3. Why is abortion such a contentious political issue?
4. How does the EITC exemplify the practical consensus on policy that sometimes emerged in the last decades of the twentieth century?
5. Describe the differing perspectives of liberals and conservatives on the issue of nonmarital childbearing.
6. What are the arguments for and against greater government support for parents who are employed?
7. What issues underlie the debate about whether the government should support marriage-promotion programs?
8. How have changes in the meaning of marriage affected the issue of whether same-sex couples should have the right to marry?

Key Terms

block grant   447
Earned Income Tax Credit
   (EITC)   445
entitlement   446
family policy   436
family wage system   439

nation   437
nation–state   437
poverty line   444
Social Security
   Act of 1935   435
state   437

Temporary Assistance to Needy
   Families (TANF)   448
welfare state   438

Thinking about Families

The Public Family	The Private Family
Many states now withhold part of a recipient's TANF benefits if she doesn't get her children inoculated against childhood diseases or if her children don't attend school regularly. Do you think this is a good policy?	Is the government inappropriately invading private life if it tries to encourage people to form one kind of family—say, a married-couple family—rather than another kind?

Families on the Internet   www.mhhe.com/cherlin7e

Note: While all the URLs listed were current as of the printing of this book, these sites often change. Please check our Web site (www.mhhe.com/cherlin7e) for updates.

The Families and Work Institute (www.familiesandwork.org) combines research and advocacy on the topic of combining work and family responsibilities. Its Web site has summaries of recent reports and surveys.

The Center on Law and Social Policy (www.clasp.org) offers balanced policy briefs on the issue of government support for marriage. Do a search on "marriage" to find several relevant reports on marriage promotion.

Many advocacy organizations have sites that argue for or against same-sex marriage. Balanced,

moderate commentary, however, is in short supply, so examine these sites critically. On the side favoring same-sex marriage, see www.freedomtomarry.org. On the other side, see www.nationformarriage.org, which urges individual action to defend traditional marriage.

The U.S. Department of Health and Human Services maintains a website with a great deal of information on "responsible fatherhood." See www.fatherhood.hhs.gov.

Glossary

1965 Immigration Act Act passed by the U.S. Congress which ended restrictions that had blocked most Asian immigration and substituted an annual quota.

active life expectancy The number of years a person can expect to live without a disability.

activities of daily living (ADLs) Personal care activities, including bathing, dressing, getting into and out of bed, walking indoors, and using the toilet.

ADLs See **activities of daily living.**

American Indian The name used for a subset of all Native Americans, namely, those who were living in the territory that later became the 48 contiguous United States.

androgynous behavior Behavior that has the characteristics of both genders.

annulment A ruling that a marriage was never properly formed.

Asian American A person living in the United States who comes from or is descended from people who came from an Asian country.

assigned kinship Kinship ties that people more or less automatically acquire when they are born or when they marry.

assimilation The process by which immigrant groups merge their culture and behavior with that of the dominant group in the host country.

assortative marriage The tendency of people to marry others similar to themselves.

asymmetry (of gender change) The greater change in women's lives than in men's lives.

authoritarian style (of parenting) A parenting style in which parents combine low levels of emotional support with coercive attempts at control of their children.

authoritative style (of parenting) A parenting style in which parents combine high levels of emotional support with consistent, moderate control of their children.

baby boom The large number of people born during the late 1940s and 1950s.

barrio A segregated Mexican-American neighborhood in a U.S. city.

bilateral kinship A system in which descent is reckoned through both the mother's and father's lines.

biosocial approach (to gender differences) The theory that gender identification and behavior are based in part on people's innate biological differences.

birth cohort All people born during a given year or period of years.

block grant A fixed amount of money that the federal government gives each state to spend on a set of programs.

blood relatives People who share common ancestors: parents and children, uncles and aunts, nephews and nieces, grandparents and grandchildren.

boundary ambiguity A situation in which people are uncertain about who is in their family and what roles these people play.

breadwinner–homemaker family A married couple with children in which the father works for pay and the mother does not.

care work Face-to-face activity in which one person meets the needs of another who cannot fully care for her- or himself.

centenarian A person who is 100 years old or older.

child abuse Serious physical harm (trauma, sexual abuse with injury, or willful malnutrition) of a child by an adult, with intent to injure.

cohabitation The sharing of a household by unmarried persons who have a sexual relationship.

cohabiting stepfamily A household in which two adults are married or cohabiting and at least one has a child present from a previous marriage or relationship.

collective ambivalence Mixed feelings across multiple children.

compadrazgo In Mexico, a godparent relationship in which a wealthy or influential person outside the kinship group is asked to become the *compadre,* or godparent, of a newborn child, particularly at its baptism.

companionate marriage A marriage in which the emphasis is on affection, friendship, and sexual gratification.

conjugal family A kinship group comprising husband, wife, and children.

consensual union A cohabiting relationship in which a couple consider themselves to be married but have never had a religious or civil marriage ceremony.

cooperative parenting An arrangement whereby divorced parents coordinate their activities and cooperate with each other in raising their children.

created kinship Kinship ties that people have to construct actively.

crisis period A period during the first year or two after parents separate when both the custodial parent and the children experience difficulties in dealing with the situation.

cultural lag The tendency for attitudes and values to change more slowly than the material circumstances that underlie them.

domestic violence Violent acts between family members or between women and men in intimate or dating relationships.

donor insemination A procedure in which semen is inserted into the uterus of an ovulating woman.

early adulthood Period between mid-teens and about 30 when individuals finish their education, enter the labor force, and begin their own families.

Earned Income Tax Credit (EITC) A refundable tax credit to low-income families with a child or children in which at least one parent is employed.

EITC See **Earned Income Tax Credit.**

elder abuse Physical abuse of an elderly person by a nonelderly person.

entitlement A program in which the government is obligated to provide benefits to anyone who qualifies, regardless of the total cost of the program.

era of divorce tolerance The time of a tolerant approach toward divorce, from the middle of the nineteenth century until, in the United States, 1970; the grounds for divorce were widened, and divorce was made more accessible to women.

era of restricted divorce The time of a restrictive approach toward divorce, until about the middle of the nineteenth century; divorces were usually granted only on the grounds of adultery or desertion, and generally only to men.

era of unrestricted divorce The time of a virtually unrestricted access to divorce, from, in the United States, 1970 to the present; divorces are usually granted without restriction to any married person who wants one.

exchange theory A sociological theory that views people as rational beings who decide whether to exchange goods or services by considering the benefits they will receive, the costs they will incur, and the benefits they might receive if they were to choose an alternative course of action.

expressive individualism A style of life that emphasizes developing one's feelings and emotional satisfaction.

extended family A kinship group comprising the conjugal family plus any other relatives present in the household, such as a grandparent or uncle.

externalities Benefits or costs that accrue to others when an individual or business produces something.

extramarital sex Sexual activity by a married person with someone other than his or her spouse.

family inequality The extent to which some families obtain more income and wealth than do others.

family of choice A family formed through voluntary ties among individuals who are not biologically or legally related.

family policy Political beliefs about how the government should assist families in caring for dependents.

family wage system A division of labor in which the husband earns enough money to support his family and the wife remains home to do housework and child care.

feminist theory A sociological theory that focuses on the domination of women by men.

fertility The number of births in a population.

flextime A policy that allows employees to choose, within limits, when they will begin and end their working hours.

formal sector The part of the economy in which workers have labor contracts and legal protections and employers are regulated.

foster care The removal of children from their parental home and their placement in another home.

free-rider problem The tendency for people to obtain public goods by letting others do the work of producing them—metaphorically, the temptation to ride free on the backs of others.

frustration–aggression perspective The theory that aggressive behavior occurs when a person is blocked from achieving a goal.

gender The social and cultural characteristics that distinguish women and men in a society.

generalized exchange The provision of assistance to one member of a family with the expectation that someone in the family will reciprocate at a later time.

gerontologist A social/biological scientist who specializes in the study of aging.

gestation Nine-month development of the fetus inside the mother's uterus.

globalization The increasing flows of goods and services, money, migrants, and information across the nations of the world.

Hispanic A person living in the United States who traces his or her ancestry to Latin America.

hooking up A sexual encounter with no expectation of further involvement.

hunter-gatherers People who wander through forests or over plains in small bands, hunting animals and gathering edible plants.

hypothesis A speculative statement about the relationship between two or more factors.

ideal type A hypothetical model that consists of the most significant characteristics, in extreme form, of a social phenomenon.

immigrant enclave A large, dense, single-ethnic-group, almost self-sufficient community.

incest Sexual relations with one's child, brother, or sister.

income-pooling model A model of the marriage market in which both spouses work for pay and pool their income.

individualism A style of life in which individuals pursue their own interests and place great importance on developing a personally rewarding life.

individualized marriage A marriage in which the emphasis is on self-development, flexible roles, and open communication.

informal sector The part of the economy in which workers have no labor contracts and no legal protections and employers are not regulated.

institutional marriage A marriage in which the emphasis is on male authority, duty, and conformity to social norms.

integrative perspective (on sexuality) The belief that human sexuality is determined by both social and biological factors.

interactionist approach (to gender differences) The theory that gender identification and behavior are based on the day-to-day behavior that reinforces gender distinctions.

intergenerational ambivalence Socially structured contradictory emotions in an intergenerational relationship.

intergenerational conflict Discord among family members that pulls family members apart.

intergenerational solidarity The characteristics of family relationships that knit the generations together.

internal economy The way in which income is allocated to meet the needs of each member of a household, and whose preferences shape how income is spent.

intersectionality (of black women's experience) The extent to which black women's lives are affected by overlapping systems of class, race, and gender-based disadvantage.

intersexual A person who is born with ambiguous sexual organs.

intimate outsider A person, such as a stepparent, who plays a role in a family that is somewhere between that of a parent and that of a trusted friend.

intimate terrorism A pattern in which a man seeks to control the behavior of his partner through repeated, serious, violent acts.

joint legal custody (of children after a divorce) The retaining by both parents of an equal right to make important decisions concerning their children.

joint physical custody (of children after a divorce) An arrangement whereby the children of divorced parents spend substantial time in the household of each parent.

Kinsey Report A 1948 book by zoology professor Alfred Kinsey detailing the results of thousands of interviews with men about their sexual behavior.

labor force All people who are either working outside the home or looking for work.

late modern era The last few decades of the twentieth century and the present day.

legal custody (of children after a divorce) The right to make important decisions about the children and the obligation to have legal responsibility for them.

life chances The resources and opportunities that people have to provide themselves with material goods and favorable living conditions.

life-course perspective The study of changes in individuals' lives over time, and how those changes are related to historical events.

lineage A form of kinship group in which descent is traced through either the father's or the mother's line.

living apart together A relationship in which two people define themselves as a couple but do not live together.

longitudinal survey A survey in which interviews are conducted several times at regular intervals.

lower-class families Families whose connection to the economy is so tenuous that they cannot reliably provide for a decent life.

marriage market An analogy to the labor market in which single individuals (or their parents) search for others who will marry them (or their children).

married stepfamily A stepfamily in which the partners are married.

masculinity The set of personal characteristics that society defines as being typical of men.

mass incarceration Extremely high rates of imprisonment, particularly of African American males.

matrilineage A kinship group in which descent is through the mother's line.

mediating structures Midlevel social institutions and groupings, such as the church, the neighborhood, the civic organization, and the family.

Medicaid The government program of health insurance for people with incomes below the poverty line.

Medicare The government program of health insurance for all older people.

mestizo A person whose ancestors include both Spanish settlers and Native Americans.

middle-class families Families whose connection to the economy provides them with a secure, comfortable income and allows them to live well above a subsistence level.

mortality The number of deaths in a population.

multigenerational households Households in which at least three generations of family members reside.

multiple-partner fertility Having children with more than one partner during one's lifetime.

nation A people with shared economic and cultural interests.

nation-state A term that combines the governmental and cultural connotations of the two words it comprises.

negative externalities The costs imposed on other individuals or businesses when an individual or business produces something of value to itself.

neo-traditional A style of family life centered on marriage but which may be preceded by cohabitation and in which wives work outside the home.

no-fault divorce The granting of a divorce simply on the basis of marriage breakdown due to "irreconcilable differences."

non-Hispanic whites People who identify their race as white but do not think of themselves as Hispanic.

nonmarital birth ratio The proportion of all births that occur to unmarried women.

norm A widely accepted rule about how people should behave.

objectivity The ability to draw conclusions about a social situation that are unaffected by one's own beliefs.

observational study (also known as field research) A study in which the researcher spends time directly observing each participant.

olderly population The group of people aged 65 years and over.

oldest-old The group of older people 85 years of age and over.

old-old The group of older people 75 to 84 years of age.

parallel parenting An arrangement whereby divorced parents gravitate toward a more detached style, going about their parenting business separately.

parental leave Time off from work to care for a child.

patrilineage A kinship group in which descent is through the father's line.

peer group A group of people who have roughly the same age and status as one another.

permissive style (of parenting) A parenting style in which parents provide emotional support but exercise little control over their children.

physical custody (of children after a divorce) The right of a divorced spouse to have one's children live with one.

polarization (of the labor market) A growth of job opportunities at the top and bottom of the job market but a lessening of opportunities in the middle.

polyandry A form of polygamy in which a woman is allowed to have more than one husband.

polygyny A form of polygamy in which a man is allowed to have more than one wife.

poly-victimization Experiencing multiple types of child maltreatment.

positive externalities Benefits received by others when an individual or business produces something, but for which the producer is not fully compensated.

poverty line A federally defined income limit defined as the cost of an "economy" diet for a family of four, multiplied by three.

primary analysis Analysis of survey data by the people who collected the information.

private family Two or more individuals who maintain an intimate relationship that they expect will last indefinitely—or in the case of a parent and child, until the child reaches adulthood—and who usually live in the same household and pool their income and household labor.

public family One adult, or two adults who are related by marriage, partnership, or shared parenthood, who is/are taking care of dependents, and the dependents themselves.

public goods Things that may be enjoyed by people who do not themselves produce them.

pure relationship An intimate relationship entered into for its own sake and which lasts only as long as both partners are satisfied with it.

queer theory The view that sexual life is artificially organized into categories that reflect the power of heterosexual norms.

racial-ethnic group People who share a common identity and whose members think of themselves as distinct from others by virtue of ancestry, culture, and sometimes physical characteristics.

reflexivity The process through which individuals take in knowledge, reflect on it, and alter their behavior as a result.

remittances Cash payments sent by immigrants to family members in their country of origin.

responsive workplace A work setting in which job conditions are designed to allow employees to meet their family responsibilities more easily.

role overload The state of having too many roles with conflicting demands.

scientific method A systematic, organized series of steps that ensures maximum objectivity and consistency in researching a problem.

secondary analysis Analysis of survey data by people other than those who collected it.

selection effect The principle that whenever individuals sort, or "select," themselves into groups nonrandomly, some of the differences among the groups reflect preexisting differences among the individuals.

self-identity A person's sense of who he or she is and of where he or she fits in the social structure.

serial cohabitation Living with a series of partners without marrying them.

service sector Workers who provide personal services such as education, health care, communication, restaurant meals, legal representation, entertainment, and so forth.

sex The biological characteristics that distinguish men and women.

sexual identity A set of sexual practices and attitudes that lead to the formation in a person's mind of an identity as heterosexual, homosexual, or bisexual.

sexual monogamy The state of having just one sex partner.

situational couple violence Violence that arises from a specific situation in which one or both partners act aggressively in anger.

skipped-generation households Households containing grandparents and grandchildren without either parent present.

social capital The resources that a person can access through his or her relationships with other people.

social class An ordering of all persons in a society according to their degrees of economic resources, prestige, and privilege.

social constructionist perspective (on sexuality) The belief that human sexuality is entirely socially constructed.

social exchange perspective The theory that people calculate whether to engage in a particular behavior by considering the rewards and costs of that behavior and the rewards of alternatives to it.

social institution A set of roles and rules that define a social unit of importance to society.

social learning perspective The theory that individuals learn behavior they will later exhibit by observing what others do and seeing the consequences of these actions.

social role A pattern of behaviors associated with a position in society.

Social Security Act of 1935 The federal act that created, among other provisions, Social Security, unemployment compensation, and aid to mothers with dependent children (later renamed Aid to Families with Dependent Children).

social structure The fundamental set of positions that organize society as a whole.

socialization The way in which one learns the ways of a given society or social group so that one can function within it.

socialization approach (to gender differences) The theory that gender identification and behavior are based on children's learning that they will be rewarded for the set of behaviors considered appropriate to their sex but not for those appropriate to the other sex.

specialization model A model of the marriage market in which women specialize in housework and child care and men specialize in paid work outside the home.

spillover The transfer of mood or behavior between work and home.

state A government that claims the right to rule a given territory and its population and to have a monopoly on force in that territory.

status group A group of people who share a common style of life and often identify with each other.

stepfamily   A household in which two adults are married or cohabiting and at least one has a child present from a previous marriage or relationship.

survey   A study in which individuals from a geographic area are selected, usually at random, and asked a fixed set of questions.

symbolic interaction theory   A sociological theory that focuses on people's interpretations of symbolic behavior.

telecommuting   Doing work from home using electronic communication.

Temporary Assistance to Needy Families (TANF)   A federal program of financial assistance to low-income families that began in 1996, following passage of new welfare legislation. (See **Aid to Families with Dependent Children**.)

time-diary studies   Surveys in which people are asked to keep a record of what they are doing every minute during a time period.

total fertility rate (TFR)   The average number of children a woman will bear over her lifetime if current birthrates remain the same.

transnational families   Families that maintain continual contact between members in the sending and receiving countries.

two-spirit people   In Native American societies, men or women who dressed like, performed the duties of, and behaved like a member of the opposite sex.

union   A stable, intimate relationship between two people who live in the same household but may or may not be married.

union formation   The process of beginning to live with a partner through cohabitation or marriage.

upper-class families   Families that have amassed wealth and privilege and that often have substantial prestige as well.

utilitarian individualism   A style of life that emphasizes self-reliance and personal achievement, especially in one's work life.

value   A goal or principle that is held in high esteem by a society.

welfare state   A capitalist government that has enacted numerous measures, such as social security, unemployment compensation, and a minimum wage, to protect workers and their families from the harshness of the capitalist system.

Western nations   The countries of Western Europe and the overseas English-speaking countries of the United States, Canada, Australia, and New Zealand.

women-centered kinship   A kinship structure in which the strongest bonds of support and caregiving occur among a network of women, most of them relatives, who may live in more than one household.

working-class families   Families whose income can reliably provide only for the minimum needs of what other people see as a decent life.

young-old   The group of older people 65 to 74 years of age.

References

Abbey, A., & McAuslan, P. (2004). A longitudinal examination of male college students' perpetration of sexual assault. *Journal of Consulting and Clinical Psychology, 72*, 747–756.

Aber, J. L., Jones, S., & Cohen, J. (2000). The impact of poverty on the mental health and development of very young children. In C. H. Zeanah (Ed.), *Handbook of infant mental health, second edition.* (pp. 113–128). New York: Guilford Press.

Acker, J. (2000). Rewriting class, race, and gender: Problems in feminist rethinking. In M. M. Ferree, J. Lorber, & B. B. Hess (Eds.), *Revisioning gender* (pp. 44–69). Walnut Creek, CA: AltaMira Press.

Adam, B. D. (2004). Care, intimacy, and same-sex partnerships in the 21st century. *Current Sociology, 52*, 265–279.

Agree, E. M., & Glaser, K. (2009). Demography of informal caregiving. In P. Uhlenberg (Ed.), *International handbook of the demography of aging* (pp. 647–668). New York: Springer.

Alan Guttmacher Institute. (2011). Facts on American teens' sexual and reproductive health. Retrieved January 5, 2012, from http://www.guttmacher.org/pubs/FB-ATSRH.html#19

Alwin, D. F. (1988). From obedience to autonomy: Changes in traits desired in children, 1924–1978. *Public Opinion Quarterly, 52*, 33–52.

Alwin, D. F. (1990). Historical changes in parental orientations to children. In N. Mandell (Ed.), *Sociological studies of child development* (pp. 65–86). Greenwich, CT.: JAI Press.

Amato, P. R. (1996). Explaining the intergenerational transmission of divorce. *Journal of Marriage and the Family, 58*, 628–640.

Amato, P. R. (2010). Research on divorce: Continuing trends and new developments. *Journal of Marriage and the Family, 72*, 650–666.

Amato, P. R., & Booth, A. (1997). *A generation at risk: Growing up in an era of family upheaval.* Cambridge, MA: Harvard University Press.

Amato, P. R., Booth, A., Johnson, D. R., & Rogers, S. J. (2007). *Alone together: How marriage in America is changing.* Cambridge, MA: Harvard University Press.

Amato, P. R., & Gilbreth, J. G. (1999). Non-Resident fathers and children's wellbeing. *Journal of Marriage and the Family, 61*, 557–573.

Amato, P. R., Meyers, C. E., & Emery, R. E. (2009). Changes in nonresident father-child contact from 1976 to 2002. *Family Relations, 58*, 41–53.

American Bar Association. (2003). Grounds for divorce and residency requirements. Retrieved November 10, 2003, from http://www.abanet.org/family/familylaw/table4.html

Amirkhanyan, A. A., & Wolf, D. A. (2003). Caregiver stress and noncaregiver stress: Exploring the pathways of psychiatric morbidity. *The Gerontologist, 43*, 817–827.

Anderson, K. L. (2010). Conflict, power, and violence in families. *Journal of Marriage and the Family, 72*, 726–742.

Anderson, M. (1971). *Family structure in nineteenth century Lancashire.* Cambridge, England: University Press.

Andersson, G. (2002). Children's experience of family disruption and family formation: Evidence from 16 FFS countries. *Demographic Research, 7*, 343–363.

Andersson, G., & Philipov, D. (2002). Life-table representations of family dynamics in sweden, hungary, and 14 others FFS countries: A project of descriptions of demographic behavior. *Demographic Research, 7*, 67–145.

Apel, R., & Kaukinen, C. (2008). On the relationship between family structure and antisocial behavior: Parental cohabitation and blended households. *Criminology, 46*, 35–69.

Aquilino, W. S. (1991). Family structure and home-leaving: A further specification of the relationship. *Journal of Marriage and the Family, 53*, 999–1010.

Archer, J. (2000). Sex differences in aggression between heterosexual partners: A meta-analytic review. *Psychological Bulletin, 126*, 651–680.

Archer, J. (2002). Sex differences in physically aggressive acts between heterosexual partners: A meta-analytic review. *Aggression & Violent Behavior, 7*, 313–351.

Ariès, P. (1960). *L'enfant et la vie familiale sous l'ancien regine.* Paris: Librairie Plon.

Ariès, P. (1985a). Love in married life. In P. Ariès & A. Benjin (Eds.), *Western sexuality* (pp. 130–139). Oxford: Basil Blackwell.

Ariès, P. (1985b). Thoughts on the history of homosexuality. In P. Ariès & A. Benjin (Eds.), *Western sexuality* (pp. 62–75). Oxford: Basil Blackwell.

Astone, N. M., & McLanahan, S. S. (1991). Family structure, parental practices, and high school completion. *American Sociological Review, 56,* 309–320.

Autor, D. (2010). The polarization of job opportunities in the U.S. labor market: Implications for employment and earnings. *The Hamilton Project.* Retrieved December 17, 2011, from http://www.brookings.edu/~/media/Files/rc/papers/2010/04_jobs_autor/04_jobs_autor.pdf

Autor, D. H., Katz, L. F., & Kearney, M. (2006). The polarization of the U.S. labor market. *American Economic Review, 96,* 189–194.

Bailey, B. L. (1988). *From front porch to back seat: Courtship in twentieth-century America.* Baltimore: Johns Hopkins University Press.

Bailey, M. J., & Dawood, K. (1998). Behavioral genetics, sexual orientation, and the family. In C. J. Patterson & A. R. D' Augelli (Eds.), *Lesbian, gay, and bisexual identities in families: Psychological perspectives* (pp. 3–18). New York: Oxford University Press.

Bailey, M., & Pillard, R. C. (1991). A genetic study of male sexual orientation. *Archives of General Psychiatry, 48,* 1089–1096.

Bailey, M., Pillard, R. C., Neale, M. C., & Agyei, Y. (1993). Heritable factors influence sexual orientation in women. *Archives of General Psychiatry, 50,* 217–223.

Baker, E. H., Sanchez, L. A., Nock, S. L., & Wright, J. D. (2009). Covenant marriage and the sanctification of gendered marital roles. *Journal of Family Issues, 30,* 147–178.

Bandura, A. (1973). *Aggression: A social learning analysis.* Englewood Cliffs, NJ: Prentice -Hall.

Bank of Mexico. (2011). Revenues by workers' remittances, period: Jan 1995 - Oct 2011. *Balance of Payments.* Retrieved December 20, 2011, from http://www.banxico.org.mx/SieInternet/consultar-DirectorioInternetAction.do?accion=consultarCuadro&idCuadro=CE81&sector=1&locale=en

Banks, R. R. (2011). *Is marriage for white people? How the African American marriage decline affects everyone.* New York: Dutton.

Bartlett, K. T. (1999). Improving the law relating to postdivorce arrangements for children. In E. M. Hetherington (Ed.), *Coping with divorce, single parenting, and remarriage* (pp. 71–102). Mahwah, NJ: Lawrence Erlbaum Associates.

Bauman, Z. (1992). *Intimations of postmodernity.* London: Taylor and Francis Books.

Bauman, Z. (2002). Individually, together. In U. Beck & E. Beck (Eds.), *Individualization* (pp. xiv–xix). London: Sage Publication.

Baumrind, D. (1971). Current patterns of parental authority. *Developmental Psychology Monographs,* vol. 4, no. 1, pt. 2.

Bean, F. D., & Tienda, M. (1987). *The Hispanic population of the United States.* New York: Russell Sage Foundation.

Beck, U., & Beck-Gernsheim, E. (1995). *The normal chaos of love.* Cambridge: Polity Press.

Beck, U., & Beck-Gernsheim, E. (2002). *Individualization: Institutionalized individualism and its social and political consequences.* London: Sage Publications.

Beck, U., Giddens, A., & Lash, S. (1994). *Reflexive modernization: Politics, tradition and aesthetics in the modern social order.* Cambridge: Polity Press.

Becker, G. S. (1965). A theory of the allocation of time. *Economic Journal, 75,* 493–517.

Becker, G. S. (1991). *A treatise on the family (enlarged edition).* Cambridge, MA: Harvard University Press.

Becker, G. S., Landes, E. M., & Michael, R. T. (1977). An economic analysis of marital instability. *Journal of Political Economy, 85,* 1141–1187.

Belenky, M. F., Clinchy, B. M., Goldberger, N. R., & Tarule, J. M. (1997). *Women's ways of knowing* (Tenth anniversary ed.). New York: Basic Books.

Belkin, L. (2003, October 26). The opt-out revolution. *The New York Times Magazine,* p. 42ff.

Bellah, R., Madsen, R., Sullivan, W. M., Swidler, A., & Tipton, S. M. (1985). *Habits of the heart: Individualism and commitment in America.* Berkeley: University of California Press.

Bendheim-Thoman Center for Child Wellbeing. (2007). Parents' relationship status five years after a nonmarital birth. *Fragile Families Research Brief, no. 39.* Retrieved June 12, 2010, from http://www.fragilefamilies.princeton.edu/briefs/ResearchBrief39.pdf

Bendheim-Thoman Center for Child Wellbeing. (2008). Parental incarceration and child wellbeing in fragile families. *Fragile Families Research Brief, no. 42.* Retrieved March 3, 2009, from http://www.f2f.ca.gov/res/pdf/ParentalIncarceration.pdf

Benería, L. (2003). *Gender, development, and globalization: Economic as if all people mattered.* New York: Routledge.

Bengtson, V. L. (2001). Beyond the nuclear family: The increasing importance of multigenerational bonds. *Journal of Marriage and the Family, 63,* 1–16.

Bengtson, V. L., Biblarz, T. J., & Roberts, R. E. L. (2002). *How families still matter: A longitudinal study of youths in two generations.* Cambridge: Cambridge University Press.

Bennice, J. A., & Resick, P. A. (2003). Marital rape: History, research, and practice. *Trauma, Violence, & Abuse, 4,* 228–246.

Benson, M. L., Fox, G. L., DeMaris, A., & Van Wyk, J. (2003). Neighborhood disadvantage, individual economic distress and violence against women in intimate relationships. *Journal of Quantitative Criminology, 19*, 207–235.

Berger, B., & Berger, P. L. (1983). *The war over the family: Capturing the middle ground.* Garden City, New York.

Bernard, J. (1981). The good provider role: Its rise and fall. *American Psychologist, 36*, 1–12

Berry, M. F., & Blassingame, J. W. (1982). *Long memory: The black experience in America.* New York: Oxford University Press.

Besharov, D. J., & Laumann, L. A. (1997). Don't call it child abuse if it's really poverty. *Journal of Children and Poverty, 3*, 5–34.

Bianchi, S. M., Hotz, V. J., McGarry, K., & Seltzer, J. (2008). Intergenerational ties: Theories, trends, and challenges. In A. Booth, A. C. Crouter, S. Bianchi, & J. Seltzer (Eds.), *Intergenerational caregiving* (pp. 3–43). Washington, DC: Urban Institute Press.

Bianchi, S. M., Robinson, J. P., & Milkie, M. A. (2006). *Changing rhythms of American family life.* New York: Russell Sage Foundation.

Bianchi, S. M., Subaiya, L., & Kahn, J. R. (1999). The gender gap in economic well-being of nonresident fathres and custodial mothers. *Demography, 36*, 195–203.

Biblarz, T. J., & Stacey, J. (2010). How does the gender of parents matter? *Journal of Marriage and the Family, 72*, 3–22.

Bittman, M., Craig, L., & Folbre, N. (2004). Packaging care: What happens when children receive non-parental care? In N. Folbre & M. Bittman (Eds.), *Family time: The social organization of care* (pp. 134–151). London: Routledge.

Black, A. (1924). Is the young person coming back? *Harper's* (August), 340.

Black, M. C., Basile, K. C., Breiding, M. J., Smith, S. G., Walters, M. L., Merrick, M. T., Chen, J., Stevens, M. R. (2011). The national intimate partner and sexual violence survey: 2010 summary report. *National Center for Injury Prevention and Control, Centers for Disease Control and Prevention.* Retrieved February 9, 2012.

Blair-Loy, M. (2003). *Competing devotions: Career and family among women executives.* Cambridge, MA: Harvard University Press.

Blank, R. M., & Greenberg, M. H. (2008). Improving the measurement of poverty. *Hamilton Project Discussion Paper.* Retrieved March 25, 2009, from http://www.brookings.edu/papers/2008/12_poverty_measurement_blank.aspx

Blau, F. D., & Kahn, L. M. (2007). The gender pay gap. *Economists' Voice*, June, 1–5.

Blauvelt, M. T. (2007). *The work of the heart: Young women and emotion 1780–1830.* Charlottesville: University of Virginia Press.

Bledsoe, C. (1990). Transformations in sub-Saharan African marriage and fertility. *Annals of the American Academy of Political and Social Science, 501*(July), 115–125.

Bloch, R. H. (2003). Changing conceptions of sexuality and romance in eighteenth-century America. *William and Mary Quarterly, 60*, 13–42.

Blumer, H. (1962). Society as symbolic interaction. In A. M. Rose (Ed.), *Human behavior and social processes* (pp. 179–192). Boston, MA: Houghton Mifflin.

Boden, S. (2003). *Consumerism, romance, and the wedding experience.* Hampshire: Palgrave Macmillan.

Bogle, K. (2008). *Hooking up: Sex, dating, and relationships on campus.* New York: New York University Press.

Bonnie, R. J., & Wallace, R. B. (Eds.). (2003). *Elder mistreatment: Abuse, neglect, and exploitation in aging America.* Washington, DC: National Academies Press.

Booth, A., & Dabbs, J. J., Jr. (1993). Testosterone and men's marriages. *Social Forces, 72*, 463–477.

Booth, A., Johnson, D. R., Branaman, A., & Sica, A. (1995). Belief and behavior: Does religion matter in today's marriage? *Journal of Marriage and the Family, 57*, 661–671.

Booth, C. L., Clarke-Stewart, A., Vandell, D. L., McCartney, K., & Owen, M. T. (2002). Child-care usage and mother-infant quality time. *Journal of Marriage and the Family, 64*, 16–26.

Borchorst, A. (2000). Feminist thinking about the welfare state. In M. M. Ferree, J. Lorber, & B. B. Hess (Eds.), *Revisioning gender* (pp. 99–127). Walnut Creek, CA: AltaMira Press.

Bos, H. M. W., van Balen, F., & van dem Boom, D. (2007). Child adjustment and parenting in planned lesbian-parent families. *American Journal of Orthopsychiatry, 77*, 38–48.

Boss, P. (1999). *Ambiguous loss: Learning to live with unresolved grief.* Cambridge, MA: Harvard University Press.

Boswell, J. (1982). Revolutions, universals, and sexual categories. *Salmagundi, 58–59*, 89–113.

Bott, E. (1957). *Family and social network.* London: Tavistock.

Bourdieu, P. (1980). Le capital social: Notes provisaire. *Actes de la recherche en sciences sociales, 3*, 2–3.

Boushey, H. (2011a). The end of the mancession: Now it's women who are the economy's big losers. *Center for American Progress.* Retrieved July 16, 2011, from http://www.americanprogress.org/issues/2011/01/atw_mancession.html

Boushey, H. (2011b). Not working: Unemployment among married couples. Retrieved July 16, 2011, from http://www.americanprogress.org/issues/2011/05/marital_unemployment.html

Bramlett, M. D., & Mosher, W. D. (2002). Cohabitation, marriage, divorce and remarriage in the United States Series 22, No 2. Retrieved June, 2003, from www.cdc.gov/nchs/data/series/sr_23/sr23_022.pdf

Brandon, P. D. (1999). Income-pooling arrangements, economic constraints, and married mothers' child care choices. *Journal of Family Issues, 20*, 350–370.

Bratter, J. L., & King, R. B. (2008). "But will it last?" Marital instability among interracial and same-sex couples. *Family Relations, 57*, 160–171.

Bray, J. H. (1999). From marriage to remarriage and beyond. In E. M. Hetherington (Ed.), *Coping with divorce, single parenting, and remarriage* (pp. 253–271). Mahwah, NJ: Lawrence Erlbaum Associates.

Briere, J., & Elliot, D. M. (1994). Immediate and long-term impacts of child sexual abuse. *The Future of Children, 4*, 54–59.

Brodzinsky, D. M., Schechter, M. D., & Marantz, R. (1992). *Being adopted: The lifelong search for self.* New York: Doubleday.

Bronte-Tinkew, J., Moore, K., & Carrano, J. (2006). The father-child relationship, parenting styles, and adolescent risk behaviors in intact families. *Journal of Family Issues, 27*, 850–881.

Brown, S. L. (2006). Family structure transitions and adolescent well-being. *Demography, 43*, 447–461.

Brown, S., & Lin, I.-F. (2011). Divorce in middle and later life: New estimates from the 2009 American community survey. *Center for Family and Demographic Research, Bowling Green State University.* Retrieved January 28, 2012, from http://www.bgsu.edu/downloads/cas/file94173.pdf

Brown, S. L., & Manning, W. D. (2009). Family boundary ambiguity and the measurement of family structure: The significance of cohabitation. *Demography, 46*, 85–101.

Brown, S. L., & Rinelli, L. N. (2010). Family structure, family processes, and adolescent smoking and drinking. *Journal of Research on Adolescence, 20*, 259–273.

Buchanan, C. M., Maccoby, E. E., & Dornbusch, S. F. (1996). *Adolescents after divorce.* Cambridge, MA: Harvard University Press.

Budgeon, S., & Roseneil, S. (2004). Editors' introduction: Beyond the conventional family. *Current Sociology, 52*, 127–134.

Bulcroft, K., Bulcroft, R., Smeins, L., & Cranage, H. (1997). The social construction of the North American honeymoon, 1880–1995. *Journal of Family History, 22*, 462–490.

Bulcroft, R. A., Bulcroft, K., Bradley, K., & Simpson, C. (2000). The management and production of risk in romantic relationships: A postmodern paradox. *Journal of Family History, 25*, 63–92.

Bumpass, L. L., Raley, K., & Sweet, J. A. (1995). The changing character of stepfamilies: Implications of cohabitation and nonmarital childbearing. *Demography, 32*, 1–12.

Burgess, E. W., & Locke, H. J. (1945). *The family: From institution to companionship.* New York: American Book Company.

Burstein, N. R. (2007). Economic influences on divorce. *Journal of Policy Analysis and Management, 26*, 387–429.

Burtless, G., & Gordon, T. (2011). The federal stimulus programs and their effects. In D. B. Grusky, B. Western, & C. Wimer (Eds.), *The great recession* (pp. 249–293). New York: Russell Sage Foundation.

Buss, D. M., Shackelford, T. K., Kirkpatrick, L. A., & Larsen, R. J. (2001). A half-century of mate preferences: The cultural evolution of values. *Journal of Marriage and the Family, 63*, 491–503.

Butler, J. (1990). *Gender trouble: Feminism and the subversion of identity.* New York: Routledge.

Cabrera, N. J., Tamis-LeMonda, C. S., Bradley, R. H., Hofferth, S., & Lamb, M. E. (2000). Fatherhood in the twenty-first century. *Child Development, 71*, 127–136.

Cain, M. (1983). Fertility as an adjustment to risk. *Population and Development Review, 9*, 688–702.

Calhoun, A. W. (1919). *A social history of the American family from 1865–1919.* New York: Barnes and Noble.

Callendar, C., & Kochems, L. (1983). The North American berdache. *Current Anthropology, 24*, 443–470.

Camarillo, A. (1979). *Chicanos in a changing society: From Mexican pueblos to American barrios in Santa Barbara and Southern California, 1848–1940.* Cambridge, MA: Harvard University Press.

Cameron, T. (2003, September 6). A way but no will when it comes to foster care. *The New York Times,* p. A11.

Cancian, F. M. (1987). *Love in America: Gender and self-development.* Cambridge, England: Cambridge University Press.

Cancian, M., Meyer, D. R., & Han, E. (2011). Child support: Responsible fatherhood and the quid pro quo. *Annals of the American Academy of Political and Social Science, 635*(1), 163–191.

Capaldi, D. M., & Kim, H. K. (2007). Typological approaches to violence in couples: A critique and alternative conceptual approach. *Clinical Psychology Review, 27*, 253–265.

Carlson, M. J., & Corcoran, M. E. (2001). Family structure and children's behavioral and cognitive outcomes. *Journal of Marriage and the Family, 63*, 779–792.

Carlson, M. J., & Furstenberg, F. F., Jr. (2006). The prevalence and correlates of multipartnered fertility among urban U.S. parents. *Journal of Marriage and the Family, 68*, 718–732.

Carpenter, C., & Gates, G. J. (2008). Gay and lesbian partnership: Evidence from California. *Demography, 45*, 573–590.

Carrington, C. (1999). *No place like home: Relationships and family life among lesbians and gay men.* Chicago: University of Chicago Press.

Carroll, J. S., Olson, C. D., & Buckmiller, N. (2007). Family boundary ambiguity: A 30-year review of theory, research, and measurement. *Family Relations, 56*, 210–230.

Castro-Martin, T., Domínguez-Folgueras, M., & Martín-García, T. (2008). Not truly partnerless: Nonresidential partnerships and retreat from marriage in Spain. *Demographic Research, 18*, 443–468.

Cavanagh, S. E., & Huston, A. C. (2006). Family instability and children's early problem behavior. *Social Forces, 85*, 551–581.

Cavanagh, S. E., & Huston, A. C. (2008). The timing of family instability and children's well-being. *Journal of Marriage and the Family, 70*, 1258–1270.

Center for Law and Social Policy. (2006). Toward a decade of indifference: Administration ignores child care needs of working families. Retrieved March 14, 2006, from http://www.clasp.org/publications/childcare_2007budget.pdf

Center on Budget and Policy Priorities. (2010). Introduction to unemployment insurance. Retrieved July 31, 2011, from http://www.cbpp.org/cms/index.cfm?fa=view&id=1466#_ftn2

Chafe, W. H. (1972). *The American woman: Her changing social, economic, and political roles, 1920–1970.* New York: Oxford University Press.

Chalk, R., Gibbons, A., & Scarupa, H. (2002). The multiple dimensions of child abuse and neglect: New insights into an old problem (research brief). Washington, DC: Child Trends.

Chan, S. C. (2006). Love and jewelry: Patriarch control, conjugal ties, and changing identities. In J. S. Hirsch & H. Wardlow (Eds.), *Modern loves: The anthropology of romantic courtship and companionate marriage* (pp. 35–50). Ann Arbor: University of Michigan Press.

Chao, R. (1994). Beyond parental control and authorization parenting style: Understanding Chinese parenting through the cultural norm of training. *Child Development, 65*, 1111–1119.

Charles, M., & Bradley, K. (2009). Indulging our gendered selves: Sex segregation by field of study in 44 countries. *American Journal of Sociology, 114*, 924–976.

Chase-Lansdale, L., & Hetherington, M. E. (1990). The impact of divorce on life-span development: Short and long term effects. In P. B. Baltes (Ed.), *Life-span development, and behavior* (Vol. 10, pp. 105–150). Hillsdale, NJ: Lawrence Erlbaum Associates.

Chase-Lansdale, P. L., Moffitt, R. A., Lohman, B. J., Cherlin, A. J., Coley, R. L., Pittman, L. D., Roff, J. E., Votruba-Drzal, E. (2003). Mothers' transitions from welfare to work and the well-being of preschoolers and adolescents. *Science, 299*, 1548–1552.

Cheadle, J. E., Amato, P. R., & King, V. (2010). Patterns of nonresident father contact. *Demography, 47*, 205–225.

Cherlin, A. (1978). Remarriage as an incomplete institution. *American Journal of Sociology, 84*, 634–650.

Cherlin, A. J. (1992). *Marriage, divorce, remarriage.* Cambridge, MA: Harvard University Press.

Cherlin, A. J. (1999, October 17). I'm O.K., you're selfish. *The New York Times Magazine*, pp. 44–46.

Cherlin, A. J. (2004). The deinstitutionalization of American marriage. *Journal of Marriage and the Family, 66*, 848–861.

Cherlin, A. J. (2009). *The marriage-go-round: The state of marriage and the family in America today.* New York: Alfred A. Knopf.

Cherlin, A. J., Burton, L. M., Hurt, T. R., & Purvin, D. M. (2004). The influence of physical and sexual abuse on marriage and cohabitation. *American Sociological Review, 69*, 768–789.

Cherlin, A., Frogner, B., Ribar, D., & Moffitt, R. (2009). Welfare reform in the mid-2000s: How African American and Hispanic families in three cities are faring. *The Annals of the American Academy of Political and Social Science, 621*, 178–201.

Cherlin, A. J., & Furstenberg, F. F., Jr. (1992). *The new American grandparent: A place in the family, a life apart.* Cambridge, MA: Harvard University Press.

Cherlin, A. J., Furstenberg, F. F., Jr., , Chase-Lansdale, P. L., Kiernan, K. E., Robins, P. K., Morrison, D. R., & Teitler, J. O. (1991). Longitudinal studies of the effects of divorce on children in great britain and the United States. *Science, 252*, 1386–1389.

Chesley, N., Moen, P., & Shore, R. P. (2003). The new technology climate. In P. Moen (Ed.), *It's about time: Couples and careers* (pp. 220–241). Ithaca, NY: Cornell University Press.

Child Trends. (2001). Births outside of marriage: Perceptions vs. reality. Retrieved February 4, 2009, from http://www.childtrends.org/Files/rb_032601.pdf

Child Trends. (2011). Facts at a glance. *Publication no. 2011–10.* Retrieved January 5, 2012, from http://www.childtrends.org/Files/Child_Trends-2011_04_14_FG_2011.pdf

Chong, A., & La Ferrara, E. (2009). Television and divorce: Evidence from Brazilian novelas. *Journal of the European Economic Association, 7,* 458–468.

Clarke, A. Y. (2011). *Inequalities of love: College-educated black women and the barriers to romance and family.* Durham: Duke University Press.

Clarke, E. J., Preston, M., Raksin, J., & Bengtson, V. L. (1999). Types of conflicts and tensions between older parents and adult children. *The Gerontologist, 39,* 261–270.

Clearinghouse on International Developments in Child Youth and Family Policies. (2011). Maternity, paternity, parental and family leave policies. Retrieved January 22, 2012, from http://www.childpolicyintl.org/

Coates, T.-N. P. (2007, February 1). Is Obama black enough? *Time.*

Coleman, J. S. (1988). Social capital in the creation of human capital. *American Journal of Sociology, 94 Supplement,* S95-S120.

Coleman, M., Ganong, L. H., & Fine, M. (2000). Reinvestigating remarriage: Another decade of progress. *Journal of Marriage and the Family, 62,* 1288–1307.

Collier, J. F. (1997). *From duty to desire: Remaking families in a Spanish village.* Princeton: Princeton University Press.

Coltrane, S. (1994). Theorizing masculinities in contemporary social problems. In H. Brod & M. Kaufman (Eds.), *Theorizing masculinities* (pp. 39–60). Thousand Oaks, CA: Sage Publications.

Coltrane, S., & Adams, M. (2008). *Gender and families.* Lanham, MD: Rowman & Littlefied.

Comstock, G., & Scharrer, E. (2001). The use of television and other film-related media. In D. G. Singer & J. L. Singer (Eds.), *Handbook of children and the media* (pp. 47–72). Thousand Oaks, CA: Sage Publications.

Connell, R. W. (1995). *Masculinities.* Cambridge, UK: Polity Press.

Connidis, I. A., & McMullin, J. A. (2002). Sociological ambivalence and family ties: A critical perspective. *Journal of Marriage and the Family, 64,* 558–567.

Cook, K., O'Brien, J., & Kollock, P. (1990). Exchange theory: A blueprint for structure and process. In G. Ritzer (Ed.), *Frontiers of social theory: The new syntheses* (pp. 151–181). New York: Columbia University Press.

Cooke, L. P. (2006). 'Doing' gender in context: Household bargaining and risk of divorce in Germany and the United States. *American Journal of Sociology, 112,* 442–472.

Coontz, S. (2005). *Marriage, a history: From obedience to intimacy, or how love conquered marriage.* New York: Viking.

Cooper, S. M. (1999). Historical analysis of the family. In M. B. Sussman, S. K. Steinmetz & G. W. Peterson (Eds.), *Handbook of marriage and the family, second edition.* New York: Plenum.

Cott, N. F. (1977). *The bonds of womanhood: "Women's sphere" in New England, 1780–1835.* New Haven: Yale University Press.

Cott, N. F. (2000). *Public vows: A history of marriage and the nation.* Cambridge, MA: Harvard University Press.

Cox, D. (2008). Intergenerational caregiving and exchange: Economic and evolutionary approaches. In A. Booth, A. C. Crouter, S. Bianchi, & J. Seltzer (Eds.), *Intergenerational caregiving* (pp. 81–125). Washington, DC: The Urban Institute Press.

Cretney, S. (1993). *Step-parentage in English law.* Paper presented at the International Colloquium on Stepfamilies Today, Paris.

Crimmins, E. M., Hayward, M. D., Hagedorn, A., Saito, Y., & Brouard, N. (2009). Change in disability-free life expectancy for Americans 70 years old and older. *Demography, 466,* 627–646.

Cross-Barnet, C., Cherlin, A. J., & Burton, L. M. (2011). Bound by children: Intermittent cohabitation and living together apart. *Family Relations, 60,* 633–647.

Crouch, S. (2006, November 2). What Obama isn't: Black like me on race. *New York Daily News.*

Danziger, S. K. (2010). The decline of cash welfare and implications for social policy and poverty. *Annual Review of Sociology, 36,* 523–545.

Darling, C. A., Kallen, D. J., & Van Dusen, J. E. (1984). Sex in transition, 1900–1980. *Journal of Youth and Adolescence, 13,* 385–399.

Davis, J. A., & Smith, T. W. (2010). General social surveys, 1972–2010 cumulative codebook. Chicago: National Opinion Research Center.

Davis, N. J., & Robinson, R. V. (1988). Class identification of men and women in the 1970's and 1980's. *American Sociological Review, 53,* 103–112.

Davis, N. J., & Robinson, R. V. (1998). Do wives matter? Class identification of wives and husbands in the United States. *Social Forces, 76,* 1063–1086.

DeLeire, T., & Kalil, A. (2002). Good things come in threes: Single-parent and multigenerational family structure and adolescent development. *Demography, 39,* 393–413.

Demos, J. (1970). *A little commonwealth: Family life in Plymouth colony.* Oxford: Oxford University Press.

Deutsch, F. M. (2007). Undoing gender. *Gender & Society, 21,* 106–127.

DeVooght, K., Malm, K., Vandivere, S., & McCoy-Roth, M. (2011). Trends in adoptions from foster care in the wake of child welfare reforms. *Fosteringconnections.org, Analysis no. 4.* Retrieved July 9,

2012, from http://www.fosteringconnections.org/tools/assets/files/Connections_Adoption.pdf

Diekmann, A., & Engelhardt, H. (1999). The social inheritance of divorce: Effects of parents's family type in postwar Germany. *American Sociological Review, 64,* 783–793.

Dill, B. T. (1988). Fictive kin, papers sons, and compadrazgo: Women of color and the struggle for family survival. *Journal of Family History, 13,* 415–431.

D'Onofrio, B. M., Turkheimer, E., Emery, R. E., Slutske, W. S., Heath, A. C., Madden, P. A., & Martin, N. G. (2005). A genetically informed study of marital instability and its association with offspring psychopathology. *Journal of Abnormal Psychology, 114,* 570–586.

Doucet, A. (2006). *Do men mother? Fathering, care, and domestic responsibility.* Toronto: University of Toronto Press.

Dreby, J. (2010). *Divided by borders: Mexican migrants and their children.* Berkeley: University of California Press.

Dronkers, J., & Härkönen, J. (2008). The intergenerational transmission of divorce in cross-national perspective: Results from the fertility and family surveys. *Population Studies, 62,* 273–288.

Du Bois, W. E. B. (1903). *The souls of black folk.* Chicago: A. C. McClurg & Co.

Dunaway, W. (2003). *The African-American family in slavery and emancipation.* New York: Cambridge University Press.

Duncan, G. J. (1984). *Years of poverty, years of plenty.* Ann Arbor: Institute for Social Research, University of Michigan.

Duncan, G. J., & Brooks-Gunn, J. (1997). Income effects across the life span: Integration and interpretation. In G. J. Duncan & J. Brooks-Dunn (Eds.), *The consequences of growing up poor* (pp. 596–610). New York: Russell Sage Foundation.

Dunifon, R., & Kowaleski-Jones, L. (2002). Who's in the house? Race differences in cohabitation, single parenthood, and child development. *Child Development, 73,* 1249–1264.

Easterlin, R. A. (1980). *Birth and fortune: The impact of numbers on personal welfare.* New York: Basic Books.

Edin, K., & Kefalas, M. J. (2005). *Promises I can keep: Why poor women put motherhood before marriage.* Berkeley: University of California Press.

Edin, K., & Kissane, R. J. (2010). Poverty and the American family: A decade in review. *Journal of Marriage and the Family, 72,* 460–479.

Edin, K., & Nelson, T. J. (2012). *Doing the best I can: Fathering in the inner city.* Berkeley: University of California Press.

Eggebeen, D., & Dew, J. (2009). The role of religion in adolescence for family formation in young adulthood. *Journal of Marriage and the Family, 71,* 108–121.

Eggebeen, D. J., Snyder, A. R., & Manning, W. D. (1996). Children in single-father families in demographic perspective. *Journal of Family Issues, 17,* 441–465.

Ehrenreich, B., & Hochschild, A. (2003). *Global woman: Nannies, maids, and sex workers in the new economy.* New York: Metropolitan Books.

Ehrensaft, M. K., Cohen, P., Brown, J., Smailes, E., Chen, H., & Johnson, J. G. (2003). Intergenerational transmission of partner violence: A 20-year prospective study. *Journal of Consulting and Clinical Psychology, 71,* 741–752.

Eichner, M. (2005). Dependency and the liberal polity: On Martha Fineman's *The Autonomy Myth. California Law Review, 93,* 1285–1321.

Eisenstadt v. Baird, 438 405 (U.S. 1972).

Elder, G. H., Jr. (1974). *Children of the Great Depression: Social change in life experience.* Chicago: University of Chicago Press.

Elder, G. H. J., Conger, R. D., Foster, M. E., & Ardelt, M. (1992). Families under economic pressure. *Journal of Family Issues, 13,* 5–37.

Elliott, D. B., & Lewis, J. M. (2010). Embracing the institution of marriage: The characteristics of remarried Americans. *ACS Data on Marriage and Divorce* Retrieved July 15, 2012, from http://www.census.gov/hhes/socdemo/marriage/data/acs/Remarriage.pdf

Ellwood, D. T., & Jencks, C. (2004). The uneven spread of single-parent families: What do we know? Where do we look for answers? In K. M. Neckerman (Ed.), *Social inequality* (pp. 3–118). New York: Russell Sage Foundation.

Emerson, R. M. (1972). Exchange theory, part 2: Exchange relations and network structures. In J. Berger, J. Zelditch, & B. Anderson (Eds.), *Sociological theories in progress.* New York: Houghton Mifflin.

Emery, R. E. (1999). *Marriage, divorce, and children's adjustment* (Second ed.). Beverly Hills: Sage.

Emery, R. E., & Laumann-Billings, L. (1998). An overview of the nature, causes, and consequences of abusive family relationships: Toward differentiating maltreatment and violence. *American Psychologist, 53,* 121–135.

England, P. (1994). [book review: Gender play: Girls and boys in school]. *Contemporary Sociology, 23,* 282–283.

England, P. (2005). Emerging theories of care work. *Annual Review of Sociology, 31,* 381–399.

England, P. (2009). A gender lens on marriage. In H. E. Peters & C. M. K. Dush (Eds.), *Marriage and family: Perspectives and complexity* (pp. 57–74). New York: Columbia University Press.

England, P. (2010). The gender revolution: Uneven and stalled. *Gender & Society, 24*, 149–166.

England, P., Armstrong, E., & Fogarty, A. (2012). Accounting for women's orgasm and sexual enjoyment in college hookups and relationships. *American Sociological Review, 77*, 435–462.

England, P., Budig, M., & Folbre, N. (2002). Wages of virtue: The relative pay of care work. *Social Problems, 49*, 455–473.

England, P., & Folbre, N. (1999). The cost of caring. *The Annals of the American Academy of Political and Social Science, 561*, 39–51.

England, P., Shafer, E. F., & Fogarty, A. C. K. (2008). Hooking up and forming romantic relationships on today's college campuses. In M. S. Kimmel & A. Aronson (Eds.), *The gendered society reader* (pp. 531–546). New York: Oxford University Press.

England, P., & Thomas, R. J. (2007). The decline of the date and the rise of the college hook up. In A. S. Skolnick & H. H. Skolnick (Eds.), *Family in transition, 14th edition* (pp. 151–162). New York: Pearson.

English, D. J. (1998). The extent and consequences of child maltreatment. *The Future of Children, 8*(1), 39–53.

English, D. J., Widom, C. S., & Brandford, C. (2001). Childhood victimization and delinquency, adult criminality, and violent criminal behavior: A replication and extension, final report (NCJ 192291). Washington, DC: National Institute of Justice.

Ericksen, J. A., & Steffen, S. A. (1999). *Kiss and tell: Surveying sex in the twentieth century*. Cambridge, MA: Harvard University Press.

Evans, G. W., Chen, E., Miller, G., & Seeman, T. (2012). How poverty gets under the skin: A life course perspective. In V. Malholms & R. King (Eds.), *The Oxford handbook of poverty and child development* (pp. 13–36). New York: Oxford University Press.

Evans, M. D. R. (1986). American fertility patterns: A comparison of white and nonwhite cohorts born 1903–1956. *Population and Development Review, 12*, 267–293.

Fahrenthold, D. A. (2006, June 19). Statistics show drop in U.S. rape cases. *The Washington Post*.

Families and Work Institute. (2002). Highlights of the national study of the changing workforce Retrieved February 24, 2009, from http://familiesandwork.org/site/research/summary/nscw2002summ.pdf

Families and Work Institute. (2008). 2008 national study of employers. Retrieved February 23, 2009, from http://familiesandwork.org/3w/2008nse.pdf

Families and Work Institute. (2011). Workplace flexibility in the United States: A status report. Retrieved January 22, 2012, from http://familiesandwork.org/site/research/reports/www_us_workflex.pdf

Fan, M. (2007, April 7). Chinese slough off old barriers to divorce. *The Washington Post*.

Farley, R., & Allen, W. R. (1987). *The color line and the quality of life in America*. New York: Russell Sage Foundation.

Federal Interagency Forum and Child and Family Statistics. (2011). America's children: Key national indicators of well-being, 2011. Retrieved January 17, 2012, from http://www.childstats.gov/americaschildren/index.asp

Fenstermaker, S. (2002). Work and gender (from the gender factory). In S. Fenstermaker & C. West (Eds.), *Doing gender, doing difference: Inequality, power, and institutional change* (pp. 105–118). New York: Routledge.

Fergusson, D. M., Horwood, L. J., & Lynskey, M. T. (1997). Childhood sexual abuse, adolescent sexual behaviors, and sexual revictimization. *Child Abuse and Neglect, 21*, 789–803.

Fergusson, D. M., Horwood, L. J., & Ridder, E. M. (2005). Partner violence and mental health outcomes in a new zealand birth cohort. *Journal of Marriage and the Family, 67*, 1103–1119.

Fincham, F. D., Cui, M., Braithwaite, S., & Pasley, K. (2008). Attitudes toward intimate partner violence in dating relationships. *Psychological Assessment, 20*, 260–269.

Fincham, F. D., Stanley, S. M., & Beach, S. R. H. (2007). Transformative processes in marriage: An analysis of emerging trends. *Journal of Marriage and the Family, 69*, 275–292.

Fine, G. A. (1987). *With the boys: Little league baseball and preadolescent culture*. Chicago, IL: University of Chicago Press.

Fineman, M. A. (2004). *The autonomy myth: A theory of dependency*. New York: The New Press.

Fingerman, K. L., Pillemer, K., Silverstein, M., & Suitor, J. J. (2012). The baby boomers' intergenerational relationships. *The Gerontologist, 52*, 199–209.

Finkelhor, D., Ormrod, R. K., & Turner, H. A. (2007). Poly-victimization: A neglected component in child victimization. *Child Abuse and Neglect, 31*, 7–26.

Fischer, C. S., & Hout, M. (2006). *Century of difference: How America changed in the last one hundred years*. New York: Russell Sage Foundation.

Fischer, D. H. (1978). *Growing old in America*. New York: Oxford University Press.

Fisher, A. P. (2003). Still "not quite as good as having your own"? Toward a sociology of adoption. *Annual Review of Sociology, 29*, 335–361.

Fisher, K., Egerton, M., Gershuny, J. I., & Robinson, J. P. (2007). Gender convergence in the American heritage time use study (AHTUS). *Social Indicators Research, 82,* 1–33.

Flandrin, J.-L. (1985). Sex in married life in the early middle ages: The church's teaching and behavioral reality. In P. Ariès & A. Bejin (Eds.), *Western sexuality: Practice and precept in past and present times* (pp. 114–129). Oxford: Blackwell, Basil.

Fletcher, J. M., & Wolfe, B. L. (2009). Education and labor market consequences of teenage childbearing: Evidence using the timing of pregnancy outcomes and community fixed effects. *Journal of Human Resources, 44,* 303–345.

Folbre, N. (2001). *The invisible heart: Economics and family values.* New York: The New Press.

Fomby, P., & Cherlin, A. J. (2007). Family instability and child well-being. *American Sociological Review, 72,* 181–204.

Fonow, M. M., & Cook, J. A. (2005). Feminist methodology: New applications in the academy and public policy. *Signs: Journal of Women in Culture and Society, 30,* 2211–2236.

Forrest, J. D., & Singh, S. (1990). The sexual and reproductive behavior of American women. *Family Planning Perspectives, 22,* 206–214.

Foucault, M. (1980). *The history of sexuality.* New York: Vintage Books.

Fox, R. (1967). *Kinship and marriage.* Harmondsworth, England: Penguin Books.

Frazier, E. F. (1939). *The Negro family in the United States (revised and abridged edition).* Chicago, IL: University of Chicago Press.

Fuller-Thomson, E., & Minkler, M. (2000). African American grandparents raising grandchildren: A national profile of demographic and health characteristics. *Health & Social Work, 25,* 109–118.

Furstenberg, F. F. (2007). *Destinies of the disadvantaged: The politics of teen childbearing.* New York: Russell Sage Foundation.

Furstenberg, F. F. (2009). If Moynihan had only known: Race, class, and family change in the late twentieth century. *Annals of the American Academy of Political and Social Science, 621,* 94–110.

Furstenberg, F. F., Jr. (2011). Comment: How do low-income men and fathers matter for children and family life. *Annals of the American Academy of Political and Social Science, 635*(1), 131–137.

Furstenberg, F. F., Jr. (1976). *Unplanned parenthood: The social consequences of teenage childbearing.* New York: Free Press.

Furstenburg, F. F., Jr., & Cherlin, A. J. (1991). *Divided families: What happens to children when parents part.* Cambridge, MA: Harvard University Press.

Fussell, E., & Furstenburg, F. F., Jr. (2005). The transition to adulthood during the twentieth century. In R. A. Settersten, Jr., F. F. Furstenburg, Jr., &

R. Rumbaut (Eds.), *On the frontier of adulthood: Theory, research, and public policy* (pp. 29–75). Chicago: University of Chicago Press.

Fuwa, M. (2004). Macro-level gender inequality and the division of household labor in 22 countries. *American Sociological Review, 69,* 751–767.

Gamson, J. (1996). Must identity movements self-destruct? A queer dilemma. In S. Seidman (Ed.), *Queer theory / sociology* (pp. 395–420). Cambridge, MA: Blackwell.

Gamson, J., & Moon, D. (2004). The sociology of sexualities: Queer and beyond. *Annual Review of Sociology, 30,* 47–64.

Ganong, L. H., & Coleman, M. (1999). *Changing families, changing responsibilities: Family obligations following divorce and remarriage.* Mahwah, NJ: Lawrence Erlbaum.

Ganong, L. H., & Coleman, M. (2004). *Stepfamily relationships: Development, dynamics, and interventions.* New York: Kluwer Academic/Plenum Publishers.

Gans, H. J. (1962). *The urban villagers: Group and class in the lives of Italian-Americans.* New York: The Free Press.

Gatz, M., Bengston, V. L., & Blum, M. J. (1990). *Caregiving families* (3 rd ed.). Orlando, FL: Academic Press.

Gauthier, A. H., & Furstenberg, F. F., Jr. (2010). The experience of financial strain among families with children in the United States. *Working Paper 10–17, National Center for Family and Marriage Research.* Retrieved July 12, 2011, from http://ncfmr.bgsu.edu/pdf/working_papers/file89164.pdf

Gelles, R. J., & Cornell, C. P. (1990). *Intimate violence in families.* Newbury Park, CA: Sage.

Gennetian, L. M., Duncan, G. J., Knox, V. W., Vargas, W. G., Clark-Kaufman, E., & London, A. S. (2002). How welfare and work policies for parents affect adolescents: A synthesis of research. New York: Manpower Demonstration Research Corporation. Retrieved November 28, 2003, from www.mdrc.org/Reports2002/ng_adolescent/ng_adolsyn_full.pdf

Geronimus, A. T. (1991). Teenage childbearing and social and reproductive disadvantage: The evolution of complex questions and the demise of simple answers. *Family Relations, 40,* 463–471.

Geronimus, A. T., & Korenman, S. (1992). The socioeconomic consequences of teen childbearing reconsidered. *Quarterly Journal of Economics, 107,* 1187–1214.

Gerson, K. (2010). *The unfinished revolution: How a new generation is reshaping family, work, and gender in America.* New York: Oxford University Press.

Gerth, H. H., & Mills, C. W. (1946). *From Max Weber: Essays in sociology.* New York: Oxford University Press.

Ghimire, D. J., Axxin, W. G., Yabiku, S. T., & Thornton, A. (2006). Social change, premarital nonfamily experience, and spouse choice in an arranged marriage society. *American Journal of Sociology, 111*, 1181–1218.

Giddens, A. (1991). *Modernity and self-identity*. Stanford, CA: Stanford University Press.

Giddens, A. (1992). *The transformation of intimacy*. Stanford, CA: Stanford University Press.

Gilkes, C. T. (1995). The storm and the light: Church, family, work, and social crisis in the African-American experience. In N. Ammerman & C. Roof (Eds.), *Work, family, and religion in contemporary society* (pp. 177–198). New York: Routledge.

Gillis, J. R. (1985). *For better or worse: British marriages, 1600 to the present*. Oxford: Oxford University Press.

Glendon, M. A. (1987). *Abortion and divorce in Western law*. Cambridge, MA: Harvard University Press.

Glenn, E. N. (1983). Split household, small producer, and dual wage earner: An analysis of Chinese-American family strategies. *Journal of Marriage and the Family, 45*, 35–46.

Glenn, E. N. (2000a). Creating a caring society. *Contemporary Sociology, 29*, 84–94.

Glenn, E. N. (2000b). The social construction and institutionalization of gender and race. In M. M. Ferree, J. Lorber, & B. B. Hess (Eds.), *Revisioning gender* (pp. 3–43). Walnut Creek, CA: AltaMira Press.

Glenn, N., & Marquardt, E. (2001). Hooking up, hanging out, and hoping for Mr. Right. *Institute for American Values*. Retrieved February 8, 2009, from http://www.americanvalues.org/Hooking_Up.pdf

Glick, J. E., Bean, F. D., & Van Hook, J. V. W. (1997). Immigration and changing patterns of extended family household structure in the United States: 1970–1990. *Journal of Marriage and the Family, 59*, 177–191.

Glick, J. E., & Van Hook, J. (2002). Parents' coresidence with adult children: Can immigration explain racial and ethnic variation? *Journal of Marriage and the Family, 64*, 240–253.

Gold, S. J. (1993). Migration and family adjustment: Continuity and change among Vietnamese in the United States. In H. McAdoo (Ed.), *Family ethnicity* (pp. 300–314). Newbury Park CA: Sage.

Goldin, C. (1977). Female labor force participation: The origin of black and white differences, 1870 and 1880. *Journal of Economic History, 37*, 87–108.

Goldin, C., & Rouse, C. (2000). Orchestrating impartiality: The impact of "blind" auditions on female musicians. *American Economic Review, 90*, 715–741.

Goldscheider, F. K. (1990). The aging of the gender revolution: What do we know and what do we need to know? *Research on Aging, 12*, 531–545.

Goldscheider, F. K. (1997). Recent changes in the U.S. young adult living arrangements in comparative perspective. *Journal of Family Issues, 18*, 708–724.

Goldscheider, F. K., & Bures, R. (2003). The racial crossover in family complexity in the United States. *Demography, 40*, 569–587.

Goldscheider, F. K., & Goldscheider, C. (1993). *Leaving home before marriage: Ethnicity, familism, and generational relationships*. Madison: University of Wisconsin Press.

Goldscheider, F. K., & Goldscheider, C. (1994). Leaving and returning home in the 20th century America. *Population Bulletin, 48*(4).

Goldstein, J. R., & Kenney, C. T. (2001). Marriage delayed or marriage forgone? New cohort forecasts of first marriage for U.S. Women. *American Sociological Review, 66*, 506–519.

Goode, W. J. (1963). *World revolution and family patterns*. New York: The Free Press.

Goode, W. J. (1971). Force and violence in the family. *Journal of Marriage and the Family, 33*, 624–636.

Gooden, A., & Gooden, M. (2001). Gender representation in notable children's picture books: 1995–1999. *Sex Roles, 45*, 89–101.

Gordon, L. (1988). *Heroes of their own lives: The politics and history of family violence*. New York: Viking.

Goodrich v. Department of Public Health, 440 309 (Mass. 2003).

Gottman, J. M. (1998). Toward a process model of men in marriages and families. In A. Booth & A. C. Crouter (Eds.), *Men in families: When do they get involved? What difference does it make?* (pp. 149–192). Mahwah, NJ: Lawrence Erlbaum Associates.

Graham, E., & Jordan, L. P. (2011). Migrant parents and the psychological well-being of left-behind children in Southeast Asia. *Journal of Marriage and the Family, 73*, 763–787.

Green, A. I. (2002). Gay but not queer: Toward a post-queer study of sexuality. *Theory and Society, 31*, 521–545.

Griswold v. Connecticut, 381 479 (U.S. 1965).

Griswold del Castillo, R. (1979). *The Los Angeles barrio, 1850–1890: A social history*. Los Angeles: University of California Press.

Grogger, J., Haider, S. J., & Klerman, J. (2003). Why did the welfare rolls fall during the 1990's? The importance of entry. *American Economic Review, 93*, 288–292.

Grogger, J. T., & Karoly, L. A. (2005). *Welfare reform: Effects of a decade of change*. Cambridge, MA: Harvard University Press.

Grubb, W. N., & Lazerson, M. (1988). *Broken promises: How Americans fail their children*. Chicago: University of Chicago Press.

Guo, G., Roettger, M. E., & Cai, T. (2008). The integration of genetic propensities into social-control models of delinquency and violence among male youths. *American Sociological Review, 73*, 543–568.

Gupta, S. (2007). Autonomy, dependence, or display? The relationship between married women's earnings and housework. *Journal of Marriage and the Family, 69*, 399–417.

Gutman, H. G. (1976). *The black family in slavery and freedom, 1750–1925.* New York: Pantheon Books.

Guzman, L., Lippman, L., Moore, K. A., & O'Hare, W. (2003). *How are children doing: The mismatch between public perception and statistical reality.* Washington, DC: Child Trends.

Guzzo, K. B., & Furstenberg, F. F. (2007a). Multipartnered fertility among American men. *Demography, 44*, 583–601.

Guzzo, K. B., & Furstenberg, F. F. J. (2007b). Multipartnered fertility among young women with a nonmarital first birth: Prevalence and risk factors. *Perspectives on Sexual and Reproductive Health, 39*, 29–38.

Hagestad, G. (1985). Continuity and connectedness. In V. L. Bengtsen & J. F. Robinson (Eds.), *Grandparenthood* (pp. 31–48). Beverly Hills, CA: Sage.

Haldeman, D. C. (1991). Sexual orientation conversion therapy for gay men and lesbians: Scientific examination. In J. C. Gonsiorek & J. D. Weinrich (Eds.), *Homosexuality* (pp. 149–160). Newbury Park, CA: Sage.

Hall, S. (1904). *Adolescence: Its psychology and its relations to anthropology, sociology, sex, crime, religion and education.* New York: Appleton.

Hall, D. H., & Zhao, J. Z. (1995). Cohabitation and divorce in canada: Testing the selectivity hypothesis. *Journal of Marriage and the Family, 57*, 421–427.

Hamilton, L., & Armstrong, E. A. (2009). Gendered sexuality in young adulthood. *Gender & Society, 23*, 589–616.

Han, W.-j., & Fox, L. E. (2011). Parental work schedules and children's cognitive trajectories. *Journal of Marriage and the Family, 73*, 962–980.

Han, W.-j., & Waldfogel, J. (2007). Parental work schedules, family process, and early adolescents' risky behavior. *Children and Youth Services Review, 29*, 1249–1266.

Handel, G., Cahill, S., & Elkin, F. (2007). *Children and society: The sociology of children and childhood socialization.* New York: Oxford University Press.

Handler, J. (1995). *The poverty of welfare reform.* New Haven: Yale University Press.

Hans, J. D. (2002). Stepparenting after divorce: Stepparents' legal position regarding custody, access, and support. *Family Relations, 51*, 301–307.

Hansen, K. V. (1989). Helped put in a quilt: Men's work and male intimacy in nineteenth-century New England. *Gender & Society, 3*, 34–54.

Harding, S., & Norberg, K. (2005). New feminist approaches to social science methodologies: An introduction. *Signs: Journal of Women in Culture and Society, 30*, 2009–2015.

Hareven, T. K. (1982). *Family time and industrial time.* Cambridge, England: Cambridge University Press.

Harjo, S. S. (1993). The American Indian experience. In H. McAdoo (Ed.), *Family ethnicity* (pp. 199–207).

Harknett, K. S., & Hartnett, C. S. (2011). Who lacks support and why? An examination of mothers' personal safety nets. *Journal of Marriage and the Family, 73*, 861–875.

Harknett, K., & Knab, J. (2007). More kin, less support: Multipartnered fertility and perceived support among mothers. *Journal of Marriage and the Family, 69*, 237–253. Newbury Park CA: Sage.

Harmon, A. (2005, March 20). Ask them (all 8 of them) about their grandson. *The New York Times.*

Harrison, L. A., & Lynch, A. B. (2005). Social role theory and the perceived gender role orientation of athletes. *Sex Roles, 52*, 227–236.

Hartog, H. (2000). *Man and wife in America: A history.* Cambridge, MA: Harvard University Press.

Haskins, R. (2001). Giving is not enough: Work and work supports are reducing poverty. *The Brookings Review, 19*(3), 13–15.

Haub, C. (2006). Hispanics account for almost one-half of U.S. population growth. Retrieved February 22, 2006, from http://www.prb.org

Hays, S. (1996). *The cultural contradictions of motherhood.* New Haven: Yale University Press.

Heclo, H. (1986). The political foundations of antipoverty policy. In S. Danziger & D. Weinberg (Eds.), *Fighting poverty: What works and what doesn't* (pp. 312–340). Cambridge, MA: Harvard University Press.

Henrikson v. Gable, 412 N.W. 2nd 702 (Mich. app. 1987).

Herskovits, M. J. (1990). *The myth of the negro past [reissued with an introduction by Sidney W. Mintz].* Boston: Beacon Press.

Hetherington, E. M., & Clingempeel, G. (1992). Coping with marital transitions. *Monographs of the Society for Research in Child Development, 57.*

Hetherington, E. M., & Jodl, K. M. (1994). Stepfamilies as settings for child development. In A. Booth & J. Dunn (Eds.), *Stepfamilies: Who benefits? Who does not?* (pp. 55–79). Hillsdale, NJ: Lawrence Erlbaum.

Hetherington, E. M., & Kelly, J. (2002). *For better or for worse: Divorce reconsidered.* New York: W. W. Norton.

Hetherington, E. M., & Stanley-Hagan, M. (2000). Diversity among stepfamilies. In D. H. Demo, K. R. Allen, & M. A. Fine (Eds.), *Handbook of family diversity* (pp. 173–196). New York: Oxford University Press.

Heuveline, P., & Timberlake, J. M. (2004). The role of cohabitation in family formation: The United States in comparative perspective. *Journal of Marriage and the Family, 66*, 1214–1230.

Heuveline, P., Timberlake, J. M., & Furstenberg, F. F., Jr. (2003). Shifting childrearing to single mothers: Results from 17 western countries. *Population and Development Review, 29*, 47–71.

Hewitt, B., & de Vaus, D. (2009). Change in the association between premarital cohabitation and separation, Australia 1945–2000. *Journal of Marriage and the Family, 71*, 353–361.

Hewlett, S. A., & West, C. (1998). *The war against parents*. Boston: Houghton Mifflin.

Heymann, J. (2006). *Forgotten families: Ending the growing crisis confronting children and working parents in the global economy*. Oxford: Oxford University Press.

Hill, M. S., & Yeung, W. J. (1999). How has the changing structure of opportunities affected transitions to adulthood? In A. Booth, A. C. Crouter, & M. J. Shanahan (Eds.), *Transitions to adulthood in a changing economy* (pp. 3–39). Westport, CT: Praeger.

Hill, S. A. (2005). *Black intimacies: A gender perspective on families and relationships*. Walnut Creek, CA: AltaMira Press.

Hirsch, J. S. (2003). *A courtship after marriage: Sexuality and love in Mexican transnational families*. Berkeley: University of California Press.

Hochschild, A. (2012). *The second shift: Working families and the revolution at home. Revised and with a new afterword*. New York: Penguin.

Hochschild, A. R. (1979). Emotion work, feeling rules, and social structure. *American Journal of Sociology, 85*, 551–575.

Hofferth, S. (1984). Kin networks, race, and family structure. *Journal of Marriage and the Family, 46*, 791–806.

Hoffman, K. L., Demo, D. H., & Edwards, J. N. (1994). Physical wife abuse in a non-western society: An integrated theoretical approach. *Journal of Marriage and the Family, 56*, 131–146.

Holtzworth-Monroe, A. (2005). Male versus female intimate partner violence: Putting controversial findings into context. *Journal of Marriage and the Family, 67*, 1120–1125.

Hong, L. K. (1999). Chinese marriages and families: Diversity and change. In S. L. Browning & R. R. Miller (Eds.), *Till death do us part: A multicultural anthology on marriage* (pp. 23–44). Stamford, CT: JAI Press.

Hotz, V. J., McElroy, S. W., & Sanders, S. G. (1996). The costs and consequences of teenage childbearing for the mothers and the government. *Chicago Policy Review, 1*, 55–94.

Howell, N. (1979). *Demography of the Dobe Kung*. New York: Academic Press.

Hsueh, J., Alderson, D. P., Lundquist, E., Michalopoulos, C., Gubits, D., Fein, D., & Knox, V. (2012). The Supporting Healthy Marriage evaluation: Early impacts on low-income families. *OPRE Report 2012–11, Office of Planning, Research, and Evaluation, U.S. Administration on Children and Families*.

Hua, C. (2001). *A society without fathers or husbands: The Na of China* (A. Hustvedt, Trans.). New York: Zone Books.

In re Dunn, 607 N.E.2d 81 (Ohio App.3 Dist. 1992).

In re A. R. A., 919 P.2d 388 (Mont. 1996).

Inglehart, R., Basáñez, M., Díez-Medrano, J., Halman, L., & Luijkx, R. (2004). *Human beliefs and values: A cross-cultural sourcebook based on the 1999–2002 values surveys*. Mexico City: Siglo Veintiuno Editores.

Ingraham, C. (1999). *White weddings: Romancing heterosexuality in popular culture*. New York: Routledge.

Isen, A., & Stevenson, B. (2011). Women's education and family behavior: Trends in marriage, divorce, and fertility. In J. B. Shoven (Ed.), *Demography and the economy* (pp. 107–142). Chicago: University of Chicago Press.

Ishii-Kuntz, M. (2000). Diversity within Asian-American families. In D. H. Demo, K. R. Allen, & M. A. Fine (Eds.), *The handbook of family diversity* (pp. 247–292). New York: Oxford University Press.

Jackson-Newsom, J., Buchanan, C. M., & McDonald, R. M. (2008). Parenting and perceived maternal warmth in European American and African American adolescents. *Journal of Marriage and the Family, 70*, 62–75.

Jacobs, J. A., & Gerson, K. (2004). *The time divide: Work, family, and social policy in the 21st century*. Cambridge, MA: Harvard University Press.

Jacobs, S., Thomas, W., & Lang, S. (Eds.). (1997). *Two-spirit people: Native American gender identity, sexuality, and spirituality*. Champaign-Urbana: University of Illinois Press.

Joe, J. R., Sparks, S., & Tiger, L. (1999). Changing American Indian marriage patterns: Some examples from contemporary Western Apaches. In S. L. Browning & R. R. Miller (Eds.), *Till death do us part: A multicultural anthology on marriage* (pp. 5–21). Greenwich, CT: JAI Press.

Johnson, M. P. (1995). Patriarchal terrorism and common couple violence: Two forms of violence against women. *Journal of Marriage and the Family, 57*, 283–294.

Johnson, M. P. (2008). *A typology of domestic violence*. Boston: Northeastern University Press.

Johnson, S. H., & Rendall, M. S. (2004). The fertility contribution of Mexican immigration to the United States. *Demography, 41*, 129–150.

Johnston, L. D., O'Malley, P. M., Bachman, J. G., & Schulenberg, J. E. (2011). Monitoring the future national survey results on drug use, 1975–2010: Volume I, secondary school students. Retrieved January 17, 2012, from http://www.monitoringthefuture.org/pubs/monographs/mtf-vol1_2010.pdf

Jones, J. (1985). *Labor of love, labor of sorrow: Black women and the family from slavery to the present.* New York: Basic Books.

Joshi, P., & Bogen, K. (2007). Nonstandard schedules and young children's behavioral outcomes among working low-income families. *Journal of Marriage and the Family, 69*, 139–156.

Kaiser Family Foundation. (2011a). Medicare spending and financing: A primer. Retrieved January 25, 2012, from http://www.kff.org/medicare/upload/7731–03.pdf

Kaiser Family Foundation. (2011b). The uninsured: A primer. Supplemental data tables. Retrieved March 2, 2012, from http://www.kff.org/uninsured/upload/7451–07-Data-Tables.pdf

Kalil, A., & Dunifon, R. (2007). Maternal work and welfare use and child well-being: Evidence from 6 years of data from the women's employment study. *Children and Youth Services Review, 29*, 742–761.

Kalil, A., Ziol-Guest, K. M., & Epstein, J. L. (2010). Nonstandard work and marital instability: Evidence from the National Longitudinal Survey of Youth. *Journal of Marriage and the Family, 72*, 1289–1300.

Kalleberg, A. L. (2011). *Good jobs, bad jobs: The rise of polarized and precarious employment systems in the United States, 1970s to 2000s.* New York: Russell Sage Foundation.

Kalmijn, M. (1991). Shifting boundaries: Trends in religious and educational homogamy. *American Sociological Review, 56*, 786–800.

Katz, J. (1976). *Gay American history.* New York: Harper and Row.

Katz, M. B. (1989). *The undeserving poor: From the war on poverty to the war on welfare.* New York: Pantheon Books.

Katz, L. F., & Autor, D. H. (1999). Changes in wage structure and earnings inequality. In D. Card & O. C. Ashenfelter (Eds.), *Handbook of labor economics, vol. 3a* (pp. 1463–1555). New York and Oxford: Elsevier Science, North-Holland.

Kelly, J. B. (2007). Children's living arrangements following separation and divorce: Insights from empirical and clinical research. *Family Process, 46*, 35–42.

Kempe, H. C., Silverman, F. N., Steele, B. F., Droegemuller, W., & Silver, H. K. (1962). The battered child syndrome. *Journal of the American Medical Association, 181*, 17–24.

Kendall-Tackett, K. A., Williams, L. M., & Finkelhor, D. (1993). Impact of sexual abuse on children: A review and synthesis of recent empirical studies. *Psychological Bulletin, 113*, 164–180.

Kennedy, S., & Bumpass, L. (2008). Cohabitation and children's living arrangements: New estimates from the United States. *Demographic Research, 19*, 1663–1692.

Kenney, C. T., & McLanahan, S. S. (2006). Why are cohabiting relationships more violent than marriages? *Demography, 43*, 127–140.

Kertzer, D. I. (1991). Household history and sociological theory. *Annual Review of Sociology, 17*, 155–179.

Kett, J. F. (2003). Reflections on the history of adolescence in America. *History of the Family, 8*, 345–479.

Kiernan, K. (2011). *Fragile families beyond divorce.* Paper presented at the Conference on Divorce, Milan, October 27–29.

Kiernan, K. E. (1992). The impact of family disruption in childhood on transitions made in young adult life. *Population Studies, 46*, 213–234.

Kiernan, K. E. (2002). Cohabitation in Western Europe: Trends, issues, and implications. In A. Booth & A. C. Crouter (Eds.), *Just living together: Implication of cohabitation on families, children, and social policy* (pp. 3–31). Mahwah, NJ: Erlbaum.

King, V. (2003). The legacy of a grandparent's divorce: Consequences for ties between grandparents and grandchildren. *Journal of Marriage and the Family, 65*, 170–183.

Kinsey, A. C., Pomeroy, W. B., & Martin, C. E. (1948). *Sexual behavior in the human male.* Philadelphia: Saunders, W.B.

Kipnis, L. (2003). *Against love: A polemic.* New York: Pantheon.

Kitano, H. H. L., & Daniels, R. (1988). *Asian Americans: Emerging minorities.* Englewood Cliffs, NJ: Prentice Hall.

Klinenberg, E. (2012). *Going solo: The extraordinary rise and surprising appeal of living alone.* New York: Penguin Press.

Kling, J. R., Liebman, J. B., & Katz, L. F. (2007). Experimental analysis of neighborhood effects. *Econometrica, 75*(1), 83–119.

Kohn, M. L. (1969). *Class and conformity: A study in values.* Homewood, IL: Dorsey Press.

Kohn, M. L., & Schooler, C. (1978). The reciprocal effects of the substantive complexity of work and intellectual flexibility: A longitudinal assessment. *American Journal of Sociology, 84,* 24–52.

Komarovsky, M. (1940). *The unemployed man and his family.* New York: Octagon Books.

Kosterlitz, J. (2005). Inside the new Social Security accounts. *National Journal, 37, issue 1/2,* 21–23.

Kreider, R. M. (2010). Increase in opposite-sex cohabiting couples from 2009 to 2010. *U.S. Bureau of the Census, Housing and Household Economics Statistics Division* Retrieved July 23, 2011, from www.census.gov/population/www/.../Inc-Opp-sex-2009-to-2010.pdf

La Ferrara, E., Chong, A., & Duryea, S. (2008). Soap operas and fertility: Evidence from Brazil. *Bureau for Research and Economic Analysis of Development, Working Paper no. 172.* Retrieved from http://ipl.econ.duke.edu/bread/papers/working/172.pdf

Lachs, M. S., & Pillemer, K. (2004). Elder abuse. *The Lancet, 364,* 1363–1272.

Lamb, M. E. (2002). Infant-father attachments and their impact on child development. In C. S. Tamis-LeMonda & N. Cabrera (Eds.), *Handbook of father involvement: Multidisciplinary perspectives* (pp. 93–117). Mahwah, NJ: Lawrence Erlbaum.

Lamont, M. (2000). *The dignity of working men: Morality and the boundaries of race, class, and immigration.* Cambridge, MA: Harvard University Press.

Land, K. C. (2011). The 2011 child and youth well-being index. *Foundation for Child Development.* Retrieved January 17, 2012, from http://www.soc.duke.edu/~cwi/2011_FINAL_CWI_Report.pdf

Landale, N. S., & Fennelly, K. (1992). Informal unions among mainland Puerto Ricans: Cohabitation or an alternative to legal marriage? *Journal of Marriage and the Family, 54,* 269–280.

Landale, N. S., Oropesa, R., & Bradatan, C. (2006). Hispanic families in the United States: Family structure and process in an era of family change. In M. Tienda & F. Mitchell (Eds.), *Hispanics and the future of America* (pp. 138–178).

Landry, B. (2000). *Black working wives: Pioneers of the new family revolution.* Berkeley: University of California Press.

Lansford, J. E., Deater-Deckard, K., Dodge, K. A., Bates, J. E., & Pettit, G. S. (2004). Ethnic differences in the link between physical discipline and later adolescent externalizing behaviors. *Journal of Child Psychology and Psychiatry, 45,* 801–812.

Lareau, A. (2011). *Unequal childhoods: Class, race, and family life, second edition.* Berkeley: University of California Press.

Laslett, B. (1973). The family as a public and private institution: An historical perspective. *Journal of Marriage and the Family, 35,* 480–492.

Laumann, E. O., Gagnon, J. H., Michael, R. T., & Michaels, S. (1994). *The social organization of sexuality: Sexual practices in the United States.* Chicago: University of Chicago Press.

Laumann-Billings, L., & Emery, R. E. (2000). Distress among young adults from divorced families. *Journal of Family Psychology, 14,* 671–687.

Laumann, E. O., Gagnon, J. H., Michael, R. T., & Michaels, S. (1995, May 25). Sex, lies, and social science: An exchange. *New York Review of Books.*

Lawrence v. Texas, 539 (U.S. 2003).

Leaper, C., & Friedman, C. (2007). The socialization of gender. In J. E. Grusec & P. D. Hasting (Eds.), *The handbook of socialization: Theory and research* (pp. 561–587). New York: Guilford Press.

Le Bourdais, C., & Juby, H. (2002). The impact of cohabitation on the family life course in contemporary North America: Insights from across the border. In A. Booth & A. C. Crouter (Eds.), *Just living together: Implications of cohabitation on families, children, and social policy* (pp. 107–118). Mahwah, NJ: Lawrence Erlbaum.

Lee, B. A., Tyler, K. A., & Wright, J. D. (2010). The new homelessness revisited. *Annual Review of Sociology, 36,* 501–521.

Lee, J., & Bean, F. D. (2010). *The diversity paradox: Immigration and the color line in twenty-first century America.* New York: Russell Sage Foundation.

Lee, S. M., & Edmonston, B. (2005). New marriages, new families: U.S. racial and Hispanic intermarriage. *Population Bulletin, 60, no. 2,* 1–36.

Leisenring, A. (2008). Controversies surrounding mandatory arrest policies and the police response to intimate partner violence. *Sociology Compass, 2,* 451–466.

Leland, J. (2008, October 8). A spirit of belonging, inside and out, *The New York Times,* pp. D1, D6.

Lehrer, E. L. (2004). Religion as a determinant of economic and demographic behavior in the United States. *Population and Development Review, 30,* 707–726.

Lever, J. (1976). Sex differences in the games children play. *Social Problems, 23,* 478–487.

Levin, I. (2004). Living apart together: A new family form. *Current Sociology, 52,* 223–240.

Levy, F. (1998). *The new dollars and dreams: American incomes and economic change.* New York: Russell Sage Foundation.

Levy, F., & Michel, R. C. (1991). *The economic future of American families: Income and wealth trends.* Washington, DC: Urban Institute Press.

Lewontin, R. (1995, April 20). Sex lies and social science. *The New York Review of Books,* 24–29.

Lewontin, R. (1995, May 25). Sex, lies, and social science: An exchange. *New York Review of Books,* 43–44.

Li, J.-C. A., & Wu, L. L. (2008). No trend in the intergenerational transmission of divorce. *Demography, 45,* 875–883.

Lichter, D. T., McLaughlin, D. K., Kephart, G., & Landry, D. J. (1992). Race and the retreat from marriage: A shortage of marriageable men? *American Sociological Review, 57,* 781–799.

Lichter, D. T., McLaughlin, D. K., & Ribar, D. C. (2002). Economic restructuring and the retreat from marriage. *Social Science Research, 31,* 230–256.

Lichter, D. T., & Qian, Z. (2004). Marriage and family in a multiracial society *The American People: Census 2000.* New York and Washington: Russell Sage Foundation and Population Reference Bureau.

Lichter, D. T., Qian, Z., & Mellott, L. M. (2006). Marriage or dissolution? Union transitions among poor cohabiting women. *Demography, 43,* 223–240.

Lichter, D. T., Turner, R. N., & Sassler, S. (2010). National estimates of the rise in serial cohabitation. *Social Science Research, 39,* 754–765.

Liefbroer, A. C., & Dourleijn, E. (2006). Unmarried cohabitation and union stability: Testing the role of diffusion using data from 16 European countries. *Demography, 43,* 203–221.

Liker, J. K., & Elder, G. H., Jr. (1983). Economic hardship and marital relations in the 1930's. *American Sociological Review, 48,* 343–359.

Lin, C., & Liu, W. T. (1993). Intergenerational relationships among Chinese immigrants from Taiwan. In H. McAdoo (Ed.), *Family ethnicity* (pp. 271–286). Newbury Park CA: Sage.

Lippa, R. A. (2005). *Gender, nature, and nurture. Second edition.* Mahwah, NJ: Lawrence Erlbaum Associates.

Liu, K., Manton, K. G., & Aragon, C. (2000). Changes in home care use by disabled elderly persons: 1982–1994. *Journal of Gerontology, 55B,* S245-S253.

Loeb, T. B., Williams, J. K., Vargas Carmona, J., Rivkin, I., Wyatt, G. E., Chin, D., & Asuan-O'Brien, A. (2002). Child sexual abuse: Associations with the sexual functioning of adolescents and adults. *Annual Review of Sex Research, 13,* 307–345.

Loving v. Virginia, 347 1 (U.S. 1967).

Luker, K. (1984). *Abortion and the politics of motherhood.* Berkeley, CA: University of California Press.

Lundberg, S. J., Pollak, R. A., & Wales, T. J. (1997). Do husbands and wives pool their resources? Evidence from the United Kingdom child benefit. *Journal of Human Resources, 32,* 463–480.

Lundquist, J. H. (2004). When race makes no difference: Marriage and the military. *Social Forces, 83,* 731–757.

Lundquist, J. H., & Smith, H. L. (2005). Family formation among women in the U.S. Military: Evidence from the NLSY. *Journal of Marriage and the Family, 67,* 1–13.

Lüscher, K., & Pillemer, K. (1998). Intergenerational ambivalence: A new approach to the study of parent-child relations in later life. *Journal of Marriage and the Family, 60,* 413–425.

Lyall, S. (2004, February 15). In Europe, lovers now propose: Marry me a little, *The New York Times,* p. A3.

Lynd, R. S., & Lynd, H. M. (1929). *Middletown: A study in modern American culture.* New York: Harcourt, Brace, and World.

MacCallum, F., & Golombok, S. (2004). Children raised in fatherless families from infancy: A follow-up of children of lesbian and single heterosexual mothers at early adolescence. *Journal of Child Psychology and Psychiatry, 45,* 1407–1419.

Maccoby, E. E. (1992). Family structure and children's adjustment: Is quality of parenting the major mediator? In M. E. Hetherington & W. G. Clingempel (Eds.), *Coping with marital transitions* (Vol. 57, pp. 230–238): Monographs of the Society for Research in Child Development.

Maccoby, E. E. (1998). *The two sexes: Growing up apart, coming together.* Cambridge, MA: Harvard University Press.

Maccoby, E. E. (2007). Historical overview of socialization research and theory. In J. E. Grusec & P. D. Hasting (Eds.), *Handbook of socialization: Theory and research* (pp. 13–41). New York: Guilford Press.

Maccoby, E. E., & Mnookin, R. H. (1992). *Dividing the child: Social and legal dilemmas of custody.* Cambridge, MA: Harvard University Press.

Magdol, L., Moffitt, T. E., Caspi, A., & Silva, P. A. (1998). Hitting without a license: Testing explanations for differences in partner abuse between young adult cohabitors. *Journal of Marriage and the Family, 60,* 41–55.

Manning, W. D., & Smock, P. J. (2005). Measuring and modeling cohabitation: New perspectives from qualitative data. *Journal of Marriage and the Family, 67,* 989–1002.

Mare, R. D., & Winship, C. (1991). Socioeconomic change and the decline in marriage for blacks and whites. In C. Jencks & P. Peterson (Eds.), *The urban underclass* (pp. 175–202). Washington, DC: The Brookings Institution.

Markman, H. J., Whitton, S. W., Kline, G. H., Stanley, S. M., Thompson, H., & St. Peters, M. (2004). Use of an empirically based marriage education program by religious organizations: Results of a dissemination trial. *Family Relations, 53,* 504–512.

Marks, N. G., Lambert, J. D., & Choi, H. (2002). Transitions to caregiving, gender, and psychological well-being. *Journal of Marriage and the Family, 64,* 657–667.

Marquardt, E. (2005). *Between two worlds: The inner lives of children of divorce.* New York: Crown.

Marshall, J., & Smith, G. V. (2006). Human rights and social issues at the U.N.: A guide for U.S. policymakers. Retrieved February 27, 2009, from http://www.heritage.org/Research/WorldwideFreedom/bg1965.cfm

Marsiglio, W. (1992). Stepfathers with minor children living at home: Parenting perceptions and relationship quality. *Journal of Family Issues, 13,* 195–214.

Marsiglio, W. (2004). *Stepdads: Stories of love, hope and repair.* Boulder, CO: Rowman and Littlefield.

Marsiglio, W., Amato, P. R., Day, R. D., & Lamb, M. E. (2000). Scholarship on fatherhood in the 1990s and beyond. *Journal of Marriage and the Family, 62,* 1173–1191.

Martin, S. P. (2004). Women's education and family timing: Outcomes and trends associated with age at marriage and first birth. In K. M. Neckerman (Ed.), *Social inequality* (pp. 79–118). New York: Russell Sage Foundation.

Martin, S. P. (2006). Trends in marital dissolution by women's education in the United States. *Demographic Research, 15,* 537–560.

Martin, S. P., & Parashar, S. (2006). Women's changing attitudes toward divorce, 1974–2002: Evidence for an educational crossover. *Journal of Marriage and the Family, 68,* 29–40.

Martin, C., & Théry, I. (2001). The PACS and marriage and cohabitation in France. *International Journal of Law, Policy and the Family, 15,* 135–158.

Mason, M. A., Harrison-Jay, S., Svare, G. M., & Wolfinger, N. H. (2002). Stepparents: De facto parents or legal strangers? *Journal of Family Issues, 23,* 507–522.

Massey, D. S., Charles, C. Z., Lundy, G. F., & Fischer, M. J. (2003). *The source of the river: The social origins of freshmen at America's selective colleges and universities.* Princeton: Princeton University Press.

Mattingly, M. J., & Smith, K. E. (2010). Changes in wives' employment when husbands stop working: A recession-prosperity comparison. *Family Relations, 59,* 343–357.

Maxwell, C. D., Garner, J. H., & Fagan, J. A. (2002). The preventive effects of arrest on intimate partner violence: Research, policy and theory. *Criminology & Public Policy, 2,* 51–80.

May, E. T. (1980). *Great expectations: Marriage and divorce in post-Victorian America.* Chicago: University of Chicago Press.

Mazzuato, V., & Schans, D. (2011). Transnational families and the well-being of children: Conceptual and methodological challenges. *Journal of Marriage and the Family, 73,* 704–712.

McCurdy, K., & Daro, D. (1994). *Current trends in child abuse reporting and fatalities: The results of the 1993 annual fifty state survey.* Chicago: National Committee to Prevent Child Abuse.

McDermott, M., & Samson, F. L. (2005). White racial and ethnic identity in the United States. *Annual Review of Sociology, 31,* 245–261.

McGue, Matt and David T. Lykken. 1992. "Genetic Influence on Risk of Divorce." *Psychological Science* 3:368–73.

McHale, S. M., & Crouter, A. C. (2003). How do children exert an impact on family life? In A. C. Crouter & A. Booth (Eds.), *Children's influence on family dynamics: The neglected side of family relationships* (pp. 207–220). Mahwah, NJ: Lawrence Erlbaum Associates.

McLanahan, S. (2004). Diverging destinies: How children are faring under the second demographic transition. *Demography, 41,* 607–627.

McLanahan, S., Garfinkel, I., Reichman, N., Teitler, J., Carlson, M., & Audiger, C. N. (2003). The fragile families and child well-being study baseline national report, revised march 2003. Retrieved October 7, 2006, from www.fragilefamilies.princeton.edu/documents/nationalreport.pdf

McLaughlin, D. K., & Lichter, D. T. (1997). Poverty and the marital behavior of young women. *Journal of Marriage and the Family, 59,* 582–594.

McLoyd, V. C., Cauce, A. M., Takeuchi, D., & Wilson, L. (2000). Marital processes and parental socialization in families of color: A decade review of research. *Journal of Marriage and the Family, 62,* 1070–1093.

McLoyd, V. C., Kaplan, R., Hardaway, C. R., & Wood, D. (2007). Does endorsement of physical discipline matter? Assessing moderating influences on the maternal and child psychological correlates of physical discipline in African American families. *Journal of Family Psychology, 21,* 162–175.

McManus, P. M., & DiPrete, T. A. (2001). Losers and winners: The financial consequences of separation and divorce for men. *American Sociological Review, 66*(2), 246–268.

McMenamin, T. M. (2007). A time to work: Recent trends in shift work and flexible schedules. *Monthly Labor Review* (December), 3–15.

McRoberts, O. M. (2003). *Streets of glory: Church and community in a black urban neighborhood.* Chicago: University of Chicago Press.

Mead, L. (1992). *The new politics of poverty: The non-working poor in America.* New York: Basic Books.

Mead, R. (2007). *One perfect day: The selling of the American wedding.* New York: Penguin.

Meyer, D. R., Cancian, M., & Cook, S. T. (2005). Multiple-partner fertility: Incidence and implications for child support policy. *Social Service Review, 79,* 577–601.

Milan, A., & Peters, A. (2003, summer). Couples living apart. *Canadian Social Trends,* 2–6.

Milkie, M. A., Raley, S. B., & Bianchi, S. M. (2009). Taking on the second shift: Time allocations and time pressures of U.S. parents with preschoolers. *Social Forces, 88,* 487–518.

Mincy, R. B., Klempin, S., & Schmidt, H. (2011). Income support policies for low-income men and noncustodial fathers: Tax and transfer programs. *Annals of the American Academy of Political and Social Science, 635*(no. 1), 240–261.

Mintz, S. (2004). *Huck's raft: A history of American childhood.* Cambridge, MA: The Belknap Press of Harvard University Press.

Mintz, S., & Kellogg, S. (1988). *Domestic relations: A social history of American family life.* New York: The Free Press.

Mitterauer, M., & Sieder, R. (1982). *The European family.* Chicago: University of Chicago.

Modell, J. J. (1989). *Into one's own: From youth to adulthood in the United States.* Berkeley: University of California Press.

Moore, J. W., & Cuéllar, A. B. (1970). *Mexican Americans.* Englewood Cliffs, NJ: Prentice Hall.

Morello, C. (2011, January 19). Blended families more common, but the "step" in "stepmom" still carries stigma. *The Washington Post.*

Morgan, S. P., McDaniel, A., Miller, A. T., & Preston, S. H. (1993). Racial differences in household and family structure at the turn of the century. *American Journal of Sociology, 98,* 798–828.

Morin, R., & Cohn, D. V. (2008). Women call the shots at home; public mixed on gender roles in jobs. *Pew Research Center.* Retrieved February 20, 2009, from http://pewresearch.org/pubs/967/gender-power

Murray, C. (2012). *Coming apart: The state of white America, 1960–2010.* New York: Crown Forum.

Nagel, J. (1995). American Indian ethnic renewal: Politics and the resurgence of identity. *American Sociological Review, 60,* 947–965.

Nagel, J. (1996). *American Indian ethnic renewal: Red power and the resurgence of identity and culture.* New York: Oxford University Press.

Nakonezny, P. A., Shull, R. D., & Rodgers, J. L. (1995). The effect of no-fault divorce law on the divorce rate across the 50 states and its relation to income, education, and religiosity. *Journal of Marriage and the Family, 57,* 477–488.

National Center for Family and Marriage Research. (2011a). Adopted children in the U.S., 2007. *Family Profiles.* Retrieved January 14, 2012, from http://ncfmr.bgsu.edu/pdf/family_profiles/file98993.pdf

National Center for Family and Marriage Research. (2011b). First divorce rate, 2010. *Family Profiles.* Retrieved November 25, 2011, from http://ncfmr.bgsu.edu/pdf/family_profiles/file101821.pdf

Newman, K. (2012). *The accordion family: Boomerang kids, anxious parents, and the private toll of global competition.* Boston: Beacon Press.

Newman, K. S. (1988). *Falling from grace: The experience of downward mobility in the American middle class.* New York: The Free Press.

Newman, K. S. (2003). *A different shade of gray: Midlife and beyond in the inner city.* New York: The New Press.

Nicholas, D. (1991). Childhood in medieval europe. In J. H. Hawes & N. Hiner (Eds.), *Children in historical and comparative perspective* (pp. 31–52). New York: Greenwood Press.

Nobles, J. (2011). Parenting from abroad: Migration, nonresident father involvement, and children's education in Mexico. *Journal of Marriage and the Family, 73,* 729–746.

Nock, S. L. (1995). A comparison of marriages and cohabiting relationships. *Journal of Family Issues, 16,* 53–76.

Nock, S. L., Kingston, P. W., & Holian, L. M. (2008). Intergenerational caregiving. In A. Booth, A. C. Crouter, S. Bianchi, & J. Seltzer (Eds.), *Intergenerational caregiving* (pp. 279–316). Washington, DC: The Urban Institute Press.

Nock, S. L., Wright, J. D., & Sanchez, L. (1999). America's divorce problem. *Society, 36,* 43–52.

Nomaguchi, K. M. (2009). Change in work-family conflict among employed parents between 1977 and 1997. *Journal of Marriage and the Family, 71,* 15–32.

O'Brien, J. E. (1971). Violence in divorce prone families. *Journal of Marriage and the Family, 33,* 692–698.

O'Connor, T. G., Caspi, A., DeFries, J. C., & Plomin, R. (2000). Are associations between parental divorce and children's adjustment genetically mediated? An adoption study. *Developmental Psychology, 36,* 429–437.

Offer, S., & Schneider, B. (2011). Revisiting the gender gap in time-use patterns: Multitasking and well-being among mothers and fathers in dual-earner families. *American Sociological Review, 76,* 809–833.

Ogburn, W. F. (1964). Cultural lag as theory. In O. D. Duncan (Ed.), *William F. Ogburn on culture and social change: Selected papers* (pp. 86–95). Chicago: University of Chicago Press.

Oliver, M., & Shapiro, T. M. (1995). *Black wealth/white wealth: A new perspective on racial inequality.* New York: Routledge.

Olson, J. S. (1979). *The ethnic dimension in American history*. New York: St. Martin's Press.

Olson, T. B. (2010, January 8). The conservative case for gay marriage. *Newsweek*.

O'Neill, W. L. (1967). *Divorce in the progressive era*. New York: New Viewpoints.

Ono, H. (2003). Women's economic standing, marriage timing, and cross-national contexts of gender. *Journal of Marriage and the Family, 65*, 275–286.

Ooms, T. (2004, May 5). The benefits of a healthy marriage. *Committee on Finance, Subcommittee on Social Security and Family Policy, United States Senate*. Retrieved March 4, 2012, from http://s242739747.onlinehome.us/publications/Ooms_Finance_050504.pdf

Oppenheimer, V. K. (1970). *The female labor force in the United States, Population Monograph Series, 5*. Berkeley: Institute of International Studies, University of California.

Oppenheimer, V. K. (1988). A theory of marriage timing. *American Journal of Sociology, 94*, 563–591.

Oppenheimer, V. K. (2003). Cohabiting and marriage during young men's career-development process. *Demography, 40*, 127–149.

Oppenheimer, V. K., Blossfeld, H.-P., & Wackerow, A. (1995). United States of America. In H. P. Blossfeld (Ed.), *The new role of women: Family formation in modern societies* (pp. 150–173). Boulder, CO: Westview Press.

Oppenheimer, V. K., Kalmijn, M., & Lim, N. (1997). Men's career development and marriage timing during a period of rising inequality. *Demography, 34*, 311–330.

Oppenheimer, V. K., & Lew, V. (1995). American marriage formation in the 1980's: How important was women's economic independence? In K. O. Mason & A. M. Jensen (Eds.), *Gender and family change in industrialized countries* (pp. 105–138). Oxford: Clarendon Press.

Orbuch, T. L., Veroff, J., & Hunter, A. G. (1999). Black couples, white couples: The early years of marriage. In E. M. Hetherington (Ed.), *Coping with divorce, single parenting, and remarriage* (pp. 23–43). Mahwah, NJ: Lawrence Erlbaum Associates.

Orloff, A. S. (1993). Gender and the social rights of citizenship: The comparative analysis of gender relations and welfare states. *American Sociological Review, 58*, 303–328.

Oropesa, R. S., Landale, N. S., & Kenkre, T. (2003). Income allocation in marital and cohabiting unions: The case of mainland Puerto Ricans. *Journal of Marriage and the Family, 65*, 910–926.

Osborne, C., & McLanahan, S. (2007). Partnership instability and child well-being. *Journal of Marriage and the Family, 69*, 1065–1083.

Owen, J. J., Rhoades, G. K., Stanley, S. M., & Fincham, F. D. (2010). "Hooking up" among college students: Demographic and psychosocial correlates. *Archives of Sexual Behavior, 39*, 653–663.

Ozment, S. (2001). *Ancestors: The loving family in old Europe*. Cambridge, MA: Harvard University Press.

Padilla, M. B., Hirsch, J. S., Muñoz-Laboy, M., Sember, R. E., & Parker, R. G. (Eds.). (2007). *Love and globalization: Transformations of intimacy in the contemporary world*. Nashville: Vanderbilt University Press.

Pahl, R., & Spencer, L. (2004). Personal communities: Not simply families of 'fate' or 'choice'. *Current Sociology, 52*, 199–221.

Painter-Brick, C. (Ed.). (1998). *Biosocial perspectives on children*. Cambridge: Cambridge University Press.

Palkovitz, R. (2002). Involved fathering and child development: Advancing our understanding of good fathering. In C. S. Tamis-LeMonda & N. Cabrera (Eds.), *Handbook of father involvement: Multidisciplinary perspectives* (pp. 119–140). Mahwah, NJ: Lawrence Erlbaum.

Papernow, P. (1998). *Becoming a stepfamily: Patterns of development in remarried life*. Cleveland: Gestalt Institute of Cleveland Press.

Parke, R. D. (1996). *Fatherhood*. Cambridge, MA: Harvard University Press.

Parreñas, R. S. (2002). The care crisis in the Philippines: Children and transnational families in the new global economy. In B. Ehrenreich & A. R. Hochschild (Eds.), *Global woman: Nannies, maids, and sex workers in the new economy* (pp. 39–54). New York: Henry Holt.

Parsons, T., & Bales, R. F. (1955). *Family, socialization, and the interaction process*. New York: The Free Press.

Pascoe, C. J. (2007). *Dude, you're a fag*. Berkeley: University of California Press.

Patterson, C. J. (2000). Family relationships of lesbians and gay men. *Journal of Marriage and the Family, 62*, 1052–1069.

Pattillo, M. (2005). Black middle-class neighborhoods. *Annual Review of Sociology, 31*, 305–329.

Pattillo-McCoy, M. (1999). *Black picket fences: Privilege and peril among the black middle class*. Chicago: University of Chicago Press.

Pearsall, P. (1987). *Super marital sex: Loving for life*. New York: Doubleday.

Peplau, L. A. (1991). Lesbian and gay relationships. In J. C. Gonsiorek & J. D. Weinrich (Eds.), *Homosexuality: Research implications for public policy*. Newbury Park, CA: Sage.

Percheski, C. (2008). Opting out? Cohort differences in professional women's employment rates from 1960 to 2005. *American Sociological Review, 73*, 497–517.

Peterson, I. (2003, October 28). In home that looked loving, 4 boys' suffering was unseen. *The New York Times,* pp. A1, B8.

Pew Forum on Religion and Public Life. (2003). Religious beliefs underpin opposition to homosexuality Retrieved January 4, 2012, from http://pewforum.org/uploadedfiles/Topics/Issues/Gay_Marriage_and_Homosexuality/religion-homosexuality.pdf

Pew Hispanic Center. (2011a). Hispanics of Mexican origin in the United States, 2009. Retrieved January 2, 2012, from http://www.pewhispanic.org/2011/05/26/hispanics-of-mexican-origin-in-the-united-states-2009/

Pew Hispanic Center. (2011b). Unauthorized immigrants: Length of residency, patterns of parenthood. Retrieved January 12, 2012, from http://www.pewhispanic.org/2011/12/01/unauthorized-immigrants-length-of-residency-patterns-of-parenthood/

Pew Research Center. (2009a). College enrollment hits all-time high, fueled by community college surge. Retrieved March 15, 2012, from http://pewsocialtrends.org/2009/10/29/college-enrollment-hits-all-time-high-fueled-by-community-college-surge/

Pew Research Center. (2009b). Home for the holidays . . . and every other day. Retrieved July 23, 2011, from http://pewsocialtrends.org/files/2010/10/home-for-the-holidays.pdf

Pew Research Center. (2010). The return of the multi-generational family household. Retrieved January 26, 2012, from http://pewsocialtrends.org/files/2010/10/752-multi-generational-families.pdf

Pew Research Center. (2011a). Fighting poverty in a tough economy, Americans move in with their relatives. Retrieved January 26, 2012, from http://www.pewsocialtrends.org/files/2011/10/Multigenerational-Households-Final1.pdf

Pew Research Center. (2011b). The public renders a split verdict on family structure. Retrieved February 19, 2011, from http://pewsocialtrends.org/files/2011/02/Pew-Social-Trends-Changes-In-Family-Structure.pdf

Pew Research Center. (2011c). Shifting political winds: Frustration with government but less anger; more support gay marriage, abortion. Retrieved March 3, 2012, from http://pewresearch.org/pubs/1913/poll-trust-washington-anger-government-gay-marriage-support-abortion

Pezzin, L. E., Pollak, R. A., & Schone, B. S. (2008). Parental marital disruption, family type, and transfers to disabled elderly parents. *Journal of Gerontology: Social Sciences, 63B,* S349-S358.

Phillips, R. (1991). *Untying the knot: A short history of divorce.* Cambridge, England: Cambridge University Press.

Pillemer, K., & Lüscher, K. (Eds.). (2003). *Intergenerational ambivalences: New perspectives on parent-child relations in later life.* Stamford, CT: Elsevier/JAI Press.

Pillemer, K., & Suiter, J. J. (2002). Explaining mothers' ambivalence toward their adult children. *Journal of Marriage and the Family, 64,* 602–613.

Pleck, E. (1987). *Domestic tyranny: The making of American social policy against family violence from colonial times to the present.* New York: Oxford University Press.

Pleck, J. H. (2007). Why could father involvement benefit children? Theoretical perspectives. *Applied Developmental Science, 11,* 196–202.

Polgreen, L., & Worth, R. F. (2003, October 27). New Jersey couple held in abuse; one son, 19, weighed 45 pounds. *The New York Times,* pp. A1, B5.

Pollock, L. A. (1983). *Forgotten children: Parent-child relations from 1500–1900.* Cambridge, England: Cambridge University Press.

Popenoe, D. (1994). The evolution of marriage and the problem of stepfamilies: A biosocial perspective. In A. Booth & J. Dunn (Eds.), *Stepfamilies: Who benefits? Who does not?* (pp. 3–27). Hillsdale, NJ: Lawrence Erlbaum.

Portes, A., & Jensen, L. (1989). The enclave and the entrants: Patterns of ethnic enterprise in Miami before and after Mariel. *American Sociological Review, 54,* 929–949.

Portes, A., & Sensenbrenner, J. (1993). Embeddedness and immigration: Notes on the social determinants of economic action. *American Journal of Sociology, 98,* 1320–1350.

Powell, B., Bolzendahl, C., Geist, C., & Steelman, L. C. (2010). *Counted out: Same-sex relations and Americans' definitions of family.* New York: Russell Sage Foundation.

Presser, H. B. (1999). Toward a 24-hour economy. *Science, 284,* 177–1779.

Presser, H. B. (2000). Non-standard work schedules and marital instability. *Journal of Marriage and the Family, 62,* 93–110.

Preston, S. H., Lim, S., & Morgan, P. S. (1992). African American marriage in 1910: Beneath the surface of census data. *Demography, 29,* 1–15.

Preston, S. H., & McDonald, J. (1979). The incidence of divorce within cohorts of American marriages contracted since the civil war. *Demography, 16,* 1–25.

Price, R. H., Choi, J. N., & Vinokur, A. D. (2002). Links in the chain of adversity following job loss: How financial strain and loss of personal control lead to depression, impaired functioning, and poor health. *Journal of Occupational Health Psychology, 7,* 302–312.

Pugh, A. J. (2009). *Longing and belonging: Parents, children, and the consumer culture.* Berkeley: University of California Press.

Qian, Z., & Lichter, D. T. (2007). Social boundaries and marital assimilation: Interpreting trends in racial and ethnic intermarriage. *American Sociological Review, 72,* 68–94.

Qian, Z., & Lichter, D. T. (2011). Changing patterns of interracial marriage in a multiracial society. *Journal of Marriage and the Family, 73,* 1065–1084.

Qian, Z., & Preston, S. H. (1993). Changes in American marriage, 1972 to 1987: Availability and forces of attraction by age and education. *American Sociological Review, 58,* 482–95.

Quadagno, J. S. (1994). *The color of welfare: How racism undermined the war on poverty.* New York: Oxford University Press.

Queen, S. A., Habenstein, R. W., & Quadagno, J. S. (1985). *The family in various cultures* (5th ed.). New York: Harper & Row.

Raley, R. K., & Bumpass, L. L. (2003). The topography of the divorce plateau: Levels and trends in union stability in the United States after 1980. *Demographic Research, 8,* 245–259.

Raley, R. K., Durden, T. E., & Wildsmith, E. (2004). Understanding Mexican-American marriage patterns using a life-course approach. *Social Science Quarterly, 85,* 872–890.

Raley, R. K., Frisco, M. L., & Wildsmith, E. (2005). Maternal cohabitation and educational success. *Sociology of Education, 78,* 144–164.

Raley, S., Bianchi, S. M., & Wang, W. (2012). When do fathers care? Mothers' economic contribution and fathers' involvement in child care. *American Journal of Sociology, 117,* 1422–1459.

Rasmussen, B. B., Klinenberg, E., Nexica, I. J., & Wray, M. (Eds.). (2001). *The making and unmaking of whiteness.* Durham, NC: Duke University Press.

Raymo, J. M., Iwasawa, M., & Bumpass, L. (2004). Marital dissolution in Japan: Recent trends and patterns. *Demographic Research, 11,* 395–420.

Rebhun, L. A. (1999). *The heart is unknown country: Love in the changing economy of Northeast Brazil.* Stanford, CA: Stanford University Press.

Rebhun, L. A. (2007). The strange marriage of love and interest: Economic change and emotional intimacy in Northeast Brazil, private and public. In M. B. Padilla (Ed.), *Love and globalization: Transformations of intimacy in the contemporary world* (pp. 107–119). Nashville: Vanderbilt University Press.

Rector, R. E. (2007). How poor are America's poor? Examining the "plague" of poverty in America. *The Heritage Foundation, Backgrounder #2064.* Retrieved March 25, 2009, from http://www.heritage.org/research/welfare/bg2064.cfm

Reed, J. M. (2006). Not crossing the "extra line": How cohabitors with children view their unions. *Journal of Marriage and the Family, 68,* 1117–1131.

Regnerus, M. (2012). How different are the adult children of parents who have same-sex relationships? Findings from the new family structures study. *Social Science Research, 41,* 752–770.

Reinharz, S. (1992). *Feminist methods in social research.* New York: Oxford University Press.

Rendall, M. S., Weden, M. M., Favreault, M. M., & Waldron, H. (2011). The protective effect of marriage for survival: A review and update. *Demography, 48,* 481–506.

Repetti, R. L. (2001). Searching for the roots of marital conflict in uxoricides and uxorious husbands. In A. Booth, A. C. Crouter, & M. Clements (Eds.), *Couples in conflict* (pp. 47–55). Mahwah, NJ: Lawrence Erlbaum.

Ridgeway, C. L. (2009). Framed before we know it: How gender shapes social relations. *Gender & Society, 23,* 145–160.

Ridgeway, C. L. (2011). *Framed by gender: How gender inequality persists in the modern world.* Oxford: Oxford University Press.

Riley, N. E., & Van Vleet, K. E. (2012). *Making families through adoption.* Los Angeles: Pine Forge Press.

Rindfuss, R. R., Morgan, S. P., & Swicegood, G. (1988). *First births in America: Changes in the timing of parenthood.* Berkeley, CA: University of California Press.

Risman, B. J. (2004). Gender as social structure: Theory wrestling with activism. *Gender & Society, 18,* 429–450.

Risman, B. J. (2009). From doing to undoing: Gender as we know it. *Gender & Society, 23,* 81–84.

Risman, B. J., & Seale, E. (2010). Betwixt and between: Gender contradictions among middle schoolers. In B. J. Risman (Ed.), *Families as they really are* (pp. 340–361). New York: W. W. Norton.

Robb, G. (2003). *Strangers: Homosexual love in the nineteenth century.* New York: W. W. Norton.

Roberts, N. A., & Levenson, R. W. (2001). The remains of the workday: Impact of job stress and exhaustion on marital interaction in police couples. *Journal of Marriage and the Family, 63,* 1052–1067.

Rodgers, J. L., Nakonezny, P. A., & Shell, R. D. (1999). Did no-faulty divorce legislation matter? Definitely yes and sometimes no. *Journal of Marriage and the Family, 61,* 803–809.

Rodgers, W. C., & Thornton, A. (1985). Changing patterns of first marriage in the United States. *Demography, 22,* 265–279.

Roe v. Wade, 410 113 (S. Ct. 1973).

Roehling, P. V., Moen, P., & Batt, R. (2003). Spillover. In P. Moen (Ed.), *It's about time: Couples and careers* (pp. 102–121). Ithaca, NY: Cornell University Press.

Roschelle, A. R. (1997). *No more kin: Exploring race, class, and gender in family networks.* Thousand Oaks, CA: Sage.

Roseneil, S., & Budgeon, S. (2004). Cultures of intimacy and care beyond "the family": Personal life and social change in the early 21st century. *Current Sociology, 52*, 135–159.

Rosenfeld, M. J. (2001). The salience of pan-national Hispanic and Asian identities in the U.S. marriage markets. *Demography, 38*, 161–175.

Rosenfeld, M. J. (2007). *The age of independence: Interracial unions, same-sex unions, and the changing American family*. Cambridge, MA: Harvard University Press.

Rosenfeld, M. J., & Thomas, R. J. (2012). Searching for a mate: The rise of the internet as a social intermediary. *American Sociological Review*, in press.

Rosenmayr, L., & Kockeis, E. (1965). *Umwelt und familie alter menschen*. Berlin: Luchterland-Verlag.

Rossi, A. S., & Rossi, P. H. (1990). *Of human bonding: Parent-child relations across the life course*. New York: Aldine de Gruyter.

Rothbaum, F., Kakinuma, M., Nagaoka, R., & Azuma, H. (2007). Attachment and amae: Parent–child closeness in the United States and Japan. *Journal of Cross-Cultural Psychology, 38*, 465–486.

Rothman, E. K. (1984). *Hands and hearts: A history of courtship in America*. Cambridge, MA: Harvard University Press.

Rowland, D. T. (2007). Historical trends in childlessness. *Journal of Family Issues, 28*, 1311–1337.

Rubin, L. B. (1976). *Worlds of pain: Life in the working-class family*. New York: Basic Books.

Ruddick, S. (1996). Reason's "femininity". In N. R. Goldberger, J. M. Tarule, B. M. Clinchy, & M. F. Belenky (Eds.), *Knowledge, difference, and power: Essays inspired by women's ways of knowing* (pp. 248–270). New York: Basic Books.

Ruggles, S. (1994). The transformation of American family structure. *American Historical Review, 99*, 103–128.

Ruggles, S. (2007). The decline of intergenerational coresidence in the United States, 1850 to 2000. *American Sociological Review, 72*, 964–989.

Ryder, N. B. (1980). Components of temporal variations in American fertility. In R. W. Hiorns (Ed.), *Demographic patterns in developed societies* (pp. 15–54). London: Taylor and Francis.

Sandefur, G. D., & Liebler, C. A. (1997). The demography of American Indian families. *Population Research and Policy Review, 16*, 95–114.

Sarkisian, N., & Gerstel, N. (2004). Kin support among blacks and whites: Race and family organization. *American Sociological Review, 69*, 812–837.

Sassler, S., & Miller, A. J. (2011). Class differences in cohabitation processes. *Family Relations, 60*, 173–177.

Savin-Williams, R. C., & Esterberg, K. G. (2000). Lesbian, gay, and bisexual families. In D. H. Demo,

K. R. Allen, & M. A. Fine (Eds.), *Handbook of family diversity* (pp. 197–215). New York: Oxford University Press.

Sawhill, I. V., & Monea, E. (2011). An update to "simulating the effect of the 'great recession' on poverty." *Brookings Institution*. Retrieved March 15, 2011, from http://www.brookings.edu/papers/2010/0916_poverty_monea_sawhill.aspx

Sayer, L. C., & Bianchi, S. M. (2000). Women's economic independence and the probability of divorce: A review and reexamination. *Journal of Family Issues, 21*, 906–943.

Schaefer, R. T. (2007). *Sociology* (10th ed.). New York, NY: McGraw-Hill.

Schieman, S., Milkie, M. A., & Glavin, P. (2009). When work interferes with life: Work-nonwork interference and the influence of work-related demands and resources. *American Sociological Review, 74*, 966–988.

Schmeeckle, M., Giarrusso, R., Feng, D., & Bengtson, V. L. (2006). What makes someone family? Adult children's perception of current and former stepparents. *Journal of Marriage and the Family, 68*, 16.

Schneider, D. (2011). Wealth and the marital divide. *American Journal of Sociology, 117*, 627–667.

Schneider, D. M., & Smith, R. T. (1973). *Class differences and sex roles in American kinship and family structure*. Englewood Cliffs, NJ: Prentice-Hall.

Schoen, R., Astone, N. M., Rothert, K., Standish, N. J., & Kim, Y. J. (2002). Women's employment, marital happiness, and divorce. *Social Forces, 81*, 643–662.

Schoen, R., & Canudas-Romo, V. (2006). Timing effects on divorce: 20th century experience in the United States. *Journal of Marriage and the Family, 68*, 749–758.

Schoeni, R., & Blank, R. M. (2000). What has welfare reform accomplished? Impacts on welfare participation, employment, income, poverty, and family structure. Retrieved November 28, 2003, from http://www.fordschool.umich.edu/research/papers/PDFfiles/00–016.pdf

Schwartz, C. R., & Mare, R. D. (2005). Trends in educational assortative marriage from 1940 to 2003. *Demography, 42*, 621–646.

Schwartz, P., & Rutter, V. (1998). *The gender of sexuality*. Thousand Oaks, CA: Pine Forge Press.

Scott, J. W. (2000). Some reflections on gender and politics. In M. M. Ferree, J. Lorber, & B. B. Hess (Eds.), *Revisioning gender* (pp. 70–96). Walnut Creek, CA: AltaMira Press.

Sedlak, A. J., Mettenburg, J., Basena, M., Petta, I., McPherson, K., Greene, A., & Li, S. (2010). Fourth national incidence study of child abuse and neglect (NIS–4): Report to Congress. *U.S. Administration for Children and Families.* Retrieved February 8, 2012, from http://www.acf.hhs.gov/programs/opre/abuse_neglect/natl_incid/reports/natl_incid/nis4_report_congress_full_pdf_jan2010.pdf

Seidman, S. (1991). *Romantic longings: Love in America.* New York: Routledge.

Seidman, S. (Ed.). (1996). *Queer theory / sociology.* Cambridge, MA: Blackwell.

Seidman, S. (2003). *The social construction of sexuality.* New York: W. W. Norton.

Settersten, R. A., Jr., Furstenberg, F. F., Jr., & Rumbaut, R. G. (Eds.). (2005). *On the frontier of adulthood: Theory, research, and public policy.* Chicago: University of Chicago Press.

Sherman, L. W., & Berk, R. A. (1984). *The Minneapolis domestic violence experiment.* Washington, DC: The Police Foundation.

Shoemaker, N. (1991). Native American families. In J. H. Hawes & E. Nybakkin (Eds.), *American families: A research guide and historical handbook* (pp. 291–317). New York: Greenwood Press.

Silverstein, C. (1991). Psychological and medical treatments of homosexuality. In J. C. Gonsiorek & J. D. Weinrich (Eds.), *Homosexuality* (pp. 101–114). Newbury Park, CA: Sage.

Silverstein, M., & Bengtson, V. L. (1997). Intergenerational solidarity and the structure of adult child-parent relationships in American families. *American Journal of Sociology, 103*, 429–460.

Silverstein, M., & Giarrusso, R. (2010). Aging and family life: A decade review. *Journal of Marriage and the Family, 72*, 1039–1058.

Simon, R. W. (2002). Revisiting the relationships among gender, marital status, and mental health. *American Journal of Sociology, 107*, 1065–1096.

Singh, S., & Darroch, J. E. (2000). Adolescent pregnancy and childbearing: Levels and trends in developed countries. *Family Planning Perspectives, 32*, 14–23.

Skocpol, T. (1991). Targeting within universalism: Politically viable strategies to combat poverty in the United States. In C. Jencks & P. Peterson (Eds.), *The urban underclass* (pp. 411–436). Washington, DC: The Brookings Institution.

Skocpol, T. (1992). *Protecting mothers and soldiers: The political origins of social policy in the United States.* Cambridge, MA: The Belknap Press of Harvard University Press.

Smart, C. (2007). *Personal life: New directions in sociological thinking.* Cambridge: Polity Press.

Smeeding, T. M., & Carlson, M. J. (2011). Family change, public response: Social policy in an era of complex families. In M. J. Carlson & P. England (Eds.), *Social class and changing families in an unequal America* (pp. 165–191). Stanford: Stanford University Press.

Smelser, N. J., Wilson, W. J., & Mitchell, F. (2001). *America becoming: Racial trends and their consequences.* Washingon, DC: The National Academies Press.

Smith, A. (1776). *The wealth of nations.*

Smith, J. P. (1994). *Marriage, assets, and savings.* Santa Monica, CA: RAND Corporation.

Smith, K. E. (2010). Wives as breadwinners: Wives' share of family earnings hits historic high during the second year of the great recession. *Carsey Institute, Fact Sheet no. 2.0.* Retrieved July 16, 2011, from http://www.carseyinstitute.unh.edu/publications/IB-Smith-Breadwinners10.pdf

Smith-Rosenberg, C. (1975). The female world of love and ritual: Relations between women in nineteenth-century America. *Signs, 1*, 1–29.

Smock, P. J. (2000). Cohabitation in the United States: An appraisal of research themes, findings, and implications. *Annual Review of Sociology, 26*, 1–20.

Smock, P. J., & Gupta, S. (2002). Cohabitation in contemporary North America. In A. Booth & A. C. Crouter (Eds.), *Just living together: Implications of cohabitation on families, children, and social policy* (pp. 53–84). Mahwah, NJ: Lawrence Erlbaum.

Smock, P. J., Manning, W. D., & Porter, M. (2005). "Everything's there except money": How money shapes decisions to marry among cohabitors. *Journal of Marriage and the Family, 67*, 680–696.

Snipp, C. M. (1989). *American Indians: The first of this land.* New York: Russell Sage Foundation.

Snipp, C. M. (2002). American Indian and Alaska native children in the 2000 census: A kids count/prb report. Retrieved January 29, 2009, from http://www.prb.org/pdf/indian_alaska_children.pdf

Sobolewski, J. M., & King, V. (2005). The importance of the coparental relationship for nonresident fathers' ties to children. *Journal of Marriage and the Family, 67*, 1196–1212.

Sørenson, A. (1994). Women, family, and class. *Annual Review of Sociology, 20*, 27–47.

Sorenson, S. B., Upchurch, D. M., & Shen, H. (1996). Violence and injury in marital arguments: Risk patterns and gender differences. *American Journal of Public Health, 86*, 35–40.

South, S. J. (1991). Sociodemographic differentials in mate selection processes. *Journal of Marriage and the Family, 54*, 440–451.

Stacey, J. (2011). *Unhitched: Love, marriage, and family values from West Hollywood to Western China.* New York: New York University Press.

Stacey, J., & Biblarz, T. J. (2001). (how) does the sexual orientation of parents matter. *American Sociological Review, 66*(2), 159–183.

Stack, C. B. (1974). *All our kin: Strategies for survival in a black community*. New York: Harper and Row.

Stepp, L. S. (2007). *Unhooked: How young women pursue sex, delay love, and lose at both*. New York: Riverhead Books.

Stevenson, B., & Wolfers, J. (2006). Bargaining in the shadow of the law: Divorce laws and family distress. *Quarterly Journal of Economics, 121*, 267–288.

Stevenson, B., & Wolfers, J. (2007). Trends in marital stability. Retrieved October 21, 2011, from http://bpp.wharton.upenn.edu/betseys/papers/Trends%20in%20Marital%20Stability.pdf

Stewart, S. D. (2005). Boundary ambiguity in stepfamilies. *Journal of Family Issues, 26*, 1002–1029.

Stewart, S. D. (2007). *Brave new stepfamilies: Diverse paths toward stepfamily living*. Thousand Oaks, CA: Sage.

Stone, D. (2000, March 13). Why we need a care movement. *The Nation, 13*–15.

Stone, L. (1977). *The family, sex and marriage in England 1500–1800*. New York: Harper and Row.

Straus, M. A. (1979). Measuring intrafamily conflict and violence. *Journal of Marriage and the Family, 41*, 75–88.

Straus, M. A., & Gelles, R. J. (1986). Societal change and change in family violence from 1975 to 1985 as revealed by two national surveys. *Journal of Marriage and the Family, 48*, 465–479.

Straus, M. A., Hamby, S. L., Boney-McCoy, S., & Sugarman, D. B. (1996). The revised conflict tactics scales (CTS2): Development and preliminary psychometric data. *Journal of Family Issues, 17*, 283–316.

Straus, M. A., & Stewart, J. H. (1999). Corporal punishment by American parents. *Clinical Child and Family Psychology Review, 2*, 55–70.

Strohm, C. Q., Seltzer, J. A., Cochran, S. D., & Mays, V. M. (2009). "Living apart together" relationships in the United States. *Demographic Research, 21*, 177–214.

Stryker, S., & Vryan, K. D. (2003). The symbolic interactionist frame. In J. Delamater (Ed.), *Handbook of social psychology* (pp. 3–28). New York: Kluwer Academics/Plenum Publishers.

Suarez, Z. E. (1993). Cuban exiles: From golden exiles to social undesirables. In H. McAdoo (Ed.), *Family ethnicity: Strength in diversity* (pp. 164–176). Newbury Park, CA: Sage Publications.

Suarez-Orozco, C., Todorova, I., & Louie, J. (2002). Making up for lost time: The experience of separation and reunification among immigrant families. *Family Process, 41*, 625–643.

Sudarkasa, N. (1980). African and Afro-American family structure: A comparison. *The Black Scholar* (November–December), 37–60.

Sudarkasa, N. (1981). Interpreting the African heritage in Afro-American family organization. In H. P. McAdoo (Ed.), *Black families* (pp. 37–53). Beverly Hills, CA: Sage.

Suitor, J. J., Sechrist, J., & Pillemer, K. (2007). Differences in mothers' support for adult children in black and white families. *Research on Aging, 29*, 410–435.

Sullivan, A. (1996). *Virtually normal: An argument about homosexuality*. New York: Vintage Books.

Sullivan, O. (2004). Changing gender practices within the household: A theoretical perspective. *Gender & Society, 18*, 207–222.

Swartz, T. T. (2009). Intergenerational family relations in adulthood: Patterns, variations, and implications in the contemporary United States. *Annual Review of Sociology, 35*, 191–212.

Sweeney, M. M. (2002). Two decades of family change: The shift in economic foundations of marriage. *American Sociological Review, 67*(1), 132–147.

Sweeney, M. M. (2010). Remarriage and stepfamilies: Strategic sites for family scholarship in the 21st century. *Journal of Marriage and the Family, 72*, 667–684.

Sweeney, M. M., & Cancian, M. (2004). The changing importance of white women's economic prospects for assortative mating. *Journal of Marriage and the Family, 66*, 1015–1028.

Swidler, A. (2001). *Talk of love: How culture matters*. Chicago: University of Chicago Press.

Tach, L., & Edin, K. (2011). The relationship contexts of young disadvantaged men. *Annals of the American Academy of Political and Social Science, 635* (1), 76–94.

Takahashi, N. (2000). The emergence of generalized exchange. *American Journal of Sociology, 105*(1105–1134).

Tamis-LeMonda, C. S., Shannon, J. D., Cabrera, N. J., & Lamb, M. E. (2004). Fathers and mothers at play with their 2- and 3-year-olds: Contributions to language and cognitive development. *Child Development, 75*, 1806–1820.

Tasker, F. (2005). Lesbian mothers, gay fathers, and their children: A review. *Journal of Developmental & Behavioral Pediatrics, 26*, 224–240.

Tasker, F., & Golombok, S. (1995). Adults raised as children in lesbian families. *American Journal of Orthopsychiatry, 65*, 203–215.

Teachman, J. (2007). Race, military service, and marital timing: Evidence from the NLSY-79. *Demography, 44*, 389–404.

Teachman, J. (2008). Complex life course patterns and the risk of divorce in second marriages. *Journal of Marriage and the Family, 70*, 294–305.

Teachman, J. D., & Tedrow, L. (2008). Divorce, race, and military service: More than equal pay and equal opportunity. *Journal of Marriage and the Family, 70*, 1030–1044.

Telingator, C. J., & Patterson, C. (2008). Children and adolescents of lesbian and gay parents. *Journal of the American Academy of Child and Adolescent Psychiatry, 47*, 1364–1368.

The New York Times. (2007, July 24). Transcript: Fourth democratic debate.

Therborn, G. (2004). *Between sex and power: Family in the world, 1900–2000*. London: Routledge.

Thompson, N. J., Potter, J. S., Sanderson, C. A., & Maibach, E. A. (1997). The relationship of sexual abuse and HIV risk behaviors among heterosexual adult female STD patients. *Child Abuse and Neglect, 21*, 149–156.

Thorne, B. (1992). Feminist rethinking of the family: An overview. In B. Thorne & M. Yalom (Eds.), *Rethinking the family: Some feminist questions (revised edition)* (pp. 3–30). Boston, MA: Northeastern University Press.

Thorne, B. (1993). *Gender play: Girls and boys in school*. New Brunswick, NJ: Rutgers University Press.

Tienda, M., & Mitchell, F. (Eds.). (2006). *Hispanics and the future of America*. Washington, DC: National Academies Press.

Tolnay, S. E. (2004). The living arrangements of African American and immigrant children, 1880–2000. *Journal of Family History, 29*, 421–445.

Toshio, T. (1993). U.S. Child substitute care flow data for FY 92 and current trends in the state child substitute care populations. Washington D.C.: American Public Welfare Association.

Trask, B. S. (2010). *Globalization and families: Accelerated systemic social change*. New York: Springer.

Tribe, L. (1990). *Abortion: The clash of absolutes*. New York: W.W. Norton.

Tronto, J. C. (1993). *Moral boundaries: A political argument for an ethic of care*. New York: Routledge.

Turner, C. F., Forsyth, B. H., O'Reilly, J. M., Cooley, P. C., Smith, T. K., Rogers, S. M., & Miller, H. G. (1998). Automated self-interviewing and the survey measurement of sensitive behaviors. In M. P. Couper, R. P. Baker, J. Bethlehem, C. Z. F. Clark, J. Martin, W. L. Nicholls II, & J. M. O'Reilly (Eds.), *Computer assisted survey information collection*. New York: Wiley.

Turner, C. F., Ku, L. C., Rogers, S. M., Lindberg, L. D., Pleck, J. H., & Sonenstein, F. L. (1998). Adolescent sexual behavior, drug use, and violence: Increased reporting with computer survey technology. *Science, 280*(May 8), 867–873.

Twine, F., & Gallagher, C. (2007). The future of whiteness: A map of the "third wave". *Ethnic and Racial Studies, 31*, 4–24.

Udry, J. R., Morris, N. M., & Kovenock, J. (1995). Androgen effects on women's gendered behavior. *Journal of Biosocial Science, 27*, 359–368.

Uhlenberg, P. (1979). Demographic change and the problems of the aged. In M. W. Riley (Ed.), *Aging from birth to death* (pp. 153–166). Boulder, CO: Westview Press.

Uhlenberg, P. (1980). Death and the family. *Journal of Family History, 5*, 313–320.

Uhlenberg, P. (2004). Historical forces shaping grandparent-grandchild relationships: Demography and beyond. *Annual Review of Gerontology and Geriatrics, 24*, 77–97.

Uhlenberg, P., & Hammill, B. G. (1998). Frequency of grandparent contact with grandchild sets: Six factors that make a difference. *The Gerontologist, 38*, 276–285.

Umberson, D. (1987). Family status and health behaviors: Social control as a dimension of social integration. *Journal of Health and Social Behavior, 28*, 306–319.

UNICEF. (2011). Convention on the rights of the child. Retrieved March 15, 2012 from http://www.unicef.org/crc/index_30160.html

United Nations. (2009). International migration report 2009: A global assessment. *Department of Economic and Social Affairs, Population Division*. Retrieved March 15, 2012, from http://esa.un.org/migprofiles/

U.S. Administration for Children and Families. (1996). Fact sheet: Personal responsibility and work opportunity reconciliation act of 1996. Retrieved 6 March, 1998, from www.acf.dhhs.gov/programs/opa/facts/prwora96.htm

U.S. Administration for Children and Families. (2009). Temporary assistance for needy families: Eighth annual report to Congress. Retrieved February 29, 2012, from http://www.acf.hhs.gov/programs/ofa/data-reports/annualreport8/ar8index.htm

U.S. Administration for Children and Families. (2011a). The AFCARS report: Preliminary FY 2010 estimates as of June, 2011. *Report no. 18*. Retrieved February 9, 2012, from http://www.acf.hhs.gov/programs/cb/stats_research/afcars/tar/report18.pdf

U.S. Administration for Children and Families. (2011b). Caseload data 2011. Retrieved February 29, 2012, from http://www.acf.hhs.gov/programs/ofa/data-reports/caseload/caseload_current.htm

U.S. Administration for Children and Families. (2011c). Trends in foster care and adoption — FY 2002–FY 2010. Retrieved February 9, 2012, from http://www.acf.hhs.gov/programs/cb/stats_research/afcars/trends_june2011.pdf

U.S. Bureau of Justice Statistics. (1995). Violence against women: Estimates from the redesigned survey. Washington, DC: U.S. Government Printing Office.

U.S. Bureau of Justice Statistics. (2007). Intimate partner violence in the United States Retrieved March 24, 2009, from http://www.ojp.usdoj.gov/bjs/intimate/ipv.htm#contents

U.S. Bureau of Justice Statistics. (2011a). Criminal victimization, 2010. *National Crime Victimization Survey*. Retrieved February 8, 2012, from http://www.bjs.gov/content/pub/pdf/cv10.pdf

U.S. Bureau of Justice Statistics. (2011b). Criminal victimization in the United States, 2008—statistical tables. Retrieved February 8, 2012, from http://bjs.ojp.usdoj.gov/index.cfm?ty=pbdetail&iid=2218

U.S. Bureau of Justice Statistics. (2012). Intimate partner violence in the United States. Retrieved February 10, 2012, from http://bjs.ojp.usdoj.gov/content/intimate/ipv.cfm

U.S. Bureau of Labor Statistics. (1988). Labor force statistics derived from the current population survey, 1948–1987. Washington, DC: U.S. Government Printing Office.

U.S. Bureau of Labor Statistics. (2005). National compensation survey: Occupational wages in the United States, July 2004 supplementary tables. Retrieved February 25, 2009, from http://www.bls.gov/ncs/ocs/sp/ncbl0728.pdf

U.S. Bureau of Labor Statistics. (2009). Work-at-home patterns by occupation. *Issues in Labor Statistics, Summary 09–02*. Retrieved January 22, 2012, from http://www.bls.gov/opub/ils/pdf/opbils72.pdf

U.S. Bureau of Labor Statistics. (2010). Long-term unemployment experience of the jobless. *Issues in Labor Statistics, Summary 10–5*. Retrieved July 16, 2011, from http://www.bls.gov/opub/ils/summary_10_05/long_term_unemployment.htm

U.S. Bureau of Labor Statistics. (2011a). Highlights of women's earnings in 2010. Retrieved November 16, 2011, from http://www.bls.gov/cps/cpswom2010.pdf

U.S. Bureau of Labor Statistics. (2011b). Household data annual averages: Employed persons by detailed occupation, sex, race, and Hispanic or Latino ethnicity. Retrieved November 5, 2011, from www.bls.gov/cps/cpsaa11.pdf

U.S. Bureau of Labor Statistics. (2011c). How long before the unemployed find jobs or quit looking? *Issues in Labor Statistics*. Retrieved July 31, 2011, from http://www.bls.gov/opub/ils/pdf/opbils89.pdf

U.S. Bureau of Labor Statistics. (2011d). School's out. *Spotlight on Statistics*. Retrieved July 23, 2011, from http://www.bls.gov/spotlight/2011/schools_out/

U.S. Bureau of Labor Statistics. (2011e). Table 5. Employment status of the population by sex, marital status, and presence and age of own children under 18, 2009–10 annual averages. *Economic News Release*. Retrieved January 19, 2012, from http://www.bls.gpv/news.release/famee.t05.htm

U.S. Bureau of Labor Statistics. (2011f). Women in the labor force: A databook. *Report 1034*. Retrieved January 20, 2012, from http://www.bls.gov/cps/wlf-databook2011.htm

U.S. Bureau of the Census. (2001). The 65 years and over population: 2000. Retrieved March 6, 2009, from http://www.census.gov/prod/2001pubs/c2kbr01–10.pdf

U.S. Bureau of the Census. (2002). The American Indian and Alaska native population: 2000. Retrieved February 2, 2009, from http://www.census.gov/prod/2002pubs/c2kbr01–15.pdf

U.S. Bureau of the Census. (2006). We the people: American indians and Alaska natives in the United States Retrieved June 16, 2012, from http://www.census.gov/prod/2006pubs/censr-28.pdf

U.S. Bureau of the Census. (2008a). All parent/child situations, by type, race, and Hispanic origin of householder or reference person: 1970 to present. *Table FM-2*. Retrieved February 2, 2009, from http://www.census.gov/population/socdemo/hh-fam/fm2.xls

U.S. Bureau of the Census. (2008b). Living arrangements of children: 2004. *Household Economic Studies, P70–114*. Retrieved February 23, 2012, from http://www.census.gov/prod/2008pubs/p70–114.pdf

U.S. Bureau of the Census. (2008c). Percent distribution of the projected population by selected age groups and sex for the United States: 2010 to 2050 (NP2008-T3). Retrieved August 15, 2008, from http://www.census.gov/population/www/projections/summarytables.html

U.S. Bureau of the Census. (2008d). Table 12. Projections of the population by age and sex for the United States: 2010 to 2050. *U.S. Population Projections NP2008-T12*. Retrieved January 24, 2012

U.S. Bureau of the Census. (2009a). American factfinder. Retrieved February 2, 2009, from http://factfinder.census.gov/home/saff/main.html?_lang=en

U.S. Bureau of the Census. (2009b). Table A2. Family status and household relationship of people 15 years and over, by marital status, age, and sex: 2008. *America's Families and Living Arrangements*. Retrieved March 7, 2009, from http://www.census.gov/population/socdemo/hh-fam/cps2008/tabA2-all.xls

U.S. Bureau of the Census. (2009c). Who could afford to buy a home in 2004? Retrieved December 2, 2011, from http://www.census.gov/prod/2007pubs/h121–07–1.pdf

U.S. Bureau of the Census. (2010a). FINC-01. Selected characteristics of families by total money income in 2009. *Current Population Survey, Annual Social and Economic Supplement.* Retrieved January 2, 2012, from http://www.census.gov/hhes/www/cpstables/032010/faminc/new01_000.htm

U.S. Bureau of the Census. (2010b). Table A2. Family status and household relationship of people 15 years and over, by marital status, age, and sex: 2010. Retrieved October 21, 2011, from http://www.census.gov/population/socdemo/hh-fam/cps2010/tabA2-all.xls

U.S. Bureau of the Census. (2010c). Table MS-2. Estimated median age at first marriage, by sex: 1890 to the present. Retrieved October 21, 2011, from http://www.census.gov/population/socdemo/hh-fam/ms1.xls

U.S. Bureau of the Census. (2010d). Young adults living at home: 1960 to present. *Current Population Survey, Table AD-1.* Retrieved July 22, 2011, from http://www.census.gov/population/socdemo/hh-fam/ad1.xls

U.S. Bureau of the Census. (2011a). 2010 census shows America's diversity. *Newsroom.* Retrieved January 2, 2012, from http://www.census.gov/newsroom/releases/archives/2010_census/cb11-cn125.html

U.S. Bureau of the Census. (2011b). The 2012 statistical abstract. Retrieved from http://www.census.gov/compendia/statab/

U.S. Bureau of the Census. (2011c). Custodial mothers and fathers and their child support: 2009. *Consumer Income, P60–240.* Retrieved February 11, 2012, from http://www.census.gov/prod/2011pubs/p60–240.pdf

U.S. Bureau of the Census. (2011d). Historical income tables—families, table F-2. Retrieved September 16, 2011, from http://www.census.gov/hhes/www/income/data/historical/families/index.html

U.S. Bureau of the Census. (2011e). Historical poverty tables -- families, table 4. Retrieved September 16, 2011, from http://www.census.gov/hhes/www/poverty/data/historical/families.html

U.S. Bureau of the Census. (2011f). Income, poverty, and health insurance coverage in the United States. *Current Population Reports, Series P60–239.* Retrieved September 17, 2011, from http://www.census.gov/prod/2011pubs/p60–239.pdf

U.S. Bureau of the Census. (2011g). Living arrangement of children: 2009. *Household Economic Studies, P70–126.* Retrieved February 23, 2012, from http://www.census.gov/prod/2011pubs/p70–126.pdf

U.S. Bureau of the Census. (2011h). Marital events of Americans: 2009. *American Community Survey Reports, ACS-13.* Retrieved February 13, 2012, from http://www.census.gov/prod/2011pubs/acs-13.pdf

U.S. Bureau of the Census. (2011i). Overview of race and Hispanic origin: 2010. Retrieved December 21, 2011, from www.census.gov/prod/cen2010/briefs/c2010br-02.pdf

U.S. Bureau of the Census. (2011j). POV01. Age and sex of all people, family members and unrelated individuals iterated by income-to-poverty ratio and race. *Poverty.* Retrieved 2012, January 25, from http://www.census.gov/hhes/www/cpstables/032011/pov/new01_100.htm

U.S. Bureau of the Census. (2011k). Poverty thresholds for 2011 by size of family and number of related children under 18 years. Retrieved February 28, 2012, from http://www.census.gov/hhes/www/poverty/data/threshld/thresh11.xls

U.S. Bureau of the Census. (2011l). Primary child care arrangements of preschoolers living with employed mothers by selected characteristics: Spring 2010. *Who's Minding the Kids?* Retrieved January 26, 2012, from http://www.census.gov/hhes/childcare/data/sipp/2010/tab02A.xls

U.S. Bureau of the Census. (2011m). Same-sex couple households. *American Community Surveys Briefs 10–03.* Retrieved January 16, 2012, from http://www.census.gov/prod/2011pubs/acsbr10–03.pdf

U.S. Bureau of the Census. (2011n). Table 1. Detailed living arrangements of children by race, Hispanic origin, and age: 2009. *Children.* Retrieved February 22, 2012, from http://www.census.gov/hhes/socdemo/children/data/sipp/living2009/tab01.xls

U.S. Bureau of the Census. (2011o). Table 1. Intercensal estimates of the resident population by sex and age for the United States: April 1, 2000 to July 1, 2010. *Population Estimates US-EST00INT-01.* Retrieved January 24, 2012, from http://www.census.gov/popest/data/intercensal/national/tables/US-EST00INT-01.xls

U.S. Bureau of the Census. (2011p). Table 1A: Child care arrangements of preschoolers under 5 years old living with mother, by employment status of mother and selected characteristics: Spring 2010. *Who's Minding the Kids?* Retrieved January 17, 2012, from http://www.census.gov/hhes/childcare/data/sipp/2010/tab01A.xls

U.S. Bureau of the Census. (2011q). Table 4. Poverty status of families, by type of family, presence of related children, race, and Hispanic origin: 1959 to 2010. Retrieved February 28, 2012, from http://www.census.gov/hhes/www/poverty/data/historical/hstpov4.xls

U.S. Bureau of the Census. (2011r). Table C4. Children with grandparents by presence of parents, sex, race, and Hispanic origin for selected characteristics: 2011. *America's Families and Living Arrangements.* Retrieved January 26, 2012, from http://www.census.gov/population/socdemo/hh-fam/cps2011/tabC5-all.xls

U.S. Bureau of the Census. (2011s). Table F2. Family households, by type, age of own children, and educational attainment of householder: 2011. *America's Families and Living Arrangements.* Retrieved January 14, 2012, from http://www.census.gov/population/socdemo/hh-fam/cps2011/tabF2-all.xls

U.S. Bureau of the Census. (2011t). Table F-7. Type of family, all races by median and mean income: 1947 to 2010. *Income.* Retrieved November 24, 2011, from http://www.census.gov/hhes/www/income/data/historical/families/2010/F07AR_2010.xls

U.S. Bureau of the Census. (2011u). Table F-13. Work experience of husband and wife—all married-couple families by median and mean income: 1976 to 2010. Retrieved January 17, 2012, from http://www.census.gov/hhes/www/income/data/historical/families/2010/F13AR_2010.xls

U.S. Bureau of the Census. (2011v). Table FG1. Married couple family groups, by labor force status of both spouses, and race and Hispanic origin of the reference person: 2010. *America's Families and Living Arrangements.* Retrieved January 19, 2012, from http://www.census.gov/population/www/socdemo/hh-fam/cps2011.html

U.S. Bureau of the Census. (2011w). Table FG5. One-parent unmarried family groups with own children under 18, by labor force status of the reference person: 2011. *America's Families and Living Arrangements.* Retrieved February 12, 2012, from http://www.census.gov/population/socdemo/hh-fam/cps2011/tabFG5-all_one.xls

U.S. Bureau of the Census. (2011x). Table FM-2. All parent/child situations by type, race, and Hispanic origin of householder or reference person: 1970 to present. *America's Families and Living Arrangements.* Retrieved February 12, 2012, from http://www.census.gov/population/socdemo/hh-fam/fm2.xls

U.S. Bureau of the Census. (2011y). Table UC1. Opposite sex unmarried couples by labor force status of both partners: 2011. Retrieved January 9, 2012, from http://www.census.gov/population/socdemo/hh-fam/cps2011/tabUC1-all.xls

U.S. Bureau of the Census. (2011z). Table UC3. Opposite sex unmarried couples by presence of biological children under 18, and age, earnings, education, and race and Hispanic origin of both partners: 2011. Retrieved January 9, 2012, from http://www.census.gov/population/socdemo/hh-fam/cps2011/tabUC3-all.xls

U.S. Bureau of the Census. (2012a). The Asian population: 2010. *2010 Census Briefs* Retrieved June 6, 2012, from http://www.census.gov/prod/cen2010/briefs/c2010br-11.pdf

U.S. Bureau of the Census. (2012b). Table B10001: Grandchildren under 18 years living with a grandparent householder by grandparent responsibility, presence of parent, and age of grandchild. *2005 American Community Survey.* Retrieved January 26, 2012, from http://factfinder2.census.gov

U.S. Bureau of the Census. (2012c). Table PCT14: Presence of multigenerational households. *2010 Census Summary File 1.* Retrieved January 27, 2012, from http://factfinder2.census.gov

U.S. Department of Housing and Urban Development. (2011). The 2010 annual homeless assessment report to Congress. Retrieved November 21, 2011, from http://www.hudhre.info/documents/2010HomelessAssessmentReport.pdf

U.S. Department of Justice. (2012). An updated definition of rape. *The Justice Blog.* Retrieved January 6, 2012, from http://blogs.usdoj.gov/blog/archives/1801

U.S. Food and Nutrition Service. (2011). Supplemental nutrition assistance program participation and costs. Retrieved July 31, 2011, from http://www.fns.usda.gov/pd/SNAPsummary.htm

U.S. House of Representatives Committee on Post Office and Civil Service. (1994). Hearings: Review of federal measurements of race and ethnicity. *Serial no. 103–7* (pp. 105–106). Washington, DC: U.S. Government Printing Office.

U.S. National Center for Health Statistics. (1995). Births to unmarried mothers: United States, 1980–92. *Vital and Health Statistics, Series 21, no. 53.* Retrieved February 2, 2009, from http://www.cdc.gov/nchs/data/series/sr_21/sr21_053.pdf

U.S. National Center for Health Statistics. (1999). Adoption, adoption seeking, and relinquishment for adoption in the United States. Advance Data, Number 306. Retrieved October 16, 2003, from http://www.cdc.gov/nchs/data/ad/ad306.pdf

U.S. National Center for Health Statistics. (2000). Nonmarital childbearing in the United States, 1940–1999. *National Vital Statistics Reports, Vol. 48, no. 16.* Retrieved February 4, 2009, from http://www.cdc.gov/nchs/data/nvsr/nvsr48/nvs48_16.pdf

U.S. National Center for Health Statistics. (2002). Cohabitation, marriage, divorce and remarriage in the United States. *Vital and Health Statistics, Series 22, no. 2.* Retrieved January 9, 2012

U.S. National Center for Health Statistics. (2005). Number and percent of births to unmarried women, by race and Hispanic origin: United States, 1940–2000. Retrieved October 21, 2011, from http://www.cdc.gov/nchs/data/statab/t001x17.pdf

U.S. National Center for Health Statistics. (2009). Births: Final data for 2006. *National Vital Statistics Reports, Vol. 57, no. 7.* Retrieved January 31, 2009, from http://www.cdc.gov/nchs/data/nvsr/nvsr57/nvsr57_07.pdf

U.S. National Center for Health Statistics. (2010). Births: Final data for 2007. *National Vital Statistics Reports Vol. 58, no. 24.* Retrieved October 21, 2011, from http://www.cdc.gov/nchs/data/nvsr/nvsr58/nvsr58_24.pdf

U.S. National Center for Health Statistics. (2011a). Births: Preliminary data for 2010. *National Vital Statistics Reports, Vol. 60, no. 2.* Retrieved February 21, 2012, from http://www.cdc.gov/nchs/data/nvsr/nvsr60/nvsr60_02.pdf

U.S. National Center for Health Statistics. (2011b). Deaths: Leasing causes for 2007. *National Vital Statistics Report, vol. 59, no. 8.* Retrieved January 2, 2012, from http://www.cdc.gov/nchs/data/nvsr/nvsr59/nvsr59_08.pdf

U.S. National Center for Health Statistics. (2011c). Sexual behavior, sexual attraction, and sexual identity in the United States: Data from the 2006–2008 National Survey of Family Growth. *National Health Statistics Reports, no. 36.* Retrieved January 4, 2012, from http://www.cdc.gov/nchs/data/nhsr/nhsr036.pdf

U.S. National Center for Health Statistics. (2011d). Teenagers in the United States: Sexual activity, contraceptive use, and childbearing, 2006–2010 national survey of family growth. *Vital and Health Statistics, Series 23, no. 31.* Retrieved January 5, 2012, from http://www.cdc.gov/nchs/data/series/sr_23/sr23_031.pdf

U.S. National Center for Health Statistics. (2011e). United States life tables, 2007. *National Vital Statistics Reports, vol. 59, no. 9.* Retrieved January 24, 2012, from http://www.cdc.gov/nchs/data/nvsr/nvsr59/nvsr59_09.pdf

U.S. National Center for Health Statistics. (2012). First marriages in the United States: Data from the 2006–2010 national survey of family growth. *National Health Statistics Reports, no. 49.* Retrieved March 20, 2012, from http://www.cdc.gov/nchs/pressroom/data/NHSR49.pdf

U.S. National Center on Elder Abuse. (2006). The 2004 survey of state adult protective services:

Abuse of adults 60 years of age and older. Retrieved March 25, 2009, from http://www.ncea.aoa.gov/NCEAroot/Main_Site/pdf/2–14–06%20FINAL%2060+REPORT.pdf

U.S. National Institute of Justice. (1998). Prevalence, incidence and consequences of violence against women: Findings from the national violence against women survey. Retrieved March 24, 2009, from http://www.ncjrs.gov/pdffiles/172837.pdf

U.S. National Institute of Justice. (2000). Extent, nature and consequences of intimate partner violence: Findings from the national violence against women survey. *NCJ 181867.* Retrieved March 15, 2012, from http://www.nij.gov/pubs-sum/181867.htm

U.S. Office of Immigration Statistics. (2011). 2010 yearbook of immigration statistics. Retrieved 2012, January 14, from http://www.dhs.gov/xlibrary/assets/statistics/yearbook/2010/ois_yb_2010.pdf

Van Gelderen, L., Bos, H. M. W., Gartrell, N., Hermanns, J., & Perrin, E. C. (2012). Quality of life of adolescents raised from birth by lesbian mothers: The U.S. national longitudinal family study. *Journal of Developmental Behavioral Pediatrics, 33,* 1–7.

Vandell, D. L., Belsky, J., Burchinal, M., Stenberg, L., Vandergrift, N., & NICHD Early Child Care Research Network. (2010). Do effects of early child care extend to age 15 years? Results from the NICHD study of early child care and youth development. *Child Development, 81,* 737–756.

Vandivere, S., Malm, K., & Radel, L. (2009). *Adoption USA: A chartbook based on the 2007 national survey of adoptive parents.* Washington, DC: U.S. Department of Health and Human Services, Office of the Assistant Secretary for Planning and Evaluation.

Waite, L. J. (1995). Does marriage matter? *Demography, 32,* 483–507.

Waite, L. J., & Joyner, K. (2001). Emotional satisfaction and physical pleasure in sexual unions: Time horizon, sexual behavior, and sexual exclusivity. *Journal of Marriage and the Family, 63,* 247–264.

Waite, L. J., & Lehrer, E. L. (2003). The benefits from marriage and religion in the United States: A comparative analysis. *Population and Development Review, 29,* 255–275.

Wallerstein, J. S., & Blakeslee, S. (1989). *Second chances: Men, women and children a decade after divorce.* New York: Ticknor and Fields.

Wallerstein, J. S., & Kelly, J. B. (1980). *Surviving the breakup: How children and parents cope with divorce.* New York: Basic Books.

Wallerstein, J. S., Lewis, J. M., & Blakeslee, S. (2000). *The unexpected legacy of divorce.* New York: Hyperion.

Ward, R. A. (2008). Multiple parent–adult child relations and well-being in middle and later life. *Journal of Gerontology: Social Sciences, 63B,* S239-S247.

Ward, R. A., Spitze, G., & Deane, G. (2009). The more the merrier? Multiple parent-adult child relations. *Journal of Marriage and the Family, 71,* 161–173.

Wardlow, H. (2006). All's fair when love is war: Romantic passion and companionate marriage among the Huli of Papua New Guinea. In J. S. Hirsch & H. Wardlow (Eds.), *Modern loves: The anthropology of romantic courtship and companionate marriage* (pp. 51–77). Ann Arbor: University of Michigan Press.

Wardlow, H., & Hirsch, J. S. (2006). Introduction. In J. S. Hirsch & H. Wardlow (Eds.), *Modern loves: The anthropology of romantic courtship and companionate marriage* (pp. 1–31). Ann Arbor: University of Michigan Press.

Webster v. Reproductive Health Services, 109 3040 (S. Ct 1989).

Watkins, S. C., Menken, J. A., & Bongaarts, J. (1987). Demographic foundations of family change. *American Sociological Review, 52,* 346–358.

Wax, E. (2008, September 19). In tradition-bound India, female, divorced, and happy. *The Washington Post.*

Weeks, J., Heaphy, B., & Donovan, C. (2001). *Same sex intimacies: Families of choice and other life experiments.* London: Routledge.

Weil, E. (2006, September 24). What if it's (sort of) a boy and (sort of) a girl? *The New York Times Magazine.*

Weinrich, J. D., & Williams, W. L. (1991). Strange customs, familiar lives: Homosexualities in other cultures. In J. C. Gonsiorek & J. D. Weinrich (Eds.), *Homosexuality: Research implications for public policy* (pp. 44–59). Newbury Park, CA: Sage Publications.

Weiss, J. (2000). *To have and to hold: Marriage, the baby boom, and social change.* Chicago: University of Chicago Press.

Weitzman, L. J. (1985). *The divorce revolution: The unexpected social and economic consequences for women and their children in America.* New York: The Free Press.

Welter, B. (1966). The cult of true womanhood. *American Quarterly* (Summer), 151–174.

West, C., & Zimmerman, D. H. (1987). Doing gender. *Gender and Society, 2,* 125–151.

West, C., & Zimmerman, D. H. (2009). Accounting for doing gender. *Gender & Society, 23,* 112–122.

Western, B. (2006). *Punishment and inequality in America.* New York: Russell Sage Foundation.

Western, B., Bloome, D., & Percheski, C. (2008). Inequality among American families with children, 1975 to 2005. *American Sociological Review, 73,* 903–920.

Western, B., & Wildeman, C. (2009). The black family and mass incarceration. *The Annals of the American Academy of Political and Social Science, 621,* 221–242.

Weston, K. (1991). *Families we choose: Lesbians, gays, kinship.* New York: Columbia University Press.

Wetzstein, C. (2008, September 7). Covenant marriage keeps more couples together. *The Washington Times,* p. M20.

White, L. (1990). Determinants of divorce: A review of research in the eighties. *Journal of Marriage and the Family, 52,* 904–912.

White, L. (1994). Stepfamilies over the life course: Social support. In A. Booth & J. Dunn (Eds.), *Stepfamilies: Who benefits? Who does not?* (pp. 109–137). Hillsdale, NJ: Erlbaum Associates.

White, L., & Gilbreth, J. G. (2001). When children have two fathers: Effects of relationships with stepfathers and noncustodial fathers on adolescent outcomes. *Journal of Marriage and the Family, 63,* 155–167.

Whitehead, B. D., & Popenoe, D. (2001). Who wants to marry a soul mate? In National Marriage Project (Ed.), *The state of our unions, 2001* (pp. 6–16). Retrieved February 12, 2004, from http://marriage.rutgers.edu/Publications/SOOU/NMPAR2001.pdf.

Whyte, M. K. (1990). *Dating, mating and marriage.* New York: Aldine de Gruyter.

Wickes, R., & Emmison, M. (2007). They are all "doing gender" but are they are all passing? A case study of the appropriation of a sociological concept. *Sociological Review, 55,* 311–330.

Wilcox, W. B. (1998). Conservative Protestant childrearing: Authoritarian or authoritative? *American Sociological Review, 63,* 796–809.

Wilcox, W. B. (2004). *Soft patriarchs, new men: How Christianity shapes fathers and husbands.* Chicago: University of Chicago Press.

Wilcox, W. B. (2011). The great recession and marriage. *National Marriage Project Report Web Release.* Retrieved July 11, 2011, from http://www.virginia.edu/marriageproject/pdfs/NMP-GreatRecession.pdf

Wilcox, W. B., & Nock, S. L. (2006). What's love got to do with it? Equality, equity, commitment and women's marital quality. *Social Forces, 84,* 1321–1345.

Wildeman, C. (2010). Paternal incarceration and children's physically aggressive behaviors: Evidence from the Fragile Families and Child Wellbeing study. *Social Forces, 89,* 285–310.

Williams, W. L. (1986). *The spirit and the flesh: Sexual diversity in American Indian culture.* Boston, MA: Beacon Press.

Williams, J. C. (2010). *Reshaping the work-family debate: Why men and class matter.* Cambridge, MA: Harvard University Press.

Willson, A. E., Shuey, K. M., & Elder, G. H., Jr. (2003). Ambivalence in the relationship of adult children to aging parents and in-laws. *Journal of Marriage and the Family, 65,* 1055–1072.

Wilson, J. Q. (2002). *The marriage problem: How our culture has weakened families.* New York: HarperCollins.

Wilson, K. L., & Portes, A. (1980). Immigrant enclaves: An analysis of the labor market experiences of Cubans in Miami. *American Journal of Sociology, 86,* 295–319.

Wilson, W. J. (1987). *The truly disadvantaged: The inner city, the underclass, and public policy.* Chicago: University of Chicago Press.

Wilson, W. J. (1996). *When work disappears.* New York: Knopf.

Wolfe, A. (1998). *One nation, after all.* New York: Viking.

Wolfers, J. (2006). Did unilateral divorce laws raise divorce rates? A reconciliation and new results. *American Economic Review, 96,* 1802–1820.

Wolff, J. L., & Kasper, J. D. (2006). Caregivers of frail elders: Updating a national profile. *The Gerontologist, 46,* 344–356.

Wong, M. G. (1988). The Chinese American family. In C. H. Mindel, R. W. Habenstein & J. W. Roosevelt (Eds.), *Ethnic families in America: Patterns and variations* (pp. 230–257). New York: Elsevier Science Publishing.

Wood, R. G., McConnell, S., Moore, Q., Clarkwest, A., & Hsueh, J. (2010). Strengthening unmarried parents'

relationships: The early impacts of building strong families. *Mathematica Policy Research.* Retrieved June 23, 2011, from http://www.mathematica-mpr.com/publications/pdfs/family_support/BSF_impact_execsumm.pdf

Wootton, B. H. (1997). Gender differences in occupational employment. *Monthly Labor Review* (April), 15–24.

Wright, L. (1994). One drop of blood. *The New Yorker,* pp. 46–55.

Xie, Y., Raymo, J. M., Goyette, K., & Thornton, A. (2003). Economic potential and entry into marriage and cohabitation. *Demography, 40,* 351–368.

Xu, X., Hudspeth, C. D., & Bartkowski, J. P. (2005). The timing of first marriage: Are there religious variations? *Journal of Family Issues, 26,* 584–618.

Yamaguchi, K., & Wang, Y. (2002). Class identification of married employed women and men in America. *American Journal of Sociology, 108,* 440–475.

Yanagisako, S. (1985). *Transforming the past: Tradition and kinship among Japanese Americans.* Stanford, CA: Stanford University Press.

Yanagisako, S. J., & Collier, J. F. (1987). Toward a unified analysis of gender and kinship. In J. F. Collier & S. J. Yanagisako (Eds.), *Gender and kinship: Essays toward a unified analysis.* Stanford, CA: Stanford University Press.

Yount, K. M., & Li, L. (2010). Domestic violence against married women in Egypt. *Sex Roles, 63,* 332–347.

Zelizer, V. (1985). *Pricing the priceless child: The changing social value of children.* New York: Basic Books.

Zhou, M., & Bankston III, C. L. (1998). *Growing up American: How Vietnamese children adapt to life in the United States.* New York: Russell Sage Foundation.

Acknowledgments

Chapter 2: Figure 2.2—Ellwood, David T. and Christopher Jencks, Figure 1.1, "U.S. Children Not Living with Their Own Parents at Age 16 Because a Parent Died or for Other Reasons, 1910s to 1990s." In *Social Inequality.* © 2004 Russell Sage Foundation, 112 East 64th Street, New York, NY 10021. Reprinted with permission.

Chapter 4: Figure 4.1—Fischer, Claude S. and Michael Hout, Figure 6.4, "Adjusted Family-of-Four Income Medians, by Education." In *Century of Difference: How America Changed in the Last One Hundred Years.* © 2006 Russell Sage Foundation, 112 East 64th Street, New York, NY 10021. Reprinted with permission.

Figure 4.2—Table 9, page 1682, Adapted from Sheela Kennedy and Larry Bumpass, "Table 9: Relative risk of mother's cohabitation and mother's marriage for children by mother's characteristics. U.S. Children ages 0–12, period Cox model estimates and period life-table estimates of proportions, from 1990–94 and 1997–2001a." *Demographic Research, 19* (2008), 1663–1692.

Figure 4.4—Adapted from Alice S. Rossi and Peter H. Rossi, *Of Human Bonding: Parent-Child Relations Across the Life Course.* © 1990 by Aldine Publishers. Reprinted by permission of AldineTransaction, a division of Transaction Publishers.

Chapter 5: Figure 5.4—Reprinted with permission from the National Academies Press. © 2006, National Academy of Sciences.

Quotation p. 165—Portes Alejandro, and Alex Stepick, *City on the Edge: The Transformation of Miami.* © 1993, The Regents of the University of California.

Chapter 6: Quotation pp. 184–185—Lewontin, Richard, "Sex, Lies, and Social Science: An Exchange," in *New York Review of Books*, May 25, 1995, p. 44. Used by permission.

Chapter 7: Figure 7.1—Rosenfeld, M.J. "Percentage of Young Unmarried Men and Women Ages 20–29 who Headed their own Household, 1880–2000," in *The Age of Independence: Interracial Unions, Same-Sex Unions, and the Changing American Family.* © 2007, Harvard University Press. Reprinted with permission.

Quotation pp. 218–219—Smock, Pamela J., Wendy D. Manning, and Meredith Porter. "Everything's There Except Money: How Money Shapes Decisions to Marry Among Cohabitors." *Journal of Marriage and the Family, 67,* (2005), 689, 690.

Quotation p. 220—Cherlin, Andrew. "The deinstitutionalization of American marriage," *Journal of Marriage and the Family, 66/4,* (2004), 848–861.

Figure 7.2—Table 3, page 1672, Adapted from Sheela Kennedy and Larry Bumpass, "Table 3: Percentage of women ages 19–44 who have ever cohabited and percentage change: 1995–2002, from 1990–94 and 1997–2001a." *Demographic Research, 19* (2008), 1663–1692.

Chapter 8: Figure 8.2—With kind permission from Springer Science+Business Media: *Social Indicators Research*, "Gender Convergence in the American Heritage Time Use Study (AHTUS)," Vol. 82/1, May 2007, p. 1–33, Fisher, K., Egerton, M., Gershuny, J.I., and Robinson, J.P., figure 4.

Figure 8.3—Republished with permission of Oxford University Press Journals, from "Taking on the Second Shift: Time Allocations and Time Pressures of U.S. Parents with Preschoolers," by Milkie, Melissa, Sara Raley, and Suzanne Bianchi, in *Social Forces, 88,* no. 2, Dec. 2009; permission conveyed through Copyright Clearance Center.

Chapter 9: Figure 9.1—From THE MARRIAGE-GO-ROUND: THE STATE OF MARRIAGE AND THE FAMILY IN AMERICA TODAY by Andrew J. Cherlin. © 2009 by Andrew J. Cherlin. Used by permission of Alfred A. Knopf, a division of Random House, Inc.

Figure 9.2—Carlson, M.J. and M.E. Corcoran. "Family Structure and Children's Behavioral and Cognitive Outcomes." *Journal of Marriage and the Family, 63,* (2001), 779–792. Reprinted with permission.

Chapter 10: Figure 10.2—Sweet, James A., and Larry L. Bumpass. Table 8.8, "Living Arrangements of Persons Aged 60 and Over, By Sex, 1940–1980." In *American Families and Households.* © 1987 Russell Sage Foundation, 112 East 64th St., New York, NY 10021. Reprinted with permission.

Figure 10.3—Pew Research Center. (2010). The return of the multigenerational family household. Retrieved January 26, 2012, from http://pewsocialtrends.org/files/2010/10/752-multi-generational-families.pdf; and Pew Research Center. (2011a). Fighting poverty in a tough economy, Americans move in with their relatives. Retrieved January 26, 2012, from http://pewsocialtrends.org/files/2011/10/multigenerational-households-final1.pdf.

Photo Credits

Chapter 1: Opener: © Digital Vision/PunchStock RF; p. 11 (top): © Purestock/PunchStock RF; p. 11 (bottom): © Corbis RF; p. 19: © U.S. Census Bureau, Public Information Office (PIO); p. 28: © Reed Kaestner/Corbis RF

Chapter 2: Opener: Courtesy of Library of Congress Prints and Photographs Division [LC-DIG-ppmsca-08762]; p. 41: © Bridgeman Art Library; p. 43: © Dynamic Graphics/Creatas/PictureQuest RF; p. 45: Courtesy of Library of Congress Prints and Photographs Division [LC-USZ62-101169]; p. 50: © North Wind Picture Archives; p. 54: © Purestock/PunchStock RF; p. 55: Courtesy of Library of Congress; p. 61: © Hulton Archives/Getty; p. 66: © Historicus, Inc.

Chapter 3: Opener: © Stockbyte/Getty RF; p. 83: © Smithsonian American Art Museum, Washington, DC/Art Resource, NY; p. 86: © PhotoAlto/Laurence Mouton/Getty RF; p. 88: © S. Olsson/PhotoAlto RF; p. 94: © Colin Young Wolff/PhotoEdit; p. 97: © Roy McMahn/Corbis RF

Chapter 4: Opener: © Alison Wright/Corbis; p. 117: © Comstock Images/Jupiter Images/Alamy RF; p. 121: © Michael Newman/PhotoEdit; p. 123: © Image Source/PunchStock RF; p. 127: © Steve Mason/Getty RF; p. 131: © Rob Levine/The Image Bank/Getty RF; p. 132: © Brand X Pictures/PunchStock RF; p. 135: © Siri Stafford/Getty RF

Chapter 5: Opener: © Stewart Cohen/Getty RF; p. 143: © Mark Richards/PhotoEdit; p. 146: © BananaStock/PunchStock RF; p. 155: © Ariel Skelley/Blend Images LLC RF; p. 159: © Ingram Publishing RF; p. 162: © Dennis MacDonald/Alamy RF; p. 164: © The McGraw-Hill Companies, Inc/Andrew Resek, photographer; p. 166: © David Butow/SABA/Corbis

Chapter 6: Opener: © Stockbyte/PunchStock RF; p. 179: © Historicus, Inc.; p. 183: © Bettmann/Corbis; p. 187: © The McGraw-Hill Companies, Inc/Christopher Kerrigan, photographer; p. 197: © Gilles Peres/Magnum Photos; p. 200: © Purestock/PunchStock RF

Chapter 7: Opener: © Brand X Pictures/PunchStock RF; p. 216: © Ryan McVay/Getty RF; p. 219: © BananaStock/PunchStock RF; p. 224: © William Gottlieb/Corbis; p. 226: © Keith Brofsky/Getty RF; p. 233: © Buccina Studios/Getty RF; p. 234: © Tom Grill/Corbis RF; p. 242: © Lucidio Studio, Inc/Corbis RF

Chapter 8: Opener: © Ryan McVay/Getty RF; p. 252: © Photodisc/Getty RF; p. 256: © Corbis RF; p. 262: © Jose Luis Pelaez Inc/Blend Images LLC RF; p. 263: © Dynamic Graphics/Creatas/PictureQuest RF; p. 265: © Photodisc Collection/Getty RF

Chapter 9: Opener: © Stockbyte/Getty RF; p. 277: © Getty RF; p. 280: © BananaStock/PunchStock RF; p. 282: © Photodisc/Getty RF; p. 284: © Digital Vision/PunchStock RF; p. 294: © BananaStock/PunchStock RF

Chapter 10: Opener: © Corbis RF; p. 307: © Stockbyte/PunchStock RF; p. 313: © Susan See Photography RF; p. 314: © Keith Thomas Productions/Brand X Pictures/PictureQuest RF; p. 316: © Mel Curtis/Getty RF; p. 328: © Creatas/PictureQuest RF; p. 330: © Design Pics/Don Hammond RF; p. 334: © Tanya Constantine/Brand X Pictures/Jupiterimages RF

Chapter 11: Opener: © Jack Star/PhotoLink/Getty RF; p. 345: © Lorenzo Ciniglio/Sygma/Corbis; p. 348: © Comstock/PunchStock RF; p. 354: © BananaStock/PunchStock RF; p. 357: © Emma Lee/Life File/Getty RF; p. 360: © Nanine Hartzenbusch/AP/Wide World Photos; p. 363: © Bob Mahoney/The Image Works; p. 368: © David R. Frazier Photolibrary RF

Chapter 12: Opener: © The McGraw-Hill Companies, Inc/Jill Braaten, photographer; p. 380: © Photodisc/Getty RF; p. 388: © The McGraw-Hill Companies, Inc/Andrew Resek, photographer; p. 393: © Keith Brofsky/Getty RF; p. 395: © Purestock/PunchStock RF

Chapter 13: Opener: © Fancy Photography/Veer RF; p. 414: © Comstock Images RF; p. 416: © Digital Vision/PunchStock RF; p. 419: © Corbis RF; p. 421:

© 2003 Charles Walker/Topfoto/The Image Works;
p. 427: © Corbis RF

Chapter 14: Opener: © AP/Wide World Photos;
p. 436: © Glow Images RF; p. 439: © The New York
Times/Redux Pictures; p. 442: © The McGraw-Hill
Companies, Inc/Andrew Resek, photographer;
p. 446: © BananaStock/PunchStock RF; p. 452: ©
Comstock/PunchStock RF; p. 459: © Keith Brofsky/
Getty RF

Name Index

Page numbers in *italics* indicate illustrations. An *f* indicates figures, *n* indicates footnotes, and *t* indicates tables.

Aber, J. L., 286
Acker, J., 101, 121
Adam, B. D., 179
Adams, M., 84, 102
Agree, E. M., 317, 318, 331, 332
Agyei, Y., 187
Alderson, D. P., 454
Allen, W. R., 168
Alwin, D. F., 130, 131
Amato, P. R., 250, 254, 258, 261, 279, 281, 352, 387, 390, 398
Amirkhanyan, A. A., 326
Anderson, K. L., 349, 357
Anderson, M., 313*n*
Apel, R., 423
Aquilino, W. S., 424
Aragon, C., 325
Ardelt, M., 286
Aries, P., 40, 49
Armstrong, E., 212
Armstrong, E. A., 212, 213
Astone, N. M., 289, 384
Autor, D., 169
Autor, D. H., 111
Axxin, W. G., 228
Azuma, H., 276

Bachman, J. G., 296
Bailey, B. L., 210, 211
Bailey, M., 187
Bailey, M. J., 187, 285
Baker, E. H., 374
Bales, R. F., 231
Banks, R. R., 169
Bankston III, C. L., 165
Bartkowski, J. P., 234
Bartlett, K. T., 389
Basena, M., 355
Bates, J. E., 276
Batt, R., 264
Bauman, Z., 28
Baumrind, D., 275

Beach, S. R. H., 352
Beal, J. F., 178
Bean, F. D., 159, 161, 167, 169
Beck, U., 8, 15, 27, 28, 29*n*, 194
Becker, G., 22
Becker, G. S., 22–23, 231, 237, 384
Beck-Gernsheim, E., 8, 15, 27, 28, 29*n*, 194
Belenky, M. F., 92
Belkin, L., 253
Bellah, R., 6, 383
Beneria, L., 119
Bengtson, V. L., 130, 310, 327, 329, 330, 333, 413
Bennice, J. A., 351
Benson, M. L., 352
Berk, R. A., 368
Bernard, J., 240
Berry, M. F., 156
Besharow, D. J., 359
Bianchi, S. M., 259, 260, 292, 319, 384
Biblarz, T. J., 284, 333
Bittman, M., 292
Black, A., 211*n*
Black, M. C., 362
Blair-Loy, M., 264, 267
Blakeslee, S., 394, 396, 397, 421
Blank, R. M., 351, 449
Blassingame, J. W., 156
Blau, F. D., 96
Blauvelt, M. T., 50
Bledsoe, C., 53
Bloch, R. H., 50
Bloome, D., 114
Blossfeld, H.-P., 239
Blumer, H., 23, 90
Boden, S., 232
Bogen, K., 265
Bolzendahl, C., 191
Bongaarts, J., 318

Booth, A., 234, 250, 254, 352, 366, 398
Borchorst, A., 438
Bos, H. M. W., 284
Bourdieu, P., 164
Boushey, H., 254
Bradatan, C., 157, 159
Bradley, K., 99, 232
Bradley, R. H., 280
Braithwaite, S., 363
Bramlett, M. D., 62, 234, 386, 414, 415
Branaman, A., 234
Brandford, C., 357
Brandon, P. D., 259
Bray, J. H., 417, 418, 420, 421
Briere, J., 356
Brodzinsky, D. M., 281
Bronte-Tinkew, J., 280
Brooks-Gunn, J., 287
Brown, S., 332
Brown, S. L., 14, 289, 423
Buchanan, C. M., 276, 389, 395
Buckmiller, N., 14
Budgeon, S., 15, 194
Budig, M., 256
Bulcroft, K., 232
Bulcroft, R. A., 232
Bumpass, L. L., 69, 115*f*, 216, 217, 291, 374, 385, 386, 411
Bures, R., 152
Burgess, E. W., 62, 224
Burstein, N. R., 384
Burtless, G., 451
Burton, L. M., 220, 352
Bush, G. H. W., 447
Bush, G. W., 312, 453
Buss, D. M., 238

Cabrera, N. J., 280
Cahill, S., 87, 88, 89
Cai, T., 399
Cain, M., 12*n*

Calhoun, A. W., 62
Callendar, C., 82, 83, 84
Camarillo, A., 57
Cameron, T., 359
Campbell, A., 202
Cancian, F. M., 226
Cancian, M., 239, 285, 290, 458
Canudas-Romo, V., 374
Capaldi, D. M., 349
Carlson, M. J., 289, 290, 290t, 450, 453, 458
Carpenter, C., 221
Carrano, J., 280
Carrington, C., 192, 221
Carroll, J. S., 14
Caspi, A., 363, 398
Castro, F., 161
Castro-Martin, T., 192
Catlin, G., 82, 83
Cauce, A. M., 275
Cavanagh, S. E., 289
Chafe, W. H., 103
Chalk, R., 357
Chan, S. C., 228
Chao, R., 276
Charles, C. Z., 154
Charles, M., 99
Chase-Lansdale, L., 394
Chase-Lansdale, P. L., 452
Cheadle, J. E., 390
Chen, F., 287
Cherlin, A. J., 4n, 7f, 60, 62, 152, 217, 220, 230n, 288, 289, 317, 328, 352, 357, 395, 407, 409, 413, 417, 450
Chesley, N., 268
Choi, H., 331
Choi, J. N., 287
Chong, A., 229
Clarke, A. Y., 169
Clarke, E. J., 330
Clarkwest, A., 454
Clinchy, B. M., 92
Clingempeel, G., 396
Clinton, B., 140, 447
Coates, T.-N. P., 140
Cohen, J., 286
Cohn, D. V., 250
Coleman, J. S., 164
Coleman, M., 407, 412, 415, 417, 418, 420, 422, 423, 424

Collier, J. F., 27, 229
Coltrane, S., 84, 102
Comings, E., 208–209
Comstock, G., 89
Conger, R. D., 286
Connell, R. W., 102
Connidis, I. A., 330, 331
Cook, J. A., 92
Cook, K., 23
Cook, S. T., 290
Cooke, L. P., 385
Coontz, S., 60, 425
Corcoran, M. E., 289
Cornell, C. P., 344
Cott, N. F., 48n, 50, 52
Cowell, W. H., 55
Cox, D., 319
Craig, L., 292
Cranage, H., 232
Cretney, S., 408, 421
Crimmins, E. M., 308
Cross-Barnet, C., 220
Crouch, S., 140
Crouter, A. C., 89
Cuéllar, A. B., 57
Cui, M., 363

da Vinci, L., 420
Dabbs, J. J., Jr., 366
Daniels, R., 59
Danziger, S. K., 449, 451, 460
Darling, C. A., 198
Daro, D., 356
Darroch, J. E., 203
Davis, J. A., 62, 122, 167, 197n, 263, 442, 447, 455
Davis, N. J., 122
Dawood, K., 187, 285
Day, R. D., 279
de Montaigne, M., 40
de Vaus, D., 387
Deane, G., 413
Deater-Deckard, K., 276
DeFries, J. C., 398
DeLeire, T., 322
DeMaris, A., 352
Demo, D. H., 352
Demos, J., 40, 47, 434
Deutsch, F. M., 95
Dew, J., 234
Dill, B. T., 53

Dix, D., 224
Doane, W., 62
Dodge, K. A., 276
Dominguez-Folgueras, M., 192
Donovan, C., 221
Dornbusch, S. F., 389, 395
Doucet, A., 102
Dreby, J., 294, 295
Droegemuller, W., 345
Dronkers, J., 387
Du Bois, W. E. B., 168
Dunaway, W., 56
Duncan, G. J., 25, 287
Dunifon, R., 289, 452
Durden, T. E., 158
Duryea, S., 229

Easterlin, R. A., 67n
Edin, K., 115, 231, 232, 287, 458
Edmonston, B., 167, 168
Edwards, J. N., 352
Egerton, M., 258f
Eggebean, D., 234
Eggebeen, D. J., 393
Ehrenreich, B., 293
Ehrensaft, M. K., 365
Eichner, M., 257
Elder, G. H., Jr., 64, 72, 286
Elkin, F., 87, 88, 89
Elliot, D. M., 356
Ellwood, D. T., 69f, 114
Emerson, R. M., 23
Emery, R. E., 347, 390, 396, 398, 402
Emmison, M., 92
England, P., 10, 26, 93, 98, 100, 212, 256
English, D. J., 357
Epstein, J. L., 265
Ericksen, J. A., 202
Esterberg, K. G., 221
Evans, G. W., 287
Evans, M. D. R., 67

Fahrenthold, D. A., 350
Farley, R., 168
Favreault, M. M., 235
Fein, D., 454
Feng, D., 413
Fennelly, K., 160
Fenstermaker, S., 93, 94

Fergusson, D. M., 346, 356
Fincham, F. D., 213, 352, 363
Fine, G. A., 90
Fine, M., 415, 418, 420, 423, 424
Fineman, M. A., 257
Finkelhor, D., 356
Fischer, C. S., 63, 69, 113*f*
Fischer, D. H., 329
Fischer, M. J., 154
Fisher, A. P., 281
Fisher, K., 258*f*
Fletcher, J. M., 201
Fogarty, A., 212
Folbre, N., 10, 256, 292
Fonow, M. M., 92
Forrest, J. D., 199
Forsyth, B. H., 185
Foster, M. E., 286
Foucault, M., 181, 182
Fox, G. L., 352
Fox, L. E., 265
Fox, R., 43
Franklin, B., 6
Frazier, E. F., 54
Friedman, C., 86
Frisco, M. L., 289
Frogner, B., 450
Fromby, P., 289
Fuller-Thomson, E., 323
Furstenberg, F. F., Jr., 72, 112,
    149, 152, 201, 202, 288*f*,
    290, 290*t*, 317, 328, 413,
    417, 458
Fussell, E., 72
Fuwa, M., 96

Gable, J., 406, 409
Gallagher, C., 145
Gamson, J., 189
Ganong, L. H., 407, 412,
    415, 417, 418, 420, 422,
    423, 424
Gans, H. J., 21, 134
Gates, G. J., 221
Gauthier, A. H., 112
Gebhard, P. H., *183*
Geist, C., 191
Gelles, R. J., 344, 346, 354
Gennetian, L. M., 452
Geronimus, A. T., 201

Gershuny, J. I., 258*f*
Gerson, K., 257, 262–263
Gerstel, N., 153
Gerth, H. H., 120
Ghimire, D. J., 228
Giarrusso, R., 323, 331, 413
Gibbons, A., 357
Giddens, A., 27, 28, 29*n*
Gilbreth, J. G., 281, 422
Gilkes, C. T., 156, 234
Gillis, J. R., 48, 210
Glaser, K., 317, 318, 331, 332
Glavin, P., 268
Glendon, M. A., 379
Glenn, E. N., 58, 255, 257
Glenn, N., 212
Glick, J. E., 159, 163
Gold, S. J., 163, 164
Goldberger, N. R., 92
Goldin, C., 56, 97
Goldscheider, C., 64, 424
Goldscheider, F. K., 64, 152, 424
Goode, W. J., 58, 146, 163, 352
Gooden, A., 89
Gooden, M., 89
Gordon, L., 344, 367
Gordon, T., 451
Gottman, J. M., 278
Goyette, K., 239
Graham, E., 295
Graham, S., 144
Green, A. I., 189, 190
Greenberg, M. H., 351
Greene, A., 355
Griswold del Castillo, R., 57
Grogger, J., 449
Grogger, J. T., 449
Grubb, W. N., 448
Gubits, D., 454
Guo, G., 399
Gupta, S., 260, 386
Gutman, H. G., 54, 55
Guzman, L., 295
Guzzo, K. B., 290

Habenstein, R. W., 44*n*
Hagestad, G., 334
Haider, S. J., 449
Haldeman, D. C., 187
Hall, G. S., 210

Hamilton, A., 178, *179,* 180
Hamilton, L., 212, 213
Hammill, B. G., 317, 332
Han, E., 458
Han, W.-j., 265
Handel, G., 87, 88, 89
Handler, J., 449
Hans, J. D., 408
Hansen, K., 178
Hansen, K. V., 178
Hardaway, C. R., 276
Harding, S., 92, 93
Hareven, T. K., 313*n*
Harjo, S. S., 166
Harknett, K., 290
Harknett, K. S., 128
Härkönen, J., 387
Harmon, A., 306
Harrison, L. A., 91
Harrison-Jay, S., 409
Hartnett, C. S., 128
Hartog, H., 48, 62
Haub, C., 158
Hays, S., 277
Heaphy, B., 221
Heclo, H., 448
Heming, S., 140
Henrikson, D., 406
Henrikson, G., 406
Henrikson, N., 409
Henry VIII, King of England, 48
Herskovits, M. J., 53
Hetherington, E. M., 394, 395,
    396, 397, 409, 417, 418,
    419, 423
Heuveline, P., 217, 288*f*
Hewitt, B., 387
Heymann, J., 120
Hill, J. P., 350
Hill, M. S., 79
Hill, S. A., 154
Hirsch, J. S., 227, 228, 229
Hochschild, A., 260, 293
Hochschild, A. R., 278
Hofferth, S., 153, 280
Hoffman, K. L., 352
Holian, L. M., 319
Hong, L. K., 58
Hoover, H., 435
Horwood, L. J., 346, 356

Hotz, V. J., 201, 319
Hout, M., 63, 69, 113*f*
Howell, N., 42
Hsueh, J., 454
Hudspeth, C. D., 234
Hunter, A. G., 386
Hurt, T. R., 352
Huston, A. C., 289

Inglehart, R., 234
Ingraham, C., 232
Isen, A., 116, 169
Ishii-Kuntz, M., 164
Izquierdo, E., 342

Jackson, J., 140
Jackson-Newsom, J., 276
Jacobs, J. A., 262–263
Jacobs, S., 82
Jefferson, T., 140
Jencks, C., 69*f*, 114
Jensen, L., 162
Jerome, Saint, 209
Jeter, M., 167
Jodl, K. M., 409, 418, 423
Joe, J. R., 46
Johnson, D. R., 234, 250,
    254, 352
Johnson, M. P., 347, 348, 352
Johnson, S. H., 158
Johnston, L. D., 296
Jones, J., 56
Jones, S., 286
Jordan, L. P., 295
Joshi, P., 265
Joyner, K., 209

Kahn, L. M., 96
Kakinuma, M., 276
Kalil, A., 265, 322, 452
Kalleberg, A. L., 111
Kallen, D. J., 198
Kalmijn, M., 73, 116
Kaplan, R., 276
Karoly, L. A., 449
Kasper, J. D., 325
Katz, J., 178, 179
Katz, L. F., 111
Katz, M. B., 444, 448

Kaukinen, C., 423
Kearney, M., 111
Kefalas, M. J., 115, 231, 232
Kellogg, S., 62
Kelly, J., 394, 395, 396, 397
Kelly, J. B., 389, 391, 394, 397*n*
Kempe, H. C., 345, 348
Kendall-Tackett, K. A., 356
Kenkre, T., 160
Kennedy, S., 115*f*, 216, 217,
    291, 374
Kenney, C. T., 352
Kephart, G., 150, 239
Kertzer, D. I., 44
Kett, J. F., 210
Kiernan, K., 118
Kiernan, K. E., 217, 424
Kilpatrick, D., 350
Kim, H. K., 349
Kim, Y. J., 384
King, V., 280, 390
Kingston, P. W., 319
Kinsey, A. C., 183, 186
Kirkpatrick, L. A., 238
Kissane, R. J., 287
Kitano, H. H. L., 59
Klempin, S., 392
Klerman, J., 449
Klinenberg, E., 145, 214
Knab, J., 290
Knox, V., 454
Kochems, L., 82, 83, 84
Kockeis, E., 316
Kohn, M. L., 130, 277
Komarovsky, M., 65
Korenman, S., 201
Kosterlitz, J., 312
Kovenock, J., 86
Kowaleski-Jones, L., 289
Ku, L. C., 185

La Ferrara, E., 229
Lachs, M. S., 360
Lamb, M. E., 279, 280
Lambert, J. D., 331
Lamont, M., 257
Land, K. C., 296
Landale, N. S., 157, 159, 160
Landes, E. M., 384

Landry, B., 154
Landry, D. J., 150, 239
Lang, S., 82
Lansford, J. E., 276
Lareau, A., 132, 277
Larsen, R. J., 238
Lash, S., 29*n*
Laslett, B., 63, 68
Laumann, E. O., 184, 196, 356
Laumann, L. A., 359
Laumann-Billings, L., 347, 398
Laurens, J., 178
Lazerson, M., 448
Leaper, C., 86
Lee, B. A., 125*f*
Lee, J., 167, 169
Lee, S. M., 167, 168
Lehrer, E. L., 234
Levenson, R. W., 264
Lever, J., 90
Levin, I., 15, 192, 193
Levy, F., 134, 147, 298
Lewis, J. M., 394, 396, 421
Lewontin, R., 184, 185
Li, L., 352
Li, S., 355
Lichter, D. T., 150, 151, 158,
    168, 220, 239
Liebler, C. A., 167
Liker, J. K., 286
Lim, N., 73
Lim, S., 56
Lin, C., 163
Lin, I.-F., 332
Lippa, R. A., 89
Lippman, L., 295
Liu, K., 325
Liu, W. T., 163
Locke, H. J., 62, 224
Loeb, T. B., 356
Louie, J., 294
Loving, R., 167
Lowenstein, A., 332
Luker, K., 442
Lunday, G. F., 154
Lundberg, S. J., 119
Lundquist, E., 454
Lundquist, J. H., 150
Lüscher, K., 330, 331
Luther, M., 41

Lynch, A. B., 91
Lynd, H. M., 223
Lynd, R. S., 223
Lynskey, M. T., 356

Maccoby, E. E., 89, 98, 389, 395, 396
Madsen, R., 6, 383
Magdol, L., 363
Maibach, E. A., 356
Malm, K., 281, 282
Manner, J., 376
Manning, W. D., 14, 193, 218, 219, 232, 393, 423
Manton, K. G., 325
Marantz, R., 281
Mare, R. D., 116, 151
Markman, H. J., 234
Marks, N. G., 331
Marquardt, E., 212
Marshall, J., 299
Marsiglio, W., 279, 280, 409, 418, 419, 420
Martin, C. E., 183, 186
Martin, S. P., 69, 114, 149t, 381, 383
Martin-Garcia, T., 192
Mason, M. A., 409
Massey, D. S., 154
Mather, C., 343
Mattingly, M. J., 254
May, E. T., 60, 62, 224
Mazzuato, V., 295
McConnell, S., 454
McCurdy, K., 356
McDaniel, A., 56
McDermott, M., 145
McDonald, J., 378
McDonald, R. M., 276
McElroy, S. W., 201
McHale, S. M., 89
McLanahan, S. S., 25, 289, 298, 352
McLaughlin, D. K., 150, 151, 239
McLoyd, V. C., 275, 276
McMenamin, T. M., 264, 266
McMullin, J. A., 330, 331
McPherson, K., 355
Mead, G. H., 23, 90
Mead, L., 449

Mead, R., 232
Menken, J. A., 318
Mettenburg, J., 355
Meyer, D. R., 290, 458
Meyers, C. E., 390
Michael, R. T., 384
Michalopoulos, C., 454
Michel, R. C., 134
Milan, A., 193
Milkie, M. A., 259, 260, 268, 292
Miller, A. J., 217, 218
Miller, G., 287
Mills, C. W., 120
Mincy, R. B., 392
Minkler, M., 323
Mintz, S., 46, 62
Mitterauer, M., 420
Modell, J. J., 211, 212
Moen, P., 264, 268
Moffitt, R., 450
Moffitt, T. E., 363
Moon, D., 189
Moore, J. W., 57
Moore, K., 280
Moore, K. A., 295
Moore, Q., 454
Morello, C., 421
Morgan, S. P., 56, 64
Morin, R., 250
Morris, N. M., 86
Mosher, W. D., 62, 234, 386, 414, 415
Muñoz-Laboy, M., 227
Murray, C., 441
Musgrove, J. F., 179, 182

Nagaoka, R., 276
Nagel, J., 141
Nakonezny, P. A., 383
Neale, M. C., 187
Newman, K., 320
Newman, K. S., 110, 333, 443
Nexica, I. J., 145
Nicholas, D., 41
Nims, B., 178, 180
Nixon, R. M., 443
Nock, S. L., 261, 319, 374, 409
Nomaguchi, K. M., 263
Norberg, K., 92, 93

Obama, B., 140, 141, 144, 299, 457
Obama, M., 141
O'Brien, J. E., 342
O'Connor, T. G., 398
Ogburn, W. F., 99
O'Hare, W., 295
Oliver, M., 155
Olson, C. D., 14
Olson, J. S., 58, 59
Olson, T. B., 460
O'Malley, P. M., 296
O'Neill, W. L., 60, 63n, 378
Ono, H., 239
Ooms, T., 460
Oppenheimer, V. K., 73, 237n, 239, 251
Orbuch, T. L., 386
Orloff, A. S., 438
Oropesa, R., 157, 159
Oropesa, R. S., 160
Osborne, C., 289
Owen, J. J., 213
Ozment, S., 41, 49

Padilla, M. B., 227
Pahl, R., 15, 191, 192
Painter-Brick, C., 86, 277
Palin, B., 202, 203
Palin, S., 202
Palkovitz, R., 281
Papernow, P., 417, 419
Parashar, S., 383
Parke, R. D., 102
Parker, R. G., 227
Parreñas, R. S., 101
Parsons, T., 231, 237
Pascoe, C. J., 100
Pasley, K., 363
Patterson, C. J., 282, 284
Pattillo, M., 155
Pattillo-McCoy, M., 156
Pearsall, P., 209
Peplau, L. A., 221
Percheski, C., 114, 253
Peters, A., 193
Peterson, I., 342
Petta, I., 355
Pettit, G. S., 276
Pezzin, L. E., 332

Phillips, R., 376, 377, 377*n*
Pillard, R. C., 187
Pillemer, K., 318, 330, 331, 360
Pleck, E., 343, 344, 367
Pleck, J. H., 279
Pliny the Elder, 420
Plomin, R., 398
Plutarch, 182
Polgreen, L., 342
Pollak, R. A., 119, 332
Pollock, L. A., 41
Pomeroy, W. B., 183, 186
Popenoe, D., 231
Porter, M., 219, 232
Portes, A., 161, 162, 165
Potter, J. S., 356
Powell, B., 191
Presser, H. B., 265
Preston, M., 330
Preston, S. H., 56, 239, 378
Price, R. H., 287
Pugh, A. J., 277
Purvin, D., 352

Qian, Z., 158, 168, 239
Quadagno, J. S., 44*n*, 448
Queen, S. A., 44*n*, 57, 58

Radel, L., 281, 282
Raksin, J., 330
Raley, R. K., 69, 158, 289, 385, 386
Raley, S., 259
Raley, S. B., 259, 260
Rasmussen, B. B., 145
Raymo, J. M., 239
Rebhun, L. A., 182, 228, 229
Rector, R., 350
Rector, R. E., 351
Reed, J. M., 218
Reinharz, S., 92, 93
Rendall, M. S., 158, 235, 236
Repetti, R. L., 352
Resick, P. A., 351
Rhoades, G. K., 213
Ribar, D., 450
Ribar, D. C., 151
Ridder, E. M., 346
Ridgeway, C. L., 98, 99

Riley, N. E., 282
Rindfuss, R. R., 64
Rinelli, L. N., 423
Risman, B. J., 95
Rittenhouse, I. M., 208–209
Roberts, N. A., 264
Roberts, R. E. L., 333
Robinson, J. P., 258*f*, 292
Robinson, R. V., 122
Rodgers, J. L., 383
Roehling, P. V., 264
Roettger, M. E., 399
Rogers, S. J., 250, 254, 352
Roosevelt, D., 435
Roosevelt, F. D., *439*
Roosevelt, T., 62–63
Roschelle, A. R., 153
Roseneil, S., 15, 194
Rosenfeld, M. J., 69, 73, 143, 212, 213*f*, 214, 214*n*
Rosenmayr, L., 316
Rossi, A. S., 128, 129*f*, 153, 310, 317
Rossi, P. H., 310
Rothbaum, F., 276
Rothert, K., 384
Rothman, E. K., 196, 211*n*
Rouse, C., 97
Rowland, D. T., 223
Ruddick, S., 92
Ruggles, S., 44, 315
Rumbaut, R. G., 72
Rutter, V., 186
Ryder, N. B., 310

Samson, F. L., 145
Sanchez, L., 374
Sanchez, L. A., 374
Sandefur, G. D., 167
Sanders, S. G., 201
Sanderson, C. A., 356
Sarkisian, N., 153
Sassler, S., 217, 218, 220
Savin-Williams, R. C., 221
Sawyer, T., 144
Sayer, L. C., 384
Scarupa, H., 357
Schaefer, R. T., 18
Schans, D., 295

Scharrer, E., 89
Schechter, M. D., 281
Schieman, S., 268
Schmeeckle, M., 413
Schmidt, H., 392
Schneider, D., 155
Schneider, D. M., 128
Schoeni, R., 449
Schone, B. S., 332
Schone, R., 374, 384
Schooler, C., 277
Schulenberg, J. E., 296
Schwartz, C. R., 116
Schwartz, P., 186
Scott, J. W., 85
Sechrist, J., 318
Sedlak, A. J., 355
Seeman, T., 287
Seidman, S., 182, 189, 208, 221
Seltzer, J., 319
Sember, R. E., 227
Seneca, 209
Sensenbrenner, J., 165
Settersten, R. A., Jr., 72
Shackelford, T. K., 238
Shakespeare, W., 420
Shannon, J. D., 280
Shapiro, T. M., 155
Sherman, L. W., 368
Shoemaker, N., 45, 166
Shore, R. P., 268
Shull, R. D., 383
Sica, A., 234
Sieder, R., 420
Silva, P. A., 363
Silver, H. K., 345
Silverman, F. N., 345
Silverstein, C., 181
Silverstein, M., 323, 327, 329, 331
Simon, R. W., 235
Simpson, C., 232
Simpson, O. J., 342
Singh, S., 199, 203
Skocpol, T., 62, 434, 439, 457
Smart, C., 191
Smeeding, T. M., 450, 453, 458
Smeins, L., 232
Smith, A., 438
Smith, G. V., 299

Smith, H. L., 150
Smith, J. P., 235
Smith, K. E., 254
Smith, R. T., 128
Smith-Rosenberg, C., 52, 179, 180
Smock, P. J., 69, 193, 218, 219, 232, 386
Snipp, C. M., 45
Snyder, A. R., 393
Snyder, M., 350
Sobolewski, J. M., 280
Sorenson, A., 122
South, S. J., 239
Sparks, S., 46
Spencer, L., 15, 191, 192
Spitze, G., 413
Stacey, J., 283, 284, 456
Stack, C. B., 128, 153
Standish, N. J., 384
Stanley, S. M., 213, 352
Stanley-Hagan, M., 417, 418, 419
Steele, B. F., 345
Steelman, L. C., 191
Steffen, S. A., 202
Stepp, L. S., 212, 213, 364
Stevenson, A., 102, 103
Stevenson, B., 116, 169, 383
Stewart, J. H., 352
Stewart, S. D., 410, 411, 418, 422
Stone, D., 255
Straus, M. A., 346, 352, 354
Stryker, S., 23
Suarez, Z. E., 161
Suarez-Orozco, C., 294
Sudarkasa, N., 53
Suitor, J. J., 318
Sullivan, A., 460
Sullivan, O., 258
Sullivan, W. M., 6, 383
Svare, G. M., 409
Swartz, T. T., 128
Sweeney, M. M., 239, 285, 422, 423
Swicegood, G., 64
Swidler, A., 6, 153, 242, 243, 383

Tach, L., 458
Takeuchi, D., 275
Tamis-LeMonda, C. S., 280
Tarule, J. M., 92
Teachman, J., 150, 415
Teachman, J. D., 386
Tedrow, L., 386
Therborn, G., 48, 377
Thomas, R. J., 212
Thomas, W., 82
Thompson, N. J., 356
Thorne, B., 26, 91, 92, 93
Thornton, A., 228, 239
Tienda, M., 161
Tiger, L., 46
Timberlake, J. M., 217, 288*f*
Tipton, S. M., 6, 383
Todorova, I., 294
Tolnay, S. E., 298
Trask, B. S., 31, 119, 120
Tribe, L., 441
Tronto, J. C., 26, 255, 257
Turner, C. F., 185
Turner, R. N., 220
Twine, F., 145
Tyler, K. A., 125*f*

Udry, J. R., 86
Uhlenberg, P., 306, 308, 310, 317, 332
Umberson, D., 235

van Balen, F., 284
van dem Boom, D., 284
Van Dusen, J. E., 198
van Eyck, J., 41
Van Hook, J. V. W., 159, 163
Van Vleet, K. E., 282
Van Wyk, J., 352
Vandell, D. L., 292
Vandivere, S., 281, 282
Veroff, J., 386
Vinokur, A. D., 287
Voss, P., 291
Vryan, K. D., 23

Wackerow, A., 239
Waite, L. J., 209, 234, 235

Waldfogel, J., 265
Waldron, H., 235
Wales, T. J., 119
Wallerstein, J. S., 394, 396, 397, 397*n*, 421
Wang, W., 259
Wang, Y., 122
Ward, R. A., 332, 413
Wardlow, H., 228, 229
Watkins, S. C., 318
Watson, J., 62
Weber, M., 120, 122
Weden, M. M., 235
Weeks, J., 221
Weil, E., 84
Weinrich, J. D., 182
Weiss, J., 68
Weitzman, L. J., 389
Welter, B., 51
West, C., 92, 94, 95
Western, B., 114, 150, 291
Weston, K., 191, 192, 194, 221
White, L., 332, 387, 409, 422
Whitehead, B. D., 231
Whyte, M. K., 211*n*, 232
Wickes, R., 92
WIdom, C. S., 357
Wilcox, W. B., 261, 278, 397
Wildsmith, E., 158, 289
Williams, J. C., 268
Williams, L. M., 356
Williams, W. L., 82, 84, 182
Wilson, J. Q., 440
Wilson, K. L., 161
Wilson, L., 275
Wilson, W. J., 148, 151, 156, 237
Winship, C., 151
Wister, S. B., 179, 180, 182
Wolf, D. A., 326
Wolfe, A., 5
Wolfe, B. L., 201
Wolfers, J., 383
Wolff, J. L., 325
Wolfinger, N. H., 409
Wood, D., 276
Wood, R. G., 454
Wood, T., 168
Wootton, B. H., 100

Worth, R. F., 342
Wray, M., 145
Wright, J., 141
Wright, J. D., 125*f*, 374
Wright, L., 144

Xie, Y., 239
Xu, X., 234

Yabiku, S. T., 228
Yamagisako, S. J., 27
Yamaguchi, K., 122
Yeung, W. J., 79
Yount, K. M., 352

Zelizer, V., 343
Zhou, M., 165

Zimmerman, D. H., 92, 94, 95
Ziol-Guest, K. M., 265

Subject Index

Page numbers in *italics* indicate illustrations. An *f* indicates figures, *n* indicates footnotes, and *t* indicates tables.

abortion
  conservative viewpoint, 441
  rights, 442
  social change, 240
  teenage pregnancy, and, 199
abstinence, 455
abuse. *See* child abuse; domestic
    violence; intimate partner
    violence
acting-out behavior, and parental
    divorce, 394
active life expectancy, 308
activities of daily living
    (ADLs), 325
Administration for Children and
    Families, 371
adolescents
  age at marriage, 385
  recognition, as stage
    of life, 210
  sexual behavior changes,
    198–199
  sexuality, and pregnancy,
    198–202
  stepfamilies, 423
  teenage mothers, 200–202
  teenage pregnancy "problem,"
    199–200
adoption, 281–283
  domestic, 281
  foster care policy, 358–359
  transnational, 282–283
Adoption Assistance and Child
    Welfare Act of 1980, 358
adult children, *330*
adultery
  era of restricted divorce, 377
  Mexican culture, 228
advocacy
  care work, 255
  contraception, adolescents, 202

reduced sexual activity,
    adolescents, 202
  sexual abuse, 350
  single parents, support for, 456
  teenage pregnancy
    "problem," 203
AFDC. *See* Aid to Families with
    Dependent Children (AFDC)
affinity-seekers, 417
Affordable Care Act, 457
Africa
  marriage, 53
  polygyny, 44
African Americans, 53–56
  African heritage, 53
  churches, and emphasis on
    marriage, 234
  culture, 151–152
  extended family, 53
  extended kin ties, *54*
  family trends, 149–154
  gender, 154
  grandparenting, 152–153
  kinship networks, 153–154
  marital separation/divorce, 386
  marriage market, 237
  marriage rates, 150–151
  marriage/childbearing, 148–149
  married women, labor force
    participation, 253, *262*
  mass incarceration, 291
  men, "caring self," 257
  middle-class families, 154–156
  multiracial self-identification, 168
  physical discipline of
    children, 276
  poverty line, 444
  remarriage rates, 415
  single-parent families, 149
  slavery, 54–56
  stepfamilies, 411

age
  historical *vs.* individual time,
    71–72
  mandatory schooling, 13
  at marriage, 114, 211, 240,
    241*t*, 385
  retirement, 10–11
  young adults, leaving home, 64
aggression levels, 87
Aid to Dependent Children
    program, 439
Aid to Families with Dependent
    Children (AFDC), 435, 446
Alan Guttmacher Institute, 205
Alaska natives, 141
altruism, 319
ambivalence, 331
American Indians, 166–167.
    See also Native Americans
  defined, 45
  family lineages, *45*
  interracial marriages, 168
  primacy of the tribe, 45–46
"America's Children: Key
    National Indicators of
    Well-Being," 302
androgens, 86
androgynous behavior, 279
annulment, 377
anti-abortion forces, 441
Apache traditions, 46
Arizona, covenant marriage, 374
Arkansas, covenant marriage, 374
arrest, domestic violence
    legislation, *368*
Asian Americans
  category defined, 143
  interracial marriages, 168
Asian immigrants, 58–59
assigned kinship, 15
assimilation, 161

assortative marriage, 116
asymmetry of gender change, 100
audio computer assisted self-interview, 185
Australia, premarital cohabitation, 387
authoritarian style (of parenting), 275
authoritative style (of parenting), 275

baby boom, 67, 72
barrio, 57
"beanpole family," 310
behavior, 29
bilateral kinship, 59, 411
biological predispositions, 33, 87
biosocial approach (to gender differences), 86
biosocial theory, *86*
birth cohort, 67
birth control pill
  early days, 202
  marital/nonmarital sexual activity, 195
birthrate
  early 1900s, 63
  Mexican Americans, 158
  1950s, 67–68
  1960s–1990s, 68
  teenage pregnancy "problem," 199–200, 202–203
"black middle class," 154
Black Thursday, 18
block grant, 447
blood relatives, 411
blue collar workers, 110
Bonds of Womanhood, The (Cott), 52
boundary ambiguity, 14
boys
  acting-out behavior, and parental divorce, 394
  androgynous character, and family types, 284
  elementary school play settings, 91

physical aggression, biosocial theory, *86*
sexual orientation, 100
Brazil
  racial distinctions, 141
  television, influence of, 228–229
breadwinner-homemaker family, 23, 225

California
  no-fault divorce, 379
  paid parental leave, 267
  same-sex marriage legislation, 454, 455
care work, 255–259
caregiving, 325–327
Census Bureau, 173, 337
centenarians, 309
Center on Law and Social Policy, 463
child abuse, 353–359
  defined, 354
  foster care, 358–359
  incidence, 354–355
  physical abuse, 357
  poly-victimization, 357–358
  sexual abuse, 356–357
child care
  government assistance, *446*
  time apart from parents, 292
child custody, 389
child rearing
  college-educated parents, 134
  social class, and, 130–133
child support obligations, 392
childbearing
  African Americans, 148–149
  nonmarital, 455–456
  outside of marriage, 114–116
  teenage mothers, 19–20
childhood
  gender construction, 88–91
  recognized as life stage, 40–41
children
  adoption, 281–283
  adults, caring for parents, *330*
  cohabiting couples, and, *219*
  family complexity, 289–291

family instability, 287–289
language acquisition, 276
same-sex partner households, 283–285
socialization, 275–278
stepfamilies, and, 422–424, 428
support factors of importance, 278–281
time apart from parents, 292–293
transnational families, 293–295
unemployed parents/poverty, 286–287
well-being, 295–300
China
  patrilineage, 43, 44
  transnational adoption, 282–283
Chinese Exclusion Act, 58
Chinese immigrants, 58
churches, 156
class. *See* social class
Coalition for Marriage, Family, and Couples Education, 246
coercive cycles, 394
cognitive indicators, 296
cohabitation, 214–222
  class, and, 217–222
  college-educated cohabitants, 217–218
  consensual union, 160
  current trends, 196
  dating, and, 211
  defined, 69, 214
  domestic partnerships, 215
  early adulthood, 72, 74
  first marriages, and, *216*
  gay men, 221
  least-educated cohabitants, 219–220
  lesbians, 221
  marriage, compared, 215
  mid 20th century, 6
  moderately-educated cohabitants, 218–219
  premarital, 6, 386–387
  Puerto Ricans, 160
  serial, 219
  Sweden, 217
  United States, 217

cohabiting stepfamily, 410
collective ambivalence, 331
college education
    cohabitation, and, 217–218
    constrained opportunities, 73
    developed countries, 118
college-educated cohabitants,
    217–218
commercial capitalism, 51
communication
    electronic, 267–268, 293
    gender differences, 90
    individualistic marriage, 226
    marriage as an ongoing
        project, 243
    as a valued quality, 243
compadrazgo, 57
companionate marriage, 224–225
companionship, 223
computer-based
    communication, 293
concerted cultivation, 277
conflict, 330–331
    children's exposure to, *395*
    parental, post-divorce, 394–395
conjugal family, 44
Connecticut
    same-sex marriage legislation,
        454, 455
consensual union, 160
conservative viewpoint
    abortion, 441, 442
    EITC, 445
    family policy, 440–442
    paid parental leave, 459–460
    vs. liberal viewpoint, 461*t*
contraception
    early days, 202
    marital/nonmarital sexual
        activity, 195
    teenage pregnancy "problem,"
        202–203
Convention on the Rights of the
    Child, 299
cooperative parenting, 391
co-parenting, 389–391
courtship, 210
covenant marriage, 374
created kinship, 15
crisis period, 394

Cuban Americans, 160–162
    business start-up loans, 165–166
    household statistics, 157
cultural lag, 99
custody, of children, 389

"Dance to the Berdache"
    (Catlin), 83
dating, 211–212
demographic change
    age at marriage, 114
    childbearing outside of
        marriage, 114–116
    divorce rates, 116
    early adulthood, 116–117
    globalization of love, 229
Department of Health and Human
    Services, 463
Department of Housing and
    Urban Development, 137
Depression. *See* Great Depression
developed countries, 118–119
developing countries, 119–120
disabled persons, 325–326
division of labor, in marriage,
    255–261
divorce, 373–403. *See also*
    separation
    child custody, 389
    child support obligations, 392
    children, and, 388–400
    contact/co-parenting, 389–391
    economic support, 391–394
    effects of, 332–333
    era of divorce tolerance,
        378–379
    era of restricted divorce,
        377–378
    era of unrestricted divorce,
        379–382
    individual factors, 382*t*, 385–388
    post-crisis period, 396–400
    psychosocial effects, 394–396
    societywide factors, 382*t*,
        383–385
divorce rates
    baby boom cohort, 72
    cross-sectional rate, 375
    early 1900s, 60
    education, and, 116

era of divorce tolerance,
    378–379
era of restricted divorce,
    377–378
era of unrestricted divorce,
    379–382
measuring, 375
1960s–1990s, 69
remarriages, 415
divorce reform, 62–63
domestic adoption, 281
domestic violence
    child abuse, 353–359.
        See also child abuse
    defined, 342
    early history, 343–344
    elder abuse, 360, 361*f*
    frustration-aggression
        perspective, 365–366
    intimate partner violence,
        346–353. *See also* intimate
        partner violence
    mandatory arrest
        legislation, *368*
    public policy, and, 367–369
    reasons for, 364–367
    social exchange
        perspective, 366–367
    social learning
        perspective, 365
    20th century, 344–346
    young adult relationships,
        361–364
Dominicans, 157
donor insemination, 283
door-to-door interviewing, *19*
dual-earner families, *117,* 122

early adulthood
    defined, 72–74
    diverging demographics,
        116–117
    sexual aggression/violence,
        361–364
Earned Income Tax Credit (EITC),
    445–446
earnings. *See* family income;
    income
economic support, post-divorce,
    391–394

education
    importance of, 113–114
    role of, 72–74
egalitarian partnerships, 258
Eisenstadt v. Baird, 195
EITC. *See* Earned Income Tax
    Credit (EITC)
elderly. *See also* grandparenthood
    abuse, 360–361
    disabled persons, 325–326
    men, living arrangements,
        316–317
employment. *See* work
employment opportunities
    college-educated couples, 134
    current trends, 111
    education, and, 72–73
    women, in developing
        countries, 119–120
England
    Children's Act, 408
    civil unions, 454–455
    no-fault divorce legislation, 380
entitlement, 446
era of divorce tolerance, 378
era of restricted divorce, 377
era of unrestricted divorce, 379
ethical considerations
    ethical training, 279
    ethics of care, 257
ethnicity. *See also* race
    divorce risk factors, 386
    kinship ties, 169–171
    racial-ethnic groups, 141–147
    racial/ethnic intermarriage,
        167–169
    socialization, and, 275–276
    "whiteness," 145–147
Europe
    premarital cohabitation, 387
    universal child allowances, 457
European colonists, 47–48
European immigrants, 145–146
exchange theory, 22, 319
expressive individualism, 7, 8
extended family
    African Americans, 53
    American Indians, *166*
    defined, 44
    Hispanics, 159

return of, 323–325
working class *vs.* middle
    class, *135*
externalities, 10
extramarital sex, 197

factory jobs, 110
Failure to Launch, 321
families
    breadwinner-homemaker
        family, 23
    defined, 9
    dual-earner, 117
    extended. *See* extended family
    gender, and, 81–107
    globalization, and, 30–32
    multiracial, 144–145, *146*
    private, 13–17
    public, 10–13, 15–17
    single parent *vs.* married
        couple, 5
    sociological theory,
        and, 22–30
    sociological viewpoint
        on, 33–34
    stepfamilies. *See* stepfamilies
    theoretical perspective, 30*t*
    transnational, 293–295
    work, and. *See* work
families–historical
        perspective, 39–78
    African Americans, 53–56
    American Indians (pre-1776),
        45–46
    Asian immigrants, 58–59
    early adulthood, emergence
        of, 72–74
    European colonists
        (pre-1776), 46–47
    family/kinship origins, 42–45
    Mexican Americans, 56–58
    "modern" American family
        (1776–1900), 49–52
    private family rise
        (1900–present), 60–69.
        See also private family
    20th century social
        change, 71–72
Families and Work Institute,
    270, 463

Family and Medical Leave Act,
    266, 267
family complexity, 289–291
family diversity, 48
family inequality, 111
family instability, 287–289
family life
    globalization, and, 118
    household chores, *28*
    household types, 288–289
    sexuality, and, 202–204
    social class differences, 126
    work, and, 263–264
    work stress, *263*
family national guard, 333–335
family of choice, 191
family policy
    conservative viewpoint,
        440–442
    current debates, 453–457
    defined, 436
    EITC, 445–446
    family policy in 2010s, 460–461
    family wage system, 438–440
    liberal viewpoint, 443
    marriage promotion, 453–454
    national health insurance, 456
    1996 welfare reform, 446–452
    nonmarital childbearing,
        455–456
    poverty, 444
    responsible fatherhood,
        457–460
    same-sex marriage, 454–455
    single-parent families, 456
    welfare state, 438
family wage system, 438–440
family-work balance, 261–268,
    458–460
farming, 51
fathers. *See also* parenting
    authority undermined,
        commercial capitalism, 51
    authority undermined, Great
        Depression, 58
    bilateral kinship, 59
    child support obligations, 392
    Chinese immigrants, 58
    divorce, and co-parenting, 390
    East Asian heritage, 58

Hopi traditions, 46
Japanese immigrants, 58
lineages, 42, *45*
living standard,
    post-divorce, 392
noncustodial, *vs.*
    stepfathers, 422
patrilineage, 42
responsible
    fatherhood, 457–458
single-father families, 393
stepfather, cohabiting *vs.*
    married, 412
Feminist Majority Foundation
    Online Web, 106
feminist movement
    domestic violence, 345–346
    power/inequality issues, 103
feminist research methods, 92
feminist theory, 26–27
fertility, 310
fetal development, 86
field research, 20
Filipino immigrants, 59
financial crisis of 2008.
    See Great Recession
financial pressures, *226*
"flapper" girls, 60
flextime, 266
Food Stamps. *See* Supplemental
    Nutrition Assistance Program
    (SNAP)
formal sector, 119
foster care, 358–359
Fragile Families and Child
    Wellbeing Study, 25
France, civil unions, 454–455
free-rider problem, 12
friendship-based family
    networks, 191–192
frustration-aggression
    perspective, 365–366
Futures without Violence, 371

gay men
    cohabitation, 221
gay parenthood, 283–285
gay pride celebration, *187*
gender
    childhood construction of, 88–91
    continual construction of, 91–95

defined, 26, 84
gender differences today,
    98–101
gender studies, 102–103
gestational construction of,
    85–87
masculinity, 101–102
social class, and, 121–122
as social structure, 95–98
socialization, and, 277–278
two-spirit people, 82–85
vs. sex, 84
*Gender Play: Girls and Boys in
    School* (Thorne), 92
gendered behavior, *94*
generalized exchange, 320
genital development, in fetus, 86
gerontologists, 309
gestation, 85
girls
    elementary school play
        settings, 90–91
    physical aggression, biosocial
        theory, *86*
    sexual orientation, 100
globalization
    defined, 30
    families, and, 30–32, 118
    of love, 227–229
    Western nations, 31
glossary of terms, 464–469
Godey's Lady's Book, 77
godparent, 57
*Goodrich v. Department of
    Public Health,* 454
government assistance, *446*
GrandFamilies of America, 337
grandparenthood
    African Americans, 152–153
    grandparents as family national
        guard, 333–335
    intergenerational ties,
        327–333, *328. See also*
        intergenerational ties
    modernization of old age,
        308–318
Great Depression, 64–68, *66*
    divorce rates, 378
    economic downturn, and family
        relationships, 254
    social change, 71

Great Recession
    disrupting family life, 18
    divorce rates, 65
    family planning delays, 223
    job losses/financial strain, 112
    unemployment, and
        marriage, 254
    young adults, living
        at home, 320
Griswold v. Connecticut, 195

Head Start Program, *436*
health insurance, 457
Healthy Marriage Initiative, 454
Henrikson v. Gable, 408
heterosexuality, medical category
    definition, 181–182
Hispanics, 156–162
    category defined, 142
    Cuban Americans, 160–162
    Mexican Americans, 157–159
    poverty line, 444
    Puerto Ricans, 159–160
    remarriage rates, 415
homelessness, 124–125, 137
homosexuality
    biological influences, 187–188
    cohabitation, 221
    gay pride celebration, *187*
    Kinsey Report, 183
    medical category definition,
        181–182
    parenthood, 283–285
    queer theory, 189–190
    Smith-Rosenberg same-sex
        intimacy study, 179–180
    social constructionist
        perspective, 182
    two-spirit people, 83
hooking up, 212–213
Hopi, 46
hormones, 86–87
household income, 110
households
    multigenerational, *43,* 322–323
    skipped-generation, 323
housing affordability, 134
hunter-gatherers, 42
husbands
    division of labor, 255–261
    divorce, and co-parenting, 390

earnings, compared to
wives, 253
era of divorce tolerance,
378–379
era of restricted divorce,
377–378
household chores, 28
household decision making,
250–251
time-diary studies, 258–259
unemployment, and
marriage, 254
weekly work activities
statistics, 260f
wives' earnings, and domestic
work distribution, 259
hypothesis, 18

ideal type, 122
immigrant caregivers, 293
immigrant enclave, 161
immigration
Asians, 163–164
Puerto Ricans, 159–160
U.S. citizenship oath, 143
Vietnamese, 163–164
Immigration Act of 1965, 59
imprisonment
African Americans, 150
mass incarceration, 291
In re A.R.A., 408
In re Dunn, 408
incarceration. See imprisonment
incest, 356
income
household, 110
wives, and domestic work, 259
income-pooling model, 238–240
independent living, 213–214
individualism
defined, 6
expressive, 6
marriage, and, 6–9
"modern" American family,
49–50
private family, rise of, 63–64
utilitarian, 6
women's/men's spheres, 51
individualistic marriage, 226–227
infidelity. See adultery
informal sector, 119

information, sources of. See
Internet information sources
institutional marriage, 222–224
integrative perspective (on
sexuality), 186
interactionist approach (to gender
differences), 92, 94
intergenerational
ambivalence, 331
intergenerational conflict, 330–331
intergenerational solidarity, 327
intergenerational
support, 318–327
caregiving,
rewards/costs, 326–327
extended family,
return of, 323–325
generalized exchange, 320
Great Recession, 320
multigenerational
households, 322–323
mutual assistance, 318–322
older persons with
disabilities, 325–326
skipped-generation
households, 323
intergenerational ties, 327–334
international migrants, 31–32
Internet, 36, 212
Internet information sources
Administration for Children and
Families, 371
Alan Guttmacher Institute, 205
Census Bureau, 173, 337
Center on Law and Social
Policy, 463
Coalition for Marriage, Family,
and Couples Education, 246
Department of Health and
Human Services, 463
Department of Housing and
Urban Development, 137
Families and Work
Institute, 270, 463
Feminist Majority Foundation
Online Web, 106
Futures without Violence, 371
GrandFamilies of America, 337
Minnesota Center Against
Violence and Abuse, 371
Monitoring the Future, 302

National Academy of
Sciences, 173
National Campaign to Prevent
Teen and Unplanned
Pregnancy, 205
National Center for Children in
Poverty, 302
National Stepfamily Resource
Center, 430
Population Reference
Bureau, 337
Prevent Child Abuse
America, 371
Sexuality Information and
Education Council of the
United States, 205
Stepfamily Foundation, 430
Survey of Income and Program
Participation, 430
Women's Bureau, 106
Work and Family Researchers
Network, 270
interracial marriage, 167–169
intersectionality (of black women's
experience), 154, 169
intersexual, 84
interview, 20
intimacy at a distance, 315
intimate outsider, 419
intimate partner violence, 346–353
intimate terrorism, 347
prevalence, 349–350
rape, 350–351
risk factors, 352–353
situational couple violence, 347
trends, 352
intimate terrorism, 347
Iowa, same-sex marriage
legislation, 454, 455
Italy, young adults, living at
home, 320

Japan, children
socialization, 276, 277
Japanese immigrants, 59
joint legal custody (of children
after a divorce), 389
joint physical custody (of children
after a divorce), 389
Journal of Marriage and the
Family, 342

Kinsey Report, 183
kinship care, 359
kinship groups, 43
kinship ties
   African Americans, 153–154
   American Indian tribes, 166
   assigned kinship, 15
   chronic poverty, 127–128
   created kinship, 15
   divorce/remarriage, 426
   fertility decline, and, 310
   historical perspective, 42
   kin network limitations, 128
   nonpoor families, 128–130
   poor/near poor families,
      126–127
   postmodern perspective, 29–30
   race/ethnicity, and, 169–171
   stepfamilies, 411–412, *416*
   wheel of obligation, 129–130
   women-centered kinship,
      127–128

labor force, 72, 251
language acquisition, 276
LAT. *See* living apart together
   (LAT)
late modern era, 27
Latinos. *See* Hispanics
Lawrence v. Texas, 7
legal custody (of children after a
   divorce), 389
legislation. *See* family policy
lesbian parenthood, 283–285
lesbians
   cohabitation, 221
   gay pride celebration, *187*
liberal viewpoint
   EITC, 445
   family policy, 443
   marriage promotion, 453
   paid parental leave, 459
   time-unlimited welfare, 449
   vs. conservative viewpoint, 461*t*
life chances, 120
life expectancy, 308–309
   early 1900s, 63
   healthy living, current
      trends, *307*
   married *vs.* divorced/never-
      married individuals, *234*
life-course perspective, 71

lineage, 42
living apart together (LAT),
   192–193
living arrangements, 314–317
longitudinal survey, 24–25
love, 208–209, 227–229
Loving v. Virginia, 167
lower-class families, 124–133

"mail order brides," 246
Maine, same-sex marriage
   legislation, 454, 455
managers, 111, *121*
*Manners, Customs, and
   Conditions of the North
   American Indians* (Catlin), 82
marital bargain, 241–242
marriage. *See also* family life
   Africa, 53
   African Americans, 148–149,
      150–151
   age trends, 114, 385
   as an ongoing project, 242–243
   Apache traditions, 46
   benefits of, 235–236
   as the capstone experience,
      231–232
   childbearing outside
      of, 114–116
   cohabitation, compared, 215
   companionate, 224–225
   covenant, 374
   division of labor, 255–261
   domestic violence risk
      factors, 352
   global historical perspective, 75
   globalization of love, 227–229
   historical trends, 225–227
   historical trends (1950s),
      66–67, 67*f*
   historical trends (1960s–1990s),
      68–70
   household decision
      making, 250–251
   individualism, and, 6–9, 226
   institution *vs.*
      companionship, 62
   institutional, 222–224
   marriage market, 236–240
   Mexican Americans, 158
   19th century, 50–51
   public policy, 453–454

Puerto Ricans, 160
   racial/ethnic intermarriage,
      167–169
   reasons for, 230–231
   religion, and, 233–234
   same-sex, 5
   sexual attraction/activity, 195,
      197–198
   sexual infidelity, 226
   2006 legislation, 5
   wedding as status symbol,
      232–233
marriage market, 236–240
   defined, 236
   diverging demographics, 116
   income-pooling
      model, 238–240
   specialization model, 237
*Marriage of Giovanni Arnolfini
   and Giovanna Cenami*
   (van Eyck), *41*
married individuals.
   See husbands; wives
married stepfamily, 410
married women. *See* wives
masculinity, 101
mass incarceration, 291
Massachusetts, same-sex marriage
   legislation, 454, 455
Massachusetts Bay Colony, 343
matrilineage, 42, 46
media
   gender socialization, and, 89
   globalization of love, 228
mediating structure, 156
Medicaid, 311, 326
medical model of domestic
   violence, 344–346
Medicare, 311, 312, 313, 326
men. *See also* husbands
   asymmetry (of gender
      change), 100
   divorce, and, 426
   domestic violence theories, 364
   elderly, living arrangements,
      316–317
   gender differentiation,
      interactionist
      approach, 94–95
   hooking up, 213
   household decision
      making, 250–251

life expectancy, married *vs.* divorced/never-married, *234*
lower-class families, 124
marital bargain, 241
masculinity, 101–102
middle-class families, 123
occupations, and stereotype, 99
parental socialization, 88
potential partners' characteristics, 238t
time-diary studies, 258–259
two-spirit people, 83–84
unemployment, and divorce, 383–384
working-class families, 123
mestizo, 57
Mexican Americans, 56–58, 157–159
marriage, 158
population statistics, 156–157
TFR, 158
middle-class families
African Americans, 154–156
concerted cultivation *vs.* natural growth, 132–133
defined, 123
parental values, 131
migration flows, 229
Minnesota Center Against Violence and Abuse, 371
moderately-educated cohabitants, 218–219
"modern" American family, 49–52
modern views, family life, 5
Monitoring the Future, 302
mortality, 308–310
mothers. *See also* parenting
bilateral kinship, 59
child support obligations, 392
divorce, and co-parenting, 390
Hopi traditions, 46
lineages, 42, *45*
living standard, post-divorce, 392
matrilineage, 42
teenagers, 200–202
women-centered kinship, 127
working outside of home, 99
multigenerational households, 43, 322–323
multiple partner fertility (MPF), 289–291

multiracial category, 144–145, *146*
mutual assistance, older persons/ adult children, 318–322

nation, 437
National Academy of Sciences, 173
National Campaign to Prevent Teen and Unplanned Pregnancy, 205
National Center for Children in Poverty, 302
national health insurance, 457
National Stepfamily Resource Center, 430
nation-state, 437
Native Americans. *See also* American Indians
racial-ethnic groups, 141
two-spirit people, 82–84
Navaho, 83
negative externalities, 10
neglect, 360
neo-traditional, 118
New Jersey
paid parental leave, 267
New York, divorce legislation, 62
1965 Immigration Act, 59
no-fault divorce legislation
California, 379–381
covenant marriage, 374
early days, 62
England, 380
societal risk factors, 383
Western nations, 380
non-Hispanic whites, 144, 146–147
nonmarital birth ratio, 199
nonmarital childbearing, 455–456
nonmarital sexuality, 195–197
nonparental care, 292, *294*
nonstandard work hours, 264–265
norms, 276
nursing home, 326

objectivity, 17
observational study, 20–22
older population, 309
oldest-old, 309
old-old, 309
online information sources. *See* Internet information sources

Panel Study of Income Dynamics, 25
Papua New Guinea
"family houses," 228
Western values, introduction, 229
parallel parenting, 391
parental divorce, 387
parental leave
California, 267
defined, 266
New Jersey, 267
Washington State, 267
Western Europe, *265*
work-family balance, 459
parental socialization, 88–89
parental values, 130–132
parenting. *See also* fathers; mothers
adoption, 281–283
authoritarian style, 275
authoritative style, 275
cooperative, 391
declining parental control, 73–74
divorce, and, 388–400
family instability, 287–289
fathers' influence, 279–281
homelessness, 124
lesbian/gay parenthood, 283–285
obligations towards children, 274–285
parallel, 391
permissive style, 275
Protestantism, 278
socialization of children, 275–278
time apart from children, 292–293
transnational families, 293–295
unemployment/poverty, 286–287
Patient Protection and Affordable Care Act, 313
patrilineage, 42, 46
peer groups, 89–91
permissive style (of parenting), 275
personal fulfillment. *See* self-fulfillment
persons with disabilities, 325–326

physical abuse, 357
physical aggression, *86*, 87
physical custody (of children after a divorce), 389
physical discipline
    of children, 276
Plymouth Colony, 47
polarization (of the labor market), 111
polite outsider, 417–418
political model of domestic violence, 344
polyandry, 44
polygyny, 44
poly-victimization, 357–358
Poor Richard's Almanack (Franklin), 6
Population Reference Bureau, 337
positive externalities, 10
poverty
    abuse, and, 358–359
    American Indians, 167
    Great Recession, 110
    parenthood, and, 286–287
    well-being of children, 297
poverty line, 444
predisposition, 33
pregnancy
    abortion rights, 442. *See also* abortion
    accidental, 385
    adolescence, 198–202
    cohabitation, and, 218, 219
    National Campaign to Prevent Teen and Unwanted Pregnancy, 203
    premarital, 240, 241*t*
premarital cohabitation, 386–387
premarital sex, 197
Prevent Child Abuse America, 371
primary analysis, 24
private family, 13–17, 60–70
    Depression generation, 64–65
    divorce reform, 62–63
    early 1900s, 60–64, 61
    1950s, 66–68
    1960s through the 1990s, 68–70
    primacy of, 425–426
professionals, 111
Protestantism, 278
psychosocial effects, of divorce, 394–396

public family, 10–13, 15–17
public goods, 10
public policy. *See* family policy
Puerto Ricans, 156, 157, 159–160
Puritans
    child abuse, 353
    childhood, recognition of, 46
    houses, Plymouth Colony, 47
    marriage laws, 48
    moral behavior, 343
    women's sphere, 52

queer theory, 189–190

race. *See also* ethnicity
    African American families, 147
    American Indian families, 166–167
    Asian American families, 163–164
    divorce risk factors, 386
    Hispanic families, 156–162
    kinship ties, 169–171
    Obama, and public opinion, 140–141
    racial-ethnic groups, 141–147
    racial/ethnic intermarriage, 167–169
    social capital, 164–166
    social stratification, 100–101
racial-ethnic group, 141–147
random-sample survey, 20
rape, 350–352, 362–363
reflexivity, 28
religion
    marriage, and, 233–234
    socialization, and, 278
remarriage, 332–333, 413–416. *See also* stepfamilies
remarriages, 413–416. *See also* stepfamilies
remittances, 58
research methods
    door-to-door interviewing, *19*
    feminist, 92–93
    field research, 20–22
    observational study, 20–22
    random-sample survey, 20
    scientific, 92
    survey, 20
resources, 236–237

responsive workplace, 265–268, 459
Roe v. Wade, 441, 442
romantic love, 208–209
rule-altering behavior, 29
rule-directed behavior, 29

same-sex couples, 29
same-sex marriage
    legislation, 215
    Massachusetts 2004 legislation, 5
    public policy, 454–455
same-sex peer groups, 90
scientific method, 18
scientific research methods, 92
secondary analysis, 24
selection effect, 200
self-development
    current context of marriage, 230
    increased emphasis on, 243
    individualistic marriage, progression towards, 226
self-fulfillment, 379, 383, 425
self-identity, 28
"separate spheres" ideology, 50, 51, 52
separation. *See also* divorce
    African Americans, 382*t*, 386
    era of restricted divorce, 377
    physical, transnational families, 293
    single-parent families, 149
serial cohabitation, 219
service sector, 251
sex, *vs.* gender, 84
sex hormones, 86
sexual abuse
    awareness of, *363*
    consequences, 356–357
    prevalence, 362–363
sexual activity
    adolescents, 198–199
    hooking up, 213
    marital, 195, 197–198
    nonmarital, 195–197
sexual acts, 181
sexual assault, 350–352
sexual behavior, adolescence, 198–199
sexual fulfillment, 223
sexual identity, 180–190

defined, 181
determinants of, 182–188
heterosexuality *vs.*
        homosexuality, 181–182
integrative perspective, 186–188
queer theory, 189
questioning, 188–190
sexual acts, compared, 181
social constructionist
        perspective, 182–186
sexual infidelity. *See* adultery
sexual monogamy, 197
sexual orientation
    asymmetry of gender
        change, 100
    genetic influences, 186–187
    household (family) type,
        and, 285
sexuality
    adolescence, and pregnancy,
        198–202
    current trends, 190–195
    family life, and, 202–204
    marital/nonmarital, 195–198
    1700s–1800s, 170–180
    sexual identity, 180–190. *See
        also* sexual identity
Sexuality Information and
    Education Council of the
    United States, 205
Singer Sewing Machine
    Company, 110
single-earner families
    companionate marriage,
        224–225
single-father families, 393
single-parent families, 456
    African Americans, 149
    family instability, 288–289
situational couple violence,
    347, 347t
skipped-generation
    households, 323
slavery, 54–56
sleeper effect, 421
SNAP. *See* Supplemental
    Nutrition Assistance
    Program (SNAP)
soap operas, 228–229
social capital, 164–166
social class
    child rearing, 130–133

defined, 120
demographics, 114–118
developed countries, 118–119
developing countries, 119–120
domestic violence risk factors,
    352–353
education, importance of,
    113–114
family, and, 133–135
family inequality, 111–113
gender, and family, 121–122
globalization, 118
job losses/financial strain, 112
kin networks, assistance from,
    126–130
life chances, 120–121
social stratification, 100–101
socialization, and, 276–277
status group, 121, 122–126
U.S. economic trends, 110–111
social constructionist
    perspective, 182
social exchange perspective, 366
social institution, 33
social learning perspective, 365
social programs, 368–369
Social Security, 311, 312, *314*, 441
Social Security Act of 1935,
    435, 439
social stratification, 100
social structure, 95
socialization
    ethnicity, and, 275–276
    gender, and, 277–278
    religion, and, 278
    social class, and, 276–277
    as support and control, 275
socialization approach (to gender
    differences), 88
socioemotional indicators, 296
sociological research. *See* research
    methods
sociological theory
    exchange theory, 22–23
    feminist theory, 26–27
    late modern era, 27–30
    symbolic interaction theory,
        23–26
South Asians, 143
South Carolina, divorce
    legislation, 62
spanking/slapping, 276, *354*

specialization model, 237
spillover, 264
spiritual love, 208
spouse's similarity, 387–388
standard of living, 311–313
state, 437
status group, 121
stay-at-home wives, *256*
stepfamilies, 405–430
    age at leaving home, 424
    children, and, 422–424, 428
    cohabiting *vs.* married, 410, 423
    defined, 410
    demography/remarriages,
        413–416
    diversity, 410–411
    as incomplete institutions,
        407–409
    kinship ties, 411–412, 426–428
    later life, 412–413
    lessons learned, 424–429
    primacy of private family,
        425–426
    stabilization period, 419–421
    stepmother *vs.* stepfather,
        421–422
    transitional period, 417–418
Stepfamily Foundation, 430
stepfathers, 412
    alliance with biological father,
        420
    cohabiting *vs.* married, 412
    roles of, 421–422
stepmothers, roles of, 420–422
stepparents' rights/
    responsibilities, 408, 409
stress, 263, 264
Supplemental Nutrition Assistance
    Program (SNAP), 450, 451
supply (of potential marriage
    partners), 236
survey, 20–22
    longitudinal, 24
    national, 24
    newspapers, 24
Survey of Income and Program
    Participation, 430
symbolic interaction theory, 23–26

TANF. *See* Temporary Assistance
    for Needy Families (TANF)
task size, 264

task stress, 264
teenage childbearing, 19–20
teenage mothers, 200–202
teenage pregnancy "problem,"
   199–200, 202
teenagers. *See* adolescents
telecommuting, 267
Temporary Assistance for Needy
   Families (TANF)
   AFDC, compared, 447*t*
   current trends, 435
   defined, 448
   MPF, 290
   policy reversal, 448–449
   welfare reform effects, 449–452
terminology (glossary of terms),
   464–469
time-diary studies, 258
total fertility rate (TFR), 158
traditional views, family life, 5
transnational adaption, 282–283
transnational families, 293–295
TRF. *See* total fertility rate (TFR)
tribal societies
   family ties, 43
   matrilineage, 46
   patrilineage, 46
True Womanhood cult, 51
2008 financial crisis. *See* Great
   Recession
two-earner families. *See* dual-
   earner families
two-spirit people, 82–85

understanding, 243
*Unemployed Man and His Family,
   The* (Komarovsky), 65
unemployment
   marriage, and, 254
   parenthood, and, 286–287
Unemployment Insurance, 450
union, 209
union formation, 209–214
   American courtship, 210
   dating, 211–212
   defined, 240
   historical trends/changes,
      240–242
   hooking up, 212–213
   independent living, 213–214

United Nations Convention
   on the Rights of the
   Child, 299
United States
   American courtship, 210
   bilateral kinship, 59
   divorce rates, 381
   family diversity trends, *11*
   family instability, 288
   intermarriages, and racial
      divide, 168–169
   mandatory schooling age, 16
   manufacturing outsourcing, 31
   same-sex marriage legislation,
      455
   teenage birthrates, 203
University of Rochester, 77
upper-class families, 122–123
urbanization, 228
utilitarian individualism, 6

values, 276
Versailles Village, 165
violence. *See* child abuse;
   domestic violence; intimate
   partner violence

wage gap, 96, *97*
wage labor, 51
Washington State, paid parental
   leave, 267
Web search, 36
*Webster v. Reproductive Health
   Services*, 442
wedding, as a status symbol,
   232–233
welfare reform, 446–452
welfare state, 437–440
Western Europe
   maternal partnerships statistics,
      288*f*
   parental leave, *268*
Western nations
   defined, 31
   economic trends, 96
   era of restricted divorce, 377
   kinship groups, 44
   no-fault divorce legislation, 380
"whiteness," as ethnicity, 145–147
widowers, *316*

wives
   division of labor, 255–261
   divorce, and co-parenting, 390
   earnings, and domestic
      work, 259
   earnings, compared to
      husbands, 253
   era of divorce tolerance,
      378–379
   era of restricted divorce,
      377–378
   household chores, *28*
   household decision
      making, 250–251
   stay-at-home, 256, *256*
   time-diary studies, 258–259
   unemployment, and
      marriage, 254
   weekly work activities
      statistics, 260*f*
women. *See also* wives
   asymmetry (of gender
      change), 100
   childbearing outside of
      marriage, 114
   cohabitation, and education,
      219–220
   developing countries, 119–120
   divorce, and, 426
   employment, and divorce, 384
   employment discrimination,
      96–97
   employment outside of home
      (1920s), *61*
   employment outside of home
      (current trends), *61, 131*
   feminist theory, 26–27
   gender differentiation,
      interactionist
      approach, 94–95
   hooking up, 213
   household decision making,
      250–251
   intimate partner violence, *348*
   intimate partner violence rates,
      348
   life expectancy, married *vs.*
      divorced/never-married, *234*
   living arrangements, historical
      trends, 314–317

marital bargain, 241
married, labor force
    participation, 251–254
middle-class families, 123
MPF, 290
occupations, and stereotype, 99
parental socialization, 88
potential partners'
    characteristics, 238t
sexual abuse, and sexual
    activity, 356
Smith-Rosenberg's same-sex
    intimacy study, 179–180
social class, and employment,
    121–122
time-diary studies, 258–259
two-spirit people, 83
wage gap, *97*

workforce participation
    (1960s–1990s), 70
working-class families, 123
women-centered kinship,
    127, 134
Women's Bureau, 106
work
    care work, 255–259
    family life, and, 263–264
    labor force, 251
    marriage, and division of labor,
        255–261
    married women's labor force
        participation, 251–253
    nonstandard work hours,
        264–265
    progressive workplace, 265–268
    service sector, 251

unemployment, and
    marriage, 254
wives' earnings, and domestic
    duties, 259
Work and Family Researchers
    Network, 270
work stress, *263*
work-family balance, 261–268,
    458–460
working-class families
    concerted cultivation *vs.* natural
        growth, 132–133
    defined, 123
    parental values, 131

young adulthood. *See* early
    adulthood
young-old, 309